PENGUIN HANDBOOKS

THE PENGUIN CARE

Anna Alston read English _____ _____ _____ as a careers officer. She was Senior Careers Officer in Waltham Forest for several years before becoming a freelance careers writer. She has co-authored several careers books and contributed articles to the *Daily Telegraph*, *The Times*, *Woman*, *Good Housekeeping* and various other magazines. She was careers counsellor on *Company* and *New Woman* magazines and since 1987 has edited the Independent Schools Careers Organization's magazine, *CareerScope*. She also works part-time as a careers adviser at a 'new' university. She has a daughter studying at university.

Anne Daniel was born and educated in the USA. After taking a degree in English, which included a year in Oxford, she married an Englishman and returned to England. For many years she ran the *Daily Telegraph* Careers Information Service and edited six editions of *The Daily Telegraph Careers A–Z*. She writes on careers and higher education for the *Independent* and works as an admissions officer in an Oxford college. She lives with her husband and three children in Buckinghamshire.

As a freelance journalist in the fifties, Ruth Miller began to specialize in writing about careers, because she had become fascinated by how and why the people she interviewed had chosen or drifted into their careers. Since then she has written about careers and related subjects for a wide variety of publications, including *The Times,* the *Daily Telegraph*, the *Independent*, *The Times Educational Supplement*, *Good Housekeeping* and *Woman*, as well as ISCO's *CareerScope* and specialist publishers, such as CRAC.

All three collaborated on *Hours to Suit*, a guide to flexible working, and have served on the committee of the Careers Writers Association.

THE PENGUIN CAREERS GUIDE

Anna Alston
and
Anne Daniel

CONSULTANT EDITOR: RUTH MILLER

Tenth Edition

PENGUIN BOOKS

PENGUIN BOOKS

Published by the Penguin Group
Penguin Books Ltd, 80 Strand, London WC2R 0RL, England
Penguin Putnam Inc., 375 Hudson Street, New York, New York 10014, USA
Penguin Books Australia Ltd, Ringwood, Victoria, Australia
Penguin Books Canada Ltd, 10 Alcorn Avenue, Toronto, Ontario, Canada M4V 3B2
Penguin Books India (P) Ltd, 11 Community Centre, Panchsheel Park, New Delhi – 110 017, India
Penguin Books (NZ) Ltd, Cnr Rosedale and Airborne Roads, Albany, Auckland, New Zealand
Penguin Books (South Africa) (Pty) Ltd, 24 Sturdee Avenue, Rosebank 2196 South Africa

Penguin Books Ltd, Registered Offices: 80 Strand, London WC2R 0RL, England

www.penguin.com

First published as *The Peacock Book of Careers for Girls* 1966
Second edition published as *Careers for Girls* 1970
Third edition 1973
Fourth edition 1975
Fifth edition published as *Equal Opportunities:
A Careers Guide for Women and Men* 1978
Sixth edition 1981
Reprinted with revisions 1982
Seventh edition 1984
Reprinted with revisions 1985
Eighth edition 1987
Ninth edition published as *The Penguin Careers Guide* 1992
Reprinted with updating material 1993
Tenth edition 1996
11

Printed in England by Clays Ltd, St Ives plc
Filmset in Monophoto Times

Contents

Acknowledgements

This tenth edition would not have been possible without the invaluable advice and hard work of our researcher, Jan Widmer. She has been tireless in her efforts to track down the most accurate and up-to-date information available. It has not always been easy and we acknowledge our debt to her.

We would also like to thank the countless organizations who answered our many questions, especially about the details we wanted for the 'Position of women' paragraphs. Special thanks are due to Aline Cumming for helping with the computing section, to Shiona Llewellyn for advising on the TV, film and radio chapter and to Dianah Ellis for help on developments in higher education. A special mention, also, to the Department for Education and Employment, the Central Statistical Office and the Equal Opportunities Commission.

Foreword

Changes in the title of this book mirror changes in society in the last thirty years, at least as it affects the female half. When it was first published in 1966, it was called *Careers for Girls* and it was a trailblazer. It is probably difficult for today's young readers to believe, but nursing, teaching and secretarial work were still considered the main good jobs for a girl. *Careers for Girls'* purpose was, unambiguously, to encourage girls to widen their career choice: to squeeze through doors which seemed shut and to make intelligent use of back doors. For example, the way into publishing and advertising was as a secretary. Equal opportunities was nothing but a pious hope and a glint in feminists' eyes. The top professions were male-dominated and tried to remain so: medical schools imposed a quota (15%) on female applicants; barristers said they couldn't accept women into chambers because there were no ladies' lavatories; policewomen knew their place, dealt only with women and children and didn't expect to rise far up the ranks; female chartered accountants were a rarity and, like lawyers, were often mistaken for their secretaries. Companies' interviewers asked female applicants about their marriage and child-rearing plans; employers could be quite open about not training women in their twenties because they were expected to leave before investment in their training had been recouped; and they hesitated about promoting female thirty- and forty-somethings because they were expected soon to reach a difficult age. It really was like that, just 30 years ago. Terms like 'returner', 'career break' and 'family-friendly' were totally unknown.

Legislation

In 1976 the Sex Discrimination Act was passed and the book was retitled *Equal Opportunities: a Careers Guide for Women and Men*. Important and welcome as the legislation was, it could not instantly change attitudes. Few of us who since the sixties have been concerned with improving women's job prospects anticipated how many intractable hurdles would have to be negotiated before equal opportunities would be more than something to look forward to. Women who did make it into top or nearly top jobs in the seventies and early eighties (and there were some) did so 'in the male mode'. They worked very full time indeed, without a career break. The vast majority were childless, and they were more often unmarried (or unpartnered) than their less successful sisters (and their successful male colleagues).

In 1992 we retitled the book *The Penguin Careers Guide*. Courses and careers were by then open to applicants whatever their sex, while many career concerns were the same for everybody: less job security than in the past; no jobs for life; downsizing in organizations; the need for transferable skills. But women's deliberations at the career-choosing stage and their subsequent job and promotion problems and progress were still – and will remain – different, which is why we still retain the paragraphs on 'Position of Women'. Lack of adequate and affordable childcare facilities is possibly top of the list of concerns for today's ambitious career women. A man may leave work to fetch his car from the garage, but a woman who says she can't work late because she has to fetch her child is quite a different matter.

In the nineties labour market, however, women may well be the flavour of the decade. Employers now realize that, if they want their share of the best, they have to look at women who now make up half of those in higher education and have overtaken boys at A-level. In the next ten years the proportion of women in the workplace will rise from the present 47% to over half. Most of the increase is expected to be in the service sector, where women outnumber men even now. Job segregation exists still: there are far fewer women than men, for example, in the City and industrial management. However, it is the occupations in which women predominate – health care, education, retailing, social services – which are increasing in size, while manufacturing – always a male preserve – is decreasing.

Most of the increase in the labour force is expected to be at professional and management levels, which is encouraging for women in higher education.

Role models

One difficulty is still the lack of suitable role models for young women. So many successful women are those who had to 'make it' in the male mould, working long hours, proving their commitment by behaving like men, socializing after work etc. But more younger role models are beginning to appear: thirty-somethings who have taken a break for child-rearing and/or worked part-time for some of the years after their return. Flexible, family-friendly or parent-friendly working patterns have become accepted. Job-sharing, which took a very long time to be tried in the private sector (it has worked in the public sector for some time) is at last taking off. Employers are beginning to find that making women-friendly working arrangements is actually economically sound, saving on recruitment and retraining costs.

Changing working patterns

Another change in the labour force is the continuing growth in part-time working, increasingly popular with employers who use part-timers to cope with the peaks and troughs in most work areas. Part-time employment protection has diminished the drawbacks of part-time work. Women with children under 16 are now more likely to work than not work (59%) but probably part-time. In 1994 46% of all women working were in part-time work, against 34% in 1971. Most women work part-time because they *want* to, but it is assumed that they don't want to work full-time because of inadequate child care.

Survey

The Institute of Employment Studies at the end of 1995 produced a survey on changes in 'Women in the Labour Market' over the last twenty years or so. Their findings are most encouraging on the whole: for example, the percentage of women economically active increased from 57% in 1971 to 71% in 1994, and that despite the fact that fewer younger (16–19) women are at work because they are remaining in education.

You can't have it all

However, within the last few years this has probably changed again, according to a general feeling or opinion, but one not yet statistically confirmed. Some women nearing senior management appear to have come to the perhaps disappointing conclusion that you can't have it all. Rather than have *very* full-time nannies and stay at work long after normal hours to socialize or discuss vital matters, these women decide that there comes a point in the hierarchy beyond which they don't want to rise. The minus points outweigh the plus points. The most intractable problem, worrying especially the successful thirty-somethings in higher-middle management is: just how far do they want to go? Although women account for only around 5% of senior management (nobody knows exactly because 'senior' is interpreted in different ways), they account for 30% of what the Institute calls 'corporate management'. 11% of all women in employment are managers or administrators, but only 5% of part-time women are in these occupations, even though professional and managerial jobs are increasingly seen as suitable for part-time and job-sharing. Lack of part-time work at this level even now is believed to be the reason for the 'downgrading' experienced by women managers after a career break, who often find it hard to find suitable work. According to the survey, 'These patterns suggest that it is not sufficient simply to provide flexible working patterns ... Issues concerning workplace and household cultures also need to be addressed.'

In other words, things look good on paper, but an increasing body of evidence suggests that practical and cultural obstacles will remain, for example the 'can't have it all' problem. Has discrimination ended? That depends on what you mean by discrimination. No employer could say, and probably doesn't even *want* to say, 'I prefer a man to fill this job.' It is subtler than that. For example, women are often much more reticent than men about advertising their achievements to people in a position to help their career progress. Informal networks, which it is hard for women to join, can influence recruitment and promotion decisions. *Starting* to work with women at the same level is probably a bit more of an effort for men who have always worked with other men; this might change soon when men who were at university with equal numbers of women reach influential positions. In the meantime, there are still a lot of men who, with Professor Higgins in *My Fair Lady* really do think 'Why can't a woman be more like a man?' – at work only, of course.

Examples of progress

Yet this decade has seen some significant 'firsts'. In the early nineties we were thrilled when women were appointed for the first time to the posts of both the Director of Public Prosecutions and

*Women as a percentage of (home) applicants accepted for university:**

	1966	1994
Medicine	26	52
Law	13	55
Engineering and technology	2	13
Veterinary science	19	63
Total of students	30	51

Women as a percentage of:

	1966	1994
Solicitors	6	29
Called to the Bar	8	43
General practitioners	12 (1974)	29
Hospital consultants	7	18
Chartered accountants	1	15
		(35 student members)

the Head of MI5. Five years later we have the first female Chief Constable, the first female Chief Economist at the Confederation of British Industry. The all-important Treasury's panel of advisers has, for the first time, two women among its seven members. This *Guide* can drop the 'Position of Women' paragraphs when such 'firsts' are no longer worth mentioning – and when mediocre women can get as high up the career ladder as mediocre men. We haven't reached that stage yet, or have we?

The tables show just some examples of the strides women have made in higher education and in occupations in the last thirty years. This *Guide*, we believe, can take some of the credit.

Ruth Miller
January 1996

Introduction to the *Guide*

What are Its Aims?

Firstly, to provide unbiased accurate careers information. Hard facts like entry and training requirements are checked with relevant organizations. Descriptions of the work involved – necessarily brief and only highlighting vital aspects – and descriptions of the sort of person likely to be good at/happy in the work are based on practitioners' experiences and views and on our own observations over many years of interviewing people at work. We believe this is the most important difference between this *Guide* and organizations' own careers literature.

Who is It For?

The *Guide* is likely to be used mainly by young people between 14 and 20. However, it is also valuable for the increasing number of people in their twenties, thirties or forties who want to, or have to, change their occupation. Some made the wrong choice the first time around or have developed new interests; others face lack of demand for their existing knowledge and skills, or redundancy. It is important to realize that most people could be happy in several different careers. What you enjoy at 40 may well be different from what you enjoyed at 21. Some people, in fact, take a long time to find out what they really want to do. For many occupations maturity is seen as an asset; education and training facilities may well be available; and standard entry requirements may be relaxed for older people (see individual entries, 'Late Start in Education and Training', pp. xxxv–xxxviii, and 'Higher Education', p. xxx).

More than ever before, individuals are expected to take charge of their own careers. This applies to everyone, from those working for large organizations to unemployed people on government training schemes. From time to time we all need to assess where we are in job terms, decide what we are aiming at, and what we need to achieve our aims. 'Buzz' phrases today are 'personal portfolio' – the individual's package of knowledge, skills and experience – and 'transferable skills' – those which can be put to good use in any work situation. The man or woman who is prepared to be flexible, to take advantage of (increasingly compulsory) continuing professional development (CPD), and who doesn't assume that any job is immune to change, is the one most likely to weather times of high unemployment.

How to Use This *Guide*

Careers in this *Guide* are listed alphabetically. However, many if not most careers are really 'areas of work'. Look at the index and you see how many more jobs than careers sections there are. Usually one kind of training leads to jobs in a variety of settings and you can normally mould training plus experience to the kind of job you will want to do when you know more about the whole spectrum and about your own likes, dislikes, strengths and weaknesses.

We could not hope to include all occupational areas in one book, so we have had to make arbitrary choices. Since the future demand is expected to be for more highly skilled, highly trained people, we have left out jobs requiring few, if any, educational qualifications, concentrating instead on those which need formal training or which lead to the widest range of options. School-leavers needing information on other jobs and training opportunities should contact their careers service. Adults should consult the Jobcentre or local guidance centre (see 'EGSAs', p. l). Use this *Guide* in conjunction with 'Some Useful Sources of Reference' (p. lii), combined with discussions with careers advisers, family, friends who know you well and, if possible, with people doing the jobs you'd like to do.

Look at job advertisements. If you are a mature job-seeker you may be baffled by some of the newer or rarer job titles. Often it is only by reading the job specification that you discover it is something you know under a different name. Some are genuinely new occupations and you may need to dig more deeply to find out if your background and possible future training would make you a good candidate. Be adventurous, look at as wide a range as possible, using the 'Related Careers' sections as signposts.

Prospects

We do not mention prospects, for the following reasons: firstly, within the book's lifetime the job market is likely to change – who would have forecast even 5 years ago that there would now be a surfeit of solicitors? Secondly, there are always regional variations.

Thirdly, and perhaps most importantly, it is frequently a mistake for a 16-year-old choosing A-levels or an 18-year-old choosing a degree subject to do so with the aim of entering a 'shortage' occupation 5 or 7 years later, as the marketplace may change dramatically meanwhile. Lastly, the term 'prospects' does not mean the same thing to all people – for some it means high salaries and/or early promotion, others link it with job security or the chance to follow the occupation anywhere in the country.

A Word to Parents

It is likely that today's generation of mothers who value themselves and their own careers can, as they always have, influence their daughters' attitudes. Parents have always been the major influence on their children's choice of career: boys and girls who have followed non-traditional paths nearly always say that their parents' support has meant a great deal. Until the far-off day when all occupations are equally shared by men and women, parents will need to continue to encourage their sons and daughters to look for occupations in which they will be happy and successful, *regardless* of whether they are thought by others to be 'suitable' only for men or women.

Checklist

GCSE

The General Certificate of Secondary Education is the main qualification awarded at 16+ to pupils in England and Wales. Grades are on a scale from A* to G; grades C and above are equivalent to the former O-level grades A, B and C (or CSE grade 1). Four or five GCSEs at grades A–C is a common starting point for most of the careers and courses in this book. From 1996 GCSE (Short Course) qualifications will begin to accredit National Curriculum short courses in modern foreign languages, design and technology and information technology. They will be graded on the A* – G scale; the standard will be the same as GCSE, but they will take less time and cover less.

A-levels and AS-levels

A-levels are normally taken 2 years after GCSEs. Traditionally students have studied 2 or 3 complementary subjects (e.g. maths/physics/chemistry or English/history/French), but 'mixed' A-levels are becoming much more common and acceptable to higher education.

AS-levels were introduced to give A-level students the opportunity to broaden their education. An AS-level is studied to the same depth as an A-level but has only half the content. AS-levels may be chosen to complement or contrast with A-levels (for example, a science student can keep up a foreign language, or an arts student maths).

Standard entry to higher education (but see 'Higher Education', p. xxx) usually requires 2 or 3 A-levels, or 2 A- and 2 AS-levels. Some institutions may accept 1 A- and 4 AS-levels. Courses may require passes in specific subjects.

Scottish Certificate of Education

The Scottish equivalent to GCE O-level, the SCE Ordinary or O-grade, is being replaced by a new Standard grade. This examination caters for a much wider ability range, so far more pupils are able to gain a Certificate.

Grades are awarded on a scale from 1 to 7. Pupils take

individual subjects at different levels, according to their ability in that subject. Grade 3 is considered to be the equivalent of C in the former O-grade and C in GCSE.

The SCE Higher grade is taken by the most able pupils after a further 1 year's study. Others take it after 2 years. For entry to degree courses in England and Wales candidates need passes in 4 or 5 H-grade subjects, 3 or 4 for entry to (4-year) Scottish degrees. Three Highers are equivalent to 2 A-levels, 5 Highers are equivalent to 3 A-levels.

The 1-year Certificate of Sixth Year Studies can be taken following a 1-year Higher course.

(Scottish secondary education is currently under review.)

National Vocational Qualifications (NVQs)/Scottish Vocational Qualifications (SVQs)

1. Job-specific vocational qualifications
NVQs/SVQs make up a training revolution which is beginning to affect employees at all levels of work. They are based on standards of competence agreed by industry. Each competence is made up of units setting out the standards of skill, knowledge and understanding that must be reached. For each unit the individual gains a credit and the NVQ certificate shows which unit credits have been collected.

Competence means the ability to perform tasks, and this is assessed 'on the job'. How or where you acquire this competence is immaterial. It may be through a full- or part-time course, by open learning (see p. xxxv) while at work, or in your own time.

NVQs/SVQs are awarded in 11 broad occupational areas covering, it is estimated, around 80% of occupations. They are at 5 levels. Level 1 is the most basic, level 3 broadly equates to 2 A-levels, while level 5 represents higher professional qualifications. Levels 1–4 are now in place in most sectors. Because each NVQ/SVQ fits into a framework it should now be possible to relate one vocational qualification to another, regardless of what organization has awarded it, making it easier to move up the qualifications ladder. For example, an NVQ level 2 in retailing awarded by City and Guilds could be followed by an NVQ level 3 awarded by the RSA.

NVQs are awarded by established organizations, such as City and Guilds (see p. xxii), BTEC (see p. xxi) and various professional bodies. In England and Wales the qualifications are approved by the National Council for Vocational Qualifications, in Scotland by SCOTVEC (which unlike NCVQ is also the awarding body). These qualifications are not graded, since candidates are deemed to be either competent or not yet competent.

People working towards NVQs/SVQs can obtain a National Record of Achievement (Record of Education and Training (RET) in Scotland): this is a personal record of achievement, experience, qualifications gained and plans for future training. It can help individuals to manage their own careers, while giving employers a good idea of what they can do.

Where NVQs/SVQs are known to be in place we have indicated this in the individual chapters.

2. General vocational qualifications

General national vocational qualifications (GNVQs)/General Scottish vocational qualifications (GSVQs) were introduced in 1993. They cover broad occupational areas: in England and Wales and Northern Ireland these currently are business, leisure and tourism, art and design, health and social care, manufacturing, science, construction and the built environment, hospitality and catering. Engineering, information technology (IT), media: communication and production, retailing and distributive trades, land and environment and management studies (Advanced level only) are due to be piloted between 1995/7. GNVQs are available at 3 levels: Foundation, Intermediate and Advanced. Foundation does not require any qualifications; Intermediate equates with 4 GCSEs and Advanced with 2 A-levels. Foundation and Intermediate are designed to take 1 year full-time, but could be longer part-time, whereas Advanced is a 2-year full-time programme. GSVQs are based on SCOTVEC National Certificate modules and are awarded at levels I, II and III. They cover business administration, hospitality, leisure and tourism, care, technology, arts and social science, design, IT, science and land-based industries.

GNVQs are awarded at 3 grades: pass, merit and distinction. In principle, universities will accept Advanced GNVQs and level III GSVQs as an alternative to A-levels for entry, but it is still too early to say exactly how students with this qualification will fare in comparison with their counterparts with 3 A-levels. However, early evidence from UCAS suggests that they have had considerable success in obtaining offers. Many students take an A-level alongside GNVQ.

From 1995 Part 1 GNVQs are being piloted. These are 2-year courses for 14–16-year-olds and can be taken at either Foundation or Intermediate level. They will take up 20% of curriculum time.

All GNVQs/GSVQs include the 'core' skills of communication, application of number and IT.

Further information

National Council for Vocational Qualifications, 222 Euston Road, London NW1 2BZ (Tel.: 0171 728 1914)

SCOTVEC, Hanover House, 24 Douglas Street, Glasgow G2 7NQ (Tel.: 0141 242 2214)

BTEC (Business and Technology Education Council)

BTEC offers nationally recognized qualifications in a wide range of subjects. These include: agriculture, business and finance, caring, computing, construction, design, distribution, engineering, hotel and catering, leisure and science.

BTEC courses may be taken in colleges of further and higher education, some approved training centres and companies and in schools. Courses are modular, with a range of compulsory 'core' and optional subjects so students can tailor-make programmes to suit their needs and interests. There are two types of qualification, Certificates and Diplomas. Certificates are usually studied on a part-time basis, Diplomas normally on a full-time basis. They are of the same standard, but Diplomas cover more ground.

There are several levels of course and qualification:

First awards
No minimum qualifications required, but some colleges may set some. Certificate courses last 1 year part time, Diploma courses 1 year full time or 2 years part time. Full-time Diplomas are being phased out and replaced with Intermediate GNVQs. Available in some schools.

National awards
Minimum 4 GCSEs (A–C) or acceptable pass in First Certificate/ Diploma or at the discretion of the college. National Certificate takes 2 years part time, National Diploma 2 years full time or 3 years part time or sandwich. Roughly equivalent to A-levels and acceptable (at the right standard of pass) for entry to degree courses.

Higher National awards
Minimum 1 A-level plus supporting GCSEs (A–C) *or* BTEC National award. Higher National Certificate takes 2 years part time, Higher National Diploma 2 years full time or 3 years part time or sandwich. Generally accepted as equivalent of pass degree.

Continuing education
BTEC also offers a range of individual units and programmes for adults wishing to update and acquire new skills.

BTEC GNVQ: No specific entry requirements for BTEC Foundation, Intermediate or Advanced GNVQ. Colleges and schools can advise which is most appropriate. BTEC GNVQs will gradually replace existing BTEC qualifications.

BTEC NVQ: Related to specific jobs and based on standards set by the industry. Anyone can be assessed for NVQs. Many are also recognized by professional bodies for entry and/or exemption purposes.
(NOTE: on 1 January 1996, BTEC merged with the University of London Examinations and Assessment Council (ULEAC).)

Further information

BTEC, Central House, Upper Woburn Place, London WC1H 0HH (Tel.: 0171 413 8400)

SCOTVEC (Scottish Vocational Education Council)

SCOTVEC administers a comprehensive and highly flexible system of vocational education. It is based on free-standing units, which can be taken on their own or built up to a group award.

National Certificate modules can be achieved by various modes of study, at school, college or place of work. A coherent group of modules at appropriate levels can lead to National Certificate Group Awards; to Scottish Vocational Qualifications (SVQs, see p. xix); or entry to SCOTVEC Higher National Certificate and Diploma courses or entry to higher education; to recognition by professional bodies for entry and/or exemption purposes.

Higher National Certificates and Diplomas, which are broadly equivalent to BTEC HNC/D, have been reorganized on a unit or modular basis. Entry is with a relevant group of National Certificate modules, appropriate passes in S- or O- and H-grades, or at the discretion of the college.

Further information

SCOTVEC, Hanover House, 24 Douglas Street, Glasgow G2 7NQ (Tel.: 0141 242 2214)

City and Guilds

Awards qualifications in over 400 different subjects in a wide range of vocational areas, including hotels and catering, construction, engineering, printing, travel and tourism, agriculture and horti-culture, media, retail and distribution and care. City and Guilds does not run courses itself; these are held in centres such as col-leges of further education, adult education institutes and training centres. Courses may be part-time, full-time or a mixture. Some are available by distance learning or through flexible learning programmes.

In the main, no specific time limits or entry requirements are laid down for qualifications. Many certificates are awarded jointly with an industry body and City and Guilds has been closely involved in developing NVQs/SVQs and GNVQs (see p. xix).

All City and Guilds awards are normally available at several levels and individuals usually progress from one to the next. In addition, there are several senior awards that people can work for and which depend on experience and demonstrated ability, not on conventional academic study: *Licentiateship* (higher technician or master craftsman level); *Graduateship* (equivalent to first degree); *Membership* (Master's degree or full corporate membership of a professional body); *Fellowship* (outstanding at the highest level).

Further information

City and Guilds, 1 Giltspur Street, London EC1A 9DD (Tel.: 0171 294 2468)

RSA (Royal Society of Arts) Examinations Board

RSA Examinations Board, one of the largest awarding bodies in Britain, offers a wide range of qualifications in many areas of education and training. Schemes range from the pre-vocational level for people still at school to postgraduate qualifications. The schemes are open to anyone and are available in many different centres, such as colleges of further education and training centres.

The main areas of qualification include accounting, administration, bookkeeping, customer service, information technology, languages, management, marketing, retailing, sales, secretarial, teaching and training, wholesaling and warehousing. RSA is a major provider of NVQ and GNVQ (see p. xix) awards.

Further information

Telephone RSA Customer Information Bureau on 01203 470033, *or* write to RSA, Westwood Way, Coventry CV4 8HS

Training and Enterprise Councils (TECs) and Local Enterprise Companies (LECs)

TECs (England and Wales) and LECs (Scotland) were set up in 1991; there are now 81 in England and Wales and 22 in Scotland. They are independent companies led by local business people, with representatives from trade unions, education, etc. They have operating agreements with the Secretary of State for Education and Employment which lay down how they are constituted and conditions they must meet to receive funding for their activities. Central government gives strategic guidance to them in line with what it sees are the priorities for improving local economies and raising the skills of the workforce. However, within limits it is very much up to each TEC/LEC to decide how to spend its funds, as it is expected to respond to the needs of the local labour market. A TEC may provide a service itself or contract some or all services out to 'providers'.

From the job-seeker's point of view the most important schemes run by *all* TECs and LECs are:

Youth Training (YT)

This is for 16–17-year-olds and most of the training is contracted out to approved training organizations. The aim is to provide broad vocational education and training. Young people's training needs are assessed and an individual training plan agreed with each trainee. The plan specifies the sort of training they will receive from the training organizations they are placed with. For example, all trainees must have the chance to gain an NVQ or SVQ (see p. xix). This is usually at level 2 or above, but may be level 1. Not all those on YT are unemployed; many trainees take part in the programme as employees of firms.

Youth credits

These are a way of delivering Youth Training, but the actual title, system and money available varies from area to area. Basically, each trainee is given credits with a monetary value which represents an entitlement to train. It is up to the trainee to 'spend' them as he or she wishes, by giving them to an employer, another training provider or a college (for a course or for open learning) in exchange for training.

Modern Apprenticeships

The first Modern Apprenticeships were launched in September 1995. They are a national initiative, underwritten by the TECs and are designed to equip young people with the range of flexible skills needed in today's changing employment market. The aim is to ensure that more young people obtain higher level vocational skills. They differ from old-style (and fast-disappearing) apprenticeships in three main ways: they are not 'time-serving'; they are not male-dominated; they are available not only in traditional industries but in occupational areas which never had apprenticeships.

A modern apprenticeship is an individually tailored training programme agreed between the apprentice, employer and local TEC, who also agree on payment. Employers must follow strict guidelines and training must lead to at least NVQ level 3. Time taken is flexible, depending on the apprentice's educational qualifications and experience at the start, but is expected to be between 18 months and 3 years. For 18–21-year-olds with A-levels/GNVQ there is a fast-stream route, the Accelerated Modern Apprenticeship, lasting up to 18 months. All apprenticeships must end by the 23rd birthday.

Modern Apprenticeships are expected to take off fast and will cover areas as diverse as accountancy, childcare, arts and entertainment and engineering.

At the time of going to press some details had yet to be finalized. For information on the schemes, contact the careers service, Jobcentre or local TEC office.

Training for work
This is for 18-year-olds and over and has replaced previous employment training schemes for adults. It is a programme offering a mix of activities including training, temporary work, work towards vocational qualifications, job specific training and work preparation. It is open to people who have been unemployed for 6 months or more; in some cases, people with disabilities or special needs can enter straight away. Participants have an individual participation plan similar to those drawn up for YT trainees.

Business and enterprise services
TECs and LECs provide help for unemployed people who want to become self-employed or to set up their own business (see WORKING FOR ONESELF, p. 551). They also provide access to a wide range of business development services.

Further information   Local TEC/LEC office, *or* TEC National Council Ltd, 10th Floor, Westminster Tower, 3 Albert Embankment, London SE1 7SP (Tel.: 0171 735 0010)

Degrees: See 'Higher Education' (p. xxx)

Diploma of Higher Education (Dip. H.E.) – England and Wales Only

Dip. H.E. courses take 2 years full-time, some 3 years part-time at higher education institutions. Entry requirements for school-leavers: 2 A-levels (but A-level grades accepted are lower than for most degree students).

Courses are comparable in standard and sometimes similar or identical in content to the first 2 years of an honours degree. Most are vocationally related, for example in health care and social work, and may be an integral part of professional training. Many diplomates go on to degree courses towards which their Dip.H.E. may count; some universities award a Dip.H.E. after successful completion of two years of a degree course.

Financing Your Studies

There are 2 main kinds of state financial awards: mandatory and discretionary. Mandatory ones are those to which students are legally entitled provided they are personally eligible and are attending an eligible course. In Scotland there are no mandatory awards, but in practice the system is the same. The main difference is that in Scotland these awards are given by the Scottish Office Education Department, while in England and Wales they are the responsibility of local education authorities. Discretionary awards are those which an LEA (or, in Scotland, the education authority of the Regional or Islands Council) can choose whether or not to give.

Non-advanced courses
These include A-level, GNVQ/SNVQ, National Diploma/Certificate, secretarial and art foundation courses. Generally they are free to those up to the age of 18 or 19 living in the area of the college. Any support for living expenses (maintenance) is discretionary and varies widely from area to area. Some LEAs will give Education and Maintenance Awards (depending on parents' income) to those under 19. In Scotland regional education authorities will give eligible students of all ages means-tested bursaries. To find out what might be available contact your LEA.

Some TECs/LECs fund vocational training courses for unemployed people. It is worth checking what is available locally.

'Eligible' advanced courses
Full-time or sandwich first degree, Higher National, Diploma of Higher Education, PGCE and comparable courses are eligible or 'designated' courses for which eligible students are given mandatory awards. These cover fees (normally paid direct to the college) and the maintenance grant which is means-tested (i.e. the amount depends on your own and, in most cases, your parents' or spouse's income).

Student physiotherapists, radiographers, occupational therapists and orthoptists are normally funded by the National Health Service via health authorities. The amount of grant is identical to that given to LEA-funded students. Where health authority funding is not available, i.e. where places additional to those funded by the health authority are offered, students should be eligible for LEA awards. Contact the college in the first instance.

In 1990 a student loans system was introduced to make up the difference between the grant and what the student needs to live on. Loans are *not* means-tested. The existing level of grant was frozen as from 1991/2 and loans are being increased annually until they account for 50% of funding (by 1996/7). Students (maximum age 50) decide at the start of each year how much they wish to borrow (up to a laid-down maximum) and have 5 or 7 years (depending on length of course) to pay the loan off, starting from the April following graduation. Loans are index-linked to inflation: the outstanding amount is adjusted annually in line with the Retail Prices Index. Repayments can be deferred for a year at a time if the individual's income is less than 85% of national average earnings.

'Non-eligible' advanced courses
Include postgraduate (except PGCE, see p. 522) and part-time (except initial teacher training) courses; also most dance and drama non-degree courses. For these there is a decreasing supply of discretionary awards. The situation for post-graduate awards (except for teaching) is particularly complicated as a number of bodies are responsible for different kinds of courses. For information consult the college where you are studying or one of the publications listed below.

Access funds
These are distributed by government to colleges to pass on to some students who are in financial difficulties or who might not be able to take a further or higher education course without help. Further education students must be 19 or over. There is no upper age limit for higher education students. For information contact the college.

Career Development Loans
These are available for people wishing to take a vocational course – full- or part-time or by open learning (see p. xxxv) – lasting at least a week and no more than 2 years, for which no other grant is available. Loans can be between £200 and £8,000 to cover up to 80% of course fees plus other expenses. They are made by 4

banks (Barclays, the Co-operative, Clydesdale and Royal Bank of Scotland) in conjunction with the Department for Education and Employment. No repayments are required for up to 1 month afterwards or up to 6 months if unemployed, and the DFEE pays the interest during this time. At the end of the period the borrower repays the loan plus further interest within an agreed time limit, usually 3–5 years. For details contact the Jobcentre or one of the banks concerned.

Tax relief
Since April 1992 some tax relief has been available for people who finance their own training through courses leading to level 4 NVQs/SVQs. Basic rate tax is deducted automatically from the fees for qualifying courses, so non-taxpayers as well as taxpayers can benefit. Students should check when enrolling that fees quoted take this into account.

Further information

'Student grants and loans: a brief guide' from the Department for Education and Employment, Publications Centre, PO Box 2193, London E15 2EU (Tel.: 0181 533 2000)

'Post-graduate awards: State bursaries for postgraduate study on designated, professional and vocational courses' and 'Post-graduate awards: librarianship and information science student-ships and fellowships', both from the DFEE above

'Students' Grants in Scotland' from the Students' Awards Agency for Scotland, Gyleview House, 3 Redheughs Rigg, Edinburgh EH12 9HH

Department of Health, Student Grants, Room 109, North Fylde, Central Office, Norcross, Blackpool FY5 3TA (only once accepted on to a health authority funded course)

Educational Grants Advisory Service, 501/5 Kingsland Road, London E8 4AU, (provides information on money for students)

Students' Money Matters, published by Trotman

Part Time and Job-Sharing

Many women and some men choose to work part time for at least some of their working lives, e.g. when their children are small or they are caring for an elderly relative. Part-time work now ac-counts for an increasing share of job vacancies. Yet the higher the position, the less likelihood there is that it is held by a part-timer. 'Conventional' part-timers are often perceived as less valuable than full-timers, and people going part time often have to accept a more routine job with less responsibility. According to government figures people in full-time employment are twice as likely as part-timers to be given training.

Job-sharing is a different concept, of particular interest to people wanting to stay on the existing rung of the career ladder. In job-share schemes 2 people with the same qualifications and similar experience take full responsibility for one job. They share pay, holidays and fringe benefits on a pro rata basis. Job-sharers may work half a week each or alternate weeks or fortnights, according to the needs of the job and the people sharing it. In some cases the sharers overlap, either to cover busy periods or to 'hand over'. For the scheme to work, sharers have to be compatible, conscientious and flexible. They pay for the privilege of working part time in a job of their choice by giving a little extra time and commitment. Employers who have tried such a scheme tend to be enthusiastic, realizing the benefits of having 2 brains for virtually the price of one; higher productivity (energy levels drop towards the end of the working week) and little time lost through holidays, sickness, etc. Although there are many more examples of job-sharing than there were, especially in the public sector, the concept has not caught on as widely as many people hoped. The initiative still has often to come from job applicants themselves.

Further information

For more information on job-sharing contact:
New Ways to Work, 309 Upper Street, London N1 2TY

Training Access Points (TAPs)

Responsibility for providing information on training and educational opportunities for individuals and employers has been given to TECs. In some cases they maintain TAPs: these are user-friendly computer terminals linked to national databases such as ECCTIS (see p. lii) and PICKUP (p. xxxvi), which may be located in libraries, careers centres, colleges, etc.

Higher Education

The traditional route to a degree is through a 3- or 4-year full-time or 4-year sandwich course. Students may specialize in a single subject, or in 2 major subjects in a 'joint' degree, or take various combinations of subjects in a 'combined' degree. Increasing numbers of institutions are organizing courses on a modular basis in order to allow students greater flexibility in developing a coherent course of study.

Entrance Requirements – Widening Access

Previously, to enter a degree course one normally needed 2 or 3 passes at A-level (or equivalent AS-levels, see p. xviii) plus supporting GCSEs. However, an increasing proportion of students – nearly a third in 1994, up from 20% in 1991 – enter with qualifications other than A/AS-level. Common acceptable alternatives are SCE (see p. xviii), International Baccalaureate, European Baccalaureate and BTEC National (see p. xxi). Candidates for entry in 1994 were the first to offer GNVQ (see p. xx).

Many courses require that candidates have an adequate foundation in specific subjects, but there is increasing flexibility here too. For example, a number of universities run *conversion* courses to enable those without the usual maths and physics A-levels to study engineering.

Mature Entrants

There are increasing numbers of mature students studying for degrees: in 1994 more than 1 in 4 new university students was over 21.

If you are over 21 and have the standard entry qualifications (see above), you will be considered in the same way as school-leavers. If not, institutions will look for evidence of your commitment, motivation and ability to study at a high level. That evidence might be, for example, an A/AS-level or two taken at evening classes or study for professional or vocational qualifications. Candidates who can present convincing evidence may be admitted as direct entrants. However, there is a range of developing schemes and initiatives to help smooth the way for mature candidates.

Access Courses

These are specially designed to prepare mature entrants for higher education. Courses may be full or part time and are offered by adult, further and higher education institutions. Many are designed to meet the needs of specific groups, e.g. women, ethnic minorities or the unemployed. Some are connected with a specific course and institution, guaranteeing a place on a degree course to those who successfully complete their access studies; others have wider applications.

Residential Courses

These are intended for adults (over 21 usually, but many are in their thirties and forties, some even older) who missed out on educational opportunities and now want to catch up – either to go on to higher education or into professional training, or simply to stretch their minds. Courses are usually 1, occasionally 2 years. They may lead to a certificate or diploma but they are above all yet another type of 'access' course. (Colleges also run short 1- or 2-week courses, but these are usually 'special interest' ones.) Course content is varied; most courses cover liberal arts and/or social studies, but computing, languages and environmental subjects, etc. may be covered.

Once accepted, students qualify for grants to cover tuition and maintenance.

Other Preparatory Programmes

These range from courses which help students to improve A-level grades, to those which update special areas of knowledge, to those which deal with study skills.

Associate Student Schemes

Associate students are not formally enrolled on degree programmes but sample some units of degree courses. Assessment is optional. When associate students are assessed, the outcome can lead to formal admission.

Credit Accumulation and Transfer Schemes (CATS)

The *principle* behind credit accumulation and transfer is simple: students should be given 'portable' credit for all types of learning – on courses, at work or through 'life experiences' – which they can accumulate to enable them to move flexibly through further studies and achieve recognized academic awards. The *implementation* is quite complex, based as it is on individuals and on maximizing their flexibility and choice.

CATS schemes are run nationally, regionally and in individual institutions. The kinds of learning assessed include units of recognized courses, in-company training, professional studies and training, and experiential learning (provided the applicant can offer evidence of the learning, not just the experience). By transferring credits students may then be able to negotiate entry with alternative qualifications; admission with exemptions or advanced standing; transfer from one course or institution to another; additional or alternative courses at a different institution from the one the student has registered at.

As already mentioned, CATS schemes are many and varied, but the original CNAA scheme was a trailblazer and set the framework for many individual schemes. CNAA established a UK-wide system of credit-rating courses (known as the tariff) which assigns both a number and level of credits to courses or units. To give a simple example of application, to achieve an honours degree one must accumulate 360 credits with a maximum of 120 at level 1 and a minimum of 120 at level 3. It is not simply a numbers game, however, with students cobbling degrees together out of all their experiences: credits accumulated and transferred must represent a coherent programme of study. They are really a basis for negotiation; for example, a student may accumulate 120 credits, but only 60 may be transferable to the next stage of his or her programme of study.

There are also opportunities for international credit transfer through, for example, ECTS (European Community Course Credit Transfer System) which was instigated on an experimental basis in 1989 by ERASMUS (European Community Action Scheme for the Mobility of University Students).

Further information

ECCTIS, see p. lii.

Assessment of Prior (Experiential) Learning (AP(E)L)

Integral to many initiatives to promote wider access and increasing flexibility are APL and APEL, which give people recognition and sometimes credit for learning already achieved. The titles and formality of this process vary. It is, in fact, the basis on which institutions of higher education have always considered mature candidates, but the development of credit-based learning is extending its use. APL is generally regarded as a global term dealing with all sorts of prior knowledge and learning experiences; APEL normally excludes any certificated learning.

NOTE: CATS and APL principles are applied not just in higher education, but more widely throughout further education and training.

Part-time Courses

The number of part-time students is increasing, but provision varies. Some institutions limit part-time opportunities to mature students and/or particular subjects; others are redesigning courses to provide the option of part-time study much more widely. Birkbeck College of the University of London specializes in part-time degrees.

The Open University

The Open University is Britain's largest institution of higher education. No academic qualifications are required for admission (except for higher degrees), but places are limited and students are admitted on a first-come basis. Students study at home in their own time, through a programme that includes specially prepared materials, set books, radio and television broadcasts, and other audiovisual materials. There are also residential summer schools.

Most students are undergraduates working for a BA degree (with or without honours). Courses are rated as full- or half-credit, depending on the amount of work involved, and are at various levels. The equivalent of 6 credits is needed for a BA, 8 credits, including 2 at higher levels, for Honours. It is possible to complete a degree in 3 years, but most people take 4–6 years. One OU credit is worth 60 CATS (see above) credits.

Many people study as Associate Students, taking undergraduate courses but not registering for a degree. There are also facilities for research and higher degrees, courses for professional development, scientific and technological updating, modern language studies, family, community and personal interest, and, through the Open Business School, a range of management courses at different levels, culminating in an MBA (Master of Business Administration).

Since 1992 the Open University has accepted students from European Community countries and, at its discretion, other parts of Europe.

Further information   The Open University, Walton Hall, Milton Keynes MK7 6AA

University of London External Degrees

Open University and London External degrees do not overlap. They serve different types of students and have fundamental differences. Whereas the Open University offers interdisciplinary courses, open entry and a paced system of support, London External degrees offer in-depth study in a single subject and set entry requirements. The University acts only as an examining body; tuition is offered by a number of correspondence colleges and a few other colleges, both maintained and private. Though it is possible for students to study totally independently, most receive tuition of some sort.

The basic entry requirement is 2 A-levels and 3 GCSE or O-levels (A–C); there may also be specific course requirements. Mature students are assessed on an individual basis. Most students are between the ages of 25 and 45.

Further information   Secretary for External Students, University of London, Senate House, Malet Street, London WC1E 7HU

NOTE: Flexibility invariably implies complexity. It is *vital* that mature and other non-traditional potential students seek help in finding their way through the maze of proliferating new opportunities to find the best way forward for them. The institutions themselves should be only too pleased to advise, but there are other sources of help (see p. lii).

Late Start and Return to Work

A Variety of Routes for Returners, Career Changers and Late Starters

There have never been as many or as flexible opportunities for catching up on missed educational and training opportunities as there are now. Adults who need educational or vocational qualifications – or simply more knowledge – for courses or careers they want to start or return to after a gap of some years can choose from an ever-increasing variety of courses and methods of study. For details of what is available nationally and locally see guides listed under 'Especially for Job-Changers and Late-Starters' on p. liv.

Preparatory Courses

Most re-entry courses were started by women, for women wishing to return to work, but men are rarely excluded. These preparatory courses have various titles, such as 'Women into Work', 'Ready for Work' and 'New Opportunities for Women'.

Courses vary in content, organization, level and quantity of work expected. Some are mainly confidence-restoring and 'diagnostic': they help students to sort out their aims, motivation, level of confidence, circumstances, and then balance these with the available job opportunities, and the obstacles which may arise. Others include work experience or work-related skills training, introduction to new technology and job-hunting techniques.

Open Learning

(The terms *open learning* and *distance-learning* are often interchangeable.)

What is *open learning*? Essentially it is a system which enables more people to make use of educational and training facilities. Flexibility and accessibility are the key-words. All colleges are trying to attract more adults to their courses, whatever their chosen method of study. Open learning aims to remove traditional barriers to education and training, such as rigid entry requirements, the need for full-time attendance, fixed-length courses, and the need to live or work within daily travelling distance of college or training centre.

Flexibility is provided in 2 ways: by making entry requirements less rigid and by giving students a choice of study methods to fit in with their work or domestic commitments. For example, *distance-learning* courses have been steadily increasing in recent years. These are a kind of 'souped up' correspondence course with study by post being supplemented by audio and videotapes and/or computer programmes, plus personal or telephone contact with a tutor. One of the best-known providers is the National Extension College; over half of its students are women, studying because they need qualifications for career progression or to return to work or study. (NEC, 18 Brooklands Avenue, Cambridge CB2 2HN)

Accessibility partly depends on where courses are held – some areas are much better provided for than others. Students can generally enrol on open-learning courses at any time and work at their own pace. Many courses require attendance on 1 or 2 days a week or even less, making it possible for many more people to participate than in the past. The growth of multi-media provision and the potential offered by the Internet have given a boost to open learning and should open it up to many more people.

Open learning is increasingly used to train people who are in work. PICKUP is a Department of Education and Science programme which has been running for 10 years and enables colleges of all kinds to provide updating courses for employees, in collaboration with employers. Many of its training packages are designed for open learning, since many users can only study at home. Some TECs and LECs (see p. xxiii) support open-learning initiatives in response to local industry's needs.

The definition of the term 'open learning' is complicated by the fact that it refers both to a concept and to specific institutions and initiatives.

Open College Networks

These should not be confused with the Open University or the Open College. Open College Networks do not themselves run courses, but consist of groups of colleges which collaborate to provide accreditation for adult learning in their geographical area. This is carried out through a system of credits and levels (see CATS, p. xxxii). These can help individual learners plan their pathways through their local further and higher education system and, in many cases, enable them to have their achievements recognized by other Open College Networks. Although the 32 Networks differ in the way they work, they all adhere to a framework giving 4 levels of award, ranging from entry to A-level/NVQ level 3.

Further information   National Open College Network, University of Derby, Kedleston Road, Derby DE22 1GB

The Open College

The Open College is an independent, self-financing charity which provides open learning material. Its aims are encouraging employers to provide more effective training for their workforce, and helping individuals, both in and out of work, to gain work-related skills. Courses focus on 5 main areas: management and supervisory management; education and training; health care and nursing; technical and personal development; basic work skills. Many courses lead to NVQs (see p. xix). Of particular interest to women returners and job-changers are 'Moving into Management' and 'Moving On – Career Change and Development'. There is now a nationwide network of Preview Centres at further education colleges where employers and prospective students can find out details of courses. The Open College sells courses to employers and colleges, but not to individuals wanting to take courses.

Further information   Open College, St Paul's, 781 Wilmslow Road, Didsbury, Manchester M20 2RW

The Open College of the Arts

This was set up in 1987 to provide training in the arts by open-learning methods to people wishing to develop their artistic and creative abilities at home. It is affiliated to the Open University (see p. xxxiii). Courses currently available are in painting, drawing, sculpture, textiles, art and design, interior design, garden design, photography, creative writing, video production, music, singing, understanding Western art, understanding opera. The 2 main elements of a course are books, tapes and videos and tutorial support. Students can choose to study either by correspondence, with help and guidance from a personal tutor, or by face-to-face study, in which case they attend group tutorials at one of over 120 centres in England, Wales, Scotland and Ireland. Many tutors are based in colleges and art centres, while others are practitioners with an interest in teaching. Optional summer schools, life classes, visits, etc., are arranged by many tutors.

Courses do not at present lead to recognized qualifications, but students on many of the courses who so wish may be assessed for an OCA award. Negotiations with universities for academic credits are in progress. The OCA can be particularly useful for people who think they might want to work in the arts, but need to test their abilities and build up a portfolio, including those who have to study at home because of domestic circumstances.

Further information

Open College of the Arts, Houndhill, Worsborough, Barnsley, South Yorkshire S70 6TU

The Open Learning Foundation

This was set up in 1990 by 20 former polytechnics as the Open Polytechnic. When these became universities the title changed to the Open Learning Foundation, but its mission remained the same: to increase the accessibility of higher education to individuals, companies and public sector organizations by improving flexible learning. It now has nearly 30 members, including 25 universities. The Foundation does not itself enrol students or award diplomas or degrees. It provides a service and encourages universities to develop their approaches to flexible learning mainly by producing study packs and learning resources; developing new teaching and learning methods; conducting feasibility studies on the application of open learning in particular subjects and occupations; staff development; creating local open learning centres, including an EU-funded network of EuroStudy centres. Areas covered so far include health and nursing, social work, business studies, engineering, languages and management.

Further information

The Open Learning Foundation Group, 3 Devonshire Street, London W1N 2BA

Sex Balance in Employment and Training

Women account for about 46% of the workforce (1995). This figure increasingly includes married women who in 1994 made up 32% of the workforce, compared with 25% in 1981. Overall about 71% of women aged between 16 and 60 (1994) are 'economically active' (i.e. working or seeking work). Of these 55% work full-time, 45% part-time. 75% of those aged 30–49 and 71% of those between 20 and 29 are economically active. The proportion of women working and whether they do so full- or part-time varies with age and the ages of children (42% of all women of working age have dependent children). Of those with children 64% work, compared with 76% of those without children and 86% of all men of working age. The activity rate is 54% for those with children aged 0–4, 71% for those with youngest children aged 5–10 and 79% for those with youngest children aged 11–15.

Women working full- and part-time in main non-manual occupational groups (shown as a percentage of all employed women), September 1995

	Full-time	Part-time
Managers and administrators	17	6
Professional occupations	12	6
Associate professional and technical occupations	12	8
Clerical and secretarial occupations	29	20

(SOURCE: *Central Statistical Office Labour Force Survey.*

NOTE: occupational categories have changed since the last edition of the book, so direct comparison with the previous position cannot be made.)

There are several reasons for the steady growth in the proportion of women in the workplace. One may be the fact that they are marrying at a later age (average age 26 in England and Wales in 1993) and delaying starting their families (in 1992, for the first time, women in their early 30s were more likely to have a baby than women in their early 20s). Another reason may be the fact that young women are better educated than their mothers and grandmothers were: in 1993 over four-fifths of women aged 16–24 had some sort of educational qualification, compared with just over three-fifths of those in their 40s and just under half of those in their 50s. (SOURCES: *Labour Force Survey* and Central Statistical Office.) Just over 1 in 5 families with dependent children is headed by a lone parent, nearly always a mother (19% compared with 2% by fathers). This means that 1 in 10 women aged 20–50 is a lone parent.

According to official occupational groupings, women greatly outnumber men in catering, cleaning, hairdressing and other personal services, selling and clerical jobs. Roughly the same proportion of men and women is in manual jobs, but a far higher proportion of men is in craft or similar occupations. Because women tend to be concentrated in low-paid, low-skilled jobs, overall they still earn less than men (75% of their average weekly earnings).

However, the proportion of women in the managerial professional technical groups is creeping up (31%) in 1995. This reflects the growing number who are going through higher education and professional training, and is one of the reasons women are likely to do well if and when the labour market expands in the future. As it is, their unemployment rates are lower than men's. According to the 'Labour market and skills trends 1995/6' (a Department for Education and Employment publication) higher level occupations are growing fastest. Between 1993 and 2001 almost 1.7 million extra managerial, professional and technician level jobs are expected to appear and will comprise 39% of total employment (the figure was 35% in 1993). 11% of women work in sales, another area predicted to grow slightly. However, there will be a fall in the number of clerical and secretarial jobs, where 26% of working women are employed. The number of full-time jobs will continue to fall and that of part-time ones to rise, another factor benefiting women, who currently hold 84% of part-time posts. Men dominate self-employment: although women have increased their share from 10% in 1991 to 24% in 1995, this figure is expected to remain much the same for the rest of the 1990s.

Proportion of women in selected occupations

Institute of Chartered Accountants	Full members 15%	Student members 35%
Chartered Institute of Management Accountants	Full members 13%	Student members 37%
Institution of Civil Engineers	Full members below 1%	Student members 10·5%
Institution of Electrical Engineers	Full members below 1%	Student members 7·2%
Institution of Mechanical Engineers	Full members below 1%	Student members 6·6%
Medicine: general practitioners (principals)	29%	Entrants to medical
All consultants	18%	school 1994
All hospital doctors	29·5%	50%
Dentists, practising	30%	First-year students 46·7%
Optometrists	50%	First-year students Over 50%
Law: solicitors with practising certificates	29%	New traineeships 1993/4 53%
Barristers, practising	21·6%	Called to the Bar 1994 43·5%
QCs	5·9%	
Circuit judges	5·5%	
Royal Institution of Chartered Surveyors	Full members 14%	Student members 14%
Society of Surveying Technicians	Below 1%	
Architects, practising	8%	Students 30%
Veterinary surgeons	33%	Students 63%
Advertising account planners and researchers	41%	
Driving examiners	8%	
Directors of social services	21%	
Health service management:		
General and senior managers	42%	
Top managers	19%	
Local authority chief executives	4%	
Town planners: RTPI members	20%	Students 42%
Education:		
University professors	5%	
Readers and senior lecturers	12%	
University lecturers	27%	
Chief education officers	19%	
Primary heads	49·5%	
Secondary heads	22·5%	

Proportion of women in selected occupations (cont.)

Civil Service:	
Grades 1–3 (top grades)	9·3%
Administration trainees (high-flyer graduates)	43%

NOTE: Statistics on their own do not tell the whole story and can be misleading. These figures should be looked at in conjunction with the 'Position of women' sections in each chapter.

Sex Balance in Education

Absolute equality in education is essential if women are to be equal at work. For many years more girls than boys have achieved 5 or more A–C grades at O-level/GCSE, and a much greater proportion of girls goes on to further education. In recent years girls have caught up with boys at A-level, and in 1994 50% of accepted entrants to university were girls. In terms of level and number of qualifications, girls are doing well, so well that *boys'* under-achievement is now making news and causing concern.

However, if one looks at the subjects these new female under-graduates have opted for, the picture is anything but balanced. Girls still tend to opt for subjects which are much more competitive and/or much less vocationally relevant and in demand.

Proportion of women in various subjects, 1994 entry

Medicine	52
Subjects allied to medicine	75
Biological sciences	61
Chemistry	36
Physics	17
Mathematics	37
Civil engineering	13
Mechanical engineering	8
Electronic engineering	9
Languages and related	70
Accountancy	41
Business and management	50
Sociology	72
Economics	27
Law	54

Whatever subtle and insidious influences have been at work in terms of gender stereotyping, it is clear that many girls in the past did not opt for courses in the physical sciences and engineering because they could not: they did not have maths and physics at A-level, often because they had not laid the proper foundation at O-level/GCSE.

However, the implementation of the National Curriculum has meant that all pupils must now take maths, English and science; *and* the science syllabus must include chemistry, physics and biology. An early result is that, whereas girls previously lagged way behind boys in higher grade passes in physics and chemistry, they have now overtaken them in combined science.

It remains to be seen if, when and to what extent this will affect the A-level choices which open (or shut) doors later on. There is a long way to go. In 1993, of those getting A-levels, 14% of girls got a pass in maths, compared with 29% of boys; 5% of girls got a pass in physics, compared with 21% of boys.

Sex Discrimination Legislation

Brief Summary of Main Provisions Relating to Employment and Education

The *Sex Discrimination Act* 1975 makes it unlawful to treat anyone on the grounds of sex (and, in the case of employment, of marital status) less favourably than a person of the opposite sex.

Employment

The Act defines two kinds of discrimination:

Direct discrimination, e.g. sending boys but not girls on day-release courses when both are doing similar jobs; or *not* promoting the person next in line because she is a woman (or a man).

Indirect discrimination: applying the same conditions to both sexes which favour one sex rather than the other but are not justified. For example if an employer, when recruiting an *office* manager, demands that the candidate must have served a *technical* apprenticeship, he or she is discriminating against women because they are far less likely to have served such an apprenticeship – which is irrelevant to the job to be done; or if an employer only recruits people aged 20–30, it indirectly discriminates against women who are likely to rear children during those years.

The Act's main exemptions – as amended by the Sex Discrimination Act 1986 – apply:

1. To employment in private households where the job involves living or working in a private house where there could be a reasonable objection to someone of the other sex having physical or social contact with a person living in the house, or knowledge of intimate details of that person's life.

2. Where sex is a genuine occupational qualification e.g. in acting or modelling.

3. Where one sex is required for reasons of decency, e.g. for certain jobs in an Asian all-women's hostel.

4. In certain jobs providing care and/or supervision.

5. To jobs which genuinely involve work abroad in countries where women in such jobs are not acceptable. However, if, for

example, an employer persistently employs men because he or she claims the job *might* take them to a country where women are unacceptable, but in fact few male employees are sent to such countries, the employer would be illegally discriminating.

6. To the Churches, competitive sport and charities.

The Equal Pay Act

The Equal Pay Act stipulates equal treatment as well as equal pay for the same or broadly similar work where a woman's job has been rated as equivalent or of equal value to a man's under an existing job evaluation scheme. It covers all conditions and benefits contained in a contract of employment, e.g. holiday entitlement, access to pension schemes and the payment of bonuses.

Maternity rights, under the amended Employment Protection Act, 'Main Provisions', in force since February 1995

All women, irrespective of length of service or hours of work, are now entitled to 14 weeks' maternity leave. If they have at least 2 years' continuous service with one employer, they are entitled to up to 40 weeks' absence. It is unlawful to dismiss a woman, irrespective of her length of service or hours of work, for any reason connected with her pregnancy. For details/advice, contact the Maternity Alliance, 15 Britannia Street, London WC1X 9JN.

Positive action

Positive Action covers single-sex education or training for women only or men only to help them reach equality in the workplace if such equality does not at present exist. It also covers assertiveness training for women as well as courses or workshops to widen women's career horizons and to help 'returners' update their skills, and knowledge of the present-day job market. PA initiatives may be taken by any person or organization (i.e. not only education and training bodies), as long as certain criteria are met.

Disappointingly little use has so far been made of the 'positive action' provision. Few women probably know that they could press for 'catching-up' courses and training.

Complaints concerned with employment matters are dealt with by Industrial Tribunals. (Leaflets setting out rights and procedures in full are available from Jobcentres.)

Education

Discrimination is unlawful in admission to and provision of education facilities in both the public and private sectors. A few exceptions relate to establishments which are single-sex. All

other classes and establishments must be open to all pupils/
students regardless of sex. Girls who want to take computing, and
boys who want to do cooking, must not be discouraged; medical
schools may not operate a quota system, etc.

It is discriminatory not only to refuse entry, but also, for
example, gently to persuade girls not to choose physics or craft,
design and technology where laboratory and workshop facilities
are restricted, and instead let them take biology, which is less
useful later. It is also discriminatory to give boys more chance of
work-experience schemes than girls, or to differentiate between
the kind of schemes offered (e.g. to arrange that all girls work in
hospitals once a week, all boys in engineering works).

Careers staff have a duty to ensure that girls are fully aware of
all the opportunities, including the non-traditional ones, which
are open to them.

As sex balance in education figures (see p. xliii) show, changes
in boys' and girls' exam subject choices are not encouraging.
While the letter of the law is observed, in many schools the spirit
of the Act is ignored.

Further information and advice

Equal Opportunities Commission, Overseas House, Quay Street,
Manchester M3 3HN
EOC, Stock Exchange House, 7 Nelson Mandela Place, Glasgow
G2 1QW
EOC, Caerwys House, Windsor Lane, Cardiff CF1 1LB
Most trade unions, professional bodies and women's groups.

Working in Europe

The Treaty of Rome guarantees the freedom for every EU citizen to work, to seek work, to set up business or to provide services in any EU member state. Community citizens may not be discriminated against on grounds of nationality. The impression often given by the media during the run-up to the introduction of the Single European Market in 1992 was that people from all member states would be free to work and to practise their professions anywhere in Europe. In fact, the situation is rather more complicated, as a member state is not obliged to recognize qualifications awarded in other member states. Undoubtedly, with the spread of multi-national companies, more people will spend part of their working lives with big companies abroad. Yet many professionals wishing to set themselves up in practice or to apply for comparable posts in other member states still face barriers. While 7 of the major professions – covering doctors, nurses, dentists, veterinary surgeons, midwives, architects and pharmacists – have agreed *'sectoral' Directives* making it easier for those covered to work anywhere in the EU, many more have not.

First General Directive

Having found the sectoral approach lengthy and difficult (it took 17 years for the architects to agree!), the EU decided to tackle the remaining professions by means of a General Directive based on the principle of mutual recognition of qualifications. This came into force in January 1991. It covers those professions 'to which access is in some way restricted by the State and which require at least three years' university-level education or equivalent plus any appropriate job-related training'. In the UK there are very few professions regulated by law or public authority (state school teachers and lawyers are examples), but for the purpose of the Directive those controlled by their own Chartered bodies are included, e.g. chartered accountants, engineers, physiotherapists, psychologists, surveyors. Only the Irish Republic implemented it by the deadline, followed by the UK and Denmark, then Spain and Portugal. Implementation throughout the EU (and some EFTA countries) is happening gradually.

Second General Directive

This has recently been agreed and covers occupations for which qualifications are gained in under 3 years. Among the UK qualifications recognized under this Directive are NVQs/SVQs levels 3 and 4. Further information from: Qualifications and ITOs Branch, Department for Education and Employment, Moorfoot, Sheffield S1 4PQ.

CEDEFOP

The European Centre for the Development of Vocational Training has been undertaking a separate exercise to enable qualifications in member states to be more readily compared. This involves agreeing job descriptions against which each country lists its own national qualifications. Comparability of qualifications held by skilled workers now exists in around 150 areas, including hotels, tourism, banking and insurance, transport, agriculture, printing and media.

Certificates of Experience

EU countries mutually recognize certain jobs and trades. People wishing to practise these in other member states have to apply for a Certificate of Experience (in the UK from the Department of Trade and Industry), which is then accepted by the other country in place of its own national qualifications. Included are those self-employed in wholesaling, retailing and food manufacturing, telecommunications, insurance agents and brokers, hairdressers and people providing various services.

This section is only a guide – interested individuals must make inquiries from the Department of Trade and Industry, Internal Union and Trade Relations Division, 123 Victoria Street, London SW1E 6RB.

Sources of Help

Careers Advisory Services

The main source of information and guidance for young people is the careers service. Recent legislation has transferred the running of local careers services from local education authorities to a variety of organizations in both the public and private sectors, which means that the titles of services and their offices will vary. All have to provide a core range of free services to young people, but are free to offer additional services on a commercial basis.

The careers services are the best point of contact for information on initiatives such as youth credits and Modern Apprenticeships, as well as advice on further and higher eduction and career choice. Some careers services also provide guidance for adults.

Universities and colleges/institutes of higher education have their own guidance services tailored to the needs of their students and graduates. As well as information on local courses and career opportunities they provide a vast amount of national information produced by AGCAS (Association of Graduate Careers Advisory Services). Students of all ages are advised to make early contact with their service.

EGSAs (Educational Guidance Services for Adults)

For many years most areas have had local independent advice centres aimed mainly at adults of all ages from all educational backgrounds. Their role has been to give free information on national and local educational and training opportunities and some offer careers counselling. Most belong to the National Association for Educational Guidance for Adults, which has worked to increase the provision and quality of adult guidance.

Although independent adult guidance services still exist in some areas, recent changes to the careers services and the various funding systems mean that in many other areas this work is carried out by careers companies (former careers services), training/new start information shops or advisers based at local colleges.

It is advisable, wherever possible, to seek out an *independent* source of guidance, one which is not attached solely to one college or provider of training and which may be mainly concerned with recruiting students.

The local careers service, TEC/LEC or reference library should have information on what guidance services are available locally and whether they are free or charge fees. Alternatively, to find out the nearest available adult guidance centre, send s.a.e. to Anne Docherty, Secretary NAEGA, 1A Hilton Road, Milngavie, Glasgow G62 7DN.

Some Useful Sources of Reference

Many of those sources listed below are available in careers libraries and reference libraries. A few are too expensive for most
individuals to buy, while others may be worth investing in and
may be ordered through bookshops. There is a growing number
of computer programmes providing help with career decisions,
occupational information and course choice, and many careers
services, schools, colleges and universities will have these available
for use by clients.

Higher and Further Education Information

ECCTIS 2000, a national computerized service owned by the
Department for Education and Employment, provides information on nearly 100,000 award-giving courses in higher and further
education institutions in the UK. Users are led through a sequence
of questions to identify the type of course they are interested in –
subject(s), type of course, type of institution, method of study,
location, etc. ECCTIS then displays details of relevant courses.
ECCTIS is on CD-ROM and is in several computer versions. It
also has databases containing the *Potter Guide* (see below) and
PICKUP (see p. xxxvi). ECCTIS also provides information on
CATS (see p. xxxii), on vacancies on first degree and HND courses
during the summer 'clearing' period, and on vacancies on PGCE
courses (see p. 522) all year. ECCTIS is available in most secondary schools and in colleges, careers services, adult guidance
centres, libraries, TAPs (see p. xxix) and British Council Offices.
Further information from ECCTIS 2000 Ltd, Fulton House,
Jessop Avenue, Cheltenham, Glos. GL50 3SH

University and College Entrance: Official Guide, published
   annually by the Universities and Colleges Admissions Service
   (UCAS).
'Stepping up': a Mature Student's Guide to Higher Education, free
   from UCAS.

The Herald Entrance Guide to Higher Education in Scotland, published annually by the Committee of Scottish Higher Education Principals.

LASER Compendium of Higher Education, vols. 1 and 2, published annually by London and South-East Regional Advisory Council (LASER).

Degree Course Guides, published by Hobsons. Compare individual courses within disciplines.

Which degree, 4 vols. covering a group of related study areas; and *Which university*, a guide to institutions; both published by Hobsons.

The Potter Guide to Higher Education, published by Dalebank Books. Does not include course information, but gives profiles of universities and colleges.

The PUSH Which University Guide, published by PUSH, McGraw-Hill Companies, Wimbledon Bridge House, 1 Hatfield Road, London SW19 3RU. Gives profiles of universities and colleges and a picture of student life.

The Natwest Student Book, published by Macmillan. Contains facts as well as opinion on subjects of study and institutions.

The European Choice: a guide to opportunities for higher education in Europe, free from Department for Education and Employment, Publications Centre, PO Box 2193, London E15 2EU.

SOCRATES/ERASMUS the UK Guide. Lists more than 500 degree and diploma subjects at UK institutions which include study in other EU institutions, from ISCO Publications, 12A Princess Way, Camberley, Surrey GU15 3SP.

Sixth-former's Guide to Visiting Universities and Colleges. Lists open days and gives advice on what to ask and look out for on a visit. Also from ISCO Publications (see above).

The ISCO Directory of Independent Further Education, a guide to courses in a wide range of vocational subjects at private colleges, also from ISCO Publications (see above).

Directory of Further Education, published annually by Hobsons. Lists full- and part-time vocational courses at all levels outside universities.

Careers Information

Occupations, published annually by COIC, PO Box 348, Bristol BS99 7FE.

'Working in' series of booklets on individual career areas, also published by COIC.

Careers Encyclopedia, published by Cassell.

AGCAS (Association of Graduate Careers Advisory Services)

publishes a series of regularly updated booklets covering most
graduate career areas.

*Working Abroad: Daily Telegraph Guide to Working and Living
Overseas*, by Godfrey Golzen, published by Kogan Page.

Especially for Job-Changers and Late Starters

Second Chances, published by COIC, PO Box 348, Bristol BS99
7FE. A comprehensive guide to education and training at all
levels.

*Mature Students' Handbook: getting into higher education for
mature students*, published by Trotman.

*Returning to Work: A Directory of Education and Training for
Women*, published annually for the Women Returners' Network, 8 John Adam Street, London WC2N 6EZ.

*Manage Your Own Career: A self-help guide to career choice and
change*, published by Kogan Page.

Major careers publishers include Hobsons, Kogan Page, Trotman,
COIC, How to Books. Check catalogues for current
publications.

For details of Scottish examination equivalents to GCSE and A-level, see p. xix.

Accountancy

Professional Accountant

Entry qualifications

At least 2 A-levels and 3 GCSEs (A–C) including maths and English language. Over half the total entrants (more than 90% of chartered accountants, 30% certified and 60% public finance) are *graduates* (any discipline). (See also 'Accounting Technician' route below, p. 8.)

In Scotland, all entrants to chartered accountancy aged under 25 must be graduates.

The work

The image of accountants as deskbound figure-crunchers is quite wrong. An accountancy qualification leads to a vast variety of jobs, in virtually any environment: manufacturing industry or television; retail or merchant banking; professional consultancy; public service. There is scope for accountants interested in the intricacies of accounting procedures and their technological development, or in high finance, or as a way into general management, and also for people who intend to become entrepreneurs. (See WORKING FOR ONESELF, p. 551.)

There is a vast variety of jobs in all types and sizes of business and public enterprise. An accountancy qualification is also an excellent preparation for jobs in merchant and other banking, insurance and the City.

There are some opportunities for employment (but *not* in public practice) in the EC, and in most other countries.

Work falls broadly into three categories:

1. *Public* (illogically also called 'private') *practice*.
2. *Industrial/commercial accountancy*.
3. *Public sector accountancy*.

Public Practice Accountants

They work in firms of partners. They are consultants, and employ qualified assistants, trainees and technicians (see below). Firms vary in size from 1 to several thousand, and in type from high-powered international practices which deal mainly with large companies and are at the very centre of the country's commercial activities, to small suburban practices which function at a gentler pace and deal mainly with private clients and local 'small traders'. Normally each accountant deals with particular clients' affairs so that there is personal (at least written or telephone) contact with individuals.

As the financial scene becomes ever more complex, accountants now often specialize in one particular accountancy aspect; for example, taxation, computer systems, mergers, corporate finance. However, the bulk of public practice work is taxation and accounting-service auditing. Auditing means analysing and verifying clients' books and ensuring that the annual balance sheet presents a 'true and fair' picture of the client's financial affairs. Auditing is done on clients' premises so it involves meeting people and possibly travelling. Audits take anything from a few hours to several months, depending on the client's size and type of business. Audits may be done in streamlined offices using the latest technologies, or it may mean having to create order out of chaos when, for example, a farmer's 'office' consists of a drawerful of bills. Auditing is largely desk-work (or desk-top computer work), but it also involves discussions with clients – anyone from clerk to managing director – if specific items in the books are not clear. Apart from auditing and making suggestions about how to improve their systems and procedures, accountants also advise their clients on personal and business financial matters, from how to invest a small legacy to setting up a business or liquidating one. Large accountancy firms provide *management consultancy* services (see MANAGEMENT CONSULTANCY, p. 291).

Industrial and Commercial Accountants

They work for an employer on a salaried basis. They can be divided into *financial* accountants, concerned largely with internal audits, taxation, wage and salary structure, financial record-keeping; and *management* accountants. This is a fast-growing accountancy specialization (and it overlaps with management consultancy). Management accountants assess the relative importance, value and cost of all aspects of a business (or public enterprise), labour, raw materials, transport, sites, administration, marketing, etc. Every person's, machine's, department's, vehicle's, etc., contribution to the effectiveness of an organization, and their interdependence, can, with the help of computer systems and mathematical models, be assessed separately and as part of the whole operation. Management accountants might, for example, compare the relative cost of using a cheap new raw material which would necessitate more expensive machine maintenance and require mounting a marketing campaign to launch the changed product, against the cost of going on using the more expensive traditional raw material – taking into account, among other factors, what the competition abroad might do, and how staff would feel about the change. Or they might assess the cost of moving a factory to a cheaper site, considering increased transport cost, recruiting and training new staff. Like management consultants, their work requires interviewing all the people whose work affects the efficiency of the organization concerned. Having compared the financial results of alternative courses of action, management accountants present the information to the decision-makers at the top of the organization.

Because management accountants take part in decision-making and business control they need a broader understanding of business organization in general and of the type of business with which they are concerned than do financial accountants. They often move into consultancy sections of auditing firms, or into *management consultancy* (see p. 291).

Public Sector Accountants

Accountants and auditors working in local and central government, the health service, and national audit and other public service bodies are, like industrial and commercial accountants, concerned with all aspects of financial management. The emphasis of their work is on the efficient and effective use of funds and the need for public accountability.

In the 1990s public service organizations are becoming more commercially orientated. Involvement in the management of change, e.g. contracting out of services, and advising on alternative options for the use of limited funds are important aspects of the finance manager's job. Work in the national audit bodies involves auditing public income and expenditure, certifying accounts and carrying out value-for-money studies.

Companies providing services to the public sector increasingly seek to recruit public service accountants and auditors. Significant numbers of finance managers become top-level general managers.

Training   There are 6 main professional qualifications, each awarded by a different body:
1. Institute of Chartered Accountants in England and Wales.
2. Institute of Chartered Accountants of Scotland.
3. Institute of Chartered Accountants in Ireland.
4. Chartered Association of Certified Accountants.
5. Chartered Institute of Management Accountants.

6. Chartered Institute of Public Finance and Accountancy.

The differences between the syllabuses are small – there is a core element of accountancy knowledge which all accountants must master – but emphasis varies.

Accountancy courses all cover economics; statistics; computer applications and systems; corporate finance; financial management; taxation; trustee work; share organization; management accounting; relevant law; EC accountancy implications; auditing. The emphasis on different aspects of accountancy differs in the various professional bodies' examinations; some syllabuses overlap more than others. The reason for the existence of several accountancy bodies is historical rather than logical and merger proposals are currently being considered.

It is generally believed that chartered accountants get all the best jobs, or indeed that all qualified accountants are 'chartered'. But that is not so at all. The various qualifications, with the exception of (6), are equally marketable. Choice of one qualification rather than another only partly depends on the ultimate career aim: it also depends on what training is available locally; and on the type of training method preferred.

Main differences in various qualifications' usefulness in the job-market

Only appropriately qualified *chartered* and *certified* accountants may, by law, become registered auditors and audit limited companies' accounts. People who want to go into public practice must therefore choose one of these two qualifications. *Chartered* and *certified* accountants can also go into industry and commerce and the public sector so these two qualifications leave the widest range of options open. (More than half of all qualified accountants work in industry and commerce.)

Management accountants are the most commercial and profit-orientated. This training concentrates more on running a business and planning its future than do the others. So people who definitely want to go into industry/commerce might choose this qualification. They too can choose to work in the public sector.

The Chartered Institute of Public Finance and Accountancy qualification differs from the others in that it is specifically tailored to the very large amount of work in the public sector – public utilities; National Health Service; local and central government.

Training methods vary between the various bodies, and they are complicated. (Candidates should read carefully all the accountancy bodies' training literature.)

All non-graduates may be required to take a 'Foundation

course', usually at university. The Foundation course syllabus covers accountancy principles, law, economics, statistics, computer applications.

The essential differences between the various bodies' training methods are:

Institute of Chartered Accountants

Students enter a training contract (3 years for graduates, 4 for non-graduates, including BTEC/SCOTVEC HND/C holders) with a firm of chartered accountants or (a recent change) an approved (by the ICA) industrial or commercial organization (including some civil service departments). In England and Wales graduates with a relevant degree take 2 professional examinations; 'non-relevant' graduates and non-graduates first take a 'conversion' course (15 weeks full time, or 7–8 months combined block-release and evening classes or correspondence course) for a Foundation stage exam. A new option allows students qualifying for exemption from the Foundation stage to take the Intermediate examination before entering a training contract. Trainees are given broad practical training in all the main aspects of the work. Larger firms have their own in-house training scheme, smaller ones may join with others in a training consortium. Theoretical study is done mainly in the student's own time and is hard work. In Scotland trainees are given block release throughout training for classes. The Scottish Institute's qualification comprises a professional examination (with exemptions for those with fully accredited degrees) and 2 tests of professional competence.

Chartered Association of Certified Accountants

Training is the most flexible. Students do not have to enter into training contracts but can train while in salaried employment by various part-time methods. Alternatively, they can study for the exams full time and get practical experience afterwards. They may change employers, and type of employer, during their training and thus can get varied experience. They need not make up their mind at the outset whether they wish to go into industry/commerce or into public practice. 3 years' training in an Approved Training Practice is obligatory for those who ultimately want to become Registered Auditors in public practice. Training – called 'relevant accountancy experience' – takes 3–4 years depending on educational qualifications and method of training. This experience can be gained before, during or after passing the professional exams. Exams leading to Associate Membership (ACCA) are at 3 levels. Those with a relevant degree or a foundation course may be exempt from all or part of level 1 and some HND/HNC holders may have partial exemption. Some exemptions for certain graduates and SCOTVEC HNC/D holders are available at level 2. Study can be full time, by day- or block-release, evening classes or correspondence courses, or by the Association's own Open Learning system. Certified accountancy students are not automatically entitled to study leave, but many companies offer it. About 40% of all UK accountancy students now choose certified accountancy.

Chartered Institute of Management Accountants

To gain Associate membership, CIMA students need a minimum of 3 years' relevant practical experience and pass 4 stages of examinations. They can gain the practical experience before or after passing the examinations and they can be working in a variety of business areas, including public and private sectors, industry and commerce. They may change employers during this period. CIMA exams are in 4 stages, each covering 4 subjects. There is a strong bias towards information systems, and topics include: strategic financial management, strategic management accountancy and marketing, and organizational management and development. Students qualified above the minimum entry level may be given exemptions from parts of the syllabus. The method of study chosen will depend on the employer and the student: options include full-time, part-time, evening, weekend and correspondence courses.

Chartered Institute of Public Finance and Accountancy

CIPFA's recently revised education and training scheme incorporates a Foundation stage. Students with an accountancy degree or an NVQ in Accounting at level 4 (see Accounting Technician training, p. 9) are exempt from this stage. CIPFA students must be employed in a public service finance post with an approved employer. They follow a structured practical experience scheme integrated with theory studied through open learning packages. The whole scheme takes between 3 and 6 years to complete. Both the syllabus and work experience reflect the increasingly commercial focus of public service and the need for financial management skills.

Personal attributes   Academic ability; numeracy; ability to speak and write concisely; business sense; logical mind; ability to negotiate without self-consciousness with people at all levels within an organization; tact in dealing with employers and clients; a liking for desk work. Training demands determination, motivation and staying-power.

Accountants in public practice: A confidence-inspiring manner; ability to put things clearly to lay people.

Industrial/commercial accountancy: Ability to communicate with and extract information from people at all levels of intelligence and responsibility; enjoyment of decision-making.

Public sector accountancy: Ability to advise and explain financial matters to councillors and other public sector representatives.

Late start No significant GCSE/A-level concessions, but individual cases judged on merit. It may be difficult to find training vacancies, but there are opportunities, particularly for people willing to undertake preparatory study (see 'Training', p. 3). Approximately 12% of the ICAEW student intake in 1993/94 was over 25.

Career-break Should be no problem for ICA and ACCA members. There are lectures and journals which help to keep accountants up to date with developments. Some reduced professional membership subscriptions. It is possible to work in most parts of the country and also to run a small practice from home. More difficult with other two bodies but possible if well established first. CIPFA has a Career Break membership category and has helped promote equal opportunity policies among CIPFA employers.

Part time Opportunities increasing especially in public practice. Job-sharing should be possible. Part-time training contracts may be possible.

Position of women Proportions are still surprisingly low:

	Qualified Members	*Trainees*
Chartereds	15%	35%
Certifieds	20·4%	49%
CIMA	13%	34%
CIPFA	13%	37%

There is little prejudice in accountancy generally except perhaps in some City firms and at the top in local government (see LOCAL GOVERNMENT, p. 265). The reason for low proportions must be: (a) tradition (b) the image of accountancy as totally desk-bound work without contact with people and (c) the fact that fewer girls have taken GCSE maths. Yet accountancy training helps women to get into senior *management in industry* (see p. 275). A fair proportion have done extremely well in, for example, financial journalism, and some in *management consultancy* (see p. 291).

Further information

Institute of Chartered Accountants in England and Wales, PO Box 433, Chartered Accountants' Hall, Moorgate Place, London EC2P 2BJ

Institute of Chartered Accountants of Scotland, 27 Queen Street, Edinburgh EH2 1LA

Institute of Chartered Accountants in Ireland, 11 Donegal Square South, Belfast BT1 5JE

The Chartered Association of Certified Accountants, Student Recruitment, 29 Lincoln's Inn Fields, London WC2A 3EE

The Chartered Institute of Management Accountants, 63 Portland Place, London W1N 4AB

The Chartered Institute of Public Finance and Accountancy, 3 Robert Street, London WC2N 6BH

Related careers

ACTUARY – BANKING – CHARTERED SECRETARY – COMPUTING – INSURANCE – MANAGEMENT – PURCHASING AND SUPPLY – SCIENCE: *Statistics* – TAX INSPECTOR

Accounting Technician

Entry qualifications

There are no prescribed entry requirements for the Association of Accounting Technicians' Education and Training scheme, but students are advised that they need reasonable numeracy and literacy skills in order to cope with the qualifications.

The work

There is no legal requirement for accountants to be professionally qualified; 'accountant' is not a 'protected title' in the way 'solicitor' or 'architect' is. This 'second tier' technician qualification was created because there is so much accountancy work which while being highly responsible and requiring expertise and training, does not require the breadth of *professional* accountancy education (see above, p. 3).

Broadly, professional accountants conduct audits (which technicians are not empowered to do) and deal with high-powered financial management and advice, etc.; accounting technicians collect the information on which professional accountants base their decisions, and deal with straightforward accountancy. This involves more desk-work than does professional accountancy, but it also involves contact with clients.

The vast majority of accounting technicians work in professional accountants' offices or under the direction of professional accountants in industry, commerce or the public sector. However, some are 'sole' or 'company' accountants in firms too small to warrant employing a professional accountant, and some accounting technicians set up on their own, dealing with private clients' (individuals, shopkeepers, etc.) VAT, income tax and similar matters. Some keep small firms' books and visit such clients at regular intervals on a contract basis. Others put advertisements in local papers and do 'one-off' jobs for people who need some straightforward accountancy advice, or help with tax returns. So accounting technicians can choose whether to take on secure employment and do mainly desk-work, or to have contact with a variety of clients and be their own boss (see WORKING FOR ONESELF, p. 551).

AAT members who want to become professional accountants (see above) normally get exemption from at least the professional accountancy bodies' (see above) Foundation examinations.

Training   The AAT has introduced a new 'competence-based' scheme in 3 stages: Foundation, Intermediate and Technician. (At Technician stage students will specialize in either accounting practice, industry and commerce or the public sector.) These are accredited as NVQs/SVQs in accounting at levels 2, 3 and 4 (see p. xix).

Personal   A methodical approach; liking for figure, computer and desk-
attributes   work. There is room in this work for those who prefer to work on their own but with limited responsibility as support staff to more highly qualified/experienced colleagues, and for those who, though unable to take the professional examination, wish to do responsible work and have contact with colleagues and clients. For AAT members who want to set up on their own: confidence-inspiring manner; self-confidence; ability not to worry as work may be sporadic rather than regular (see WORKING FOR ONESELF, p. 551).

Late start   Very good scope for various kinds of older entrants such as unqualified but experienced accountancy staff, returners to office occupations, mid-career changers. Older people with relevant experience or knowledge may be exempted from some AAT examinations.

Career-   Unlikely to present any problems as long as people keep up with
break   changes in taxation and other accountancy matters. Evening classes and correspondence courses (including Open University) can act as *refresher* training. Reduced membership subscriptions for those on maternity break.

Part time   Very good scope, both in employment and working on one's own. Job-sharing should be possible.

Position of women	Women are doing well as accounting technicians, both in employment and working on their own. In 1994 40% of Members and 61% of newly registered Student Members were women.
Further information	Association of Accounting Technicians, 154 Clerkenwell Road, London ECIR 5AD

Related careers	BANKING – INSURANCE – PURCHASING AND SUPPLY – SHIP-BROKING . . . EXPORTING – STOCK EXCHANGE AND SECURITIES INDUSTRY

Actuary

Over 90% *graduate* entry, most graduates have degrees in a mathematical subject.

For school leavers:

England and Wales: 2 A-levels, one of which must be at least grade B in a maths subject, the other at least grade C, and 3 GCSEs (A–C) or equivalent including English.

Scotland: 3 H-grade passes including maths (grade A) and English.

The work   Actuaries use the theory of probability and the theory of compound interest together with statistical techniques to highlight and solve financial problems; to suggest appropriate courses of action and to predict the financial implications of such actions. In other words, they 'work out the odds'. Their work has a strong mathematical bias and is essentially desk-work performed in a variety of settings. Some 60% of actuaries work for insurance offices, concentrating on the technical side of life assurance and pension funds, investigating such matters as relative life expectancies of various groups in the population, and assessing the effects of life-styles and characteristics on premiums and policies and investment. In other insurance branches – accident, fire, motor – actuaries assess risks and pin-point variables in the light of changing conditions and life-styles, and advise on reserves necessary to cover long-term liabilities. In government departments actuaries advise on public service pensions and insurance scheme. Though they are concerned with various aspects of people's lives and welfare (cushioning the effects of old age, accident, sickness which are the reasons for insurance schemes), actuaries do not usually have much contact with people outside their own office.

About 30% of actuaries work in consultancy. Much of their work involves advising clients, usually about pension funds, but they also advise insurance companies too small to have their own actuarial department, or give specialist advice to large insurance companies.

There are also openings in merchant banks, the Stock Exchange and other financial institutions, as well as some limited opportunities (usually to do with pensions) in industry and commerce.

Actuaries can go into middle and higher business management, especially in life assurance companies and pension funds.

Training *For school-leavers*: On-the-job training (minimum 3 years) plus 6–7 years' part-time study (mainly by correspondence) and discussion classes for Institute of Actuaries' (England and Wales) or Faculty of Actuaries' (Scotland) examinations. Employers may give time off for daytime study, but considerable evening work is necessary too. The syllabus includes actuarial mathematics, economics and finance, statistics, life insurance, general insurance, pensions and investment and asset management.

For graduates: On-the-job training and 3–5 years' (depending on degree subject) part-time study as above. A good degree in mathematics, statistics or economics qualifies a student for exemption from some early parts of the professional examinations. A first degree or post-graduate diploma (1 year full time, 2 years part time) in actuarial subjects can lead to further exemptions.

Personal attributes Liking for concentrated desk-work; an analytical brain (actuaries tend to be good and devoted bridge-players); probing curiosity; pleasure in solving complicated problems; ability to interpret and express in clear English results of mathematical and statistical analysis; business sense.

Late start Only advisable for very able mathematicians because of the long training; also difficulty in finding training posts.

Career-break Possible for experienced actuaries who have kept up with developments, especially relevant legislation and data processing application (see p. 138). Temporarily retired members pay a reduced subscription which nevertheless entitles them to receive all journals and attend meetings. Correspondence courses can be adapted to form *refresher* courses.

Part time In theory work could be done part time, and by job-sharers or freelances; in practice no concentrated attempts to organize this seem to have been made by prospective part-timers.

Position of women Women comprise only 10% of fully qualified members of the Institute of Actuaries; but 30% of student members are women, so the proportion is going up. (The figures in Scotland are lower.) No special difficulties getting jobs and promotion.

Further information	Institute of Actuaries, Napier House, 4 Worcester Street, Gloucester Green, Oxford OX1 2AW
	The Faculty of Actuaries, 40/44 Thistle Street, Edinburgh EH2 1EN

Related careers	ACCOUNTANCY – BANKING – CIVIL SERVICE – INSURANCE – STOCK EXCHANGE AND SECURITIES INDUSTRY

Advertising

Entry qualifications
No rigid requirements; in practice usually at least A-level English. Most entrants are now *graduates*.
Graphic design, typography, etc., require art-school training (see ART AND DESIGN, p. 54).

The work
Advertising specialists work in:
1. Agencies.
2. Company advertising departments.
3. The media and for suppliers of advertising services (e.g. studios, film production, market research).

Agencies

Agencies plan, create and place advertisements on behalf of advertisers who appoint them to handle their 'account'. This may be a detergent, a package holiday, government information, or financial services. Only 40% of advertising expenditure is concerned with persuading people to *buy*; advertisements are also used to get money for charities, votes for political parties, support for legislation, to encourage energy saving or investment, to fill jobs.

Agencies vary in size and scope. A very few employ up to 500 people, most under 50. Some specialize: for example, in business-to-business or recruitment advertising. The largest agencies have a range of specialist services 'in house' such as package design (see p. 57), film production (see TELEVISION, FILM AND RADIO, p. 526), market research and marketing (see pp. 16, 297) and public relations (see p. 412). Others buy services in from outside suppliers.

Account Executive/Account Planner

Agency staff work in groups on individual accounts. Responsible for each account group of specialists are *account executives*. They are usually in charge of several accounts, each dealing with a different product, and are the link between clients and agency. They must acquaint themselves thoroughly with each client's product: this may involve working with a planner (see below) to identify the 'target group' (the people at whom the advertisement is to be aimed); to investigate the competition's product; to ensure the client's claims for the product can be substantiated. After the initial research, the group decide on a 'campaign theme', then the account executive discusses it with the client. When the brief and the budget are agreed, work on 'creating the advertisements' starts.

The account executives coordinate the work, control the budget and present progress reports to the client. Their work involves travelling if clients are scattered over the country or abroad.

Some agencies split the job into *account executives* and *account planners*. The executives' main responsibility is liaison with the client; the planners' with organizing and interpreting research into consumer attitudes and developing the strategy on which the advertising will be based.

The executives' job requires self-confidence and diplomacy, as clients often have to be persuaded that the type and tone of a campaign suggested by the agency will be more effective than the client's own idea. Planners' jobs tend to be more strategic and intellectual in approach.

Media Executive and Buyer

Media planners' jobs are crucial to the success of any campaign. In consultation with account handlers and creative staff they work out how best to spend the available budget in order to generate most sales/influence. They choose the channels of communication – newspapers, magazines, radio, television, posters and so on – which are most appropriate for any particular campaign and reach the target group most economically. Media planning decisions are based on information and statistics provided by *media research*. Computers are widely used to compare effectiveness and costs, but creative requirements – for colour, movement or sound – require subjective judgement.

Media buyers are responsible for the purchase of advertisement space or air time.

Planning, research and buying are the three media functions; they may be carried out by different people within the department, or the whole media operation may be the responsibility of a group of individuals assigned to a particular campaign.

Market Research (see also p. 297)

Before an advertising campaign is planned, facts are compiled about the product's uses, its advantages and limitations, competitors' products, distribution and so on. Facts and opinions are also gathered about its potential users – the target group: not just in terms of who they are, how much money they have and where they live, but in terms of their attitudes and behaviour. Some facts come from desk research, collecting information from a variety of published sources and the client's own records. Others may need specially commissioned research, ranging from statistics compiled by part-time interviewers questioning members of the public, to sophisticated behavioural studies involving trained psychologists.

Creative Department

Once the account group has been briefed and a strategy agreed with the client, the creative team of *copywriter* and *art director* together develop the advertisement.

The advertising 'message' is translated into a 'communication' that makes an instant impact on the target group. Words and pictures must complement each other.

Copywriters must be literate and imaginative, but they must choose their words under considerable constraints – from the disciplines of the brief and the restrictions of the space or time available, to the obligations of the Code of Advertising Practice and legal requirements. An interest in commercial success and an understanding of people's ways of life and priorities are far more useful than literary leanings.

Copywriters and art directors work with television producers and directors to create television and cinema commercials. There is no hard and fast rule about who exactly does what, and whether the visual or verbal aspect is the more important.

The *art director* is responsible for the visual appearance of advertisements, deciding whether to use photography, illustration, computer graphics or typography, and commissioning and supervising their production. The typographer chooses type which is easily readable, fits the layout and reflects the character of the product. The artist (only the larger agencies employ their own) may produce anything from a 'rough' to a finished 'visual' (see 'Graphics . . .', p. 57).

The atmosphere in agencies is often relaxed and informal, but the pace and pressure are very demanding indeed. The decline in the number of people in agencies means fierce competition for any openings. Considerable talent, the right kind of personality and commitment are needed to survive and succeed.

Advertisers

Many advertisers incorporate advertising into marketing (see p. 297). *Brand managers* are responsible for the marketing policy for a product, including its advertising. Relatively few have their own advertising departments, which vary in size. If a manufacturer creates and places all the advertising directly, the department may be much like a small agency. There is less scope for employees to work on different types of products simultaneously, but there may be a broader range of work.

Retailers' advertisement departments may deal with store and window displays, exhibitions, fashion shows, promotions and public relations, for example, using an advertising agency only for display advertisements.

Advertising departments are useful training grounds, giving experience in a range of work.

Media

The advertising departments of media owners are responsible for selling space or air time to advertisers, directly or through agencies. The *research section* provides information about readers or viewers; it helps advertisers pin-point target groups. The *promotions section* may have its own creative department, which works in three areas: projecting the medium to advertisers, to distributors, and to retailers on behalf of advertisers. *Sales representatives* are responsible for selling advertisement space or air time; this may include telephone selling, trying to get classified advertisements (which may involve having to put up with being rebuffed, and trying again). *Media managers* are responsible for ensuring that advertisements comply with the Code of Advertising Practice, which may involve checking copy claims and possibly asking for changes to be made before accepting copy.

*

Training   Considerable patience – apart from talent – is needed to get a job. Nearly three-quarters of jobs are in London. Once in, training is a combination of practice and theory. Agency policy varies concerning how far vocational qualifications listed below are looked for or encouraged and possession is no guarantee of a job.

Pre-entry training is not essential. The larger agencies tend to run in-service training schemes, sometimes supplemented by external courses. The Institute of Practioners in Advertising runs a phased programme of training courses designed to cater for the training needs of executives employed at IPA member agencies at each stage of their career development. Some agencies take several graduates (any discipline) each year; many advertisers have management training schemes which can lead to advertising jobs.

Secretaries occasionally progress to executive or copywriting positions; their chances are better with a small specialist agency (for example, a recruitment agency) or in an advertising department, but they are never great. Other ways into the industry are through production departments (see PUBLISHING, p. 415, and PRINTING, p. 395) and 'traffic control' (progress chasing – keeping the work flowing to schedule through all the different departments and processes).

Those wanting to take pre-entry course can choose from:

(a) A growing number of university courses – degrees and higher national diplomas – with a substantial advertising component.

(b) College Certificate (2 years), Diploma (1 year) and post-graduate Diploma (6 months) in advertising at West Herts College (formerly Watford College).

(c) Full-time, part-time or distance learning courses leading to the CAM Foundation's Certificate and Diploma (available at pre-entry stage or when in employment).

NVQs at levels 3 and 4 have been launched. These are jointly accredited by CAM and the RSA.

Personal attributes   Business acumen; interest in social and economic trends; flair for salesmanship; numeracy; communication skills; ability to work in a team; ability to stand criticism whether justified or not; ability to work under pressure; stamina; resilience; persistence; interest in popular culture.

For creative people: Discipline; originality; strong feeling for uncomplicated images and 'messages'; willingness to produce the kind of words/artwork that are best for the campaign, whether artistically first-rate or not.

For planning and research: Objectivity; a logical, analytical brain.

Late start   Little opportunity without previous relevant commercial experience.

Career-break   Prospects only reasonable for experienced planners or for successful executives who have 'kept their hand in' with freelance work.

Part time   Little opportunity.

Position of women   Although the majority of advertisements are aimed at women, until very recently their share of account executive positions was small. However, this has been steadily growing and in 1994 was 46%. Overall, women make up nearly half of agency staff and do particularly well in account planning/research (41%) and media (40%). An increasing number of brand managers (see MARKETING, p. 297) are women. They fare much worse as copywriters and art directors. Although the Women's Advertising Club keeps an eye on women's promotion, they have not been able to do much about unequal promotion at senior level. It is an area where discrimination is difficult to prove, as there is no career structure; promotion does not depend on qualification and experience but on 'suitability' for any particular job.

Further information   CAM Foundation, Abford House, 15 Wilton Road, London SW1V 1NJ

Institute of Practitioners in Advertising, 44 Belgrave Square, London SW1X 8QS

Related careers   MANAGEMENT – MARKETING AND SELLING – PUBLIC RELATIONS – RETAIL MANAGEMENT

Agriculture and Horticulture

Entry qualifications

Entry at all levels, from no qualifications to degree.

The work

Agriculture and horticulture cover a wide range of land-based industries, both traditional and, increasingly, non-traditional. Pig and poultry rearing, fish and deer farming, fruit, vegetable and flower growing, shooting, nature trails, wine-growing – these and many other activities make up an industry that in the last few years has been going through one of its biggest ever changes, more particularly on the agricultural side. This is due to a number of factors: increased efficiency leading to over-production, which in turn has led to the imposition of quotas on what a farmer can produce. Farmers' incomes have been dropping, which means fewer staff can be employed and more farmers and their families work part rather than full time. Smaller units are disappearing, while larger ones survive by becoming even more efficient. Numbers employed in general farm work have dropped dramatically and anyone looking to a career in farming in future must be prepared to develop good management and/or specialist skills. Bad publicity about chemical pollution, intensive farming and several food scares, plus pressures from a more health-conscious public, mean more farmers have been switching to less intensive, organic methods of production. All farmers are having to find other ways to use their resources, for example by diversifying into the tourism or recreation industries (e.g. bed and breakfast, golf driving ranges). About 40% of agricultural holdings now have at least one non-farming activity. This may not mean a big increase in income, and many farms are not suitable for such developments, but somehow farmers have to find ways of 'adding value' to their products or activities – perhaps making ice cream from surplus milk, or encouraging the public to 'pick your own' fruit. Government schemes to pay farmers to 'set aside' land from production and to subsidize the planting of woodlands are part of a movement towards seeing farmers not just as producers of food, but as custodians of the countryside.

Management posts in agriculture and horticulture are often held by people who started out in practical work and then became supervisors. Increasingly, though, qualifications such as HNDs and degrees are essential for such jobs as farm manager, unit manager, manager of a country park. As farms and horticultural units grow in size, the range but not the number of management jobs is increasing. A manager of, for example, an animal unit needs scientific, technological, veterinary, accounting, even computer knowledge. Marketing skills are increasingly in demand.

Research is usually concerned with a particular aspect of crop production or of animal husbandry. This could be concerned with pest control, plant disease, soil chemistry, genetics, nutrition, taste preservation (researchers work closely with technologists in the food industry – see 'Food Science and Technology', p. 462). Work may be wholly or largely theoretical, involving study of scientific journals and papers as well as collaboration with scientists from other disciplines. It often involves experimental work in the laboratory or in trial growing areas. Researchers work for research establishments, for botanical gardens, in industry, in the Civil Service (mainly the Ministry of Agriculture, Fisheries and Food (MAFF)).

Advisory work is carried out by government (through MAFF) and by commercial firms which supply agricultural and horticultural goods and equipment. Advice may be given on pest control, selection of the best variety of crop, choice of feed, marketing, finance, diversification.

Agriculture

The main branches of 'traditional' practical farm work are:

Animal Husbandry

Beef cattle: work varies according to size and type of farm. Some farms only rear calves, others fatten cattle through to slaughter.

Dairy cattle: a 100-cow herd can be worth a large sum of money, so this is highly responsible work. Tasks involve feeding, milking and following strict hygiene maintenance routines.

Pigs: Farms breed pigs for sale, or buy young pigs and fatten them for sale as bacon or pork, or they do both. Extent of automation varies.

Poultry: highly specialized holdings concentrate either entirely on egg production or on hatching chicks – often in fully automatic giant incubators – or on rearing table birds. Some poultry units resemble a cross between a laboratory and a modern factory, with indoor, clean work. Increased demand for free-range eggs means more scope for alternative forms of egg production, but there are still few farms where looking after poultry means feeding birds in the farmyard.

Sheep: hill farms usually concentrate on large flocks; on lowland farms sheep may form part of a unit and shepherds also do other work. Shepherds work with, and may train, dogs.

Working in Arable Crops

The wide variety of crops grown on British farms tends to be concentrated in the east of the country. Most arable work is highly mechanized, but requires considerable skill in operating and maintaining sophisticated machinery.

On the whole, the larger and/or more mechanized the farm, the greater the degree of specialization. Individuals need not stick to one specialization throughout their career, though some prefer to do so. Livestock workers are expected to drive tractors.

General Farm Work

People who do not want to specialize can carry out general duties, driving tractors, helping with livestock, repairing buildings, clearing ditches, etc. The range of jobs depends on the type and size of farm.

Horticulture

There are two main divisions: commercial – growing plants for sale – and amenity – making and maintaining gardens as pleasant environments. Horticulturalists, therefore, may work in different settings – as sole employee or as one of a large team; in the depths of the country or in the middle of a town.

Commercial Horticulture

This includes the production of fruit, vegetables, flowers, plants of all kinds in market gardens, nurseries, garden centres, greenhouses and fruit farms. Some sell directly to the public, while others sell only to other horticultural concerns. Some specialize in, for example, bulb production, soft fruit, cut flowers or house-plants. Others grow a wide variety of plants. Many tasks are now mechanized, but some are still done by hand – some pollination, disbudding, collecting seed, grafting, for example. Much effort now goes into producing strains that are disease-resistant and/or have a longer growing season (e.g. through genetic engineering). Computer systems are often used to control the environment in order to produce exactly the right conditions for different plants. Garden centres are a feature of most towns, offering pot-grown plants which customers can plant in their gardens at any time of year, plus a huge range of garden tools and accessories. Jobs in these offer the most contact with members of the public, who expect them to be knowledgeable. Experienced horticultural workers can become plantation assistants on fruit stations or quality inspectors for commercial canning and quick-freezing stations, or manage 'pick your own' farms (weekend work).

Amenity Horticulture

Its purpose is to provide pleasant open-air environments in town and country. It includes town and country parks; picnic areas off motorways; National Trust and similar properties; nature trails; theme parks; bowling greens; golf courses. It frequently involves nursery work and arboriculture (see 'Forestry', below). Staff have to cope with the sometimes conflicting demands of the gardening programme and events held in the park (e.g. open-air concerts). A park manager may spend a large proportion of time on such non-horticultural activities as paperwork and rubbish disposal. Current reductions in staffing levels often affect types of planting, e.g. bedding plants may give way to grass and shrubs. The work involves contact with the public and often helping with recreational activities, such as sitting at cash-desks for open-air concerts, usher and patrol duty, although in some parks these duties are carried out by keepers with no horticultural training (see also Diploma in Management Studies, under LEISURE/RECREATION MANAGEMENT, 'Training', p. 263). There may be more of a career structure (and day-release) in this type of horticulture than in commercial concerns.

Landscape and Garden Contractors

The work overlaps with landscape architecture (see p. 242) and amenity horticulture. It includes design and construction of new gardens and regular maintenance of existing gardens. Increasingly, contractors are employed by local authorities (and in future even by the Royal Parks) to maintain public gardens and parks.

*

Training   Although it may still be possible to get a job in farming and horticulture without going to college, there is much more chance of a proper career for those with formal training. Expertise and management skills are of increasing importance. The main training routes are:

Modern apprenticeships (see p. xxiv)
Available in some areas in agriculture and commercial horticulture.

NVQs/SVQs
Available in agriculture and horticulture at levels 1–4. Work-based training with part-time courses can lead to these; some full-time courses also lead to credits towards NVQs.

National Certificate route
National Certificate courses normally last 1 year full time. No set academic requirements, but students are required to have had 1 year's previous practical work, sometimes 2, on a farm or holding. (Youth Training, see p. xxiv, may be available.) Also, as competition for places is keen, those with some good GCSE grades or with other certificates, e.g. City and Guilds, have more chance of acceptance. Most NCs are in general agriculture or horticulture, but a few are specialized, e.g. in dairy farming or greenkeeping.

    Advanced National Certificate courses last 1 year and are specialized. Examples are agricultural mechanization, deer management, arable farm management, commercial fruit production. Some colleges offer a National Certificate in Farm Management – of a similar level to the ANC.

BTEC/SCOTVEC route (see pp. xxi, xxii)
BTEC National Diploma/SCOTVEC National Certificate courses can be in general agriculture or horticulture or specialized. Examples are game, wildlife and habitat management, fishery management, forestry, rural resource management, amenity horticulture. Higher National Diplomas (3-year sandwich) offer an alternative to a degree course for those looking for a career in practical farming or horticulture. A range of additional courses are available, mainly in new technologies, management and farm organization; these are especialy suitable for people who have spent some time working in the industry.

Degrees
3 or 4 years. Entry requirements normally include 1 or 2 sciences
at A-level. There is a wide variety of courses: examples of titles,
apart from general agriculture or horticulture, are crop science,
crop technology and resource management, agriculture and land
management, agricultural botany, agricultural and food marketing, agroforestry, animal production science. Little actual farm
work is included in degree courses, which are intended for future
advisers, researchers, teachers or managers. Entrants to full-time
courses are frequently required to have had 1 year's practical
experience. This is a good idea even where it is not obligatory.

Kew Diploma
3-year, degree-level course in amenity horticulture. Entry requirements are minimum 5 GCSEs, including English, maths and a
science, plus 2 A-levels, preferably in science subjects, plus at least
2 years' work in a 'recognized' horticultural establishment. A
small number accepted straight from sixth form.

Fringe Specializations

Forestry

This is a small specialization, although until recent tax changes
made it less attractive, commercial conifer planting had been
increasing. The Woodlands Grant Scheme is encouraging farmers
to plant trees instead of crops; and environmentalists would like
to see the planting of more hardwoods (which take a long time to
grow and attract a wide range of wildlife) and fewer conifers. In
commercial forestry trees are grown as a renewable resource and
harvested like any other crop. Other woodlands are maintained
for sporting or recreational purposes. Urban forestry is growing
in importance; known also as arboriculture, it covers the establishment, care and maintenance of trees for amenity purposes (see
'Amenity Horticulture', above).

Employers include the Forestry Commission, local authorities,
commercial companies that own forests all over the country,
co-operatives and individual landowners. There are opportunities to work abroad. Managers – senior forest officers – plan
afforestation programmes and may be in overall charge of a
single plantation, a group of forests or a whole district. Though

an administrative job it involves driving and walking. It includes responsibility for fire protection, wildlife protection, disease identi- fication and control, planning and control of recreational areas, possibly marketing. Forest workers carry out practical tasks under supervision usually of foresters or forest officers.

Training   Forest workers do not need formal qualifications, but may be given in-service training and/or sent on block-release for courses leading to NVQs level 1 and 2, BTEC First Diploma or City and Guilds/SCOTVEC certificates.

Most foresters or forest officers train by taking *either* a BTEC National Diploma *or* SCOTVEC-based college diploma *or* a degree in a forestry-related subject or a post-graduate course. Diploma courses normally require a minimum 2 years' practical experience. Those seeking the highest level management posts may need to take the Professional Examination of the Institute of Chartered Forestry (forestry graduates take only part 2, ND holders take parts 1 and 2).

Traditionally, diploma-holders have been taken on as super- visors, responsible for overseeing day-to-day operations, and gradu- ates as assistant or area managers. Graduates have more scientific knowledge than diplomates, but the distinction has become blurred and promotion is possible for both types of entrant.

Fish Farming and Fisheries Management

This is the breeding and rearing of various types of fish for food or sport. Most fish farms are small owner-run businesses, but there are larger ones employing several staff. Other employers of fisheries managers are water authorities, angling clubs, estate owners, fish processors. Like all animal husbandry this is usually a 7-day-a-week job and involves unsocial working hours.

Training   There is no prescribed entry and training route: the usual ways into this growing industry are through a BTEC/SCOTVEC National Award (see pp. xxi, xxii) in Fishery Studies; or a BTEC sandwich Higher National Diploma; or the Institute of Fisheries Management correspondence course for its certificate and diploma (no entry requirements). NVQs are being introduced.

For research posts: degree in biological or agricultural science, usually followed by a post-graduate course.

It is possible to progress to management from a technician post.

Agricultural/Horticultural Engineering

Agricultural engineers apply engineering principles to all kinds of agriculture and horticulture. As the world's non-renewable and slowly renewable resources are being rapidly used up, it is essential to make the most efficient use of natural resources. This involves recycling processes; exploring and using new sources of energy; and, above all, incorporating new technologies in the design and manufacture of agricultural equipment. Agricultural engineers may be involved in the sales, marketing and servicing of equipment; in designing and constructing farm buildings; in product planning; mechanizing procedures; crop storage and processing. The work is related to food technology (see p. 462) and professional engineering (see p. 181). There is scope for work abroad, especially in developing countries.

Farm/Garden Mechanic

All farmworkers must be able to cope with running repairs; many arable units which use machinery worth thousands of pounds employ their own farm mechanics who are in charge of maintenance, repairs and adaptation of all types of mechanical gadgets. On large units there may be several mechanics; usually there is only one. However, the majority of mechanics are employed by agricultural and garden machinery dealers, carrying out servicing and repairs in a workshop or in the field where the machinery is being used.

Training   For levels of engineering see p. 181.

Courses are available leading to City and Guilds, National Certificate or BTEC/SCOTVEC awards, as well as degrees in agricultural engineering. An NVQ level 3 is in place. Holders of a Higher National Diploma or a degree in a related subject (geography, science, agriculture) can take a post-graduate course in agricultural engineering.

Farm or garden mechanics may follow a formal training scheme accredited by the British Agricultural and Garden Machinery Association.

Horticultural Therapy

This covers the use of horticulture and agriculture in the treatment of certain groups of patients. It may form part of a planned rehabilitation of a physically handicapped patient or it may provide education, recreation or vocational training for people suffering from mental handicap or other disabilities. Most therapists (who may be called a horticultural instructor/organizer or project worker) work in sheltered workshops, hospitals, residential homes, training centres or specialist colleges for people with a physical handicap.

Training   There is as yet no career structure, although the majority of the work is carried out by professional care staff and horticulturalists. Horticultural Therapy (a registered charity) launched a professional development Diploma in Therapeutic Horticulture in 1992, consisting of a day-release course over 30 weeks for people with qualifications in either horticulture or occupational therapy. All take a general horticultural therapy module and then, depending on background, choose the particular horticultural or therapy module. A certificate course is now being developed for support workers in this field to provide them with a basic understanding of the principles and practice of horticultural therapy.

*

Personal   *For most jobs*: attention to detail; physical robustness and ability
attributes   to cope with irregular hours; reliability; good powers of observation; ability to work without supervision.
        For managers: ability to recruit and cope with permanent and seasonal staff; ability to take decisions, knowing that these may be subject to the vagaries of nature; enjoyment of responsibility.

Late start   On the whole this is not advisable as trainee vacancies tend to go to young applicants (partly because the pay structure is age-related), although there are no age limits on training schemes or courses. Some farmers' children return to farming as a second career when their parents wish to retire.

Career-   There should be no problem for those in management jobs before
break   the break, except that competition for jobs is fierce. The Forestry Commission has a career-break scheme for men and women who retire temporarily for domestic reasons.

Part time   Many more people than in the past are working part time, especially in agriculture.

Position   The proportion of women employees in agriculture is still low.
of   However, the proportion of women owners, partners and part-
women   time family workers is about a third and many more are taking full-time college courses. With increased mechanization there is

no reason why a healthy, fit woman should not do as well as a man, given that no one should be asked to lift exceptionally heavy loads. In horticulture, women do well at all levels. Women tend not to apply for forestry work, but some are employed, especially in the Forestry Commission.

Further information

Careers, Education and Training Advice Centre, c/o Warwickshire Careers Service, 10 Northgate Street, Warwick CV34 4SR

Royal Botanic Gardens, Kew, Richmond, Surrey TW9 3AB

Forestry and Arboriculture Safety Training Council (FASTCo), 231 Corstorphine Road, Edinburgh EH12 7AT

Institute of Horticulture, 14/15 Belgrave Square, London SW1X 8PS

Institute of Fisheries Management, 22 Rushworth Avenue, West Bridgford, Nottingham NG2 7LF

The Institution of Agricultural Engineers, West End Road, Silsoe, Bedford MK45 4DU

British Agricultural and Garden Machinery Association, 14–16 Church Street, Rickmansworth, Herts WD3 1RQ

Horticultural Therapy, Goulds Ground, Vallis Way, Frome, Somerset BA11 3DW

Related careers

LANDSCAPE ARCHITECTURE – SCIENCE: *Scientist; Technician* – ANIMALS: *Veterinary Nurse/Surgeon*

Animals

Veterinary Surgeon

Entry qualifications

A-level chemistry plus 2 others normally chosen from physics, biology and maths. The subject not offered at A-level should be included among the GCSEs offered (usually at least 6). This is the most competitive of degree courses; very high A-level grades are required. Experience of handling animals, sometimes observing a veterinary surgeon in practice, is essential.

The work

General practice

Some veterinary practices deal mainly or exclusively (except in cases of emergency) with small or 'companion' animals; others deal with farm animals or horses; some are mixed practices, but even here veterinary surgeons are likely to develop particular areas of interest and expertise. Veterinary surgeons must provide a 24-hour service, but most practices are organized so as to provide reasonable time off and holidays.

Veterinary surgeons treat animals both in their surgeries and at their owners' premises. It is important for them to be able to communicate effectively with animals' owners. This means a different approach for pet-owners, who have an emotional attachment to their 'companion animals', and for farmers to whom their animals are an investment. While always committed to the welfare of an animal, the veterinary surgeon must allow a farmer to balance an expensive new treatment against an economic return. In farm animal practice, veterinary surgeons are concerned not just with treating individual animals but with advising on the well-being and productivity of the entire stock.

Veterinary surgeons in practice often take on additional part-time appointments. Farm practitioners may be Local Veterinary Inspectors for the Ministry of Agriculture, testing cattle for tuberculosis or brucellosis or carrying on inspections at cattle markets. Some practices carry out supervision of meat hygiene in abattoirs or poultry slaughterhouses; others work at licensed greyhound tracks. District councils need veterinary surgeons to inspect the riding establishments, zoos, pet shops and dog-breeding and boarding kennels which they license.

Newly qualified veterinary surgeons normally start as assistants in established practices, moving on to a more senior assistantship and then to a partnership in an existing practice or setting up a new practice.

State Veterinary Service

The State Veterinary Service is concerned not with individual animals but with the 'common herd'. Its responsibilities include: the control and eradication of notifiable disease; diagnostic and consultancy work on notifiable and non-notifiable disease; epidemiological studies; disease monitoring and surveillance; special investigations and surveys; public health liaison and human diseases related to animals; red meat and poultry hygiene; the operation of animal health schemes; improved farm animal health.

Veterinary surgeons are employed as *Veterinary Field Officers* or *Veterinary Investigation Officers*. They work closely together, with the field officer generally carrying out a major part of the statutory work while the investigation officer provides diagnostic services based on laboratory tests. The Central Veterinary Laboratory contracts (as a Civil Service agency) to carry out research into conditions of economic importance to British farm livestock. Immediate practical farming problems as well as long-term applied and fundamental research projects are dealt with. It also provides services for the State Veterinary Service.

Other opportunities

Veterinary surgeons are also employed in research institutes of the Agricultural Research Service and Medical Research Council; animal welfare societies; the Royal Army Veterinary Corps; industry, mainly pharmaceutical companies and those making animal feeds and fertilizers; universities; the Animal Health Trust, a voluntary organization for veterinary research and the promotion of post-graduate veterinary education. There are also opportunities in developing countries, and British qualified veterinary surgeons may practise in any EC member state.

Training   Degree courses usually last 5 years (6 at Cambridge) and are divided into pre-clinical (anatomy, physiology, biochemistry, pharmacology) and clinical (animal husbandry, medicine and surgery, veterinary public health). During the vacations of the clinical years of the course students must spend 6 months gaining experience in aspects of veterinary work under the supervision of veterinary surgeons in practice, in veterinary laboratories and in other areas of veterinary work.

In some veterinary schools training is shortened by 1 year for science graduates.

Personal attributes Scientific interest in animals and their behaviour and development, rather than sentimental fondness for pets; powers of observation; a firm hand; the ability to inspire confidence in animals (i.e. total absence of nervousness) and in their owners; self-reliance and adaptability; indifference to occasional physically disagreeable conditions of work.

For some posts: organizing ability and powers of leadership; for others, ability to work as one of a team.

Late start As there is such stiff competition for degree course places, it is unlikely that anyone over 30 would be accepted, though there is no official upper age limit.

Career-break In general practice, would have to be negotiated with partners. A retraining course has been organized every other year for those wishing to return to practice. Veterinary surgeons in the State Veterinary Service are civil servants (see p. 123).

Part time Opportunities to work part time or as a locum.

Position of women The proportion of female registered veterinary surgeons is 33% overall, but much higher for those under 30. In 1994, 63% of those accepted on to veterinary degree courses were women. It used to be thought that women, particularly small women, would have difficulty coping with some of the heavy work. The increasing numbers of women entering show that they cope well enough.

Further information Royal College of Veterinary Surgeons, Belgravia House, 62–64 Horseferry Road, London SW1P 2AF

Veterinary Nurse

Entry qualifications 4 GCSEs (A-C), including English language and a physical or biological science or mathematics.

The work Veterinary nurses assist veterinary surgeons in their surgery and occasionally on visits. They hold and pacify animals during examination and treatment; in the surgery they also sterilize and look after instruments. They collect and analyse specimens, prepare medicines, take out stings and stitches, clean out cages, and clear up after operations. They may also assist in the reception of patients. They work mainly in 'small-animal' practices, i.e. those dealing with domestic animals, and for the RSPCA and other animal welfare and research organizations.

The hours are usually long and irregular. Animals have to be cared for at weekends, which may mean going to work on Saturday and Sunday, perhaps just to feed them.

Some veterinary surgeons' practices employ only one veterinary nurse who may then have little companionship. Most of the working day will be spent with the employer.

Training

Minimum age for enrolment as trainee is 17; practical work may start earlier.

Training is on the job, plus study by correspondence or day- or block-release courses.

A potential trainee must first find a job with a veterinary practice or hospital approved by the RCVS as a training centre and must then enrol with the British Veterinary Nursing Association (BVNA) as a trainee. The syllabus covers anatomy and physiology, hygiene and feeding, first aid, side-room techniques (analysing specimens and preparing slides), and the theory and practice of breeding and nursing. Finals may be taken after at least 2 years' traineeship.

Trainee vacancies are sometimes advertised in the *Veterinary Record*, and prospective trainees may themselves advertise for jobs. Letters to local veterinary surgeons and animal research and welfare societies may also bring results; and the BVNA will provide a list of those veterinary practices and centres which are approved as training centres.

Personal attributes

A love of animals and a scientific interest in their development, behaviour, and welfare; lack of squeamishness; a willingness to take orders, and yet to act independently when necessary; readiness to work well both alone and with others; a sure, firm, but gentle grip; patience. Ability to type and drive is helpful.

Late start

There is no upper age limit, but most trainees are young. This is to some extent dictated by the low wages received during training.

Career-break

Any career-break would have to be negotiated with employer. However, this is basically a young person's job.

Part time

There are opportunities for part-time work. Most trainees work full time.

Position of women

This is still a female preserve. The numbers of male veterinary nurses and students are barely in double figures.

Further information   British Veterinary Nurses Association, Seedbed Centre, Coldharbour Road, Harlow, Essex CM19 5AF

Horses

Entry qualifications

4 GCSEs, including an English subject, for riding instructors, but requirements waived for entrants over 18. None for grooms and stable managers. But see 'Training', below.

The work

Looking after horses nearly always means hard physical work that has to be carried out daily in all weathers. Hours tend to be long, especially in summer, and most people work a 6-day week. Most new entrants have had experience of working as unpaid helpers or have had their own pony/horse while at school, so they know what is involved. Staff may live in or out, but grooms and stable managers usually live on the premises because of the early-morning start. Meals may be provided.

Riding Instructors

They teach children and adults, both in private lessons and in classes, and accompany riders out on 'hacks'. Classes may be held early in the morning or late in the evening, to suit pupils coming before or after work. Some instructors work for one establishment full time, others work freelance or part time. Many combine teaching with general stable work. Setting up one's own riding school requires considerable capital, experience and business knowledge.

Groom/Stable Managers

They work in and may eventually manage a variety of establishments, e.g. hunt, racing, show jumping and eventing stables, livery yards (which look after other owners' horses), riding schools, studs. They clean stables, feed and water horses, watch out for and report any symptoms which indicate a horse may be sick, clean and maintain tack. They prepare horses for competition – eventing, showjumping, dressage, driving, polo, showing, etc. At a stud, grooms also look after the brood mares and care for their foals. They may also assist with breaking and training. This is highly skilled work. Opportunities are increasing for 'skilled' –

not necessarily 'qualified' – workers. 'Plum' jobs like travelling with show horses are rare. However, British grooms are in great demand abroad.

Training   *Instructors*
The 2 main examining bodies in the horse industry are the British Horse Society and the Association of British Riding Schools. The BHS exams consist of 2 parallel streams, riding, and horse knowledge and care. Intending instructors must take both, together with teaching tests. The route is:

Stage I (minimum age 16).

Stage II. Candidates for Stage II must first have passed the separate BHS Riding and Road Safety Test.

Stage III (minimum age 17). This together with the Preliminary Teaching Test (minimum age 17$\frac{1}{2}$) leads to the Preliminary Teaching Certificate. (On completion of 500 hours of teaching experience, the full *Assistant Instructor* Certificate (AI) is awarded.)

Stage IV (minimum age 20). This, together with the Intermediate Teaching Examination and a full Health and Safety at Work first aid certificate, leads to the *Intermediate Instructor* (II) award.

Stable Manager's Certificate (minimum age 22). Those who pass this plus the Equitation/Teaching exam gain the full *Instructor's Certificate*.

BHS instructional qualifications are currently recognized in 27 countries through the International Group for Qualifications in Training Horse and Rider.

Grooms
People who want to become grooms and stable managers, but have no particular riding ambitions, can take either the BHS horse knowledge and care tests, Groom's Certificate, Intermediate Stable Manager's Certificate and Stable Manager's Certificate (without the riding tests) or the ABRS exams. These consist of *Preliminary Horse Care and Riding*, the *Assistant Groom's Certificate* (minimum age 17) and *Groom's Diploma* (minimum age 18). No educational qualifications are required for the ABRS exams.

The National Pony Society runs examinations for stud workers.

Training for horse exams is normally as a working pupil, an arrangement by which the pupil is given instruction and pocket money in exchange for work. Courses for Preliminary Teachers last around 1 year. It is also possible to work for these exams while working as a groom. There are also some fee-charging schools. It is important to check that any training establishment is approved by the BHS and/or is a member of the ABRS.

Increasingly, equestrian studies courses are being offered at colleges of agriculture and further education colleges, leading to BTEC National and Higher National awards and incorporating BHS qualifications. Degree courses are now also available, as is youth training. It is anticipated that in future people with qualifications will have the most opportunities in managing equestrian establishments of all kinds.

NVQs (see p. xix) are awarded jointly by the National Horse Education and Training Council and the BHS, City and Guilds, and the Racehorse Thoroughbred Breeding Training Board.

Personal attributes Physical stamina and ability to work outside in all weathers; indifference to getting dirty; willingness to work 'unsocial' hours and sometimes by oneself.

For instructors: authority; ability to express oneself clearly; patience; a liking for children.

Part time There may be some part-time work for riding instructors at local riding establishments. Part-time work is on the increase.

Position of women The proportion of women is probably around 80%. This is largely a young woman's field, as far as jobs are concerned, but quite a few women own their own riding schools or stables.

Further information British Horse Society, The British Equestrian Centre, Kenilworth, Warwickshire CV8 2LR

Association of British Riding Schools, Office No. 2, Queens Chambers, 38–40 Queen Street, Penzance TR18 4BH

National Pony Society, Willingdon House, 102 High Street, Alton, Hants GU34 1EN

Other Work with Animals

There is a wide range of other opportunities to work with animals. They range from guide dog trainer to gamekeeper, pet shop assistant to RSPCA inspector, zookeeper to dog beautician. Some of these fields offer a very limited number of openings. Often no specific academic qualifications are needed and training is on the job. Most are essentially practical, manual occupations with limited prospects. (None is a suitable alternative for anyone who narrowly misses becoming a veterinary surgeon.)

Further information
Universities Federation for Animal Welfare, 8 Hamilton Close, South Mimms, Potters Bar, Herts. EN6 3QD. A very wide range of opportunities is covered in their leaflet *Careers with Animals* – send an s.a.e.

Archaeology

Entry qualifications
Degree course requirements. Maths or a science and modern language at GCSE normally required. For *classical archaeology*, Latin or Greek at either level. For *conservation*, chemistry at A-level. Archaeology GCSE and A-level are available, but are not required.

The work
Archaeology is the science of gaining knowledge from the past from the study of ancient objects. Excavations tend to be the most publicized aspects of the work, but the actual digging up and recording work is becoming less centre stage as emphasis on preservation and limiting of damage to sites increases. Though archaeologists need a broad knowledge of the whole field, they normally specialize in one geographical area or period, for example landscape, regional, prehistoric, Anglo-Saxon or theoretical archaeology. Some archaeologists also specialize in particular artefacts, for example coins, weapons or inscriptions.

Among the many broad archaeological specializations are archaeological science, conservation, heritage management, underwater archaeology, environmental archaeology, geophysical survey, archaeological computing and landscape archaeology. These can be studied through a wide variety of post-graduate courses.

Many archaeologists work in museums (see MUSEUMS AND ART GALLERIES, p. 320). Others work for English Heritage, the Royal Commission on Historical Monuments in England, Scotland and Wales, Historic Scotland, Cadw in Wales, the National Trust, Forestry Commission, British Gas. There are many more archaeologists than related jobs.

Training
BA or BSc in archaeology as a single subject or in combination with a wide variety of other disciplines. These can be followed by a 1-year Masters degree in various specializations. NVQs in archaeology should be available in 1996.

The Institute of Field Archaeologists is the professional institute for archaeologists with various membership levels.

**Personal
attributes**
Deep curiosity about the past; intellectual ability well above
average; artistic sensibility; patience; manual dexterity (for handling delicate and valuable objects). For excavation, physical stamina.

Late start
Advisable only for people who already have a relevant degree or
scientific skills and/or hobby experience. Archaeological degrees
tend to attract mature students.

**Career-
break**
Prospects for returners depend on previous experience.

Part time
See below.

**Position
of
women**
The Institute of Field Archaeology now has an Equal Opportunities Committee. A 1995 survey of the quality of work and lifestyle
in archaeology showed that there are still fewer women in this
area than men, despite the fact that they take up half the degree
places. It also showed, however, that pay scales were equal,
except in senior positions (over £21,000), where women represent
only 22% of the sample. Across all employers, flexible working
patterns were rare, although most local authorities offered flexi-
time. About a third offered job-share and day-release
opportunities.

Publication, the main route to success, is still dominated by
men and, although women still do a lot of the key specialist
analysis, they are rarely cited as key authors.

**Further
informa-
tion**
The Council for British Archaeology, Bowes Morrell House, 111
    Walmgate, York YO1 2UA
The Institute of Field Archaeologists, Manchester University,
    Oxford Road, Manchester M13 9PL

**Related
careers**
ARCHIVIST – MUSEUMS AND ART GALLERIES

Architecture

Architect

Entry qualifications Some schools of architecture require specific GCSE and A-level passes. The Royal Institute of British Architects (RIBA) recommends students should have minimum 2 academic subjects at A-level and 5 GCSEs (these to include English, maths and double award science).

The work Architecture is a multi-disciplinary profession requiring a combination of artistic, technological and sociological expertise. The challenge of architecture is to produce, within a given budget, an aesthetically pleasing design which will stand up to wear and tear and is the kind of building in which people will want to live or work. Architects must fully understand traditional and new building methods and materials and appreciate their potential and limitations. They must also understand and be interested in contemporary society and changing lifestyles, the community's expectations and needs, and social problems which may lead to loneliness, mugging and vandalism. They need to question householders, office workers, teachers, hospital staff, managers, social workers, etc. to come up with a design for a building that is 'user friendly' and which works. Some of the architectural disasters of the postwar period are due to lack of consultation and lack of imagination. For example, the design and layout of a housing estate and its walkways can provide a haven for muggers; a redesign can mean a dramatic drop in antisocial behaviour. This, together with strict financial constraints, makes architecture today a more demanding discipline than it has ever been. Tasks range from converting houses into flats to designing hospitals, retirement homes or factory complexes.

Architects receive instructions (the 'brief') from their clients or employers on the type, function, capacity and rough cost of the building required. Then they do their research – and at that stage they may question some assumptions on which the client based the brief.

When the type of the building has finally been decided upon, the design work begins. This starts with producing, perhaps jointly with colleagues, a sketch scheme of the floor plans, the elevations, and perspective drawings. Several designs may have to be produced before one is finally approved.

The next stage is to prepare contract documents, which will include detailed drawings and specifications; estimates of cost; and applications for necessary planning consents from the local authority. At this stage, especially if the scheme is a big one, consulting engineers (see p. 186) and quantity surveyors (see p. 502), may be appointed. When the contract for the work has been awarded to a building contractor, the architect is in overall charge of the project, with responsibility for certifying payment to contractors, and for inspecting the work in progress. This involves regular visits to the building site, issuing instructions to the contractor's agent or foreman and discussing any problems that might arise. Site visits may involve walking through mud and climbing scaffolding.

The architect is normally also responsible for the choice or design of fittings and the interior design of the buildings. (See ART AND DESIGN, p. 57.)

An architect can work in different *settings*: in private practice; in the architects' and planning departments of a local authority; in a cooperative; with a public body; with a ministry; or in the architect's department of a commercial firm large enough to have a continuous programme of building or maintenance work.

In private practice the client may be an individual, a commercial firm, a local authority or other public body. It is usual for private practices to specialize, but not exclusively, in houses, schools or offices, etc. In private practice architects normally work only on design and not, as in other categories, on design and maintenance.

In local authorities architects may work on a wide variety of buildings, such as one-family houses, blocks of flats, schools, sports centres and clinics. They also collaborate with private architects employed by the authority for specific schemes.

For other public bodies such as government departments, the architect's work is less varied and is largely confined to the organization's particular building concern: e.g. hospitals for the Department of Health.

The same applies to architects working for a commercial concern. Their work is confined to that organization's particular type of building: e.g. hotels and restaurants for a large catering organization; shops for a retail chain.

The majority of architects are salaried employees, but they may become junior partners and later principals in a firm, or set up on their own. But to start a firm requires a good deal of experience, capital and contacts. 48% of practices employ 5 or fewer full-time architects.

Since 1982, architects have been permitted, under RIBA rules, to become directors of building and development companies, so they can now combine professional work with running their own business. Architects' prospects can be badly affected by recessions and they have to be prepared to take on any work they can find. There are reasonable opportunities to work abroad.

Training

The normal pattern of training is a 5-year full-time course, with 1 year of practical experience after the third year and a second year of practical experience at the end of the course, making a minimum of 7 years. Besides full-time courses, some schools of architecture offer part-time (day release) courses, but this method of training is not suitable for everyone, as it takes even longer than the normal training; however, it does provide a route to qualification for self-funding students. Subjects studied include history of architecture, design and construction, town planning, environmental science, materials science, building control, some sociology, economics, law. The development of design skills through projects is central to an architect's education and increasingly involves CAD (computer-aided design).

For interior designers, architectural training need only be up to degree level. It must be followed by a specialized art-school course (part or full time) and practical experience.

NOTES: 1. Architecture, planning and landscape architecture are related disciplines. There are some courses which start with a combined studies year so that students can delay specialization until they know more about the whole field. But courses must be chosen with care: practising architects whether in private practice or public employment must be on the Register of the Architects Registration Council of the United Kingdom and only courses recognized by the RIBA lead to Registration. Up-to-date lists of recognized courses are available from the RIBA. Course titles can be misleading, e.g. 'Architectural Studies' may or may not be a recognized course.

2. For candidates who are not quite certain whether to commit themselves to a 7-year training it is useful to know that the first 3-year stage of training, on most courses, leads to an honours degree in its own right, and therefore to all the graduate jobs for which no particular discipline is specified.

Personal attributes

A practical as well as creative mind; an interest in people and their changing lifestyles; self-confidence to put over and justify new ideas; mathematical ability; drawing skills; the ability to deal with legal and financial questions; a reasonably authoritative personality; an aptitude for giving clear instructions and explanations.

Late start The RIBA has a well-established system of external examinations offering a route to qualification for mature students who have at least 6 years' practical experience.

Career-break Opportunities for those who have kept up by way of reading journals, attending occasional lectures and seminars. The RIBA's Women Architects' Group is helping to set up returners' courses. Architects are strongly advised to 'keep their hand in' and do *some* work throughout the break, however sporadic.

Updating courses are a feature of the profession under its CPD (Continual Professional Updating) scheme for all architects. There is currently one refresher course, but normally ad hoc arrangements are made for returners to work in architectural offices. Some returners take one of the post-graduate courses available and specialize in, for example, urban design, planning or conservation of historic buildings.

Part time A fair proportion of women architects work part time, virtually all of them in private practice. They predominate in 'agency' (temporary contract) work which may combine well with domestic responsibilities but rarely improves career prospects. There is little opportunity for part-time work in the public sector, but up to middle-level jobs it should be possible to organize job-sharing and other flexible working.

Position of women 8% of registered architects and 30% (higher in Scotland) of first-year students are women. Proportions have risen slowly in recent years.

At present, far fewer women than men are principals in private practice. Most women remain assistant architects; in public service women seem to progress further, but still the vast majority remain in middle-level jobs. However, this may change as more women qualify.

Further information Royal Institute of British Architects, Education and Practice Standards Department, 66 Portland Place, London W1N 4AD
Royal Incorporation of Architects in Scotland, 15 Rutland Square, Edinburgh EH1 2BE
Society of Architects in Wales, Midland Bank Chambers, 75a Llandennis Road, Rhydypennau, Cardiff CF2 6EE
Royal Society of Ulster Architects, 2 Mount Charles, Belfast, N. Ireland BT7 1NZ

Architects Registration Council, 73 Hallam Street, London W1N 6EE

Related careers	*Architectural Technologist (see below)* – ART AND DESIGN – ENGINEERING – LANDSCAPE ARCHITECTURE – SURVEYING – TOWN AND COUNTRY PLANNING

Architectural Technologist (formerly Technician)

Entry qualifications	These are in a transitional stage. For associateship membership of BIAT, the British Institute of Architectural Technologists (formerly Technicians), a degree in architectural technology or in the built environment will become the minimum entry requirement. Meanwhile, a BIAT approved HNC/HND in Building Studies with Architectural options will continue to be accepted.
The work	The impact of advanced technology in the construction process and the complexity of the problems that have to be solved when designing, planning and constructing 'the built environment' has led to a change in the status of technicians. The new title of technologist reflects the greater amount of knowledge they need to be able to work alongside and often in partnership with other professionals, such as architects and planners. A number of degrees in architectural technology have recently been introduced.

Architectural technologists work in architects' and planners' offices both in private practice and in public employment as well as with large firms of building contractors. Duties vary considerably according to the size and structure of the office. They may include any or all of the following: collecting, analysing and preparing technical information required for a design; preparing technical drawings for the builder and presentation drawings for the client; administration of contracts; liaison with clients and with specialists such as quantity surveyors; taking notes at site meetings; site supervision; collecting information on performance of finished buildings (which means contact with satisfied and possibly dissatisfied clients); office management. Technicians do responsible work but on the technical rather than the creative side. Those with a few years' experience in employment can set up on their own and, working for private clients or building contractors, design conversions; or help out in architectural firms which need occasional extra staff. Prospects vary according to economic climate but during the recession technicians suffered less than architects: many architectural technicians do much the same work as architects in junior positions but they are paid less than fully qualified architects. Contractors and individuals often now employ technicians rather than architects for the more routine type of work. Technicians who want to become architects must take the full architectural training; their BTEC award is normally accepted in lieu of A-levels. Few technicians, however, switch to architectural training: if they are good enough to take the architectural training, they usually do very well as technicians.

Training   See entry qualifications.

Training can be *either* full-time: A-levels/GNVQ advanced level or National Diploma in Building Studies followed by a degree in Architectural Technology or the Built Environment (with a technology base) *or* part-time: BTEC National Certificate in Building Studies, followed by Higher National Certificate while working as a trainee with day-release *or* a mixture of the two.

NOTE: the HNC/HND qualification will eventually not be acceptable for membership of the BIAT.

Personal   Accuracy; ability to draw; technical ability; interest in architecture
attributes   and environment; liking for teamwork; some design flair.

Late start   Not advisable because of low salary while training. Young trainees tend to be preferred, but previous experience in construction is an asset. BIAT offers a non-standard route for those aged 30-plus who have a minimum of 10 years' experience.

Career-   Theoretically no reason why qualified technologists should not
break   return.

Part time   Not much opportunity in employment, but possible as self-employed.

Position   Only about 4% of BIAT members are women; figures for trainees
of   are about 5%. The job is highly suitable for women who are
women   interested in housing and the environment but are put off by the long full architectural training. It is largely lack of role-models (women technicians who can talk about their work) which keeps the proportion of women so low. The few women who have taken this training are doing very well, both in jobs and in their own small practices. They have no special problems getting training vacancies or places on full-time courses.

Further information   The Education Officer, British Institute of Architectural Technologists, 397 City Road, London EC1V 1NE

Related careers   SURVEYING: *Surveying Technicians* – ENGINEERING: *Engineering Technicians*

Archivist

Entry qualifications

Good honours degree (usually in history). Preference given to applicants with GCSE-level Latin.

The work

Archivists' work combines scholarly research with the selection, preservation, arrangement and description of documents, such as official records of central and local government and courts of law, or private documents such as title deeds, business records, family papers. Archivists assess the value for posterity of papers being currently produced and preserve and put in order, for reference purposes, all types of records which were produced in the past. They help members of the public with their research, whether they are professors of history, solicitors in search of evidence, students working on projects, or genealogists. They must understand methods of preservation and repair, of microfilming and new technologies.

Most archivists work in central and local government record offices. Other posts are in professional institutions, universities, and a wide variety of other establishments, including ecclesiastical foundations, hospitals, charitable organizations, specialist museums, libraries and research bodies. There is considerable scope for trained archivists who prefer to specialize in the management of current records, especially in business and industry. Some of these posts require scientific or other specialist knowledge, and computer technology is increasingly important in many areas of the work. The work involves contact with a vast variety of members of the public. The supply and demand for archivists are about even. It is usually necessary to go wherever there is a vacancy, both for the first job and later for promotion. Vacancies are very scarce in some parts of the country.

Training

Nearly all posts now require formal training: 1-year post-graduate full-time course for an MA or Diploma in Archives Administration. Subjects include palaeography, record office management, research methods, conservation methods, editing, some history and law. The Society of Archivists runs a correspondence course for graduates in professional archival posts. It is possible, but difficult, for a graduate to work up from an unqualified assistant post to a professional appointment.

Personal attributes   A strong sense of history; liking for painstaking research; curiosity; ability to communicate with a wide variety of people.

Late start   Probably difficult, for above reasons; see 'Career-break', below.

Career-break   Return difficult, as there are always sufficient young job applicants and vacant posts may not occur in a particular area for several years. However, 'retired' members can pay reduced subscriptions to the Society of Archivists.

Part time   Training: correspondence course normally available only to working archivists. Work: some part-time posts available, but with few promotion prospects. Job-sharing should be possible.

Position of women   Just over half of Britain's archivists are women; but twice as many men as women are county archivists.

Further information   Executive Secretary, Society of Archivists, Information House, 20–24 Old Street, London EC1V 9AP

Related careers   ARCHAEOLOGY – INFORMATION WORK – MUSEUMS AND ART GALLERIES

Armed Forces (Officer Entry Only)

Entry qualifications
Minimum 5 GCSEs. See individual forces.

The work
The main purpose of the armed forces is the defence of the country. Following recent world events there have been, and probably will continue to be, cutbacks in defence spending and a reduction in the numbers required to serve throughout the forces. However, there will always be a demand for new entrants to ensure continuity, as many officers serve for only a few years. All the forces contribute to European defence through NATO and in addition may from time to time be involved in peace-keeping missions or disaster relief anywhere in the world.

Jobs are varied. As well as providing increasingly sophisticated technical expertise the three services have to be self-sufficient, i.e. they have to house, feed, clothe, equip, transport, select, train and provide medical and welfare services to servicemen and service-women at home and overseas. Many jobs are unique to the services, but some are also relevant to civilian life. Recruiters look for a particular mix of abilities and personal qualities to try to select people who will fit in and enjoy the way of life. Although the majority will spend their time without experiencing combat, nevertheless they can never forget that at any time they might have to take part in action against an enemy.

Most officers have a dual responsibility: as a leader and manager of a group of men and women, and as a specialist.

As jobs are so diverse, and training for them is so specific, it is not possible to give more than an outline of the various entry routes in this book. A great deal of information and help is available to people considering joining any one of the services; they should contact their school's or university liaison officer, or local recruiting office, or write to the addresses given below.

NOTE: Women are gradually being integrated into all three services, so a greater variety of jobs are open to them than in the past.

The Army

Regiments and corps are divided into Arms (those involved in battle) and Services (those providing many kinds of services to the Arms). Each has its own responsibilities, e.g. the Royal Signals handle communications (often using very advanced technology); the Royal Engineers handle engineering and construction, as well as running mapping services for all three forces. Would-be officers apply to a corps or regiment, though not all are open to all entrants. Age limits vary, as do entry requirements. (Nearly 75% of recently commissioned officers are graduates.)

Main entry routes and types of commission
Regular commission (to age 55, but may apply to leave after 3 years' service):

Main school-leaver entry: for men and women aged 17¾–25 and with 5 GCSEs (A–C), including English language, maths and either a science or foreign language, and 2 A-levels.

Graduate entry (any subject) or with certain professional qualifications. Upper age limits vary.

Short-service commission (minimum usually 3 years and can be extended up to 8 years):

Minimum age 17¾ and up to 25, depending on regiment or corps. Minimum 5 GCSEs (A–C) including English and, for some regiments or corps, maths or science.

There are various scholarship schemes to give financial support to sixth-formers and undergraduates; boys and girls are eligible for scholarships while doing A-levels, and there is a separate scheme for boys and girls to take science A-levels at the Army's own sixth-form college at Welbeck. Undergraduate cadetships and bursaries are available for men and women reading for a degree in any subject and lead to a Regular or Short Service Commission. Short Service Limited Commissions are available for men and women who want to spend time in the Army (4–18 months) before starting degree courses, i.e. in their 'gap' year.

Royal Navy

Over half the Navy's officers are graduates, who can be from almost any discipline. There are several branches, each providing a specialist service:

Seamen officers are responsible for the safe and efficient handling of a ship while on watch and they may also train to operate weapons systems. They can go on to 'sub-specialize' in aviation, either in aircraft control, as airborne observers or as helicopter pilots (a few are selected to fly the Sea Harrier jump-jet). Other specializations open to seamen officers are on submarines, as hydrographic surveyors (see SURVEYING, p. 505) and as divers (for mine clearance).

Engineer officers work with highly advanced technology and its complexity means that they specialize as one of the following: weapon engineer officers (surface ships), weapon engineers (submarines), marine engineers (surface ships), marine engineers (submarines) and air engineers.

Supply and secretariat officers work in ships and also at shore establishments. They are concerned with both the technical and the personnel aspects of a ship's organization. Their main duties are: administration; correspondence; welfare and personnel matters; naval stores; catering; pay and cash. While at sea, supply and secretariat officers also have quite separate operational duties.

Instructor officers are responsible for education and much of the training, from general academic studies to advanced technical training.

The Royal Marines are the Navy's amphibious infantry and they have their own entry and training requirements. The training is the physically hardest of all in the forces and includes a very demanding commando course.

Main entry routes for men and women

Full career commissions (serve up to age 50). (1) *Seaman or Supply and Secretariat*: For direct entry to Naval College: aged 17 to under 23 with 2 A-levels and 3 GCSEs, including English and maths. Graduate entry for those with a degree (and GCSE (A–C) English and maths) aged under 26. (2) *Engineering*: University cadetship entry: a place on a mechanical, electrical, electronic or aeronautical degree course. Age under 22. An Engineering Sponsorship scheme is available for those with 18 UCAS points, including at least grade C A-levels in mathematics and physics. Graduate entry with a degree in mechanical, electrical, electronic or aeronautical engineering or acceptable equivalent. Age limits as in (1). (3) *Royal Marines*: Full career entry: 2 A-levels and 3 GCSEs (A–C), including English and maths, aged $17\frac{1}{2}$ to under 22. Graduate entry with a degree and with GCSE (A–C) in English and maths, aged under 25.

Short and Medium Commissions (from 8 to 16 years depending on specialization and personal choice). For *seaman* and *engineering officers* entry qualifications as above, but upper age limit 25 for seamen, up to 32 in some cases for engineers. *Supply and Secretariat* direct entry to Naval College possible with 2 A-levels and 3 GCSEs (A–C), including English and maths, or as a graduate. *Pilots, observers* and *air traffic control*: with 2 A-levels and 3 GCSEs (including English and maths) or as a graduate. *Instructor*: mainly with a degree or professional qualification in engineering, physics, maths or computing. A few arts graduates taken each year. Must be aged under 34. *Royal Marines* (men only!): entry with 2 A-levels and 3 GCSEs (including English and maths), aged 17½ to under 23, or as a graduate aged under 25.

Women in the Navy
Entry and conditions of service are now mainly the same as for men. However, although they can become helicopter pilots and observers, they do not fly commando helicopters or Sea Harriers, or serve in submarines or in the Royal Marines.

Sixth-form scholarships, university cadetships and bursaries are available to male and female candidates.

Royal Air Force
As in the other forces, officers in the Royal Air Force are leaders, managers and specialists. Aircrew – pilots and navigators – provide the front line. Air traffic controllers are responsible for directing the movements of aircraft in the air and of aircraft and vehicles on the airfield. Fighter controllers report on radar pictures and control what goes on in the air by planning air operations and guiding aircraft to their targets. Intelligence officers gather and interpret data largely obtained from sensors in reconnaissance aircraft to help those planning operations. Engineers specialize in work either on aircraft or on communications and radar systems. Supply officers are responsible for provisions of all kinds and the movement of cargo and personnel by all means of transport. In the administrative branch, officers work in accountancy, estates management, personnel and welfare services. Others work as education and training officers, station catering managers and physical education officers. There are two types of commission in the RAF: *permanent* (up to age 38 or for 16 years, whichever is the longer, with possible extension to age 55) and *short service* (3–6 years, varying from branch to branch; for pilots and navigators it lasts 12 years, with the option to leave after 6 years' 'productive service'). For most branches both types of commission are available.

Main entry routes
For all commissions the minimum academic standard is 2 A-levels and 5 GCSEs. (A–C) or equivalent, including English and maths. There is a large graduate intake.

Aircrew: aged 17½ to under 24 (pilots) or under 26 (navigators). *Air traffic control, fighter control* and *intelligence officers*: aged 17½ to under 30. *Engineering Officer*: aged under 39 and must have an acceptable engineering degree or Higher National award. *Supply Officer*: aged under 30 (exceptionally under 39) with degree or Higher National award in business studies, public administration or computer studies preferred. *Catering Officer*: aged under 39 with Higher National award, degree or professional qualification in catering. *Education Officer*: aged under 30 (exceptionally 39) with a degree (occasionally Higher National) in science, engineering or similar subject. *Administration Officer*: aged under 30 (exceptionally 39), needs a degree or Higher National award in business studies or relevant professional qualifications, e.g. accountancy. *Physical Education Officer*: aged under 27 (exceptionally 39) and must be qualified PE teacher.

Sixth-form and flying scholarships are available, as well as university cadetships and bursaries.

Personal attributes   Depend very much on the branch or job, but all officers need certain qualities of leadership, initiative, ability to get on with people from all kinds of background, liking for teamwork, adaptability, physical fitness. Must enjoy and be willing to contribute to community life.

Further information   Your local Army, Royal Navy or RAF Careers Office or Jobcentre or Careers Service.

Art and Design

Entry qualifications   See 'Training', below.

The work   Covers 2 distinct fields: art, which is largely painting and sculpture and is not a career in the usual sense; and design, which could be called applied art: it covers design for industrial and commercial application and industrial engineering. The terminology can be confusing. For example *industrial design* (engineering) is also called *product design*, and comes under the broader heading *3-dimensional design*. Similarly, *graphic design*, with all its subcategories – illustration, typography, photography, etc. – is also called *visual communication* or *communication design*.

In the Art and Design degree (see below), the areas of specialization are: (1) fine art; (2) graphic design; (3) 3-dimensional design; (4) textiles/fashion. Within these broad categories there are many specializations.

Fine Art

An extremely small number of artists are talented enough to make a living by painting and sculpting alone. Anyone determined to paint or sculpt for a living must have a private income, a second string to their bow, or be prepared for a precarious existence.

Commissions for murals and sculptures for public buildings are extremely rare, and private commissions even more so.

The majority of painters and sculptors also teach, and for that they need art teacher training. Part-time teaching is now *very* difficult to get. Others combine fine art with design in overlapping areas, for example, studio-based craft, or such graphics specialization as book illustration or advertising. But in these areas opportunities are also rare. A few artists do picture-restoring or copying, but again there are few openings.

Design
(see also ENGINEERING, 'Design', p. 183)

The function of the designer, who is, broadly, a specialist combining artistic talent and training with sufficient technical and business knowledge to appreciate the requirements of an industry, is still evolving. Design careers tend not to be structured, although the last 20 years have shown that there are certain employment patterns that new entrants can aspire to. Most designers start as assistants and work first in the area of specialization in which they trained. Later, with experience and evolving interests, they can switch specializations, or at least sub-specializations. For example, a 3-dimensional designer might switch from light engineering to furniture or interior design; a graphic designer from typography to photography; a fashion/textile designer from fashion (see p. 60) to floor-covering or wallpaper, etc. Sometimes 3-dimensional-trained designers switch to visual communication – but the switch the other way round is less likely. A few later combine several design categories.

Titles in industry are arbitrary and mean little; an assistant designer may have more scope for creativity and decision-making than a designer or even design director. Many industrial employers are not yet used to working with designers; the contribution the designer is expected or indeed allowed to make varies from one job to another. For example, sometimes the bias is towards technical expertise: the designer is expected to state, through design, exactly how a product is to be manufactured or printed. Sometimes the bias is towards creativity, and the designer is expected to put forward ideas for totally new products. Usually, the visual appearance of the product is the most important aspect of the designer's brief.

Designers usually work with a team of experts from different disciplines, both technical (engineers, printing technologists, etc.) and business (buyers, marketing people, etc.). This teamwork is one of the important differences between artists and designers. Designers cannot just please themselves: their ideas on what is good design and what is not have to be adapted to fit in with commercial and technical requirements.

Though the designer's work varies from one field of design to another, the end-product always has to fulfil at least 3 demands: it must look up-to-date, perform its function adequately, and be economically produced so that it is profitable. For example, a poster must attract attention and be easily readable; a tin-opener or a fridge must work well, look good and last; a biscuit pack must attract attention, fit into shelf-displays, keep its contents fresh, and open easily; a machine tool must serve the engineer's stated purpose, be easy and safe to handle and clean; and all these products must be manufacturable within given cost-limits. Designers must fully understand the purpose of the product they are designing and its marketing and manufacturing problems. They must know the limitations and potentialities of materials and machines available for production. Sometimes a change in technology allows the designer to develop a revolutionary design: e.g. the removal of buffers from the high-speed train allowed the design of a totally different engine shape.

Starting as design assistant, the trained designer gains useful experience when carrying out simple 'design-technician' rather than design tasks. For example, the beginner may translate a designer's idea for a product into detailed working drawings: this requires technical know-how rather than creativity. In furniture design, for example, the task might be specifying how to fix A satisfactorily to B in manufacturing terms without spoiling the appearance.

One designer is usually responsible for several design assistants (now sometimes called design technicians); the size of design teams varies greatly. Designers and design assistants work in various settings: in advertising agencies; manufacturing concerns' design departments; architects' offices; interior design studios; design consultancies, and many others. Organizing freelance work either on one's own or with colleagues on a design consultancy basis is complex and requires experience: newly trained designers should try and gain experience as staff designers first. They need to know a lot not only about production problems and organization, but also about how to deal with clients and finance.

The ratio of opportunities to qualified applicants is more favourable in the less glamorous and more technical field of *product design* than in *interior*, *set*, or *textiles* and *fashion design*.

There will never be as many creative top-level jobs as there are aspiring designers, but there is scope for design assistants or 'technicians' whose work varies in creativity and responsibility; for example, making working drawings from designers' scribbled outlines; model-making; or, in communication design, trying to get as near the designer's intended effect as possible with a restricted number of colours and within printing constraints. There is a vast range of jobs in product design which require technical competence, an appreciation of what constitutes good design and *some* creativity rather than creative genius.

Prospects are reasonable for people who *want* to design for industry and appreciate that it is teamwork, but *not* for failed artists. Many of the best product and fashion designers go abroad where British training is greatly appreciated.

Graphics or Graphic Design or Visual Communication

This is concerned with lettering; illustration, including photography; the design of symbols or 'logos'. It ranges from the design of books, book jackets, all kinds of advertisements (posters, packaging, etc.), to the visual corporate identity symbol of organizations, i.e. presenting the image of that organization in visual, instant-impact-making terms. For example, a logo might be required for use on all of an airline's, hotel chain's, local authority's or company's equipment and property; from planes to cutlery, letter-heads to delivery vans and perhaps even items of clothing.

Visual communication includes 'visual aids' for industrial and educational application. This is an expanding area: instructions and/or information are put over in non-verbal language, with symbols taking the place of words. Symbols are used as teaching aids in industrial training; as user-instructions in drug and textile labelling; as warning or information signs on machinery; on road signs. Symbols may be in wall-chart or film-strip form, or on tiny labels as on medicine and detergent packages, or on textile labels, or on huge posters. Symbol design, whether single or in series, requires great imagination, social awareness, logical thinking.

Visual communication also includes TV graphics: captions, programme titles, all non-verbal TV presentation of information, such as election results, trade-figure trends, etc.; packaging, publicity and advertising; stamp and letter-head design. Computers are being used increasingly to produce graphics. Graphic designers work in advertising agencies, in design units, or in manufacturing firms and other organizations' design departments. Television absorbs only a tiny proportion.

There are few openings in general book and magazine illustration and design, but there is considerable scope in technical and medical graphics, which require meticulous accuracy rather than creative imagination. There is also some scope in the greeting-card trade and in catalogue illustration. Much of this is considered hackwork by creative artists.

3-Dimensional Design

This can be divided conveniently into *product design* and *interior design*.

Product design

This covers the design of all kinds of consumer goods (e.g. domestic appliances, or suitcases) and of machine tools, mechanical equipment, cars, as well as pottery, furniture, etc.

There is pressure on manufacturing industry to pay more attention to design than it has in the past. But there is no general agreement on how this is to be brought about. Many engineers and manufacturers still believe that with a bit more design training, engineers can cope with the aesthetics and ergonomics (ease of handling and cleaning, convenience in use, legibility of instructions). But most progressive manufacturers now agree that engineers must work *with* design specialists who, for their part, must have a thorough understanding of engineering principles and production constraints.

The proportion of 'design input' and 'engineering input' varies from product to product. Designers talk about a 'spectrum' – for example, in the manufacture of a plastic cup the 'engineering input' is very small, the 'design input' large; at the other end of the spectrum is a gas turbine, where the design input may be confined to the lettering of the instructions and the colour (which is, however, important, as it affects the 'work environment', which affects industrial efficiency). In between the two extremes are appliances such as food processors and CD players. The engineer designs the components and says how they must be arranged to do the job; the industrial designer is primarily concerned with the appearance and ergonomics of the product.

Between the first sketch and the final product there may be many joint discussions, drawings, modifications, working models and prototypes. The designer negotiates with the engineer; design technicians develop the product through the various stages. Designers and engineers work in teams – whether the team leader is an engineer or a designer varies according to the type of product, the firm's policy and, last but by no means least, the engineer's and designer's personalities.

Product designers need such extensive knowledge of relevant engineering and manufacturing processes that they tend to stay within a particular manufacturing area. The greatest scope is in plastics, which cover a wide range of products, from toys to complex appliances and equipment.

Interior design

Interior designers work in specialized or general design consultants' studios; large stores; for a group of hotels or supermarkets; in private practice or local authority architects' offices. A considerable knowledge of architecture is required in order to know how to divert drains, move walls safely, or enlarge a shop window satisfactorily. The job of the interior designer, besides being responsible for such things as the management of contracts, is to specify the nature of an interior – how it is made, built and finished – as well as selecting the finishes and fixtures and fittings.

Planning interiors for a hotel, shop, aircraft, etc., needs research before designing starts. Beginners often spend all their time on fact-finding: the different items of goods to be displayed; the number of assistants required in a new shop; the kind of materials suitable and safe for furnishing a plane. They also search for suitable light fittings, heating equipment, furnishing materials, and they may design fixtures and fittings.

The term 'interior design' is often interpreted rather loosely, and some jobs require less training and creativity. This applies particularly to work done by assistants in the design studios of stores or architects' offices; in showrooms of manufacturers of paint, furniture, furnishings, light fittings, wallpaper, etc.; in the furnishing departments of retail stores, and in specialist shops. In these settings, interior designers may advise customers or clients on the choice and assembly of the items needed. This may mean suggesting colour schemes, matching wallpaper and curtains, sketching plans for room decoration, or advising on the most suitable synthetic fabric for a particular furnishing purpose. As stores estimators and home advisers, they may go to customers' houses to give advice or even only to measure up for loose covers and curtains. Some stores and specialist shops employ interior designers as buyers in furniture and furnishing departments, and paint, wallpaper and furnishing fabric manufacturers may employ them as sales representatives. In these jobs 'interior designer' is a courtesy title rather than a job description.

Set design
The work requires a knowledge of period styles, structures and lighting techniques, and a wide range of interests, to help visualize the right kind of set for any particular play or TV programme. Limited scope.

Design for exhibitions and display
Combines some of the work of interior and set designer with model-making and graphic design. Exhibition design is usually done by specialist firms. Exhibitions are often rush jobs, and designers may help put up stands and work through the night before opening. Exhibition designers also work in museums (see p. 320). Limited scope. See also TELEVISION, FILM AND RADIO, p. 529.

Display design

Closely allied to exhibition design, but can be a specialization on its own. The essence of window and 'point-of-sale' design is communication: the display designer must present the store's or shop's image, attract attention and persuade the passer-by to buy. Window display can consist of merely putting a few goods in the window or a show case, or it can be a highly sophisticated exercise in marketing, using specially designed models (see 'Model-making', below) and specially chosen merchandise to convey a 'theme' and marketing policy. In stores there may be a *display manager*, a *display designer* and several *display assistants* or *technicians* who make/arrange the props and merchandise. Reasonable scope.

Studio-based design (glass, jewellery, silverware, stained glass, etc.)

Design and production by designer-craftspeople who run their own small-scale studios or workshops where each article is made individually. This is a fairly precarious way of making a living. However, some studios survive, especially in tourist areas, selling to local shops and individual customers. They have 'studied the market', and perhaps compromised, producing designs which sell rather than those which they would ideally like to produce.

Model-making

This includes the design and/or making up of models for window and exhibition display, and the making of scale models for architects, planners, and interior-design and product-design studios. Many designers, architects, etc., find that their clients are better able to judge a design if they see it in 3-dimensional model form rather than as drawings.

   Model-makers use the traditional materials – wood, plaster, fabric, etc. – and also the new synthetics. They usually work in specialist studios and firms, but some work in other types of design studio. There is more scope here for manual work requiring some creative ability than for pure artistic design. It is an expanding field.

Textiles/Fashion
(see also FASHION AND CLOTHING, p. 207)

Textile design includes printed and woven textiles, carpets and other floor coverings, wallpapers, and plastic surface coverings and decoration. There are few openings in manufacturing firms. One of the difficulties is that thorough knowledge of manufacturing methods is essential, but it is difficult to get a job with suitable firms.

Textile designers work on their own more frequently than do other designers. They usually work through agents who show their designs to manufacturers. Fashion collections are held two or more times a year, furnishing collections usually twice.

Training   Courses fall into one of two groups, lower level/further education and higher level/higher education. It is perfectly possible to take a lower level course and then look for a job; however, many people take a lower level course as a means of getting on to a Higher National Diploma or degree.

Lower level courses
Progression to art and design higher education usually depends on successful completion of a suitable preparatory course. The choice is:

Pre-Foundation/GNVQ Intermediate, normally 1-year full-time. No specified entry requirements.

1-year full-time (occasionally 2-year part-time) Art Foundation (not available in Scotland), for students aged 17 or more, most of whom have several GCSEs and have studied in the sixth form. This course should be 'diagnostic' to help students decide on their eventual specialization. There are many aspects of design which school-leavers cannot know about, and by taking a Foundation course students may be drawn to one of the less well-known design fields. However, Foundation courses are not all the same, so students need to look carefully at what is on offer. In practice, though, students normally have to attend their nearest course, as funding is not generally available from local education authorities for lower level courses taken outside their area.

BTEC/SCOTVEC National awards and Advanced GNVQs
Nearly all of these are 2-year full-time courses for people aged 16 or more. For those with no particular educational qualifications there is a BTEC Intermediate GNVQ in Art and Design (this having replaced the First Diploma); the National Diploma in Design is for those who already know in which area they want to become involved. In some cases students with A-level art (or mature entrants) may enrol for the second year of these courses. There are very few National Certificate courses.

The National Diploma has been replaced in many colleges by the Advanced GNVQ/GSVQ in Art and Design. This is a broad-based course equivalent to A-level standard and acceptable for degree entry; however, as it is still new it has yet to establish the same sort of success rate for progression as that shown by the well-established courses.

Access courses (see p. xxxi)
These are designed for adults returning to education after a break. They usually last 1 year and may be full- or part-time.

Portfolio courses
There are a number of courses, mainly part-time, which do not lead to particular qualifications, but are to help students prepare the portfolio of work which they need when applying for Foundation courses and similar.

The Open College of the Arts
Set up 10 years ago as a charitable trust, the Open College of the Arts provides home-based education in the arts using similar methods to those of the Open University (see p. xxxiii), to which it is affiliated. Courses that can be taken by distance learning, with or without tutorial support provided by one of a network of tutorial centres, include basic art and design, drawing, painting, graphic design, textiles and photography. OCA courses do not lead to nationally recognised qualifications, but they are very useful to mature entrants needing to gain basic knowledge and a portfolio before applying to mainstream courses.

Higher level courses
These consist of Higher National Diplomas, Higher National Certificates, degrees and postgraduate awards.

HNDs/HNCs
These vary considerably. Some are almost indistinguishable from degree courses, but they do not necessarily contain so many complementary studies, and can therefore devote more time to professional design studies. Many vocational courses are approved by the Chartered Society of Designers (the professional association for designers), and they may be as useful in career terms as degree courses (possibly even more so). The Society approves only courses which have up-to-date equipment at their disposal and which include 'professional practice'.

Other courses are chosen for their relevance to the student's objectives. Some are suitable for the student who wishes to concentrate on, for example, lettering or typography, costume jewellery, glass decoration, photography, model-making, interior decoration, window display, book-binding, picture restoring, etc., but who does not aim to be a designer responsible for the creative conception of projects and products.

National Certificates and Higher National Certificates, and National Diplomas and Higher National Diplomas, are intended to lead to the same level of achievement, but the two types of award emphasize the different design aspects. Certificate and Higher National Certificate courses each teach technical skills and procedures within one, or possibly two, sub-specializations. For example, within graphic design, typography and photography; within 3-dimensional design, model-making and window display. A Higher National Certificate holder who specialized in photography, for example, would be able to brief photographers to carry out work required for a mail-order catalogue, as requested by the chief designer, but would not be a top-rank photographer.

National Diploma and Higher Diploma courses are more broadly based than Certificates, and they place more emphasis on creative aspects and design problem-solving. A Higher National Diploma holder in graphic design would be expected, for example, to see through the production of a mail-order catalogue from the marketing manager's brief right up to the finished product.

Courses are usually industry-orientated. Students are taught by staff with industrial experience (though how recent that experience is varies from one course to another). All courses include 'professional practice'. That covers 'client-contact', i.e. communication with people who want work done (and who do not necessarily understand art jargon); business administration; design management. Colleges which cannot guarantee work experience in a commercial studio must simulate such real world-of-work pressures as working to absolute deadlines; coping with late or non-delivery of materials; absence of vital colleagues; last-minute changes in design-brief; working to stringent cost-limits.

In future there are probably going to be more courses which integrate business and design practice, and courses which move across the traditional design specialisms, training 'multi-skilled' designers who can adapt to changing industrial demands. Students will also all have to learn to work with the many new visual-communication technologies.

Choosing the right course is difficult, terminology is very vague and course-titles can be misleading. For example, a graphic design and a visual communication course could both cover exactly the same ground. Equally, graphic design could be much narrower, or indeed much broader, than visual communication; also the approach to the work and sub-specializations and options within courses vary enormously.

Degrees
Normally 3-year full-time, 4-year sandwich. 4–5-year part-time courses are on the increase to attract mature students.

NOTE 1: at present there are two higher education admissions systems for art and design: UCAS (Universities and Colleges Admissions Service) and ADAR (Art and Design Admissions Registry). They will combine to form a single system for entry after 1997.

NOTE 2: London's art, design and some specialist colleges now form the London Institute.

Entry requirements: Either 5 GCSEs (A–C) plus Foundation course lasting 1 or 2 years; or 1 A-level and 3 GCSEs (A–C) plus – normally but not invariably – a 1-year Foundation course; or BTEC/SCOTVEC National Certificate or Diploma. Individual colleges vary in their precise requirements; some demand, for example, GCSE (A–C) maths or craft design and technology and English. Acceptance also very much depends on applicant's portfolio, i.e. on proof of creative ability.

Degrees are normally awarded in 4 separate areas of specialization: fine art, graphic design, 3-dimensional design, and textiles/fashion. Within their specialization, students normally study 1 principal and 1 or 2 subsidiary subjects. In graphic design, for example, typography may be the principal subject, with photography and lettering as subsidiaries. In 3-dimensional design, product design may be the principal, with ceramics and/or silversmithing as subsidiaries.

Students sometimes work for some weeks in a studio or design department industry. Contact with whatever branch of design they hope to take up should play a vital part throughout the course. All students spend 15% of their time on complementary studies which may include history of art and/or management.

Within these broad outlines, individual courses vary greatly. Courses are normally preceded by a full-time Foundation course (not in Scotland) which should be 'diagnostic' to help students decide on the specialization in which to qualify. There are many aspects of design which school-leavers cannot know about, and this course is expected to lead many students to one of the less well-known design fields. However, not all Foundation courses give such broad training and candidates should find out something about the courses. Acceptance for the Foundation course is no guarantee of acceptance for the degree course itself. Art and design can also be studied as part of a joint/combined/modular degree. For example, there are degrees in design and computer studies, design and business management, creative arts.

Postgraduate training
Although a degree or HND is the basic requirement for anyone

wanting to get on in the design world, it is usually necessary these days for artists and designers to update their skills or acquire new ones at some stage, often between 3–10 years after gaining their first degree or HND. There are postgraduate courses in most design specializations, for example in film, in TV graphics, computer-assisted art and animation, conservation, theatre design. The highest qualification is the Royal College of Art's Master's degree.

Art Therapy

Work and training

This is a growing field. Its purpose is twofold: painting and other art forms help withdrawn patients to express themselves and relieve tension, and seeing patients' work helps psychiatrists pinpoint patients' thoughts and problems. The majority of art therapists work – usually on a sessional basis – in psychiatric and mental handicap hospitals with children and with adults, individually and in groups; some work with children with special needs. Art therapy is not so much a career in itself as a field in which practising artists with the necessary human qualities can do useful work. Post-graduate 1-year full-time or 2-year part-time courses are essential.

*

Personal attributes

All careers in art and design require resilience, self-confidence and exceptional talent.

Especially for design: Ability to work as one of a team; creative sensibility and imagination coupled with a logical analytical mind; an interest in science and technology; curiosity and a desire to solve technical problems; perseverance; an interest in the social environment and in the community's needs, tastes and customs; the ability to take responsibility and criticism; willingness at times to lower one's artistic standards in the interests of economic necessity or technical efficiency.

For freelances and senior staff jobs: Business sense (see Design Enterprise Programme, p. 66); the ability to communicate with employers and clients who commission the work but are possibly not themselves interested in art.

For 'technician' jobs: Considerable manual dexterity, technical ability and some creativity.

Late start   The majority of students are in their 20s when they start their courses.

Career-   If experienced and established, designers can set up on their own;
break   some return to outside employment, but competition from recent art-school leavers is likely to be stiff.

Part time   As freelance.

Position   In 1994 more women applied, and were accepted, for degree and
of   HND courses. Women painters and sculptors are doing as well
women   (or as badly) as men, but fewer women than men are in senior jobs or consultancies in design. However, that is due not to discrimination but to the fact that men choose their specialization more realistically and for that reason are more likely to succeed. For example the Art and Design Admissions Registry in 1994 received 702 applications for Theatre Design from women, 151 from men; 3,504 applications for Fashion from women, 544 from men. Yet 1,658 applications for Industrial/Product design were from men, just 251 from women; and 7,071 applications for Graphic Design were from men, 3,702 from women. Yet in these two areas prospects for at least getting a foothold are far better than in Theatre Design and Fashion.

In the Chartered Society of Designers, women form 50% of students and of Diploma members (those with design qualifications and within 5 years of leaving college), but only 20% of full members – proportions which have not changed for several years.

Further   National Society for Education in Art and Design (NSEAD),
informa-   The Gatehouse, Corsham Court, Corsham, Wilts. SN13 0ES
tion   Design Council, 1 Oxenden Street, London SW1 4EE
Chartered Society of Designers (formerly SIAD), 29 Bedford
      Square, London WC1B 3EG
Art and design degrees and BTEC HNDs: Art and Design Admissions Registry, Penn House, 9 Broad Street, Hereford HR4
      9AP
British Association of Art Therapists, 11A Richmond Road,
      Brighton, Sussex BN2 3RL
British Display Society, 70A Crayford High Street, Dartford,
      Kent DA1 4EF
BTEC and SCOTVEC (see pp. xxi, xxii)
The Design Enterprise Programme, London Enterprise Agency, 4
      Snow Hill, London EC1A 2DL (offers small business course

with training grant for qualified artists/designers, see WORKING FOR ONESELF, p. 551)

Open College of the Arts, Houndhill, Worsborough, Barnsley, South Yorks. S70 6TU

Related careers	ADVERTISING – ARCHITECTURE – CARTOGRAPHY – ENGINEERING – FASHION AND CLOTHING – LANDSCAPE ARCHITECTURE – MUSEUMS AND ART GALLERIES – PHOTOGRAPHY – TEACHING – TELEVISION, FILM AND RADIO

Banking

Banking has gone through a period of rapid and dramatic change. Competition has intensified, spurred on by new technology and legislation. Distinctions between different institutions have blurred with activities and services formerly offered by one particular kind of institution now being offered by others. For example, banks offer mortgages and insurance, while building societies (see p. 84) offer cheque accounts. The clearing banks have investment banking divisions or subsidiaries, while the investment banks (as well as the clearers) have bought stockbroking firms. More and more one hears the term 'financial services group' to convey the range of financial activity.

Banking can be broken down into services to individuals and services to companies, though there may be overlap (especially in the clearing banks) in terms of both activity and career opportunity. For example, a high street branch manager may be involved with individuals and with corporate clients; a trainee might have a spell in a department marketing corporate services and then move into a role as a personal accounts executive.

Retail/Personal Banking

Entry qualifica-tions Most banks do not now set minimum academic requirements. Those with A-levels, Advanced GNVQ, a BTEC National award or a degree will normally be recruited to an accelerated training programme. In Scotland, three Highers at grades A–C are required.

The work Banks provide a wide range of financial services to personal customers, largely through their branch networks. They take deposits and make loans, transmit money from one account to another, exchange foreign currency and travellers' cheques, offer mortgages, insurance policies, pensions and investment schemes. They also offer financial advice on a range of matters.

Staff at all levels in a branch deal with people as well as money and figures. From an early stage in training considerable emphasis is placed on the ability to relate to customers, identify their needs and promote the bank's services.

Trainees normally start in the general office, where they learn basic procedures such as sorting and listing cheques so that they can be 'read' electronically and operating the terminal linked to the central computer on which customers' accounts are updated. Trainees usually commence duties as a cashier. Cashiers are in the front line of the intensifying battle for customers so they must make a good impression. Courtesy, efficiency and helpfulness are important.

After a spell at the counter, trainees undertake other customer service duties, for example, setting up standing orders/direct debits and opening accounts. Promotion to senior clerical duties involves the development of supervisory skills and the more specialized technical knowledge needed to deal with, for example: customers' investments; the sanction of small personal loans and analysis, with the management team, of more detailed lending propositions; or executor and trust work, dealing with trusts and wills in which the bank may look after customers' or their dependants' interests, advise people who have been left money on investment, or explain complex money matters to bewildered heirs. As clerical officers are promoted to junior management grades they take on increased responsibility for customer service and the smooth running of the branch.

Managers may be responsible for one branch or several. Within policy laid down by the bank, they have considerable responsibility for approving loans, dealing with business customers from the small to, sometimes, the very large, overseeing the smooth running of their branches and marketing the bank's growing range of services and 'products'.

Those on accelerated management training programmes might spend only very short periods in the clerical functions. They are not necessarily expected to master the tasks but need to appreciate their importance in the overall service the bank offers its customers. There are also opportunities in regional and head offices where, for example, specialist advice is available and new 'products' are developed. A career with a bank can also develop into non-banking functions, e.g. personnel.

The combination of recession and new technology has led to large cuts in staff among the banks. The impact is more marked in lower-level jobs; in an intensely competitive climate, the banks continue to recruit and train those who have the potential to become senior managers. The banks all have well-developed graduate recruitment and training programmes, but in theory it is still possible to reach senior levels from a modest start. (Many graduates also opt to develop their careers on the corporate side of the business.)

Training   Largely on the job, with residential courses at more senior levels. Day-release may be available for those preparing for the exams of the Chartered Institute of Bankers, but it is often restricted to Associate Examination candidates and those on accelerated programmes. There are evening and correspondence courses for other candidates.

Personal   Meticulous accuracy; the interpersonal skills to deal with
attributes   customers; a clear, logical mind; tact; courtesy; a feeling for figures and interest in work with data-processing equipment.

Late start   No precise figures are available for the profession overall. In the past the proportion of full-time late entrants has been small, but banks are now looking very seriously at mature applicants with experience and the right personal qualities.

Career-   Most of the major banks operate a career-break/return-to-work
break   scheme. They vary in detail but, broadly speaking, are open to male and female staff, for a period of 2–5 years. Some guarantee a return to the organization at one's previous grade. Normally the member of staff is expected to undertake refresher training for 2–4 weeks a year and to keep abreast of developments.

Position   About 60% of staff employed are female. About 30% of junior
of   managers, 12% of middle managers and 5% of senior managers
women   are women. Nevertheless, it is estimated that the figure has probably doubled in the last 5 years. Approximately 50% of graduate trainees are women. Though, according to Women in Banking, 'theory is well ahead of practice', all the banks are concentrating on the barriers to promotion for women and looking into childcare, flexible hours, job-sharing and so on. Some banks run special management development courses for female staff which deal with such issues as assertiveness and women's expectations. Approximately 30% of female staff work part time; at present these are mainly at clerical and secretarial level.

Wholesale/Corporate Banking

Entry   There are some opportunities for school-leavers with GCSE or
qualifica-   A-level or equivalent, but their prospects may be limited. Most
tions   banks recruit mainly graduate trainees.

The work   Companies and governments require financial services broadly equivalent to those offered to individuals, but the scale and complexity are much greater. Among the services offered by the banks to their corporate customers are: banking, which is basically taking deposits, transferring funds and lending money; corporate finance, which includes advising on mergers and acquisitions, raising capital, business strategy, competitors and outside factors; and treasury, which involves buying and selling foreign currency to protect against disadvantageous currency movements. The banks are also involved in investment management on behalf of institutional investors of large sums of money, such as pension funds and investment trusts, and the securities business (see p. 495) – making issues and buying and selling shares. Government work on the privatization of nationalized industries has been a feature of recent years.

Corporate banking can start with the local branch manager, but the more complex work will be done in the corporate divisions of the clearing banks, their investment banking subsidiaries, and the investment banks. Not all banks offer the same range of services. Staff are required for a range of tasks from analysis to sales. In most jobs staff should be capable of analysing, researching and selling the results, but team work is a common feature of this area of banking.

An important related activity is dealing – in currencies and various financial 'products' designed to help firms finance their businesses. Banks may deal speculatively on their own account to make a profit, or on behalf of clients to help them manage financial risks.

After the rapid expansion of the mid-1980s, numbers have been steadily declining, affected by both fierce competition and recession. However, though the level varies, the larger banks will maintain some regular recruitment as a long-term investment. For those who are successful, the financial rewards are high, but, as recent years have shown, high rewards are often balanced by high risks, especially on the dealing side. It is not a business that carries 'passengers'.

Most 'bankers' and corporate financiers will be graduates, but dealers are often non-graduates who start in a support function. Specialist staff, e.g. experts in a particular industry, have good opportunities to move between banks.

Training   Largely on the job with the opportunity and encouragement to obtain relevant qualifications.

Personal   High intelligence; ability to work as a member of a team and to
attributes   relate to clients at a high level; flexibility; competitive drive; ability to think analytically and practically. *For dealers*: confidence, quick wits, entrepreneurial flair, independence.

Late start   Some 20% of entrants are over 30, with relevant industrial/professional experience. A 'fresh' start for job changers without such experience is unlikely.

Careerbreak   Most of the major high street banking groups operate a careerbreak/return-to-work scheme (see p. 70). Formal schemes are rare, if not non-existent, among the other banks.

Position of women   Women are not yet seen in large numbers in top positions. However, at the entry level they have been very successful in recent years, with some banks reporting a higher success rate among women graduate applicants. Job-sharing and part-time work are not widespread and mainly confined to clerical/secretarial areas and possibly support functions like personnel. Employers claim resistance from clients who want continuity of service from their bankers.

Further information   Banking Information Service, Education and Careers, 10 Lombard Street, London EC3V 9AT

Chartered Institute of Bankers, Membership Services Unit, Emmanuel House, 4–9 Burgate Lane, Canterbury, Kent CT1 2XJ

Institute of Bankers in Scotland, 19/20 Rutland Square, Edinburgh EH1 2DE

London Investment Banking Association, 6 Frederick's Place, London EC2R 8BT

Related careers   ACCOUNTANCY – ACTUARY – BUILDING SOCIETY WORK – INSURANCE

Beauty Specialist

Entry qualifications
For school-leavers, 2 or more GCSEs depending on course, but some schools ask for biology or chemistry; see 'Training', below. Minimum age for employment as beauty therapist, 18 +; as consultant, usually about 24.

The work
Practitioners may use one of several job-titles, but the two most common terms are *beauty therapist* and *beauty consultant*.

Beauty Therapist

Most *beauty therapists* use the full range of available treatments on the face and body. These extend from make-up, facials and wax or electric depilation (removal of superfluous hair) to massage, saunas, diet and exercise. They know when to deal with a skin complaint themselves or when to advise the client to see a doctor. It is possible to learn one or two techniques only, e.g. a *beautician* works on the face and neck only; a *manicurist/pedicurist* on the hands/feet; the *electrologist* (or *epilationist*) uses various means to remove unwanted hair; a *masseur/masseuse* performs face/body massage. (*Aromatherapists* massage with aromatic oils.)

Beauty therapists work in private high street salons (sometimes combined with hairdressers), in their own, or clients' homes, in health farms or cosmetic firms' salons. Clients may be of all ages, male or female.

It is not always easy for students to find jobs, but generally beauty and fitness treatments are becoming more popular. Some beauty specialists set up on their own: the initial financial outlay on equipment depends on the treatments offered. The town hall will advise on necessary licences (see WORKING FOR ONESELF, p. 551). For those trained in hairdressing there are some opportunities in television (see p. 531) and with psychiatric and other patients for whom beauty care can be part of their rehabilitation.

Beauty Consultants (Sales Consultants, Sales Representatives)

Usually work in the perfumery department of large stores,

occasionally in luxury hotels (at home or abroad), on liners, or at airports. They are usually under contract to a cosmetics firm and travel round the country, working for a week or two each in a succession of stores or shops.

They sell and promote the firm's products and try to win regular customers. They answer questions on skin-care and make-up problems, and may give talks and demonstrations.

Top jobs are as cosmetic buyers for stores, at the head offices of cosmetic firms, and as training consultants.

Training   *Professional training*

For jobs in a reputable salon or health farm, it is important to take a course leading to one of the mainstream qualifications. NVQs (see p. xix) are available at levels 1 to 3 and students should make sure that courses lead to these qualifications, as they are likely to become very important in the future (e.g. for getting insurance cover). Courses are available in both local education authority colleges and private schools. The advantage of maintained college courses is that they are free for younger students, although they generally last longer than private ones. Most good private courses last from 5 to 12 months (some are longer). Fees for private colleges range from a few hundred pounds to several thousand, depending on range of skills taught. Syllabus includes theory – anatomy, physiology, diets, salesmanship, salon organization – and practical work: giving facials, different types of massage, make-up, sometimes electrical treatments, etc.

Main courses are:

1. 2-year (1-year for over-21s) full-time course for City and Guilds Beauty Therapist's Certificate. *Entry requirements*: 3 GCSEs (A-C), preferably including a science. (Separate Certificate in Electrical Epilation may be available as part of the course.)

2. 2-year full-time BTEC National Diploma in Beauty Therapy. *Entry requirements*: 4 GCSEs, including biology or SCOTVEC National Certificate.

3. BTEC/SCOTVEC Higher National Diploma in Beauty Therapy. Courses last 2 years full time; special emphasis on TV make-up requirements, and remedial aspects. *Entry requirements*: 4 GCSEs and 1 A-level in approved subjects which must include at least 1 science subject (some colleges ask for A-level science).

4. Courses leading to awards of one of the national or international beauty therapy examining bodies, for example the International Health and Beauty Council, the Confederation of International Beauty Therapy and Cosmetology and ITEC

(International Therapy Examination Council). Minimum age usually 18.

NOTE: It is important to check the usefulness of courses not included above with one of the organizations mentioned under 'Further information'.

Courses given by cosmetics houses for sales consultants
Minimum age depends on age range at which product is aimed, e.g. teenagers or mature people. Majority need to be 24+ and must have several years' selling experience and must be good salespeople. Training is mainly in-store and lasts a few weeks. Subjects dealt with are facials, simple massage, eyebrow shaping and make-up, for both day and evening. These courses qualify students as sales consultants, but not as beauty therapist.

It is useful to take a hairdressing training as well as beauty training. It widens the choice of jobs later.

Personal attributes A liking for people of all ages; a friendly, confident manner; tact; courtesy; an attractive, well-groomed appearance; naturally good skin; cool, dry hands; good health; business sense; ability to express oneself easily; foreign language sometimes an asset.

Late start Beauty specialists' work is very suitable for late entrants. Many salons prefer women who are nearer in age to the majority of clients than young school-leavers are. Nurses and physiotherapists sometimes choose this work as a second career.

Career-break No special problem, except for need to find new clients.

Part time Fairly easy for experienced people.

Position of women Up to now this has been a 100% female occupation, but some male students are now on courses.

Further information City and Guilds of London Institute (see p. xxii)
BTEC and SCOTVEC (see pp. xxi, xxii)
IHBC, 46 Aldwick Road, Bognor Regis, West Sussex PO21 2PN
ITEC, James House, Oakelbrook Mill, Newent, Glos. GL18 1HD
Confederation of International Beauty Therapy and Cosmetology (CIBTAC), Parabola House, Parabola Road, Cheltenham, Glos. GL50 3AH

Related careers TELEVISION, FILM AND RADIO: *Make-up artists/Designers*

Booksellling

Entry qualifications	None laid down, but good general education essential.
The work	All bookselling is a branch of retailing, but there is a difference between a specialist bookshop, where customers expect to find knowledgeable staff, and non-specialist bookshops with a limited range of titles and various non-book products on sale. The latter are more suitable for people interested more in a retailing career than in books. Specialist bookshop staff must be well read in order to be able to advise customers and answer queries. Reading should cover a wide field rather than only one's own interests, but in large bookshops staff usually specialize in one or two subjects. Customers are often left to browse undisturbed amongst the stock and are offered help and advice only when they want it.

Assistants' duties include daily dusting and filling and tidying shelves and display-tables. This also helps them to learn the stock and remember where titles are shelved. Assistants also write out orders, keep records and may do some bookkeeping. In many bookshops, ordering, stock control, etc. is now computerized. Assistants may pack and unpack parcels and carry them to the post; bookshop work is physically quite hard.

One of the most interesting and most skilled parts of the job is helping customers who have only a vague idea of what they want or cannot explain what they have in mind. It may involve tracing titles in bibliographies and catalogues.

Book-buying – selecting a small proportion of the vast number of new titles published each month – is a highly skilled and often tricky task. Several members of staff may be responsible for buying within one or more subject areas. They have to be able to judge what will interest their particular customers, whether to buy a new title at all and how many copies to order. New titles are ordered before reviews have appeared so staff must trust their own judgement. They must also judge how much reliance to place on the recommendation of publishers' representatives.

Managers may take part in or do all the buying – it depends on how experienced their staff and how large the shop. Above all, the manager tries to give the shop an 'image' to attract a nucleus of regular customers. This is done partly by the choice of books in stock and partly by the method and type of display and arrangement of the shop as a whole. The manager is also responsible for the stock-control system (as would be the case in any other kind of shop).

Far more people want to work in bookshops than there are vacancies. Bookshops thrive only at Christmas; nevertheless some owner-managers of small bookshops do reasonably well if they have researched the market thoroughly before setting up shop (see WORKING FOR ONESELF, p. 551).

Training

Staff learn mainly on the job, although some large shops and chains have formal training schemes. Good bookshops and departments encourage staff to take the Booksellers' Association's qualification, the Certificate in Bookselling Skills. The syllabus includes computerized ordering and cataloguing systems, up-to-date marketing and customer-relations principles. It therefore contains 'transferable skills' which may be useful in other retail spheres. On-the-job training is complemented by distance-learning packages. Students may have a tutor, seminars and tutorials; self-help groups complement the training. An outside examiner assesses students' work before the Certificate is awarded. A new Diploma in Professional Bookselling has been introduced by the Booksellers' Association.

Personal attributes

An excellent memory; commercial sense; wide interests and extensive general knowledge; pleasure in reading and handling books; a liking for meeting people with various interests; a helpful friendly manner and the knack of making diffident customers who are not well-read feel they are welcome; the ability to work well in a large team or in a very small shop or department; a calm temperament.

Late start

No greater problem than young entrants.

Career-break

Should not present any problems.

Part time

Good scope.

Position of women

A large proportion of staff and managers, but not of owners, are women. The proportion of part-time staff – mainly women – has increased recently, but their pay is low.

Further information	The Booksellers' Association of Great Britain and Ireland, 272 Vauxhall Bridge Road, London SW1V 1BA
Related careers	INFORMATION WORK – RETAIL MANAGEMENT

Building

Entry qualifications

For degree in building: 2–3 A-levels, to include maths/science for some courses. *For technician training*: see BTEC/SCOTVEC National and Higher National, pp. xxi, xxii. *For craft training*: none specified.

The work

The building industry is made up of companies ('contractors') of all sizes, from international giants employing thousands of skilled craft workers and professional staff, including architects, chartered builders, surveyors and chartered engineers, to small 'jobbing builders' employing one or two craftsmen/women and taking on additional people as required. Many small builders work part of the time on their own and part of the time as sub-contractors to larger firms, sometimes providing a specialist skill which the main contractor may not be able to offer. Large companies have their own design departments and execute large-scale projects such as housing estates, large office blocks, hospitals, etc. Smaller firms – and often large ones too – work to plans drawn up by the client's architect and may sub-contract work to specialist firms of plumbers, tilers, smaller general builders, etc. On large projects the client, or the client's representative, appoints a *clerk of works* (see p. 81).

The building trade (particularly, but not only, firms concerned with large projects) is very dependent on the economic climate. Traditionally, when there is plenty of work, especially large-scale projects, there is a shortage of skilled, trained people at all levels. There are still too few building graduates, so experienced managers are usually in demand.

Levels and organization of work are very much less well-defined than, for example, in the engineering industry. Many contractors start at craft level and build up their own business, but they need to understand the new technologies and materials, know how to work to given standards and how to organize work efficiently (i.e. ensuring that workforce, plant and materials are at the right place at the right time and that there is a regular flow of work). There is, therefore, increasing scope for people with specialist and management qualifications, but there will always be scope for craftsmen and craftswomen who are good at their job and also have organizing ability to build up their own business. Knowledge of basic crafts like bricklaying, carpentry and plumbing is useful even for managers; knowledge of new materials and technologies is essential in all parts of the industry.

Building Managers

Managers are responsible for co-ordinating the wide variety of activities and processes involved on a project. They must see that work is carried out in the right sequence with the right materials – which must be available at the right time – and at the right cost. They organize the labour force, so must understand the work of bricklayers, carpenters, etc. Depending on the size of the firm, work may include organizing the financial side (paying wages, paying for materials, etc.). Some building management jobs are site-based (there may be a site office), some are office-based; nearly all jobs involve some site visits; and many jobs, at least for large firms, involve working away from home at times, occasionally overseas.

Usual job titles and specializations (which vary very much between firms) are:

1. *Buyer* (*purchasing officer*): Selects from the design drawings the materials and services needed; contacts suppliers and sub-contractors to obtain the most competitive prices; ensures materials are available at the right time.

2. *Estimator*: Calculates the likely cost of materials (from door handles to concrete), labour and plant, and the time needed for the project when the firm is tendering for a contract. Also analyses costs of existing projects to provide guide to future estimates.

3. *Planner*: At pre-tender stage is involved in the decision about how the tender can be adjusted. When tender is accepted, produces charts showing sequence of operations. Works closely with contract manager. In large companies will use computer for this. Planners need experience of estimating, buying or contracts management.

4. *Site engineer*: In charge of technical side of an individual project. Sets out the positions and levels of the building to ensure it is placed in the correct position in accordance with the designs. Oversees all the work on site, including quality control (see 'Civil Engineering' and 'Structural Engineering', pp. 187–8).

5. *Site manager/site agent* (used to be called 'general foreman'): In charge of the contract. Ensures the designs and specifications are understood by the foremen/women; plans and coordinates materials and labour. Sees that building keeps to the plan and time schedule (see 'Building Technicians', below, and 'Surveying Technicians', p. 508). May control work of young engineers.

6. *Production controller*: Works on incentive schemes; measures work done by operatives as part of productivity control; takes part in construction planning at site level. Some specialize in work study and/or industrial relations.

7. *Contract manager*: Oversees several projects. Moves from site to site ensuring that work is progressing according to plan. Plans movement of machines and labour to minimize delays and time-wasting. Has overall responsibility for completion of projects to correct standard at the right time.

8. *Clerk of works*: Other building management specialists work for the contractor; the clerk of works is employed by the client (or client's representative). May be employed full-time on a contract basis or on a self-employed private practice/consultant basis. Works from an office on site and is responsible for seeing that the work is carried out according to the specification. As the only person on site not working for the contractor the clerk of works can be rather isolated, so needs to be confident and self-sufficient. On large schemes duties may include supervising several other clerks of works specializing in, for example, heating and ventilating or electrical installation.

9. *Building control officers*: They are responsible for checking sites to see that work complies with building regulations. In certain circumstances they may advise contractors on alternative methods of construction. Up until recently they worked only for local and other public authorities, but they can now work in the private sector.

Building Technicians

The work of technicians overlaps with that of managers and, in fact, many managers start as technicians (see 'Training') and do not gain any higher qualification. Technicians may be involved in any of the specializations mentioned above. They do many of the detailed costings, work out quantities and prepare drawings. On site they may be involved in surveying, measuring and detailed planning of the work.

The work of building managers and technicians overlaps and both overlap very much with that of chartered surveyors/surveying technicians and civil/structural engineers/technicians.

Building Crafts

Craftsmen and craftswomen are skilled in one, occasionally more than one, occupation or trade: the most common are bricklaying, carpentry, joinery, plastering, plumbing and electrical installation, tiling and roofing.

Training   *Manager*

Either on the job by training first as a technician (see below) and then taking BTEC/SCOTVEC Higher National awards. Successful completion plus appropriate experience leads to exemptions from various examinations of the Chartered Institute of Building.

Or (for jobs with big organizations) 3-year full-time or 4-year sandwich degree in building/building technology/building construction and management. Most give full exemption from Chartered Institute of Building's Final examination.

Clerk of works: As above followed by evening or correspondence course for Institute of Clerk of Works' Intermediate and Final examinations. (BTEC National awards give some exemptions.) Membership of the Institute is compulsory before sitting the examinations. Some local authorities give day-release.

Building control officers qualify in building, surveying or relevant engineering subjects at BTEC/SCOTVEC or degree level.

Technician

Either via the Construction Industry Training Board's youth training programme (see below) *or* as a trainee with a company and day- or block-release (both may lead to BTEC/SCOTVEC National awards) *or* by studying full time for BTEC National Diploma (or SCOTVEC equivalent) (see pp. xxi, xxii). Courses can be in building studies, construction or building services engineering (see ENGINEERING, p. 188).

Craft

The CITB has introduced a new policy to take effect in 1995/6, under which it recognizes a range of flexible training routes to meet the needs of young and older entrants and may involve full- or part-time or block-release. All are aimed at enabling trainees to gain NVQs level 2. These routes are:

1. 2-year apprenticeship or traineeship foundation courses under the agency of either the CITB or a training contractor followed by employment as an apprentice or trainee.

2. Full-time courses (normally 2 years) at further education colleges.

3. Direct employment on an industry-based training scheme.

4. On-the-job training for jobs for which this is the only method (e.g. tunnelling).

5. Adult training.

6. Modern apprenticeships (similar to 1) but lasting 3 years and leading towards NVQs level 3.

Personal attributes *Building crafts*: Some manual dexterity; an inquiring and logical mind; willingness to work with the minimum of or no supervision with potentially dangerous equipment; a reasonably careful nature or at least awareness of dangers unless basic rules are observed.

Building management: Ability to work with all kinds of people and help them work as a team; technical and practical aptitudes; good at organization; willing to work outdoors in all weathers; commercial sense.

Late start No age limit for traineeships as there used to be for apprenticeships, but in practice young school-leavers are given preference. There may be training and retraining schemes for adults (see p. xxv) with or without related experience and/or qualifications, e.g. as surveying technician, p. 508.

Career-break Probably difficult without retraining. So far nothing is known about returners (see WORKING FOR ONESELF, p. 551).

Part time Possible if working for small contractor or shop or for oneself.

Position of women There are as yet few craftswomen (less than 1%); more women have entered building management and are proving very successful. In 1995 2% of the Chartered Institute of Building membership were women, following a 16% rise over the previous 12 months.

Further information Construction Careers Service, Construction Industry Training Board, Bircham Newton, King's Lynn, Norfolk PE31 6RH (for England and Wales); or 4 Edison Street, Hillington, Glasgow G52 4XN (for Scotland)

Chartered Institute of Building, Englemere, King's Ride, Ascot, Berks SL5 8BJ

Institute of Clerks of Works, 41 The Mall, London W5 3TJ

Institute of Building Control, 21 High Street, Ewell, Epsom, Surrey KT17 1SB

JT Ltd, Head Office, South Block, Central Court, Knool Rise, Orpington, Kent BR6 0JA

Scottish Electrical Charitable Training Trust, Bush House, Bush Estate, Penicuik, Midlothian, Edinburgh EH26 0SB

Women and Manual Trades, 52–54 Featherstone Street, London EC1Y 8RT

Related careers AGRICULTURE AND HORTICULTURE – ARCHITECTURE – ENGINEERING: *Civil Engineering* – SURVEYING

Building Society Work

The traditional function of building societies has been, on the one hand, to encourage people to save and invest with them, and, on the other, to use this money to lend out as mortgages to house-buyers. However, since 1986 building societies have been widening their activities and have become more directly competitive with the banks. Many now operate bank-type cheque accounts, make unsecured loans, offer estate agency services, insurance services, pension plans, stock market investment schemes. Not all societies have developed all options but most have diversified in some way. Some societies are likely to follow the lead of the Abbey National and become public limited companies to enable them further to develop as 'personal financial services' groups.

Entry qualifications

For *clerical staff*, who take the Chartered Institute of Bankers Certificate in Financial Services Practice, no formal entry qualifications. For *trainee managers*, aiming for the Associateship of the Chartered Institute of Bankers (ACIB), at least one A-level and GCSE English language at grades A–C *or* accepted equivalent *or* a recognized degree or professional qualification.

The work

In the past, most managers started as clerks and were promoted within the society. It is still possible to reach a management position from a humble start, especially in a small society, but in practice most large and medium-size organizations now have 2-tier entry.

Clerical staff carry out routine office tasks such as filing, accounting and data-processing. *Cashiers* or *customer advisers* deal with clients at the counter, handling routine transactions and giving advice and information. They have a key role in promoting new services and 'products'. Some may be promoted to a management development programme.

Trainee managers, who must have the minimum qualifications for the Associateship examination (see above), do some counter work to learn how to deal with customers, but most of their time is spent on such work as mortgage principles and processing, assessing applicants' suitability for mortgages, and liaising with surveyors, estate agents, conveyancers and investment specialists.

Some time may be spent in head office functions. After 2–3 years trainee managers are expected to be fully fledged managers of small branches or assistant managers of larger branches.

Much of *managers'* time may be spent on routine mortgage processing or on some of the new activities, but marketing is one of their key functions. Not only are managers responsible for selling *their* society and branch to the local community, but they have an important role in talking and listening to customers about their needs and feeding this information back to head office, where new products are developed. Managers may be promoted through a succession of larger branches, to an area or regional office management role, or to a head office function such as marketing or systems development.

To compete in the highly competitive financial services market, there is a growing need for people with specialized skills and knowledge in, for example, accountancy, law, marketing, economic planning. Most of the major societies now run graduate training schemes.

Building societies vary in size, structure and the kind of career they offer. There are still small local societies without organized management and training structures. People interested in a more varied career in personal financial services should try for a job in one of the large or medium-size organizations.

Training
Largely on the job. Study for relevant qualifications may be by part-time day or evening classes, correspondence courses, flexible learning, revision courses, private study. It should take about three years to complete the Associateship exams. A range of 'top-up' courses can lead to an honours degree in financial services after further part-time study, usually by distance learning.

There are also opportunities to work towards NVQs/SVQs, not only in building society specific work, but also in areas such as IT, secretarial administration and accounts.

Personal attributes
Communication skills; flexibility; ability to learn quickly; organizing ability; numeracy; liking for routine desk work; good business sense.

Late start
Trainee managers may be taken on up to about 30, branch staff later. Retail banking, office or retail experience may be useful. Academic entry requirements may be waived.

Career-break
Not as common as in the banks, but schemes do operate in some organizations and are likely to grow over the next few years. Rapidly developing technology, services and products can make a return more difficult.

Position
of
women

80% of staff in the industry are women, but at higher levels and in management, males predominate.

Societies vary greatly in their policies. Some are introducing parental breaks, term-time working, part-time and job-sharing opportunities, though these innovations are not common at management level. Some organizations are running assertiveness courses to encourage female staff to be more career-minded. Career-minded girls should shop around for a good employer.

Further
informa-
tion

Chartered Institute of Bankers, Membership Services Unit, Emmanuel House, 4–9 Burgate Lane, Canterbury, Kent, CT1 2XJ

Building Societies Association (for member societies), 3 Savile Row, London W1X 1AF

Individual societies (and the Abbey National plc)

Related
careers

BANKING – INSURANCE – MANAGEMENT

Careers Work

Recent legislation has transferred the running of local careers services from local education authorities to a variety of organizations in both the private and public sector. The new careers services are contracted to the Department of Education and Employment to provide a core range of services to young people, schools and employers, but will offer additional services on a commercial basis (though fees are not always met by clients). The role of some careers advisers is likely to change as a result of these developments, but it is too early to know exactly how.

Careers Adviser

Entry qualifications

Degree, Dip. H.E., teaching qualification or acceptable alternative of comparable standard.

The work

The traditional role of careers advisers in careers services is to help young people to make sound and realistic career choices and to implement those choices. This covers a wide range of activities from helping an unemployed school-leaver find a job to helping a school to plan an on-going programme to suit various age and ability groups. Recent developments in education and training have broadened the scope of careers advisers' work so that they have a more active role in, for example, helping to plan work-related areas of the school curriculum and liaising with training organizations on the provision of appropriate training. In addition, work with adults has increased; a growing number of careers services throughout the country have become all-age guidance services, developing their work with adults who might be unemployed, looking for a change of career, or returning to education or work after a break.

Interviewing individuals at various points in their education is an important part of careers work. Advisers must be objective is impartial in helping the clients come to understand their own interests, abilities and personalities and show them how to plan their future work/training strategy. The result of these discussions is likely to be a guidance summary and an action plan. Advisers must not push or favour one particular option or route. This demands both guidance and counselling skills and a sound knowledge of all the options.

Careers officers work closely with schools and further education colleges and their role is expanding. They work with careers teachers to plan and implement a programme of careers education and guidance which can span several age groups and decision points. It is now common for individual careers advisers to negotiate formal school-level agreements about the kind of service they will provide during an academic year.

This work in schools can include work with individuals or groups; arranging for people to come in and talk about their work; arranging visits to work places; or work experience for pupils. Careers advisers also have a key role in promoting and establishing closer links between education and industry. For example, they might arrange courses and conferences which bring teachers into industry, liaising with schools to select suitable teachers, helping employers to develop appropriate programmes, assisting both sides in the evaluation of the exercise and helping teachers to relate what they have learned to the curriculum. Careers advisers may help schools organize and keep up-to-date the information in their careers libraries. These days this information is not simply in the form of leaflets, books and videos. Most schools have computers which can run a whole range of careers software, including ECCTIS (for higher education courses), and various programs to help with self-analysis and occupational choice. Careers advisers are expected to be knowledgeable about all of these and they themselves increasingly make use of laptop computers.

A good deal of careers advisers' time is spent gathering information. They need to keep up to date with developments, trends and impending changes in education, training and the jobs market. They visit employers, talking both to training and personnel officers about their needs and to people actually doing jobs about the nature, demands and satisfactions of their work. They contact colleges and other educational institutions to keep themselves informed about courses, entry qualifications and employment prospects and advise colleges on suitable courses to run for young people.

Much of this work takes careers advisers out and about, but there is a certain amount of essential office-based administrative work. Good record-keeping is very important, and the information collected must be made accessible to colleagues and clients.

Often this involves writing brief summaries or more detailed information sheets on, for example, a particular occupational area or topics like choosing a course.

After a period of general experience careers advisers may specialize. Opportunities include work with ethnic minorities, with special-needs pupils, with adults or with more academically able pupils.

Training   1-year full-time (2-year part-time) course plus a probationary year in service leading to the Diploma in Careers Guidance. Courses are offered by a number of universities and the College of Guidance Studies in Kent (which also offers an open learning course). Trainee careers advisers may be seconded on a course by their employing organizations. The syllabus includes organization of education services; occupational and social psychology; public and social administration; organization of industry; counselling aims and methods; practical work with pupils; visits to a variety of places of work and talks with/by employers.

Psychometric testing is increasingly being used within careers services, and careers advisers using such tests are usually required to have a certificate of competence from the British Psychological Society. NVQs/SVQs levels 2–4 in advice and guidance are currently being developed; the Institute of Careers Guidance, in conjunction with the Local Government Management Board, has been accredited as one of the awarding bodies.

Personal attributes   Ability to get on with and understand people of all levels of intelligence and temperament; interest in industrial and other employment trends and problems; sympathy with rather than critical attitude towards other people's points of view; organizing ability; willingness to work in a team; ability to put facts across clearly and helpfully; ability to gain people's confidence and to put them at ease however shy and worried; insight and imagination to see how young people might develop and to understand adults' particular difficulties; ability to communicate with individuals, with groups and in writing.

Late start   Those over 25 with 5 years' relevant work experience are exempted from normal entry requirements, but must demonstrate ability to cope with post-graduate level course. Relevant jobs are those which involve dealing with a variety of people, preferably in a work situation. Maturity and variety of experience can be an asset: approximately a quarter of students are 'mature'.

Career-break   Should not present any problems.

Part time   Some opportunities. Job-sharing and other flexible work patterns are now common.

Position of women   Women careers officers outnumber men, but a very much smaller proportion are in senior management jobs. As in many other professions, women have felt that they have had to be better qualified and experienced than men for the same type of promotion. Recent years have seen more women making it to more senior roles.

Further information   Institute of Careers Guidance 27A Lower High Street, Stourbridge, West Midlands DY8 1TA

Local Government Management Board, 4th floor, Arndale House, The Arndale Centre, Luton LU1 2TS

Other Careers Work

There are opportunities for careers work in a number of other organizations, but they are limited in number and the entry qualifications of practitioners are very varied. In some cases careers officers have diversified into another area; in most cases previous employment experience is a prerequisite.

In *higher education*, careers advisers carry out a range of activities similar to those in careers services but at a level appropriate to the age, maturity, sophistication and educational level of their clients. A degree and employment experience are essential; beyond that, backgrounds vary enormously. There is no pre-entry training; in-service training may be arranged by the employer or by the Association of Graduate Careers Advisory Services.

A network of educational guidance services for adults, which had gradually been established over a number of years, now falls under the TEC/LEC umbrella (see p. xxiii). Advisers working in these aim to help adults understand and take full advantage of the full range of educational and training opportunities available. The work includes information, assessment, advice and counselling, so, again, a wide variety of backgrounds may be appropriate.

Other employers of careers advisory staff include *professional bodies*, *charities* and *vocational guidance organizations*. Again, backgrounds vary widely. Some people have experience in the

Careers Service, in teaching, in personnel or in the relevant profession. Vocational guidance organizations often look for psychology graduates.

Related careers	PERSONNEL / HUMAN RESOURCES MANAGEMENT – PSYCHOLOGY – TEACHING – YOUTH AND COMMUNITY WORK

Cartography

Entry qualifica- tions
For *cartographer*: degree or Higher National award: A-levels in geography, maths or science often required. For *cartographic draughtsmen/women*: 4 GCSEs (A–C) including maths and English.

The work
Cartographers are concerned with map-making. A map in this context covers any type of chart, plan, 3-dimensional model or computer image representing the whole or sections of the earth, or of other parts of the universe. While their work in producing 'traditional' maps and wall charts with which everyone is familiar, such as those used in schools and universities, by walkers and motorists and for land and air surveying, is as important as ever, there is steady demand for more specialist maps and charts. Planning professionals may need maps showing traffic flow or the distribution of housing, employment or industry; forest officers need to see areas of planning, thinning and felling; highly accurate details of the sea bed are needed by scientists looking for oil or minerals. There are increasing calls for charts showing the spread, or contraction, of animal and plant populations and human habitation. The penetration of space and of the earth's crust has extended cartographers' horizons and set new challenges in finding new ways of representing the results of such exploration.

Cartographers are concerned with every stage of preparation and interpretation. They have to determine what data are needed for any particular map, discuss how to collect it, evaluate the information that comes in and apply it to map production. This is the *editorial* function. The actual collection of data is done by other specialists such as surveyors (see p. 499), specialist photographers (see p. 378), computing people (see p. 138) or by historical or archaeological researchers. Infra-red photography, often taken from satellites, remote sensing and seismic measurements are techniques widely used in data collection. Information technology is having enormous impact on the way cartographers work, as shown by increasing use of GIS – Geographical Information Systems. These enable the storage, processing and display of information on a computer screen. GIS consist of a database, a statistical/mathematical analysing capacity and a means of graphic display. One of the many benefits of GIS is that they enable data to be scanned from existing 'hard copy', manipulated and processed before being displayed in new and graphic ways on screen or printed out. Cartographers are developing electronic map forms which are replacing at least some products previously printed on paper.

This is a fairly small profession and entry and training opportunities have changed very much in the last few years. While editing is done by cartographers, production is usually the responsibility of the cartographic draughtsman/woman, although there is often overlap. The cartographic draughtsman/woman's traditional skill with hand and pen is now supplemented or replaced by the manipulation of computer images. Traditionally, the Ordnance Survey was the largest employer of cartographic staff; owing to re-organization and the introduction of GIS, staff here have been cut and at the time of writing there is no recruitment of new staff. Other government departments, such as the Ministry of Defence, that used to use large numbers of staff are in a similar situation. The main civilian employers are BT, the Civil Aviation Authority, British Gas, electricity companies and, of course, map publishers. There are some openings in universities and with local authorities.

Training

Trainee posts with part-time study are very rare; pre-entry training is normally required, often to be followed by further study.

There are a very few single honours degree courses in cartography. It is more common is to study it as part of a degree in Topographic Science (the collection, analysis and presentation of geographical information), or in combination with subjects such as geography, maths, computer science or surveying. There are a growing number of degrees and Higher National Diplomas in Geographical Information Systems (GIS).

Cartographic draughtsmen/women can take one of the handful of BTEC/SCOTVEC National Diploma courses in cartography, surveying and topographical studies.

Personal attributes

Patience; diligence; great accuracy; good colour vision; powers of observation; willingness to experiment; sense of design useful.

Late start

Very few opportunities.

Career-break

In principle, should be no problem for qualified cartographers who have kept up to date, but likely to prove difficult when jobs are decreasing.

Part time   Possible, but again affected by job situation.

**Position
of
women**   Comparatively few women have qualified, but those who have had no special problems.

**Further
informa-
tion**   Mr R. W. Anson, President, British Cartographic Society, School of Construction and Earth Sciences, Oxford Brookes University, Gipsy Lane Campus, Headington, Oxford OX3 0BP.

**Related
careers**   ARCHITECTURE: *Architectural Technologist* – ART AND DESIGN – SURVEYING

Catering

Entry qualifica-tions

All educational levels. Considerable *graduate* entry. See 'Training', below.

The work

The industry can be divided into two areas, *commercial services* and *catering services*. Under *commercial* come hotels – vast number of small ones, small number of large and/or luxury ones, motels, clubs, pubs and restaurants. *Catering services* include what is traditionally called institutional management: the provision of meals in schools and colleges, hospitals, etc., as well as industry, local and central government, passenger transport. Contract caterers may work in either area. There is not necessarily any greater difference between jobs in commercial and in non-profit-making catering than there is between individual jobs *within* each area.

Catering skills are highly transferable and there is considerable overlap between the different sectors. But for senior hotel management, experience in food and drink services as well as in accommodation services is necessary; for non-residential catering, experience of accommodation services is *not* necessary.

Job titles often tell one very little: 2 jobs with the same title may involve totally different tasks and levels of responsibility. Much depends on the size of establishment and the level of service it provides. It is an industry in which it is still possible to start at the bottom and, with aptitude, hard work and willingness to gain qualifications, reach the top, and/or start one's own business.

In senior management, work often overlaps with other managerial jobs and involves less contact with the public (the reason which brings most entrants into this industry). Senior managers in a fast food chain may, for example, work entirely at head office with visits to units where they meet customers; in industrial catering they may be responsible for a group of catering units, visiting individual managers and liaising with head office; or they may investigate latest 'catering systems' (see below).

The majority of catering jobs involve working when customers are at leisure, as do so many jobs in service industries. This can make a 'normal' social life difficult at times, but there are compensations to be had in being able to shop, play sport, etc. at less crowded times.

Success in most management jobs depends largely on motivating others to do their jobs well, and on efficient utilization of equipment and deployment of staff.

As in other industries, technology is 'de-skilling' some jobs and introducing new skills in others. Large industrial and institutional catering concerns and some chain restaurants increasingly use *systems catering* or *catering systems* instead of letting the chef decide what is for dinner and then getting the staff to prepare the meal. There are variations on the catering systems theme, but broadly this is how it works. Market research (see pp. 16, 297) identifies the most popular dishes within given price-ranges for given consumer-groups. Dishes are part- or fully prepared, and sometimes even 'trayed up' in vast production kitchens. Then they are transported, frozen or chilled, to the 'point of consumption', which may be many miles away. Finally, at the point of consumption, food is 'reconstituted', perhaps in a microwave oven. An example of this new technology is in a large hospital: here patients' food is put into covered trays similar to those on an aircraft; different materials are used in different sections of the tray so that when they have been transported from the kitchens the hot dishes can be heated up in large ovens in ward kitchens while the cold food, such as salad, stays chilled.

Managers must understand the technologies involved and their effects on ingredients, and they must be good organizers.

Hotel Manager

The work   The manager's work varies enormously according to size and type of hotel. In large hotels, the general manager is co-ordinator and administrator, responsible for staff management, marketing and selling, financial control, provision of services, quality control and customer care. Departmental managers are in charge of specialist services: reception, sales, food and bar service, housekeeping, banqueting, etc. The manager deals with correspondence, has daily meetings with departmental managers and may be in touch daily or weekly with head office. Although managers try to be around to talk to guests (not only when they have complaints), most of their time is spent dealing with running the business side, making decisions based on information obtained from the accountant, personnel manager, sales manager, food and beverage manager, etc.

Managers do not normally have to live in, though they may have a bedroom or flat on the premises. Working hours are long, and often busiest at weekends and during holidays. They must be able to switch from one task to another instantly, and change their daily routine when necessary – which it often is.

Among managers' most important tasks: creating and maintaining good staff relations, as success depends entirely on the work done by others under their overall direction; giving the hotel the personality and the character which either the manager, or more often the employer, intends it to have; and being able to make a constantly changing clientele feel as though each of them mattered individually. However, the extent of emphasis on personal service varies according to the type of hotel. .

In small hotels the manager may have a staff of about 15 to 30, and instead of several departmental managers, possibly 1 general assistant. Living in may be necessary, and off-duty time may be less generous than in large hotels. There are *far* more small (and unpretentious) hotels than large or small luxury ones. Many small and medium-sized country hotels are owned by companies and run by couples.

General Assistant – Assistant Manager

The work   This varies according to the size and type of hotel. In small hotels, assistant managers help wherever help is needed most – in the kitchen, in the bar, in housekeeping. Although the work is extremely hard, it is the best possible experience – an essential complement to college training.

In large hotels, assistant managers may be the same as departmental managers (see above). They may take turns at being 'duty manager' available to deal with any problem that occurs on a particular shift. Trainee managers may spend some time as assistants in different departments before deciding to specialize.

Personal attributes   *For top jobs*: Exceptional organizing ability and business acumen; outgoing personality; the wish to please people, however unreasonable customers' demands may seem; an interest in all the practical skills – cooking, bar-management, housekeeping, etc.; willingness to work while others play; ability to shoulder responsibility and handle staff; tact.

For assistants/managers of small hotels: Partly as for managers, but exceptional organizing ability is not necessary; instead, a liking for practical work is essential, and willingness to work hard and get things done without taking the credit.

Receptionist/'Front Office'

The work   The reception desk is always near or at the entrance to the hotel. Receptionists are always at the centre of activities. Since they are usually the first contact guests have with the hotel on arrival it is essential that they make a good impression.

Head receptionists are assisted in large and medium-sized hotels by junior receptionists. They check bookings and deal with inquiries over the telephone or by post. To steer a course between unnecessary refusal of bookings and over-booking is skilled work. Receptionists deal with correspondence; they must be able to do straightforward book-keeping, type and compose their own letters: they notify other hotel departments of arrivals and departures, and keep the customers' accounts up to date by collating chits handed to them by the restaurant, hall porter, bar, etc., and entering them on to guests' accounts. Almost all hotels have computerized reservations and accounts systems, which give instant information on a whole hotel group's vacancies, on guests' accounts, and possibly on the supply position regarding clean linen, beverages, etc. Reception also acts as general information office: staff answer guests' queries about, for example, train times, local tourist attractions or the address of a good hairdresser.

Receptionists work shifts, for example from early in the morning to mid-afternoon or from mid-afternoon to late at night. Especially in country hotels, they may live in; meals on duty are supplied free.

Head receptionists are usually responsible directly to the manager; theirs is considered one of the most important posts in the hotel business and can be a stepping stone to general management.

Personal   A friendly, helpful personality; an uncritical liking for people of
attributes all types; a good memory for faces – visitors appreciate recognition; ability to take responsibility and to work well with others; considerable self-confidence; a methodical approach; a liking for figures; meticulous accuracy; especially in tourist areas, modern language skills. *For top jobs*: business acumen; good judgement of people; leadership.

Housekeeper

The work   Except in small hotels, housekeepers do not do housework, but supervise domestic staff (mainly room-service attendants, formerly called chambermaids). Other duties include: checking rooms, seeing that they are clean, comfortable and that all the amenities are working (e.g. tea-makers and fridges); supervising laundry and ordering linen; pass-key control; room-service organization and supervision; liaison with other departments such as reception and maintenance; training and engaging staff and arranging work schedules. In a large hotel a head housekeeper may be in charge of a staff of 200.

In small and medium-sized hotels the housekeeper may be responsible for choosing and maintaining the furnishings, decoration and general appearance of bedrooms and lounges. In large hotels there may be one assistant or floor housekeeper to every floor, or every two floors; the executive housekeeper, who is immediately responsible to the manager, therefore has considerable overall responsibility.

Personal attributes Organizing ability; practical approach; an eye for detail; ability to handle and train staff.

Hotel Sales Management

A fringe hotel management career. Hotel sales managers work for large hotels and hotel groups. They sell 'hotel facilities' – efficiency, service, atmosphere, as well as conference and banqueting facilities. A hotel sales manager working for a group may approach large business concerns and try to fix contracts for business executives to stay regularly at the group's hotels. Jointly with tour operators (see TRAVEL AGENT/TOUR OPERATOR, p. 546) and airlines, etc., they build package tours.

Hotel sales managers come either via hotel management, or marketing (p. 297) or any other type of business experience.

Personal attributes Business acumen; numeracy; extrovert, friendly personality.

*

Restaurant Management

Eating places range from wine bars to large 'popular' and to exclusive *haute cuisine* restaurants. Restaurant managers must know how to attract and keep customers.

Catering for fluctuating numbers of customers with the minimum of waste is a highly skilled job, as is arranging staffing rosters to cope with busy periods without being over-staffed in slack ones.

Managers' responsibilities vary greatly according to type and size of restaurant. For example, if the restaurant is one of a chain, overall planning and ordering may be done at head office; in other places the manager may be given a very free hand to 'give the restaurant that personal touch', as long as menus keep within a given price-range and reach the profit target. The responsibility for menu-planning is usually the chef's (except in chain restaurants), but the manager must have considerable understanding of food and also of wine.

According to type of restaurant, managers spend varying amounts of time on 'customer contact'. Chef-proprietors have to spend some time away from their kitchens talking to customers. Except in lunch-only restaurants, working hours, though not necessarily longer, are more spread out, with some evening and weekend work.

Professional Cooks

Cooking always involves some physically hard work – the busier the kitchens, the tougher the job often is. Even with modern design and equipment, kitchens still tend to be hot, noisy and damp, and at times very hectic.

There are a variety of openings at various levels of skill and responsibility. For example, in large-scale *haute cuisine*, a chef heads a hierarchy of section chefs or *chefs de partie*, each responsible for one area of activity – larder, vegetables, pastry, etc. The chef may be responsible for budgeting, buying, planning – or this may all be done by a food and beverage manager, or at head office; responsibilities depend on type and size of organization worked for. In small restaurants, 2 or 3 cooks may do all the work. In simpler restaurants, convenience foods are used extensively and cooks' ability to produce palatable, inexpensive yet reasonably varied menus is the most important aspect of the work. It is no easier than, but very different from, *haute cuisine*. Production kitchens (see p. 96) leave little scope for creative cooking; every dish is prepared to recipes specifying such details as the size, weight, colour and often even the position on the plate of meat or cucumber slices, of sprouts or strawberries. But in experimental kitchens where new dishes and technologies are tried out, the work combines creative cooking skills, an understanding of the effects on the ingredients of being prepared in these unorthodox ways and, above all, managerial skills. There is also scope for creativity in small proprietor-run restaurants.

In large kitchens there are many cooking jobs without managerial responsibilities, but anyone who wants to progress beyond the kitchen-hand stage must take systematic training; home-cooking experience is not enough.

It is important to distinguish between courses for professional cooks, largely run by colleges of further education and some universities, and for *haute cuisine* for home cooking, mainly found in private schools. Cookery classes and schools do not always make this difference clear.

Freelance Cooks

Many people, both those professionally trained and gifted amateurs, make a living by freelance cooking. Clients range from company directors hosting lunches for a dozen clients to individuals wanting someone to cook for dinner or cocktail parties at their home. Some cooks specialize in party food for large or small gatherings. They need their own car or van to transport equipment and shopping. They must be able to budget and cook within various price-ranges.

Sometimes they cook for families on holidays abroad, or for travel agents' chalet-party package tours, working in ski resorts all winter, at the seaside all summer. This type of work usually includes general housekeeping.

Food and Drink Service – 'Waiting'

Food service can range from working behind a self-service food counter to highly skilled 'silver service' in a directors' dining-room or luxury hotel. *Beverage service* includes working behind a bar in a hotel or public house and, as *wine waiter*, helping a customer choose a suitable wine. Like cooking, waiting is at times physically hard and hectic, although the working environment is usually much pleasanter. In a restaurant the quality of the meal service is often as important to the customer as the quality of the food and can help to make or break its reputation.

Fast Foods

The products of this expanding part of the industry range from fish and chips to curry, pizzas to hamburgers. Outlets may be independent businesses, part of a large chain or franchises (the parent company, or franchisor, supplies materials and services and the right to use a trade name, in return for which the franchisee invests capital and pays a levy). Some sell takeaway food only, others also provide table service; all resemble small food-factories with a retail counter. All operations can be learnt quickly and staff often take turns cooking and serving; most chains train 'on the job' and in their own training centres. In what is very much a young person's environment, promotion from school-leaver entrant to supervisor level can be rapid. Management posts are filled either by very successful supervisors or by people with degrees or diplomas in catering, business studies or even arts subjects. The latter have to learn all the basic operations at first hand before undergoing management training. The fast food industry is highly competitive and requires considerable business expertise in order to maintain cash flow and to control stock. Success depends on high turnover, which in turn involves very long hours, but there are real opportunities for people to run their own business.

Pub ('Licensed House') Management

There are over 77,000 pubs in Britain, of which nearly half are independent, about a third owned by national companies and the balance by regional companies. Although the British pub has a traditional image, most now offer food, some with a separate restaurant, a few even have a theatre. Children are now allowed in parts of many pubs, while the loosening of licensing hours restrictions means that pubs can choose to open all day, including Sundays. Those who run pubs are proprietors, managers employed by the owner, or tenants or lessees, who rent or lease the pub for a given period. The work is best suited to couples, many of whom take up the work in middle age. It is a way of life rather than a job, as it means being tied to the bar during licensing hours, 7 days a week. Work involves purchasing, stock-keeping and record-keeping as well as bar service. Thorough knowledge of licensing laws is essential. Interest in entertainment trends and more than just a 'liking for people' of all kinds are essential. Specialist training and experience in bar and cellar work is required by anyone hoping eventually to become a licensee.

An important area of employment for people working in the licensed trade is leisure and recreation: sports clubs, leisure centres, private clubs, race courses, holiday centres nearly all have bars. Bar staff are the licensees and have their own 'franchise' – instead of working for a salary they 'rent' the bar on the premises and run it.

Industrial and Contract Catering

This covers the provision of meals at places of work and is often called 'employee feeding'. Service is provided either by staff employed by the organization itself, or, increasingly, by *catering contractors*. These run 'catering units' on clients' premises in factories, offices, old people's homes, hospitals, schools, colleges, and, with mobile units, at special/outdoor events. They may also operate vending machines. Contractors' staff can change the setting in which they work without having to change employers. Area and disrict managers are in charge of a number of units; unit managers and chef/managers work on the same premises regularly for a period.

Unit managers themselves usually only cook if fewer than about 50 meals are being served. Their main task normally is trying to achieve as even a flow of work as possible. Other tasks include: *menu-planning* – the complexity of this varies according to the range of meals to be provided, from a narrow range of standard dishes to a wide selection including directors' dining-room 'specials', and according to the importance attached to nutritional values and tight budget control. Expertise includes being able to provide at least 2 weeks' changing menus within several given price-ranges and at different grades of sophistication; *costing* – ingredients, labour costs, etc.; *purchasing*, which includes negotiating with suppliers and specifying, for example, the uniform size and weight of each lamb chop in an order of several hundreds.

Managers normally attend meetings with directors and/or personnel managers and also discuss improvements or complaints with staff representatives. They must keep up with technological developments and are usually responsible for, or for advising on, types of service, and purchase and maintenance of equipment. (That work may also be done by specialists.)

There is a wide choice of jobs: from preparing sophisticated snacks for a West End showroom, or a dozen *haute cuisine* lunches in a managing director's office with 1 or 2 assistants, to feeding 2,000 a day with a staff of 50 including 2 or 3 assistant managers.

In much contract catering, hours are more regular than in other parts of the industry, and staff often work weekdays only.

School Catering Service

This has undergone big changes in the last few years. Compulsory competitive tendering by local education authorities has meant that in many areas contract caterers, not the local authority itself, provide the service and, therefore, employ the school meals staff. Schools catering is basically the same as industrial catering, with special emphasis on catering for children's tastes, nutritional values and strict budget control. In some areas, only snacks are provided, in others much effort has gone into improving the standard and image of the service.

After training, caterers supervise the preparation of dinners, either at school kitchens or at centres from which up to 1,000 meals are distributed to a number of schools.

Promotion depends on the employing organization. Senior staff (who may be called school meals organizers) advise on buying, planning, staffing, kitchen management, nutrition, etc. They are also concerned with contract compliance, specifications and marketing. Cost control is very important. Organizers are responsible for geographical areas and do a good deal of travelling. Hours tend to be regular.

Hospital Catering

Hospital catering officers (now often called hotel managers) organize provision of meals for patients, staff and visitors, which means meals for between 200 and 3,000 people, many of whom need meals round the clock. Some hospitals have opened up their conference/meetings facilities to outsiders. They usually prepare diets under the overall direction but not day-to-day supervision of *dietitians*. Unlike other catering managers who may have learnt largely on the job, hospital catering staffs (management level) invariably have had systematic specialist training. At the top, *catering advisers* work as National Health Service Regional Officers (see HEALTH SERVICES MANAGEMENT, p. 215), i.e. not actually in hospitals. They advise on planning kitchens, catering technologies (see systems catering, p. 96), staff training and staffing requirements, etc. *Catering managers* are responsible for the catering arrangements in a group of hospitals. *Catering officers* or hotel managers are responsible for provision of meals in individual hospitals. (See DIETETICS, p. 166, for dietitian catering officers.)

Assistant and *deputy catering officers* are steps on the ladder to catering officer. In small hospitals, *catering supervisors* may be in charge of the whole catering operation; in larger hospitals they are responsible for a section.

Experience in hospital catering is very useful training for other specializations.

Increasingly hospital catering is contracted out to specialist firms.

Transport Catering

This is often done by contractors using *catering systems* (see p. 96) Menu planning in airlines involves taking into account climatic conditions at point of consumption; commercial facts such as air commuters' 'menu-fatigue' (business people travel the same routes regularly; frequent menu changes must be made or customers are lost to the competition); research into which dishes and wines 'travel well'.

Airline catering is very tightly cost-controlled; but in *marine catering* priorities are different: for passengers and crews at sea, meals are the highlight of the day. Proportionately more money is spent on food at sea than in the air, so sea-cooks and chefs have greater opportunities for creative cooking, and therefore for getting good shore-based jobs later.

Victualling ships – ordering supplies for trips sometimes several months long – is another catering specialization. Work is done in shipping companies' offices. Previous large-scale catering experience is essential.

Accommodation and Catering Management (previously called Institutional Management)

The work   This is management in non-profit-making, mainly residential establishments: halls of residence, hostels; the domestic side of hospitals; as well as, increasingly, in commercial conference and training centres. It also includes non-residential work: private school catering; meals-on-wheels; social service departments' day centres.

Managers may be called bursar, warden, domestic superintendent, catering manager. The range of titles makes it difficult to compare level of responsibility, status or duties.

There are almost as many different types of establishments as there are of hotels, and there is considerable overlap between catering and accommodation management. The difference is one of emphasis and setting in which the work is done. Some jobs have more in common with running a hotel – for example, running a large conference or management training centre – than with other institutional management jobs, in which residents' general well-being and emotional needs as well as their creature comforts have to be considered (such as old people's homes, where the job is part catering, part social work).

A *manager* may be wholly or partly responsible for all or some of the following aspects of community life: meals service; budgeting; purchase and maintenance of kitchen equipment; planning additional building; furnishings and decoration; the use of the buildings for conferences or vacation courses; dealing with residents' and staff's suggestions and complaints; helping to establish a friendly atmosphere both among staff and among residents; in small establishments, first aid and home-nursing (but *not* responsibility for sick residents); acting as host and as general information bureau; dealing with committees.

Most jobs are entirely administrative, but in small institutions the manager occasionally has to help out with housework or cooking. Many (by no means all) jobs are residential; accommodation varies from bedsitter to self-contained flat for couples (with partner not necessarily working in the organization concerned).

Assistant institutional managers – often means housekeepers – are usually beginners seeking experience or those unwilling or unable to take the more responsible jobs, but in large organizations, especially hospitals, it is a step on the ladder.

*

Training   The main choice is between a full-time college or university course and getting experience and training on-the-job, preferably as part of a formal training scheme, for example modern apprenticeship.

Main full-time routes

With 2/3 A-levels or equivalent: 3-year full-time or 4-year degree (titles include hotel and catering management, hospitality management). These vary in emphasis on different catering aspects, but generally include supervision of food and beverage preparation (and some practical work); catering management principles and practice; catering technologies; specialist work such as airline catering; sales management and marketing; accounting; computer application; aspects of tourism, recreation and leisure industries; international catering and languages (some courses include opportunities to study in Europe).

There are a few post-graduate qualifications for people with a relevant degree or experience or any degree plus experience/interest in catering (including 'exceptional entry' courses for the Hotel and Catering International Management Association – HCIMA – Professional Diploma, see below).

With 1 A-level or equivalent BTEC/SCOTVEC Higher National Diploma (titles similar to those for degree). Core subjects include operational techniques and procedures; work organizations; physical resource management; human resource management. Options may include accommodation management; applied nutrition; conference and banqueting management; licensed trade management; languages; sales and marketing; small business enterprise.

With 4 GCSEs or equivalent: 2-year courses for GNVQ/

GSVQ Advanced (see p. xix) (eventually replacing National Diplomas) in Hotel and Catering.

With some GCSEs or equivalent, or in some cases no qualifications, 1-year course for GNVQ/GSVQ Intermediate or NVQs/SVQs.

With the HCIMA Professional Certificate or equivalent qualification: 1-year full-time or 2-year sandwich course for the HCIMA Professional Diploma. (Full-time students must have had at least one year's experience in the industry.)

Main work-based routes

With 1 A-level or equivalent: BTEC/SCOTVEC Higher National Certificate. Takes 2–3 years. Subjects covered as for HND (above), but with fewer options.

With a combination of 4 GCSEs *or* equivalent *or* vocational qualifications *plus* experience in catering: 2-year part-time or block release course for HCIMA Professional Certificate. Distance learning course also available. Subjects studied are food and beverage and accommodation operations; human resource organization; business accounting and introduction to law; sales and marketing.

With the HCIMA Professional Certificate or acceptable alternative qualification and appropriate experience: 3-year part-time course for HCIMA Professional Diploma. Distance learning course also available. Subjects studied are food and beverage management; accommodation management; human resource, marketing and operational management.

NOTE: It is essential to check acceptability of individual qualifications and experience with the HCIMA, which will also advise on credits that may be given for previous studies through Accreditation of Prior Learning (APL, see p. xxxiii). HCIMA awards also lead to NVQs.

With no set entry qualifications: NVQs/SVQs in variety of catering subjects at levels 1–4 (see p. xix). In order to gain these it is necessary to have training and support from the employer. A formal training scheme, such as those provided by the Hotel and Catering Training Company (HCTC), or Modern Apprenticeships (see p. xxiv) are the best options. (Accommodation services, chef, fast food, and restaurant Apprenticeships are available.)

Training and qualifications for the licensed trade are also offered by the Brewers and Licensed Retailers Association, the British Institute of Innkeeping (for staff in pubs) and the Wine and Spirit Education Trust (for those in the wine and spirit trade).

Personal attributes   *For all catering* (in varying degrees): organizing and administrative ability; outgoing personality; ability to motivate staff and to communicate with all types of people – from kitchen porters to managing directors, from salespeople to a coachload of pensioners; interest in people and in their creature comforts; some practical skills; ability to work under pressure; stamina; flexibility; tact when dealing with 'difficult' customers; sense of humour. *For self-employed cooks*: as above, plus business acumen. See also 'Hotels'.

Late start   No problem. Admission to courses depends on experience and motivation rather than age and GCSEs.

Career-break   No problem in institutional management for people who can live in and/or work irregular hours; nor in industrial and schools catering. Many women set up their own small-scale catering businesses: for example, providing local firms with midday snacks, etc. (see WORKING FOR ONESELF, p. 551). Refresher training is possible.

Part time   Half the workforce is part time, but there are still very limited opportunities at management level. Opportunities exist in cooking, housekeeping, junior reception, food service and barwork, and freelance catering offers possibilities.

Position of women   Although hotel management has traditionally been a man's world, women are steadily coming through the ranks and several of Britain's top hotels are run by women. But to do really well, women must be ambitious, determined and willing to move around the country if necessary.

Some highly talented women chefs own and run their own establishments and women are less rare than they were in the large, traditionally run hotel kitchens.

In industrial catering, women have good opportunities to move up the management ladder. Just over half the managers are women. In hospitals, institutional-management-trained women have top jobs in domestic management, but top catering officers – concerned with food and drink, not housekeeping – are more frequently men. About 70% of schools and institutional catering managers are women. The fact that women do hold large-scale catering management jobs in some areas shows that it is only tradition which has kept them out of other catering management areas. Currently, the head of one of the largest local authorities' catering organizations is a woman, as is the head of catering in the House of Commons.

Further information

The Hotel and Catering and International Management Association, 191 Trinity Road, London SW17 7HN

Hotel and Catering Training Company, International House, High Street, Ealing, London W5 5DB

Brewers and Licensed Retailers Association, 42 Portman Square, London W1H 0BB

Scottish Licensed Trade Association, 10 Walker Street, Edinburgh EH3 7LA

British Institute of Innkeeping, Wessex House, 80 Park Street, Camberley, Surrey GU15 3PT

Wine and Spirit Education Trust Ltd, Five Kings House, 1 Queen Street Place, London EC4R 1QS

Related careers

DIETETICS – SCIENCE: *Food Science and Technology* – HOME ECONOMICS – TEACHING – TRAVEL AGENT/TOUR OPERATOR

Chartered Secretary and Administrator

Entry qualifica-tions

None laid down for entry to Foundation Programme of Institute of Chartered Secretaries and Administrators, but must be 17 or over. Exemptions for graduates and BTEC Higher award holders (see 'Training', below).

The work

This has nothing to do with personal secretarial work (see SECRE-TARIAL AND CLERICAL WORK, p. 464). Instead, it is general administration and management in public, private and voluntary sectors.

The main element in professional administration, wherever it is carried out, is coordinating (and possibly also controlling) various individuals and/or departments within an organization. Administrators are generalists who co-ordinate the activities of specialists. They form a link between people and their separate activities; they make sure that different sections or departments dovetail, and fit into the whole. Increased use of information technology in all organizations means they need a good grasp of information systems – how they work and what they can do. At senior level, administrators have an 'overview' over whatever their organization does; at junior level, they may, for example, co-ordinate the work of the accounts department; at middle level they ensure that, for example, production, distribution and personnel departments are informed of each other's needs. Professional administrators often work for a time in the various departments, to find out how each works and where it fits into the whole. Like other professional qualifications, professional administration can lead to the top in whatever the type of organization. The work is immensely varied, and so are the top jobs. Senior administrators may be involved in the choice and design of complicated computer systems aimed at improved decision-taking by top managers.

Qualified chartered secretaries can become company secretaries: public companies are by law required to have company secretaries, i.e. people who have either a legal, an accountancy or the ICSA qualification. According to type and size of company, company secretaries can be chief executives – possibly called director, or secretary-general – responsible only to the Board or whoever are the policy-makers; or they can be the chief administrative officer responsible to the director or chief executive.

As it is an adaptable qualification, chartered secretaries have a wide choice of jobs.

Training
The Institute's examinations consist of 3 programmes; Foundation, Pre-professional and Professional, all made up of modules. The first two programmes give a broad business education, covering law, accounting, information systems, organizations and personnel. The Professional Programme is a post-graduate level qualification and focuses on managing the affairs and protecting the integrity of the organisations.

Study can be full time or part time, by correspondence course or distance learning. Typically, students take 4 modules a year. Graduates in any discipline are exempt from the first 2 programmes, and are expected to qualify in 18 months. All students are expected to complete the examinations within 5 years. Holders of BTEC/SCOTVEC Higher National awards start with the Pre-professional Programme or, in some cases, with the Professional Programme.

People with other professional qualifications may also be given exemptions.

Personal attributes
A flair for administration; common sense and good judgement; numeracy; interest in current affairs; tact; discretion.

Late start
Good opportunities, especially now that access to ICSA examinations is 'open'.

Career-break
Should be no problem for people who had responsible jobs before the break. Because of the flexible examination structure it is possible for people to study while on a break.

Part time
Fair possibilities, particularly in small firms.

Position of women
Women are doing very well. About 16% of all Institute members and 55% of its students are women.

Further information
The Institute of Chartered Secretaries and Administrators, 16 Park Crescent, London W1N 4AH

Related careers
ACCOUNTANCY – HEALTH SERVICES MANAGEMENT – LAW

Chiropody
(Podology, Podiatry, Podiatric Medicine)

The profession is in the process of changing its title from chiropodist to podiatrist, and the professional body is now known as the Society of Chiropodists and Podiatrists.

Entry qualifications
Minimum age 18. 2 A-levels and 3 GCSEs (A–C) (or equivalent), including at least 1 science at either level, or Access course (see p. xxxi).

The work
Chiropodists diagnose and treat foot diseases and functional and constitutional foot disorders; they inspect children's and adults' feet to prevent minor ailments from growing into major ones. When patients need their shoes adapted, chiropodists give the necessary instructions to surgical shoemakers or shoe-repairers; they also construct special appliances themselves. They are unusual among the professions supplementary to medicine in that they diagnose and treat conditions without medical referral. Most can undertake invasive skin/nail surgery under local anaesthetic, and a growing number are qualified to perform minor bone surgery. Chiropodists can choose the environment in which to work:

1. *Private practice*: This is the most remunerative work and scope is growing. Chiropodists may practise in surgeries in their own homes and, occasionally, visit patients in their homes. Private practice can be lonely work (even though patients are seen all day) but many work in group practices, partners renting premises jointly or using rooms in one of the partners' homes as a surgery.

2. *Hospitals and health authority clinics*: Chiropodists are employed on a session (3-hourly) basis, part or full time.

3. *Industry*: Firms where staff are on their feet all day often employ full-time or part-time chiropodists.

In both (2) and (3) chiropodists enjoy the companionship and social facilities of a large organization. Some combine part-time work with private practice.

There is a shortage of chiropodists in some areas, largely because of the increased numbers of elderly people needing treatment. For opportunities in the EU, see p. xlviii.

Training   Traditional diplomas have been replaced by degrees. Only graduates will in future be eligible for State Registration, which is essential for all public jobs, and for membership of the Society of Chiropodists and Podiatrists. All courses are inspected by the Chiropodists Board of the Council for Professions Supplementary to Medicine. Much of the course content is practical and includes treatment of patients under supervision. Theory includes the basic medical sciences, anatomy, physiology, medicine and surgery, and local anaesthesia. Courses are at schools within higher education institutions.

Courses which do not lead to degrees, do not lead to State Registration and Membership of the Society of Chiropodists and Podiatrists. All recognized courses last at least 3 years, full time, and qualify students for mandatory grants.

Personal attributes   A high degree of manual dexterity; ability to get on with people greatly enhances chances of promotion and of having a flourishing private practice. However, unlike many other careers with patients, shy, retiring people may get on well, providing they are even-tempered.

Late start   Good opportunities, with some relaxations in entry requirements. 20% of entrants are over 25.

Career-break   No problem if kept up with developments. *Ad hoc* arrangements for *refresher* courses can usually be made.

Part time   Ample scope for work (although not for promotion), no part-time training. Job-sharing possible.

Position of women   At present, 65% of practising chiropodists and 75% of students are women. Proportionately there are more men than women in senior jobs and in private practice.

Further information   The Society of Chiropodists and Podiatrists, 53 Welbeck Street, London W1M 7HE

Related careers   NURSING – PHYSIOTHERAPY

Civil Aviation

Air Traffic Control Officer

Entry qualifications

Study to A-level standard of 2 subjects (preferably maths, geography or science) and 3 GCSEs (A–C). Must include English language and maths at either level. Graduates or people with other qualifications welcomed. High standard of physical fitness, eyesight and hearing required.

The work

Teams of ATCOs control and monitor the movements of aircraft taking off, landing and when *en route* in designated controlled airspace. An aircraft leaving a controller's area of responsibility is co-ordinated with the next ATC unit, which may be an airfield or an air traffic control centre in the UK or in Europe. Pilots of aircraft are, in fact, in 2-way radio communication with controllers from the time they request permission to start engines until the engines stop at their destination.

The work is responsible and highly skilled: it may involve the safe 'stacking' of aircraft in an airfield's 'holding area' while awaiting approach; the 'sequencing' of aircraft using radar to maintain a safe distance between them, and ensuring that aircraft flying the same routes at varying speeds, heights and directions are always safely separated horizontally and vertically. ATCOs use computers in their calculations. After gaining operational experience, a small proportion of ATCOs specialize in ATC computer work.

ATCOs spend most of their time – normally wearing earphones – monitoring data about relevant aircraft, either looking at a radar display unit or out over an airfield. The international language of ATC is English, so UK ATCOs talk and are talked to in their own language. Foreign pilots sometimes have problems expressing themselves clearly, especially when under pressure. Although ATCOs must make quick decisions, they can ask pilots to repeat anything which is not quite clear.

The great majority of operational ATCOs work shift duties, and all ATCOs must be prepared to do so; as far as possible shifts are planned well in advance, but last-minute changes are sometimes necessary.

Training Cadets (trainee ATCOs) follow an initial 72-week course for their air traffic control licence. This consists of periods of academic and simulation training at the College of Air Traffic Control near Bournemouth, with some periods of practical training at operational units. Training is given in all aspects of ATC, and in basic meteorology, navigation, telecommunications and principles of radar and associated techniques; an 'introduction to flying' course is also given in which cadets normally reach 'solo' standard.

Personal attributes Good eyesight (including normal colour vision) and high level of physical fitness; a calm cool temperament; ability to conceal and control excitement in emergencies; ability to concentrate both in busy and in quiet periods; a good quick brain, with quick reactions and the ability to be decisive; the ability to work as part of a team.

Late start Normal maximum age 26; with substantial relevant experience, this is raised to 34. Suitable applicants may be offered deferred entry so that they can complete a professional training or a degree course before joining the service.

Career-break Not easy; the number who have done so is tiny.

Part time None. but might consider some flexible working.

Position of women The number of women who apply for ATCO posts is increasing. Of new cadets, about one third are women.

Further information Civil Aviation Authority Personnel Services, Room T1, Gate 3, CAA House, 45–59 Kingsway, London WC2B 6TE

NOTE: Air Traffic Control Assistants (ATCAs) assist ATCOs in their tasks by undertaking certain routine functions, particularly with data preparation and display, at both airfields and airways control centres. None being recruited at present.

Cabin Crew (Stewardess and Steward)

Entry qualifications

Minimum age usually 20. Upper age limit for trainees about 34. Minimum height requirements vary between airlines. No set educational qualifications, but good GCSE standard, preferably including English and maths, and conversational ability in a foreign language. Some catering or nursing experience, or minimum 1 year in a responsible job which involved dealing with people, e.g. in a travel agency.

The work

The cabin crew welcome passengers, supervise seating and safety-belt arrangements, and look after air-sick travellers, babies, and children travelling alone. Stewards and stewardesses serve meals (but do not cook them), and sell drinks, cigarettes, etc. in a variety of currencies.

They 'dress the plane' to see that blankets, head-rests, magazines, cosmetics, etc. are available and in good order, and make necessary announcements over the public-address system. They deal with any emergencies and write reports after each flight, with comments, for instance, on the behaviour of unaccompanied children.

Most of the time cabin crews are airborne waiters and waitresses. From the moment the plane is airborne they are continuously busy, working at great speed in a confined space.

Duty hours vary from one airline to another and are likely to be changed at the last minute because of weather and other 'exigencies of the service'. Normally on European routes cabin crews are 'on' for 4–6 days with a good deal of night duty; they are then off-duty for 2–4 days. On long-distance trips they may be away from home for 3 weeks, but that would include several days' rest at a foreign airport.

The farther the destination, the more chance of sightseeing. On short routes cabin crews may fly backwards and forwards for a month without seeing more than the airport at their destination. On long-distance trips crews often change planes at 'slip-points' and stay for a few days' rest, living in luxury hotels at their airline's expense.

British-trained crews are in demand by American and other foreign airlines if they speak the appropriate language.

Training

About 6 weeks with Europe-only airlines to about 8 with trans-atlantic ones. Subjects include meal-service, first aid, documentation, airborne procedure, foreign currency exchange, emergency drill with swimming-pool lesson in the use of the inflatable dinghy and life-jacket, practical fire drills, customer service, grooming and deportment.

Personal attributes   A likeable personality; calmness in crises; common sense; efficiency; sensitivity to anxious passengers' needs; well-groomed appearance.

Position of women   See p. 119.

Further information   Individual airlines.

Ground Staff
(some examples)

Passenger Service Assistant/Agent
(titles vary)

Entry qualifications   Usually good GCSE-standard English, maths, geography and foreign language. Minimum age usually 18.

The work   Passenger service assistants see that passengers and luggage get on to the right plane, with the minimum of fuss. They check-in luggage, which involves checking travel documents, and check-out passengers at boarding gates. They answer passengers' questions on travel connections and similar matters.

Other duties carried out by experienced PSAs include: load-control – preparing information for aircraft loaders on luggage weight; cargo documentation for customs clearance; checking that planes leave with the right meals, cargo, baggage.

PSAs work in uniform, and do shift work. They move about the airport all day, rarely sit down.

Training   Several weeks' induction and on-the-job training.

Sales Staff
(titles vary)

Entry qualifications

Usually good GCSE-standard English, maths, geography, a foreign language.

The work

Sales staff sit in airport and city offices and answer questions on international flight connections; make fare calculations (in various currencies); sell tickets over the counter and over the phone. Bookings are made to and from all over the world; each reservation must be related to reservations made elsewhere and reservation vacancies available for any particular flight at any given moment. This is called 'space control'. Reservations staff use computerized information systems: at the push of a button they can see, on their computer terminal, exactly what the present reservation situation is on any flight of their airline.

Senior sales staff may call on travel agents, business houses and other important customers to explain ancillary services such as car hire, hotel accommodation, package holidays, and 'sell' their own particular airline, both passenger and cargo services.

Sales staff may do shift work, though less so in senior positions.

Training

Short on-the-job training with some lectures.

Personal attributes

For all 'public contact' jobs: an orderly mind; communication skills; a liking for meeting many people very briefly; a calm, helpful manner; good speech and appearance.

Position of women

See p. 119.

Commercial Management, Flight Operations and Flight Planning

Entry qualifications

Vary with different airlines and according to supply and demand. Some promotion from sales staff; most entrants have A-levels; many have degrees or BTEC/SCOTVEC HND in Business Studies (see pp. xxi, xxii).

The work

The administration of flight programmes, which cover many thousands of flight-miles, millions of tons of freight and ever-growing 'passenger throughput', is a highly complex undertaking. Staff organize the airline's fleet of planes over its network, making the most efficient use of each aircraft, e.g. ensuring that as far as possible outgoing freight is replaced with return-flight freight, and that the 'turn-round' time in airports is as short as possible, while allowing time for maintenance, loading, etc. 'Aircrew management' involves arranging individual crew members' schedules, taking into consideration maximum flying hours allowed; rest-days ('stop overs') abroad, etc.

Apart from this planning work, staff are also responsible for ensuring that at all times aircrew have all the information they need before each take-off, throughout the planned itinerary. This involves discussions with a variety of departments and individuals; keeping detailed records; being prepared for emergencies.

Training   Through airlines' own training schemes, lasting 2 to 3 years, or BTEC/SCOTVEC Higher awards or degree, followed by shorter airline training. Schemes vary between companies and according to expansion or contraction of airline industry.

Personal attributes   Drive; organizing ability; liking for working under pressure.

Late start   Good opportunities for cabin crew, passenger service assistants and sales staff (see 'Entry qualifications', above).

Career-break   Possible, but depends on vacancy situation. Also, returners have to start again with basic training.

Part time   Possible in some jobs, for example cabin crew, passenger services, but this affects promotion. Also some short-term contracts with 'package tour' companies for cabin crews.

Position of women   *Air stewardesses and stewards are all 'cabin crew'*; a woman is quite often in charge of an aircraft's cabin crew. *Ground staff* examples: traditionally mainly women, but more men joining. *Commercial management*: so far very few women have tried. Equal chances of promotion.

Further information   Individual airlines.

Related   CATERING – LANGUAGES – TRAVEL AGENT / TOUR OPERATOR
careers

Pilot

Entry   None is laid down by the Civil Aviation Authority for
qualifica-   the Commercial Pilot's licence, but 5 GCSEs (A–C) including
tions   English, maths and a science are assumed.

The work   The pilot's most taxing task is assimilating a mass of separate bits
of information presented by an array of indicators on the instru-
ment panel and by colleagues, to 'process' all this in the mind,
and to take whatever action may be necessary. Procedures during
the flight and especially during take-off and landing are complex
enough, but what makes pilots' jobs so arduous is the fact that
they must at all times be prepared for the unexpected. Instrument
failure may require the pilot instantly to override the computerized
equipment's instructions and perhaps take evasive action to avoid
a mid-air collision. Though individual pilots may never have to
cope with such 'incidents', they must be ready and able to do so.

In an airline, the first job is as *co-pilot*. Promotion to *captain*,
which is not automatic, would come about half-way through a
pilot's career. The captain has total responsibility for the aircraft,
crew and passengers. *Navigators* are no longer employed, and
flight engineers not on all aircraft: the pilot must in any case be
able to perform navigating and engineering tasks.

Work starts at least an hour before take-off, studying the
detailed flight plan. This gives such information as exact height at
various stages on the precisely defined route; meteorological information; take-off and landing weights which are vital data in case
of emergency action.

On 'short hauls' (in Europe) pilot and crew are busy all the
time. On long hauls there can be long hours with only routine
checks to go through. This can be difficult in an unexpected way:
pilots get bored, because there is no real work to do, yet the need
for alertness is as great as ever.

UK pilots are increasingly working in Europe. There is some
small demand for other types of pilots (plane or helicopter): on
air taxis; crop spraying; aerial photography; oil rig supplying;
weather and traffic observation; flying privately- or company-
owned planes and helicopters, and especially for instructors in
flying clubs.

Training   *Fixed wing – i.e. planes*
In the past the overwhelming majority of students at the recognized air training schools were sponsored; the major sponsor of pilots in the UK was British Airways. At the time of going to press, BA had just announced it was to start recruiting cadets again – the first time since 1990.

Basic training lasts at least 12 months. The syllabus includes aerodynamics, meteorology, electrical engineering and electronics, aircraft design and systems, flight procedures and aviation law. Flight training is carried out both in aircraft and in simulators.

The first qualification is the Commercial Pilot's Licence (CPL), but to fly in an airliner as co-pilot the basic requirement is the CPL plus Instrument Rating. Ratings are qualifications in particular aspects of flying and in flying particular types of aircraft; the type of aircraft a CPL holder may co-pilot depends on individual Ratings. To become qualified as captain of an airliner a pilot must have the Airline Transport Pilot's Licence (ATPL) and many thousands of flying hours.

Full-time, non-sponsored training to CPL costs about £42,000 but many people now qualify by first getting a Private Pilot's Licence (PPL). They then gain sufficient hours to take an Instructor's Course; as Instructors they are paid and they can accumulate the 700 hours' flying-time necessary to qualify for exemption from the full-length, full-time CPL training. This roundabout way of qualifying is very much cheaper and can be done while, most of the time, earning a living in part-time employment. With the harmonization of European pilot licensing, this route will eventually disappear.

Helicopter
At present most commercial helicopter pilots are recruited from the Services, where they are trained while holding a short service or similar commission. Commercial operators run sponsorship schemes from time to time to provide co-pilots.

Personal attributes   Above-average intelligence; ability to fight boredom and be alert at all times; mental agility; high standard of fitness; self-confidence; leadership qualities; ability to take instant decisions; total unflappability; very well-balanced personality.

Late start   30% of newly qualified pilots are late entrants (see 'Training', above), but there are upper age limits to airline sponsorship schemes, typically 27 on entry.

**Career-
break**   Should be possible as all pilots need retraining throughout their
career.

Part time   Should be possible, but hours often irregular.

**Position
of
women**   Only about 1% of pilots are women. Once trained they have no
greater difficulty getting work (outside large airlines) than
men. The sponsorship schemes are open to women as well as
men. British Airways employs about 30 women pilots. The British
Women Pilots Association has over 300 members and helps with
advice and (small) scholarships.

There are now several women helicopter pilots; up until
now, as the Services have not trained them, their only avenue has
been through commercial sponsorships or by paying for the
training themselves (current cost around £40,000).

NOTE: The RAF (see p. 52) is now training women pilots.

**Further
informa-
tion**   British Helicopter Advisory Board, Building C2, West Entrance,
Fairoaks Airport, Chobham, Woking, Surrey GU24 8HX
British Women Pilots Association, Rochester Airport, Chatham,
Kent ME5 9SD
Civil Aviation Authority, Flight Crew Licensing, Aviation House,
South Area, Gatwick Airport, Gatwick, West Sussex RH6
0YR (licensing inquiries only)

**Related
careers**   *Air Traffic Control Officer (see above)* – ENGINEERING – SUR-
VEYING

Civil Service

The Civil Service exists to administer the business of the government. This covers a vast range of activity from defence procurement to the issue of driving licences, and the Civil Service is one of the largest employers in the country with more than half a million staff.

Opportunities exist at all educational levels. There is a strong tradition of and commitment to training to enable staff to function effectively and progress up a well-defined career structure. Training may be on the job, at the Civil Service College or on outside courses as appropriate, and may cover anything from time management to print buying to the most up-to-the-minute computer techniques.

Over the last few years the Civil Service has been undergoing major changes with far-reaching developments still taking place. The aim is to make the Civil Service more efficient, businesslike and responsive.

Although by definition the Civil Service is an administrative organization and its careers in administration are well recognized, within its vast and varied structure it offers opportunities in virtually every career area. Approaching half of its staff are specialists, some of whom were recruited after their specialist training, while others were given the opportunity to acquire specialist qualifications after joining the Civil Service. There are also increasing opportunities for mature entrants and job changers, at all levels.

The work of government departments – and their staff at all levels – is immensely varied. It affects virtually every aspect of modern life – health, education, the environment, transport, agriculture, defence, foreign affairs, social security, energy policy, taxation and so on. These broad headings cover a vast and complex range of activities and concerns of which it is possible here to give only a few examples.

The Ministry of Agriculture, Fisheries and Food offers opportunities for senior staff to participate in meetings in Brussels on the development, negotiation and implementation of EU agricultural policy, but it is also responsible for the management of sea fisheries and consumer protection. The Ministry of Defence is one of the largest consumers of the products of British industry with vast annual expenditure to manage. In the Gulf War of 1991 it had the awesome task of supplying and arming tens of thousands of British troops, thousands of miles from the UK. It is also responsible for the Meteorological Office. In the Home Office staff might be concerned with the administration of prison management and reform or with how the Data Protection Act is working. The Scottish and Welsh Offices, with their regional responsibilities, embrace a range of activities handled by different departments elsewhere, e.g. education, agriculture and fisheries, transport, health.

Across all departments and levels there is a broad spectrum of functions, both strategic and operational. Some civil servants advise ministers; others deal direct with members of the public; some research the implications of policy options; others provide support services in, for example, computer operations, personnel, finance or general support work.

Civil servants face similar pressures to those in industry, and the work is no less stimulating. Efforts continue to make the Civil Service more 'businesslike' with all the demands and satisfactions for its staff which that implies. Management is increasingly decentralized, allowing more flexibility in decision-making and managing budgets and staff.

Many civil servants now work in 'executive agencies' which operate like businesses under a Chief Executive who is set financial and quality of service targets and given the financial and management freedom to pursue them. The idea is to make managers more accountable and visible and for the new ethos to filter down through the staff, with financial rewards for outstanding performance.

Administration

Administration Trainees
(The Fast Stream)

Entry qualifications
A first- or second-class honours degree in any subject. Arts graduates have traditionally predominated in the higher grades of the Civil Service, but science, technology and business graduates are particularly welcome as the Civil Service recognizes the need for relevant, expert knowledge in high-level administration. There is a shortage of top-quality applicants, especially those with science and technology degrees.

Method of entry and training

An annual recruitment scheme is organized by the Recruitment and Assessment Services Agency. Candidates undergo a qualifying test and 2 days of written tests, group exercises and interviews conducted by the Civil Service Selection Board in London. Successful candidates are told the initial estimate of their potential at the time of selection; this assessment is progressvely revised. (Unsuccessful candidates may be offered a post as an Executive Officer without further interview.)

Applicants can state their preferences for particular departments or agencies during the selection process.

Successful Administration Trainees (and newly appointed HEODs) spend 2–4 years (including a probationary period, its length determined by the employing department) in this grade. During this time they will have several carefully selected 'postings' involving different types of work and modular courses at the Civil Service College. Throughout the trainee period ATs are supervised and their progress monitored.

Some ATs are given the opportunity to gain accountancy qualifications. Others, in the 'European Fast Stream', are helped to prepare for competitions for posts in European Community institutions.

The work

Senior civil servants are responsible, under ministers, for formulating and implementing the policy of the government of the day. As indicated above, the subject matter of the work varies considerably, but the work of civil servants at this level falls into several broad categories. It includes researching and analysing policy options; developing the organization and procedures necessary to translate policy objectives into practice; dealing with parliamentary business, including briefing ministers and drafting replies to Parliamentary questions; drafting legislation; dealing with operational matters affecting the day-to-day responsibilities of a department; working in a minister's Private Office. There is scope for liaison and negotiation at a senior level within and between departments, with outside organizations, and with foreign governments. The balance of tasks varies between different postings.

As mentioned above, the Civil Service is moving towards greater accountability and responsibility for individual managers. Ultimately, however, ministers make final decisions. These decisions (including the nuts and bolts of legislation) are made on the advice and recommendations of their civil servants, so there is a real opportunity to contribute to matters of national and international importance from an early stage of a fast-stream career. There is also considerable intellectual challenge in mastering complex issues and giving impartial advice, whatever one's own politics or those of the government of the day.

Fast-stream administrators are selected for their potential to reach the top grades of the Civil Service. For both ATs and HEODs there is a probationary period, its length determined by the employing department. After the successful completion of this period, ATs are normally promoted to Higher Executive Officer (Development). Further promotion is based on performance, which is regularly assessed against objectives; an HEOD performing to expectations could expect further promotion in 2–4 years. Fast-streamers who do not perform satisfactorily may have their appointments terminated or be offered an appointment in the main stream. Though those in the fast stream are recruited and trained for accelerated career development, they compete for promotion on merit against those who joined the Civil Service through other routes.

Personal attributes

High intelligence; capacity to grasp all issues involved in a problem, to weigh up facts, conflicting opinions and advice and to make a decision; ability to extract the main points from a mass of detail and to write balanced and concise reports; ability to hold and delegate authority; enjoyment of responsibility; the ability to manage both people and resources; the ability to communicate and work well with other people at all levels – junior staff, colleagues, outside organizations and ministers.

Executive Officers

Entry qualifications

2 A-levels and 3 GCSEs (A–C), including English language; or acceptable Scottish equivalents; or equivalent GNVQs or a good BTEC/SCOTVEC National award; or a degree. About 50% of entrants are graduates or have BTEC Higher awards.

Method of entry and training

Entry is by competitive tests and interview. Recruitment schemes may be organized individually by departments or agencies, or on their behalf by the Recruitment and Assessment Services Agency. For the latter candidates may state preferences for departments and/or location; these are met as far as possible.

The majority of training for executive officers is given on the job and may be supplemented by courses at the Civil Service College. There are also opportunities for more specialized training leading to external qualifications as appropriate (e.g. in accountancy and computing). Many departments organize their own management development programmes for EOs.

The work

Executive officers are the first line of management in the Civil

Service. Their role is more operational than strategic and is generally concerned with applying policy. The subject matter obviously varies a great deal from one department or agency to another, but executive officers may be involved in several broad types of work. In carrying out their duties EOs *manage staff and resources*, allocating, monitoring and controlling the team's work, motivating them and helping them to develop their potential. Many EOs *handle casework*, making decisions on the basis of often complex law, regulations and precedent. A major part of the work of many EOs involves *dealing with the public*; EOs are the civil servants who often have a public face and sometimes specific job title – as customs officers, immigration officers, revenue executives, in the Department for Education and Employment or Department of Social Security. *General administrative duties* are an essential part of EOs' work and essential to the smooth running of a department or agency; they may include finance, personnel, estate management, purchasing and support for senior colleagues, including arranging meetings and writing reports.

Some EOs have more specialized responsibilities and are recruited and trained accordingly. Examples are the Immigration Service, Inland Revenue, Customs and Excise and the Diplomatic Service (see p. 128). There are also opportunities for EOs to train in accountancy (see p. 1) or information technology (see p. 138).

Successful EOs (there is annual appraisal) are promoted to Higher Executive Officer and Senior Executive Officer. After their probationary period, however, EOs may be considered, along with graduate entrants, for selection to the 'fast stream' with prospects for accelerated promotion to the higher grades.

Personal attributes
Practical intelligence; organizing ability; enjoyment of a measure of responsibility; a liking for paper work and for dealing with people; ability to manage staff.

Administrative Officer

Entry qualifications
5 approved GCSEs (A–C), including English language; *or* a written test; *or* relevant previous experience. Many candidates have A-levels or a BTEC/SCOTVEC National award. Recruitment is usually carried out by departments or agencies advertising posts locally and at Jobcentres. The Recruitment and Assessment Services Agency also undertakes some recruitment on behalf of agencies and departments.

The work
Administrative officers are employed in most government departments and executive agencies. They do much the same wide range

of jobs as office staff and administrative assistants in industry and commerce. They deal with incoming correspondence, see that it is distributed to those concerned, write letters or draft them for their manager, handle correspondence with and telephone inquiries from the public, assemble statistics and keep records, often on computer.

There is often more variety of work than in comparable jobs in a private firm. For example, in the Immigration Department of the Home Office, an administrative officer may deal with students visiting this country, with permits for employment, and with aliens whose residence permits have expired. Administrative officers may also interview the general public who call in for information or papers.

There are opportunities for promotion to executive officer. Administrative officers may be given day-release to study for appropriate examinations.

Personal attributes   Accuracy; reliability; a liking for desk work and for meeting the public. There is room both for good mixers and for those who prefer to work on their own.

Administrative Assistants

Entry qualifications   *Either* GCSE (A–C) in English language and one other subject; *or* a short test; *or* relevant previous experience. In practice most entrants have several GCSEs (A–C) or a BTEC/SCOTVEC National award. Recruitment is local.

The work   Administrative assistants do routine clerical work for administrative officers: filing, sorting, keeping records. They may also deal with inquiries from the public, and they may learn to use computers or electronic mail equipment. They are encouraged to take appropriate day-release classes and examinations. There are good prospects for promotion to administrative officer.

The Diplomatic Service

Entry qualifications   1. For Grade 8/7D, the fast stream, as for administration trainee. Any degree subject welcome. Linguistic aptitude is assessed as part of the selection process, but will not necessarily be the deciding factor, except possibly in borderline cases.

2. For Grade 9, mainstream entry, as for executive officer. The majority of successful applicants at this grade are graduates.

3. For Grade 10, clerical entry, as for administrative officer. Entrants must be at least 17 and under 20 on 1 January in the year in which they apply.

4. There is also a secretarial branch as well as occasional openings for research officers, economists, legal advisers, architects, surveyors, engineers and other specialist staff.

The work   Staff spend about a third to a half of their career working at the Foreign and Commonwealth Office in London. For the remainder of their time they are serving overseas in any of the more than 160 countries with which the UK maintains diplomatic relations. During a working lifetime anything from 6 to 10 'tours' of 2–4 years each are spent working at British embassies, high commissions and other missions in a variety of countries. The willingness to serve anywhere in the world is, therefore, vital.

Work is very varied. In the course of their careers staff may work on trade promotion, political reporting and analysis (especially in the fast stream), consular services to British nationals living or travelling overseas, immigration work, aid administration, or personnel and financial management.

Promotion is generally on the basis of performance on the job. There are special competitions involving written tests and interviews to secure accelerated promotion or to transfer to the fast stream, where promotion is most rapid (though opportunities for promotion to senior levels exist for all entrants, including schoolleavers).

Training   The Diplomatic Service attaches great importance to proper training. New entrants at all levels usually undertake a short induction course which acquaints them with the organization and working of the service and its place in the machinery of government. Specialized job-related courses are arranged for staff who are going to take up jobs in, for example, commercial or consular work, and there are also courses designed to develop individual skills and potential, for example in management, effective speaking or international economics. The Diplomatic Service, not surprisingly, attaches great importance to language training. For some jobs full-time language training for up to 2 years is provided; all staff, even when it is not essential for their jobs, are encouraged to learn something of the local language and are entitled to at least 100 hours of free tuition. Language allowances are paid to staff who reach a certain level of proficiency. Diplomats can master several languages during their careers.

Personal attributes   Members of the Diplomatic Service must combine the skills of salespeople, political analysts and public relations officers. They must have a calm and reliable personality; a persuasive, confidence-inspiring manner; the ability to make friends easily and put down roots instantly; and the adaptability and resourcefulness to cope with the constant upheaval of moving from one place to another. The Diplomatic Service is not so much a job as a way of life. It demands balance, staying power, curiosity about the way other nations live and the confidence to put forward the British point of view.

Specialists and Professionals in the Civil Service

The Civil Service employs a wide range and substantial number of specialists and professionals. There are opportunities for those with considerable previous experience outside the Civil Service; the newly qualified; and those seeking opportunities to obtain professional qualifications.

The basic entry and training structures of these careers and their different functions and applications are discussed in detail in other sections of this book. This section looks at their roles within the Civil Service.

Scientists
(see SCIENCE, p. 438)

Scientists in the Civil Service may be involved in research and development; providing scientific services; statutory advisory and inspection duties; scientific contributions to the formulation of government policies. Within these broad areas of work is a vast range of activity and interest covering aspects of life as diverse as the food we eat, the air we breathe and the weapons that defend us.

For example, scientists in the Ministry of Agriculture study problems caused by animals, from insect damage to stored foodstuffs to bird collisions with aircraft. Others are concerned with food additives and the evaluation of new food products and processes, especially biotechnology. The Ministry of Defence's Chemical Defence Establishment carries out research to evaluate the hazard to the armed services of biological and chemical agents, work which gained widespread attention during the Gulf War. At the Royal Mint metallurgists and chemists control the composition of the coinage alloys at a number of stages in the manufacturing process. The Home Office maintains the Forensic Science Service, which provides the scientific backing to the search for criminal evidence, using sophisticated techniques to analyse a wide range of materials such as blood, fibres, glass, paint and soil. The National Physical Laboratory of the Department of Trade and Industry has developed spectroscopic techniques for the analysis of the atmosphere and carries on investigation into noise and its effect on hearing.

There are opportunities in most scientific disciplines, both major areas like chemistry, physics and computer science, and smaller, more specialized fields like animal nutrition, meteorology and plant pathology.

Entry qualifications

1. Science Management Training Scheme: first- or upper-second-class degree in relevant subject plus interest in and aptitude for senior science management. This is an accelerated promotion scheme to groom high-calibre scientists for a role in complex policy formulation and the management and implementation of those policies. Selection is by written and group exercises, tests and interviews.

2. Scientific Officer: a degree or BTEC/SCOTVEC Higher award in a relevant subject. Recruitment is carried out centrally and departmentally, regularly and as vacancies arise. All posts are advertised nationally, usually in *New Scientist*. Some departments offer sponsorship and sandwich placements to students.

3. Assistant Scientific Officer: 4 GCSEs (A–C) (or acceptable Scottish alternative), including English language and maths or a science. Preference may be given to those with a science *and* maths or with a relevant A-level. Recruitment is carried out locally as vacancies arise. There are opportunities for further study and promotion.

Engineers
(see ENGINEERING, p. 181)

There are opportunities for every type of engineer in the Civil Service. The Ministry of Defence has the greatest requirement, and for example needs engineers to design test software for combat simulators and develop improved helicopter rotor blades. At the Department of Transport, while civil engineers might design new roads and bridges and manage huge projects, electrical engineers develop computer-based traffic control systems. Department of the Environment engineers work in multi-disciplinary teams seeking an integrated approach to pollution control over a range of industries. Recent projects for the Property Services Agency's engineers have included the new British Library and the renovation of the Palm House at Kew Gardens.

Entry qualifications

1. Defence Engineering Service Fast Stream: a first- or upper-second-class degree in a relevant subject plus aptitude for management. This is an accelerated training and promotion scheme run by the Ministry of Defence to groom good graduates for the most senior posts in both engineering and general management. Selection is by written and group exercises, tests and interviews.

2. Graduate Engineer: honours degree in relevant subject. Relevant training leads to chartered status.

3. There may be opportunities for those with A-levels or Scottish Highers to be sponsored on a degree course, and for those with technician and craft qualifications to join an appropriate grade and obtain training for further qualifications and promotion.

Surveyors
(see SURVEYING, p. 499)

The majority of opportunities for surveyors in the Civil Service lie with four main departments. The Valuation Office Agency is concerned with acquisitions and disposals, renewals, and rent reviews and valuations for capital gains tax. The Property Services Agency is the largest design and construction organization in the country with responsibility for conservation and restoration as well as new building. Surveyors in the Defence Estate Service are responsible for all the property owned by the Ministry of Defence, one of the largest landowners in the UK; there are also overseas projects to be managed. The Agricultural Development and Advisory Service offers advice, often as a chargeable service, to farmers, growers and landowners on all aspects of land and estate management. Smaller numbers of openings are available in other departments including the Department of Health, the Department for Education and Employment, Ordnance Survey and national museums. All types of surveyor are needed, but different departments have different requirements.

Entry qualifications

There are opportunities for qualified professionals; for graduate trainees; and, in the Property Services Agency, for *Cadet Valuers*. The latter must have at least 3 GCSEs (A–C) and 2 A-levels (subjects at either level to include English and maths) *or* a noncognate degree. Distance-learning and day-release courses plus practical training lead to professional qualification.

Economists
(see ECONOMICS, p. 178)

Economists work in about 20 government departments, analysing the economic implications of virtually every aspect of government policy. A key part of this work is the interpretation of economic and other statistics. In some departments, for example the Treasury, economists specialize; in others they apply economic principles to a variety of different situations.

Entry qualifications
A first- or second-class honours degree in economics or agricultural economics, or in a subject including major elements of these. There are also opportunities for graduates in other subjects to undertake post-graduate courses in economics.

Statisticians
(see SCIENCE, p. 451)

Across the range of government activity statisticians collect, analyse and interpret data on a variety of subjects and for a variety of purposes. Statistics on subjects as diverse as transport, health, education, trade and household expenditure are used both to shape and reflect policy and to inform industry, the academic world and the general public on aspects of modern life.

Entry qualifications
A good degree. Those who have at least a second-class degree which includes formal training in statistics are appointed as assistant statisticians. There is a special trainee scheme for those whose degrees are not in maths or statistics, who should have at least a good maths A-level or equivalent.

Press and Publicity

The Civil Service is one of the largest employers of press and public relations specialists. Overall their job is to explain government policies and measures to the public. This might involve advising a minister on dealing with the news media; planning a publicity and information campaign on, for example, drink-driving; organizing an exhibition to promote British trade overseas; working on a range of publications dealing with subjects as diverse as recruitment, overseas aid or detailed statistics on social trends. The Central Office of Information offers the greatest number of opportunities, but there are openings in most departments.

Entry qualifications

There are openings both for new graduates and for experienced professionals.

Lawyers
(see LAW, p. 250)

Lawyers in government service have a great number of roles, many of which mirror work done in private practice and industry, some of which are unique to government. Lawyers have a key role in drafting legislation and assisting ministers in steering it through Parliament. They are also advisers on the formulation and implementation of policy. Many are involved in prosecution and litigation over, for example, serious VAT fraud. Lawyers working on the administration of justice might be advising on the discipline, conduct and welfare of the judiciary or settling cases before the European Court. There are also opportunities to advise on a range of matters concerning the Civil Service as a large organization – employment legislation, employee accidents at work, conveyancing and pay agreements.

Entry qualifications

There are opportunities for both qualified lawyers and for graduates who wish to qualify through government service.

Architects
(see ARCHITECTURE, p. 40)

There are 2 main areas of work: advising ministers on the building aspects of policy and then putting policy into effect; and designing new buildings or project-managing the work of private contractors. Work embraces schools, hospitals, historic buildings and defence establishments.

Entry qualifications

There are currently very limited opportunities for fully qualified architects.

Accountants
(see ACCOUNTANCY, p. 1)

Accountants in the Civil Service are at the forefront of many developments designed to promote accountability and introduce financial management disciplines. They are also involved with government's dealings with industry and commerce and with tax matters.

Entry qualifications

There are openings for those with a professional accountancy qualification and opportunities for some administration trainees and executive officers to train and qualify as accountants.

Research Officers

Research officers study the impact of government policies and provide information on which policy is based. Most opportunities are with the Resource and Planning Research Group and the Social Sciences Research Group.

Entry qualifications

A first- or upper-second-class honours degree or post-graduate degree in an appropriate subject, e.g. geography, economics, social anthropology, psychology.

Information Systems and Technology

Computers are in widespread use throughout the Civil Service. Applications range from sophisticated weather forecasting and research into climatic change, through a new Home Office electronic photofit system to help catch offenders, to the Department for Education and Employment's administration of the country's largest and most complex pension scheme (for teachers).

Entry qualifications

All levels and types of computer personnel are needed. Specialists are recruited, but there are also opportunities for executive officers to train in administrative computing.

*

Late start (Civil Service generally)

There is no upper age limit (except for a few schemes which involve long-term training). There may be increasing opportunities for mature candidates, especially those with managerial, professional, technical or scientific qualifications and/or experience.

There is a fast-stream administrators' recruitment scheme for experienced managers and professionals.

**Career-
break**
Formal career-break schemes of up to 5 years are available to staff. Many include 'keep in touch' programmes. It is also possible for former staff with a good track record to apply at any time after resigning for reinstatement in the same grade and at the same salary level as when they left.

Part time
See 'Position of women'.

**Position
of
women**
Since 1984 the Civil Service has had a programme of action to promote equality of opportunity for women. It has been a pioneer among employers in developing a range of measures such as career-breaks, part-time working, job-share, childcare and keep-in-touch schemes. (These are not exclusive to women employees.)

In 1993/94 women represented 52% of all new entrants to the Civil Service. The majority are in the administrative grades; 69% of administrative officers and 70% of administrative assistants are women. The percentages of women at middle and senior management grade levels seem still to be relatively small, but must be looked at in the context of the rate of improvement and the age profile of the grades. The percentage of women at the most senior levels (grades 1–3), where the pyramid really narrows, has increased from 3·3% in 1984 to 9·3% in 1994. Civil servants are normally well into their forties by the time they reach this stage, so may have embarked on their careers *before* equal opportunities legislation, initiatives to help women take advantage of the opportunities, and high education and career expectations for girls. The women who reach these grades at present actually do so earlier than do men. At Grade 3 women are, on average, 1 year younger than their male counterparts, and at Grade 5, 4 years younger.

Slightly lower down the career structure, where younger women can be expected to have been more influenced by the factors mentioned above, the percentages are higher. The presence of women with high potential in the grades which 'feed' the Senior Open Structure is important.

There is an Opportunity 2000 benchmark that by the year 2000 women will constitute 15% of the top three Civil Service grades; this is expected to be achieved. Women's representation at Grades 1 to 7 is currently as high as 30% to 51% in 5 departments.

During the period 1986–90 women consistently formed some 47% of those attending the qualifying test stage of the Administration Trainee selection process, while their success rate at the final stage was lower, ranging from 31% to 43%. By 1993 a new structured questionnaire was introduced to use alongside cognitive tests. First results were encouraging, with women making up 38% of first stage successes compared with 30% in 1992.

The Civil Service is continuing to look at other, perhaps less immediately obvious, barriers to women. Some years ago it did away with upper age limits for most categories of entrants; these were seen to discriminate against women who had given time to domestic commitments. Now it has abolished the 'seniority' (the term used to indicate how long a member of staff has remained in a particular grade) needed to get promotion. Women are also encouraged to be more assertive and career-minded by, for example, asking for 'hard'or 'crunchy' (Civil Service jargon) jobs, e.g. finance rather than personnel. Getting as wide a range of experience as men is bound to stand them in good stead at promotion boards.

The percentage of men working part time has trebled to 0.9% since 1984, and the percentage of women has almost trebled (from 6.2% to 18.4%). The highest-level part-timers are at grade 3. 15% of women at grade 7, and 17.5% at grade 5, work part time.

Further information	Graduate and Schools Liaison, Room 127/2, Office of Public Service and Science, Horse Guards Road, London SW1P 3AL

Related careers	*See those mentioned in the text* – LOCAL GOVERNMENT

Computing/Information Technology (IT)/Information Systems

Entry qualifications

Nothing rigid: depends on job-type (see below). Ability to think logically and communicate effectively is more important than specific GCSEs and A-levels. For trainee programming jobs, in practice, at least 2 A-levels or degree (any subject); for software programming/engineer, usually computing science degree – computing science A-level not required for most of these courses. Sandwich computing science or IT degrees more helpful than full-time degrees.

The work

Wanting to work with computers is by no means a reason for choosing a computing career. In virtually any job, whether it is clerical, technical, professional; whether it is in banking, manufacturing, retailing or medicine, computers are used extensively. They are tools with which to process information, measure, assess, monitor facts, figures, progress, procedures. They are information-processing devices. The information or 'data' may be in the form of numbers, words or graphs. Strictly speaking, the term 'computer' is out of date. It was correct when, in the early days, computers merely performed complex arithmetical operations with phenomenal speed and complete accuracy – when they were merely 'number crunchers'. Now that their capacity and use have widened so dramatically, 'information technology' or IT is becoming the accepted term. IT describes the 'convergence' of office automation, telecommunications and computing. However, 'computing' and 'computer' have become part of the language, and the terms have stuck. For most major organizations computing has become an integral part of doing business. This has raised computing and IT to strategic importance as far as the business is concerned. Terminology is not always specific. Computer science is a generic term often used by academics running courses, while lay people more often use IT. In Europe *informatics* tends to be the generic term. Information systems – the name given to a combination of hardware, software and people – is in widespread use.

People usually want to work with computers because they are fascinated by their versatility, their capacity to cut out drudgery and to achieve results which in pre-computer days were either impossible to achieve, or took a vast amount of time and trouble. Thanks to microprocessors, robots now perform repetitive manufacturing tasks; while office automation systems have already transformed much of business practice. Word processors eliminate repetitive typing; databases help solicitors keep track of case-law without having to search through heavy tomes; management can gather information from various sources spread over various sites via communication networks to help it make decisions based on facts and figures rather than hunch. In all these spheres people who use computers need not understand any more about the working of the computing device than car drivers need to understand about engines – and they are no more computer professionals than car drivers are engineers. There is a vast and sometimes underrated difference between amateurs who program their computers and computer professionals.

To perform its information-processing tasks, the actual device, the 'hardware' (which is designed by engineers and computer scientists), relies entirely on 'software', the instructions or 'programs' also designed by engineers. It is the software which enables the computer to enter into a dialogue with the people who want to use it, and to respond to their needs. There are two kinds of software: *systems software*, that runs the actual computer, and *applications software*, that makes it perform various functions, such as word processing and computer aided design. The versatility of the tasks which can be performed depends on the complexity and quality of the software, and on the size and sophistication of the computer. Many of today's PCs, workstations and laptops are approaching the power of yesterday's mainframes – and the power and complexity of the network to which they are commonly connected. The communication between user and professional remains vital.

PCs have seen the growth of software solutions to business problems, communications within and between offices (email) and integrated packages comprising spreadsheets, word processors and databases. These have given rise to many new support jobs within organizations.

Computing Jobs

Computing and IT professionals comprise a range of highly

skilled specialists who have to acquire their expertise just as any
other professionals have to. The demarcation between the various
computer specialisms is constantly changing, and the emphasis is
on team work, because devices are becoming ever more sophisticated, demanding new skills or newly combined skills. Until
recently, a big growth area was computer-integrated manufacture,
CIM, which brings together systems used for design, manufacture,
marketing and finance. Teams of computer staff are headed
by project leaders, who now have a well-defined planning and
monitoring management role. Now the big growth area is
communications.

Systems Software Programmers/ Software Designers/Software Engineers
(titles are interchangeable)

These people produce the software which enables the otherwise
inert hardware to provide the basic facilities – the 'controlling
programs'. This has been likened to the electric power system into
which users 'plug' various devices – it is the 'computer workhorse'.
Whether it is PC, a robot controller, or a system with 100
workstations, the controlling program, designed and developed
by the *systems programmer*, makes the whole thing function. The
work is a combination of applying *computer science* and *telecommunication* principles, creativity, high technology expertise and
analytical reasoning. *Software programmers* work jointly with
other highly trained professionals. They are the only computer
people who (a) must have a technological/scientific background
(a degree normally) and who (b) work almost entirely with other
highly qualified experts and have little contact, at work, with non-
computer people. Their work is basically Research and Design
(see 'Design' and 'Research and Development', pp. 183, 184,
under ENGINEERING).

Some develop existing operating systems, updating, extending,
refining them; others work on software which will be ready for
general use in the future. Theirs can be very much pushing-out-the-
frontiers-of-science work. Most of the work requires high-calibre
brains, but there is also scope for support staff (see 'Incorporated
Engineers and Engineering Technicians', p. 195). *Systems
programmers/software designers/software engineers/systems inte-
grators* work mainly for computer manufacturers and software
houses, but companies which have large computer networks
either employ some systems programmers or bring in outside
consultants. Of all computing jobs, theirs is the most theoretical/

academic, and a rapidly diminishing portion of the computer jobs market.

A few years ago all big companies, such as retailers and banks, had their own large IT departments. These have now been 'downsized', i.e. reduced in terms of type of equipment and number of IT staff employed, and contract staff are brought in as and when needed (a process known as 'outsourcing').

Network and Telecommunications Specialists

This growing group of specialists design and support the Local Area Networks (LANs) which allow computerized workstations to 'talk' to each other. Networking has become a means of integrating both computer applications and business functions. Jobs in this area cover network design, implementation, support and management. This is one of the most rapidly growing areas of IT and suitable staff are in short supply.

Systems Analysts and/or Designers

They identify the problem and design the solution to it. There are three stages to the job. First, they investigate and analyse the existing system – or lack of it – in the organization which is intending to install or update a computer system. In many organizations patterns of work have evolved haphazardly and, in the process, have become inefficient. For example, in a chain-store which has increased its volume considerably over the years, the method of recording sales, ticketing goods, making out bills, stock control and dealing with suppliers may be totally unsuited to the size of the organization today. The *systems analyst* spends several months getting to know the intricacies of the business, observing and talking to staff in all departments and at all levels – from junior clerk or packer to buyer or marketing and managing directors – to assess routines, bottlenecks, objectives. The work requires business acumen, knowledge of commercial practice and an ability to get people to talk freely about their work and to accept changes in old-established routines. When the old system has been translated into a logical sequence of procedures, the systems analyst writes a report on how computerization would affect the organization's staff, and how it would improve efficiency and profitability, and at what cost. If the report is accepted by the management, the systems analyst completes the analysis and design, using structured procedures, hands over the program specification to the programmers, and probably supervises the subsequent implementation, troubleshooting if necessary.

The systems analyst's role will often overlap with that of a business analyst, someone without a computing background, probably with a business degree, who analyses the problem from a business and financial perspective. They frequently work together.

Analyst/Programmers

In commercial computing – the vast majority of jobs are in this field, rather than in science or engineering – the jobs of *analyst/ designers* and of *programmers* are normally merged into *analyst/ programmers*, who are currently much in demand. They see the whole project through, in teams under a project manager, until it is completed and validated. The vast majority of analysts and designers work for computer users; 'in-house' analysis and design used to be more usual than having the work done by software houses, i.e. consultancies which provide professional services for a number of clients. However, computing and IT skill shortages, downsizing and outsourcing have reversed this trend and many firms now employ consultants. Some analyst/designers (with ample experience) work as freelances.

Analyst designers' work also covers advising employers, or clients, on what systems to buy; so they must be knowledgeable about and critical of the various systems available. They must be very good at explaining complicated matters to lay people – the computer users.

The attraction and challenge of this computing job is the mixture of tasks and of talents required: applying highly specialized technical knowledge; improving an organization's efficiency; assessing competing computer manufacturers' claims for new products. On top of applying technical know-how, systems analysts/ designers must be very good at dealing with people: communication skills are vital. They must make the computer acceptable to staff and design the interface to be acceptable to the clients; traditional working methods and hierarchies may have to change; re-training has to be arranged and accepted, and staff reductions may have to be faced.

Applications Programmers

There is a spectrum of *applications programmers*; some work to a 'loose specification', using great expertise and ingenuity; others work to a 'tight specification', need less expertise and have less scope for ingenuity. Most now become *analyst/programmers* (see above). The relationship between *systems analyst/design* and *applications programming* has been likened to that of architecture and building. Applications programmers work to 'program specifications' – a description of what the program is to achieve – provided by the systems analyst/designer.

Applications programming covers various stages. Applications programmers roughly assess the time needed to complete the program, break it down into separate components, and then break down each component into individual step-by-step sequences of instructions upon which the computer can act. All this needs logical, analytical reasoning, but not mathematical skills. Then comes the translation into an appropriate language, which is usually typed directly into a computer terminal. Applications programmers may produce programs to instruct particular machines to perform particular tasks: for example, to enable a chain of hotels to keep a constantly updated record of vacancies, or a hospital group to keep a constantly updated record of the lengths of waiting lists within the various specialities and the various hospitals within the hospital group. In large organizations teams of applications programmers would deal with a variety of programs – writing for new applications; updating existing programs. Applications programmers with considerable experience, working for software/systems houses, manufacturers, consultancies, users and, increasingly, as freelances, can also specialize in 'applications packages'. These are programs, or 'program systems' produced 'for stock', to be bought off-the-shelf by users with run-of-the-mill. requirements: programs for stock control; payrolls; video games; office applications like word processing; spread-sheets and databases for personnel systems. As 'tailor-made' programs are very expensive – they take a long time to write – off-the-shelf programs are being produced in ever-growing numbers as more and more computers are being installed and therefore more users with similar requirements are catered for. Writing applications package programs requires special skills: the programs must be 'user-friendly' (easy for laypersons to understand), well documented and flexible enough to be adaptable to particular users' differing needs.

There is usually a hierarchy of programmers, from trainee right up to *project team leader*, and then on to various management jobs. Most work in mixed-project teams with systems designers and other specialists as required.

As virtually everybody in computing, however high up, has to have had some programming experience, programmers have a choice of ladders. Most large installations have two branches: one dealing with developing systems and with those in the planning stage, employing the above staff plus specialists, e.g. *database adminstrators*; and another one dealing with the actual functioning of the system in use.

Database Administration/Information

Data is now viewed by most organizations as a valuable corporate resource. These organizations usually see data as a separate area for control and management. Database administration personnel (often called information officers) design, manage and maintain the company's data and control access to it. This is a highly specialized and technical area. Considerable experience of database systems and business needs are required.

Computer Engineers/Scientists and Information Technologists
(various disciplines)

They design and develop computers and related products ('peripherals') for computer manufacturers (see ENGINEERING, p. 189). Various specialists are involved, mainly but not only *electronic engineers, physicists, mathematicians. Information technologists* are emerging as specialists in their own right. At the moment titles of relevant degree courses vary (for example, IT or Computers and Communications); computing hardware professionals of the future must carefully study degree course syllabuses. Terminology of job-titles and specific functions vary, too. Hardware manufacture is a declining industry in Britain; major companies that once concentrated on this are now moving into selling software instead.

Some 'Spin-off' Jobs

With 'orthodox' (i.e. *applications* or *software programming, systems/software design/analysis*) qualifications and experience, there are a growing number of opportunities in rapidly changing and expanding computer careers, suiting individuals with various bents, abilities, expertise. *Information technology*, including as it does telecommunications (and office automation), is developing faster than any industry ever has done: new jobs are constantly emerging – but beware: the unskilled or semi-skilled ones may be short-lived: a few years ago there was a vast demand for computer operators and for so-called 'service engineers' who were often narrowly trained. Now, users themselves rather than specialist operators operate the majority of workstations; and some large computers can diagnose and rectify their own faults: *service engineers* now are thoroughly trained to cope only with serious faults (see 'Incorporated Engineers and Engineering Technicians', p. 195).

User Support Staff

As the users now include senior management, this is now a much more high-powered and expanding area than it was. Support staff provide a 'hand-holding' service to users who have bought a new system or updated and extended an existing one. Job content varies greatly. Support staff may be asked to provide training for everyone who will use or be affected by the new systems, from clerk to managing director; they may suggest additional or more efficient application of the system; or, if they work for manufacturers or software houses, they may visit at regular intervals to see all goes well – and possibly keep the customer informed of new equipment or software. The job combines ability to communicate and establish good relations with people at all levels in an organization, with technical expertise to keep up with technological developments.

Service Engineers

They work either for large users 'in-house' or for manufacturers, and visit customers – often irate and impatient – whose equipment has broken down (or apparently broken down: often it is simply wrongly used). Service engineers must thoroughly understand the complexities of hardware and software to be able to diagnose and rectify the trouble. This usually means plugging in a replacement part rather than actual repair. Unlike engineers at the hardware/ software production end, service engineers get out and about and meet the users (see 'Incorporated Engineers and Engineering Technicians', p. 195).

Sales and Marketing

For details of general *sales and marketing*, see p. 297. However, in the computer hardware and software area specialist knowledge is vital. Computing is not only technologically the most sophisticated industry, it is also a highly competitive, cut-throat industry. Sales people usually specialize in systems for specific markets – i.e. commercial, scientific or educational.

Knowledge Engineers

This is one of the newest and fastest-growing areas of work, involving the application of '*expert systems*' to commerce, industry and service industries. A knowledge engineer designs the computer system to perform tasks normally associated with a human expert, e.g. medical diagnosis or an oil rig's safety system.

Technical Writing

Writing manuals for – especially – workstations and PCs is a growing job area. It requires the ability to put over complex information clearly, succinctly and unequivocally, and it requires thorough understanding of what the device described can and cannot do, and how it functions. Manual-writers have to know very much more about their subject than the people for whom they are writing. Existing manuals are often criticized; manufacturers say they have difficulty finding people who combine the necessary technological expertise with the necessary communication skills. Technical writers may be employed by manufacturers or by consultancies or work as freelance or 'in-house'. 'End-user documentation' production is becoming a sophisticated area. Writers have to produce material – both in print and 'screen dialogue' – which is 'user-friendly', i.e. easily understood by amateurs, as well as documentation for experts.

Consultants

Systems analysts and *designers* can ultimately become independent consultants – advising prospective users on whether a system would be of use to them and, if so, which one. Considerable experience of the computer-scene, plus specialist knowledge in a commercial, banking, retailing, etc., or industrial or educational area, is essential.

Training   This is still evolving. Experience is, on the whole, more important than paper qualifications, but experience is often difficult to get without qualifications. It is still just possible to start with a few good GCSEs as an operator or network manager and, with in-house training and preferably day-release, become an *applications programmer* and then a *systems analyst* – if the conditions and the personality and ability are right. Because of the quick expansion and rapid developments in the whole computer area, training is still disorganized and haphazard, with several overlapping types of qualifications. Many people at the top of the profession now have no formal computing qualifications, because when they started their careers there were no relevant qualifications. Others have got on without qualifications because of the shortage of computer staff, but new entrants must aim at a qualification (though the only work for which a degree is invariably demanded is *software/systems programming/software engineering*). Training is also continuous, with the need for continuous updating (known as continuing professional development or CPD). Yet still far too few IT employers are prepared to train staff. Anyone joining the industry is advised to look for companies which participate in the BCS's comprehensive Professional Development Scheme (PDS) which companies buy into. Small companies may not have the resources to do this, but instead may have an arrangement whereby the BCS will 'authenticate' the CPD undertaken by their staff (who keep a record of their training).

Courses are at all levels from post-graduate to those for people with few educational qualifications. Non-degree qualifications are awarded by a number of different organizations, some specializing in a particular branch of the industry. The following are the main entry and training routes, but individuals should look very carefully at syllabuses to ensure that they choose a course to suit their particular interest and academic level. They need also to decide whether to take a full-time, part-time or distance-learning course (many can be taken by any of these methods).

1. Degree (full time or sandwich) in a computing subject (titles include computing science, software engineering, information engineering, business computing, information processing, computer systems). Science A-levels (physics and/or maths) are required for some, but not all, courses.

NOTE: see ENGINEERING, p. 194, for introductory/foundation courses for people with arts A-levels who want to take a degree normally requiring science A-levels.

2. Degree in business studies with a computing option.

3. Post-graduate or post-HND computing course following a humanities degree, particularly languages.

4. BTEC/SCOTVEC (see pp. xxi, xxii) Higher National awards in computer studies, business information technology, software engineering, maths studies (with computing options).

5. British Computer Society: the main professional body; awards its own qualifications, from applications programming upwards. Candidates must have had at least 1 year in relevant employment. Part 1 is equivalent to an HND and Part 2 to an

Honours degree. Degree and Higher National courses accredited by the BCS lead to exemptions from part or all of its examinations.

6. Institute of Data Processing Management (emphasis is on business applications): offers a Diploma qualification and a Certificate in Applications Programming for people with 4 GCSEs or who have completed the IDPM Foundation course (no entry qualifications). There is also a Higher Diploma for those with *either* the Diploma *or* BTEC National in relevant subjects *or* 2 A-levels *or* 4 years' relevant experience if over 21. There is also a Graduate Diploma in Management Information Systems (various entry qualifications including degree and BCS Part 1).

7. BTEC/SCOTVEC National awards in computer studies.

8. City and Guilds (see p. xxii) offers a flexible scheme covering most aspects of IT, from introduction to programming to advanced applications programming. There is also a scheme for microcomputer technology. Some parts of the scheme contribute towards NVQs (see p. xix).

9. The Royal Society of Arts (see p. xxiii) offers a Certificate, Diploma and Advanced Diploma in IT.

NOTE: The IT Industry Training Organization (ITITO) has been set up to oversee future IT awards. NVQs/SVQs are awarded by the BCS, BTEC and other organizations.

NOTE: Private schools' diplomas (full-time courses) vary enormously in value. Check with the British Computer Society (see p. 151) before enrolling.

Computing is the fastest expanding career area. Old – in computing terms – job categories are breaking down, but for computing professionals who are flexible and prepared to continue learning new skills and for constant change and challenge, scope is immense. Computing is expanding in two dimensions: (1) It is penetrating ever more areas of activity, with more and more workplaces within each area installing or expanding systems; and (2) devices and systems are getting ever more sophisticated and versatile; for example, electronic mail and network services are widely used; voice input is in use in a number of specialized areas. As one generation of computers comes on to the market, the next one is in production, and the one after that on the drawing-board (or rather the researcher/designer's VDU). So computing professionals of all kinds have a promising future.

About 85–90% of computing professionals now work with users or consultants installing, programming, analysing/designing systems, controlling, managing, setting up project teams or computing departments, liaising with other staff, training existing staff to use systems. So *systems programmers, systems analysts/ designers, analyst/programmers*, well-qualified *applications programmers, technical writers, user support staff* are all likely to be in demand for the rest of this century (see display advertisements in the press for variety of job-titles, tasks to be performed and levels of responsibility/expertise). But the demand for *operators* and for not-very-highly-skilled programmers is dwindling fast, as these tasks are increasingly performed by non-specialist staff – the users. Manufacturers and software houses employ the remaining 10–15%.

Broadly, then, prospects are excellent for highly skilled, highly trained people and for support staff – i.e. *technicians* (see 'Incorporated Engineers and Engineering Technicians', p. 195); but prospects are not so good for run-of-the-mill professionals who are lured into computing merely by the novelty of the work, and by the advertisements.

The prospects for people with engineering/science background plus computing experience/training are excellent. There is increasing scope for specializing within a work area: people with experience in, say, *retail, banking*, the *law* or *agriculture* may become computing professionals by grafting computing skills on to their particular expertise.

Personal attributes   *All professionals*: Communication skills, written and spoken; flexibility, willingness to adapt to new methodologies and to continue learning.

Systems analyst/designer: Well-above-average intelligence and powers of logical reasoning; numeracy; imagination to put themselves into the shoes of the people whose jobs they may be 'analysing away' or at least changing; tact and diplomacy; ability to get on well with people at all levels in an organization's hierarchy; a confidence-inspiring manner; curiosity; creativity to visualize how old-established methods might be changed; ability to explain complicated procedures in simple language; ability to listen; ability to take an overall view of a situation and yet see it in detail; business acumen, at least for many jobs.

Applications programmers/programmers/analysts: Powers of logical thinking; numeracy; powers of sustained concentration; great patience and willingness to pursue an elusive problem till solved; liking for concentrated desk-work; ability to communicate easily with people in computing as well as with lay people.

Programmers who hope to progress to systems analysis should note the different personal qualities required.

Systems programmers/software engineers: Very high intellectual ability; originality; research-inclined mind; imagination; interest in high technology and its implications and rapid developments.

Network managers: Practicality; liking for routine work; organizing/administrative ability for those wanting to get promotion.

Late start Good opportunities, especially for people with business or related experience and for mature students, who may take full- or part-time degree or other relevant courses.

Career- See below.
break

Part time See below.

Position There are outstanding opportunities for women. The 85–90% +
of computing professionals who work with computer users (see
women above) are in 'dealing-with-people' jobs. Their computing expertise is the essential background for the job. So the vast majority of computer people are doing work which even the most traditionally minded would consider eminently suitable for women. It requires an interest in what makes people tick, to understand and know how to allay people's fear of new – and jargon-ridden – technologies. Women have shown that they appreciate employees' resistance to change and know how to work out changed working patterns which are both efficient and acceptable to staffs. In systems analysis/design women's knack of gaining staff's confidence at the investigation stage has proved particularly useful.

As the whole area is so new, there have been no traditional barriers to break down. Nevertheless, there is evidence now that a disproportionate number of senior project leader and other management jobs are being filled by men, and that women are 'dropping back' A 1995 survey by WIT (Women into Information Technology Foundation) showed that women made up only 20% of senior posts such as those of development manager and project manager, compared with 27% of trainee programmers and 28% of junior analysts/designers. 29% of senior programmers and 20% of senior analysts were women. Interestingly, the nearer the job to the user, the higher the proportion of women – rising to well over 50% on 'help desk' support. This pyramid structure could be due to senior managers' traditional attitudes to women in management jobs (see MANAGEMENT, p. 272). But there may be another reason: of the first generation of specially trained computing professionals, a sizeable proportion is at present either taking a child-rearing career-break, or experiencing the adverse effects of having taken such a break. In this fast-changing profession, it is essential to work continuously, or at least to keep one's hand in during the break. Women who take off more than a few months will inevitably be left behind. But as there are good opportunities for part-time or project-based work there is no need for a complete career-break. The same survey showed that 78% of companies surveyed offered part-time working, 61% flexible hours and 45% job-sharing.

So opportunities for women are excellent. But there are worrying signs that women are not making full use of these opportunities, and that computing is becoming a male-dominated area at an early stage. Parents are buying computers as toys for their young sons, not for their young daughters; in schools far more boys join computer clubs, and take (are persuaded to take?) computing at GCSE and A-level, although neither is generally required for degree courses. At degree level, the proportion of girls taking computing science has actually declined. In *old* universities it dropped from 15% in 1984 to 13.6% in 1991, while in 'new'; universities (former polytechnics) it was 22% in 1990. Applications statistics for 1994 entry showed the proportion to be 13% for old and new universities combined. (However, 16% of those *accepted* were girls.) There is no simple explanation for girls' apparent decline of interest. One reason, computing professionals – both sexes – say, is that computer advertisers are projecting a false image. The main emphasis, as computing skills are needed in virtually every area of work, should be on communication skills, not just on mathematical/technological skills. There is no reason whatever why girls should not see computing as a 'fun subject', just as boys do, working with people in all kinds of job areas, and why women should not match men as computing professionals at all levels. The Women into Information Technology Foundation (WIT) is trying to encourage higher education institutions and employers to run events and take other initiatives to attract girls to this area. It also provides information on refresher training, useful for women returners.

Further information

British Computer Society, 1 Sanford Street, Swindon, Wilts. SN1 1HJ

BTEC, Central House, Upper Woburn Place, London WC1H 0HH

Institute of Data Processing Management, IDPM House, Edging-
ton Way, Ruxley Corner, Sidcup, Kent DA14 5HR
WIT Foundation, Concept 2000, 250 Farnborough Road, Farnborough, Hants GU14 7LU

Related   ENGINEERING – MANAGEMENT SERVICES: *Operational Research*
careers   – SCIENCE

Dance

Teaching and performing are two separate careers. There are three kinds of performer in Western dance: (1) classical ballet, (2) contemporary, (3) musical theatre.

Performing

Entry qualifications

No specific educational requirements, but a good general education is essential for ballet dancers. Many dance schools offer A-levels and GCSEs, and A-levels are essential for students interested in the growing number of degree courses in dance performance or teaching.

Ballet Dancer

The work

Ballet dancers lead dedicated lives. Their days are spent practising, rehearsing and performing. They have little spare time and may not indulge in such activities as cycling, riding, etc., lest they develop the wrong muscles. They meet few people who are not in some way involved with ballet.

They are usually attached to one particular company and may be on tour for much of the year.

Ballet companies have only a few vacancies each year so opportunities are limited. Once a member of the *corps de ballet*, a talented dancer has a chance of rising to solo parts and understudying bigger roles, but it is rare indeed to rise to principal dancer status. Even a successful dancer's professional life is short; only the very exceptional still get engagements in their middle thirties. There are some opportunities abroad – dance is a very international activity.

Training

Serious training must have started by the age of 11 and certainly no later than 16 with a professional teacher who prepares pupils systematically for one of the officially recognized major dancing examinations: e.g. those of the Royal Academy of Dancing, the

Imperial Society of Teachers of Dancing, or the British Ballet Organization (RAD, ISTD, BBO).

The best training is given at professional schools which give general education for GCSEs and a thorough drama and dance training. It is advisable to apply only for courses accredited by the Council for Dance Education and Training (and for which some local education authorities will give discretionary grants).

There are part-time ballet schools all over the country but pupils from the few full-time vocational schools (some of which are attached to companies) probably stand a better chance of getting into a company when they finish.

Ballet training includes national and character dancing, mime, history, art and literature, and usually French (most technical terms are in that language).

Before accepting a pupil, good schools insist on a thorough orthopaedic examination, which is repeated at regular intervals throughout training.

Personal attributes   Suitable physique, including strong back and feet; intelligence; intuition; emotional depth; musical talent; the ability to take criticism without resentment; a strong constitution; complete dedication; a distinct personality.

Contemporary Dancer

The work   The work and lifestyle of the contemporary dancers is very like that of the ballet dancer, requiring the same degree of dedication. As contemporary dance groups are structured differently from classical ballet companies and are often much smaller, there is not the same hierarchy and route to principal dancer.

Training   This is quite different from that of classical ballet, although contemporary dancers may have started with classical training as children and may continue to take classical dance classes occasionally (as classical dancers may take contemporary classes). Their kind of dance makes different aesthetic and physical demands and requires specialized training. Students frequently take a foundation course before starting their vocational training, which should begin by age 18. Most contemporary dance courses are degrees (for example the degree in Contemporary Dance run by the London Contemporary Dance School and validated by Kent University), although they still do not attract mandatory funding (i.e. students have to apply for discretionary grants, see p. xxvi).

Musical Theatre Dancer

The work Modern stage dancers perform in musicals, pantomime, cabaret, on TV, and in light entertainment generally. They are not usually attached to a company, but appear in individual shows. As well as learning dances, they often have to learn scripts and songs. They are more likely to be on short-term contracts and to have longer periods out of work than other dancers. Even when not working, they have to keep up their practice, which means paying for private classes at a dance centre.

For the fully trained first-rate dancer prospects are fair. But like other entertainers, a dancer must be prepared for months of 'resting', meanwhile earning a living in some other way yet being available to attend auditions. If lucky, they may get a long run in the West End, a tour, or a television series.

Training 3 years full time, preferably. Most start vocational training at 16 and courses are 3 years' full-time. Over 80% of dancers currently employed in the West End have been through accredited vocational dance courses. At auditions, dancers must show potential; and do not rely on examination passes (they may be expected to have reached Elementary). The modern stage dancer should also have some training in voice production, drama and singing.

Personal attributes A strong stage appearance and presence; resilience; versatility; enterprise in tracking down jobs; sense of rhythm.

*

Teaching

Entry qualifications To teach dance in state primary and secondary schools (i.e. not dance schools) qualified teacher status is required: *either* a degree leading to QTS *or* a degree in dance *or* in performing arts (titles and content vary) followed by a Post-graduate Certificate in Education (see TEACHING, p. 522). Entry requirements may be waived for mature entrants.

The work A dancing teacher may teach both children and adults, or may specialize in teaching one or the other. Adults are taught in private schools/classes or in local authority adult education centres.

Children are taught in ordinary schools; dancing schools; specialized professional schools.

Ordinary schools
Full-time or visiting part-time teachers teach dance to GCSE, mainly to improve children's poise and deportment.

Dancing schools
These are intended for children who don't have dancing lessons at school. They may be run by a teacher who hires a hall for the purpose, or they may be in a dancing school which caters for both children and adults.

Children are usually prepared for recognized dancing examinations (see 'Ballet Dancer, Training'). This ensures that children are being properly taught even though they do not intend to become professionals.

Professional schools
Dancing is an essential part of the curriculum in what is generally an arts-orientated private school; the teacher deals with especially talented children who hope to become professional dancers.

Job prospects are good for teaching adults and children. Royal Academy of Dancing and Imperial Society of Teachers of Dancing examiners often go abroad to organize, teach and examine.

Training   *Leading to qualified teacher status*
Applicants to degrees in dance should check prospectuses very carefully before choosing a course, as the 'dance component' varies from a few hours to a substantial proportion.

The dance teaching societies (e.g. ISTD and RAD) have their own entrance requirements for student teachers and need to be contacted individually. Students can teach only the syllabus they have been trained in, and usually work in private schools and classes. A couple of degree courses are available for the ISTD and RAD syllabuses. A fast-growing area, in which there are some specialized teaching courses, is that of community dance. The emphasis is frequently on contemporary or ethnic dance.

Other courses   The following are also intended for performers, teachers and other professionals in dance, e.g. administrators and notators: the University of Surrey's Dance in Society degree; the London College of Dance/Middlesex University degree; the BTEC HND in Dance at Coventry Centre for Performing Arts.

Personal attributes   The ability to explain and demonstrate steps and movements; a fine sense of rhythm and some proficiency at the piano; a liking for people of all ages; imagination; endless tact and patience; good appearance; graceful movements. (See also TEACHING, p. 523.)

Teaching Keep Fit and Exercise

This area has expanded rapidly in the last few years. Movement classes have mushroomed, changing their style frequently in order to follow the latest (often imported) fashion. Many people have cashed in on the dance/exercise craze without a proper knowledge of how the body works and what kind of movement is suitable for each type of student. The most suitable basic training for teachers in this area is either a proper dance course; or Physical Education teacher training; or a 2-year part-time course organized by the Keep Fit Association and run in conjunction with local education authorities; or courses leading to the RSA Certificate in Exercise to Music.

Choreography

The work   The dancer who has exceptional imaginative powers and the ability to interpret music in terms of dancing may ultimately do choreography. This is dance composition: the grouping of dancers and sequence of dances which make up the entire ballet. In musical theatre, a choreographer may direct within a wide range from the production numbers on TV which involve scores of dancers, to the unexacting dances of a seaside concert party.

Choreography is not a career for which a novice can be trained unless there is a noticeable talent. Years of experience of classical or contemporary dance and a musical training are needed (see MUSIC, p. 324). However, some dance courses now include choreography or offer it as an option.

Career-break   Many dancers take up teaching after a break from performing.

Part time   Good opportunities in teaching.

Position of women   *Performing*: 89% are women. More men are coming into the profession; but there is still a far greater shortage of *first-rate* male than of first-rate female dancers.

Teaching: This is still a predominantly female occupation (especially teaching children) but there is no reason why more men should not train for teaching.

Further information   Council for Dance Education and Training, Riverside Studios, Crisp Road, London W6 9RL (for addresses of accredited dance schools)

Imperial Society of Teachers of Dancing, Euston Hall, Birkenhead
   Street, London WC1H 8BE

Central Register and Clearing House (qualified teacher status
   B.Ed. and post-graduate courses), 3 Crawford Place, London
   W1H 2BN

The Keep Fit Association, 16 Upper Woburn Place, London
   WC1H 0QG

Royal Society of Arts (see p. xxiii).

Related careers	DRAMA – MUSIC – TEACHING

Dentistry

Dental Surgeon

Entry qualifications

3 good A-levels (or equivalent) usually including at least 2 sciences (biology and chemistry are preferred). Chemistry, biology, physics and maths must usually be included at GCSE. Most dental schools accept 2 AS-levels in lieu of 1 A-level. (See 'Training' for arts A-level candidates.)

The work

Dentists (or dental surgeons) preserve teeth by filling, crowning and scaling. They extract teeth and design and fit artificial dentures. They also do surgical operations on the jaw, and orthodontics, which is the improvement of irregular teeth, mainly in children. The preventive aspects of dentistry are very important, involving regular teeth inspection for children. Prospects are good and qualifications are accepted in the EU.

General Practice

The majority of dentists are in general practice. Some treat National Health patients almost exclusively, some treat both private and NHS patients. Others treat only private patients.

Dentists in general practice have the best financial prospects and the greatest independence, but they are also likely to work the hardest. They may be in a partnership, or in practice on their own, working in their own premises with their own equipment, and employing their own dental surgery assistants (see p. 163).

It is usual to begin as an assistant or associate in a practice, with a view to becoming a partner later, but primarily to learn how a practice is run. This involves a good deal of organization, filling-in of forms, ordering stocks, and contact with technicians.

It is also possible to buy the 'goodwill' of a dentist who is retiring or moving away, or simply to put up a plate and wait for patients.

Community Dental Surgeon

The Community Dental Service is intended to foster the idea of
dental care within the whole community through the dental inspection and treatment of priority groups such as school and pre-
school children, expectant and nursing mothers and, increasingly,
elderly and handicapped people.

Hospital and University Dental Surgeon

In hospitals, a dentist looks after sick patients whose teeth need
urgent attention, and does jaw operations and complicated extrac-
tions. Outpatients may need only ordinary dental treatment.

Dental work in hospitals has the usual hospital advantages of
life in a community, colleagues to discuss difficult cases with, and
social and sports clubs. Dentists wishing to do university research
and teaching usually combine this with some hospital work.

Training 5-year course at dental schools attached to universities. The
dental course proper may be preceded by a 1-year preliminary
science course (as for medical training). Students with A-level
physics, chemistry, biology, zoology or maths are exempt from it.

Most dental schools have discontinued this course. Even when
dental schools do accept students for a preliminary year, local
authorities do not normally pay grants for what is in effect an A-
level course.

Dental training lasts for 5 years. The syllabus covers anatomy
and physiology, the uses of dental materials, design and fitting of
dental appliances, pathology, some medicine, general as well as
dental surgery, anaesthesia, orthodontics, children's and general
preventive dentistry, radiology, dental ethics, and relevant law.

Practical work on 'phantom heads' normally begins in the
second year, and work on actual patients during the second or
third year of the dental course.

Personal attributes Manual dexterity; a methodical and scientific approach; and good
health. Left-handedness is not a disadvantage.

Dentist in general practice especially: The ability to establish
easy relationships quickly with people, and give confidence to the
nervous (the growth of the practice depends almost entirely on
the patients' personal recommendations); organizing ability.

Community dental surgeon especially: The ability to get on with
children.

Hospital dentist especially: The ability to work well as a member
of a team.

**Further
informa-
tion**

General Dental Council, 37 Wimpole Street, London W1M 8DQ

**Related
careers**

DENTISTRY: *Auxiliary Work* – MEDICINE

Auxiliary Work

For people interested in dentistry but without the necessary qualifications for dental training, there are four careers: *dental therapist,
dental hygienist, dental surgery assistant* and *dental technician.*

Dental Therapist

**Entry
qualifica-
tions**

Minimum age for training 18.
   5 GCSEs (A–C), including English language, and a science
subject, preferably biology, plus the Dental Surgery Assistants'
National Certificate and minimum 1 year's experience in a dental
surgery.

The work

Dental therapists do 'operative work'; they work in hospitals and
community dental services, mainly helping dentists to give treatment to children and to teach them how to care for their teeth.
They work under the direction of a dentist who prescribes the
treatment to be given; this includes simple fillings, extraction of
deciduous teeth, and cleaning, scaling and polishing teeth. Dental
therapists always work under the direction and prescription of a
registered dentist. Their responsibility is therefore limited. Many
of the patients are very young – in welfare clinics under 5, in
school clinics mostly under 11. Dental therapists do not work for
dentists in general practice.
   There is now intense competition for the very few training
places per year.

Training

2 years full time, only in London and Wales. Practical training
(on which more time is spent than on theory) is initially on
phantom heads, so that students learn how to scale, polish, fill
and extract teeth without worrying about hurting the patient;

they also work on patients, under supervision. Theoretical training includes anatomy, physiology of the teeth and jaw, some radiography, some dietetics – enough to understand why some foods are good and some bad for the development of children's teeth.

Personal attributes   Considerable manual dexterity; conscientiousness; some interest in science; good health; a way with children.

Further information   General Dental Council, 37 Wimpole Street, London W1M 8DQ

Dental Hygienist

Entry qualifications   Minimum age for training 18.

5 GCSEs (A–C), preferably including English language and a science subject. Candidates are given a manual dexterity test, and are expected to have had experience as a dental surgery assistant (see below). They would normally hold a relevant nationally recognized certificate.

The work   Dental hygienists also do 'operative work'. They do scaling and polishing under the direction of dentists, but do not do any fillings etc. An important aspect of the work is preventive dentistry.

They work with adults as well as with children, in general practice as well as in community health clinics and hospitals.

More dentists in general practice, especially in partnership, now employ hygienists, but there are no promotion prospects.

Training   1 year full time (probably 2 years from 1996) at dental hospitals. Training is similar to that of therapists, but the extraction and filling of teeth are not included. Some time is spent in learning how to talk about oral hygiene to children and adults.

Personal attributes   As for therapists, plus the ability to express oneself lucidly.

Further information   General Dental Council, 37 Wimpole Street, London W1M 8DQ

Dental Surgery Assistant

Entry qualifications
None laid down, but most hospital training schools demand some GCSE passes, which should include English language and a science. None required for admission to the examination for the National Certificate of the Examining Board for Dental Surgery Assistants.

Minimum age for training usually 17.

The work
Surgery assistants do no 'operative work'. They act as the dentist's 'third hand', handing them the right instruments at the right time. They also look after the instruments, do sterilizing, get out patients' treatment cards, help with filling in forms and filing, do secretarial and reception work.

Surgery assistants work wherever dentists work, i.e. in general practice, in community dental clinics and in hospitals.

Training
Most dentists train their own assistants, but some prefer those who were trained at a dental hospital, for a period varying from 12 to 24 months. The type of training differs slightly from one hospital to another, but it is mainly practical, with some lectures and demonstrations.

The majority of dental surgery assistants, however, go straight from school or from secretarial college to a dentist's surgery and are trained on the job. They are advised to attend evening classes.

After the training they can take the examination for the National Certificate awarded by the Examining Board for Dental Surgery Assistants. The certificate is awarded after 2 years' work.

Personal attributes
A polite, friendly manner; some manual dexterity; a well-groomed, neat appearance; good health.

Further information
British Association of Dental Nurses, 110 London Street, Fleetwood, Lancashire FY7 6JY

Dental Technician

Entry qualifications
For BTEC National Diploma in Science (Dental Technology): 4 GCSEs (A–C), including English, maths and 2 sciences. For SCOTVEC Diploma in Dental Technology, normally 4 O-grades including English and science subject.

The work
Dental technicians construct and repair dentures, crowns and other orthodontic appliances. They work either in commercial

dental laboratories where work for individual dentists is carried out, or in hospital dental laboratories. It is highly skilled work and there is a great shortage of dental technicians.

Training *Either* (in commercial laboratories or dental practices) a 5-year apprenticeship with day-release for BTEC National award; *or* (in dental hospitals and health authorities) a 3-year training scheme with block-release for the BTEC National award; *or* (less common) 3-year full-time course for BTEC/SCOTVEC National award plus 2 years' consolidation in an approved laboratory.

Approximately 10% of successful students take a 2-year part-time course for the BTEC Higher National certificate.

Personal attributes Great manual dexterity; patience; accuracy.

Further information General Dental Council, 37 Wimpole Street, London W1M 8DQ
Dental Technicians Education and Training Advisory Board, 5 Oxford Court, St James Road, Brackley, Northants NN13 7XY

Late start 1. *Dentists*: Unusual. Dental schools vary in their attitude to mature students and judge each case on its merits – acceptance depends largely on the number of years students would have after qualifying. There is, usually, no relaxation in entry requirements. Over-35s are unlikely to be offered a place. No employment problem once qualified.

2. *Auxiliary work*: Young students are given preference for training usually, but mature entrants are also considered.

Career-break No problem: for dentists there are refresher courses. The Dental Retainer Scheme encourages women dentists to work at least 12 sessions and attend 7 education sessions a year, while paying reduced membership fees.

Part time Good opportunities for employment, none for training. Job-sharing should be possible.

Position of women 1. *Dentists*: 30% of practising dentists are women, but over 46% of students are now female. Of all the top professions, dentistry is the most promising for women. They have truly equal chances of promotion in the health service; they are usually welcomed in private practice by partners and by patients; and it is a profession which can be carried on anywhere in the country.

2. *Dental therapists, hygienists and surgery assistants*: Predominantly female professions.

3. *Dental technicians*: Although most technicians are men, more women are now training and their position is much as for other dental staff now.

| **Related careers** | MEDICINE – NURSING – SCIENCE |

Dietetics

Entry qualifications

2 to 3 A-level passes, preferably chemistry and another science subject. Also mathematics and English to GCSE standard.

BTEC National Diploma in science with an appropriate merit pass or an Access course in science or health-related studies may be acceptable.

The work

The dietitian's special skill is to translate the science of nutrition into understandable and practical information about food and health. Career opportunities have greatly diversified as healthy eating habits become increasingly recognized as a vital part of preventing disease and promoting good health.

Dietitians are concerned with food and health in its widest sense and their work is preventive and therapeutic. They have to know about food production and processing; social, economic and psychological factors that influence food choice; the digestion, absorption and metabolism of food, its effect on nutritional well-being; how to treat disease and prevent nutrition-related problems.

Dietitians work in many different settings. Currently, about half of the profession are employed in the National Health Service, where they work in hospitals or in the community as 'hands-on' dietitians or as managers.

Hospital dietitians advise people who need special diets as part of their medical treatment, e.g. a carefully controlled diet for kidney disease or an appropriately formulated liquid feed which is passed through a tube. With other health professionals they work as part of a clinical team. They also help in developing food policies and liaise with the catering services to ensure that healthy food is available for both patients and staff, and special dietary needs are met. Many hospital dietitians eventually specialize, e.g. in the treatment of children, diabetes or eating disorders. What-ever the reason for referral, the dietitian works with the patient (or carer) to plan changes to their eating patterns. As well as treating the medical condition, diets must take into account usual food habits, cultural customs and social and financial position in a non-discriminatory way. The dietitian must provide support and encouragement through sometimes difficult times of adjustment.

Community dietitians' work is more about health education, although many run clinics in doctors' surgeries and health centres for people needing specialist dietary advice. As there are so few dietitians, an important part of their job is to work closely with primary health-care teams. This includes keeping nurses, doctors, health visitors and other health professionals up to date on the latest food issues so that they in turn can communicate important health messages as widely as possible. Dietitians also work with the media and speak to groups and societies to ensure that accurate nutrition information is available to their local communities.

Another important aspect of community work is working in partnership with local people to tackle food issues that they are concerned about, e.g. cooking skills, access to affordable, healthy food. Community dietitians may also work with schools, social services, agencies involved with the under-5s, workplaces, services for elderly people and local authorities to help promote positive, enjoyable changes in food choice. This work may involve: helping to develop and implement food policies; developing educational resources; nutrition education for staff or carers; liaison with catering services and individual advice for people with special dietary needs, e.g. people with chewing or swallowing difficulties.

Outside the NHS dieticians work in rapidly expanding areas such as:

education – e.g. as educators in centres of higher and further education, for other health-care workers such as doctors and community nurses and for the media.

research, for example, into evaluating and improving dietetic treatment and developing the science of nutrition and dietetics.

industry, for example with trade associations, food retailers, food manufacturers, catering organizations, public relations and marketing companies – in a consultancy role, giving advice on nutrition to businesses and their customers.

freelance dietetics, for example in private practice, sports nutrition and the media.

Experienced dietitians are usually in demand, but getting that first job may mean moving to another part of the country. There are some openings in the developing countries and in the EU (for dietitians who speak the relevant languages). British qualifications are not automatically recognized in the USA, Canada and Australia, but reciprocity of recognition may be obtained in the future.

Training   State registration with the Council for Professions Supplementary to Medicine is essential for a dietitian wishing to work in the

National Health Service and a definite advantage when working outside the Health Service. There are alternative routes:

1. A recognized 4-year degree course. The syllabus includes: physiology; biochemistry; microbiology; nutrition and food science; diet therapy; health education; catering; psychology and sociology.

2. Graduates with degrees which include human nutrition, physiology or biochemistry may take a recognized 2-year post-graduate diploma. All courses include a period of approved practical clinical training in hospital and community settings.

Personal attributes
An interest in science, people and food; enjoyment of communicating with people from all walks of life; an ability to explain complex things in a simple manner; a positive and motivating attitude and an understanding, non-discriminatory approach; confident spoken and written communication skills; patience and a sense of humour.

Late start
No age-bar in jobs, mature students welcome on degree courses. (See Access Courses, p. xxxi.)

Career-break
Presents no problems. The British Dietetic Association organizes courses for returners to the profession. Other 'refresher' courses may be organized by hospitals and colleges.

Part time
Opportunities for part time and job-sharing at all levels of seniority. At present no part-time training opportunities, but some colleges and universities are developing more flexible study routes, including part-time courses.

Position of women
About 90% a female profession, but the proportion of male students is increasing.

Further information
British Dietetic Association, 7th Floor, Elizabeth House, 22 Suffolk Street, Queensway, Birmingham B1 1LS (please send an s.a.e.)

Related careers
CATERING – SCIENCE: *Food Science and Technology*; *Biochemist*; *Chemist* – HOME ECONOMICS – MEDICINE

Drama

Acting

Entry qualifications

No rigid requirements. See 'Training', below.

The work

A career only to be contemplated by those who feel they could not possibly be happy doing anything else. Complimentary notices for school or college plays are rarely pointers to professional success, because being the best of a group of local performers is irrelevant when competing with the best from all over the country. In addition, luck plays a large part: being in the right place at the right time is as important as being good at the job.

Entry to this overcrowded profession is extremely difficult. There are 'casting agreements' between theatrical, TV, film and commercials producers which control the employment of actors and virtually restrict employment to Equity members. Equity (the actors' trade union) in turn strictly controls the entry of new members.

Television

Provides well over half the total of acting jobs, but is not easy to get into: producers can pick and choose and tend to choose players who have had repertory experience or who have done exceptionally well at drama schools or in fringe theatre work. TV drama is recorded on video tape or film in short scenes or 'takes'. Each take rarely lasts for more than a couple of minutes. The actor may be asked to film scenes out of story order, which requires a high level of discipline. Rehearsal time is scarce; the technique now widely used is the rehearse/record method. The actors rehearse each scene on set, then record it immediately. Making TV drama can be very boring. At least two-thirds of an actor's time on set is spent sitting around waiting for technical problems to be sorted out. Added to this, actors have very little control over the finished product; the director, camera operator and editor have more control than they do. However, generally TV work pays better than theatre work and exposes the actor to a wider audience.

Theatre

Performers may give eight performances a week. In repertory, there are often rehearsals during the day as well, which leaves little free time. Reasonably priced digs near the theatre are rarely luxurious; theatre dressing-rooms tend to be cramped and uncomfortable.

No actor ever has a 'secure job' – contracts may be as short as 2 weeks; rarely longer than a year.

Apart from the conventional theatre, there has in recent years been a considerable growth in 'fringe theatre'. Companies are often set up by players working as co-operatives (for a very small wage), taking plays into small halls, pubs, schools, etc. This type of acting – without a proper stage – requires adaptability, devotion and special technique: it is not much easier to get into than conventional stage work.

Commercials

Work comes through casting agencies. Work is never regular; TV commercials' producers always look for fresh faces, and an actor or actress who is currently advertising, for instance, a baby food, is unlikely to be used for some time, either for a competitor's food or for, say, a sophisticated drinks or fashion advertisement. Once established, actors and actresses sometimes appear in commercials which are written to suit their particular style, or they do 'voice overs' – the speaking but not the visual part of the commercial. Commercials are not a way into acting, but useful bread-and-butter jobs.

Films

The film industry is very small. There is very little work; nobody can hope to be *only* a film actress or actor today. The decision whether to accept a tiny part in a TV soap-opera or wait for a hoped-for break in a film is always a difficult one. A performer who has accepted a part must stick to it and not let a producer down if something better turns up – this is essential to retain all-important agents' or casting directors' goodwill.

Acting is never easy, however good a player is. It gives great satisfaction, however, to people with stamina, real talent and lots of luck. At any one time over two-thirds of professional actors and actresses are out of work. An inquiry also showed that the chances of success are best for students who have attended one of the established schools (see 'Training', below) whose courses are accredited by the National Council for Drama Training. Another advantage of accredited schools is that their graduates who get jobs are automatically given the coveted Equity (provisional) card. Most of these belong to the Conference of Drama Schools. Those who have been to one of the lesser-known schools which are totally out of touch with the changing needs and techniques of the theatre and broadcasting, or those few who somehow slipped in without any systematic training at all, are much less likely to find work. Entry to good schools, however, is very competitive (RADA, for example, auditions over 1,000 people a year for 25 places). 'Graduates' from established drama schools do not normally have great difficulty in getting their first job. They are usually fixed up within a few months of leaving drama school. It is the second step, into bigger and better repertory, or into TV, West End, etc., which is the problematical one – and which vast numbers never manage to take at all. It means coming to London, finding a good agent who will take a newcomer, and earning a living, yet being available if the hoped-for audition comes.

Entry requirements and training

No rigid academic requirements; acceptance at good drama schools depends on audition, but candidates considered suitable almost invariably have several GCSEs and often A-levels, especially in English language and/or literature. The average ratio of applicants to places for men at good schools is about 12:1; for women candidates it is about 15:1.

About 85% of players who earn their living at acting have been to accredited schools. Although grants are not mandatory (i.e. automatic), an increasing number of local education authorities will give grants for NCDT accredited courses. Some run their own auditions before deciding.

Performers' courses last 2 or 3 years. Students unlikely to succeed are asked to leave, or leave of their own accord, well before the end of the course. Courses prepare students for all types of work, but individual schools' curricula vary considerably. All cover the three main aspects: *movement*, *voice production* and *acting studies*. All students do all types of parts, from musical to mime, Shakespeare to Stoppard. Courses include general stagecraft, play-construction, etc.

Drama can also be taken as part of a first degree course, but the primary purpose of nearly all these courses is the study of literary criticism, history and literature of the theatre; not vocational acting training. Graduates from these courses usually go into teaching or possibly into drama production (mainly TV); but there are far fewer such openings than there are drama degree students.

There are a very few degree and post-graduate courses for performers.

Post-graduate drama courses are usually academic, not vocational.

Personal attributes
Good health; well-cut features, but not necessarily beauty; the ability to learn lines quickly; a good memory; great self-confidence; imagination and sensitivity to interpret any part; resilience, to ignore or benefit from the constant and public criticism from teachers, producers, directors, colleagues and the critics; an iron constitution; a sense of rhythm, at least (preferably an aptitude for dancing and singing); outstanding acting talent and a 'stage personality'; grim determination.

Late start
Not impossible, but difficult owing to stiff competition for drama school places.

Career-break
Possible, provided contacts are kept up.

Part time
Only by the very nature of the work.

Position of women
The ratio of female to male students training is 3:1. Although there are far more parts for men than for women, more women graduate every year. In this profession it is of course not a question of discrimination at the employment stage, but entrenched tradition makes even women dramatists write more parts for men than for women. Actresses are therefore strongly advised to have a second string to their bow. Secretarial or word processing training is useful here, as 'temping' and part-time jobs enable an actress to be available for auditions while earning her living. Women directors still face a great deal of discrimination, especially in the established theatre. As a result of all this, some women-only drama groups and co-operatives have been set up to provide work for women directors and actors. A 1992 Equity survey showed that women were generally paid less than men for similar work.

Drama Therapy

Drama therapy aims to use various dramatic techniques (including mime and improvisation) to provide therapeutic experiences for mentally and physically handicapped and psychiatric patients. It is practised by both specialist drama therapists and other professional staff involved in the care and treatment of such patients.

Training Either via part-time course while working in the health or community services (for details write to the British Association for Drama Therapists, 7 Hatfield Road, St Albans, Herts) or via the 1-year full-time course, Drama and Movement in Therapy, operated by Sesame (a charity) at Kingsway-Princeton College. Students should have had previous relevant experience, e.g. psychiatric nursing, teaching, social work or drama. For details write to the Department of Creative and Vocational Studies, Kingsway-Princeton College, Hugh Myddelton Centre, Sans Walk, Rosoman Street, London EC1R 0AS.

Stage Management

The work Stage managers and their teams are responsible to the director, during rehearsals, for the implementation of her/his instructions. This usually includes such things as the recording of actors' moves and other stage directions in the prompt book; collecting props, sound effects, etc., for the director's approval; relaying the director's requirements to the scenic, costume and lighting departments; ensuring that the actors are in the right place at the right time for rehearsals, costume fittings, etc. During the run of the play stage managers are in charge of everything on stage and backstage, and are responsible for seeing that each performance keeps to the director's original intention. Stage managers may also conduct understudy rehearsals. They often work all day and are in the theatre until the lights go out. Stage managers are engaged by theatrical managements for one particular production, or for a repertory season, or occasionally on a more permanent basis.

There is a shortage of trained and experienced stage managers. Many directors start as stage managers. First jobs are the most difficult to find.

Training Full-time stage management courses at drama schools for 2–3 years. Admission to the courses is by interview and only those who are interested in stage management for its own sake or as preparation for work as a producer or director, but not as a stepping-stone to acting, are accepted. As with acting, those who have attended courses accredited by the National Council for Drama Training have the best prospects.

The subjects studied include history of drama and theatrical presentation; literature; the elements of period styles; stage management organization and routine: play study; carpentry; stage lighting; voice; movement; make-up.

NOTE 1: Stage management training does not lead immediately to work in television and films, but, if supplemented with experience, it may do so.

NOTE 2: There are also a very few full-time courses for theatre *electricians* and *sound engineers*.

Personal attributes
Organizing ability; natural authority and tact for dealing with temperamental and anxious actors; a practical approach; ability to deal with emergencies from prop-making to mending electrical equipment; calmness during crises; interest in the literary and technical aspects of theatrical production; the ability to speak well – both lucidly and concisely; visual imagination; a genuine desire to do stage management in preference to acting: frustrated actors do not make good, or happy, stage managers.

Late start
Should be fair opportunities for people with amateur dramatic experience; maturity helps in a job which involves organizing others.

Career-break
Should be no problem if good experience before the break – and if willing to work all evening and often during the day.

Part time
Sporadic rather than part time.

Position of women
Proportions of men and women have always been fairly equal; women are welcome in this branch of the profession and do well in it.

Further information
National Council for Drama Training, 5 Tavistock Place, London WC1H 9SS (no reply without an s.a.e.)
Conference of Drama Schools (a quicker response with s.a.e. for list of member schools), c/o Central School of Speech and Drama, 64 Eton Avenue, London NW3 3HY
Local theatre; drama schools

Related careers
LAW: *Barrister* – LEISURE/RECREATION MANAGEMENT – SPEECH AND LANGUAGE THERAPISTS – TELEVISION, FILM AND RADIO

Driving Instructor and Examiner

Driving Instructor

Entry qualifications

4 years' full (not provisional) car driving licence without disqualification: The minimum age someone can accompany a learner driver is 21.

The work

The majority of instructors work on their own. This is more lucrative, but also more precarious, than working for one of the big driving schools. Hours are irregular and long: far more pupils want lessons at lunch time, after work or at weekends than during normal working hours. Most instructors teach between 6 and 12 pupils a day.

Being a good driver is not the most important aspect of instructing: instructors must like teaching and have the natural ability to do so; they must be able to put themselves into the position of a nervous, possibly not very talented, learner. They usually drive all day and every day through the same streets, which can be dull. The attractions of the work are, largely, being one's own boss; developing learners' road sense and driving technique; talking, during lessons, to a variety of people.

Business depends on area: it is essential, before investing in a dual-control car, to find out whether or not the area is already saturated with instructors.

Personal attributes

Organizing ability, business acumen, ability to get on with all types of people and to put them at their ease; complete unflappability and fearlessness; some mechanical aptitude; teaching talent; endless patience; ability to criticize tactfully and explain lucidly.

Training

Instructors must pass the Department of Transport's 3-part examination: a written test (Part 1), a practical driving test (Part 2) and a test of instructing ability (Part 3). Parts 2 and 3 must be completed within 2 years of passing Part 1. Only 3 attempts at each of these two parts are permitted. The syllabus for Part 1 includes principles and applications of road safety, driving techniques, and theory and practice of learning, teaching and assessment. Part 2 is a stringent test at advanced level. In Part 3 the examiner plays the part first of a new learner and then of a pupil at about test standard. After passing Part 2, trainees are allowed to hold a 6-month training licence and charge for instruction, but they must pass Part 3 before being registered as an Approved Driving Instructor.

Examiners

Entry qualifications and training

Driving examiner
Minimum age 25; must have held a driving licence for 5 years without conviction for a serious motoring offence; wide experience of driving in the last 3 years; should be physically fit; active interest in, and knowledge of, all motoring/road/traffic trends and problems; some mechanical knowledge of cars and other vehicles; preferably some experience of driving a variety of vehicles including motorcycles. Selection is based on driving experience, a special driving test and interview, followed by a 4-week course.

Traffic examiner
Some experience of law enforcement as it affects heavy goods and public service vehicles. Selection is by interview.

Vehicle examiner
Automotive engineering training at City and Guilds, National Certificate, or Higher National Certificate level and total of minimum 4 years' formal training (which can include up to 3 years' full-time study).

The work

Driving examiners are Civil Servants. They work as members of a team under a senior examiner, attached to one of over 300 test centres throughout the country. They test learner drivers of cars and other vehicles to ensure that candidates are competent to drive without endangering other road-users and that they drive with due consideration for other drivers and pedestrians. To do this the examiner takes drivers over an approved route and asks them to carry out various exercises. While doing this the examiner must take notes without distracting the driver's concentration and must make a fair assessment. The work is highly concentrated and, for work as responsible as this, can be fairly repetitive.

Traffic examiners, also Civil Servants, investigate, by observation on the road, by inquiry of operators and by examination of drivers' records, whether laws concerning operation of vehicles (such as the hours a driver may be in charge of a vehicle without rest period) are being observed. Examiners do not have to examine vehicles' mechanical conditions.

Recruitment is only sporadic. For promotion, examiners may have to move to another area.

Vehicle examiners are employed by the Vehicle Inspectorate to carry out a variety of mechanical testing and inspection tasks, including checking of HGVs; supervising the tachograph scheme; checking operators' maintenance arrangements; inspecting vehicles and preparing reports following road accidents. They may appear in court as expert witnesses.

Personal attributes   Air of authority; friendliness; tact; ability to concentrate constantly; unflappability.

Late start   Most instructors and examiners have had some other job before; maturity is an asset.

Career-break   *Instructors*: There is a danger that, during the break, another instructor may set up in the area. Continued driving during the break would be essential.

Examiners: Too early to know what the opportunities for returners would be, but returners would be encouraged.

Part time   It is possible to have a small number of pupils, but it is never possible to work during school-hours only. Summer months are the busiest time. So far no part-time examiners, but part-time work and job-sharing is possible.

Position of women   *Driving instructors*: About 12% now are women. Women instructors have no special problem getting pupils.

Driving examiners: This is a relatively new career for women. They now form 8% of the total, up from just over 5% in 1987.

Traffic examiners: there are now 15 women out of a total of 179.

Vehicle examiners: There are as yet no women doing this work.

Further information   *Driving instructors and driving examiners*: Driving Standards Agency, Stanley House, Talbot Street, Nottingham NG1 5GU

Traffic and vehicle examiners: Vehicle Inspectorate Executive Agency, Berkeley House, Croydon Street, Bristol BS5 0DA

Related careers   TEACHING

Economics

Entry qualifications
Degree in economics; A-level maths or statistics preferred, but not essential, for all courses.

The work
Economics is concerned with the organization, utilization and distribution of productive and financial resources, nationally and internationally. This includes the study of political, industrial and social relationships and interactions.

Economics comes under the Social Sciences umbrella (but is not a 'science' in the same sense as physics or chemistry). Economic theories are 'applicable' or 'inapplicable' rather than 'correct' or 'incorrect'. Even if worked out on mathematical models and tested on the computer, premises are based on sweeping simplifications rather than on unassailable facts and figures. Hence the variety of 'schools' of economists (e.g. Keynesian, monetarist), each with different answers to the same economic problems. Economics therefore involves making judgements, choosing to adhere to one set of principles rather than another.

Economists work in a wide variety of settings – in urban and regional planning, in industry, commerce, the City, the Civil Service (the largest employer), in financial and industrial journalism, as organizers or researchers in trade unions and in management consultancies and overseas in development programmes. They try to identify the causes of problems like inflation or traffic congestion and suggest courses of action which might solve or ease the problem. Some economists specialize in, for example, the economics of energy resources, the car industry, agriculture, transport.

Extent of specialization varies enormously. Some economists become very knowledgeable about a particular aspect or part of an industry; others in an area of economics. One assignment required an economist with a background in the catering industry to suggest sites for and types of new hotels which a major company wanted to build. Work involved research: what makes hotels successful at home and abroad? In what proportion do food, accommodation, hotel location, service, pricing, affect a hotel's profitability? What constitutes 'good' food, accommodation, etc.? The economist spent a year asking questions in hotels – of guests and staff and management – analysing relevant companies' accounts, and then presented the report. Another economist who specialized in 'agricultural economics' prepared a report on measures to improve the productivity of an underdeveloped Third World country. New specializations emerge as society's needs, priorities and problems change. For example, economists in the Civil Service are concerned with all aspects of our lives, from energy conservation to services for the disabled, from monitoring the performance of the higher education system to cost/benefit analysis of a new motorway scheme.

Economists who take jobs as *economists* act as advisers, whatever type of employer they work for. They do not normally take or implement decisions, and they have to be prepared for their advice to be ignored. Economists who want to be involved more directly with the work of the organization that employs them would be wise to go into management in industry or commerce (see MANAGEMENT, p. 275; BANKING, p. 68; ACCOUNTANCY, p. 1).

An economics degree can be a general graduate qualification; and it can be a 'specialist' qualification – for work in systems analysis, statistics, market research, investment analysis, cybernetics, operational research (see under relevant headings).

Training   Most degree courses include, as 'core' studies, micro- and macroeconomics. Specializations to choose from include agricultural economics, monetary theory and policy, economics of less-developed countries, public sector management, econometrics, economic forecasting, economic geography, transport studies. Economics can be combined with almost any other discipline including accountancy, geography, computing, law, sociology, languages, maths, philosophy and a physical science. The content of individual courses and the emphasis given to the many aspects of the subject vary greatly from one to another, but quantitative methods are of increasing importance.

Personal attributes   Numeracy; interest in political and social affairs; analytical powers; resilience, to be able to persevere when events prove research and theories wrong, and when suggestions are being ignored; ability to explain complex research findings to lay people.

Late start   Should be no problem for people who have commercial, financial or similar experience.

Career-break   It is essential to maintain contact through reading journals, going to meetings and reading reports, etc.

Part time   As freelance for established consultants. Job-sharing is possible, but not widely available as yet.

Position of women   Nearty 40% of economics students are women. They do not seem to have any special difficulties getting jobs. A comparatively large proportion do well in financial journalism and in investment analysis. The subject is adaptable enough to enable women to work in some area at all stages of their career. Instead of part-time work they may do sporadic freelance work, if established and experienced.

Further information   No central organization.

Related careers   ACCOUNTANCY – COMPUTING/IT – INFORMATION WORK – JOURNALISM – MANAGEMENT – MANAGEMENT SERVICES : *Operational Research* – TOWN AND COUNTRY PLANNING

Engineering

Qualified engineers are divided into three sections on The Engineering Council's Register: *Chartered Engineer, Incorporated Engineer* and *Engineering Technician*.

Chartered Engineers
(see p. 195 for Incorporated Engineers and Engineering Technicians)

(see p. 195 for Incorporated Engineers and Engineering Technicians)

Entry qualifications

Degree: 2, often 3 A-levels, normally including maths and physics, and at least 3 GCSEs (A–C) which should include English language and often a foreign language and chemistry. Chemistry A-level is essential for chemical and, usually, agricultural engineering. BTEC/SCOTVEC National Certificates and Diplomas are accepted for many degrees if appropriate units were taken; their acceptance by universities is not automatic. (Introductory courses for people with the wrong A-levels are available at many institutions.)

The work

Engineering is not so much one career, more an expertise which opens doors into a vast range of jobs. Engineers probably have a wider choice of environment in which to work, and of type of job, than any other professionals.

The purpose of engineering is the design and manufacture of the 'hardware' of life. Engineers have a hand in the creation of anything in use anywhere – from chips (both kinds) to chairs; cable TV to toys; motorways to kidney-machines; robots to milk bottles. They are the wealth creators without whom the country's economy cannot improve, and they are also a twentieth-century type of missionary: by designing irrigation and similar schemes for the Third World they reduce famine and poverty. So engineering can be the right choice as much for the person who wants to improve the quality of life all round as for the person who wants a prestigious top managerial or professional job.

There is a range of engineering functions (see below), each appealing to different temperaments and talents. Engineers can concentrate on, for example, creative design; on developing ideas, seeing them translated into the end-product and sold at a profit; on managing people and/or resources and/or processes; on research into, say, laser beam applications or into robotics.

Apart from the many aspects of practical 'active' engineering, there is the vital commercial exploitation of ideas and products. Technical sales and marketing (see below) are now often considered the sharp end of the profession, and engineers do well in both these areas.

It is estimated that most engineers spend about one third of their time discussing work with colleagues, customers or clients, staff, bosses; but there are backroom jobs for loners.

An engineering qualification is much underrated as a way into more glamorous-sounding and more difficult-to-get-into careers – e.g. marketing (see p. 297), industrial management (see p. 275), public relations (see p. 412), television (see p. 526) and other graduate employment. Engineering is, in fact, very much a 'transferable skill' – and that is immensely useful at a time when everybody is likely to change jobs several times in a working life.

Even non-engineering employers who recruit graduates often now prefer science and engineering to arts graduates. Their specific knowledge can be useful in an age when technology has a bearing on virtually any type of business; their analytical approach to problem-solving is invariably useful, even when the problem is not a technical one. So even young people who are not planning to spend their lives as engineers, but want to go into anything from merchant banking to journalism, might well consider taking an engineering degree as a stepping-stone. Engineering need be no more a vocational course than an arts degree (and engineering courses are much easier to get into than arts degree courses).

There are post-graduate courses in business management, systems analysis, transport, etc., which can be taken either immediately after qualifying or a few years later (after the *career-break*, p. 200). New-style courses in 'information engineering' (combining computing and electronic engineering) and 'mechatronics' (combining mechanical and electronic engineering) aim to train engineers to manage computer-based engineering systems.

Job prospects are good on the whole, because engineering is such an adaptable skill; the broader the areas of application of the discipline, the better the prospects; for example, mechanical and electronic engineers are needed in very many more areas of employment than are naval architects. Within electrical, electronic, mechanical and manufacturing engineering it is possible to switch from one branch to another. This usually requires taking a post-graduate course (possibly part time, while working). Many engineers, from any discipline, go into industrial and commercial management (see MANAGEMENT, p. 275) and into management consultancy (see p. 291). Others, especially electronics engineers, go into computing (see p. 138). Chartered engineers can become maths, physics and engineering science teachers. There are opportunities in the EC and elsewhere abroad. The new title 'European Engineer' (Eur/Ing) will become a 'passport' enabling greater mobility and recognition for engineers working in Europe. To gain this title, professional engineers must show they have completed a package of degree, training and experience lasting not less than 7 years. Competence in a second European language will soon be a requirement, too.

Engineers normally specialize in two dimensions: in one *branch* or *discipline*, and then, after training, in one *function*, or type of activity. The main functions within each branch are:

Design

This is the most creative of the engineering functions and is the core of the engineering process. Design engineers create or improve products which can be manufactured and maintained economically, perform satisfactorily, look good and satisfy proven demand. Looks matter more in consumer goods – microwave ovens, telephones – than, for example, in machine tools. Design engineers may also design a new, or improve an established, engineering process. Most designers work to a brief. For example, a car manufacturer's marketing department may request that next year's model within a given price range should incorporate fuel-saving and/or safety devices (which may have been perfected in Research or which Research may be asked to work on); and that the model should incorporate certain visual features which seemed to 'sell' a competitor's model; design engineers may add their own, totally new ideas.

Their job is to find efficient and economic solutions to a set of problems. They must investigate materials and processes to be used in the manufacture of the product, which means they have to consult experts from other disciplines; but it is the design engineer who specifies what goes into the manufacture of the product and what processes are to be used.

Because the work of design engineers varies so enormously, the job is impossible to define precisely. Designing an aircraft which is a team effort has little in common with adding a feature or two to an established type of machine tool or TV component. Most work is done in 'design offices', where several graduates assisted by technicians work under a *chief design engineer*. Some designing, in electronics for example, is done in the laboratory. CAD – computer-aided design – is now used extensively. An experienced design engineer can choose whether to be part of a team that designs, say, a whole new airport, or whether to work alone on simple, straightforward design.

Personal attributes High academic ability; an urge to put new technologies to practical use; creativity; imagination and interest in problem-solving; ability to co-ordinate the work of others; interest in marketability of product; ability to work as one of a team or to lead it.

Research and Development (R and D)

In some organizations research and development are two separate departments; in some the two, plus design, go together. But most typically, research and development form one department, with design a separate, but very closely linked one.

R and D engineers investigate, improve and adapt established processes and products, and they may create new ones. The work is essentially experimental, laboratory-based, but the 'laboratory' could be a skid-pan on which new tyre-surfaces are tried out, or a wind-tunnel in which to experiment with aircraft models.

While there is some extending-the-frontiers-of-knowledge kind of research, most engineering research is 'applied', i.e. aimed at maximizing sales and profits; or at saving precious resources; or exploiting newly discovered materials or processes.

Work comes from several sources: *design engineers* may want to use a new material, but they need to know more about its 'behaviour' before using it; *manufacturing engineers* may ask R and D to investigate why there is a recurrent fault in a particular production process or product; the *marketing department* may complain that a particular aspect of a competitor's fridge or carphone makes the competitor's product sell better: R and D would investigate the better-selling product, and come up with suggestions. Research and development is very much team work.

Personal attributes Practical bent; high academic ability; imagination; perseverance in the face of disappointing research results; interest in following up ideas which have profitable application; ability to work well with colleagues from other departments; willingness to switch from one project to another if Marketing or Manufacturing have urgent problems.

Manufacturing (previously known as Production)

The manufacturing function broadly covers changing raw materials into all types of articles. This involves the selection of the most suitable material and the application of the manufacturing process and system in order to manufacture the products.

Products can range from pizzas to cars, CDs to beer cans. The engineer must see that labour, equipment and materials are used efficiently and that the product is completed at the correct quality and cost, in the right quantity, at the right time. The work environment could be a huge (and noisy) heavy engineering plant; it can be a large, but very quiet, highly automated workshop.

In the past, manufacturing engineering was usually done by practical people with some knowledge of engineering processes. As manufacturing processes become ever more sophisticated, and as industry has begun to recognize the need for greater efficiency and streamlining, this activity has grown in importance (and status). It is now an important equal of other engineering branches and functions.

Production managers' work has much in common with personnel management: smoothing out problems on the shop-floor before they flare up into disputes; dealing with unions and with staff problems which might affect the department's productivity.

Personal attributes Organizing ability; practicality; ability to get on well with people of all types at all levels in the hierarchy – from operatives to heads of research and managing director; ability to keep calm under pressure and in inevitable crises; liking for being very much at the centre of action and solving problems.

Technical Sales and Marketing

Sales engineers use engineering expertise in a commercial context. They spend most of their time away from the office, meeting people. Selling engineering products ('specialist selling'), which may be selling anything from machine tools to oil rigs, domestic freezers to road maintenance equipment and service, combines sales techniques with technical knowledge. Customers may be lay people to whom the virtues of a product have to be explained, or highly professionally qualified people (more so than the sales engineer, possibly) who ask searching questions about the product's performance and properties. Sales engineers also act as links between prospective customers and manufacturers, passing on criticism of and requests for products and changes. They must find out, for example, what features – design, after-sales service, cost – make a competitor's product sell better in other countries or at home. (See also MARKETING AND SELLING, p. 297.)

Searching out new customers is an important part of selling. Some sales may take months of meetings and negotiating. Sales engineers may travel abroad a good deal, or they may have their own 'territory' near home – it largely depends on the type of product.

Personal attributes   Outgoing personality; adaptability to use the right approach with different types of customers; perseverance, and indifference to the occasional rebuff; commercial acumen; interest in economic affairs; communication skills.

Consultancy

This function absorbs significant numbers only in civil and structural engineering, but numbers in other branches – notably mechanical, electronic and production engineering – are increasing. Consulting engineers work in partnerships in private practice, rather like accountants or solicitors. A few set up on their own. Firms vary in organization and extent of specialization. Basically, consultants provide specialist services for clients in charge of large projects who may be public authorities, architects, other engineers or quantity surveyors. Consultants advise, provide feasibility studies, design to a brief, and, sometimes, organize projects. They are not in the construction/manufacturing business but may be in charge of putting work out to contractors and, as their client's agent, may then be responsible for supervising contractors' work, including authorizing payment.

Consultants may specialize: for example, civil engineers may specialize in motorway or in oil rig design, or in traffic management; electronic engineers may specialize in telecommunications or in medical electronics or in instrumentation and systems. Consultants are usually *design engineers* (see above), but as they move up the ladder they spend more time dealing with clients and getting business – i.e. on the commercial side of the job. Some go into or specialize in *management consultancy* (see p. 291). Civil and structural consulting engineers work abroad a lot, especially in the Middle East, usually on contract for a fixed number of years.

Personal attributes   As for design engineers, plus a confidence-inspiring manner, persuasive powers for dealing with clients and contractors; for senior jobs: commercial sense.

Other functions

Apart from these specializations, there are many jobs which are, usually, carried out within one of the main functions. Titles and the work they describe vary. They include *maintenance* (work on employer's premises) and *service* (work carried out on customer's premises), *test*, *installation*, *quality assurance*, *systems*, *control* engineers. These functions may be carried out by graduates early in their career, they may be top jobs or they may be carried out by technicians (see p. 195).

Considering the need for precision in engineering, job and function titles are often surprisingly vague and can, therefore, be misleading.

Engineering Disciplines

The main *branches* or *disciplines* are:

Mechanical Engineering

Mechanical engineers work in all branches and all functions; they are concerned with the application of the principles of mechanics, hydraulics, thermodynamics, to engineering processes. They have a vast choice of end-product to work with and environment to work in: literally no industry is closed to them; they work in hospitals; in computer manufacture; robotics; all types of research establishments. Engineers who want to help humanity as directly as possible, who want to see the application of their efforts to the alleviation of suffering and discomfort, can work in *medical engineering* (see below); engineers who want to go into technical sales or into marketing, or general management can take their mechanical engineering training into anything from mobile phones to agricultural machinary, oil extraction to food processing.

Civil Engineering

Civil engineering covers the design, planning, construction and maintenance of, firstly, the 'infrastructure': transport systems, water supplies and sewage plants; and, secondly, large-scale structures, ranging from oil platforms to power stations. Transport systems include roads, bridges, tunnels (including the vast Channel Tunnel project), ports and airports. Transport planning and management is another, growing, activity. Providing water supplies may involve building reservoirs; controlling the flow of rivers; ensuring safe drinking water and effective irrigation systems in developing countries; and the disposal and treatment of waste to prevent pollution.

Civil engineers work for local and central government, in industry and for international organizations. Many work as *consulting engineers*, called in by large organizations to design and carry out a project. Others work for civil engineering contractors supervising construction projects and dealing with building contractors; they may also do design work. Many British firms work on overseas contracts.

Structural Engineering

This is a specialized branch of civil engineering. Structural engineers are particularly skilled in non-traditional construction materials and techniques. Those working for civil engineering firms might design large-scale constructions such as grandstands and bridges. Those called in as consultants by architects might design the foundations and skeletal framework of large buildings such as skyscrapers and hospitals.

Environmental Engineering (Heating and Ventilating Engineering/Building Services Engineering)

Environmental engineers are concerned with heating, lighting, acoustics, ventilation, air conditioning, noise and air pollution and its control. They are called in as consultants by civil engineers and architects on building projects from hospital to airport, office block to housing estate, chain store to underground station. This branch straddles mechanical, electrical and structural engineering.

Electrical and Electronic Engineering

The two overlap. Broadly, *electrical engineering* is concerned with the use and generation of electricity to produce heat, light and mechanical power: electrical engineers work in generating stations, distribution systems and on the manufacture of all kinds of electrical machinery from tiny motors for powered invalid chairs to heavy motors for industrial plant. They are also concerned with research into the more efficient use of, and new sources of energy for, electrical power.

Electronics is mainly concerned with *computers, telecommunications, automation/instrumentation and control.*

(a) *Computers*: The electronic engineering industry is concerned with producing the machinery – the 'hardware' – which gives house-room to the software, i.e. the programs, and with producing the components and products which 'computer systems' need to perform their tasks. This includes microprocessors, visual display units, printers, mainframe and desktop computers. (For details of software/programming jobs see COMPUTING/INFORMATION TECHNOLOGY, p. 138).

The proportion of design, research and development engineers is greater in electronics than in other branches. (Mechanical, electrical and chemical engineers, physicists, and computer scientists also work in computer manufacture.)

(b) *Telecommunications*: Include, for example, the extension of old-fashioned telephony into 'multi-facility' services such as 'conference calls': facilities for telephone conversations between several participants in different locations; and for 'confravision': centres in various towns equipped with closed-circuit television as well as with 'conference call' services are rented by the hour to business people who then 'hold meetings' with colleagues or customers without having to travel. Other telecommunications developments include optical fibre systems; the extension of radio networks; satellite and cable television.

Telecommunication technologies used in offices, and, increasingly, at home, include electronic mail – devices which enable keyed-in messages and reports to be transmitted instantly from one computer to another – fax machines and facilities like Ceefax, etc. The Internet is the latest example of the 'information explosion'.

(c) *Automation, instrumentation and control*: This is concerned with automatic control devices, from the operation of automatic flight control systems in aircraft to nearer-home gadgets such as automatic ovens and central-heating time-clocks, and robotics.

Then there is the vast area of computer-controlled equipment which has become possible as a result of the development of *microelectronics*: the design, development and production of scaled-down, minuscule electronic circuitry – the 'chip' – and with its application. The chip affects virtually every industrial, commercial, scientific and professional activity but it can do nothing by itself: electronics specialists develop its potential and 'program' (instruct) it to perform the precisely defined task for which it is intended.

Examples are hotel, aircraft and theatre seat reservations; supermarkets (bleeping checkouts that keep the warehouse management informed of the precise level of stock of every item in every store at any time); document storage and retrieval systems (see INFORMATION WORK, p. 227). In manufacturing, 'robotics' – assembly-line work done by programmed robots – is developing fast. Scientific applications include weather-forecasting; computer-aided design in civil and structural engineering; dating archaeological discoveries.

Medical or Biomedical Engineering

This is a combination of electronic, electrical and mechanical engineering and physics. Medical engineers at the moment usually take a degree in either mechanical, electronic or electrical engineering (but there are also medical engineering options in electronic and mechanical engineering degrees) and then either take a postgraduate course or join a team working on medical engineering projects. These are often carried out jointly with consultants in hospitals, who specify what they want any particular equipment to do. Kidney transplants, heart surgery, and many less spectacular procedures are only possible thanks to the imaginative cooperation of doctors and engineers.

Medical engineers also design aids for severely handicapped people – e.g. artificial, remarkably usable, replacement limbs or custom-built 'transport'.

Medical engineering is often overlooked as an alternative to medicine for people who want to be closely involved with alleviating disabilities.

Chemical Engineering

Chemical (or process) engineers are concerned with the design and development of laboratory processes, and with their translation into large-scale plant, for the production of chemicals, dyes, medicines, fertilizers, plastics, etc. Their expertise in designing and managing plant in which chemical processes take place is also used in food processing, brewing, paper, textile and other industries. Biochemical engineers specialize in the design and development of industrial plant in which biochemical processes can take place (see 'Biotechnology', p. 448), e.g. developing alternative sources of energy and converting noxious waste into useful byproducts or at least into harmless substances. Chemical engineering has far wider application than is often believed: many chemical engineers do work in oil refineries and other heavy industry, but there is wide scope elsewhere, for example in textiles and electronics. 'Green' issues are of increasing importance.

Manufacturing Engineering
(see p. 185)

This branch covers all aspects of manufacture. It embraces knowledge of many aspects of engineering and ensures that labour, equipment and materials are used efficiently.

Manufacturing engineers need both technical and 'people management' skills, so that goods of the right quality are produced at the required time at the right price. They plan the production methods and systems (which nowadays often involve computer-controlled tools) and may modify machinery to suit a particuar task. They liaise with other departments such as design, R and D, purchasing and sales.

Naval Architecture

Despite the title, the work is engineering rather than architecture. It is concerned with the design, repair, construction and economic operation of craft which float on or under or hover just above the water. Craft can be of any size from sailing dinghy to supertanker, hydrofoil to oil rig. Naval architects work for the Services as well as for ship- and boat-building firms. A small branch.

Aeronautical/Aerospace Engineering

Concerned with aircraft design and construction and space and satellite research, as well as with planning, operation and maintenance of airlines' fleets of aircraft and aircraft components. They work for aircraft manufacturers, airlines and the Ministry of Defence. This is a small branch of engineering; a greater proportion work in R and D, fewer on production. People who want to work in this area can take electronics or physics degrees and leave more options open.

Agricultural Engineering
(see AGRICULTURE AND HORTICULTURE, p. 27)

Mining Engineering

Mining engineers' training is very much more vocational than that of other engineers. The majority of mining engineers (it is a small branch) in this country work in the coal industry; a few in quarrying, rock, salt, and potash mining. There are opportunities abroad in ore extraction and other types of mining and minerals processing, usually after some experience at home.

Other branches

Some engineering specializations described elsewhere (or advertised) have different titles from all those mentioned here. They may be small branches, or offshoots of, or options within, established engineering branches. Titles may describe jobs which can be done by people from various disciplines (e.g. in robotics). Or they may describe emerging new branches which are also still under the umbrella of an established branch.

Engineering can no longer be neatly categorized into the traditional disciplines. It is a fast-changing profession, developing as a result of scientific discovery (scientists discover; engineers exploit discoveries and make them work productively as well as in response to need). For example, new sources of energy will be needed next century: engineers are working on the development of wind, wave and solar energy – and become *energy engineers*. Technological tasks are so complex now that people from various disciplines have to pool their expertise: at the same time, some disciplines are becoming so unwieldy that they sub-divide. That applies specially in *electronics* and *mechanical engineering*. New titles do not have as precise meanings as have traditional engineering disciplines.

Here is a very brief (and superficial) guide to some of the current engineering job-titles and the – probable – umbrella discipline, or function, which should be the first port of call for information on what knowledge is required and what work involved:

Computer systems, control engineering: umbrella discipline – *Electronics*.

Offshore, oil, fuel, energy engineering: umbrella disciplines – *Mechanical, Electrical, Electronic* or *Chemical Engineering*. (Energy engineering can also describe the energy-saving function in large organizations.)

Nuclear engineering: umbrella disciplines – *Physics* and *Electronics*.

Industrial engineering: umbrella discipline – *Manufacturing Engineering*, but can also be combination of *Management* and *Engineering*.

Process engineering: umbrella discipline – *Chemical Engineering*.

Plant, installation, test and commissioning engineering: umbrella disciplines – could be *Mechanical, Production* or *Chemical Engineering*, but also used for functions carried out by *Mechanical* or almost any other specialist engineer.

Training   Engineers who undergo 'accredited' training are registered in the appropriate category by The Engineering Council's Board for Engineers' Registration (BER).

Professional engineers are commonly called Chartered Engineers, although strictly speaking to use the title Chartered Engineer requires corporate membership of one of the Chartered Engineering institutions.

One institution asks for a first- or second-class honours degree, which is a higher standard than that set by The Engineering Council. The situation is confusing, so anyone considering professional engineering should look carefully at each institution's requirements.

The Engineering Council recognizes several routes to qualification as a professional engineer:

1. The mainstream route: an honours degree in engineering jointly accredited by The Engineering Council and relevant engineering institution, leading to the award of Bachelor of Engineering (B.Eng.), not, as in the past, a B.Sc. (with a few exceptions). These 'enhanced' B.Eng. courses closely integrate theory and practice. In addition to the study of fundamental scientific principles, to be accredited they must include engineering applications such as design practice, production techniques, fabrication and financial applications.

They are normally 3 years full time, or 4 years sandwich. Some offer a general first year before specialization. A recent initiative has increased the number of courses specializing in, or offering options in, manufacturing systems engineering; these concentrate on the manufacturing process, its specification, design, maintenance, etc.

2. 'Extended' (plus enhanced) degree courses leading to Master of Engineering and lasting 4 years full time, 5 years sandwich. These cater for 'high-fliers' and are of three kinds, providing either study in greater depth than the B.Eng. of one branch of engineering or study of a range of engineering disciplines or engineering study plus a grounding in finance and management.

3. One of the new 'integrated' engineering degree programmes, leading to B.Eng. or M.Eng. The difference between these and (1) and (2) is that they emphasize the interdisciplinary nature of engineering. The syllabus may include civil, electrical, electronic,

manufacturing and mechanical engineering, business and management studies, and, optionally, a foreign language. Their other feature is that they offer flexible entry requirements and are therefore suitable for people without A-level physics.

4. Other engineering courses – general or specialized – designed for people without maths and physics A-levels: these provide a foundation year after which students go on to take a 3- or 4-year degree course.

Candidates should always look carefully at different syllabuses and check whether courses have been accredited.

5. Students take a 'part-accredited' engineering or science honours degree and add sufficient 'bolt-on' modules to make good the academic gaps. This must not take longer than 1 academic year.

6. Graduates with an ordinary or unclassified engineering degree who first register as Incorporated Engineers (see p. 195) can add modules as in (5).

7. Science or maths honours graduates who can satisfy The Engineering Council that their subsequent training and experience compensate for any deficiency in vocational background may register.

8. Technicians who follow the part-time BTEC route (p. 197) can take The Engineering Council's own 2-part examination leading to registration as Chartered Engineer.

Sandwich courses are particularly suitable for students wanting to enter industry, as they are able to sample the industrial scene. Some large companies sponsor students for all or part of their course (i.e. pay them while they are studying), who thus gain work experience in that organization. College-based students work for a range of employers during their course. 'Thin' sandwich courses last 4–5 years, alternating 6 months' study with 6 months' work experience. 'Thick' sandwich courses last 5 years, with a year at the beginning and end spent with an employer and 3 years' full-time study in between.

Incorporated (formerly Technician) Engineers and Engineering Technicians

Entry qualifica- tions

In practice normally 4 GCSEs (A–C) including maths and science, but see 'Training', below, and BTEC/SCOTVEC (pp. xxi, xxii). Technicians can also start by training as craftsmen/women through Modern Apprenticeships or government-backed youth training schemes (see p. xxiv).

The work

The technician scene is very confusing indeed to anyone outside the industry. There are, officially – that is according to the Board for Engineers Registration – two levels: *Incorporated Engineers* are those whose work overlaps with graduates and whose breadth of knowledge enables them to take responsibility for a wide range of tasks; *engineering technicians* are those who take responsibility for jobs in a more narrowly defined area. In practice, however, the distinction is blurred. The term 'technician' is loosely used to cover a whole range of job levels. Very many 'technician' jobs are in fact done by graduates. Technicians become 'senior technicians' rather than 'Incorporated Engineers' in some organizations. Some go on to qualify as Chartered Engineers (see 'Training', below). Manpower studies have shown that in electronics there are more technicians than professional engineers/scientists and probably four times as many civil engineering technicians as there are professional civil engineers.

Chartered and Incorporated Engineers' work overlaps in all branches, but more in electrical, electronic, mechanical and produc- tion engineering than in the others. It also overlaps in all functions (see above) but much less in design and research where graduates' depth and breadth of training, and their creativity, are usually essential. After a few years' work, though, applicants' experience and ability rather than their qualifications count. At that stage, experienced technicians are on a par with *average* graduates (not with high-fliers). Degrees for Chartered Engineers became the normal qualifications about 25 years ago, when new technologies increased the complexities of engineering tasks (and as higher education became more accessible). But for every engineer who has the chance to make full use of degree-level knowledge – who is, say, responsible for the safe design of an oil rig or for a research project into the application of laser beams in surgery – there are hundreds of engineers whose jobs require sound profes- sional expertise, but not the depth and breadth of knowledge needed for top jobs. Hence the increasing scope for technicians.

Incorporated Engineers have never managed to put themselves across as a professional entity, although in most branches they have their own professional institutions, and, within the engineering profession, they are fully recognized as vital experts in their field and essential colleagues. According to experience and training, they are either left to get on with tasks on their own, or are support staff with limited responsibility (both apply to average graduate engineers as well). Job titles such as, for example, *plant*, *project*, *production*, *commissioning*, *development* or *sales* engineer can describe *either* a Chartered *or* an Incorporated Engineer. There is nothing precise about titles and demarcation by qualification in the engineering profession which depends so much on expertise and/or experience.

Work is as varied as that of Chartered Engineers.

Tasks include, for example:

In all branches: Draughtsmanship (usually computerized) which may be routine work, but may involve using initiative and special knowledge, and producing working drawings from designers' rough notes and/or instructions; or assisting professional engineers in research, design, development, perhaps building prototypes; *production* (see 'Manufacturing', p. 185); being responsible, for example, for one or several production lines or for continuity of supplies, or dispatch. *Estimating*: costing projects or parts of projects; supervision of installation of equipment on customer's premises or in firm's own factory; *repair and maintenance* in anything from garage to hotel, hospital to factory; *after-sales service* investigating complaints, for example. (Greatest scope in electrical and electronic engineering.)

Settings include:

Broadcasting (see p. 526).

Telephone companies.

Newspaper production.

Hi-fi, television and video servicing.

Commercial recording studios – for example, as *balancing engineers* (who must be able to read music and have a good ear) are responsible for producing the required levels of sounds from various sources.

Civil and structural engineering sites: technicians help cost projects; supervise construction work; work out what equipment is required on bridge or road works; liaise with clients and, in municipal work, with local residents. In traffic management they may be in charge of compiling a 'street inventory' prior to the installation of traffic signals (finding out where gas and electricity mains are; what shops/schools and other 'traffic generators' there are) or organize traffic counts. They may also become *building control officers* for local authorities.

In *manufacturing* technicians work at all levels, from monitoring or servicing machinery to, jointly with personnel (see p. 368), working on job evaluation schemes. In *Marketing and sales* where (see above) engineering knowledge is only one of the necessary skills, experienced technicians do very well indeed and can rise to the top. Finally, experienced technicians can set up their own workshops/business (see WORKING FOR ONESELF, p. 551).

Prospects are good, especially for electronics, electrical and mechanical technicians. Even during recessions the demand for technicians often exceeds supply. Experienced technicians are also often able to get work *abroad*. Technician training is broadly based and, once trained, technicians can switch type of work.

Personal attributes

A practical and methodical approach and an interest in technology are needed in all technician jobs. There is room for backroom types who like to get on with their work on their own, for those who like to work in a team, those who like to work in a drawing office or laboratory, and for those who enjoy visiting clients and customers. For some jobs (the minority) manual dexterity. For others, ability to explain technical points in plain language and liking for meeting people.

Training

Training can be as a full-time student at college or part time while employed as a trainee technician.

Trainee technician route

The Engineering Training Authority (EnTra) has developed a framework for Modern Apprenticeships in engineering manufacture which is approved by the government and supported by employers and trade unions. These became available in September 1995 and are the recommended work-based route for trainee technicians and craftspeople. Entry can be with appropriate GCSEs (see 'Entry Qualifications'), p. 195). A-levels, GNVQs or BTEC/SCOTVEC certificates or diplomas. Length of training depends on initial qualifications and eventual aim, but it will lead to an NVQ level 3 in a selected area. On average it will take three years of combined theory and practical skills development, but each apprentice follows an individual programme agreed at the start and set out in a written agreement or 'pledge' signed by the apprentice and the employer and underwritten by the local TEC (see p. xxiii). All apprenticeships will be based on the following structure:

A *foundation stage* spent 'off the job' and lasting up to one

year: subjects covered include health and safety, engineering drawing, materials and use of tools, specific vocational training and six
core skills – working with others, improving one's own learning
and performance, IT, application of number, communication
and problem-solving. Apprentices work towards various NVQ/
GNVQ units and may achieve NVQ level 2.

A *post-foundation stage*, mostly 'on-the-job' but with 'off the
job' periods and day-release to college to cover theory. Many will
follow BTEC courses, some City and Guilds. The main aim is to
cover the skills and knowledge needed for NVQ level 3, but
apprentices are also expected to reach advanced level in core skills
(as specified for GNVQs). Modern apprenticeships are designed
to prepare people for a range of career opportunities and can lead
to university entrance for suitable candidates.

Until Modern Apprenticeships become universally accepted by
industry, many employers will continue to offer training programmes for technicians in manufacturing industry which combine theory with practical experience. Length of training varies
according to the entrant's qualifications and ambitions. They will
normally work towards BTEC/SCOTVEC National Certificate
or Diploma, which, together with training and responsible experience, leads to registration with The Engineering Council as Engineering Technician. Those who go on to take a BTEC/
SCOTVEC Higher National Certificate or Diploma and have the
required training and responsible experience become registered as
Incorporated Engineers.

Civil Engineering technicians follow similar part-time or full-
time education and training routes leading to BTEC/SCOTVEC
awards in either Civil Engineering or Construction, before registration with the Engineering Council. Their training is overseen not
by EnTra, but by the Institution of Civil Engineers (see p. 203 for
address of the Civil Engineering Careers service).

Full-time college route
Either a 2-year full-time or a 3-year sandwich BTEC National
Diploma (or SCOTVEC equivalent). With training and responsi-
ble experience this can lead to registration as Engineering
Technician (as above).

Students can then take a 2-year full-time or 3-year sandwich
course for a BTEC/SCOTVEC Higher National Diploma.

Entrants with at least 1 relevant A-level (usually maths or
physics) and appropriate GCSEs (A–C) or GNVQ can go straight
into a BTEC Higher award course.

Craft Level Entry

Entry qualifications

Average ability in maths, science, technical/practical subjects. Employers normally test applicants' aptitudes. Many ask for GCSE pass in maths.

The work

Engineering craftsmen/women do skilled work and need sufficient theoretical knowledge to understand the principles behind the operations they carry out and to solve basic problems. They work in all branches and may be in charge of semi- and unskilled workers. Their work, and their scope, is changing as a result of new technologies. First of all, the distinction between craftspeople and technicians is narrowing, with craft-trained people becoming technicians more frequently than in the past; and second, as a result of automation in all engineering spheres, the distinction between the specialist trades is blurring. Traditional crafts or 'trades' continue to be practised, including:

Machine-shop Crafts

Toolmaking: The use of precision machinery and tools to make jigs, fixtures, gauges and other tools used in production work. Apprentices may start in the toolroom, or they are upgraded from other trades.

Toolsetting: Setting of automatic (such as computer/tape numerically controlled) or semi-automatic machines for use by machine operators in mass production.

Turning: Operating lathes which use fixed cutting tool(s) to remove metal/material from a rotating workpiece.

Milling: Operating milling machines where metal/material is removed from a fixed workpiece by rotating cutter(s).

Jig-boring: Highly skilled work in which very heavy articles are machined to a high degree of precision.

Grinding: Obtains a very accurate finish by removing small amounts of metal with rapidly revolving abrasive wheels. It is also used to sharpen tools.

Fitting

Fitters, whether working in mechanical, electrical or electronic engineering, combine the basic skills of the machine-shop craftsperson with the ability to use hand tools. In production work they may assemble cars, generators, TV sets, etc. They carry out maintenance and repair work on domestic appliances and office machinery either on customers' premises – private houses, factories, offices, etc. – or in workshops. Gas fitters install, service and repair gas-powered domestic appliances or industrial plant; marine engine fitters put together and repair ships' engines, etc.

Craftspeople may switch trades more easily than in the past, as well as learn new ones, but overall prospects are not as good as those for technicians.

Training

See Modern Apprencticeships, p. xxiv.

Many employers offer craft training programmes which combine practical skills, training and further education. A typical programme would consist of:

1-year ('Basic Engineering Training') 'off the job', i.e. in a Training Centre, learning basic engineering skills. These include hand and machine skills, manipulation of sheet metal, welding and electrical/electronic skills.

2–4 years spent in the employing company on a package of skill training and experience 'on the job' to nationally agreed standards. An EnTra Certificate of Validated Achievement (CVA) is awarded after each stage showing what the individual trainee has achieved.

During both Basic Engineering Training and the in-company training period trainees attend a College of Further Education by day- or block-release to learn relevant theory, working for City and Guilds or BTEC/SCOTVEC awards.

This pattern of training can lead on to technician work and training (see above).

In civil engineering, contractors employ craftsmen/women and operatives. N/SVQs are available and apprentices can follow the Civil Engineering Apprenticeship Training Scheme (CEATS). Details from the Federation of Civil Engineering Contractors (see under 'Further information', p. 203).

Late start (all levels)

Chartered Engineers: Possible for technicians and people with related degrees or at least good, and recently acquired, science A-levels, or who have taken a foundation course (see pp. 197–8).

Technicians: Good opportunities for people who have taken appropriate courses, especially in electronics and related fields or such specialized areas as TV and other electronic equipment servicing.

Craft level: Not advisable.

Career-break

Because of the pace of technological change, a complete gap of even a few years would be difficult to bridge. But there are various schemes for enabling people on a domestic break (mainly women) to keep in touch. These include encouraging women to visit their former employers regularly during the break and, on their return, for them to have a 'mentor' or 'industrial tutor' who, in an informal way, helps them to catch up. During the break, women technicians and Chartered Engineers are encouraged to take the Open University (see p. xxxiii) 'Women in Technology' Associate Student programme. This has been specially designed for women who want to return to work after a child-rearing break. A further initiative is the Women's Fellowship Scheme aimed at providing part-time research posts for women scientists and engineers wanting to re-enter academic life after a break.

Part time Few part-time jobs at present, but some opportunities for engineers who have specialized or can specialize in computing and related work. Others work on 'one-off' contracts. Job-sharing schemes do not seem to have been tried on any scale, but there is no reason why they should not work.

Position of women (all levels) The proportion of women engineers is still very small. A survey of engineering employees by EnTra, which compared the situation in 1993 with that in 1990, showed that 2% of professional engineers (up 1%), 1% of engineering supervisors (the same), 1% of Engineering Technicians and Incorporated Engineers (down 1%) and 2% of craftspeople (up 1%) were female.

The proportion of girls studying engineering at university had been slowly rising since the 1970s but has recently declined. In 1991 14.7% of university and 12.5% of polytechnic first degree places were taken up by girls; in 1994 they took up only 10% of first year places in old and 'new' universities (ex-polytechnics). As ever there are quite wide variations between disciplines. 20% of chemical, 10% of civil and 9% of general engineering first year places went to girls, but only 7.5% of mechanical, 4% of electrical and 6.7% of electronic. This last figure is especially disappointing: it had been thought that good job prospects and the mainly clean, hi-tech environment in which the dealing-with-people element is very great indeed would appeal to girls not otherwise attracted to engineering.

The small proportion of women cannot be entirely explained by the still relatively small proportion who take A-level physics and maths (see p. xliii for GCSE and A-level male/female proportions); 55% of students accepted for ophthalmic optics in 1994 are women, and they normally also need A-level physics and maths (and ophthalmic optics courses are usually more difficult to get into than engineering courses). Yet engineering generally, and electrical engineering especially, leads to a far wider job choice and hence smaller risk of unemployment, than ophthalmic optics. Women's career-choices cannot be blamed just on poor careers information; it must also be due to the fact that women are still less long-term career-minded than men.

At technician level (see p. 195) the situation is even worse, with very few women, and not all trainees seem to be working for qualifications. However, 9·2% of students enrolling on first year HND engineering progammes in 1994 were women. The largest technician institution, many of whose members work in information technology, the Institution of Electrical and Electronics Incorporated Engineers, has a tiny number of women among its 30,000 members. Yet the Institution has for many years now run an annual Young Woman Technician of the Year competition which always gets widely publicized and shows the wide range of jobs women do. (It is possible that women technicians are less willing to join institutions, but even allowing for that, the proportion is dismal indeed.)

Women who have gone into engineering are doing well. Many have found that being female and therefore more noticeable may have helped in gaining sponsorship (for training) and jobs. Recruitment officers say they usually have 'more good and fewer average and plain hopeless' women than men applicants. They genuinely want more women Chartered and Incorporated Engineers. The fact that a woman has the initiative to step off the tramlines and choose a non-traditional career shows she is more determined and interested than the average male who may have chosen engineering 'because it is there', and the obvious next step after school.

Promotion prospects, according to various surveys of women engineers, are reasonable in the early stages, but opportunities at management level, and for management training, could be better (see MANAGEMENT, p. 275, for hurdles in women's promotion paths). Nevertheless, the small but growing number of women in senior-middle and senior jobs (including non-technical work such as marketing) say that attitudes are changing and that opportunities *are* there – especially in the wide-ranging electronics area where 'people-related' skills are specially important.

Another good sign is that individual membership of the Women's Engineering Society has risen from 495 in 1984 to 770 in 1996.

There is no shortage of initiatives from industry, The Engineering Council, polytechnics and universities to attract more women. Conferences, seminars, residential weeks for sixth-formers, have all been running for several years and there are now many more young women engineers to act as 'role models'. The WISE

(Women Into Science and Engineering) campaign has encouraged more girl pupils to consider engineering.

A booklet is available from The Engineering Council which gives details of awards, courses, visits and other initiatives designed to encourage girls and women to consider careers in science and engineering.

Further information

The Engineering Council (for list of individual Institutions as well as general information), 10 Maltravers Street, London WC2R 3ER (Freephone 0800 282167)

Engineering Training Authority (EnTra), Vector House, 41 Clarendon Road, Watford WD1 1HS (for manufacturing branches of engineering)

Civil Engineering Careers Service, 1–7 Great George Street, London SW1P 3AH

The Federation of Civil Engineering Contractors, 6 Portugal Street, London WC2A 2HH

For list of special courses (conversion and technician) for women: Engineering Council, Women's Engineering Society, c/o Imperial College, Dept of Civil Engineering, Imperial College Road, London SW7 2BY

BTEC/SCOTVEC (see pp. xxi, xxii)

Related careers

AGRICULTURE AND HORTICULTURE – ART AND DESIGN – BUILDING: *Building Managers* – COMPUTING/IT – SCIENCE – SURVEYING

204

Environmental Health Officer

Entry require ments
5 GCSEs (A–C) and 2 A-levels. Passes must include maths, English language and 2 sciences; one of the sciences must be at A-level. BTEC alternatives (plus English language) may be acceptable.

The work
Environmental health officers ensure that people are protected from a wide range of hazards in the environment in its widest sense – houses, shops, workplaces, leisure facilities, the air we breathe, our water supplies. Increasing public concern about the environment is reflected daily in the news: a leak of toxic chemicals; salmonella in eggs; contaminated water supplies; the effects of lead on children living near busy motorway junctions; an outbreak of legionnaire's disease; deaths from contaminated yoghurt; housing unfit through damp for human habitation. Environmental health officers deal with all these problems.

The majority of environmental health officers work in local authorities. Their role is both to advise on safety and hygiene and to enforce legislation. This involves visiting a great variety of sites; a high proportion of EHOs' time is spent out of the office.

EHOs ensure that safe and hygienic standards are met in the preparation, manufacture, transport and sale of *food*. This can mean visiting high-technology plants or market stalls, restaurants or slaughterhouses, to check on the cleanliness of equipment and staff, storage facilities and handling procedures. EHOs have powers to enter and inspect *housing* if they 'have reason to believe that the premises are not fit for human habitation' or they may be called in by the residents. They advise on repairs, improvements and sometimes demolition. Responsibility for *places of work* overlaps with that of factory inspectors (see p. 212). EHOs check on working conditions, for example sanitary arrangements, overcrowding, temperature, ventilation, lighting and hours of work for juveniles.

Noise, pest control, water and waste, air pollution and *communicable diseases* are also the responsibilities of EHOs. They may also deal with caravan and camping sites, houseboats and leisure boats, swimming pools and leisure centres, and some aspects of animal welfare.

Some EHOs have a general role covering a wide range of responsibilities; others specialize in, for example, food hygiene, housing or atmospheric pollution.

Some work in industry, e.g. food manufacturing.

Training   1. 4-year sandwich degree course. Syllabus includes the basic sciences as applied to environmental health (control of infectious diseases and of vermin, for example); physical aspects of housing (dilapidations, unfitness); public cleansing; water supply; drainage, sewerage and sewage disposal; procedures under Housing Acts; hygiene of buildings (standards of heating, ventilation and lighting); food (hygiene and inspection), etc.

2. 2-year sandwich post-graduate course for graduates with appropriate degree.

The above courses include a period of integrated professional training with a local authority.

3. *In Scotland.* 4-year degree in environmental health at Strathclyde University, in conjunction with 48 weeks' practical training in a local authority, followed by a Professional Interview for the Diploma in Environmental Health.

Personal attributes   Interest in people's living and working environment; ability to take decisions; sufficient self-confidence to go where one is not necessarily welcome, to be firm when necessary and to discuss complicated problems intelligently.

Late start   There is scope for late entry, though the older one is, the more difficult it could be to get the necessary practical training. Degree courses may relax the academic entry requirements for mature entrants.

Career-break   Should be no problem for those who keep in touch.

Part time   Should be possible to organize. EHOs' major employers, local authorities, have been among the most forward-looking on flexible working.

Position of women   Previously a male-dominated field, but more women are coming in. Entry is about 50/50 male/female. Those in senior positions are usually men, but there are increasing numbers of women of the right age and experience. In the past women were assumed not to be able or willing to do the rougher parts of the work in, for example, slaughterhouses or unfit-for-habitation dwellings, and so they did not get all-round experience. Now that there are more women, and changing attitudes and legislation enable them to broaden their experience, time will tell if they take their fair share of senior appointments in future.

| **Further information** | The Chartered Institute of Environmental Health, Chadwick Court, 15 Hatfields, London SE1 8DJ |
| | The Royal Environmental Health Institute of Scotland, 3 Manor Place, Edinburgh EH3 7DH |

| **Related careers** | SCIENCE: *Food Science and Technology* – HEALTH AND SAFETY INSPECTORS – HOUSING MANAGEMENT – TRADING STANDARDS OFFICER |

Fashion and Clothing

The fashion and clothing industry is one of the largest in the country. Even at its highest fashion end it is concerned with business, not art. The vast majority of the industry is concerned with producing garments that large numbers of people want to wear, at a price they can afford. In the UK about three-quarters of production is for high street chain stores, with the retailers closely involved at all stages to ensure the right look and the right quality for their markets. Increasingly fashion and clothing is an international industry. Designs may be produced, patterns and lay plans developed, fabrics 'sourced', and garments made with each stage taking place in a different country; the finished garments may then be sold through shops in many parts of the world.

Entry qualifications
Vary according to level and type of training.

Main Sectors of the Industry

In *haute couture*, garments to an exclusive design are cut and made up for individual customers almost entirely by hand. *Upmarket ready to wear* follows couture trends but makes more garments in more sizes for sale through exclusive shops. These are the glamour end of the market, but are extremely small. They are fairly insignificant in employment terms, though not in influence.

Most employment opportunities are in the mass-production sector. It covers a huge variety of garments for different markets and for a multitude of purposes: clothing is about far more than fashion.

Womenswear is the largest sector of the market, but *menswear* has become very much more fashion-conscious, as has *childrenswear*, a growing area with its own special demands from babywear to teenage fashion (and still including a significant amount of school uniform). *Leisurewear*, including dancewear, sportswear and ski-wear, is a very lively market that has been enormously influenced by the development of special fabrics and finishes.

Workwear is a varied sector of the market, ranging from simple

overalls for canteen staff to heavy-duty specialist protective clothing, e.g. for the chemical industry and oil rig workers. The
technical and design problems for specialist applications may be
very complex and must usually take health and safety legislation
into account. *Uniforms* (for the police, armed services and so on)
are a specialized sector of workwear and range from dress uniforms to gas-tight suits. *Corporate wear* (e.g. for bank, airline and
hotel staff) is a growing market.

The work   A very, very few *designers* become 'names' in *haute couture* or up-
market ready to wear (or in 'diffusion ranges', which are good-
quality wholesale production of designer name garments and
have successfully brought good design down market in the last
few years). Some young designers set up on their own, designing
and making clothes for boutiques (sometimes their own), perhaps
occasionally getting orders from store buyers. Most work in
wholesale manufacturing, where high fashion is adapted for
the high street.

Designers do not work in isolation but as members of a team
with fabric designers or buyers, marketing specialists, production
specialists, buyers from retail outlets. Very rarely is design an
artistic 'gut feeling'. It is marketing-led, based on research. The
designer almost always works within a trend (e.g. an ethnic
influence) and within a firm's particular 'hand-writing', incorporating both into garments which will sell to a given type of market
(for example, trendy, classic, young, elegant, country). The designer's skill is in adapting something for a new market, making
it look fresh while retaining the features that made it popular.
A recent example is the waxed jacket, taken from the country to
the high street, and skinwear, taken to the youth leisurewear
markets.

Different kinds of garments present different kinds of design
challenges. For example, the designer of uniforms for paramedics
is not concerned with high street trends but with considerations
like how the garment will stand up to the weather, how to make
sure it won't get in the way of the wearer's work, how to make it
as hygienic as possible.

Some designers do their own pattern cutting, or it may be the
job of a specialist *pattern cutter* or *technologist*. Pattern cutters
cut an accurate pattern from which the 2-dimensional designer's
sketch can be formed into a 3-dimensional sample garment.

Garment technologists are the bridge between design and manufacture. They take the sample and plan the way in which the
garment will be made. They decide on, for example, what thread
will be used, what seam and stitch types, what machinery will be

needed, the costs at every stage. Sometimes a design proves too complicated or expensive, so the garment technologist will work with the designer to reach a compromise, perhaps changing some details in a way which will reduce the number and complexity of the manufacturing operations but still retain the designer's concept. Some garment technologists work for the large retailers, ensuring that the designs, quality and costs meet the retailer's specifications.

When the design is finalized, it returns to pattern cutters, who will return it to a 2-dimensional pattern suitable for mass production. A *pattern grader* then takes a standard size pattern and makes patterns to fit a range of different sizes. *Lay planners* work out how to place the pieces on the fabric in the most economical way. All these processes now make extensive use of computers.

The *production manager* is in charge of working out and managing production flow systems, ensuring that the manufacturing process, once it is broken down into a number of operations, will run smoothly, without bottlenecks, and keeping all the operators and equipment evenly busy.

The clothing industry invests very heavily in sophisticated machinery, so *engineers* are very important, ensuring that the machines are working effectively and advising on crucial investment decisions.

This industry is extremely varied. Job titles and functions are not clear-cut. People with different titles can be doing the same job and vice versa. People with different levels of qualifications can also be doing the same job. In smaller companies an individual may carry out several elements of the design/production process; in a larger company he or she may specialize in one particular function. There are also a number of liaison roles between retailers, designers and manufacturers.

Training   There is a wide range of courses available at a number of levels. Titles include: textiles/fashion; fashion; clothing technology; fashion design with technology; design (fashion); fashion technology; knitwear design. Course title is little indication of course emphasis and content; for example, one BTEC HND in fashion/fashion marketing focuses on the design and development of leisure and sportswear garments with career options ranging from creative design to fashion forecasting. Another, in clothing technology, offers work experience in local manufacturing companies *and* TV and theatre wardrobe departments. Basically, most courses will include elements of design, pattern technology, garment technology, production management, business studies and raw materials. The balance and emphasis will differ, but most lead to a range of overlapping jobs. Some graduates start work at a lower level than their qualifications would seem to warrant, but they should be able to find a way up with experience. People who start with modest qualifications can also work their way up; prospects are better on the production than on the creative side.

Courses available:

1. Post-graduate degrees and diplomas: 1–2 years, full time or sandwich; entry requirements – degree or equivalent.

2. Degrees: 3–4 years, full time or sandwich; entry requirements – 2 or 3 A-levels plus supporting GCSEs *or* BTEC/SCOTVEC National Diploma *or* foundation course.

3. BTEC/SCOTVEC Higher awards: 3 years full time for the Diploma, 2 years part time for the Certificate (the SCOTVEC Certificate is 2 years full time); entry requirements – 1 A-level and 4 GCSEs (A–C) *or* Advanced GNVQ *or* level 3 NVQ or National Diploma.

4. BTEC/SCOTVEC national awards: 2 years full time; entry requirements – 4 GCSEs (A–C) *or* Intermediate GNVQ or level 2 NVQ *or* BTEC First Certificate or Diploma.

5. Engineering: a few specialist degrees but other engineering qualifications suitable (see p. 181).

6. S/NVQ's are available at levels 1 to 3. No formal entry requirements.

Local colleges may offer City and Guilds courses at craft and operative level.

Personal attributes
Depends on particular job. *For top-level designers*, visual imagination, creative genius *and* exceptional business flair. *For others*, visual imagination and colour sense; adaptability; willingness to discipline creative flair to the technical and economic necessities of design for a popular market; self-confidence; some manual dexterity; ability to work as part of a team. *For production specialists*, interest in the technology of fashion; organizing ability; creative approach to problem-solving; eye for detail; ability to delegate and deal with people.

Late start
Depends on talent and drive. Competition from young college leavers is very stiff.

Career-break
Designers: Depends on how established before break. *Production*: Probably no problem for those who have had good experience before the break. Changing technologies can easily be coped with by well-trained production managers.

Part time   Not normally, except as freelance designer or, very occasionally, as relief (holiday) cutter, etc.

Position of women   Women can do well in this field. An increasing proportion of designers are women. More would be welcome in production.

Further information   CAPITB plc, 80 Richardshaw Lane, Pudsey, Leeds, LS28 6BN
For S/NVQs, Qualifications for Industry Ltd, at the same address.

Related careers   ART AND DESIGN – JOURNALISM – PHOTOGRAPHY – PUBLIC RELATIONS – TELEVISION, FILM AND RADIO

Health and Safety Inspectors

Entry qualifications: For *factory* and *agricultural inspectors*, normally an honours degree in any subject; for agricultural work, a relevant subject may be preferred. GCSE (A–C) in maths and a driving licence essential. For *specialist inspectors*: normally a good degree, several years' industrial experience and a professional qualification where relevant (e.g. Chartered Engineer).

The work The Health and Safety Executive is concerned with minimizing death, injury and disease stemming from work activities. Inspectors, who are civil servants, are concerned with the health, safety and welfare not only of workers, but of any of the public who may be affected by their work. They have been closely involved investigating recent disasters such as those at the Hillsborough stadium, King's Cross station and the Piper Alpha oil rig, but most of their work deals with prevention. They act as advisers, investigators, enforcement officers and sometimes prosecutors, collecting evidence, preparing and presenting cases. They deal with everything from a small workshop where disabled people may make toys to huge projects like the Channel Tunnel.

The majority of inspectors are *factory inspectors*. They cover a large range of industries and workplaces, not only factories but, for example, hospitals, construction sites, shipyards, offices and shops. Depending on where they work, factory inspectors may deal with a limited number of industries or with a broad range. *Agricultural inspectors* are concerned with agricultural, horticultural and forestry establishments. There are also specialist inspectorates for railways, offshore safety, nuclear installations, mines and explosives.

Generally the work may be divided into 3 types or levels. Inspectors are the 'GPs' who carry out the day-to-day work, visiting sites across the whole range of industry to ensure that conditions, machinery and equipment, procedures and safeguards meet the requirements of legislation. For particular problems inspectors may call on the advice of specialists (analogous to consultants in medicine) who may be experts in very narrow areas. When required, Health and Safety Laboratories provide sophisticated research, investigation and analysis; for example, after the King's Cross fire one HSL forensic lab constructed a 1/2-scale model of the escalator to investigate how the fire spread.

Inspectors are out of the office for as many as 3 days a week. They have considerable freedom to plan their work.

Training *Factory* and *Agricultural Inspectors*: 2-year post-entry programme combining work experience and formal training leading to a post-graduate diploma in occupational health and safety.

Specialist Inspectors: 1-year post-entry programme to gain inspectorial competence.

Personal attributes Self-reliance; interest in technical matters and in people; diplomacy; ability to get on well with all kinds of people at all levels in the work hierarchy; fitness; initiative; ability to take responsibility; ability to communicate easily; curiosity.

Late start Very good opportunities. People with experience are needed, especially as the work is expanding. Track record may make up for lack of academic qualifications; each case is treated on its merit. Specialist inspectors always have previous experience.

Career-break No problem. Inspectors are civil servants, see p. 123.

Part time Again, as civil servants, prospects are good. Job-sharing, part-time, even term-time-only working are possible.

Position of women In the Factory and Agricultural Inspectorate nearly 50% of entrants are female. In the specialist inspectorates there are very few women; but it is hoped that this will change as more women graduate and gain experience in appropriate areas.

Further information Personnel Operations, Health and Safety Executive, St Hugh's House, Trinity Road, Bootle, Merseyside L20 3QY

Graduate and Schools Liaison, Room 127/2, Office of Public Service and Science, Horse Guards Road, London SW1P 3AL

The Private Sector

Many firms have their own safety officers whose job, broadly, is to ensure that all legal requirements are being met, and to advise management generally on all aspects of health and safety in the organization. There are no specific requirements for this work. Some practitioners are former health and safety inspectors or environmental health officers (see p. 204). The National Examination Board in Occupational Safety and Health offers certificates and diplomas leading to membership of the Institution of Occupational Safety and Health. Study is by part-time, block-release or distance-learning.

Further information   Institution of Occupational Safety and Health, 222 Uppingham Road, Leicester LE5 0QG

Related careers   ENGINEERING – ENVIRONMENTAL HEALTH OFFICER – SCIENCE

Health Services Management

The National Health Service is the largest employer in Europe with more than 1·2 million staff. It has been going through a period of unprecedented change, a key feature of which is the 'internal market'. This separates the Health Service into 'providers' and 'purchasers'. The providers, hospitals or other units, offer direct services to patients. The purchasers, health commissions or fund-holding GPs (i.e. those who manage their own budgets), buy the services patients require from providers. The idea is that patients and those purchasing care on their behalf will have more choice, and thus the providers will be forced to be more efficient, cost-effective, and concerned for the needs of patients. Patients will no longer want to go to hospitals where there are long waiting lists for operations or where out-patients are never seen on time, while purchasers will not want to pay for inferior services.

It is too early to assess the full impact of these changes, but they are likely to affect the ethos and content of managers' jobs. They will need to develop an eye for value as well as service; they will need to calculate how much things actually cost and set up new monitoring systems; contracts negotiation and management will be important for both purchasers and providers; both sides will need new research on better services and ways of measuring and monitoring quality of service. Career patterns and the range of opportunities are also likely to change, with lateral moves becoming more common and varied.

Entry qualifications
Entry is at all educational levels. There are formal training schemes for those with A-levels or degrees. There is also direct entry with relevant professional qualifications and experience, and some managers move over from the clinical side.

The work
Health services managers provide the framework within which patients are treated by doctors and other clinical and paramedical staff. Their wide range of responsibilities includes strategic planning; financial and human resource planning; the maintenance of buildings; the purchase and control of supplies and equipment; personnel management; contracting support services such as laundry,

catering, and other patient services. The internal market means that managers have to be more entrepreneurial in selling their services to purchasers and think innovatively about developing new services.

Most jobs are with the 'providers' of health services, i.e. hospitals or community units, e.g. for the elderly or mentally ill. Work varies according to the size and structure of the unit as well as the individual manager's specific job. Thus one manager might be working on improving services to the ethnic community, arranging for translators and seeking advice on cultural expectations, while another works on the funding of a new consultant's position – what paramedical and other support staff will he or she need, when and where can an out-patient's clinic be fitted in, what about extra equipment? Increasingly managers work in interdisciplinary teams (including doctors and other professional staff) to plan and develop new services, implement change (which is caused not just by legislation and reorganization but by medical and technological advances, changing population and so on), and manage staff, budgets and facilities. Negotiating skills are essential since resources are finite and various interests often conflict; for example, the cost of advances in one clinical speciality might mean a reduced budget in another.

Health commissions' primary role will increasingly be as purchasers of health care. In the short term this is likely to result in fewer jobs at this level. The basic function of purchasing managers is to assess the health needs of their population, identify ways of meeting those needs, enter into contracts with providers, and monitor the contracts and quality of provision. Regional officers of the NHSE have a strategic role. They are responsible for long-term financial and manpower planning and helping to develop the role of the other tiers of the structure. Traditionally, able, ambitious managers moved from unit to district to regional management, but the NHS changes have upset that pattern. For example, to head a trust, with the new management freedom and demands might offer a more attractive challenge. Family health services authorities, which are responsible for the family doctor, dental, pharmacy and optician services, have merged with districts to form health commissions.

New careers for managers are emerging in primary care. GPs employ practice managers to run their practices. When the GPs are fundholders this may involve responsibility for a large budget and for monitoring contracts.

Careers in health service management are not confined to the NHS. It is increasingly common for people to move between the private and voluntary health service sectors and the NHS, and there is also increasing exchange between the social services and the health services. The large pharmaceutical and health supplies companies also look to recruit managers who have a good understanding of the health service.

Training   Training for health services management is in a state of transition, as is the NHS itself. There is enormous flexibility and variety, but this can be confusing for prospective entrants. Training opportunities are both considerable in number and different in kind. They are multi-level and multi-mode. Schemes may be run nationally, regionally, by commissions and possibly, in future, by larger trusts. Entry qualifications include degrees, A-levels and, for lower-level administrative work which can nevertheless lead to management, GCSEs. Trainees can work towards post-graduate qualifications (including MBA and diplomas in management); relevant business/ professional qualfications (e.g. in finance, personnel, purchasing); Institute of Health Services Management award. There is an increasing number of undergraduate degrees in health studies. Modes of study include full-time pre-entry courses, day-release, distance-learning and open learning. An individual's choice may be influenced not only by personal preferences and circumstances, but by what provision is available locally and the needs of a particular employer.

The National Management Training Scheme (NHS MTS) is intended to groom candidates for rapid promotion to senior management. Entrants must have a degree or acceptable professional qualification; in-service candidates may also apply. The Scheme, which normally takes 22 months (though there is flexibility), includes work attachments in a range of settings, formal management training, a real management post, projects and investigations which can take the trainee on a secondment into industry. Throughout, the trainee has as mentor a senior manager who helps him or her to plan development and assess progress. The training leads to a nationally recognized management qualification – there are various options.

In Scotland: Scotland has its own training schemes for health services managers. Major schemes for graduates and suitably qualfiied internal candidates are in general management, financial management, supplies management.

Because so many qualifications are appropriate and training opportunities exist at many levels, anyone interested should contact the regional health authority.

The Institute of Health Services Management also provides continuing professional development to help managers adapt to the rapid changes and new developments going on in the health service.

Personal attributes   Numeracy; flexibility; ability to discuss complex issues with specialists at all levels; organizing ability; ability to work as member of team; communication and negotiating skills; commitment to patient care.

Late start   Good opportunities for those with appropriate qualifications and experience – the NHS does recruit managers from outside, usually from other parts of the public sector. The flexible training opportunities, for example the MESOL (Management Education Scheme by Open Learning) programme (for those already in the health service) which offers three modes of study leading either to Open University or to IHSM qualifications, make the transition to or progress in health services management easier.

Career-break   Should be no problem, successful schemes have been running, but see 'Position of women', below.

Part time   Most part-time opportunities are at lower levels; some job-sharing has worked at higher levels, but see 'Position of women', below.

Position of women   A major study of health service managers with particular emphasis on gender has recently been carried out by IHSM Consultants for the NHS Women's Unit. It shows that 42% of general and senior managers and 19% of top managers are women. They are better qualified, but marginally less well-paid, than their male counterparts. Women are more likely to develop their careers within provider (trust) organizations, particularly community, elderly and learning disability trusts, whereas men predominate in purchaser organizations.

   The survey also shows that managers at the top are working very long hours and change jobs very quickly, on average every three years. As in other fields, these are the kind of factors that hinder women's careers far more than men's. But the NHS Executive is concerned to promote equal opportunities and has established the NHS Women's Unit which has a women's career development register which provides support for women aiming for top manager posts.

Further information   Institute of Health Services Management, 39 Chalton Street, London NW1 1JD

Related careers   CHARTERED SECRETARY AND ADMINISTRATOR – CATERING: *Institutional Management* – MANAGEMENT

Home Economics

Entry qualifications None laid down; depends on 'Training' (see below).

The work Home economists act as a link between producers of household goods and services and their consumers. This covers a wide range of jobs. Within industry they also act as link between technologists who design and develop new products but often know little about consumer preferences and requirements, and marketing and general management staffs. So home economics, at least at senior level, requires communication skills as well as an understanding of technological and of social trends.

Home economists work in various settings: industry, social services, public relations, public utilities, consumer advice and protection, retailing, hotels and catering. Increasingly they are working in community care and in health and welfare fields. Home economics teachers are involved in health and design and technology education. There is nothing clear-cut about the professional home economist's work: people with related kinds of training may do the same, or similar, jobs; and qualified home economists branch off into related fields such as catering, marketing, consumer and trade magazines, and books.

The majority work in manufacturing industry on development, quality control, promotion and marketing of products, appliances and equipment used, or services provided in the home. Before new or improved food and washing products, dishwashers, cookers, central heating systems, etc. are put into production, home economists discuss details of design and performance with engineers, scientists, designers, marketing people. They put the customers' point of view; they test prototypes in the laboratory under 'ideal conditions', and they also use them in the same way as the customer might – being interrupted in their work and not always following the instructions as they should. For instance, they test whether a new type of butter-substitute creams easily, even if kept in the fridge too long and if clumsily handled; how a washing machine behaves if switches are turned on in the wrong order, or how easily a new cooker cleans when it is really dirty.

As a result of laboratory and 'user' tests, alterations are often made before a product is put into production. In the retail industry, home economists work in, or manage, food- and textile-testing laboratories, some become management trainees and then go into retail management (see RETAIL MANAGEMENT, p. 431).

For gas, electricity and solid fuel suppliers they work as 'home service and energy advisers' (titles vary). They visit consumers in their own homes: this may be a straightforward 'after-sales service'; more often it is to investigate a complaint, maybe about a central heating installation which is not working properly. The home economist must be able to diagnose the fault and perhaps then to explain tactfully that the instructions have not been followed. Increasingly they are involved with educating the public in the need for, and methods of, energy conservation (for example, home insulation and other fuel-saving devices). The work combines dealing with lay people who have much less technical knowledge, and with experts who have very much more.

Under the heading *customer relations* or *marketing*, work involves writing clear, concise user-instructions for explanatory labels and leaflets which accompany fish-fingers, freezers, synthetic fibre carpets, babyfoods, etc., as well as dealing with inquiries and complaints correspondence.

Home economists also identify demand for new products or changes in existing ones. This may involve field work – interviewing potential customers in their homes (see 'Market Research', p. 16, and MARKETING AND SELLING, p. 297) and thinking up innovations which could be marketed profitably.

In the *media* home economists prepare features and programmes: they cook and cost elaborate as well as very cheap dishes, or arrange and cost domestic interiors which are then photographed and described, or demonstrated on TV. They also use their skills in assessing and reporting on equipment and on issues relevant to the consumer at home and at work.

In local authority *social services departments* home economists advise low-income families on budgeting and general household management; and they may run the home-help service and advise on the efficient running of the authority's residential homes. Those who have studied a housing option may work in local authority or private *housing management*. There are also openings in health education.

In *hospitals* home economists become domestic administrators at top management level.

They may also work in the *Trading Standards Department* (see p. 543) in consumer services.

Experienced home economists can work as freelance consultants: firms may wish to research and/or promote a new product and need a home economist for a particular project rather than permanently. For example, home economists work as freelances, writing explanatory leaflets, developing and checking recipes and equipment, etc. Some prepare food for magazine photography or TV commercials; some write books and articles for consumer magazines.

Job prospects are good, especially for graduates, although competition for top jobs (most are in cities) is keen. However, the combination of technical knowledge and understanding of family and consumer needs can be useful in a variety of jobs; home economists willing to be adaptable can find work in a wide range of organizations. Greatest scope in food and domestic appliance manufacturing, in retail, fuel and energy industries.

Training

No particular qualification leads to any particular type of job. It is possible for anyone with basic approved training or related training (see 'Accommodation and Catering Management', under CATERING, p. 105) and the right experience and personality ultimately to do as well as a graduate. But the more thorough the training, the wider the scope of job.

1. *Degree*: Entry requirements: 2 A-levels and 3 GCSEs (A–C) (no specific A-levels, although home economics preferred, but maths, English language and a science at least at GCSE level). Degree courses in Home Economics or related subject such as Food, Textiles and Consumer Studies; Home Economics and Resource Management; Applied Consumer Studies; B.Ed. (Home Economics) (see TEACHING, p. 517).

2. *BTEC/SCOTVEC Higher National awards in Home Economics* or related subject, e.g. Food and Consumer Studies: Entry requirements: 1 A-level (preferably home economics) and 3 GCSEs to include English language, maths or a science. Diploma and degree courses include varying amounts of nutrition, food preparation and science; design and performance of equipment and materials, including textiles; business and marketing studies; consumer and social studies; communications and the media; information technology. Students can choose from a range of options, for example the carer in the community, ergonomics, housing and community health, product development, press and public relations.

3. *BTEC/SCOTVEC National awards in Home Economics* or related subject: Syllabus covers broadly the same subjects as HND but not in such depth; some courses concentrate more on practical skills such as cooking; home management; care of textiles, etc.

4. *City and Guilds*: For candidates without any or only a few GCSEs who prefer a course which concentrates entirely on practical skills: City and Guilds 2-year full-time course in Home Economics for Family and Community Care *or* NVQs in Food Preparation and Food Service/Health and Social Care/Leisure and Hospitality *or* GNVQ in Food Manufacture.

Not all types of courses are available in all areas.

Personal attributes
Practicality and organizing ability; interest in consumer affairs, ability to understand both consumers' and manufacturers' points of view; ability to communicate easily both with more highly qualified professional and with often poorly educated, possibly illiterate consumers; liking for people; humour.

Late start
Mature entrants are welcome on all courses and may be given exemptions if they have relevant experience.

Career-break
Should be no problem for people who keep up with developments.

Part time
Good opportunities; no reason why job-sharing should not be tried. Some part-time courses are being developed.

Position of women
This is a virtually 100% women's occupation, though there are now a few men in the profession and there are more male students. Industrial and media employers of home economists still tend to think of customers for whose benefit home economists work as housewives. Anyone who feels strongly about equality might not fit into many of the jobs done by home economists.

Further information
BTEC, Central House, Upper Woburn Place, London WC1H 0HH

City and Guilds of London Institute, 1 Giltspur Street, London EC1A 9DD

Institute of Home Economics, Hobart House, 40 Grosvenor Place, London SW1X 7AE

National Association of Teachers of Home Economics Ltd, Hamilton House, Mabledon Place, London WC1H 9BJ

Related careers
CATERING – DIETETICS – PUBLIC RELATIONS – TEACHING – TRADING STANDARDS OFFICER

Housing Management

Entry qualifications

Various levels. Considerable graduate entry.

The work

Traditionally, housing managers are responsible for the administration, maintenance and allocation of accommodation let for rent. In recent years their scope has expanded enormously and it is still expanding. It now also includes, for example, the running of Housing Aid Centres; the administration of rent rebate, and rent allowance and housing benefit schemes; housing research and the formulation of housing policy. The majority of housing managers and housing assistants still work for local authorities, but as local authority housing stock has diminished (more council houses are sold than new ones built) and the number and scope of housing associations has increased, the proportion working for housing associations has grown. A small number work for building societies, property companies and voluntary bodies.

Day-to-day housing management adds up to an unusual combination of dealing with people, using technical knowledge and getting out and about. Duties may include interviewing applicants for homes; visiting prospective tenants in their homes to assess their housing needs; finding and monitoring bed and breakfast accommodation and trying as quickly as possible to move tenants into something more satisfactory; inspecting property at regular intervals and arranging, if necessary, for repairs to be carried out; dealing with tenants' complaints about anything from noisy neighbours and lack of play facilities for children to lack of maintenance. Rent collecting, which used to be the most important and time-consuming task, has all but died out: most tenants now take or send rent to the housing office.

Housing staff try to establish or maintain good tenant-landlord relationships and try to forge a conglomeration of dwellings into a community. To this end they may try to involve tenants in managing their block of flats or estate, or they may set up tenants' management committees. In Housing Aid Centres, housing staff advise on any problem related to housing, from how to cope with an eviction order or how to get a rent allowance, to where to apply for a mortgage.

At senior level, the work involves top-level general and financial management using modern management techniques; the purchase of properties; the allocation of accommodation (which is the most onerous task); research into housing needs and into such questions as 'How can we retain the neighbourliness of the slums in new developments?', 'What is a good environment?', etc.; advising architects and planners on social aspects of siting, design and lay-out of new developments.

The fact that there has been a considerable increase in owner-occupiers and a decrease in accommodation let for rent by local authorities has not diminished the importance of housing management, but it has changed its role. As stock for rent is reduced more, and more tenants are poor and on benefits, so the welfare element has become more important. The emphasis now is more on efficient management, and on exploring innovative ways of coping with housing need. New approaches to the problem include shared ownership; rent-into-mortgage schemes; leasing short-life property from private landlords; more cooperation between local authorities, housing associations, and building societies and private property companies. There is also now more movement between housing associations and local authorities than there used to be. It is still easier, though, to move from local authority to housing association than the other way around.

Many housing managers prefer to stick to day-to-day management throughout their careers, because they enjoy dealing with people. At senior level the jobs can be controversial. Directors of Housing may have to implement policies with which they do not agree, e.g. sale of council houses.

In local authority departments which manage thousands of dwellings, staff usually specialize in one aspect of the work at a time. In housing associations, which manage a smaller number, one housing assistant or housing manager may deal with everything concerning a number of tenancies. Housing associations increasingly provide facilities for special groups, e.g. for the elderly, single-parent families, the disabled. Some run hostels for such 'special needs' groups as ex-prisoners or people who have been psychiatric patients and still need support while adjusting to living in the community.

The profession is not expanding, but the proportion of graduates is increasing. Housing associations also often employ people without specific housing qualifications but other relevant ones, or simply with useful experience. This could be in general management, or accountancy, or with a degree in social science/administration or in surveying. As the stock of property increases, maintenance and conversion need more people with relevant knowledge. A new, as yet small, housing specialism is housing consultancy. Consultants are people with housing experience who set up as freelances and advise on or help with state-of-the-art financial or general management, setting up rent-into-mortgage or other innovative schemes in which private and public sector organizations cooperate. They also help with in-house training.

Training   There are several routes to the professional qualification, the Chartered Institute of Housing's Professional Diploma:

1. The recommended route: Entry with at least 1 A-level and 4 GCSEs (A–C), for on-the-job training with day-release for the BTEC Higher National Certificate in Housing Studies. The HNC is followed by a further 2 years part-time training for the Institute's Professional Diploma. Both the HNC and Professional Diploma are available by distance learning.

2. Candidates with 4 GCSEs (A–C) can first take the BTEC National Certificate in Housing Studies.

Training for full professional status thus takes 4 years for A-level entrants and 6 for GCSE entrants. Candidates who do not aim at senior management jobs can stop after taking the National Certificate. At that level there are several specialized courses in, for example, Caretaking and Estate Services; Tenant Participation; role of wardens.

3. Graduates, any discipline, either take the 2-year part-time course for the Professional Diploma, or they can take one of several full-time university post-graduate courses in housing.

4. A number of degrees in housing (titles vary) have been recognized by the Chartered Institute of Housing.

5. The Royal Institution of Chartered Surveyors (General Practice Division) qualification also leads to substantial exemption from the Professional Diploma.

The Institute's PD covers such varied areas of study as social policy; building construction and maintenance (to a standard which any interested person can cope with); law relating to housing; management studies; housing finance. Before finally qualifying for the award candidates must pass the Institute's Test of Professional Practice.

While housing associations often take graduates and do not expect them to train for the Professional Diploma, for career moves the PD is increasingly required.

NOTE: There are no BTEC Diploma (i.e. full-time) courses in Housing Studies.

NVQs/SVQs levels 2, 3 and 4 are now in place.

Personal attributes   Getting on well with all types of people; an interest in social, practical and economic problems, and in planning; tolerance; ability to be firm; indifference to being out in bad weather; organizing ability and diplomacy for senior people.

Late start   Late entrants welcome in theory, but training vacancies are often difficult to find for mature entrants. More opportunities in housing associations where aptitude and relevant work, as well as 'life experience', are sometimes more important than qualifications.

Career-break   Returners are very welcome indeed. Short courses and workshops are arranged through HERA (see below) and by individual housing organizations. The Institute has reduced membership fees for the temporarily retired.

Part time   Excellent opportunities, especially, but not only, in housing associations, for part-time work and job-sharing.

Position of women   The proportion of women and men entering housing is fairly even, but *very* few local authority housing managers are women (see 'Position of women', under LOCAL GOVERNMENT, p. 268). There is no reason whatever why women should not do better. They do very well in housing associations.

Further information   The Chartered Institute of Housing, Octavia House, Westwood Business Park, Westwood Way, Coventry, Warwickshire CV4 8JP

HERA, 2 Valentine Place, London SE1 8QH

Related careers   ENVIRONMENTAL HEALTH OFFICER – LOCAL GOVERNMENT – TOWN AND COUNTRY PLANNING

Information Work
(Librarianship/Information Science)

It has been said that we live in an information society. The sheer weight of information available increases all the time and impinges on every facet of modern life. We need information on which to base decisions on a whole range of issues. The fifth-former wants to find out where various A-level combinations could lead him or her. A doctor needs to know the possible side-effects of a new treatment. An investor might look into the performance of various shares. A marketing manager wants to keep abreast of what the competition is up to. Information is vital to our education, our work, our leisure, our health.

Developments in technology have had an enormous impact on the 'information industry'. Not only has technology led to new ways of collecting, organizing and retrieving information, but it has also led to more information! The information specialist has to deal with a range of sources far beyond books and other printed material.

Entry qualifications

For professional work, a degree; for paraprofessional work, nothing rigid, but 4 GCSE passes, including English, may be asked for.

The work

Distinctions between the librarian and the information scientist have blurred. Differences are often a matter of the emphasis of their work, rather than a fundamental difference of role or purpose. Job titles are not necessarily an indication of job content or emphasis. Information scientists may be chartered librarians; a librarian in a specialist library may work with highly technical information; some specialists have dual membership of the Library Association and the Institute of Information Scientists. Information officer and research officer are other titles that may crop up in job adverts.

The common basic purpose of the librarian/information specialist is to see that relevant information is available and used effectively. For whatever purpose, the job of the information specialist is to *acquire*, *organize* and *exploit* information. This covers a vast range of activity. *Acquiring* might range from maintaining as broad and balanced a collection as possible to cater for a wide range of general interests, within a given budget, to trawling the international market to build up a highly specialist collection of academic or technical interest. *Exploiting* might mean inviting a children's author to read his or her stories to pre-schoolers or preparing a newsletter to keep specialists aware of developments in their field.

The *public library* service is vast and provides a wide range of services to the public. Librarians are responsible for the selection, purchase, cataloguing and arrangement of a wide variety of materials – books and periodicals, videos, cassettes, records, slides, compact discs and information packs, for example. Many libraries run special services, such as 'books-on-wheels', children's activities, services to business or the ethnic community. All provide information, sometimes in specially produced packs, and answer inquiries. Many libraries have computerized information systems.

In a smaller library, and early stages of their careers, librarians' work may cover several functions, but many jobs involve some degree of specialization. More senior positions involve managing staff and resources. As in most jobs, routine work is inevitable, but many of the routine tasks associated with libraries – issuing books, filling and tidying shelves – are not done by professional librarians but by library assistants. Most public librarians will be chartered librarians (see below).

Academic libraries in universities, polytechnics and colleges offer a service to both staff and students, and sometimes to outsiders. In consultation with academic staff, librarians carefully select materials to support the teaching and learning going on in the institution. Many academic librarians are specialists in a particular subject area and often have a degree in that subject. Others may manage special collections, e.g. early printed books, manuscripts, music or computer software. Important aspects of the work in academic libraries are helping students to understand and use effectively the facilities available (including the latest technology) and helping academic staff to keep up to date with developments in their subjects. Many posts in academic libraries are open only to those who have a post-graduate qualification (see below).

Industry and commerce need good information to make good decisions. As in other areas, the information specialist is responsible for selecting material; this could demand considerable specialist knowledge of the organization's area of operations in, for example, science or engineering, as well as information skills. Computer technology has had an enormous impact on the storage and retrieval of information, as well as on the range available, and information specialists will be expected to exploit this to fulfil their company's needs, whether it involves designing and implementing a system to catalogue all the company's information resources, or buying in the latest database. The provision of information for specific purposes is an important task and might involve compiling a list (perhaps from a computerized system) of key references on a particular topic; exploiting a network of outside contacts, e.g. trade associations, learned societies, other company libraries; preparing summaries or abstracts of new information. A reading knowledge of a foreign language can be very useful.

Information specialists are also employed in government departments, museums, research and professional bodies, and the media. There are some opportunities to work as a freelance consultant.

In public and academic libraries, where services are affected by public-spending policies, openings are not increasing in numbers. In information departments and special libraries the number of jobs is increasing. Graduates in physics, chemistry, computer studies and related science/technology fields are keenly sought; there is also a need for specialists in accountancy, economics, finance, law and management. (However, any degree subject can lead to work in this field.)

Training   1. For membership of the Library Association (chartered librarians): a 3- or 4-year degree course in library/information studies *or* a degree in any subject followed by a 1-year full-time or 2-year part-time post-graduate course *plus* a minimum of 1 year's post-course training. Most post-graduate courses prefer students to have had some experience as a trainee or assistant in a library before starting a course.

2. For membership of the Institute of Information Scientists: a degree in any subject plus a period of practical experience. An approved post-graduate qualification in library and information studies/information science/information management can reduce the period of qualifying experience by up to 3 years.

3. For library and information assistants: part-time courses leading to City and Guilds, BTEC and SCOTVEC National and Higher National Certificates in librarianship and information studies. There is also a 2-year full-time BTEC National Diploma course.

Employers' requirements and preferences can vary. For some jobs a relevant first degree can be more important than further qualifications. Some people take relevant post-graduate courses, but do not go on to professional membership. Others have dual membership of both professional bodies.

Personal attributes	Good communication skills; curiosity; an interest in a variety of related topics without the desire to delve too deeply into any one; a methodical approach; a high degree of accuracy; organizing ability; a retentive memory; staying power for long, possibly fruitless search; resourcefulness; interest in electronic information systems; capacity to switch instantly from one topic to another; ability to cope with frequent interruptions when doing jobs requiring concentration; ability to anticipate users' needs. Because library and information work has so many different aspects, practitioners' relative strengths in these areas may vary.
Late start	No upper age limit. Educational institutions may relax normal requirements for mature students, but finance is more difficult after 40 – part-time courses could help. Good prospects for unqualified assistants.
Career-break	Should be no problem if well qualified and up to date. Short courses, can be used as refresher courses, though not intended as such. Formal schemes are increasing, particularly in the private sector.
Part time	Reasonable opportunities at junior and up to middle-management level, but more difficult at senior levels.
Position of women	A high proportion of library and information professionals are women. Previously women were not very successful in getting senior posts, but the position is radically changing. Increasingly women *are* now getting top jobs.
Further information	Aslib (The Association of Information Management), 20–24 Old Street, London EC1V 9AP The Library Association, 7 Ridgmount Street, London WC1E 7AE The Institute of Information Scientists, 44–5 Museum Street, London WC1A 1LY

Related careers	ARCHIVIST – BOOKSELLING – MUSEUMS AND ART GALLERIES – PUBLISHING

Insurance

Entry qualifications

For the qualifying exam of the Chartered Insurance Institute, *either* BTEC/SCOTVEC National award (see pp. xxi, xxii) *or* 2 A-levels and 2 GCSEs (A–C), including English at either level. Graduate entry is increasing, and some degrees give exemption from part of the CII exams. GCSE entrants with commitment and the willingness to study part-time (often with employer's help) can move up the ladder, but the best prospects are for people with A-levels, BTEC/SCOTVEC National, HND or degree.

Foreign languages are useful as insurance is an international activity and some jobs involve considerable travel.

The work

Insurance is a method of compensating for losses arising from all kinds of misfortunes, from the theft of a video to an airliner crash, from a holiday cancelled through illness to the abandonment of a major sporting event. It is based on the principle that many more people pay regularly into a common fund than ultimately draw from it, and thus the losses of the unlucky few may be made good. The organizers of the system are the *insurers*, i.e. the *insurance companies* or *Lloyd's underwriters*. Lloyd's itself is not an insurance company, but a society whose individual members are grouped together into syndicates to accept and underwrite 'risks'. Each syndicate is administered by an agency which employs a *professional underwriter* (see below) to carry out the business. Banks (see p. 68) and building societies (see p. 84) are also now moving into insurance. It is usual to specialize in one of the main branches of insurance: *marine and aviation*, *life and pensions*, *property*, *accident*, *motor and liability* and *reinsurance* (where very large risks are 'farmed out'), although transfers are possible. Occupational pension schemes are a growth area.

Underwriters are responsible for assessing risks, deciding whether they are insurable, and on what terms and conditions they can be accepted. Some underwriting decisions are routine and based on guidelines laid down by the company for dealing with standard cases (for example, ordinary motor insurance). Others are highly complex and/or unusual and demand specialized skill or judgement (for example, the Channel Tunnel or an art treasure on special exhibit).

In the case of buildings, industrial plant and other commercial operations, underwriters may call on the advice of *surveyors*. The surveyor prepares a factual report on any aspects that might affect the underwriter's assessment of the risks (e.g. fire protection or security arrangements). Some surveyors go into risk management, which is concerned with identifying, assessing and minimizing the risks a company may face in its day-to-day activities. Insurance surveyors are often selected from existing staff and trained internally; they are not necessarily chartered surveyors. When risks are very complex, science or technology graduates might be recruited for this work.

When a claim is received *claims staff* assess the loss and determine the amount to be paid. As with underwriting, some cases are straightforward (though you might be dealing with people whose loss demands your tact and sympathy), while others are complex and require technical, legal and medical knowledge. For large or disputed claims insurance companies may call in independent *loss adjusters* to examine the claim and help to reach a settlement. Some loss adjusters come from the claims department of an insurance company, but others have relevant qualifications, e.g. in law, surveying, accountancy, engineering.

Inspectors (or *sales-agents*) have a good deal of independence. They are responsible for obtaining new business and ensuring that existing clients' cover is adequate as circumstances change. They may deal with 'agents' (e.g. brokers, solicitors, estate agents, building society managers) or direct with the public.

Insurance brokers act as intermediaries, bringing together the insurers and those who wish to be insured. Jobs include finding new business, looking after and advising existing clients, and placing the risks in the market (i.e. finding insurers to underwrite the policy). Brokers may be small High Street firms or international giants employing thousands of staff. Only accredited brokers ('Lloyd's brokers') are allowed to do business with Lloyd's underwriters.

Training

On the job, with day-release for 3 years (evening study is also necessary) for Associateship of Chartered Insurance Institute, followed by 2 years (approximately) for Fellowship of CII. A BTEC/SCOTVEC National award in Business Studies can lead to partial exemption from CII examinations, and leaves options open for work in other commercial fields. For some specializations, e.g. investment and pensions management, the CII exam is followed by Fellowship exams of a relevant institute. Graduate trainees may follow an accelerated training programme.

Loss adjusters may take the Chartered Institute of Loss Adjust-

ers exams after insurance company experience if they already hold
a previous professional qualification such as ACII.

Personal attributes Some mathematical ability; a liking for paperwork; ability to
grasp the essentials of a problem; sound judgement; determination
and a certain amount of push; tact; a persuasive, confidence-
inspiring manner; ability to communicate with people, often in
difficult circumstances. For brokers, extrovert manner and entrepreneurial flair.

Late start Many employers are adopting a more relaxed attitude towards
the age of recruits, but training vacancies can be more difficult to
obtain after the age of 30. Mature entrants would be expected to
follow the same training routes as young recruits, but the minimum academic requirements might be relaxed. In sales, maturity
is an advantage.

Career-break Employers are introducing schemes; details vary.

Part time Part time, job-sharing, working from home are becoming more
popular within the industry.

Position of women The proportion of women members of the CII is rising. Though
only 1 in 4 members is female, among the under-25s the propor-
tion is nearly 50%.

Further information The Careers Information Officer, The Chartered Insurance Insti-
tute, 20 Aldermanbury, London EC2V 7HY
The British Insurance and Investment Brokers' Association,
BIIBA House, 14 Bevis Marks, London EC3A 7NT
Chartered Institute of Loss Adjusters, Manfield House, 376 The
Strand, London WC2R 0LR

Related careers ACCOUNTANCY – ACTUARY – BANKING – BUILDING SOCIETY
WORK – COMPUTING/IT – STOCK EXCHANGE AND SECURITIES
INDUSTRY

Journalism

Entry qualifications
Newspapers: 5 GCSEs (A–C) including English language for traineeship, but nearly all school-leaver entrants have at least 2 A-levels. 55% of entrants are graduates. For pre-entry course: 2 A-levels in practice.

Magazines: Depends on editor; for pre-entry course: 1 A-level, 4 GCSEs (A–C). About three-quarters of new entrants come from some kind of higher education course.

The work
Journalism covers a variety of jobs in a variety of settings (or 'media', which really should be 'media of communications'). Broadly, the main job groups are *reporter*; *correspondent or specialist reporter*; *feature writer*; *news editor*; *editor*; *freelance*. Division of duties depends on paper's size and organization.

Newspapers

Most newspapers now have computerized editorial systems, i.e. journalists input their copy through a keyboard directly into a computer. Virtually every journalist starts as trainee reporter. Reporters cover any kind of event: from council or Women's Institute meeting to political demo, fire, or press conference for visiting film star or foreign statesman. Reporters 'get a story' by asking questions and listening to other journalists' questions and interviewees' answers at press conferences, or in one-to-one interviews with individuals. For such interviews, reporters have to do some preliminary 'homework' – to interview a trade union secretary or famous novelist, for example, requires some background knowledge.

Reporters must compose stories quickly and meet tight deadlines. Accuracy, brevity and speed are more important than writing perfect prose: reporting is a fact-gathering and fact-disseminating rather than a creative job.

Occasionally, reporters may be on a particular story for several weeks, researching the background and/or waiting for developments. They work irregular hours, including weekends.

Specialist Reporter or Correspondent

'Hard news' is broadcast more quickly than it can be printed; to fight TV and radio competition, newspapers have developed 'interpretative' or specialist reporting. Specialists' titles and precise responsibilities and scope vary; the aim always is to interpret and explain news, and to comment on events, trends, causes and news behind the news. The number (and the expert knowledge of) specialists varies according to the type and size of newspaper. On the whole, only the nationals have specialists who concentrate entirely on one speciality; on other papers and in news agencies, reporters with a special interest in a particular field (or several) may do specialist along with general reporting. The main specializations are: parliament and/or politics generally; industry; finance; education; foreign news; local government and/or planning; social services; sport; science and technology; agriculture and food; motoring; fashion, women's/home interests; theatre; films; broadcasting. Financial correspondents tend to be economics graduates, science correspondents are science graduates, but education correspondents are not normally teachers: there are no hard-and-fast rules about how specialists acquire their specialist knowledge (and how much they need).

News Editor

Journalists with organizing ability may become news editors, controlling reporting staffs, allocating stories to individual reporters and attending senior staff's daily editorial conferences. It is an office job and normally involves no writing. The title usually applies on daily papers; but titles and organization of work vary considerably from one paper to another.

Sub-editors

Sub-editors do the detailed editing of copy; they re-write stories to fit in with required length, re-write the beginning, and may 'slant' stories. They write headlines and, in consultation with the night or assistant editor, may do the layout of news pages. On large papers there are several specialist subs. Subbing is team-work and entirely desk-bound; it always has to be done in a hurry.

Feature Writers

Usually experienced journalists who can write lucidly and descriptively on any topic; but specialists may also write features. Reporters may combine reporting with feature writing.

Columnist

Like feature writing, a job for experienced journalists; there are specialists, for example financial or consumer affairs columnists, and general columnists. The work requires a wide range of interests and contacts.

Leader-writers

Leaders may be written by the editor, or specialist correspondent, or other experienced journalists.

Editor-in-chief, Assistant Editor, Deputy Editor

Editors (including departmental editors) are co-ordinators, policy-makers. The number of top jobs, and the amount of writing editors do, vary greatly: some editors write leaders on specific subjects, some write in crises only; some on a variety of subjects, others not at all.

The amount of freedom editors-in-chief have to run the paper in the way they want depends on the proprietor; policies vary enormously.

There is no set promotion structure on newspapers. Some journalists do all or several types of newspaper work in succession in preparation for senior editorial jobs (subbing is a vital step on the ladder), others become heads of departments (finance, fashion, home affairs, chief sub, etc.) fairly quickly. Many remain reporters.

Titles, functions and division of labour are not consistent throughout the industry and often change with a change of editor-in-chief or proprietor.

*

Freesheets

Locally distributed 'giveaway' papers are the fastest-growing advertising medium. Free newspapers vary enormously in the proportion and variety of their editorial content. A few are much like small local weekly papers; most carry very little editorial matter. Some are published by established newspaper houses, some by members of the Association of Free Newspapers, yet others are run individually from tiny offices by a man/woman and a boy/girl. Jobs on free newspapers with varied editorial content may be acceptable as traineeships (see below), but work on the majority is unlikely to lead to jobs on national or other prestigious local newspapers.

Magazines

Broadly there are two types:

1. Professional and business to business; and also 'house' journals, geared to a particular profession, trade or organization.

2. 'Consumer' magazines: they cater for all types of leisure interests and include women's, teenage and hobby magazines and comics.

On (1) journalists often work closely with experts in the particular field of which they must have/develop some understanding. They write features, report developments, and re-write experts' contributions. Magazine work, however specialized, can be a way into newspaper work – especially for graduates (particularly science or technology) with writing ability. It often requires broader skills than newspaper journalism: e.g. knowing about sub-editing and layout.

Consumer magazines employ feature writers, sub-editors and departmental editors more than reporters, but organization varies enormously. Consumer magazines use freelances more than do newspapers. Editors' work includes originating feature ideas and selecting and briefing outside contributors, both freelance journalists and specialists who are not journalists.

Freelance Journalism

Freelances are either 'generalists' – feature writers who write on any subject – or specialists. On the whole, only experienced journalists with staff experience, and particularly those with specialist knowledge which is in demand (technology, consumerism, child development, education, for example), succeed.

Specialists – teachers, engineers, lawyers, with writing ability and topical ideas – also do freelance journalism as a sideline, but this is becoming more difficult.

Training *Newspapers*
These are the most common methods:

Direct entry traineeship: 2 years, including 6 months' probation. Acceptance depends as much on paper's policy and candidate's suitability as on academic qualifications. Competition for trainee posts at any stage is fierce. Candidates must apply direct to editors of provincial (including suburban) dailies and weeklies.

The London-based nationals rarely take trainees. (Previous experience in student or freelance journalism is essential. Candidates need to submit samples of work done: an article or report specially written for the particular paper, which shows the editor that the applicant has identified the paper's style, is important, as is work done for school or university paper.)

Trainees complete a foundation distance-learning package during probation and attend a 12-week block-release course later in their training. All trainees must pass preliminary examinations in law, public affairs (local and central government), newspaper journalism and shorthand and have a set period of work experience before being allowed to sit the National Council for the Training of Journalists' National Certificate Examination (NCE). The syllabus for this includes, English usage; relevant law; public affairs; interpretative reporting (interviewing, fact-gathering methods, etc.); current affairs; sub-editing skills. Also still necessary is shorthand (100 w.p.m.), which reporters still use alongside tape recordings to take notes, even though they will use computers to write their copy.

Practical training should cover work in all departments, including new technology production methods. Quality and thoroughness of training schemes vary, so it is essential to find out as much as possible about them before accepting a traineeship. 1 or 2 groups now run their own training schemes independently of the NCTJ.

NVQs/SVQs: the industry has agreed in principle that there should eventually be a single qualification for journalism with NVQ hallmarking. NVQs/SVQs have been introduced at level 4 in newspaper journalism in 3 subjects: writing, production journalism and press photography. Eventually, the NCE and NVQ frameworks are likely to be combined. Meanwhile it has been agreed: 1. that the NCTJ preliminary examinations can provide the necessary evidence of underpinning knowledge needed for NVQs/SVQs; 2. that candidates who have the NVQ (writing) can sit the NCE without further proof of qualification (i.e the preliminary examination). However, basic training courses remain essential; the actual qualifications taken will probably depend on the employing paper's policy.

1-year full-time pre-entry courses: 2 A-levels required. Over one-third of entrants to newspaper journalism now take such courses, at colleges of further and higher education. Courses shorten subsequent traineeship by 6 months. A few candidates are sponsored by newspapers; the majority are accepted after having taken a written test and been interviewed by the NCTJ, to which applications must be made. Grants are not mandatory (see

p. xxvi). Courses do not guarantee employment. There are also *2-year Higher National Diploma courses* at a few institutions.

Post-graduate courses (20 weeks to one year): Graduates from these courses also have to start as trainees, but they take the NCE after 18 months' training.

Some national papers are taking on trainees without previous experience and – *very rarely* – doing this through the NCTJ training scheme.

NOTE: The NCTJ also now runs a distance-learning course in sub-editing, open to journalists and non-journalists: this can contribute towards an NVQ in newspaper journalism (production).

Magazines

The Periodicals Training Council accredits a number of vocational courses for intending periodical journalists. These include:

Three courses at the London College of Printing and Distribution (part of the London Institute):

    1. *2-year BTEC HND in Journalism.*

    2. *BA Hons in Journalism.*

    3. *1-term postgraduate course in periodical journalism.*

3-year BA degree in Promotion focusing on fashion and beauty journalism at the London College of Fashion.

The post-graduate courses at City and Cardiff universities include a periodical journalism option.

Full-time 13-week training course run by Reed Business Publishing includes work experience on their magazines (no fee). Only a handful of students accepted for each course. Successful students may be offered jobs within the group or in other publishing companies. 9-week post-graduate course run by PMA Training (fee approximately £2,000 in 1995).

The PTC can provide the full list.

An industry-wide Editorial Training Scheme which was run by the Periodical Training Council for large publishing houses was discontinued due to the recession, but may re-start in 1996.

NVQs in periodical journalism are available at levels 3 and 4. The National Council for the Training of Journalists offers a distance-learning course in periodical journalism: this is suitable for would-be magazine writers, or those who are working part-time in this field and/or are wanting to prepare for NVQs.

NOTE: First degrees in journalism have been introduced. Although these will be very attractive to school-leavers they are unlikely to give their graduates any real advantage over entry routes outlined above for either newspaper or periodical journalism. The same applies to media studies courses. Most editors prefer to take candidates who have shown breadth of interest by studying disciplines other than journalism/communications/media. Vocational training then follows the degree.

Magazine journalism training is much less tightly structured than newspaper training and entry is still largely with specialist knowledge (especially scientific/technical/computing, but also other expertise, from drama to sport, education to law) and with writing/editing ability. Quite a few arts graduates are editing technical journals.

Competition for trainee posts on magazines is fierce. Previous experience in student or freelance journalism is essential. Work on a journal dealing with one particular subject, whether electronics or municipal affairs, is good experience and can be a stepping stone to more general journalism. There is some scope in broadcasting (see p. 526) for experienced reporters. Science and engineering graduates have reasonable scope on the increasing number of publications which deal with various aspects of science and technology (especially information technology/computing) and which try to attract both specialist and lay readers.

Personal attributes   The different jobs demand different talents and temperaments, but all journalists need a feeling for words; the ability to express themselves lucidly and concisely; wide interests; an unbiased approach; a pleasant easy manner so that shy, inarticulate people will talk to them easily; a certain presence so that busy, important people do not feel they are wasting their time answering questions; powers of observation; ability to sift the relevant from the irrelevant; ability to absorb atmosphere and to sum up people and situations quickly; an inquiring mind; great curiosity; the ability to become temporarily interested in anything from apple-growing to Zen Buddhism; resourcefulness; resilience; tact; willingness to work very hard; punctuality; a fairly thick skin (interviewees can be rude). For *senior jobs*: organizing ability.

Late start   *Newspapers*: Late entrants account for 25% of the intake and follow the normal training programme (though this is not compulsory for those aged over 30).
   Magazines: Quite normal for specialists.

Career-break   Near-insurmountable problems as reporter on *newspapers*. Only well-above-average women who have proved their value to the paper before the break have much hope of returning after several years away. Many women turn to freelancing or edit, on a freelance basis, small organizations' or professional magazines: this is almost a cottage industry and badly paid. Fewer problems for feature writers, sub-editors.

Few problems on *magazines*.

Part time   Mainly as freelance. Up to 80% of magazine copy may be written by freelances. Some job-sharing possibilities.

Position of women   *Newspapers*: Half of qualified journalists are women and the proportion of women trainees is 50%. However, their share of senior jobs, though increasing, is still very little indeed; yet there is no shortage of applicants (as there is in some other careers where women do badly). Women have no more difficulty than men getting traineeships, but there seems to be discrimination at subsequent levels (on newspapers, not magazines). Women also still tend to have 'women's stories' allocated to them. They are not given the varied experience (foreign correspondent; assistant to news editor; sub-editor, etc.) which is vital for top jobs. However, this is slowly changing; but women still have to be considerably better journalists, more determined and more un-daunted than their male colleagues, to get beyond middle-level jobs.

Magazines: No problem. Approximately 55% of editorial staff and several editors are women.

Further information   National Council for the Training of Journalists, Latton Bush Centre, Southern Way, Harlow, Essex CM18 7BL

Newspaper Society, Training Department, Bloomsbury House, Bloomsbury Square, 74–7 Great Russell Street, London WC1B 3DA

The Scottish Newspaper Publishers' Association, 48 Palmerston Place, Edinburgh EH12 5DE

Periodicals Training Council, Imperial House, 15–19 Kingsway, London WC2 6UN

Reed Business Publishing, Quadrant House, The Quadrant, Sutton, Surrey SM2 5AS

PMA Training, The Old Anchor, Church Street, Hemingford Grey, Cambs. PE18 9DF

Related careers   ADVERTISING – INFORMATION WORK – PHOTOGRAPHY – PUBLIC RELATIONS – TELEVISION, FILM AND RADIO

Landscape Architecture and Design

Entry qualifications

Vary according to training, but for student membership of Landscape Institute: 3 GCSEs (A–C), 2 A-levels (or equivalent). Mix of science and arts subjects at both levels preferred. See 'Training', below, for graduate entry.

The work

Landscape architects plan and design the outdoor environment. Working with architects, civil engineers, planners or landscape contractors, their task is to reconcile the demands made on the environment by developments such as industrial or housing schemes or new roads with aesthetic and environmental needs. Their aim is to create landscapes which are pleasing, but at the same time functional, economic to build and manage, able to accommodate buildings. They must also take account of the natural environment and nature conservation. In urban areas the work is mainly concerned with the layouts of housing schemes, road works, shopping and pedestrian precincts, business and recreation parks, city regeneration schemes and almost any public space. In the countryside landscape architects plan industrial sites such as power stations and reservoirs and determine how best to blend new roads into their surroundings so that they are as unobtrusive as possible. They work on the restoration of derelict land caused by industrial processes, quarrying or mining. They design layouts for open spaces, anything from spacious grounds for new hospitals to small private gardens, play – and recreation grounds. They may site and design picnic areas in country parks or lay-bys on main highways.

Once the design is agreed with the client, landscape architects invite tenders from contractors, arrange the contract and supervise the subsequent work, to ensure that it is carried out satisfactorily and within the budget. They are also responsible for specifying the right type of plants to achieve the desired appearance at all times of the year and at all stages of growth: this means balancing the amount of maintenance funds available in a public park, for example, with the amount of maintenance needed by the particular plant. An increasingly important part of their work is concerned with environmental assessments. Landscape architects frequently act as expert witnesses at planning and other inquiries affecting the landscape.

Many landscape architects work in private practice, and a large proportion work in the public sector, mainly in local authorities. In public employment they are usually responsible to planning officers or architects, with less freedom than in private practice to carry out their own designs.

Prospects are good. The demand for qualified landscape architects is growing as the need to make the best of our environment is becoming more widely appreciated. Some opportunities in EU countries.

Training

The recommended route
Either: 4-year full-time course at a school of landscape architecture attached to a university or polytechnic plus 1 year's practical experience (which may come between years 3 and 4).

Or: Course in related subject, for example architecture, geography or agriculture, followed by a university diploma or Master's course in landscape architecture, either 2 years full time or longer part time. Both these lead to graduate membership of the Landscape Institute.

Graduate members must gain 2 years' professional experience and pass the Institute's professional practice examination in order to become associate members.

Alternative method of entry
There is no technician grade or qualification in landscape architecture, but it is possible to get into this work by training in a variety of allied disciplines – for example, geography, geology, planning, soil science, plant sciences, rural environment studies, art and design, horticulture – and then learn on the job, working in a landscape architect's or developer's office. Initial training should preferably be at degree level, but there is always some limited scope for people with a flair for design and horticulture who are willing to combine some practical work with designing. This overlaps with gardening/garden design. (See 'Horticulture', p. 22). For membership of the Landscape Institute it is essential to take one of the Institute-recognized courses. Some private courses, which do not lead to membership of the Landscape Institute, are available.

Personal attributes

Visual imagination; flair for design; a keen interest in design and environment; a knowledge of how people live in town and countryside; ease of expression, both in drawing and writing; the ability to work well with other people; a good business head (for private practice).

Late start As vacancies on landscape architecture courses are scarce, young applicants are given preference (but see alternative method of training). With the right initial qualifications it should be possible to make this a second career.

Career-break People who have kept up with developments should have no problems. Reduced subscription available for members temporarily unemployed.

Part time Reasonable opportunities in employment; possibility of running small consultative practice – but part-time work likely to be sporadic rather than regular.

Position of women Women were among founder members of the Institute. Now 40% of members are women. There has never been much discrimination in this career.

Further information The Director General, Landscape Institute, 6–7 Barnard Mews, London SW1 1QU

Related careers AGRICULTURE AND HORTICULTURE – ARCHITECTURE – ART AND DESIGN – ENGINEERING: *Civil Engineering* – TOWN AND COUNTRY PLANNING

Languages

The British notoriously lack foreign language competence and the implications are likely to grow more serious with increasing European integration. In the European market, British companies could be at a real disadvantage compared with European competitors with a polyglot workforce. As one European businessman put it, 'We are happy to sell to you in English, but we like to buy in our own language.' Individuals could also lose out as increased labour mobility within the European Union will favour those with language skills.

Nevertheless, it must still be emphasized that language skills on their own are of very little value. Saying that you can speak German or Italian is, on its own, about as useful to an employer as saying that you can speak English. What matters is the framework of technical, professional or practical skills within which you can apply your languages.

There are very few careers for which languages are the primary skill required, and even these require other skills and qualities. For a growing number of careers, however, languages are a useful, sometimes essential, secondary skill.

Languages as a Primary Skill

Interpreting

The work   *Conference interpreters*
At international conferences interpreters may do either 'simultaneous' (the main type) or 'consecutive' interpreting. They must be exceptionally proficient in at least 2 major languages; an additional knowledge of 1 or more less common languages is a help. *Simultaneous interpreters* relay the meaning of a speech, often on complicated subjects, almost instantaneously. The technique can be learned, but the talent and temperament are inborn. *Consecutive interpreters* relay a speech as a whole, or in large chunks, after each speaker. This requires as much skill as simultaneous interpreting.

Conference interpreters invariably interpret into their own language.

Some interpreters are employed by international agencies; others are freelances and are booked for a particular conference. Most of the year is spent travelling to and from New York, Geneva, Strasbourg, Brussels and London, living in hotels. The life may be luxurious, but it is extremely hectic, with very long irregular hours. Most conference interpreters now are specialists.

Conference interpreting is an extremely small profession. The professional association has only about 2000 members, in all languages, worldwide.

Business and specialist interpreters

Business organizations of many kinds may need interpreters, for example when receiving trade delegations, negotiating international contracts and at trade fairs. Some of these interpreters may need specialist knowledge (such as engineering, information technology, computing, physical science or economics). Translators, both staff and freelance, may undertake this type of work. There are also opportunities working for conference organizers.

Public service interpreters

They are employed mainly by local authority social services departments to help members of ethnic communities whose first language is not English deal with officials in departments. For example, they help them to communicate with social security and housing officials, teachers and medical staff. They may also work in the courts. Employment is usually part time.

Interpreters in the last two groups use ad hoc or liaison interpreting, in which they interpret into and out of two languages, for example in a conversation between speakers of different languages.

Translating

The work Translators must be able to translate idiomatically and to write lucidly and concisely – being bilingual is not sufficient. They translate into their mother-tongue, so the prevalence of English has increased rather than reduced work for English translators.

They need a very good education and specialist knowledge of preferably a range of related subjects, though this may be acquired on the job. Most translations have some specialist content – contracts require some legal knowledge; scientific articles some understanding of the subject-matter; specifications (for construction work, of anything from ships to atomic power stations) need some technical knowledge. Translators often have to discuss phrases and technical jargon with engineers, scientists, lawyers, etc., to get the sense absolutely right; translating is therefore often team-work.

Government departments, and industrial, commercial and research organizations, often have translating departments which employ specialists in particular fields, and sometimes non-specialists, who have, for instance, Chinese or Arabic, as well as 1 or 2 of the more usual languages.

Translating agencies employ specialists, and people who have unusual languages, often on a freelance basis. They like to have on their books a large number of people with widely different specialities and languages, on whom they can call at a moment's notice. There is increasing scope in translating instruction manuals for consumer goods manufacturers.

Much is rushed deadline work, especially for freelances.

Training

It is increasingly important for interpreters and translators to have formal training and qualifications. The main courses and qualifications are:

1. Post-graduate courses, usually lasting 1 year, in technical and specialized translation/interpreting. Candidates must normally have a degree in 2 languages at the same level. Different courses offer different languages; Arabic, Czech, Slovak, Danish and Norwegian are among the more unusual options.

2. A few 4-year degree courses include emphasis on translating and interpreting skills.

3. The Institute of Linguists offers examinations (but not courses) leading to a Diploma in Translation. It is a post-graduate level qualification open to graduates and others who can demonstrate a high level of language competence (e.g. gained by living and working in a foreign country). They also offer a Diploma in Public Service Interpreting. (A number of institutions offer courses; distance-learning is available through the National Extension College and City University.)

4. The Institute of Translation and Interpreting offers practical exams leading to their Diplomas for those with at least 3 years' experience in translating or interpreting.

Personal attributes

An agile mind; interest in current affairs; a knowledge of cultural and social structures not only of their own country but of any country in whose language they specialize; ability to concentrate for long stretches and to work under pressure; ability to work well with others.

Conference interpreters need a calm temperament and the ability to snatch a few hours' sleep at any time.

Teaching
(see TEACHING, p. 517, for details)

Late start   Translating and teaching (see p. 517) possibly; interpreting unlikely.

Career-break   Unless very well established, return might be difficult for interpreters, as competition very keen.

Translating: No need to give up all contacts while raising family.

Part time   Theoretically there should be a good deal available as translating and interpreting are so often done by freelances. However, much of the work has to be done quickly – which means it may not be regular part-time work, but could be a few days' or weeks' rushed full-time work every now and then.

Position of women   Women who have the right knowledge and aptitude do well; women tend to be better than men at languages, but may fall down on the necessary specialist knowledge which sometimes requires long training.

Languages as a Secondary Skill

There are a number of areas in which a knowledge of a foreign language can be a requirement or an asset, though it is not the primary skill and may not be a day-to-day part of the work. They include broadcasting (see p. 526); bilingual secretarial work (see p. 464); librarianship and information work (see p. 227); the Diplomatic Service (see p. 128); travel and tourism (see p. 546); patent agents (see p. 364); banking (see p. 68); law (see p. 250). In industry and commerce languages are undoubtedly becoming more important, but it is impossible to generalize about the roles in which they are most useful. Export marketing is an obvious example, but engineers, computer staff, general managers could all, in some circumstances, need languages. Receptionists and switchboard operators are often the first point of contact with a foreign supplier or customer. You should not consider any of these careers simply as a way to 'use my languages'. Rather, you should recognize competence in a foreign language as a skill that can enhance almost any career, giving an entrée to more interesting prospects, at home and abroad.

General language training

There are many ways in which people may become proficient in a foreign language. Recent education initiatives aim to give more young people at least a starting-point at school. Under the National Curriculum all pupils will have to study a foreign language until the age of 16. GCSEs in languages concentrate much more on oral skills than previous courses did.

No matter which direction your education takes at this point, there will almost certainly be the chance to further develop language skills. Some people will go on to A-levels and then language degrees; the options include a traditional literature-based course, an 'applied' language course with emphasis on oral fluency and the economy, institutions and social climate of the relevant countries, or a degree combining languages with another subject such as law, engineering, business studies, marketing, computer studies and so on. There are also a number of college courses for A-level entrants which offer languages for business, as well as language options in Dip. H.E. and BTEC courses.

Examinations in languages at different levels, and for different purposes, are also offered by the Royal Society of Arts, the London Chamber of Commerce and the Institute of Linguists. NVQs are being developed.

A spell abroad is an extremely useful way to refine language skills. Most schools run exchanges, and most language degree courses include a year abroad. There are also a number of European Community schemes under SOCRATES to encourage young people to work or study in other member states.

Further information

Institute of Linguists, 24a Highbury Grove, London N5 2EA
Institute of Translation and Interpreting, 377 City Road, London EC1V 1NA

Law

Barrister (Advocate in Scotland)

Entry qualifications

First- or second-class honours degree (any subject).

The work

Barristers plead in courts and give advice on legal matters. They clarify points of law and use their critical judgement in deciding what legislation and what precedents are relevant in any particular case. Their expertise helps clients, but barristers are first and foremost concerned with points of law, not with helping individuals: their relation with clients is far more formal than that of solicitors.

Barristers are normally consulted by solicitors on behalf of their clients and do not normally see clients without a solicitor being present. In some instances barristers may be instructed by members of other professions, e.g. accountants, surveyors, architects and overseas lawyers.

Though it is no longer required, most barristers work from 'chambers', sharing overheads and administrative back-up with other barristers. However, each barrister is self-employed; they may not go into partnership or be employed by other barristers. Once in practice, a barrister must wait for briefs by *solicitors* or be given work by the *barristers' clerk* (see p. 254), who 'distributes' work which comes to the set of chambers rather than to a particular barrister in the chambers.

Barristers normally specialize either in *common law*, which includes criminal work (the greatest proportion: it covers any case of law-breaking, however minor the offence), divorce, family, planning, personal injuries litigation and commercial law; or in *chancery work*, a much smaller branch which covers conveyancing, trusts, estate duty, taxation, company law.

In common law the emphasis is on pleading in court ('advocacy'); in chancery on work in chambers, drafting 'opinions' and advising. Common law work appeals, therefore, more to people who enjoy verbal battles and the court's somewhat theatrical atmosphere; chancery work appeals to those who enjoy the challenge of intellectual problem-solving.

Common law barristers usually join one of the six 'circuits' into which England and Wales are divided for legal administration purposes; they may then plead in provincial courts as well as in London. About a third of barristers in independent practice work from provincial chambers.

Barristers earn very little at first and often supplement their income by coaching, or other work, unless they have enough money to live on for the first year or so. Many barristers never attempt to practise at the Bar (others try to, but cannot get into chambers or get work); instead they become legal advisers in industry, or in local or central government. Such work is usually more easily available. It is far less precarious than the Bar, and in industry and commerce can lead to board-level jobs, but the work is not as varied as, nor has it the glamour of, being at the Bar.

The *Civil Service* offers a variety of work (see p. 134). *Justices' Clerks* advise the lay justices (JPs) in magistrates' courts, and have close day-to-day contact with the public.

The *Crown Prosecution Service* is responsible for deciding whether or not to prosecute cases in the criminal court; where they decide to prosecute it is the solicitors and barristers employed at headquarters or in one of the 31 area offices who conduct the case, not, as previously, the police. In Scotland, *Procurators Fiscal*, assisted by Deputes, are the public prosecutors in the sheriff courts. Legal staff at the Crown office deal with more serious crimes.

Barristers, after at least 7 years' practice, are eligible for appointment (by the Lord Chancellor) as Chairpersons of Industrial Tribunals. These Tribunals deal with unfair dismissal, redundancy payments and other matters relating to employment generally. Under the Sex Discrimination Act they also hear complaints from individuals who believe they have been discriminated against in terms of equal pay, promotion, acceptance for a particular job and other employment matters. Other Tribunals involve mental health and social security. Chairpersons are appointed to regional panels and sit on Tribunals within a given area. Appointments can be full time or part time (i.e. some lawyers carry on with their practice as well).

It takes a good deal of determination, and sometimes good contacts, to succeed at the Bar. Now that solicitors have increased rights of advocacy, things could become more difficult for barristers.

Training   Training consists of an *Academic Stage*, a *Vocational Stage* and a *Practical Stage*.

1. The Academic Stage: Students take *either* a qualifying law

degree, which is basically one that covers the 6 'core' subjects (see 'Training', under 'Solicitor', p. 257), *or* a non-law degree followed by a 1-year course for the Common Professional Examination (the CPE) at an approved institution.

Law degree courses vary greatly in emphasis on particular aspects of law. Most include the core subjects, but these are not always compulsory, so students must make sure they take the appropriate subjects in order to fulfil the requirements of the Academic Stage. It is also important to relate content to one's interests and plans: for example some courses concentrate more on international and/or EU law; some on family and welfare law; some on tax and/or company law; some are geared more to private practice, some more to public service. Consult *CRAC Degree Course Guide*, see p. liii.

2. The Vocational Stage: This consists of a 1-year Vocational Training Course at the Inns of Court School of Law. The emphasis is on the practical application of knowledge and advocacy skills. Students develop skills in, for example, negotiation, legal research, problem-solving, opinion-writing, drafting documents, oral and written communication, and presentation. Assessment is continuous and takes into account practical work, tests and examinations. On successful completion of this stage students are 'called to the Bar'. At present the Bar Council Vocational Course is only available at the Inns of Court School of Law. However, it is proposed that other institutions should offer the course from the autumn of 1997. Details of these institutions should be available from the Bar Council from the summer of 1996.

3. The Practical Stage: Barristers wishing to practise at the Bar (or represent business employers in court) must serve 1 year's pupillage. During the first 6 months the pupil takes a background role, reading papers, drafting documents, attending court, helping to prepare cases, and becoming familiar with the rules of conduct and etiquette of the Bar. This period must be spent in chambers. During the second 6 months (which may be spent in commerce or government) a pupil may take cases on his or her own account. In the past the year of pupillage was often a time of financial hardship as pupils were not allowed to earn at all during the first 6 months. Many chambers guarantee a minimum income throughout pupillage. The Bar Council operates a system which identifies chambers with vacancies for pupils and provides this list to possible pupils. It is proposed that a formal clearing house to process applications for pupillage should be in place in January 1997.

Before enrolling on the Vocational Course all Bar students must join one of the four Inns of Court and 'keep terms' by dining in the Hall of their Inn a certain number of times. The purpose of this is to make contacts with practising barristers and to be initiated into the traditional ways of the Bar.

Training (Scot-land)

This is radically different. Scottish barristers, called advocates, must be members of the Faculty of Advocates in order to practise at the Bar. Candidates, known as 'intrants', qualify in 4 stages:

1. *Either* take a law degree from a Scottish university, giving subject-for-subject exemptions from the Faculty examinations *or* (very unusually) take all the Faculty's own examinations. (Many intrants take 1 or 2 Faculty papers because it gives them greater freedom to choose other subjects in their degree courses.)

2. They then take a 1-year full-time course at a Scottish university for the Diploma in Legal Practice (in common with Scottish solicitors).

3. For those wishing to practise: 21 months' (reduced by 9 months in certain cases) traineeship in a solicitor's office, followed by $9\frac{1}{2}$ months' pupillage (known as 'devilling') with a member of the Bar. Solicitors with at least 5 years' experience need to serve only 8 months' pupillage.

4. Pass the Faculty examination in evidence, practice and procedure.

English barristers who have completed a full period of pupillage may be admitted on passing an Aptitude Test.

Personal attributes

A confidence-inspiring personality; power of logical reasoning; gift of expression; a quick brain; capacity for very hard work; tremendous self-confidence; some acting ability, or at least a sense of drama and relish for verbal battles in front of critical audiences; physical stamina; a good voice; resilience.

Late start

Only for the very determined and able. *Exceptional* non-graduates over 25 may be accepted for a special CPE route (details from the Inns of Court School of Law at the Council of Legal Education address, below), but this is very rare. A law degree might be a better bet as it gives a degree more generally accepted in the jobs market. In Scotland, between 1984 and 1988, the average age of persons starting practice at the Bar was 32. About 60% of those admitted to the Faculty have at least 2 years' experience in another career, usually as solicitors.

Career-break

Opinions differ as to how easy this is. Certainly one must be very well established before any break. There is also evidence that a break may damage a woman's career prospects (but not a man's).

Part time   Barristers in practice at the Bar are self-employed practitioners and have some scope in arranging their workloads to suit themselves, but regular part-time work is impossible to arrange. Employed barristers may have more scope, especially in the Civil Service (see p. 134).

Position of women   This has traditionally been one of the most difficult fields for women to succeed in. It was only in the 1970s that women began entering the profession in any numbers at all. Since then the numbers have been rising quite dramatically. In 1969–70, 8% of those called to the Bar were women; in 1979–80, 28%; in 1990–91, 41%. Currently, 22% of barristers practising at the Bar are women. Of those obtaining a tenancy in a set of chambers in 1994, 36% were women. However, 12% of male barristers are QCs (senior advocate and adviser), but less than 3% of women are. This can be important for judicial appointments, where women are also under-represented. Time out for domestic commitments is given as a reason why women take longer to reach senior appointments, but surveys have shown that most of the women who do reach them have *not* had time off; women seem simply to need more time and experience to reach the same levels as men.

Further information   General Council of the Bar, 3 Bedford Road, London WC1R 4DB
Council of Legal Education, 39 Eagle Street, London WC1R 4AJ
Faculty of Advocates, Advocates Library, Parliament House, Edinburgh EH1 1RF

Related careers   ACCOUNTANCY – CIVIL SERVICE – *Legal Executive/Solicitor (see below)*

Barristers' Clerk (England and Wales only)

Entry qualifica tions   4 GCSEs (A–C), including English language and maths.

The work   This small profession has changed little over the past 100 years or so. Barristers' clerks 'manage' chambers and the barristers working in them (see Barrister, p. 250). The job of senior clerk (or Clerk to Chambers) is a unique mixture of power-behind-the-throne and humdrum clerking, involving negotiating fees and other matters relating to briefs coming to chambers with solicitors (from whom the briefs come). Clerks play a particularly important role in 'building up' young barristers: some briefs come to Chambers rather than to individual barristers and it is the senior clerk who decides which of the young barristers is to be given the brief.

Senior clerks usually have junior clerks who make tea, carry barristers' books and robes to court, type opinions and pleadings. There is no career structure and no hope whatever of progressing to becoming a barrister, but as senior clerks get a commission on all their Chamber's barristers' earnings they often earn more than some of the barristers for whom they are clerking.

Training On the job, with lectures. Clerks can take the BTEC course recommended by the Institute of Barristers' Clerks examination, after 4 years' clerking.

Personal attributes Very great self-confidence and presence; tact; willingness to tackle any kind of menial office job; respect for tradition and the established professional and social pecking order, in which barristers are a long way above clerks; interest in the law.

Late start Upper age for starting is normally 20; people who worked as barristers' secretaries very occasionally switch to clerking at any age: i.e. barristers are not willing to train late entrants, secretaries would know what clerks' duties are.

Career-break Return to work would be very difficult.

Part time Limited opportunities, and none for senior clerk. (No logical reason for this.)

Position of women About 25% of clerks are women. A few women have become senior clerks.

Further information Institute of Barristers' Clerks, 4a Essex Court, Temple, London EC4Y 9AJ

Related careers CIVIL SERVICE – *Legal Executive* – SECRETARIAL AND CLERICAL WORK

Solicitor

Entry qualifications A degree *or* fellowship of the Institute of Legal Executives (see p. 257) (90% of entrants are graduates). In Scotland non-graduates need high grades in the SCE Highers, which must include English and either maths or science or foreign language.

The work A solicitor is a confidential adviser to whom people turn for legal advice and information in a vast variety of personal and business matters. As everyday life becomes more complex, the solicitor is increasingly asked to help in matters where common sense, wisdom and an objective approach are as important as legal knowledge. Whenever possible solicitors try to settle matters out of court.

Solicitors have full rights to represent clients personally in magistrates' and county courts and now have the right to appear as advocates also in the Crown and High Courts (Scottish solicitors have somewhat greater rights in the equivalent courts). Increasing numbers of solicitors practise advocacy. When a barrister is briefed to appear for a client, the preparatory work and the liaison with the client is still undertaken by the solicitor.

The majority of solicitors work in private practices, ranging from large multi-partner departmentalized city firms to small general or even sole-practitioner firms. Work content, conditions and remuneration are correspondingly wide-ranging. A city solicitor will generally specialize immediately, working for corporate clients in mainly commercial fields such as banking, taxation, company law and property development. Solicitors in smaller practices tend to handle a wider range of tasks, usually for individual clients, but everywhere there is a trend to earlier and greater specialization. Typical areas of work in smaller firms are crime, family law, personal injuries, conveyancing, landlord and tenant matters, and smaller-scale commercial work. There are now several small firms which concentrate on providing an expert streamlined service in just 1 or 2 areas, for example medical negligence, entertainment law, immigration.

Most social welfare law, civil and human rights cases, and almost all legally aided cases are undertaken by smaller firms and to some extent by publicly funded law centres, usually in inner-city areas.

Relaxation of traditional rules has enabled solicitors to become involved also in financial services and estate agency and to advertise their services. Solicitors are now required to attend post-qualification continuous education courses.

A solicitor with 3 years' experience can establish a practice but will need capital and contacts to succeed. Securer employment opportunities are available at all levels in local government and the civil service. For those interested exclusively in criminal work there are opportunities in the Crown Prosecution Service or the Procurator Fiscal Service in Scotland. Many commercial, industrial and other organizations employ legal advisers where the nature of the work will depend on the activities of the employer.

After substantial experience solicitors can apply to become

registrars, stipendiary magistrates, recorders or circuit judges. There are also opportunities for appointments to chair industrial and other tribunals.

Training (England and Wales)

There are 3 routes to qualifying:

1. The law degree route (about 75% of solicitors qualify this way). After successfully completing a qualifying law degree (one covering the 7 'core' subjects – constitutional and administrative law, criminal law, contract, tort, trusts, land law and European Law) graduates go on to the new Legal Practice Course. This replaced the Law Society Finals Course in 1993, lasts about 1 academic year, and is more skills-based than the Finals course. Successful completion of the Legal Practice Course is then followed by a 2-year training contract ('articles'), which includes training in at least 3 different areas of law taken from a list of subjects laid down by the Law Society. There is a degree of specialization at this stage so it is important to choose carefully. Most people train in private practice, but there are some opportunities in the Civil Service, local government, the Crown Prosecution Service, the Magistrates' Courts Service, and industry and commerce.

2. The non-law degree route. Graduates take a 1-year course leading to the Common Professional Examination (CPE) or a Diploma in Law before proceeding to the Legal Practice Course and articles as above. Qualifying therefore takes 1 year longer than for law graduates.

3. The non-graduate route. Candidates first become Fellows of the Institute of Legal Executives (see p. 258). They then take the Legal Practice Course and the training contract may be waived.

NOTE: All routes are very competitive. There are nearly 7,000 places in the Legal Practice Course; in 1995, 11,000 applications were made. In the same year fewer than 4,000 training contracts were registered, and the Law Society does not expect these numbers to increase in the foreseeable future. Good grades are essential at both A-level and degree stages. Relevant work experience can also be useful.

Training (Scotland)

Either a law degree at a Scottish university followed by 1-year full-time course for the Diploma in Legal Practice *or* a 3-year training contract with a firm of solicitors leading to the Law Society of Scotland's professional examinations, followed by the Diploma. The law degree route is the most popular. All 'intrants' undergo a 2-year post-Diploma practical training with a practising solicitor, either in private practice or a public service.

Personal attributes Capacity for absorbing facts quickly; logical reasoning; ability to see implications which are not obvious; ability to come to grips with an intricate problem; a good memory for facts and faces; tact; patience; clear and concise expression in writing and in speech; sound judgement of character; an understanding of human behaviour; a personality that inspires confidence.

Late start Mature entrants are advised to take the ILEX route or take a law degree (most academic institutions make concessions for mature students). It is easier than in the past for mature trainees to get articles, but not in prestigious City firms.

Career-break Some firms of solicitors are now instituting formal career break schemes. The Association of Women Solicitors runs courses for returners and is helping universities and colleges to develop courses in this area.

Part time Part-time opportunities are improving in private practice, the Civil Service and local government. The last two also offer job-sharing, but it is very rare in private practice, where part-time work is seen to be more acceptable.

Position of women More than half of trainee solicitors are now women. Women's position within the profession has improved greatly in recent years as a result of market forces (i.e. a shortage of solicitors), but this has now changed dramatically (see NOTE, p. 257). Women do tend to become partners later than men, but to some extent this is probably correlated with their temporary absences. The City of London is perceived as having more liberal attitudes than some provincial firms.

Further information The Law Society, 227 Strand, London WC2A 1BA
Law Society of Scotland, 26 Drumsheugh Gardens, Edinburgh EH3 7YR

Legal Executive (England and Wales only)

Entry qualifications 4 GCSEs (A–C) or equivalent, including NVQ level 3 and GNVQ Intermediate. (A-level law shortens the training.)

The work Legal executives work for a solicitor in much the same way as junior executives work for a managing director: they are responsible for a strictly limited section of work. Solicitors are in overall control, make contact with clients and lay down policy. Legal executives usually specialize in one particular branch of the law – probate, conveyancing, litigation, company law, etc. Their day-to-day work will include: looking up references in law books, preparing documents, interviewing clients and witnesses and conferring with clients on points of detail. In small practices, or when managing a branch office, they may also be involved with the whole spectrum of work.

Although they cannot speak in open court, legal executives undertake advocacy before judges of the County Court and Masters of the High Court on preliminary, or interlocutory, matters. They also have some limited rights of audience in the County Court, particularly on family matters.

Legal executives may become solicitors in 1 or 2 years after becoming Fellows (see p. 257).

Training
On the job, together with part-time training at day-release or evening classes, or by approved correspondence course, for the 2-part Institute of Legal Executives' Membership Examination. The syllabus includes general legal subjects and practice and procedure, and allows for specialization in one branch of the law. Training time varies from 2 to 4 years, but each part *normally* takes 2 years. There are a small number of full-time courses for Part 1. After 5 years' relevant employment (2 of which must follow Part 2) members can become Fellows.

NVQs in legal work will become available by the end of 1996.

Personal attributes
Sufficient powers of concentration to detect relevant details in a mass of complex documentation; patience and perseverance; self-confidence and ability to discuss matters with all types of people from criminals to judges. Common sense and good practical skills.

Late start
Over-21s do not need specific educational qualifications: many decide to become legal executives after having worked as legal secretaries. It is possible to prepare for the Membership Examination without being in relevant employment.

Career-break
Should be no problem for people who keep up with legislative changes.

Part time
Some opportunities for jobs and also for training, but promotion is difficult. Job-sharing should be possible.

Position of women	This used to be an all-male profession; now over 60% of student members of the ILE are women and they hold about half of senior posts. Many women have taken the ILE examinations while being employed as clerk or secretary, and have progressed to a more responsible job once they have passed.
Further information	The Institute of Legal Executives, Kempston Manor, Kempston, Bedford MK42 7AB

Related careers	*Barrister/Barristers' Clerk/Solicitor (see above)/Licensed Conveyancer (see below)* – CHARTERED SECRETARY

Licensed Conveyancers (England and Wales only)

Solicitors no longer have a monopoly in conveyancing property. Independent conveyancers may work on their own or in solicitors' or local government offices.

Entrants need to have 4 GCSEs (A–C), including English. Mature students over 25 may be accepted with relevant experience only. Training is in 2 parts:

1. Part-time or correspondence study for the Council for Licensed Conveyancers examinations Foundation and Finals. Certain exemptions are available to those who have legal qualifications and experience in conveyancing.

2. 2 years' supervised full-time practical training, full-time, part-time, before, after or whilst studying for the examinations.

Further details, including information on approved courses and possible exemptions from Part 1, from the Council for Licensed Conveyancers, 16 Glebe Road, Chelmsford, Essex CM1 1QG.

Leisure/Recreation Management

Though we may not have become the 'leisure society' as predicted some years ago, people are spending more time and money on leisure activities. The leisure industry is enormous and employs 13·5% of all UK employees. At its broadest it includes everything from hotels and catering to zoos and safari parks, taking in pubs, wine bars, cinemas, theme parks and heritage sites, sport and leisure centres, museums, art galleries and theatres, parks and playgrounds, even libraries. Though this may suit economists and industry analysts, it is not a practical starting-point for career-choosers. Running a pub is almost certainly not what someone turning to this chapter has in mind; nor is your average librarian likely to consider himself or herself as part of the leisure industry. Many people who will find themselves in this broad-sweep leisure industry are likely to have interests and motivations that lead them to other chapters in this book. Nevertheless, it is helpful for people who see leisure as primarily sport and physical recreation to recognize that the opportunities are very much wider than is commonly realized.

Entry qualifications None specified. In practice professional qualification and/or administrative experience.

The work The leisure industry has developed piecemeal, but it is characterized by growth, diversity and increasing integration. It is generally recognized that leisure and recreation are an important aspect of the well-being of both individuals and the community; it is also recognized that well-run leisure facilities can be profitable. So more facilities are being developed. They are increasingly sophisticated in response to market demand. Where once you had swimming pools you now have 'leisure pools' with waves, water slides, deck-chairs, and interior landscaping.

Integration occurs on several levels. Local authorities (who used to be the largest employers of leisure management staff, though they have now been outstripped by the private and voluntary sectors) have established integrated, multidisciplinary departments to cover indoor and outdoor sports, parks and countryside, the arts, community and children's play facilities, entertainments and libraries and tourism. Large-scale complexes are being developed where people can, for example, shop, eat, swim, bowl, or take in a film or concert. Increasingly, leisure facilities are a partnership of public and private sectors with, for example, an authority providing finance for a development, while a private concern manages it on a contract basis. In addition to local authority facilities there are opportunities in, for example, company sports and social clubs, countryside and theme parks, the Sports Council and governing bodies of individual sports, the Arts Council, arts centres, theatres and concert halls.

The work involved obviously varies a great deal and it is possible to give only a few examples. *Senior managers*, whatever their title, are responsible for financial management, marketing, promotion, and management and motivation of staff who might include administration, catering, maintenance and specialists, e.g. coaches or instructors. *Assistant managers* generally look after a particular function (bookings and administration, for example), a facility (e.g. the swimming pool and all associated activities) or a range of activities (e.g. all outdoor sports or entertainments in an authority's parks). *Supervisors* are concerned with the day-to-day running of activities and the work of staff such as poolside staff, gardeners or entertainment centre staff. There are variations on this pattern: in a smaller centre a manager will have to take on a broader range of responsibilities, while in a larger facility there may be more specialized roles. Depending on the size and nature of the organization there may also be central roles in policy formulation, budgeting and planning.

By definition 'leisure' is when you are not working, so leisure staff at operational levels must work when most other people are not working.

The leisure industry is a very broad-based pyramid with many more jobs at basic than at senior levels. Its relative lack of structure, however, makes it a fairly easy pyramid to climb for those with the right motivation and qualifications. On the other hand entrants often have to start at a level lower than their paper qualifications seem to warrant.

Some areas of this vast field are obviously more specialized. *Arts administration*, for example, has a particular character and appeal, especially for graduates. It entails enabling artistic events (plays, concerts, etc.) to take place. This may involve planning, publicity, engaging performers, booking venues, handling ticket sales, finance (often including negotiating grants and sponsorship), maintenance of buildings and general administration. The actual range of tasks will depend on the size and nature of the organization – in a small company managers might have to sell tickets at the door, at the Barbican they won't! There are a few relevant degrees and post-graduate courses, as well as options on more general leisure courses (see 'Training', below). There is still, however, a large foot-in-the-door element in this field and many people develop careers from spare-time activities and voluntary work.

Training   It is becoming increasingly necessary to have relevant educational or professional qualifications. Nevertheless, particularly in commercial leisure centres, successful managers may have few qualifications but lots of flair and entrepreneurial skills. Generally speaking, however, and certainly for local authority posts, systematic training is advisable.

The Institute of Leisure and Amenity Management offers four qualifications achieved through a work-based practical research project:
  1. The ILAM First Award – pre-entry requirements are 4 GCSEs (A–C) or equivalent; GNVQ/GSVQ Intermediate in Leisure and Tourism; N/SVQs in appropriate leisure fields at Level 2; a relevant City and Guilds qualification.
  2. ILAM Certificate in Leisure Operations – pre-entry requirements are 2 A-levels or equivalent; N/SVQs in appropriate leisure related fields at level 3; or relevant BTEC, City and Guilds or relevant management qualification.
  3. ILAM Certificate in Leisure Management – pre-entry requirements are N/SVQs in appropriate leisure fields at level 4; BTEC Continuing Education Certificate in Leisure Management or HNC/D in Leisure Studies or other leisure-related field; relevant management qualifications; a leisure-related or business and finance degree.
  4. ILAM Diploma in Leisure Management – pre-entry requirements are the ILAM Certificate in Leisure Management; a recognized degree or postgraduate qualification.
An individual wishing to enter the ILAM Qualification Scheme who has worked in the industry but does not have the required qualifications, may apply to ILAM for recognition of their prior experience.

Personal attributes   Good organizing ability; practicality; ability to make different specialists work as a team; interest in the needs of all sections of the community; confidence in dealing with members of the public (even when they are impatient or boisterous).

Late start   No reason why not.

Career-break   Should be possible, but keen competition for jobs.

Part time   Should be possible – also job-sharing – as there is considerable shift-work in some jobs.

Position of women   As there are few traditions, there are no barriers against the promotion of women to be broken down. There are, though, still comparatively few women managers.

Further information   ILAM, Lower Basildon, Reading, Berks. RG8 9NE

Institute of Sport and Recreation Management, 36–38 Sherrard Street, Melton Mowbray, Leicestershire LE13 1XJ

Scottish Sports Council, Caledonia House, South Gyle, Edinburgh, EH12 9DQ

BTEC, SCOTVEC, City and Guilds (see pp. xxi–xxiii)

Related careers   AGRICULTURE AND HORTICULTURE – LOCAL GOVERNMENT – MUSEUMS AND ART GALLERIES – PUBLIC RELATIONS – SPORT – TEACHING

Local Government

Local government is not a career but an employer. More precisely it is more than 500 employers throughout England, Scotland and Wales. Together they employ about 2 million people and spend more than £30 billion every year providing services, many of which are required by law, to the local communities.

In recent years there have been great changes in the way local services are managed. Increasingly services are put out to competitive tender with the council's own workforce in many instances competing with outside firms. Some council departments are run as external consultancies, selling their services to other departments. The idea is that the providers of the service will have to improve efficiency, while the 'purchasers' will develop a keener eye for quality of service and value for money, both of which local residents and businesses are entitled as Council Tax payers to expect. As in other public-sector areas, new management skills are required of those responsible for bringing a more businesslike approach to the provision of public services, e.g. contract management and quality assurance.

Entry qualifications

Most local authority employees hold qualifications relevant to the work they do. Some openings for those with a good general education, usually in administrative posts.

The work

This varies enormously. Local government is enabled or required by law to provide a wide range of services. The larger employers of staff include: education, which includes schools, colleges, the youth service and the careers service; social services; public protection, which includes the work of the police and fire services, consumer protection and environmental health; leisure services, which can include sports and community facilities, libraries, museums, theatres and the promotion of tourism; highways, housing, buildings and planning, which ranges from strategic planning to provision and maintenance of a range of community buildings. Obviously the scope of such activities involves a large number and wide range of people doing different things!

Among the scores of careers in local government are a number which can be pursued both inside and outside of local government.

These include accountancy, law, engineering, computer work, librarianship, public relations and human resources management. Local government is one option within these career areas. For another group of careers local authorities are the exclusive or major employers. These include teaching, social work, town planning, careers advisory work, environmental health and trading standards (consumer protection). Another large group is involved in general administration, advising on policy formulation and procedures and co-ordinating the implementation of policies agreed by the elected councillors. Their work may include servicing committees, research and report-writing, as well as the day-to-day administration ensuring the smooth running of departments and services.

Many of the professionals employed by local authorities provide services directly to the public, e.g. teachers and librarians. Others, however, are part of the vast, essential support structure. Computing and for the most part legal services, for example, are not offered direct to the local community, but they are essential to the provision of education and social services. In fact departments and services are not self-contained and projects usually involve multidisciplinary teams. For example, the building of a new school would involve not only the education department, but architects and surveyors, lawyers, planners, finance, possibly the fire services, even the leisure department if, say, it were intended that the school's sports facilities be used by the community outside school hours.

People may be promoted within a department and authority, but it is common to move among employing authorities, and being willing and able to move can aid rapid progress. It is also becoming increasingly easy, especially for those with good management skills, to move across departments.

Training   Local authorities provide extensive training for all levels of staff, with opportunities to study for appropriate qualifications in a range of areas. The entry point, length and structure of training may vary. In some cases local authorities offer graduate entrants the opportunity to gain the practical training and experience necessary for professional qualification; in others they offer A-level (or equivalent) entrants sponsorship on an appropriate degree course. Other entrants may be sponsored for day-release for relevant qualifications. Among the fields in which training schemes are offered are: personnel (human resources management), IT, environmental health, town planning, trading standards, accountancy, engineering, surveying, careers work, social work, leisure management, architecture, housing management, law.

For individual professions: see individual entries. (Some professionals train with local authorities; others join after qualifying.)

For general administration: entry qualifications vary. An increasing number of administrative officers are *graduates*, with some authorities running special graduate-training schemes. The professional qualification for senior administrators is membership of the Institute of Chartered Secretaries and Administrators, for which day-release may be available. *A-level entrants* may also study for this qualification or for a BTEC Higher award in public administration. Those with *4 GCSEs (A–C)* can begin work and study for BTEC National awards in public administration; those who are motivated and able can continue on to a related BTEC Higher award, a degree and/or ICSA membership. (It is probably best for those who are ambitious to aim for educational qualifications that will take them to the highest entry point possible for them.)

It is difficult to draw lines about who is an administrator and who is not. Many of the professionals mentioned above are part of the administrative structure (for example, personnel), and many qualifications can lead to senior management. In some departments it is very common for the senior management to have grass-roots experience; for example, senior education administrators commonly have teaching experience.

NVQs are increasingly being implemented by local authorities, mainly in Business Administration, Care, and Sport and Recreation, and Modern Apprenticeships are rapidly becoming available to young people.

Personal attributes   Depends on the particular type of work, but generally interest in local affairs; ability to deal with people; organizing ability; ability to work as one of a team. *For senior management*, willingness to carry into effect decisions taken by councillors, whether or not one agrees with them.

Late start   Good for those with relevant experience and, as seen above, so much is relevant. Authorities' policies and practices vary.

Career-break   May be possible. Local authorities have been among the most forward-looking employers on flexible working arrangements. Arrangements vary from authority to authority.

Part time   Over the last few years local authorities have made a virtue of necessity and been among the first to implement job-sharing and other flexible work patterns on a wide scale. Opportunities vary somewhat with type and level of work.

**Position
of
women**
In spite of large numbers of women employed, relatively enlight-ened policies on recruitment, retention and flexible working, very few women have made it to the top in local government. One factor may well be that fewer women are willing or able to move to different authorities to get the breadth of experience required for top jobs. Yet there are doubtless other less obvious barriers, the so-called 'glass ceilings'. METRA (the Metropolitan Authori-ties Recruitment Agency, a consortium of metropolitan and a few other authorities) has established a national working group to identify the real barriers and promote the extension of good practice including courses for returners, work-shadowing, re-fresher courses, support networks, childcare provision and asser-tiveness courses for women.

**Further
informa-
tion**
'Local Government Opportunities' at:
Local Government Management Board, Arndale House, Arndale
  Centre, Luton LU1 2TS
Or:
METRA Services Limited, P O Box 1540, Homer Road, Solihull,
  West Midlands B91 3QB

**Related
careers**
CIVIL SERVICE

Logistics, Distribution and Transport Management

See 'Training'.

Logistics is a relatively new term to describe the management of the 'supply chain', from raw materials right through to the point at which the product is sold, used or consumed. Logistics is a vital part of manufacturing, retailing, local and central government departments and the armed forces. The final product could be anything from a loaf of bread in a supermarket, a car in a high street showroom, military supplies in a war zone, a pint of beer in the pub, petrol in a filling station, or a pair of surgical gloves in an operating theatre. Some estimates show that over a quarter of the UK population works in a logistics-related job.

There are two main reasons why logistics has become a specialist function, both concerned with giving companies a competitive edge. The first is the rapid development of microcomputers and information technology and their applications to logistics and distribution. For example, when the checkout operator's scanner 'reads' the label on a tin of dog food, a message is sent by computer to the supplier to say that the item has been sold and needs replacing. Similar systems enable a car manufacturer to monitor the exact level of stock of components and to order more to arrive 'just in time' – storage space is costly, so this system saves money. The second is the drive to provide better customer service: customers not only want basics, such as the right amount of raw materials arriving at the right time, but may be attracted by extra services, for example after-sales support or disposal of waste products.

The aim of all those involved in logistics is to ensure that the right resource is in the right place at the right time. All managers need an understanding of the issues involved, but, increasingly in larger organizations, logistics specialists are employed to oversee every link in the chain. Companies and organizations may have their own logistics department or they may use outside logistics services. These services may manage the whole supply business or may deal solely with *transport* or *storage*.

Job titles in logistics and distribution management vary between employers. Logistics manager, transport manager, supply officer, operations manager, warehouse manager, materials planner, inventory controller, commodity manager are some of the most usual. Associated disciplines/functions are MARKETING AND SELLING (see p. 297), PURCHASING AND SUPPLY (see p. 420), RETAIL MANAGEMENT (see p. 431), MANAGEMENT (see p. 275) and finance.

Examples of logistics jobs

Logistics planner/strategist: Planners analyse the various links of the supply chain and try to find ways of making the whole work ever more smoothly and efficiently. The key is the flow of information at every stage and this is where sophisticated computer systems can be so effective. Planners working in logistics consultancies will work with managers in the client's organization to look at logistics issues such as warehousing, supply, materials handling, transport and IT systems.

Road transport manager (freight): The vast majority of goods in Britain (and only slightly fewer in Europe) are carried by road. Movement of goods can be carried out by suppliers/manufacturers/retailers' own transport fleets (known as 'own account' operations) or by 'third party' operations. These specialists include small local hauliers and huge national and international carriers whose lorries are a common sight on motorways and at ports. A transport manager will oversee a fleet of vehicles and their drivers, making sure that deliveries reach customers on time and in good condition. The many aspects of running a transport business include finance, purchase and maintenance of vehicles, recruitment and training of drivers, safety (both of vehicles and in the loading and unloading of dangerous substances), looking for ways of making lorries more environmentally friendly (for example by changes in design and limiting of speed). Movement of lorries needs to be planned to ensure the lowest mileage and, wherever possible, 'backloading' – collecting a load for the return journey.

Warehouse manager: Many manufacturers and retailers own and operate their own warehouses. Others use specialist distribution companies who may offer both transport and storage services. Warehouse managers may operate a warehouse dedicated to one customer's goods or provide storage, packaging and handling services to several different customers. The efficient use of space, the use of sophisticated systems for the checking in and out of goods means fewer people are employed in warehouses than in the past, but managers still have to oversee people, vehicles and systems.

Training   Entry to trainee management posts is *either* with a degree/HND in transport/logistics/distribution, *or* a degree/HND in another discipline with or without a relevant postgraduate qualification, *or* into a junior post as a school-leaver (A-levels in geography or economics useful) followed by study on-the-job for professional qualifications. Many people working in this area have not gained formal qualifications, but these are becoming more important, especially where recognition by other European countries is necessary.

The two main professional organizations are the Chartered Institute of Transport (CIT) and Institute of Logistics and Distribution Management. Both offer routes to membership for school-leavers and for graduates/HND holders.

The Chartered Institute of Transport
The Certificate is the junior qualification. Study is part-time, by distance learning or through an in-company training scheme. Trainees may take further courses to give access on to the degree-level Diploma (the qualifying examination for membership) which contains core subjects (transport economics, management accounting and finance, management of transport operations, human resource management), various options and a project. Full or partial exemptions are given to entrants with relevant degrees/HNDs. Transport managers have to be given an operating licence for which they have to show they are professionally competent (usually through the RSA Certificate of Professional Competence, see RSA, p. xxiii).

Institute of Logistics and Distribution Management
The introductory Foundation course is for supervisors and provides entry to the Certificate: this is for first line managers and students specialize in either warehousing, transport or inventory management as well as studying core modules in managing people, managing resources and logistics management. The Diploma (degree level) is for potential senior managers: the course covers materials handling, warehousing, transport, materials management, financial management, human resource management and planning the logistics function. The Advanced Diploma is accepted as a recognized qualification across Europe (through the European Logistics Association). There are various study options for all three awards.

NVQs/SVQs are being introduced.

Personal   Practical, analytical mind; interest in problem-solving; ability to
attributes see the large picture as well as attending to detail; independence
and willingness to take responsibility; good communication and
negotiation skills; for many jobs, willingness to move from one
function to another; ability to cope with pressure and frequent
changes; ability to motivate and lead others.

Late start Many people have moved sideways into logistics functions or
moved up from clerical or operational roles (many transport
managers started as drivers). This *may* become less common as
graduate entry grows, but it will depend on whether or not the
candidate has relevant previous experience.

Career-   Too early to say, but it would be essential to keep up to date with
break   developments.

Part time No reason why it should not be possible.

Position This type of work has tended to be male-dominated, but certainly
of   at graduate entry level women are very successful, not least
women   because of their good negotiating skills.

Related Specializations

Freight Forwarding

Freight Forwarders: arrange transport of all types of freight to
and from anywhere in the world. They search out the most
efficient method or combination of methods of transport in each
particular case, evaluating respectively the need for speed, security,
refrigeration, the fragility of the goods, etc. Goods may be sent by
rail, road, air or sea, or by a combination of several modes of
transport. Freight forwarders must be well acquainted with the
advantages and disadvantages of the various methods of transport
(which they are likely to learn by experience and from colleagues
rather than from the transporters themselves), and with the intricacies of freight handling and storage and the different techniques
and arrangements in the various ports and airports all over the
world. They must make it their business to find out routes which,
though possibly longer in mileage, may be more efficient because

turn-round arrangements in some ports and airports are quicker than in others.

They are also responsible for documentation, such as Bills of Lading, import and export licences, and for specialized packing and warehousing.

Some freight forwarders specialize in certain commodities or geographical areas; others in certain methods of transport and/or types of packing or warehousing.

Training   On the job with part-time or distance learning study leading to membership of the Institute of Freight Forwarders.

The Advanced Certificate in Overseas Trade is the first-stage professional exam. This is followed by 4 modules: geography in transportation (compulsory) and 3 options, including advanced customs, dangerous goods (surface), foreign languages for industry and commerce.

The IFF also recognizes the NVQ/SVQ level 2 in International Trade and Services; levels 3 and 4 are being introduced. The GNVQ in Retail and Distributive Services (see p. xx) has options in International Trade.

Shipbroking

Shipbrokers: match up empty ships with cargoes and negotiate terms on behalf of their clients. This process is known as 'fixing', and is rather like solving a giant jigsaw puzzle. Shipbrokers may use a regular cargo run or charter a ship for a single voyage or a series of voyages, or a part of a ship's freight space. They also act as agents for shipowners when their ships are in port and deal with customs formalities, loading documentation, arrangements for the crew and any problems that may crop up. Shipbrokers also buy and sell ships for their clients. Some specialize in one activity, others are involved in several.

Shipbrokers often work long and irregular hours, as they have to be in telephone contact with people all over the world during their working hours.

Training   Trainee shipbrokers take a correspondence course (there is only one college course, at Guildhall University) leading to membership of the Institute of Chartered Shipbrokers. For the Foundation Diploma in Shipping they take one compulsory subject, Introduction to Shipping, and one other. For the Qualifying examinations they take 3 specialist subjects of their choice: these include Ship Sale and Purchase, Marine Insurance, Tanker Chartering, Dry Cargo Chartering and (in conjunction with the Chartered Institute of Transport) International Through Transport. Partial exemptions may be given to entrants with relevant qualifications.

Further information

Chartered Institute of Transport, 80 Portland Place, London W1N 4DP

Institute of Logistics and Distribution Management, Douglas House, Queen Square, Corby, Northants NN17 1PL

Institute of Freight Forwarders, British International Freight Association, Redfern House, Browells Lane, Feltham, Middlesex TW13 7EP

Institute of Chartered Shipbrokers, 3 Gracechurch Street, London EC3V 0AT

Related careers

MANAGEMENT – MARKETING AND SELLING – PURCHASING AND SUPPLY – STOCK EXCHANGE AND SECURITIES INDUSTRY – TRAVEL AGENT / TOUR OPERATOR

Management

Entry qualifications   Nothing specific (see 'The work' and 'Training', below), but a degree or professional qualification is advisable.

The work   Management is a vast and confusing field, with vague terminology. It is not so much one structured career as an activity, the purpose of which is to make the best use of available resources – human, money, material, equipment, time – in order to achieve a given objective. It is becoming much more professionalized, with specific, though varied, theories, techniques and training leading to various qualifications (or none). It is also a 'transferable skill': managers now often take their expertise from one type of organization – say manufacturing industry – to another, say tourism. Any system which provides a product, or a service, has to be managed. Someone has to see that things actually happen and that policies are carried out effectively and economically. Traditionally, this has been implemented through a hierarchy of managers sandwiched between the policy-makers at board or equivalent level and the 'doers'. Now, however, the pattern is less one of rigid hierarchies with policy emanating from the top. Companies cannot afford to carry the costs of too many 'non-productive' managers; instead they are beginning to 'empower' staff at all levels and encourage them to create and act on their own initiative. Companies are, therefore, ripping out layers of management and flattening the hierarchy (which can be as few as 4 levels from top to bottom in a large international company) and giving managers considerable autonomy. At all levels, managers must enthuse their subordinates into doing things as efficiently as they – the managers – would wish to have done them themselves.

One of the most important aspects which applies to all types and levels is, therefore, communication: managers spend between 70% and 90% of their time talking to people – in conference, on the phone, in one-to-one discussion. That applies whether a manager manages a whole or part of a supermarket; an international sales force; a large export department or a small section of one; an engineering workshop; a manufacturing company.

There are basically two ways into management: *either* by first becoming a specialist in something, *or* by starting as 'management trainee' in an organization with a management training scheme. But trainee schemes which give broad-based, systematic training are not easy to get for people without qualification, so pre-entry training for a qualification is advisable (see 'Training', below).

Levels of management: There is no clear-cut distinction between junior, middle and senior management. Designations vary between organizations. Rising from one level to another does not necessarily depend on gaining further qualifications. However, qualifications are very useful and may be essential, especially when changing employers.

Most people who choose a management career think of senior, and general, managers – but they are the smallest management section.

Junior managers are the easiest to define. They are usually responsible for controlling the work of a number of people who are all doing the same work – usually work in which the junior managers are trained (or at least which they are able to do) themselves. For example a supervisor fitter is a skilled fitter; a word processing supervisor is a word processor operator or secretary (see p. 464), though he/she is now often a graduate management trainee; a factory production line supervisor has worked on the production line (though possibly as a graduate engineer gaining experience). Junior managers organize the flow of work, and sort out minor problems (often including subordinates' personal ones). In the office of, say, an export department, a junior manager might be responsible for ensuring that documentation relating to goods for one or two countries is dealt with correctly; on the shop-floor junior managers might be responsible for one or two production lines, which could mean about 100 people. Junior managers are also the link with middle management. However, there is a slow but growing trend to 'self-managed work groups', where there is either no manager, or the management element is a small part of the job. Some companies are experimenting with the concept of teams electing their own leaders on an annual basis.

Middle managers co-ordinate and implement policies; increasingly they also set policies. This level of management spans a wide range of jobs and levels of responsibility. The step from junior to middle management is the most crucial on the management ladder: while junior managers are usually responsible for people all doing the same kind of work, middle managers are responsible either for the work of a number of junior managers who are all doing different jobs, or for a larger group of people in the same field. Junior managers who want promotion must therefore broaden their experience and 'move sideways' before moving up. This experience-broadening is part of 'management development' (see PERSONNEL ... MANAGEMENT, p. 368) and should be built into managers' training, but in very many firms young managers have to plan their own career-paths rather than rely on personnel managers to do it for them. This is partly what makes 'management' such a difficult career to plan and to describe. It is not so much qualifications as varied experience, luck, drive and initiative, which matter.

The majority of managers remain middle managers always, gradually taking responsibility for a wider range of activities or for bigger departments. For example a sales manager in charge of a regional sales force is a middle manager and remains so even when responsibility covers a larger sales force, or becomes more important in cash-terms or regions. A manager in charge of a mail order firm's dispatch department, responsible for a large sum of money and for the firm's reputation for reliability, is a middle manager, and might still be a middle manager when, say, also overseeing the dispatch and the packing departments. However, in another firm the job might be designated 'senior manager': it depends on a firm's organization, and their interpretation of what senior management is.

A vital and growing 'senior-middle management' area is '*management of change*'. Typically this is the result of automation. Introduction of new technologies – whether robots in a factory or desk-top computers in an office – is a 'socio-technical' problem. There is as yet no single tried and tested way of tackling this development and its implications. In some companies consultants in 'organizational change' or 'organizational behaviour' (usual backgrounds: social or behavioural science degree plus/or extensive business experience) may be called in to advise; more often managers (departmental, office, production, personnel – it varies enormously) have to cope. These managers may have to deal with employees' fears of new and unknown working practices; with the 'de-skilling' of some jobs and retraining staff for others; with 'slimming down' the workforce and with the search and training for new job opportunities for redundant employees. 'Planning for change' is evolving into a management specialism or at least a new management task (see MANAGEMENT CONSULTANCY, p. 291). Change does not result only from automation. A growing trend is for companies to re-examine how they do things by looking at processes (a chain of activities that delivers value to a customer) rather than functions (bits of processes that represent the way a company is typically organized). This gives much greater scope for rationalization and avoidance of duplication, as well as brand-new ways of working. This is what is usually called 'business process re-engineering or redesign'. Technology may enable this change to happen, but it is not the 'driver' and is only one component of the change. '*Planning for change*' involves close co-operation with computer and other specialists.

Senior managers innovate and lead. They are concerned with strategy. They may plan far ahead and base planning and policy decisions on information and advice from specialist managers. The higher up the ladder, the more creativity, imagination and understanding of economic and social trends and the environment in which an organization operates is required. Senior managers also initiate changes in both the structure and the direction of an organization, and they are responsible for establishing effective lines of communication to ensure that policies are known and understood (and discussed) right down the line. They must also ensure that the effects of policy-implementation are monitored.

There is, however, no strict dividing line between middle and senior managers. Anyone responsible to the board is definitely a senior manager. That usually includes heads of departments – personnel, production, finance, marketing, etc. And 'general managers', who do the co-ordinating, are usually considered senior managers.

Some terms used in management jargon

Line management: A line manager is the manager in charge of whatever the organization's principal activity and main purpose is. In a manufacturing industry it is the production manager; in retail it is the store manager; in an air freight charter company it is the person selling aircraft space. (The term 'line' is apparently derived from 'being in the firing line' – the line manager is the one who tends to get shot at when things go wrong.)

General management: General managers co-ordinate the work of several specialist departments (or functions), for example personnel, production, accountancy, etc. By training they are usually specialists in one of the functions for which they are responsible, which one is immaterial.

Executives and managers: The distinction is vague. Broadly, managers are responsible for controlling other people's work, whereas executives are not necessarily: for example, a legal adviser is a senior executive, but not a manager. But middle or senior managers may also be called executives.

Managers and administrators: Again the distinction is vague. What is called management in industry is often called administration in the public sector. The terms are often interchangeable (in terms of activity), particularly in the forces, but 'administrators' are more likely to be concerned with the smooth running of a department or organization without making any changes; whereas 'managers' are expected to choose the most efficient (or 'cost-effective') of various alternative routes to achieve an objective. Management implies more decision-making. But as in the whole of the management field, different people mean different things by the same terms.

Management covers such a vast range of jobs that it is impossible to generalize about prospects. However, there is a serious shortage of good managers (especially with a technical background). Nevertheless, entry to management trainee jobs is very competitive. Graduate and HND candidates on the whole stand a better chance than others. Over one-third of vacancies are for 'any discipline' graduates; where the discipline is specified, engineering/technological degrees are most in demand with computing subjects and then business/management studies next. First jobs are often in large firms' *manufacturing* (see p. 185), *marketing and sales* (see p. 297), *purchasing and supply* (see p. 420) departments, and in small and medium firms where specialisms are not so clearly defined. There are numerically more openings in small and medium-sized firms than in the large, household name 'first choice' companies and all-round experience in small firms can be very good training.

Employers prefer management trainee applicants who have had some work-experience – if not on a sandwich placement, then in holiday or temporary employment. Having worked abroad – in whatever capacity – can also be an advantage. It follows that it may be advisable to take almost any job even if it is not a 'management' one, to gain experience of the 'real world' work environment.

Training   Paths into management and progress once in are nothing like as clear-cut as they are in established professions – because of the diversity of management tasks, environment and objectives; of levels of responsibility and of 'management styles' (and because there is no precise, universally agreed definition of 'management'). What has become clear over the last few years is that getting *in* requires a very different combination of qualities and qualifications than getting *on* afterwards. That makes description and definition of training rather difficult. However, here are some guidelines and trends:

There has been a 'qualification inflation': jobs once done by people with O-levels now tend to be done by people with A-levels; jobs once done by people with A-levels now tend to go to graduates or HND holders (though there are some exceptions: in some cases employers are switching back and are now asking for

A-level leavers for jobs for which a few years ago they wanted graduates).

To be considered for a management trainee job, qualifications certainly matter in the majority of cases, but they must be accompanied by the right personal qualities (which vary from one employer to another – for broad guidelines see 'Personal attributes', below). Later, the balance and combination of requirements are different. For promotion, paper qualifications are less important; track record is more important. For example, a person with a degree but unimpressive work experience has fewer promotion/job-change chances than a person who proved managerial ability in a previous job, and somehow acquired the necessary theoretical knowledge. But the relatively few organizations with elaborate management training schemes cannot train all the managers required; so for the majority of potential managers these are the usual ways of qualifying for management in industry, commerce and elsewhere:

Senior management

1. Degree in business or management studies (titles vary). Courses usually include practical experience in industry or commerce (or public authority) which gives students an insight into the real world of work. This enables those who do not enjoy the atmosphere, or find the pace too exacting, to change to some other graduate career. Employers welcome business/management studies graduates because they have had work experience, know what to expect, and have a basic understanding of business. All universities and many colleges of higher education run business/management degrees. These may be full-time or sandwich (i.e. with spells of work experience). There are also part-time business/management degrees, mainly for people in relevant employment, though people who have had previous relevant experience may be accepted. These courses are useful for people who want to return to work after a break or want to switch to a business career while still in other employment. Some 'mixed mode' courses enable students to combine 1 or 2 years' full-time study with 2 or 3 years' part-time study.

Syllabuses vary. Titles vary too, and do not necessarily indicate any specific content or structure. 'Management Science' does not involve more management science than does 'Business Studies', for example. All courses contain a systematic introduction to management theories and techniques and to the various business functions; most courses specialize and many offer options in a particular branch or management function – for example, marketing or international marketing; industrial relations; export management; manpower planning; finance; organizational behaviour, etc.

Some courses are more suitable for people interested in, for example, 'human resources management'; others for those interested in business economics/finance; or in transport or distribution or engineering management. Students should look carefully at course content and options before applying.

Entry requirements: Normally any 2 – or now often 3 – A-levels and 3 GCSEs (A–C), including English and maths. Only a few courses require A-level maths; and a few (those which specialize in international marketing or European business administration) a modern language. Most courses accept good BTEC/SCOTVEC National awards (see pp. xxi–xxii) in lieu of A-levels. Mature candidates are often accepted with experience in lieu of qualifications.

2. A degree in any discipline or specialist qualification (see 'The work', above), e.g. in accountancy (p. 1), engineering (p. 181), work study (see MANAGEMENT SERVICES, p. 294).

3. *Post-graduate or post-experience courses*. These fall into two main groups: (i) courses in general management; and (ii) courses leading to specialist qualifications such as personnel management, international marketing, transport, production, export management, etc. Both types of courses can be either full time, part time while in relevant employment, or, possibly, while preparing to go back to work after a break. The best-known courses are at the graduate business schools in London, Warwick, Cranfield and Manchester, but there are a great number of others. Most courses last 1 or 2 years full time or 2–4 years part time. Many are suitable also for people who have been working for a few years but have no academic or professional qualifications, and for people who have been out of employment for some time (women who raised families mainly) as well as for mid-career changers.

Courses may lead to higher degrees (Master of Business Administration – MBA, M.Sc. or M.Phil.) in management sciences, administrative management, industrial management, international management, etc. Titles vary and do not necessarily indicate a particular emphasis or content. Prospective students should look at graduate study guides and carefully study course prospectuses. MBAs especially have proliferated recently.

Another type of course is the Diploma in Management Studies (DMS), the largest single management training scheme. The course structure is very flexible. The DMS can take 9 months full time; but most courses take 2 or 3 years' day- or block-release or evening study. (A few DMS courses are organized to suit people with children to look after, with 10-to-3 attendance. Inquire at local higher education institution about existing or planned short-day courses.) The scheme is intended primarily for people with at least 2 years' middle-management experience. Entry qualifications are *either* HND/C, degree, equivalent professional qualifications; and, often, minimum age 23, *or* minimum age 27 with, usually, at least 4 years' relevant experience in lieu of academic qualifications.

DMS courses update students' knowledge of management techniques and aim to improve their management skills. Most courses also specialize either in a 'management function', for example, personnel; export marketing; production management; or in an 'operational area', for example, recreation/leisure management; transport management; public administration; education administration. Like other vocational training (rather than academic education) courses, DMS course content is constantly changing to meet employers' and students' requirements.

Some business degrees, post-graduate and post-experience courses offer options in 'small business' management, mainly for people who want to set up and run their own small show (see WORKING FOR ONESELF, p. 551) and for those who particularly want to work in small firms.

Below degree-level training

BTEC/SCOTVEC (see pp. xxi, xxii), Higher National Diplomas and Certificates. Higher National Diploma courses are usually 2 years full time or 3 years sandwich. Higher National Certificates are usually taken by day- or block-release while in appropriate employment (see Employers' Training Schemes, below).

All BTEC courses cover what are called 'central themes': (i) money – basically financial consequences and implications of decisions taken; (ii) people – how to get on with and manage them; (iii) communication – overlaps with (ii) and broadly means making sure everybody in an organization understands what others are doing and why. It involves explaining actions and proposals clearly, in writing and verbally; (iv) numeracy and application of new technology to problem solving. This involves learning how to 'quantify' plans, problems and situations, and developing an analytical approach. BTEC's 'central themes' approach should enable students to be flexible and adapt to the different kinds of jobs everyone is likely to be doing throughout their working lives.

On top of the 'central themes', BTEC students specialize in a career group. Some of the main business-related ones are business and finance, business administration, distribution, leisure management, management services, international business, personnel management.

SCOTVEC (see p. xxii) titles are similar and cover much the same ground as BTEC courses.

BTEC/SCOTVEC Higher National awards may lead to complete, and certainly lead to partial, exemption from relevant professional bodies' 'intermediate' examinations; for example, BTEC Business and Finance HND leads to the Chartered Institute of Bankers' and Chartered Institute of Insurance's final examinations. Increasingly, professional bodies in the commercial field accept, or require, BTEC Higher National awards instead of their own 'Stage 1' or 'intermediate' examinations. The advantage from the students' point of view is that they can postpone narrow specialization till they know more about all the related specializations, and that they can more easily switch specializations in mid-career.

Qualifications leading to junior management which can be stepping stones to middle management:

(i) BTEC National Diploma or BTEC National Certificate.

(ii) BTEC Certificate in Management Studies (CMS). A 1-year part-time course for managers and potential managers. Minimum age usually 21, but most students are older; candidates normally have either 5 GCSEs (A–C) or a BTEC National Award, or extensive experience. (Candidates over 25 who have had at least 3 years' supervisory or management experience may be admitted without academic qualifications.) Most courses are 'generalist' – but there are some specialist ones, e.g. National Health Service, Local Government, Recreation/Leisure Management. The course is intended for people who want to progress up the management ladder and have to acquire specific knowledge as well as general education/training to be able to analyse and understand changing management processes and practices.

Employers' training schemes: Many firms (mainly large ones) and public sector industries run training schemes. Entry is at various levels either for training, with day-release, for a professional qualification, or, for professionally qualified people – in whatever subject, but specially business/management, accountancy or engineering – as 'graduate trainee' or 'management trainee'. Schemes vary enormously in content, quality and usefulness to the trainee. In some firms, trainees learn only how to be of use to that particular organization – and thus their future job choice is more limited; in others they get a thorough management training. Detailed research before accepting management trainee jobs is essential. Large organizations often take only, or mainly, graduates for training schemes likely to lead to senior or even senior/middle management. Some organizations consider HND and degree holders on an equal footing. Some large companies –

sometimes as part of a consortium – run in-house MBA pro-grammes tailored to their particular needs.

Open or distance-learning (see p. xxxv) – primarily intended for people at work, but useful also for career-changers and returners: BTEC offers Continuing Education study units in business admin-istration, intended for people over 21 with at least 3 years' work experience (not necessarily immediately preceding the course) who want to update rusty skills or learn new ones. Units include *managing the office, information technology for managers, industrial relations*.

Units can be built up into a Certificate (CBA). Time to com-plete a unit varies from one person to another, but on average a unit is expected to take 90 hours' private study. Tuition material includes video and audio cassettes as well as printed texts. Stu-dents can study entirely on their own as on traditional correspond-ence courses, but links with local colleges are encouraged, so that students have some face-to-face contact and can use libraries. SCOTVEC arrangements are similar.

The Open Business School, part of the Open University (see p. xxxiii), works on similar lines. Courses include tutorials, week-end schools and are at 3 levels: Professional Certificate in Manage-ment, Professional Diploma in Management and MBA. The first two, which can each be completed in a minimum of 1 year, have no entry requirements. The Certificate includes compulsory courses *accounting and the PC for managers* and *managing customer and client relations*, plus either *the effective manager* or *managing health services* or *managing voluntary and non-profit enterprises*.

To gain the Diploma, Certificate holders choose a number of courses from a range that includes *personnel selection and interviewing, managing design, managing people* and *international marketing* and complete a project.

The MBA is in 2 parts: part 1 consists of either the Certificate and Diploma or, for managers aged 27-plus with an honours degree or equivalent, a 9-month foundation course for *the competent manager*. Henley Management College and some other establishments are also running, or planning, distance-learning schemes. (Southampton Institute has recently launched the first MBA by computer conferencing and the Internet.)

NVQs/SVQs

These vocational qualifications are becoming established quite fast among managers. The 'lead body' for management, respons-ible for setting standards for NVQs/SVQs, is the Management Charter Initiative (MCI). This was set up in 1990 amid concern among employers and government about Britain's poor record in management training and the damaging effect this had on the country's international competitiveness. The MCI's aim has been to encourage employers to make a commitment to a 10-point code of good management practice. It has developed a set of management standards which form a benchmark against which managers' competence can be measured at 4 levels: supervisor, first line, middle and senior. The MCI does not itself accredit NVQs/SVQs: this is done by a number of organizations, including the Institute of Management, City and Guilds and SCOTVEC. Some NVQs/SVQs are awarded together with existing qualifications. For example a level 4 NVQ can be awarded with a BTEC National Certificate. The Institute of Management's own awards – Certificate in Supervisory Management, Certificate in Management, Diploma in Management – lead to NVQs at levels 3–5.

Personal attributes Numeracy, business acumen, the ability to get on well with and be respected by people at all levels in the hierarchy, natural authority, willingness to take the blame for subordinates' misdeeds, self-confidence, unflappability in crises, organizing ability. *For senior management*: an analytical brain; creativity and imagination; ability to see implications and consequences of decisions and actions taken; ability to sift relevant facts from a mass of irrelevant information; enjoyment of power and responsibility; a fairly thick skin to cope with unavoidable clashes of temperament and opinion; resilience, courage, entrepreneurial flair; boundless ambition; ability to take snap-decisions without worrying about them afterwards; physical and mental energy.

Late start See above for post-graduate courses, DMS and Open Learning.

A few companies, so far mainly in retail and in catering, are encouraging women of 30-plus to become management trainees. Candidates are expected to have a degree, or professional qualification, or relevant experience which is usually selling or secretarial; but a few companies realize that women who have managed a home, family, voluntary work and/or hobbies of some kind have in fact been 'project managers', i.e. they know how to bring different strands together.

Career-break See below.

Part time Few opportunities at present; there could be more in future, *if* women present their own proposals for job-shares or other arrangements.

**Position
of
women**

Women should have a great future in management, but they are actually faring worse in industrial/commercial management than in the professions. Only 8·75% of the Institute of Management's members are women. (However, of the 1994/5 intake 40% were women!) BIM members are middle and senior managers and normally must have degrees or professional qualifications to be eligible for membership. (This figure is a far better indicator of women's share of responsible management positions than census and labour force survey figures which give women's share of management jobs variously as between 6% and 22%. These figures include supervisory and junior management jobs.) The majority of women managers – all levels – are in service industries like retail or catering rather than in wealth-creating manufacturing, and in personnel rather than in 'sharp end' functions like production or financial management. Yet manufacturing industry is desperately short of *good* managers, and for today's 'participative' management style establishing and maintaining good personal relationships with a wide variety of types of people is considered one of the most important management qualities. Women are supposed to be 'good with people', so it is illogical that so few are managers. As industry now realizes that it cannot afford to waste half the nation's management potential simply because it happens to be held by females, several research projects (and many conferences) have been funded in recent years by government and industry to find out (a) why women are making such slow progress in industry (it is not just discrimination; it is clearly more complicated than that), and (b) what can be done to get more women managers.

Various research projects have identified (or, perhaps, confirmed?) that there are three basic and interrelated reasons why women do badly in this traditionally male area:

1. *Organizational causes*: Traditional career paths were designed for men, and have not been sufficiently adapted to take account of the fact that most women want to have children and a career.

2. *Assumptions* which do not stand up when tested: for example it is still widely believed that women management trainees/managers leave their first employer sooner than their male colleagues, and before they have 'paid off' the money invested in their training. But this is not so. Statistics show that women leave to have babies after 5 to 7 years; men switch employers after 5–7 years. Many women who leave cite poor career prospects as the reason.

Another false assumption is women's alleged worse absentee record. Women employees *as a whole* take more time off, it is true. But, for all employees, the lower the level of responsibility, the higher the level of absenteeism: *far* more women have lowly jobs, so far more take time off. What the statistic obscures is that at middle and senior management level, women's record equals men's. Other assumptions which research has disproved include: women are more emotional at work; men do not want to work for women. Broadly, research has proved that discrimination, founded on false assumptions, persists, but is *very* slowly diminishing.

3. The third and most intractable reason why women do badly in management lies in *women themselves*: their attitudes, aspirations, qualifications. Women lack confidence and hence ambition; they need to do more strategic career-planning than men and in fact they do less. This ties up closely with (1) above: career structures are planned for men: in most companies young men are *assumed* to want to go up the ladder – their careers are almost automatically 'developed'; they are sent on courses and given broadening experience which fits them for promotion. Women have to *ask* for 'career development', to be sent on courses and given broadening experience (this applies at all levels of management, but especially junior management). Women therefore have to be much more highly motivated in order to get as far as men do automatically.

Women find themselves in two kinds of chicken-and-egg situations: (a) If they push themselves forward, they are dubbed aggressive – and that is unacceptable in women managers. If they do not push themselves forward, they are far less likely than men to be noticed and given the training/experience essential for promotion. (b) Women have few 'role models'. As so few women are in top jobs, few girls know, or know of, anyone with whom they can identify, whom they can emulate. They feel they will not be promoted anyway; so they do not try. They do not try, so they do not get promoted.

Women are also less likely than men to have the kind of qualifications which help to get on the management ladder. Fewer women than men have technology- or business-based qualifications. Lower down the ladder fewer girls than boys have the sort of qualifications which enable them to start as technicians and get day-release for technical qualifications which can then lead to supervisory work and junior management.

Research has also found that women's careers 'take off' later than men's. Only when the employer *and the woman herself* seem sure that she takes her career seriously is she considered for appropriate 'career development'. Generally, women's careers lag behind those of men shortly after graduation, long before childbearing becomes an issue. Despite many years of equal opportunities legislation and pressure groups' efforts, women are still less likely to apply for promotion or training than men with equal qualifications and/or experience. There is evidence that recruitment ratios now reflect application ratios. Again, lack of self-confidence and of role-models means that women need stronger personalities or more ambition (and push) than their male colleagues to do equally well.

The most important, though not startling, proposal for attracting more women into industry and commerce is that career structures must take account of women's 'broken career-pattern'. Maternity leave provisions have not solved the problems of combining career and family responsibilities. Fewer women than expected want to return to full-time work after the statutory maternity leave. Many are returning to jobs below their qualification and pre-break status because these are the only jobs they can do part time, or as job-shares (see p. xxviii). An increasing number (though still few) employers now want to minimize this 'waste of human resource' – especially where they have invested heavily in the training of highly qualified women. A number of schemes to encourage and enable women managers to return to work at a level commensurate with their experience have, therefore, emerged. Two types, or levels, of arrangements are being made: (a) Women are encouraged to keep in touch during the *career-break* by, for example, working a few weeks a year, or a day or half day a week. (b) Returners are allowed to work part time (often called 'less than full time') for a few years after the break. This may take the form of, for example, working half a week, or fewer weeks a year than normal (perhaps during term-time only). In as yet a *very* few cases women are connected to the office by computer – not to do computing work but using the computer merely as a communication tool – and visit the office only occasionally. Such schemes may well become more numerous (for both men and women, incidentally).

No blueprint for action has been produced, but, for women with relevant qualifications or with ambition and self-confidence, prospects are now good. Employers like to be seen to be complying with equal opportunities legislation and they also realize that women, as they still have to prove themselves, tend to work harder and be more committed to succeeding than men of comparable ability. The – regrettably few – women who go into the 'sharp end' business functions such as finance or production do particularly well, probably because only women with above-average self-confidence and ability take up jobs in areas which are still very much male preserves.

At present, women are more likely to do well in large than in medium-sized and small companies, and they do well in managing their own business (see WORKING FOR ONESELF, p. 551).

To help women gain the confidence and the social skills needed to progress, many kinds of courses for women have been set up. Some are short day or weekend courses/seminars organized by the Industrial Society and other, smaller organizations. Course titles vary from 'Putting Yourself Across' to 'Getting Going' or 'Assertiveness Training'. All courses stress the need for women to learn how to be assertive without being aggressive, and they explain the vital difference between being aggressive which is a Bad Thing for women in business and being assertive (broadly, confident and polite yet firm) which is a Good Thing. Courses include role-playing and workshops. Then there are longer general management courses, some of which offer special bursaries to women; some are specially for women. Some companies sponsor women to attend. The women's training scene is changing constantly. Some of the post-graduate and post-experience (including post-senior secretarial experience) courses (see 'Training', above) give special scholarships to women and want to attract more women students. Post-graduate and post-experience courses are useful for potential returners and usually accept women who have been away from their jobs for some time: returners' maturity, life-experience and having managed home, family (and especially voluntary work) are recognized as being valuable in management jobs. The Diploma in Management Studies (see 'Training') can be particularly useful for returners.

The Open University runs an 8-week course 'Women into Management' (see also 'Open Learning', p. xxxv). Some post-graduate and post-experience courses still have relatively few women applicants. Approximately 20% of the Association of MBA's members are women (and membership ensures that graduates can keep in touch with developments in business). So while at present a career-break still hinders women's promotion prospects considerably, women do not seem to do as much as they could to ease their return.

Further information

No one specific information point; see specific careers; higher education guides (see p. lii); CRAC Degree Course Guides: BTEC; SCOTVEC

Institute of Management, Management House, Cottingham Road, Corby, Northants NN17 1TT (can supply BIM members with list of management courses, including those specifically for women)

Management Charter Initiative, Russell Square House, 10–12
    Russell Square, London WC1B 5BZ
Women in Management, 64 Marryat Road, London SW19 5BN

**Related
careers**   *Virtually every career offers management opportunities*

Management Consultancy

Entry qualifications

Degree and/or professional qualification and, usually, management experience. This is essentially a '*second career*'.

The work

The term 'management consultant' is often used rather loosely. Some self-styled management consultants do not satisfy established practitioners' or the professional organization's standards. The Institute of Management Consultants – the professional body to which most practitioners belong though they do not have to – defines management consulting as 'the service provided to business, public or other undertakings by an independent and qualified person or persons in identifying and investigating problems concerned with policy, organization, procedures and methods; recommending appropriate action and helping to implement those recommendations'. To be accepted for membership, practitioners are expected to have relevant qualifications and experience.

Management consultants are called upon to improve organizations' effectiveness, diagnose faults and suggest remedies. They may, for example, be called in by a food manufacturer to investigate reasons for the company's declining market-share. Before producing a plan of action to improve matters, they thoroughly research the firm's organization, its potential, and the competition. They might then suggest the company should widen, or narrow, or completely change, its product-range; or they might recommend changes in the company's marketing strategy, its management structure, its industrial relations policy, the introduction of new technology – or a combination of any of these and perhaps other strategies. But work is by no means confined to industry. Consultants are increasingly called in by, for example, charities and public authorities. A particular growth area is 'managing change' in any type of organization – i.e. helping to implement smooth transition from traditional to new working patterns – not only new technology-based ones but also such innovations as job-sharing.

Because the field is so wide and requires so many varieties of expertise, consultants tend to specialize. They may specialize in an aspect of management – for example in information technology

(IT), financial, distribution, marketing, human resources (see PER-
SONNEL . . . MANAGEMENT p. 368), or information management.
They may also specialize in working with one type of organization
– local authorities; charities; manufacturing industry or even one
type of manufacturing such as light engineering, or one type of
service industry such as catering or retail. Others specialize as
consultants in '*change management*' (see p. 277).

Before the recession there was a boom in management consultancy. It then went into decline and has now stabilized at around
5% growth. There is a real shortage of good people at the top
and a surplus at middle and lower levels. Membership of the
Institute is increasingly seen as proof of high standards.

**Training/
experi-
ence**

A few management consultancies recruit new graduates – usually,
but not always, people with technical or business/management
degrees – and give them rigorous internal training, followed by
on-the-job training while working for a client. But the vast majority of recruits have a few years' post-graduate or post-qualification
experience. Many have an MBA. Consultancy firms may then
provide in-house training and/or send staff on external courses.
IT consultancies may be large accountancy firms or associated
companies, major hardware suppliers who are taking on this role
or independents. There is a trend away from big consultancies to
small specialist ones.

**Personal
attributes**

Ability to work as one of a team as well as independently; ability
to cope with possibly hostile attitudes on the part of staff whose
work is being scrutinized; adaptability to working in different
environments; great diplomatic skill to deal with people at all
levels and persuade them to change their ways; self-confidence
and a confidence-inspiring manner; an analytical mind; an open
mind to approach each new set of circumstances on its merits;
curiosity; patience; willingness to work long hours; ability to put
complex matters concisely and simply.

Late start   Maturity and experience are an asset.

**Career-
break**

It is essential to keep up with developments and to keep the break
short.

Part time

Theoretically possible by having small work loads or job-sharing
(see p. xxviii) but so far few women consultants have felt established enough to try unconventional, i.e. less than full-time, work.

Position of women

The proportion of women is still small, but it is increasing as more women have had the opportunity to acquire the essential management experience. Their share of Institute membership is 15–20% and growing. Women have tended to specialize in service industries consultancy and in recruitment/human resources management, though they too cover the whole range, from economists to agriculturalists to IT specialists. Recently, some have set up as specialist consultants in introducing equal opportunities programmes, and in change-to-new-technology management in office work.

Further information

Institute of Management Consultants, 5th Floor, 32–3 Hatton Garden, London EC1N 8DL

Related careers

ACCOUNTANCY – COMPUTING/IT – MANAGEMENT – PERSONNEL/HUMAN RESOURCES MANAGEMENT – MANAGEMENT SERVICES

294

Management Services

Entry qualifications

For *work study* and *organization and methods*, nothing rigid, just appropriate work experience. For *operational research*, a degree, normally in a subject requiring numeracy.

The work

'Management services' is the collective term for a number of functions concerned with the application of analytical techniques to problems concerning the efficient use of manpower, machinery or systems. They provide objective information and analysis for improved management decision-making. The 3 core management services are work study, organization and methods (O & M) and operational research (OR), but some management services departments include other specialists such as economists (see p. 178), statisticians (see p. 451), or systems analysts (see p. 141), while some work study or O & M work might come under another department, for example human resources.

Work Study and Organization and Methods

Work study had its origins in production, and organization and methods in the office, but the aims and principles are basically the same. There are 2 main aspects of the work: method study and work measurement. Method study is the analysis of how operations are carried out and how they might be improved. Work measurement means using specific techniques to measure the time and human effort involved in specific tasks so that standards of performance can be established for planning, control, payment systems and the introduction of new technologies, for example.

In addition to identifying problems, collecting the necessary data, evaluating and proposing solutions, work study and O & M practitioners often get involved in implementing the solutions, for example by training line managers or helping to design a new office layout or select new equipment. Tact, sensitivity and good communication skills are needed at every stage. People at all levels can be reluctant to admit there is a problem and can feel resentful at being 'measured' or threatened by the thought of change. Your solutions may have to be 'sold' to a range of interested parties.

Operational Research

Whereas work study and organization and methods are concerned with the detail of systems in 'the workplace, operational research applies scientific method to complex organizational and management problems at a broader policy or strategic level. The aim is to improve existing systems and methods of decision-making. Many opportunities are with large concerns with extremely complex problems. For example, OR is used by the coal industry to develop strategies which will stand up to a range of possible future prices for coal; factors taken into account are estimates of future demand, availability, and production and freight costs. At the other end of the scale OR has been instrumental in the development of computer packages which enable schools to design a timetable which satisfies the choices of as many pupils as possible.

A key tool of OR is the 'model', a computer simulation of the system to be improved. All sorts of variable factors can be incorporated to see what would happen in given situations if different courses of action were taken. The implications of alternative decisions can then be compared. The operational researcher needs good technical and analytical skills to find the right model, method or technique to suit the problem. He or she also needs good communication skills to help define the problem in consultation with management, gather the necessary information, explain the progress, often to a non-technical audience, and promote the solution at senior levels. Numeracy is important but, unlike in OR's early days when it was very 'hard' or quantitative, there has been an increasing realization that problems often have a large non-quantitative element. When the problems are 'messy', OR needs to be 'soft'.

Most operational researchers are young; OR is a good springboard to general management and to related areas such as corporate planning, marketing, finance, distribution and production.

Training   For work study and O & M, largely on the job as an assistant. Distance, day-release, evening and a few full-time courses are available for the Certificate and Diploma of the Institute of Management Services. It usually takes 3 years of part-time study to reach the Diploma via the Certificate.

For operational research a post-graduate degree may be an advantage. Employers may sponsor students on these courses. On-the-job training is also provided, often supplemented by in-house or outside short courses.

Personal attributes
Numeracy; ability to get on with people at all levels in an organization; good communication skills; methodical approach; analytical mind; tact. *For work study and O & M*, common sense and imagination. *For OR*, ability to understand and explain complicated matters clearly.

Late start
Prospects are good in work study and O & M, which are very much 'second careers'; most people entering have some previous work experience. In OR a late start is possible only for those with suitable degree and industrial experience. As mentioned above, OR is largely a young person's field; it is estimated that some three-quarters of practitioners are under 40.

Career-break
Should be no problem for those who keep in touch. Diversity of settings makes it difficult to be definite.

Part time
Part-time work is rare and likely to take the form of project or consultancy work rather than reduced hours in a regular job. Opinions differ on how job-sharing might work; keeping in touch would be vital and home computer links could help. Given the problem-solving nature of the work, the 'two minds' argument seems persuasive.

Position of women
Only about 8% of members of the Institute of Management Services are women, but at a recent Young OR Conference (for the under-30s) about 50% of the delegates were women. Women who identify these careers and enter them do well. The move from 'hard' to 'soft' OR has probably helped, but more women should recognize how much work study and O & M depend on common sense, organizing ability and establishing good relations with people.

Further information
Institute of Management Services, 1 Cecil Court, London Road, Enfield, Middlesex EN2 6DD
Operational Research Society, Neville House, Waterloo Street, Birmingham B2 5TX

Related careers
ACTUARY – COMPUTING/IT – ENGINEERING – HEALTH AND SAFETY INSPECTORS – MANAGEMENT – SCIENCE: *Mathematical Sciences*

Marketing and Selling

Entry qualifications

Nothing specific; for *Chartered Institute of Marketing's Certificates*: *either* 1 A-level, 4 GCSEs (A–C) including English *or* 5 GCSEs (A–C) plus 1 year's marketing experience *or* BTEC/SCOTVEC National *or* GNVQ Advanced (Business) *or*, if aged over 21, 3 years' experience. For *Advanced Certificate*: the Certificate *or* a degree *or* HND/C. For *Diploma*: *either* the Certificate *or* relevant degree *or* relevant Higher National award. Considerable graduate entry.

Marketing

The work

Effective marketing is the key to profitability and essential for Britain's trading position in the world economy. Marketing goods and services is as skilled an occupation, and as important, as producing them. But marketing is a rather vague term, often used loosely to cover a range of activities. Different establishments interpret the term differently, and titles include brand manager; product manager; development manager; marketing executive; marketing manager; export manufacturing manager, etc. Titles do not necessarily indicate any particular level of responsibility or scope.

The Chartered Institute of Marketing defines the purpose of marketing as follows: 'Marketing is the management process responsible for identifying, anticipating and satisfying customer requirements profitably' – at home and, vitally important, abroad.

Marketing people (sometimes called 'marketers') find out what customers want or, more important, can be persuaded to want, at what price, and then relate potential demand to the company's ability to produce whatever it is, get it to the 'point of sale', and do all that profitably.

Marketing involves *researching* the market and *analysing* research results – which involves devising and organizing surveys and interpreting the results; discussing results with accountants, production, distribution and advertising people. Marketers may suggest the company adapt its existing products to cope with the competition's better products, or with changes in buying habits, or they may think up a totally new product and help to develop and launch it, or they may introduce a better after-sales service.

All these activities have always been carried out in business, but as business has become more complex and professionalized, with decisions being based on researched facts and, above all, figures rather than guesswork and experience, the 'marketing function' has become a 'business profession' and even an academic subject. Its importance in business has grown enormously in recent years. Poor marketing in the past is blamed for poor business performance. This applies particularly to *international marketing*. As exporting is becoming more and more essential for economic survival, international marketing is becoming a vital function in many more businesses. Marketing people have good prospects of going to the top in general management.

Marketing is often split into *consumer goods and services marketing*; *industrial marketing*; and *international marketing* (which could refer to either, and is part of the export business).

In all these activities, marketing involves several types of work: detailed research to establish customers', and potential customers', needs and potential needs: what type of customers, where, might buy at what price, with how effective an after-sales service, etc. Whether it is yet another washing powder or, in industrial marketing, a new piece of office machinery or computer, a new magazine or a food product, the procedure is basically the same. In *industrial marketing*, an engineering or science background is useful, but people switch from one area of marketing to another. In *international marketing*, a thorough understanding of other nations' cultural as well as social and economic set-up is vital (and of course speaking the relevant language). Perhaps the most crucial among several other marketing activities is *sales forecasting*. How many cars with what particular features will country X be willing to buy in 2, 5, 10 years' time?

Marketing people must always base their conclusions on researched social and economic trends, which include statistics. Marketing has a glamorous image, but the basis of it is the correct interpretation of information.

Though the majority of marketing people work in large, often multinational, companies, increasingly medium and small companies are separating 'the marketing function' from general business management.

Selling

Selling is both a career in itself, and an essential part of (and sometimes the best way into) marketing. The two are closely linked: *marketing* finds out what customers want and helps to put the goods/services on the market; *selling* is concerned with finding and dealing with customers for the product/service.

There are different kinds of selling – and various ways of categorizing sales staff. A useful division is between *consumer goods selling* and *specialized selling*. In consumer goods selling (this totally excludes retail and door-to-door selling), sales representatives, or reps, sell to wholesalers and/or, more usually, to retailers. Selling to retailers involves 'merchandising', which means helping the retailer to maximize sales, by promotion campaigns, suggesting ideas for improving shop display, etc. Reps may also advise retailers on new sales techniques, shop display, etc. There is a hierarchy in consumer goods selling, with the *field sales supervisors* and *area sales managers* in charge of reps, and *sales managers* and *sales directors* at head office directing the whole sales operation.

Speciality or *technical* or *industrial selling* is usually done by staff with technical background and perhaps production management experience (see p. 185). An engineering background is particularly useful (see ENGINEERING, p. 181). The speciality selling process differs totally from consumer goods selling: purchasing decisions are made not by shopkeepers or store buyers, but by technical and financial experts. To effect one sale may take months of negotiations, and extensive after-sales service. Speciality sales staff do not necessarily sell only standard products – whether they are large pieces of machinery or machine tools – they may agree for their company to modify a product or produce a 'one-off' piece of equipment.

Sales reps may form part of a team, or be the only rep in the firm. They may have a 'territory' in this country which may require them to be away from home for several days most weeks, or it may be a territory near home – it depends on the kind of product and on how many potential buyers there are within an area.

Exporting

A wide range of companies have export departments and some staff move into the export function from another department, most obviously from sales within the UK. However, companies frequently recruit staff from outside who have particular experience and expertise in dealing with overseas markets. Job titles and functions vary, but examples are:

Export clerk in manufacturing company: checks and acknowledges orders; liaises with production and packing departments;

lets customers know of any delays; organizes necessary paperwork.

Export sales correspondent: prepares quotations, tenders and delivery schedules for customers, often within a geographical area or product range; supervises the work of the export clerk; takes part in sales promotions and deals with overseas agents.

Export area sales or *product manager*: responsible for reaching sales targets within a market or product area; visits and looks after existing customers and agents and researches openings for new business; arranges overseas promotions/exhibitions; negotiates new contracts.

Export manager/director: in charge of all aspects of export function; visits customers and agents in all the company's markets and product areas; appoints new staff; sets sales targets; liaises with UK sales and production managers.

Training   There are various ways into marketing – the most usual way to start is as sales rep. *Manufacturing* (see ENGINEERING, pp. 185, 191) people often move into marketing (which is sometimes better paid). Many graduates go straight into marketing as assistants.

While working as trainee or whatever the title, marketing staff can take part-time courses for the Chartered Institute of Marketing's examinations. These are at 3 levels, Certificate, Advanced Certificate and Diploma.

Part-time courses lead to the Certificate in Marketing or the Certificate in Selling. Both syllabuses include fundamentals of marketing and selling: business communications, promotional practice, marketing environment, management information. (In some subjects there is a common syllabus with the Institute of Chartered Secretaries, see p. 110, and the Institute of Purchasing and Supply, see p. 420.)

Part-time courses also lead to the Advanced Certificate in Marketing or the Advanced Certificate in Sales Management.

For the Diploma in Marketing there are part-time courses and a distance learning scheme. Subjects include international marketing, marketing planning and control, marketing communications, and marketing analysis and decision-making. The Diploma is now accepted by some higher education institutions as an entry qualification for post-graduate study.

For *export marketing* some trainees work for the Institute of Export's examination (see p. 301), by day-release or correspondence study. The syllabus adds export procedure and principles of export management to marketing methods, principles and procedures.

Pre-entry training for marketing is either by business studies degree with marketing option or by specialized marketing degree. These degrees either link marketing to a specific area such as chemicals or textiles or engineering; or concentrate on international marketing and export. An engineering or science degree is a good way into speciality selling.

There are also BTEC/SCOTVEC Higher awards (see pp. xxi, xxii) with marketing export options, and distribution options.

The *Advanced Certificate in International Trade* is jointly run as a first-stage professional examination by the *Institute of Export* and the *Institute of Freight Forwarders* (see p. 274). Students then go on to take part 2 of the institutes' professional exams. (People working in export departments may take the Institute of Export's Certificate in Export Office Practice before the Advanced Certificate.)

Personal attributes

Marketing: A high degree of business acumen and of numeracy; a little risk-taking instinct; self-confidence; ability to assess the effects of economic, social or political events; ability to stand perhaps unjustified criticism when forecasts turn out wrong, due to unforeseeable causes; social awareness and interest in social and economic trends; ability to communicate easily with colleagues and clients, whatever their temperament and their degree of expertise; ability to cope with change.

Selling: Numeracy; extrovert personality; ability to establish instant rapport with people; judgement; sensitivity for gauging right approach to customers; indifference to the occasional rebuff; enjoying being alone when travelling; willingness to be away from home a lot; good listening and communication skills.

Late start

People with technological or business qualifications can switch to marketing.

Career-break

It is not likely that in this competitive field it will be easy for any but the best and most determined people to return to what is essentially still a young person's career. Women with technological or science degrees or experience stand the best chances in industrial marketing.

Part time

Only in backroom research – very few openings indeed, unless able to work for oneself as a consultant.

Position of women

This has traditionally been a man's career, but it is changing. Equal numbers of men and women are joining the Chartered Institute of Marketing. Women have good prospects if they fit the

302   Marketing and Selling

employer's idea of what the 'right type' for any particular job is. Perception, analytical ability, flexibility and good communication skills, which are perceived as female attributes, will stand women in good stead for roles in sales, marketing and customer service. In *export marketing* their scope is limited because employers often claim that in some countries saleswomen and women negotiators are not acceptable. Graduate women stand much better chances than school-leavers, who tend to be offered secretarial jobs 'with a view to progressing in marketing', and then do *not* progress. Female graduate sales reps who are good at their job say they are at an advantage: they tend to be noticed and 'trained up'. So far, however, there are very few women sales directors (except in cosmetics etc.). Potentially it could be a promising area. Especially in *specialized selling*, more women would be genuinely welcome in many organizations. Companies say that not enough women graduates apply. The proportion of female graduates *accepted* is slightly higher than that of males accepted. Probably women who do apply are more highly motivated. It is too early to say, however, what women's promotion prospects to senior sales management positions are. Only about 1 in 20 qualified CIM members over the age of 35 are women. The CIM's Director of Marketing is qualified and a woman.

Further information
Chartered Institute of Marketing, Moor Hall, Cookham, Maidenhead, Berks. SL6 9QH

Institute of Export, Export House, 64 Clifton Street, London EC2A 4HB

Market Research Society, 175 Oxford Street, London W1R 1TA

Related careers
ADVERTISING – LOGISTICS . . . MANAGEMENT – MANAGEMENT – PUBLIC RELATIONS – RETAIL MANAGEMENT

Medicine

Entry qualifications

3 good A-levels (or Scottish equivalent) or 2 A-levels and 2 AS-levels are normally required for entry to medical school. Chemistry is almost always required with other subjects commonly chosen from biology, maths and physics, though an increasing number of medical schools are happy to consider candidates whose third A-level (or AS) is in non-science subjects. A small number of medical schools run a 1-year pre-medical course for candidates without the usual science A-level background (good sciences at GCSE would normally be expected).

General Practice (Family Doctor)

The work

About half of doctors qualifying go into general practice. Family doctors are in the front-line of primary health care. As self-employed practitioners GPs have considerable autonomy in deciding how best to provide the services to patients required under their NHS contracts. Under the recent NHS reforms some practices have become 'fundholders', permitted to purchase services for their patients from hospitals.

All family doctors are involved in: acute disease management, i.e. diagnosing, treating or referring for specialist treatment a range of ailments presented by patients; preventive medicine, helping patients to understand how to prevent, look for and deal with problems; counselling, i.e. dealing with patients' fears and feelings, both those that have a medical basis and those that lead to physical symptoms. General practitioners might also get involved in other work in the community, e.g. in old people's welfare, the Red Cross, nursing homes, schools and businesses. Some do sessional work in hospital out-patient clinics. There is also liaison with other sectors of the NHS, for example hospitals, on the provision of health care.

Most family doctors work in partnership with other doctors. Some practices organize themselves along specialist lines with, perhaps, one partner particularly experienced in obstetrics and gynaecology, while another may have a special interest in stress and another in heart disease.

A typical family doctor's day might consist of a morning

surgery from, say, 8.30 until 11.00 a.m.; routine office work, dealing with telephone inquiries, signing prescriptions, reading the post, dealing with letters to and from hospital consultants; home visits; lunch; visits or clinics (e.g. antenatal, minor operations, diabetic, child development); more office work; evening surgery. Doctors within a practice or several practices normally get together to provide a night and weekend emergency call rota. The larger the rota the less often any one doctor is on duty, but the busier he or she is likely to be when on call.

Recent years have seen enormous changes in general practice. New drugs are continually available; practices have direct access to investigation facilities and new equipment enabling them to provide care over a more interesting range of conditions; practice nurses handle routine procedures and extend health education and preventive work. Computerization is used for repeat prescription control, for the maintenance of registers (e.g. of all women due for cervical screening, or all under-5s due for immunization) and for the compilation of data that enables the doctors to measure and assess what they are doing for their patients as a whole. However, all these developments are merely aids to improve and monitor service. They do not replace the family doctor's traditional role of caring for patients largely by listening to and talking with them.

Hospital Service

The work   *All* doctors start their careers in hospitals, though eventually only about half as many stay there as enter general practice. Doctors who remain in hospital medicine become specialists. There are more than 50 specialities. General medicine group and surgical group are the largest; within each are many sub-specialities ranging from general medicine and general surgery to very small fields like audiological medicine, palliative medicine or paediatric surgery. Other major specialities are accident and emergency, obstetrics and gynaecology, anaesthetics, radiology group, pathology group and psychiatry group.

Both the nature and pattern of work in different fields can vary considerably. For example, general medicine and surgery and obstetrics have far more emergency work than psychiatry or dermatology, while pathology has very little. The nature of the round-the-clock demands on anaesthetists means they have evolved a more predictable shift system than other doctors.

For many years of hospital doctors' careers they are, though fully registered and in paid employment, technically in training posts. As they progress through jobs as house officer, senior house officer, the unified training grade, they take on more and more responsibility under the supervision and guidance of more senior doctors. The most junior doctors take responsibility for practical, routine day-to-day care and administration (keeping records, communicating with families and other members of the medical team), progressing to more advisory work and greater clinical responsibility. Junior doctors' hours are long and irregular; the more senior doctors become, the less they are likely to be called from their beds to an emergency, but the more complex the decision or procedure when they are.

At the head of hospital teams are consultants, who have continuing responsibility for patient care. It can take from 8 to 12 years of specialist training to reach this level, although recent changes are shortening this period.

Doctors' choices of speciality are determined not only by interest and inclination, but often by opportunity. Some fields are very much more popular and competitive than others, and it can take some time and experience before a final choice is made.

Public Health Medicine and Community Health

The work   Public health medicine is concerned with the promotion of the health of a whole community rather than of specific individuals. It is primarily about preventive medicine and there is no direct clinical contact with patients.

Most public health doctors are employed in regional or district health authorities. Their work includes the overall administration, planning and development of the 3 branches of the health service (environmental health, personal health, community care); the development of comprehensive information; and health education services. Community physicians also act as advisers to local authorities, which retain responsibility for running school, environmental and some personal health services.

Environmental health covers infectious disease control and prevention (regular immunization and special immunization campaigns); food and other hygiene inspection; prevention of insanitary conditions in restaurants, shops, housing (including overcrowding); control of noise nuisance and air pollution. The day-to-day work is carried out by environmental health officers (see p. 204).

Personal health services cover provision of antenatal, postnatal and child health clinics; midwifery; district nursing services (see separate entries); care of handicapped children.

Community care covers provision for the care of the mentally ill and handicapped who increasingly live at home or in hostels; support in the home given by social workers; day centres and social clubs for the elderly and handicapped; hostel accommodation and organization; co-operation with local voluntary organizations in the mental health field. (See District and Psychiatric Community Nursing for increase in numbers of patients cared for in the community.)

There are also opportunities for public health doctors in: the four government health departments (England, Scotland, Wales and Northern Ireland); the Public Health Laboratory Service and Communicable Disease Surveillance Centre; medical schools; international agencies such as the World Health Organization; and abroad, especially in developing countries. This is a growth area and there are more training vacancies than can be filled.

Community health clinics are not staffed by public health specialists, but by community medical officers (who probably have a Diploma in Community Health) or by GPs or by those with post-graduate training in obstetrics, paediatrics, geriatrics, etc. Community health offers opportunities for part-time sessional clinic work and mature entrants (returners) are very welcome.

Occupational Health or Occupational Medicine

The work   Occupational medical officers give medical check-ups to employees and work with personnel departments. They also do research into occupational health, studying the effects of diverse environmental conditions on health and efficiency of the staff. The scope of their work is very wide. For example, it might include studying the effects of new technology, chemical processes and underground working on employees. It also requires knowledge of conditions such as occupational asthma, dermatitis and alcoholism and how they affect workers' efficiency. They work closely with trade union representatives and may make suggestions to management about ways to improve employees' health at work.

Research and Teaching

The work   Research into new forms of treatments and new drugs and their effects is done in hospitals, research establishments and drug firms. Doctors can, and usually do, combine clinical and scientific work, but there are also research appointments, often including some teaching, for those who are interested in the scientific side of medicine rather than 'patient contact' (see SCIENCE, p. 438).

Training (all doctors)

This is in 2 parts: pre-registration and post-registration. Doctors must obtain a 'registrable qualification'. There are several, each signified by different initials; all are essentially of equal value.

The undergraduate course takes 5 or 6 years. It has traditionally fallen into 2 parts, a 2-year *pre-clinical* course, including anatomy, physiology and biochemistry, consisting of lectures, laboratory work and a great deal of reading, and a 3-year *clinical* course, when students have contact with patients, take case histories and, under supervision, make diagnoses. However, most medical schools are moving towards a better integration of 'pre-clinical' and 'clinical' subjects throughout the 5 years.

It is vital to look closely at courses since they vary greatly in organization, teaching methods and emphasis. Some include study for a B.Sc. degree, while for others this is optional. Before students get their registrable qualification they must spend a 'pre-registration year' as full-time junior house officer in hospital. (At this stage they start earning.)

Post-registration training is essential, very hard work, and rather haphazard. In some areas junior doctors have to arrange their own succession of hospital 'training posts', but many others have rotational training schemes which doctors slot into. Each training post has to be educationally approved by the relevant Royal College (for example, in England and Wales a training post in surgery has to be approved by the Royal College of Surgeons). Post-registration training, in a succession of approved training posts as senior house officer and unified training grade, can take from 8 to over 12 years before becoming a consultant (it depends mainly on the speciality chosen). During this period of full-time work, doctors study for specialist qualifications (and many fail the exams the first time). Recent changes to specialist training will shorten this period, making it more structured and geographically stable.

Doctors wishing to become *general practitioners* must take a 3-year post-graduate training, consisting of 2 years in a choice of specified full-time hospital (and, sometimes, community medicine) posts, and 1 year as a full-time trainee in general practice (or the equivalent on a part-time basis).

Doctors wishing to become *public health doctors* take the examinations of the Faculty of Public Health: subjects include epidemiology, statistics, aspects of the social services, the principles of administration and management.

Doctors wishing to specialize in *occupational health* or *medicine* take the examinations of the Faculty of Occupational Medicine.

Personal attributes
The ability to communicate with people, take responsibility and to make vital decisions after weighing up all the relevant factors; patience with people unable to express themselves clearly; sympathy without emotional involvement; understanding of and liking for all types of people and tolerance with human weaknesses; self-confidence; conscientiousness; resourcefulness; the energy and stamina to work hard for long and often irregular periods; great powers of concentration; above-average intelligence; good health.

For research: Patience for long-term projects and an inquiring mind.

Late start
Medical schools vary in their policies on accepting mature candidates, so one has to inquire from several before giving up – if determined to start; it becomes very difficult if over 30. Most schools require an upper second honours degree in a related subject, for example biochemistry, or equivalent qualification (including nursing). However, length of training is not reduced even for qualified nurses or people with other related qualifications.

Career-break
Some doctors take a complete break during their careers. It is not advised for those aiming to become consultants. It is essential to keep in touch, otherwise the continuous changes make it difficult to slot back in. Since 1972 there has been a Doctors' Retainer Scheme to enable doctors to maintain a foothold in medicine during periods when domestic commitments prevent full- or part-time work. The Scheme gives the opportunity to do a small number of specially arranged clinical sessions and attend some post-graduate medical education sessions. The doctors are paid a retainer and are required to keep up to date. The Retainer Scheme is not recognized for training purposes and doctors are advised not to remain on the Scheme longer than necessary. Part-time working at consultant level is increasingly offered and has been an option in general medical practice for many years.

Position of women
In general practice 29% of doctors are women: 26% of principals, 53% of trainees, 59% of assistants.

In public health medicine 43% and in community health 76% of doctors are women.

Since 1991 women have accounted for over 50% of medical school entrants. Studies have found that, in general, female medical students are more strongly motivated than men, do better in medical school, and progress more quickly through the early stages of their careers, up to SHO level. However, at registrar level and above, women doctors progress far more slowly than men, especially at consultant level. Women doctors are consistently under-represented at levels from registrar upwards and consistently over-represented in the lower grades. (These studies compared actual with expected achievement and are therefore not distorted by age and the lower expectations and smaller numbers of girls entering in the past.)

Some women complain of discriminatory attitudes in the health service, and there is no question that indirect discrimination is built into the traditional training and employment pyramid. The long training and arduous work conditions of junior hospital doctors disproportionately affect women's progress. Domestic responsibilities do not fit in easily with the long hours of work and study; part-time training is not widespread; and there is a feeling that the doctors who have spent longer than the norm in reaching particular grades, who have had unconventional career patterns, and who are older are regarded less favourably by appointments committees.

In 1991 the Department of Health published *Women Doctors and their Careers*, the report of a working party convened to look into the waste of the talents of women in medicine. As women form a higher proportion of entrants, the implications of failing to pay sufficient attention to their needs are considerable. Among the recommendations of the working party were: increased opportunities for part-time training (for which the Medical Women's Federation has fought for years) at all levels; more flexibility in the way the Royal Colleges assess whether candidates meet their requirements; more part-time career posts; and more flexible working arrangements, including job-sharing and shift work, which would make even full-time working more predictable. There is evidence of progress in all these areas, although women's representation at consultant grade is still worse than expected. However, it varies a great deal by speciality and geographical area.

In general practice women wishing to work part time have had relatively few problems. However, the Medical Women's Federation fears that the new NHS contract for GPs could have an adverse effect on women. By affecting the way in which part-timers are paid, practices may be reluctant to take on part-time partners.

Further information   British Medical Association, BMA House, Tavistock Square, London WC1H 9JP

Studies have commented that prospective doctors, particularly women, need more and better careers advice, especially during training. We recommend: for those considering a career in medicine, *Learning Medicine*, by Peter Richards, published annually by the BMA, £5.95 (1995 edition); for medical students, *Living Medicine – Planning a Career, Choosing a Speciality*, by Peter Richards, published by Cambridge University Press, £10.95 (1990 edition); *Making Your Career in Medicine* is available from the NHS Women's Unit, Eileen House, 80–94 Newington Causeway, London SE1 6EF

Related careers   ANIMALS: *Veterinary Surgeon* – DENTISTRY – ENGINEERING: *Medical or Biomedical Engineering* – NURSING – OCCUPATIONAL THERAPY – OPTICAL WORK: *Optometrist* – ORTHOPTICS – OSTEOPATHY – PHARMACY – PHYSIOTHERAPY – SCIENCE – SOCIAL WORK

NOTE ON COMPLEMENTARY MEDICINE: Complementary medicine is the general name for a number of therapeutic techniques which include acupuncture, osteopathy (see p. 362) and chiropractic, herbal medicine, homeopathy and naturopathy. In recent years interest has been growing in this style of medical practice, which regards health and disease in terms of the whole person. A demand for more treatment is bound to lead to a demand for more practitioners.

Because there is no statutory regulation for complementary medicine (with the exception of osteopathy and chiropractic), training has been a minefield. Courses range from those for qualified doctors only, through 4-year degree courses, to those lasting only a few days, with, in many fields, little objective guidance as to the reputableness or otherwise of courses. 'Buyer beware' has been the rule for both prospective entrants and clients/patients. The situation is rapidly changing, however. With government approval, the Institute for Complementary Medicine has set up the British Register of Complementary Medicine. To be admitted to the Register practitioners must meet standards set by scrutiny panels. Though registration is voluntary, it is beginning to have an effect; for example, some magazines accept advertisements only from registered practitioners.

NVQs are currently being developed, and as they take hold,

registration is likely to become more important for both clients and practitioners.

Further information is available from the Institute for Complementary Medicine, PO Box 194, London SE16 1QZ. Send a large s.a.e. (plus 3 loose first-class stamps), together with details of your interests and qualifications, for lists of training courses.

Merchant Navy

Entry qualifications
Engineer, Deck and Radio Officers: normally 4 GCSEs (A–C) including maths, English-based subject and physical science. *Catering Officers*: BTEC/SCOTVEC Hotel, Catering and Institutional Operations (but see 'Training', below).

The work
Although Britain's merchant navy fleet is much smaller than it used to be, there are still opportunities for those wanting to go to sea and recruitment of officer cadets has picked up after some years of decline. There is still virtually no recruitment of ratings. There are very few cruise ships; most of the fleet consists of cargo vessels, container ships, tankers and ferries.

Although the UK's fleet is older than that of some competitors, living conditions for crews are far better than they used to be. Everything is being done to minimize boredom and irritation which tends to arise when groups of people live and work together in a close community. Vessels now often have single or double cabin accommodation, TV rooms, spacious lounges. Life at sea in modern ships is a mixture of modern technology and traditional hierarchy. Modern vessels have family accommodation so that officers can bring their partners.

UK-trained officers are welcomed by foreign shipping companies.

Engineer Officers

They are responsible for ships' engines including heating, pumps, etc. They ensure that the ship sails smoothly and efficiently; supervise repairs at sea and overhauls in port. When on watch, the engineer monitors the engines, now usually done with computerized equipment. Modern ships' engine-rooms are clean, airy and contain a mass of electronic equipment. They have nothing in common with old-fashioned boiler rooms, although the work is still very practical.

Engineer Officers are in charge of and responsible for the work of engine-room staff; so managing people is part of the job, as with all ships' officers.

Deck (Navigating) Officers

They navigate the ship. In port they are responsible for efficient loading and unloading, which involves both mathematical and common-sense problem-solving, especially in ships which carry a variety of cargo, simultaneously or in succession. They are responsible for controlling large numbers of seamen; in port they may negotiate with stevedores and others concerned with loading and unloading.

Deck Officer is a step on the ladder to becoming Captain or Master.

The increasingly sophisticated technology found on board has changed the nature of much of the work done by both deck and engineer officers, so that their roles are less clear cut than before. This has led to more cadets being recruited for training as Dual Certificate Officers. 'Multi-skilling' and versatility are becoming as important in the merchant navy as in many other occupational areas.

Radio/Electro-technical Officers

The statutory requirement for all ships to carry a radio officer is being phased out, as automated communications systems are being installed. Where ships carry an officer to look after ship-to-ship and ship-to-shore communications, he/she will be called electronics officer and will be expected to look after all the electronic equipment on board, not just that used in communication. The majority of radio/electronic–technical officers who work in land-based jobs in the marine industry work for manufacturers and suppliers of the equipment.

Catering Officers (called Purser or Hotel Manager on cruise liners; sometimes Chief Steward on tankers, etc.)

Responsible for purchase, storage, preparation (supervision) of food, meal service, maintenance of accommodation. On liners, they are also responsible for passengers' banking, information and entertainment services.

Training   *Engineering Cadets* (*trainee officers employed by shipping companies*)
1. With minimum 4 GCSEs (A–C), including maths, physical science and subject involving use of English, or after full

engineering craft training; 4-year course for BTEC/SCOTVEC Higher National Certificate in Marine Engineering.

2. With A-level maths and physics studied and a pass in one: 3-year course for HND in Marine Engineering.

3. With A-level maths and physics: B.Sc. in Marine Engineering.

All cadets take the Department of Transport Class 4 Certificate of Competency examination.

Deck Cadets (trainee officers employed by shipping companies)
1. With 4 GCSEs (A–C), including maths, physical science and subject involving use of English: 3–4 years for BTEC/SCOTVEC National Diploma in Nautical Science, leading to appropriate Department of Transport Certificates of Competency. It is possible to be accepted with 3 GCSEs and to train initially for a lower level Certificate of Competency giving the holder a watch-keeping certificate on smaller ships in restricted waters.

2. With A-levels (subjects as above): 3-year 'accelerated cadetship' and study for HND.

3. With 2 or 3 A-levels (1 in physics or maths) and 3 GCSEs (A–C): full-time or sandwich course for B.Sc. Nautical Science.

Dual Certificate Cadets
Training is longer than that for engineering or deck officers only – normally 4 years – and more demanding. Cadets work for an HND in Marine Technology, and during their practical spells at sea receive training in both aspects of their work. They work for the appropriate Certificate of Competency, i.e. Class 4 (Engineering) and Class 3 (Deck).

All the above courses include periods of practical training and experience at sea.

NVQs levels 2–4 are being piloted.

Radio Officers
Unlike cadets they must gain their qualifications *before* going to sea (the Radio-telecommunications General Certificate and the Electronic Navigational Equipment Maintenance Certificate). Students need 4 GCSEs (A–C), including maths, English and, preferably, physics for a 3-year course for HNC Electronic and Communications Engineering (Telecommunications) with marine options. The most common route now is to take 4 years and gain an HND in the same subject (with marine options) or to come direct on to the HND programme after A-levels. As explained above, radio officers as such are no longer being recruited; to get a job on a ship, they need to be all-round electronics experts,

and the vast majority taking the HND find jobs elsewhere in the telecommunications industry.

Catering Officers
Entry is normally as Catering Rating, though a small number start higher up the ladder with Hotel, Catering and Institutional Operations BTEC/SCOTVEC award (see p. 106).

Other opportunities at sea (very limited)
Assistant Purser: Must be over 21, have good secretarial skills, a foreign language, 4 GCSEs (A–C). These jobs are being reduced.

Children's hostess: Must be registered nurse (see p. 335) or teacher.

Nurse: Must be experienced registered nurse (see p. 335) and over 26.

Steward and stewardess on ferries and passenger liners: Employment largely seasonal, experience of domestic work in hotels and a foreign language useful. Not a career with prospects.

Ship's doctor: Newly qualified doctors may work as ship's doctors for a few months.

Personal attributes
Practicality; resourcefulness; ability to supervise and control people at work; gregariousness; willingness to take orders and accept one's place in the hierarchy, coupled with ability to take responsibility and make instant decisions. *For women*: also self-sufficiency, as being the only woman, or 1 of 2 or 3 women among large groups of men, can be lonely; indifference to standing out in a crowd and therefore being constantly 'on show'.

Late start
Very limited except for jobs requiring previous experience/training. Possible in theory, but unusual, as engineering officers for those with an engineering background or relevant degree. Upper age limit for cadets is around 25, usually lower for dual certificate.

Career-break
Unlikely.

Part time
No.

Position of women
Women officers and cadets sail on modern ships described above. Girls are being recruited both as *Deck Officer Cadets* and *Engineering Cadets* by a number of companies, and more would be welcomed. There have been women *Radio Officers* for some years. *Catering Officers* have rather less scope, mainly because the

majority of Catering Officers come up through the ranks, after training at the Sea Training College, where there are few facilities for girls.

So far very few women are ship's doctors, but on vessels with adequate accommodation theoretically no bar.

Further information

The Chamber of Shipping, Carthusian Court, 12 Carthusian Street, London EC1M 6EB (for general information on all merchant navy careers and list of shipping companies)

The Marine Society, 202 Lambeth Road, London SE1 7JW (A charity offering range of scholarship schemes for young people wishing to go to sea. Please send s.a.e. for information.)

Individual shipping companies

Related careers

ARMED FORCES – ENGINEERING

Meteorology

Entry qualifications

Graduate entry: most graduates join the Met Office at Scientific Officer (SO) level and need *either* a good degree in mathematics, physics, meteorology, computing sciences or electronics *or* a Higher National award in mathematics, physics or computing. A few people with other graduate qualifications, e.g. in Business Studies, are recruited to fill specific posts.

Basic entry: Traditionally, the Met Office has recruited large numbers of staff at Assistant Scientific Officer (ASO) level. With the significant increases in computer power and automation since the 1980s, fewer ASOs are needed. However, from time to time there are openings for people with a minimum of 4 GCSEs (grade C or above) or equivalent including English language, maths, physics or double award science including physics. Other useful subjects include computer studies, electronics and statistics.

The work

The Met Office is an executive agency within the Ministry of Defence and is due to become a Trading Fund in April 1996. It employs over 2,000 people, about half of these at its headquarters in Bracknell, Berkshire. The Met Office is highly regarded for the production of numerical weather forecasts, climate prediction and related studies. As well as producing weather information for the general public, it covers a wide range of activities and provides services to defence and other government departments, civil aviation, commerce and industry and the media. Parts of the Met Office, such as forecasting offices and telecommunications sections, operate round the clock, every day of the year, so staff working in these areas are required to work shifts.

Scientific Officers work in the following areas, depending on the subject and level of their degree: climate, physical processes or numerical weather prediction research; forecasting; instrumentation, commercial and defence-related meteorology; information technology (IT), including operations and engineering, systems support, user services and systems strategy and consultancy. All graduates need an aptitude for, and interest in, programming. People with computer science qualifications normally work with

IT. Howeever, there are opportunities for all staff to change disciplines during their career.

Assistant Scientific Officers work anywhere in the UK and must be prepared to move as required. At Bracknell ASOs are involved in analysing and verifying climatological and statistical returns; providing support for research scientists; providing support for computer programmers. At other stations work includes making weather observations; producing climatological and statistical returns; supporting forecasters who provide weather information for a range of clients; collecting and transmitting data. In all cases they make extensive use of computers; appropriate training is given.

Training

On-the-job training is given to all staff. In addition, initial, formal residential courses are run at the Met Office College and elsewhere.

For graduates, initial training at the Met Office College lasts for up to 5 months.

Initial training for ASOs is a 2-week distance-learning package, with help from the line manager, followed by 6 weeks' residential training at the Met Office College.

There are opportunities for staff to study for relevant higher academic qualifications.

Personal attributes

Enthusiasm and genuine interest in meteorology and/or computer science; versatility and adaptability; the ability to work independently, yet be a valuable team member; good communication skills.

Late start

No age limits.

Career-break

Unpaid leave is available to men and women who wish to take time away from work to raise a family; this may also be available for other reasons, e.g. other domestic responsibilities or further education.

Part time

Some opportunities for part-time work and job-sharing, mainly at Bracknell.

Position of women

19% of staff are women (all disciplines). Of the 30 Directors, 1 is a woman. 6% of Grade 7 staff are women.

NOTE: Grade titles such as SO, ASO and grade 7 are being changed.

Further information

Meteorological Office, Personnel Management (Recruitment), London Road, Bracknell, Berks. RG12 2SZ

Related careers

SCIENCE

Museums and Art Galleries

Entry qualifications

Various (see 'Training', below); for curator-level jobs, in theory 4 GCSEs, in practice degree or equivalent.

The work

The scope of museum work has widened greatly in recent years. Established museums and art galleries have shed their image of solemn shrines devoted to earnest study of art, artefact and history; they have become more user-friendly, wanting to entertain as well as inform and thus attract a wider public. The term 'museum' is now used rather loosely and covers a more varied range of establishments than it used to. The term 'heritage centre' or 'heritage site' is increasingly used instead. Museum and heritage sector establishments overlap in terms of the work, which is basically selecting and organizing exhibits and attracting and organizing visitors.

Over half of Britain's roughly 3000 museums were started in the last 20 years, and it is these museums which have transformed the museums scene. Museums fall into 3 main groups:

1. 17 funded by the Museums and Galleries Division of the Department of National Heritage: these include large and prestigious ones like the British Museum and the National Gallery. These establishments offer the greatest scope to the traditional academic specialist type of curators who chose the job because of their interest in pursuing their specialism. These curators may or may not combine collection management with general departmental management: there is a move to divide these 2 management functions. National museum curators are normally graduates in subjects relevant to the department concerned. They usually start as assistant curators. Science/technology graduates are as likely to get a job as arts graduates. Competition is very keen indeed.

2. About 750 local authority-run museums and art galleries. They include a few large and prestigious ones and hundreds of small local museums of local history or industry. Employment prospects vary; few jobs are research-based; most involve coping with everything. Entry is usually with a degree or comparable qualification (which could be non-specific management experience).

3. The largest and fastest-growing group of around 800–900: the 'independents'. They are funded either by sponsors and entry fees or entirely by entry fees. They are 'market-led'. Their success depends on a commercially viable idea, and management, marketing and communication skills. The group includes sophisticated tourist attractions like the Yorvik Viking Centre in York and the Museum of the Moving Image in London, as well as hundreds of small special-interest ones like the Silk Museum in Macclesfield and the Freud Museum in London. Jobs go to applicants with commercial and communication skills; academic qualifications are not required, but as competition is very keen, academic qualifications in addition to the required skills help.

Both local authority and independent museums use volunteer labour fairly extensively; such volunteer experience is very useful when applying for 'real' jobs. As there are always more applicants than vacancies, only applicants with volunteer experience stand much chance of acceptance.

Apart from traditional curators, who are concerned with collection management and research, there are many other museums jobs, including a few 'museum-specific' ones:

Exhibition designers. A growing number of museums are appointing in-house designers, but the majority are self-employed or work for exhibition design consultancies; their expertise is 'bought in' by museums. The work now often includes using audio-visual and interactive video equipment (the National Gallery extension which opened in July 1991 has 'work stations' with touch-sensitive screens where visitors can 'research' pictures and artists in a computerized encyclopaedia). Designers work closely with *interpreters*. Interpretation means showing objects in their context and imaginative presentation. It overlaps with *education officers* and may involve role-playing: perhaps dressing up as a 1920s chauffeur when showing transport from that period, or as a Roman shopkeeper when interpreting shopping in ancient Rome. Interpreters also help visitors use the high-tech equipment. The National Curriculum's emphasis on hands-on experience has increased the scope for museum–school collaboration. Education officers may also give lectures which are targeted at specific audiences, from tourists to groups of scholars.

Designers usually have an art-training background at Higher National award or degree level; *interpreters* and *education officers* are usually graduates (no particular discipline), and may or may not have teaching experience.

There is now some movement between independent and other staff; experience in an independent museum may lead to work in a traditional one. Work in a heritage sector establishment or even a pure tourist attraction is useful experience in exhibit and visitor management. (A former theme park director was recently appointed development manager of a national museum.)

Other museum work, not museum-specific, includes marketing, public relations, shop management.

Conservation is a profession in its own right and is a growth area. The national and a few local authority museums and art galleries use in-house conservators, but most are self-employed or work for private firms and collectors as well as for museums and art galleries. They don't by any means deal only with paintings or other traditional exhibits; anything from agricultural machinery to dresses or first-generation computers needs conserving. Conservators see their job in three stages: examination to assess the object's properties and need for repair; preservation to arrest or prevent deterioration; and restoration. Most conservators specialize by material and/or type of object: textiles, paintings, machinery, furniture, etc.

Training

This is becoming much more flexible to take account of changes in the work. The industry's training organization is the Museum Training Institute (MTI) which administered the Museum Association's Diploma, the professional qualification for curatorial jobs. This Diploma is due to be phased out in 1996, to be replaced by S/NVQs levels 2–5 (see p. xix).

The Museum Association *has* required those wanting to become associate members to take 1 of 4 postgraduate courses. From 1995 this is no longer essential, but the relationship between professional membership, post-graduate training and S/NVQs is not yet clear. However, some post-graduate courses are starting to take note of S/NVQ standards in assessments of parts of the course.

There is a small number of post-graduate courses available in museums studies or heritage management. These may be full- or part-time and lead either to a diploma, or to a Master's degree. It is also possible to include heritage management in some first degrees and Higher National Diplomas.

On the *conservation* side, there is a variety of courses providing specialized training in a vast range of artefacts and materials, from plastics to stained glass, paper to antique clocks. Courses are at many levels from college certificate to post-graduate degree and may be full- or part-time. S/NVQs are also being introduced.

Personal attributes

Intellectual ability; a love of knowledge for its own sake; visual imagination; a lively curiosity; organizing ability; an understanding of laypeople's interests and tastes; communication skills; patience for waiting for the right job and for promotion.

Late start No objection in theory, but competition from young post-graduate candidates very strong.

Career-break In national and local authority museums Civil Service (see p. 123) and Local Government (see p. 265) conditions apply; in independent museums and the heritage sector the situation varies greatly.

Part time and job-sharing These are beginning to be widely accepted.

Position of women The ratio of men to women is about even up to senior/middle level, but so far there are very few women directors of museums, etc.

Further information Museum Training Institute, Glyde House, Glydegate, Bradford BD5 0UP

Association of Independent Museums, c/o Weald and Downland Open Air Museum, Singleton, Chichester, W. Sussex PO18 0EU

Conservation Unit, Museums & Galleries Commission, 16 Queen Anne's Gate, London SW1H 9AA

Related careers ARCHAEOLOGY – ARCHIVIST – ART AND DESIGN – INFORMATION WORK

Music

Entry qualifica- tions	Acceptance at music colleges depends on performance at audition. For most performers, except for singers, intensive musical training must have started by their teens at the latest.

For teaching, see p. 517. For degree courses, at least 2 A-levels and 3 GCSEs (A–C) with, usually, A-level music.

The work	Work with music covers a very wide field: performing, com- posing, recording, video-making, administration, teaching, criticism and journalism. Some of the traditional boundaries between what are loosely called 'serious' and 'pop' music and musicians are breaking down and fashions come and go as in any arts or entertainment area. In 'pop' and other 'non-traditional' music it is possible to reach the top without a proper musical training; success depends on many other factors. This section is concerned only with those parts of the profession that need formal training.

Performing

Some symphony orchestras and opera houses employ orchestral players on a full-time basis. Others, including smaller ensembles, are made up largely of regular but freelance musicians who may, or may not, work for other orchestras as well. Singers may be salaried members of a chorus or freelance.

Most freelance musicians, however devoted to serious music, are glad to work as 'session players' on TV commercials, film incidental music and other light music recording sessions, etc. A violinist may play in a concert at the Barbican on one evening and the following day in a TV jingle recording session.

A freelance musician has to fit in work as it comes. The work may fluctuate from 3 daily sessions (3 hours each) over a long period, to no work for many weeks. Long practice at home is always necessary. Live concerts or recording sessions are arranged well in advance, but some lucrative TV or film sessions are booked at short notice, and accepting bookings requires careful judgement. Once a date is booked, it is unwise to break it, even if a better engagement is offered.

The musician's work is physically exhausting, and may include travel over long distances, combined with rehearsals and nightly performances, often in cold or overheated halls. An engagement for a season with a ballet or opera company may involve 5 performances a week with as many rehearsals, and practice at home. The atmosphere amongst musicians is usually friendly, although the competition is keen.

Part-time teaching, either privately or in schools, gives many freelance musicians a supplementary income. However, it is often difficult to fit in performing engagements with teaching.

Prospects in music have never been good and have been made harder with cutbacks in state and local authority funding. It is estimated that only about 1 in 10 of music students who finish their full training (itself restricted to the good students) eventually makes a living as a performer. Only 1 in as many hundreds becomes a soloist. Good luck is almost as important as talent.

Composing

Making a living from composing concert repertoire is very difficult: it takes many years for composers to have a body of their music regularly performed. They normally need another source of income, mainly within the profession, sometimes outside. Some fortunate composers make a good living from writing music for different parts of the media, for example TV, films, commercials and corporate videos.

School Teaching

As the main job this is quite a different career. Teachers are employed in primary and secondary schools. They teach music either full time in one school, possibly with a second subject, or part time in various schools and/or youth clubs and evening institutes run by the local education authority.

There is scope for imagination and initiative. Music teachers' main job is to promote interest and enthusiasm, as only a minority of pupils take music examinations. They may start a choir or an orchestra, or record evenings; organize record libraries, visits to concerts, etc.

There is currently a shortage of music teachers, particularly at primary level, now that music forms part of the National Curriculum.

Private Teaching

Many people go straight into full-time private teaching after leaving music college or university. They may prepare children, and sometimes adults, for graded examinations in an instrument(s). Because of its nature, this work is mostly done after school hours, in the evenings and weekends. Some teachers prefer to do this rather than work in schools, as they have more control over what they do.

Sound Engineering/Music Technology

For broadcast sound engineering see TELEVISION, FILM AND RADIO (p. 526). Sound engineers (not to be confused with professional engineers) in recording studios are responsible for the overall recording quality and for interpreting the producer's ideas. They need a grasp of basic physics and electronics in order to understand how to work their equipment, but they do not need great technical knowledge to start with (most enter as tape operators or assistant engineers). Some highly qualified and experienced sound engineers may be called *music technologists*. They apply advanced technology to the creation and reproduction of sound. They work on the design and manufacture of equipment, as well as in recording studios and broadcasting.

It is difficult to enter this area; really good engineers, however, are always in demand and a few become producers. Limited openings as yet for music technologists as this is still a relatively 'new breed'.

Musical Instrument Technology

There is some limited scope in musical-instrument technology, which means making or repairing musical instruments – anything from harpsichords to clarinets, organs to synthesizers. The electronics side, involving the manufacture and repair of musical equipment, probably offers the best prospects. There is a steady demand for piano-tuners.

Training   *Performers*
This has been gradually changing. Most courses at music colleges/conservatoires now lead to a degree, whereas in the past many led to graduate status diploma. The choice is between a 3- to 4-year full-time course at a college of music or a university based degree. Traditionally, university music degrees were largely academic and

were not intended primarily for performers. Graduates who did not want to join the profession would (and still can) go on to a post-graduate performers' course at a music college. However, there are now many university courses which do emphasize performance; they may lead to a degree in music or in performing arts. There are also now a couple of degrees taught jointly by universities and conservatoires.

Degrees may last 3 or 4 years, they may lead to an ordinary or an honours degree and this may be called a BA Music or Bachelor of Music (B.Mus.). Where a college or university offers both degrees, the B.Mus. is intended for those students who want to concentrate almost entirely on performance, while the BA Music contains more academic studies.

The syllabus of any performers' course (degree or diploma) normally includes a principal subject and a second study subject. Instrumentalists play two instruments. Singers may take either an instrument as second study or they may take speech and drama. Other subjects included are aural training, theory and history of music, analysis, orchestral experience, choral and opera study, contextual studies and, often, a language. In addition many colleges offer a wide selection of specialist options, such as composition, contemporary or early music, electronic music, music therapy, music administration, aesthetics, ethnic music and conducting.

For people interested in non-classical music, there is now a number of courses (degrees, HNDs, a Diploma in Higher Education and BTEC National Diploma) in popular and commercial music, jazz and band studies.

Composers
The most common route is to take a music degree at university, followed by a post-graduate course in composition at either university or a conservatoire.

Teachers
Music teachers in *schools* must gain Qualified Teacher Status (see TEACHING, p. 522) by taking either a music degree (or graduate diploma) followed by a 1-year course of professional teacher training *or* a B.Ed. with music as a main subject. There is a shortened B.Ed. for people over 21 with music training. Teachers who give instrumental lessons in or out of school are not required to have Qualified Teacher Status. Some take education options within performers' courses, some take post-graduate teaching courses at music college (for example the Licentiateship of Trinity

College London (Music Education)). A number of short or part-time courses exist for practising teachers. For example the Associated Board has recently set up a 1-year part-time Professional Development Course for Instrumental and Singing Teachers; the ISM has also created a distance-learning diploma for music teachers in private practice in conjunction with Reading University.

Those wishing to be listed in the Incorporated Society of Musicians (ISM) Register of Professional Private Music Teachers must have suitable professional qualifications and experience.

Music Technology/Sound Engineering

Traditionally this has been on the job. Competition to get into the recording industry is now so great that some pre-entry training or experience is necessary. There are various ways to train: short introductory courses, evening courses, occasional day release. Recording companies often look for people with some kind of technical or engineering background, not necessarily electronics. There are now a number of degrees and HNDs available with titles such as music and technology, electronic music, music acoustics, music and physics or electronics. For classical music recording sound engineers normally need a music degree.

Musical Instrument Technology

There are full-time (usually 2 years) coures leading to City and Guilds, SCOTVEC National Certificate, BTEC/SCOTVEC Higher National Diploma, Diploma in Higher Education or a degree. *Piano tuners* can study full-time or by day- or block-release.

Other Courses

For those wanting to go into music administration or management there are one or two relevant courses. Otherwise openings tend to be for people with experience in some aspect of the music business or with specialist qualifications in, for example, accountancy or marketing.

Personal attributes *For performers*: Apart from outstanding talent, perseverance, resilience, courage, and indifference to setbacks; the ability to work as one of a team; a pleasant manner; good health; very wide musical interest; good sight-reading speed; willingness to work ouside the musical field between engagements. *For teachers*: as for teaching (p. 523), plus creative imagination and initiative.

Music Therapy

This is a small but growing field. Music therapists work with physically or mentally handicapped children and adults. They work in the fields of mental illness and mental handicap in both the health and the education services. Music can contribute to the development and treatment of disabled and maladjusted people in various ways as a medium of non-verbal communication – by helping to relax their bodies and minds, as a mental stimulus, and as an emotional outlet. Autistic children, for example, and severely withdrawn adults, who do not respond to any other form of activity and cannot form relationships, often benefit greatly from listening to, and making, music.

There are 3 1-year full-time and 1 2-year part-time post-graduate courses in music therapy. Candidates must have had at least a 3-year full-time musical education and some experience of working with disabled people. Some work full time in one hospital, some do 'sessions' in several centres. The work is extremely demanding and needs maturity and sensitivity. Many find they cannot cope with full-time therapy work.

Career-break

It is unlikely that performers can resume orchestral playing after a long gap unless they keep up with serious daily practice; but there should be no problem returning to teaching.

Part time

Performing: work as freelance is possible in many areas – but work tends to be sporadic rather than regular part time. *Teaching and music therapy*: part time or job-sharing should be possible, but not necessarily exactly where one wants it.

Position of women

Women are still under-represented in large professional orchestras, considering that they make up around half of music students. There are still only a few women conductors. Women still appear to be discriminated against, though it is probably impossible to prove this.

Further information

For early training: Local education authority music adviser

For general information: Incorporated Society of Musicians, 10 Stratford Place, London W1N 9AE

For music courses: *Music Education Yearbook* (Rhinegold Publishing), available at most libraries

For sound engineering and record companies: The British Phonographic Industry (BPI), 25 Savile Row, London W1X 1AA

For music therapy: Association of Professional Music Therapists, The Meadow, Pierce Lane, Fulbourn, Cambridge CB1 5DL
City and Guilds Institute (see p. xxii)
BTEC and SCOTVEC (see pp. xxi, xxii)

| **Related careers** | DANCE – LEISURE/RECREATION MANAGEMENT – TEACHING – TELEVISION, FILM AND RADIO |

Nursery Nurse/Nursery Officer/Nanny

Entry qualifications
None laid down, but most colleges demand at least 2 GCSEs (A–C); many entrants have more; a few have A-levels. Private training colleges demand at least 3 GCSEs (A–C).

The work
Nursery nurses look after children 8 years and under. They are primarily concerned with healthy children (they are now often called nursery officers), but, strangely, in this context 'healthy' may include children with problems and also the physically and mentally disabled.

Nursery nurses' roles cover very much more than physical care and supervision of young children. Young children learn through play and through communicating with other children and with adults; they need adequate stimuli and individual attention to ensure their healthy intellectual, emotional and social development. When nursery nurses read to children, talk to them individually, discuss, say, their painting efforts, and generally help them to enjoy nursery activities they are, in effect, teaching.

Nursery nurses work in various settings:

1. Nursery classes and schools (for 3–5s) and infant schools (5–7s), run by local education authorities (LEAs). Nursery nurses help organize play activities, read to and play with children. Usually 1 nursery nurse is responsible for a small group of children. A qualified nursery or infant teacher (see p. 518) is normally in charge.

2. Day nurseries and family centres, run by social services departments for under-5s (mainly 3–5s) who are at risk socially, physically or emotionally; and for children where both parents have to go out to work or for other reasons cannot satisfactorily look after them during the day. There are now very few places for children whose parents merely think that nursery is a Good Thing. A proportion of children in day nurseries have special needs, so work can be very demanding. Occasionally staff involve parents in the nursery's activities – largely to help parents understand the children's needs and development. Staff may also do unofficial 'casework' (see SOCIAL WORK, p. 476).

3. Private day nurseries, workplace nurseries and crèches: there is an increasing number of these, catering for parents who want their children to have the benefits of nursery experience, especially in areas where there are few LEA-run nursery places. Most cater for working parents by being open all day, and some are, in fact, attached to one or more companies and open only to their staff.

4. In hospital, nursery nurses help to look after babies in maternity wards, and on children's wards they play with and care for children. Actual nursing is done by registered nurses (see p. 338).

5. The largest single group work in private families, as 'nannies', mainly these days in homes where both parents go out to work. Unlike in the past, most nannies expect to share the care of the children with the parents.

There is a variety of working patterns: some live-in nannies take charge of a young child or 2 or 3 children all day; in addition, in between the end of the school day and a parent's return from work (and perhaps during the school holidays), they may look after several schoolchildren whose parents share the nanny's salary. Other nannies work 2 days for one family, 3 days for another if the mothers concerned are themselves part-timers and need only part-week nannies. Work in a family differs from that outside the home in that nannies are on their own: nobody to ask for help in emergencies, and much of the time no other adult to talk to. The work is both more responsible and lonelier; it may also be less rigorous. Most nannies do some housework or at least cook for the children while the parents are at work.

6. A very small proportion work in hotels and holiday camps as children's hostesses. Experienced nannies can get jobs abroad.

Nursery nurses who take the Advanced Diploma courses have fair promotion prospects and may become officers in charge of nurseries of all kinds, at home and abroad. However, the ratio of senior to junior jobs is low.

Training   1. The usual method: minimum age 16. A 2-year full-time or longer part-time course at a college of further education. Students spend three-fifths of their time at college, two-fifths on 'placements' working with children. Most placements are in public sector nurseries, etc., but colleges often include days-only placements in private families considered suitable for training purposes. Students do not normally have sole charge of children or get experience of 24-hour care, and do not get the 'feel' of being a nanny where both parents work.

The syllabus includes the social, emotional, physical and intellectual development of children from 0 to 8; children's social, emotional and physical needs to ensure normal development; children with all kinds of special needs, including physical and mental disabilities; importance and significance of play, companionship, communication; promotion and maintenance of health (including nutrition and prevention and control of infection); organizing play activities; employment issues; patterns of family life and social institutions – and changes in both; the nanny in a private family; how the social services work; arts and crafts; early years and National Curriculum.

In England and Wales courses offered by the Council for Awards in Children's Care and Education (CACHE) lead to the National Nursery Examination Board (NNEB) Diploma in Nursery Nursing. This is a 2-year full-time modular course. Part-time courses are also available.

In Scotland courses comprise SCOTVEC National Certificate modules and lead to registration by the Scottish Nursery Nurses' Board. This programme will be changed in due course with the introduction of NVQs/SVQs (see below).

The NNEB Diploma can be followed by a modular course lasting about 2 years part time or 1 year full time, leading to the Advanced Diploma in Child Care and Education. Students have to complete 6 modules or units, and can specialize in special groups, such as handicapped or disturbed children, or ethnic minorities, or in nursery management. Different modules are offered by different colleges and students study by day- or block-release. This award carries 120 CATS (see p. xxxii) points for people applying later for a degree course.

In Scotland there is a 1-year day-release Post Certificate course, but this is soon likely to be replaced in most regions by SCOTVEC HNCs and HNDs.

There is also a 1-year full-time course offered by CACHE leading to the Certificate in Child Care and Education. This can give entry into the Diploma course and in certain cases can lead to remission of teaching time for the Diploma course.

2. 18–24-month courses at the 3 private Association of Nursery Training colleges. Students must be at least 18; to make sure they like the work, most look after children privately, in between school and college. Private colleges prepare students for the CACHE awards and for their own diplomas.

3. The National Association for Maternal and Child Welfare runs Diploma courses which, though not recognized as a qualification for public sector work except in a handful of local authorities, lead to work as mothers' (or parents') help and nanny. Course structure, length and content varies.

NOTE: NVQs/SVQs (see p. xix) in Child Care and Education at levels 2 and 3 are being introduced throughout the UK and are offered by CACHE. For the time being existing CACHE awards are likely to keep their existing titles.

Personal attributes   A way with young children; patience; imagination; willingness to take responsibility and to work hard at routine chores; ability to work well in a team; interest in mental, social and physical development of children.

Late start   Entry is possible at any age. There are two centres offering very intensive 1-year Fast Track courses, suitable for those with some experience.

Career-break   Should be no problem.

Part time   Little opportunity at present in social services department nurseries and in infant nursery schools and classes, but growing opportunities as daily nanny – working for women who are themselves working part time.

Position of women   Under 1% of students are men; no reason at all why this should remain so – men welcome on courses and in jobs.

Further information   Council for Awards in Children's Care and Education, 8 Chequer Street, St Albans, Herts. AL1 3XZ (enclose s.a.e.)

Scottish Nursery Nurses' Board, 6 Kilnford Crescent, Dundonald, Kilmarnock, Ayrshire KA2 9DW (enclose s.a.e.)

National Association for Maternal and Child Welfare (NAMCW), Education Department, 1st Floor, 40–42 Osnaburgh Street, London NW1 3ND (enclose s.a.e.)

Local authority education or social services departments

Related careers   NURSING – SOCIAL WORK – TEACHING

Nursing

This section covers *hospital* and *community nurses*, *health visitors* and *midwives*, as well as 'Project 2000' (p. 342) training. Nursing, especially nurse training, has changed dramatically in recent years and is still changing. After decades of discussions and reports a blueprint for nursing in the nineties and beyond was finally agreed by the Royal College of Nursing (the professional body), the United Kingdom Central Council for Nursing, Midwifery and Health Visiting (UKCC, the statutory body) and the government. Reforms are now being implemented. This is important to know for persons who are interested in nursing but put off by what they have heard about training and working conditions.

Changes in health care and nursing philosophy affect nursing tasks. For example: increasing emphasis is put on health promotion and prevention of disease; patients are now discharged from hospital much more quickly than used to be the case. Though at home, many patients still need nursing care. More nurses are therefore needed to work in the community, away from the hospital (where there is always someone senior to ask for advice). At the same time, a far greater proportion of patients in hospital (acute/general or psychiatric) need highly skilled and time-consuming nursing care. In other words, the quicker 'patient throughput' in acute hospitals, and the trend for people with psychiatric problems/mental handicap to live in the community, have changed the nature of nursing in hospital, and changed the balance between hospital and community nurse requirements (just as it has changed the balance between near-convalescents and seriously ill patients *in* hospital).

Some changes, less easily definable than those in education, training and nursing structure, have already taken place. For example, the doctor/nurse relationship has changed. There is generally today much more joint decision-making, and more mutual respect for the other's function. The patient/nurse relationship has changed too: nurses no longer 'nanny' patients; instead the emphasis is on 'consultation between equals' in the spirit of the Patient's Charter.

To attract more mature candidates and returners, and to retain more nurses with children, both training and work have been made more flexible. Part-time and job-sharing opportunities are moving higher up the ladder, and nurses with post-Registration qualifications (see p. 350) now have wider choices and better promotion prospects. All these changes are beginning to attract more men into the profession.

'Nursing' covers a range of jobs which vary widely in terms of levels of functions, of responsibility, professional qualifications required, environment worked in. There is therefore scope for people with widely differing aims, interests, abilities.

Nurses' work is much more difficult to define than other professionals' because there are so many, and some contradictory, facets to it. For example, nurses must be able to establish relationships with their patients, they must be prepared to do basic bedside nursing tasks, and they are highly trained professionals, who take vital decisions and use highly sophisticated equipment.

Entry requirements (all registered nurses)

Minimum age UK except Scotland: $17\frac{1}{2}$; Scotland: 17. 5 GCSEs (A–C) (Scotland 5 O- or S-Grades 1–3) or equivalent, which normally includes BTEC National or equivalent SCOTVEC awards. Applicants with lower qualifications may be able to sit an entry test which assesses their potential, motivation and 'track record' (work/life experience). However, colleges of nursing often set their own entry requirements at a higher than minimum standard. Many want candidates to have at least studied (not necessarily passed) a science; most teaching hospitals (i.e. those where medical students are trained) ask for A-levels or Higher grades.

NOTE ON TITLES: All nurses are now entitled to call themselves 'registered nurses', whatever branch they opted for. Under pre-Project 2000 training they became 'Registered General Nurse', 'Registered Sick Children's Nurse', etc.

Branches of Nursing

Registered Nurse (Adult)

The work

This is concerned with physical health. Whenever possible, nurses now apply what is called 'the nursing process', a process of systematic nursing care: they have got away from the image of nursing as a collection of separate tasks – from giving out bedpans to doing the round with the consultant. Instead, 'patient care' now comprises assessing, discussing and planning for individual patients' needs, putting the plan into operation, and then monitoring and, if necessary, changing it. Normally, every nurse is, on each duty round, allocated a number of patients to look after. That involves, for example, being present when consultants visit 'their' patients, talking to relatives, as well as ensuring that the patients are washed, sent for treatment, etc. Detailed notes have to be kept to assure continuity as colleagues often have to take over when a patient's 'own' nurse is not on duty. To carry out the 'nursing process', nurses need extensive knowledge of a variety of highly complex, responsible tasks. These include: administering a vast array of drugs in the right dosages and understanding what side effects to watch out for; using highly sophisticated machines in coronary and other intensive care units; keeping records on patients and knowing at all times what changes if any have occurred in their patients' condition; organizing the ward team; discussing patients' conditions with relatives and doctors; helping distressed patients to come to terms with their situation; trying to allay anxious patients' fears. A nurse may have to assess a situation and decide whether a patient's condition warrants sending out an emergency call for the doctor, or whether to suggest in discussion with the doctor that the social worker (see p. 476) should come and help sort out a patient's domestic problems. Qualified nurses also help with the teaching of nurses in training.

The majority of staff nurses (first post-Registration job) now take one of the large variety of post-Registration courses (see p. 350). They can become clinical specialists in, for example, theatre work, intensive care, geriatric or coronary care, and eventually be 'team leaders', or be in charge of a number of wards or units within a hospital or hospital group, and act as consultant to colleagues from other specialities as well as to junior staff. They can go into teaching where innovative methods and structures of courses are changing traditional teaching methods; or they can go into management.

Nurse-managers are not as much directly concerned with patient-care as with the smooth and efficient running of a complex organization. The work resembles management in commerce and industry; a large number of people carry out a variety of vital, interrelated activities which have to be co-ordinated. These 'managers' may have greater job-satisfaction than managers at that level in industry, because the end-product is the well-being of patients. Nurse-managers normally take a succession of management courses, often at business schools together with senior managers from industry; the principles of management are the same, whatever the organization to be managed (see also HEALTH SERVICES MANAGEMENT, p. 215).

Opportunities for nurses to work in the community rather than in hospitals have increased enormously in recent years and are still increasing. Then there are opportunities in the prison service, in the services, in the private sector – both in private hospitals and in patients' homes – and in agency nursing: many nurses do agency work a year or two after qualifying (or later, as returners), either because they prefer occasional days or nights to a regular job, or because of the variety that agency work offers. As many hospitals depend fairly regularly on agency nurses to fill gaps, agency nurses can often arrange to work for a time in nursing areas of their choice, e.g. on surgical or orthopaedic wards. In that way they widen their experience and can make an informed choice before deciding on any particular post-Registration course.

Personal attributes   Common sense; practical bent; sympathy for the sick and the old without sentimentality; an interest in medicine without morbid curiosity about illness; sensitivity coupled with a certain amount of toughness so as not to get too emotionally involved; organizing ability; patience; a sense of humour to put up with the inevitable occasional short tempers and difficult people; ability to know when to be firm – and how to be firm but not rude; powers of observation; initiative; ability to take responsibility one moment and to do exactly as told the next; good health.

Registered Nurse (Children)

The work   Nursing sick children can be both more rewarding and more arduous than nursing adults. It requires a different range of skills, including the ability to work with the child's family and involve them in his or her care: Mothers or fathers often stay in hospital with their young children. Many children stay only for a very short time; others stay for longer because they are very seriously ill and/or suffer from a rare condition which has to be assessed. Increasingly, paediatrics is very concerned with detection and follow-up of physical and learning difficulty. Some paediatric nursing is highly specialized, with nurses having taken post-Registration specialized training.

Children's wards are run to resemble home conditions as much as possible. Visiting is now normally allowed at all times; rigid tidiness and regimentation is frowned upon.

Jobs for children's nurses are not as readily available everywhere as they used to be or as jobs with adults. There are now only very few jobs in hotels, boarding schools, with airlines, etc., but more as nannies at home and abroad, and as school nurses. Some take post-Registration courses in community paediatric nursing.

Personal attributes The same as for the general nurse; plus extra patience and a way with children. A sick children's nurse must be able to talk to children on their own level. Many of the best children's nurses come from big families. Good powers of observation are essential, as small children cannot explain their ailments.

Registered Nurse (Mental Health)

In hospitals

1 adult in 8 in this country at some time in his or her life needs help because of some form of mental or emotional illness. The majority don't need hospitalization, and even most of those who do stay for only a short time, probably a few weeks, and possibly return for further brief spells in hospital in between leading normal lives. Only a minority are long-stay patients. The term mental illness covers a wide spectrum. In mild cases (the majority) it can be difficult to decide whether a person is over-excited or eccentric or is actually mentally ill. In severe cases sufferers may be unable to separate fantasy from reality and react to people and situations in unreasonable, even alarming, ways. 2 groups of patients have increased in recent years: (1) people of all ages who cannot cope with the stresses and strains of modern life; (2) old people who suffer from senile dementia.

Over 90% of patients are 'voluntary' or 'informal'. Many of them are able to go out to shop or visit friends or relatives, and when in hospital busy themselves in the hospital's workshops, recreation rooms or gardens. For most patients a vital part of their treatment is the contact with a friendly, skilled nurse; the inability to communicate with other people is part of most mental illness; nurses help a great deal towards patients' recovery by talking to them and, above all, listening therapeutically.

In most psychiatric hospitals the atmosphere is relaxed and informal. Patients and staff live in a friendly so-called 'therapeutic' community. Patients are encouraged to share with the staff responsibility for running wards and for the active social life of the hospital. The aim is always to minimize the institutional atmosphere. Most wards are in small units of general hospitals.

At informal meetings with staff the patients are encouraged to discuss and even criticize treatment, to talk about their difficulties and to help each other with their problems. At staff-only meetings, after ward meetings with the patients, all nurses have a chance to discuss patients, treatments and new methods with consultants and senior staff.

Psychiatric nursing can of course sometimes be harrowing. Nurses must always remember that their patients' apparently bad behaviour is a symptom of their illness. Teamwork among the staff helps a great deal, and during their training nurses learn to recognize and handle the emotional aspect of their work.

In the community

Community psychiatric/mental health nurses are sometimes (unofficially) referred to as 'district nurses for people with psychiatric problems'. But community psychiatric nursing is much less clearly definable than district nursing. As a post-Registration profession in its own right, it is still evolving, and different health/social services authorities organize the work in different ways. CPNs have, therefore, great scope to develop their own ideas and initiatives. It is very much a growth area within nursing because of the accelerating trend for psychiatric patients to live 'in the community' rather than go into or stay in hospital. Very broadly, CPNs combine 3 main, overlapping, functions.,

1. They give practical help and counselling support (see 'Counselling', p. 410) to patients discharged from hospital and now having to adjust to living with their families, in hostels or on their own; also, to patients who right from the start of their illness are treated as out-patients and/or attend day hospitals.

2. CPNs provide a preventive service: they see people who may be referred by GPs, social workers, district nurses, health visitors, even relatives or neighbours, or they could be 'self-referred': i.e. people who realize they have problems which they cannot cope with.

3. CPNs help to 'educate' the community to understand the nature of mental illness; they also help families and foster-families (even landlords) – anyone who has a patient living in their home – to cope with disturbed people's behaviour. Supporting patients' families, etc. is a *very* important part of community psychiatric nursing.

CNPs may also run clinics, do group-work (see 'Psychotherapy', p. 408) with patients and/or their families, and help run day centres. Because of the increasing numbers of patients with psychiatric problems cared for in the community, the profession is expanding greatly.

Training for community mental health nursing is not yet mandatory, but RNs (Mental Health) interested in this work are encouraged to take one of several full- or part-time specialist courses.

Personal attributes Curiosity about what makes people behave as they do; emotional stability; patience and perseverance; the ability to listen well and to be genuinely concerned without becoming emotionally involved; interest in outside work to keep a sense of proportion; a sense of humour; a gregarious nature; good physical and mental health.

Registered Nurse (Learning Disabilities/ Mental Handicap)

In hospitals

People with learning disabilities are immature: their mental development usually stopped before birth or sometimes later, through genetic problems, severe illness or accident. Unlike mental illness, this condition is not normally curable, and some patients stay in residential care all their lives. However, the tendency today is to enable as many patients as at all possible to live in the community. This means that patients *in* hospital tend to be severely handicapped, often both physically and mentally. Nurses help patients develop their potential as far as it is possible to do so. The extent of the disability in each patient determines the degree of independence that can be achieved. It takes very great patience and perseverance sometimes to enable a patient even to dress or feed him/herself. However, once the patient has taken even one small step towards independence, both patient and nurse feel they have achieved something. Some patients are prepared for life outside the sheltered hospital atmosphere and learn to shop, use money, etc. This type of nursing is always a mixture of teaching, showing understanding, and establishing relationships of trust with patients. Nurses work in teams with doctors, psychologists, occupational therapists and physiotherapists. Like psychiatric nurses, these nurses attend meetings with other professionals to discuss patients and problems.

In the community

Over 60% of persons diagnosed as suffering from learning disabilities now do live with their families, on their own, in shared accommodation or in hostels. Their need for continued care varies enormously from the occasional chat to regular care. A client – the term now preferred to 'patient' – may, for example, have 'an eating problem'; a GP or social worker may have alerted the nurse who will then visit and teach the client to use a spoon, etc., and probably also try and persuade the client's family to encourage their client to be more independent. The nurse may find that the extent of the client's learning difficulty is much smaller than the parents assumed. Teaching relatives how to care for clients is an important part of the nurse's work. Some clients, perhaps those only recently discharged from hospital but able to live in a shared flat, may merely have to be encouraged to increase their independence: to learn such social skills as saying 'hello' to neighbours, and such 'living skills' as paying the milkman or using public transport. The aim of nurses is always to develop clients' potential as fully as their disability allows.

Nurses also hold 'information sessions' to help other community care and health professionals, as well as the community at large, understand developments and changes in the treatment of people with learning difficulties.

Training for community nursing in this branch is not mandatory, but RNs are encouraged to take one of the full- or part-time courses available.

Personal attributes

Affectionate nature; a practical approach; teaching ability; patience; gentleness; interests unconnected with the work; ability to be genuinely concerned without becoming emotionally involved. Those who like looking after small children often enjoy this work.

Training (all registered nurses)

Training for Registration is in the throes of revolutionary changes. 200 or so schools of nursing have been reduced to about 90; small ones which were not able to give students the breadth of experience required either closed or amalgamated. Schools are now called 'colleges' of nursing. Most importantly, the structure of training is changing.

Unlike the old 'apprenticeship' style training method, the new system, known as *Project 2000* (or P2000), is what is called 'education led'. It leads to a dual qualification: Registration as nurse in 1 of the 4 branches and the Diploma in Higher Education, which is an academic qualification.

Dip. H.E. holders are eligible for acceptance into the third year of some nursing degree courses (see below) or take a 'top-up' course for a degree. Once they have got their degree they can apply for that large proportion of graduate jobs which are open to 'graduates in any discipline'. The status of nursing is thus raised, and nurses' options are increased. This, it is expected, will reduce the drop-out rate from training and, together with improved pay, encourage more men to take up nursing.

P2000 students *are* students, not salaried employees. They are 'supernumerary' for all but about 20% of their course. Courses are at colleges of nursing which have links with a higher education establishment. Nursing students may share some lectures, and college facilities, with students on other higher education courses. However, the extent of integration of college of nursing/HE establishment varies, and is still developing as the system is so new.

The structure of P2000 courses differs fundamentally from the traditional pattern. All students, whichever branch of nursing they have chosen, start with an 18-month Common Foundation Programme – or CFP (this has applied in Scotland for several years). The second 18 months are devoted to the student's chosen branch. There may, at that stage, be a chance to change from the originally chosen branch if during the CFP the student changed his/her mind.

Course content has been updated to take account of changes in society and in the thinking about health and disease. Much of the course content is the same as before, covering nursing practice and theory in the relevant areas, but there is now much more emphasis on the healthy individual, and on health promotion and preventive care. More time is spent studying the social and biological sciences. Teaching is more 'student-centred', with more time for discussion of issues between students and staff. About 50% of course time is spent on practical work on the wards, or in community settings. Students spend considerably more time learning about and working in the community, to prepare them for the increasing work outside the hospital – but note that P2000 nurses are *not* qualified as community nurses (see below for community nurse work and training).

P2000 students receive non-means-tested bursaries rather than a salary. Bursaries are a little larger than student grants – nursing students work harder and have less holiday. All P2000 courses comply with EU directives so Registered nurses (who have the necessary language skills) can work in EU countries.

As before, it is important for candidates to choose their course carefully, looking not only at the *Applicants' Handbook* but also studying individual colleges' prospectuses. The emphasis on different aspects of nursing varies between courses, and so do the facilities and the extent of integration with the relevant higher education establishment. (Continuous assessment and project work are part of every course.)

Part-time training: There should be more opportunities for part-time training under P2000. Each college makes its own arrangements, but there seems to be general agreement that the CFP part can be arranged on a 'short day' basis, and that individual branch programmes can be lengthened on 'an individually negotiated basis'. However, some colleges are much more willing to make such arrangements than others.

Nursing at degree level
There is a growing number of degrees which lead to Registration.

Organization and emphasis varies from one course to another and has little to do with the course title: 2 degrees in 'Nursing Studies', for example, may have less in common than 2 degrees of which one is in 'Nursing', the other in 'Nursing Studies'. So it is essential to look at prospectuses. All degrees in Nursing and Nursing Studies lead to Registration, normally in one branch of nursing.

Degree courses originally started to attract students who were interested in nursing but also wanted – and were qualified for – a higher education qualification. As P2000 courses now lead to an HE qualification as well as Registration, the difference between degree and non-degree nursing courses is not as great as it was. Nevertheless, prospective nurses with degree course entry qualifications probably will still want to take a degree rather than a Dip. H.E. In academic jargon, a Dip.H.E. is level 2, an honours degree level 3. There are a few shortened degree courses for applicants with 'relevant' degrees, as well as a few part-time degrees for Registered nurses.

Other Nursing in the Community

Nurses who work outside the hospital, where there is always someone more highly qualified to discuss problems with, have much more independence in terms of decision-making and organizing their working days. *District nurses*, *health visitors*, *community psychiatric nurses* (see p. 340), *school nurses*, *practice nurses* and *community midwives* all come under what is now often loosely called the 'community nursing' umbrella. They are all examples of specialized 'nurse practitioners', a term inceasingly used. They are part of the multi-professional community care team, working closely with GPs, social workers and other colleagues from related professions. The proportion of community nurses is growing, as more and more patients live in the community but still need nursing care and support. It is expected that many community nurses will soon have limited prescription rights, which underlines the responsibility they have. Few community nurses wear uniform.

District Nurse

Entry qualifications

Registered nurse (adult).

The work

District nurses undertake skilled nursing duties for patients not ill enough to be in hospital but needing nursing care. They visit acute and chronically ill patients as necessary and elderly people at regular intervals to keep an eye on them. They may also help permanently disabled patients to learn to use new aids, and help relatives to learn to carry out routine nursing tasks. When necessary they put people in touch with social workers or with other members of the health care team. District nurses work closely with local general practitioners, who advise on whom to visit and, often, the treatment required, and with hospitals. As there is a tendency for patients to be discharged from hospital as early as possible, district nurses are undertaking more and more technical nursing procedures, such as changing dressings for post-operative patients, taking out stitches, observing and reporting on patients' progress. They also give moral support, helping patients and their relatives to come to terms with their situation, etc.

Experienced nurses often lead teams which include several district nurses and nursing auxiliaries. To provide a 24-hour service, nurses work shifts. Because of the close co-operation between hospital and community services, district nurses may often also do some clinic sessions in hospital. This means they have both independence of community nursing and the companionship and chance to talk shop. Some district nurses specialize, e.g. in work with diabetics, the disabled, the elderly, terminal care.

Training

At present: 1 academic year for the Certificate in District Nursing, at a higher education establishment. The course includes learning how to adapt hospital nursing procedures to nursing under often less than ideal home conditions; teaching home nursing to patients' relatives; the organization, scope and availability of the social services; counselling (see 'Counselling', p. 410). There are also a very few nursing degree courses which include district nursing. But see changes in post-Registration training, p. 350.

Personal attributes

As for general nursing, plus organizing ability. District nurses must wish to work independently and to use their experience and ability in the community rather than in the sheltered atmosphere of the hospital. They should be resourceful, friendly and good listeners. They need a wide interest in the community in which they live and work, and tolerance of other people's way of life. They should know when to be critical and when to accept patients' own standards of cleanliness, etc.

Health Visitor

Entry qualifications

Registered nurse (adult).

The work

Health visitors are professionals in their own right. They organize their own work.

The important difference between health visitors on the one hand and nurses and social workers on the other is that the latter usually meet clients when something has gone wrong. The purpose of health visiting is the promotion of health and the prevention and early detection of physical and mental ill health. Health visitors give health care advice, identify the need for and if necessary mobilize other sources of help.

They are responsible for monitoring children's health from the time midwifery care ceases (a few weeks after birth usually) until the school nurse (see p. 348) takes over checking children's development. They advise mothers on childcare, health hazards and health care both by regular home visits and in clinics. Routine home visits may act as an 'early warning system', and health visitors often notice signs of stress or disorder before these develop into problems. For example, a young mother who gave up the companionship at work just before the child was born may feel lonely, and guilty for not being a radiant mother; the health visitor helps by discussing her feelings and by suggesting ways of coping with the problem. Other matters which might develop into problems but for the health visitor's early advice are older children's health or behaviour, or marital difficulties.

Health visitors' work may overlap with that of district and community psychiatric nurses. They may visit patients recently discharged from hospital; mentally ill or handicapped people who are cared for at home; the elderly; anyone who may be referred to them by social workers, doctors, a neighbour even. They are very much involved with health education and may lecture in schools, etc.

When visiting, health visitors are concerned with the family as a whole, not only the ill or disturbed member of the family. They may be based in doctors' practices, or work from health centres.

Training

At present: 1 academic year at a higher education establishment. Subjects studied include: social aspects of health and disease and preventive medicine theories and practice; social studies with special reference to the family as a social institution; health education; organization, scope and availability of social services; counselling (see 'Counselling', p. 410). There is also a degree in Nursing Studies and a health visiting qualification. But see changes in post-Registration training, p. 350.

Personal attributes   Interest and belief in preventive medicine and social advice; understanding and sympathy with social pressures and with people, whatever their temperament, background, lifestyle, competence; desire and ability to use expertise in the community; tolerance; patience.

Occupational Health Nurse

Entry qualifications   Registered nurse (adult) plus, usually, 2 years' post-Registration experience.

The work   Occupational health nurses work in factories, stores and wherever else there is a large number of employees, with the aim of promoting health in the workplace. The work is partly preventive, advising on diets, keeping an eye on the disabled, discussing worries with individuals. Occupational health nurses also deal with accidents and sudden illness and give minor treatments, such as injections, changing dressings. They advise both on health problems generally and on those peculiar to a particular industry, e.g. skin or respiratory diseases caused by certain types of work. They are now very much involved, at least in most large and/or progressive organizations, with research into the effects of the introduction of new technologies and/or working patterns on employees' health and on their job-satisfaction. This may involve discussing the arrangements of desks in word processing stations, or checking noise levels in tool shops, as well as shift and night work arrangements and canteen facilities. An important aspect of their work is the identification of health hazards, and initiating whatever measures are necessary to eliminate or minimize such hazards. They work closely with factory inspectors (see p. 212).

They work closely with occupational health doctors (see p. 306). They usually keep medical records of all employees and assist at the medical examination of prospective employees. They often arrange for such ancillary services as chiropody, eye-testing, physiotherapy. They discuss health and safety measures on the shop-floor and in the office with management, shop steward and factory inspector (see p. 212) and work closely with the personnel department. For example, if an employee's work is deteriorating, OHNs help to find the psychological or physical cause. OHNs also help to find suitable jobs for the disabled and may discuss with management measures which should be taken in special cases.

In large concerns there may be a medical department; more often there is one occupational health nurse working for the personnel director and/or the visiting medical officer.

Unlike other nursing jobs, normal office hours usually apply.

Training   Not mandatory, but strongly advised: 1-year full-time or 2-year part-time (day-release usually) course for the Occupational Health Nursing Certificate, normally at a higher education establishment. The syllabus includes industrial organization, factory and allied legislation; toxic hazards; effects of and coping with technological and organizational change. But see changes in post-Registration training on p. 350.

Personal   As for other nursing, with a special interest in industrial health,
attributes new technologies and changing patterns of work, safety problems, and human relationships at work. The ability to work independently and to discuss matters easily both with workforce and management is essential.

School Nurse

Entry   Registered nurse.
qualifica-
tions

The work   School nurses take over the monitoring of children's development where health visitors' work stops, i.e. when children reach school age. They work in the school health service and regularly visit a number of schools. Their routine checking of vision, hearing, growth, etc. is a preventive service: they hope to detect minor problems before they develop into serious ones. Teachers and parents ask school nurses' advice when a child shows signs of not being quite 'up to scratch', physically or mentally. The school nurse may contact parents when that seems advisable.

School nursing varies very much from one area to another, according to local organization; how many schools one school nurse is responsible for; and also according to individual school nurses' initiative and interpretation of their role.

School nurses are also very much involved in health education. Again, the extent of involvement varies: in some areas health education officers (usually health visitors by qualification) are appointed and school nurses would work with them; in other areas health education is left to health visitors and/or school nurses. Increasingly, school nurses take part in a programme of lectures/talks both to schoolchildren and at parents' evenings/ meetings, on such issues as drug abuse, AIDS, etc.

In some areas school nurses hold a kind of 'surgery' at certain days in 'their' schools, when parents, children and teachers can come and discuss any problem that bothers them. School nursing is very much less structured in terms of specific duties than most other nursing specializations.

Although school rolls are falling, the need for monitoring and for health education is rising; so opportunities for school nurses may be increasing. Most school nurses are part-timers.

Training   At present: 12-week full-time or equivalent part-time course at a higher education establishment. The course covers child development; social and physiological influences on health and disease; health education and disease prevention. See changes in post-Registration training on p. 350.

Personal   As for health visitors, with particular interest in working with
attributes children and adolescents.

Practice Nurse

Entry   Registered nurse.
qualifica-
tions

The work   Practice nurses have worked in GPs' practices for some time, carrying out such routine procedures as taking blood samples, changing dressings, etc. However, recent NHS changes greatly increased the range of tasks GPs or their support staff are asked to undertake; practice nurses' numbers and their importance have therefore increased greatly. Exactly what they may and may not do is still a 'grey area'. Their duties are not as clearly defined as those of other specialist nurses, and their work varies according to their GP employers' views and their own experience. Most practice nurses now undertake such non-routine tasks as setting up and running health promotion clinics (e.g. well-women, asthma and hypertension, and baby clinics), and they may also do some screening: i.e. check patients' health. All new patients who register with a GP must be offered screening, and all over-75s at least once a year. Practice nurses may do this screening and decide whether the patient needs to see the doctor. In the case of elderly patients this may involve home visits. It is expected that practice nurses, like health visitors and district nurses, may soon have (strictly limited) prescription rights.

Training   Training is not yet obligatory but it is strongly recommended. There are short courses, plus day seminars on an on-going basis.

Post-Registration Courses

The structure of post-Registration training has been updated to take account of P2000 courses, the highly specialized types of therapy and care now available, and also of changes in patients' needs and expectations. Some courses are mandatory, i.e. people wishing to take up particular work must become qualified. Many are optional, but there is much emphasis now on professional development of nurses and they are expected to take responsibility for ensuring they keep up to date. Most courses are modular, consisting of 'core' or shared modules that everyone takes and specialist ones taken by individuals working in a particular job or wishing to move into another area. The extent of 'core' modules in the various training programmes varies, and is probably greatest on courses for community-based nurses: all of these, whether district nurses, health visitors or community psychiatric nurses, have to acquire the skills which enable them to work independently as 'nurse practitioners' and an understanding of what makes communities tick and where and how they themselves fit in. Post-Registration courses can last anything from a few days to a year. They may be part-time or full-time, for example where nurses are seconded for a year to gain a district nurse qualification. There is even a 3-year full-time degree for RNs, leading to a dual qualification in community nursing. There are a few courses offering shortened training to RNs for another branch, for example children's nursing. P2000 nurses and midwives wanting to 'convert' their qualification into a degree can take full- or part-time 'top-up' courses.

The English National Board has developed a Framework and Higher Award structure for Continuing Professional Education. Those nurses, midwives or health visitors who complete the Higher Award gain both a professional and academic qualification (first or higher degree). Preparation for the award can be by various modes: short or longer courses, open learning, private study. The emphasis is on the nurses' competence and expertise, not on theoretical exams, and they can negotiate credit for successful completion of ENB approved courses under a Credit Accumulation and Transfer Scheme (CATS, see p. xxxii).

Midwife

Entry qualifications

As for registered nurses, see p. 336.

The work

Midwives look after mother and child from early pregnancy until about 4 weeks after the birth of the child (when health visitors take over). They give ante- and post-natal advice, support and instruction, and take full responsibility during the birth in straightforward cases and call a doctor in case of complications which they are trained to spot at an early stage. They run hospitals' baby units including those for premature and sick babies. They are trained to a high professional standard and work closely with doctors. They also run clinics for pregnant women as well as training sessions for expectant fathers and mothers. As mothers' stay in hospital is often very short, midwives' home visits are vitally important. These may involve counselling women who suffer from post-natal depression, or who need advice on coping with a new-born baby without neglecting their other children. It also often involves family planning advice.

Midwifery is a unique combination of applying complex practical and high-tech skills, teaching parentcraft and counselling.

There is today much more emphasis on the psychological aspects of childbirth and its effects on the rest of the family than there used to be. The majority of births take place in hospital, but midwives are very much involved with the home-versus-hospital birth debate. To ensure continuity of care from early pregnancy until the health visitor takes over care of mother and child, the emphasis is on an integrated hospital and community midwifery service, with individual midwives working in both home and hospital. But there are also opportunities for midwives to work *only* in hospital or *only* in the community. A small number of midwives work in the private sector. There is at present a shortage of midwives.

Training

There are two routes, both (from July 1995) called *Pre-Registration*:

1. Pre-Registration midwifery programmes (shortened) for Registered nurses (adult branch) who wish to gain a midwifery qualification. These lead to either a Diploma of Higher Education or a degree. They last a minimum of 78 weeks full-time.

2. Pre-Registration courses are for those who want to go directly into midwifery, not nursing. Like nurses, they take either a 3-year course leading to midwifery qualification and a

Diploma in Higher Education, or a 4-year course combining a midwifery qualification with a degree. Midwives can – and are encouraged to – take various post-Registration courses.

Personal attributes

As for district nurses (see p. 345), plus of course special interest in babies and the self-confidence needed particularly when persuading fathers to get involved in the preparation for the birth.

Late start (all above professions and specializations)

Excellent opportunities. Mature entrants of both sexes are very welcome because their drop-out rates are lower and their stay in the profession is longer than young entrants'. Special tests assess mature entrants' potential rather than their 'school knowledge'. Work/life experience is considered more important than academic achievement. If necessary, mature entrants are advised to take an Access course (see p. xxxi). NVQs/SVQs and GNVQ Advanced level may be accepted for entry.

Career-break

Returners are very welcome indeed; Return to Nursing courses are available in most districts and can be tailored to suit individuals' needs. There are 'refreshers' for all community nurses, specialists, managers and teachers.

Promotion prospects for returners are good.

Part time

Opportunities for flexible work patterns are now available much higher up the promotion ladder than they used to be. Part time is encouraged at virtually all levels, and job-sharing is also encouraged (but the initiative still often has to come from individuals).

Part-time training is becoming more widely available.

Position of women

Still only about 10% of men in the profession, but it seems to be increasing. Men still hold far more than their share of top jobs (especially in management and teaching) but that is probably due to the fact that until recently so many women dropped out when they had families or returned part time, and promotion for part-timers above Sister is still fairly new. So women's share of top jobs is likely to increase considerably in the next few years.

Further information

From appropriate National Boards:

Careers Service, English National Board for Nursing Midwifery and Health Visitors: PO Box 2 EN, London W1A 2EN

Nursing Adviser, Scottish Health Service Centre, Crewe Road South, Edinburgh EH4 2LF

Welsh National Board: 13th Floor, Pearl Assurance House, Greyfriars Road, Cardiff CF1 3AG

Northern Ireland Board: RAC House, 79 Chichester Street, Belfast BT1 4JR

Royal College of Nursing, 20 Cavendish Square, London WIM 0AB

| **Related careers** | MEDICINE — NURSERY NURSE — OCCUPATIONAL THERAPY — PHYSIOTHERAPY — SOCIAL WORK |

NOTE: Since the launch of P2000 a new grade of staff has been introduced to the NHS. These are Health Care Assistants who combine the non-nursing duties otherwise carried out by nursing auxiliaries with some of the routine nursing tasks previously carried out by student nurses when working on the wards (under P2000 student nurses are 'supernumerary' and not nearly so available on the wards). Health care assistants work in all kinds of hospitals and units (including psychiatric), in care homes and in the community. No formal educational qualifications are required (although this is up to the employer) but minimum age is at least 17/18. There is no formal training scheme but health care assistants can work for NVQs/SVQs in Care up to level 3. People considering this type of work are advised where possible to apply to authorities that do offer training and assessment for NVQs/SVQs.

There is no direct route into Registered nurse training. However, there may be some recognition of NVQs/SVQs level 3 as an alternative entry qualification (see Late Entry, p. 352).

Occupational Therapy

Entry qualifications

3 GCSE (A–C) passes and 2 A-levels (or equivalent, including Scottish Highers) in different subjects. At least 1 science is required; biology is useful and is required for some courses. Alternative qualifications (for example, BTEC National Diploma in appropriate subject) may be acceptable. Courses may ask for more than the minimum. English is commonly required.

The work

Occupational therapists are concerned with helping people with physical and mental disorders to live as full a life as possible by overcoming as much as possible the effects of their disability. This covers a very wide range of activities concerned with physical, psychological, social and economic well-being. Some occupational therapists feel that the title conjures up out-of-date images of patients weaving baskets or doing jigsaws during long days of convalescence, and that 'rehabilitation therapist' would better convey the essence of their work. Others feel the title is fair enough, given that they are concerned with all the things that 'occupy' patients day-in, day-out – basic everyday care, work, leisure, social interaction. The work covers a spectrum that borders physiotherapy at one end and social work at the other.

Occupational therapists work with people of all ages and various kinds of problems. *Physical disability* may be the result of accident, illness or old age. It may be the kind of problem that gets better – or one that gets progressively worse. It may be part of a complex combination of multiple handicaps. Together with other members of the health care team, the occupational therapist assesses the problem and devises a programme of treatment to help the patient regain as much independence as possible. The emphasis is on patients' ability, not disability. Treatment might involve strengthening exercises – or shopping expeditions. Occupational therapists devise new ways for patients to perform old tasks, e.g. cooking from a wheelchair, dressing, getting in and out of bed and bath. They may take patients on a trial visit home from hospital so they can advise on how the environment may need to be adapted. The solution is sometimes as simple as rearranging a room, or as complicated as building an extension. Sometimes there is no solution but rehousing, so the occupational therapist may have to liaise with the housing department. They also assess patients for various kinds of aids and equipment, from those which open jars to sophisticated hoists.

The problems of people with *mental health* needs are very different, but the aim is the same – to give them the confidence and ability to live as independent a life as possible. The work varies and might include just visiting and talking with acutely ill patients who are too ill to join a structured programme; devising games and exercises to improve, for example, concentration or memory; art or dance therapy to help patients become aware of their immediate environment and express themselves; planning 'paired' or group activities to encourage patients to socialize. Interests and hobbies are encouraged so that patients will be able to use their leisure and reduce isolation. The practical skills that they will need for living in the community are taught and practised – daily care and personal hygiene, cooking, shopping, using public transport, budgeting. Occupational therapists also help patients rediscover and practise the skills they need for their jobs. This may involve liaison with employers.

Occupational therapists treat patients in hospitals, special centres, schools and in their homes. The main employers are the National Health Service and local authority social services departments. There are also opportunities in prisons, industry, special schools, GP practices and residential homes. An increasing number of occupational therapists are in private practice.

Courses are broad-based, but after qualification occupational therapists may specialize in work with particular groups, e.g. children, orthopaedic patients, stroke patients, alcoholics, drug abusers, elderly people, those with learning disabilities or mental health needs.

Occupational therapists are important members of the health team. They are practical problem-solvers and have enormous involvement in people's lives at a critical time. The success of their work depends on winning people's confidence, establishing a relationship, being able to work as part of a team but also independently. There is a shortage of occupational therapists and increasing demands with limited time and resources can lead to frustrations.

Occupational therapy support workers are generally employed in health and social services departments. They work under the supervision of occupational therapists, who provide the in-service training in their own specialist areas. They can also work towards NVQs; achievement of a level 3 NVQ can lead to a degree course.

Training   1. 3-year full-time course or 4-year part-time course leading to a degree.
        2. 2-year accelerated courses for graduates.
        3. 4-year part-time in-service courses for mature entrants already working in OT.

Personal   Organizing ability; the ability to explain things clearly to all types
attributes   of patient; adaptability and judgement to find the right approach to psychiatric patients; resourcefulness, patience, cheerfulness, good powers of observation; some dexterity; an interest in practical work; and a fairly strong scientific bent.

Late start   Good opportunities – about 30% of students are mature entrants. Applicants must check individual schools' requirements. Mature students may be accepted without the standard academic qualifications, but they are normally expected either to have considerable work experience or to show evidence of recent academic study (e.g. an A-level, Open University Foundation Course (see p. xxxiii) or Access course, see p. xxxi). There are also special courses – see (3) under 'Training', above.

Career-   No problem. Refresher courses available.
break

Part time   Good opportunities for basic-grade and senior practitioner positions as well as job shares, but this is dependent on employer requirements.

Position   Traditionally an all-female profession, with men making up 5%
of   of the workforce, although this is increasing.
women

Further   College of Occupational Therapists, 6–8 Marshalsea Road, South-
informa-   wark, London SE1 1HL
tion

Related   PHYSIOTHERAPY – NURSING: *Psychiatric Nurse*
careers

Optical Work

Optometrist (Ophthalmic Optician)

Entry qualifications

2, or more often 3, A-levels or 4 or 5 Scottish Highers: in both cases 2 must be in mathematics or science. GCSEs (minimum grade C) to include English, maths and physics or physics with chemistry.

The work

The main duties of an optometrist are examining eyes; measuring vision defects with the help of optical instruments; and working out lens-prescriptions for short- or far-sightedness and astigmatism.

Some optometrists now test sight with computerized equipment. They are also trained to dispense ophthalmic prescriptions. The training is broad based and is both scientific and medical. The work combines dealing with people and applied science; much of the work is clinically based and the optometrist has to see the patient as a human being, not simply as a pair of eyes. Optometrists are concerned with the correction and treatment of visual errors and the health of the visual system. They do not treat patients with diseased eyes. If they find any abnormality or signs of disease in the eye they refer the patient to his or her general practitioner.

Optometrists work either in general practice, doing mainly sight-testing, or in hospital, where they see more intricate eye conditions and assist ophthalmic surgeons with investigations and treatment of eye disease, and with research.

General practice may mean seeing patients in 'rooms' – possibly in the optician's own home; it may mean managing and/or owning an optician's practice and doing all the dispensing work as well; frequently it means doing the ophthalmic work in a shop managed and/or owned by a firm of ophthalmic or dispensing opticians which owns several practices.

There is a steady demand for optometrists.

Training

3 years for a B.Sc. degree (in Scotland 4 years) plus 1 year's clinical experience in paid employment. The syllabus includes physical optics, optical instruments, anatomy and physiology, abnormal and pathological conditions of the eye, refraction. The

British College of Optometrists is the examining body for ophthalmic optics. After passing the College's Professional Qualifying Examination and completing a pre-Registration year, students apply for Registration with the General Optical Council. Registration is obligatory for practitioners.

Personal attributes

An interest in physics and maths; patience; manual dexterity; a liking for briefly meeting a flow of new people; a confident manner especially with old people and children; business ability.

Late start

This is a long training and courses are oversubscribed, therefore only applicants with up-to-date knowledge of science likely to be accepted. Approximately 7% of entrants are over 30. Once trained there should be no problem getting jobs.

Career-break

If one has kept up with developments, no problem. *Refresher* courses available for all optometrists.

Part time

Good opportunities at all levels. Job-sharing possible.

Position of women

Women have been accepted for a long time and have no problems getting good jobs. The proportion of registered practitioners who are women is nearly 50%. In recent years over half the UK students accepted for optometry degree courses at university have been women. Optometry is well-suited to part-time work and women optometrists have also found it relatively easy to return to full-time work after a spell of part-time work.

Further information

The College of Optometrists, 10 Knaresborough Place, London SW5 0TG

Dispensing Optician

Entry qualifications

5 GCSEs (A–C) including maths or physics, English, plus 1 other science subject.

The work

Dispensing opticians do not do any sight-testing or other eye-examination. They interpret the prescription of the ophthalmic surgeon or ophthalmic optician using complex apparatus to measure for, fit and supply spectacles, contact lenses and artificial eyes. All such work requires calculations of distance and angles, etc. Equally important are the selling and 'cosmetic' aspects of the work. Dispensing opticians discuss with patients (a term opticians use in preference to customers) which type of frame is the most flattering in each case.

Most dispensing opticians also deal with other types of optical instruments, supplying apparatus to ophthalmic surgeons, opticians and laboratories, and selling sunglasses, opera glasses, microscopes, etc. to the general public.

Dispensing opticians can also get managerial jobs in 'prescription houses' (firms which make lenses to prescription) and in firms of dispensing opticians which manufacture optical instruments.

Dispensing opticians usually start as assistants but later may manage a shop, or practice, in which optometrists or surgeons do the eye-testing.

They have at least as great a variety of jobs and settings to choose from as optometrists. In relation to their educational qualifications and the length of their respective trainings, they do better financially – a dispensing optician manager may in fact earn more than a practising optometrist.

Training   *Either* (and recommended): a 2-year full-time course at a technical college, plus 1 year's practical experience; *or*: 3 years' work as a trainee with a dispensing optician, plus theoretical instruction, either by day-release or by correspondence course (which must be approved by the General Optical Council) with some attendance at a college.

All methods of training lead to the qualifying examinations for Fellowship of the Association of British Dispensing Opticians.

The syllabus covers optical physics, the anatomy and physiology of the eye, the interpretation of ophthalmic prescriptions, the necessary measurements and adjustments for frames, and the recording of facial measurements. The full-time course also includes business practice.

Personal attributes   Some manual dexterity; interest in salesmanship and in fashion; ability and enjoyment in dealing with flow of people.

Late start   No special problems, except for competition from young entrants. Science graduates may be exempt from part of the course.

Career-break   No problem: *refresher* courses exist and may increase.

Part time   Good opportunities also for job-sharing at all levels up to managing a high street shop.

**Position
of
women**

Steady increase of women entrants over last few years; now women account for about half of practitioners and many are in senior management jobs.

Orthoptics

**Entry
qualifica-
tions**

5 GCSEs (A–C) including English language, maths and a science subject, and 3 A-levels, preferably including a science subject.

The work

Orthoptists are responsible for the diagnosis, investigation, treatment and progress-monitoring of patients who have defects of binocular vision, e.g. squint, double vision or related vision conditions. The orthoptist's role is expanding. The importance of early diagnosis and treatment of children is increasingly recognized. Orthoptists therefore work on screening programmes for pre-school-age children. Special equipment and special skills enable orthoptists to assess the visual abilities of even very young children – some patients are under a year old. Orthoptists also deal with children who have reading difficulties. They must be able to build up relationships with children of all ages and with their parents.

Other patient-groups include the physically and mentally handicapped; people who have had accidents or strokes; multiple sclerosis sufferers; and the elderly who can be helped to achieve their maximum visual potential, for example in glaucoma clinics. The latter client group is increasing in size as the proportion of elderly people in the population is increasing.

Orthoptists thus deal with a very wide age-range; with a wide range of conditions, and in a range of settings – in hospitals, in paediatrics, school, geriatric and neurological clinics or departments. Patients are referred by ophthalmic surgeons, neurologists, general physicians, paediatricians, and other specialists.

Equipment used for diagnosis and treatment is highly sophisticated. Its use requires great technical knowledge and skill. The need for getting clients of all ages to co-operate and do exercises – both in the clinic and at home – requires orthoptists to understand and communicate well with people of all ages and temperaments.

There are opportunities for experienced orthoptists to become clinical teachers of orthoptics, and to work in private practice. British qualifications are accepted in most countries and there is scope for orthoptists in the EU if they speak the relevant language.

Training

This is via a 3-year degree course. Syllabus includes general anatomy and physiology; child development; anatomy and physiology of eye and brain; optics; diseases of the eye and the principles of eye surgery; practice of orthoptics.

Students gradually gain clinical experience working with patients of all ages.

Personal attributes   A scientific bent; powers of observation, deduction and persuasion; understanding of people of all ages and temperaments; ability to work as one of a team, and also independently; communication skills.

Late start   The orthoptists insist on normal entry qualifications. However, determined candidates in their 20s or 30s may be admitted for training especially if they have had experience of dealing with children. Approximately 5% of entrants are mature (see 'Access courses', p. xxxi).

Career-break   Depends on (a) whether orthoptist kept up with developments, and (b) on level of vacancies. Short 'up-dating' *refresher* courses are available.

Part time   Fair opportunities; promotion to head of department possible; job-sharing schemes can be arranged by enterprising practitioners.

Position of women   This is still a virtually all-female profession, but no reason why it should remain so. About 5% of orthoptists are male.

Further information   British Orthoptic Society, Tavistock House North, Tavistock Square, London WC1H 0HX

Related careers   MEDICINE – SCIENCE

Osteopathy

Entry qualifications See 'Training', below.

The work An osteopath uses manipulative methods both in the diagnosis and the treatment for the correction of derangements of the bony and muscular structures of the body, and makes a special study of the spine in relation to health and disease. Osteopathy does not include the curing of organic disease but it covers the treatment of some organic functional disorders. The majority of patients need treatment because of stiff joints, slipped discs, etc. Patients are often referred to osteopaths by GPs who recognize the value of osteopathic treatment for certain disorders, but the majority of patients come through personal recommendation.

The majority of osteopaths work in private practice, but increasingly they are working within the NHS (with fund-holding GPs and Trust hospitals) to make osteopathy more widely available.

Osteopathy was granted statutory recognition under the Osteopathy Act 1993 (the first statutory body in primary health care to be set up since the 1930s). A General Osteopathy Council (GOsC) is due to be set up, and this will accredit courses and qualifications for the profession. This will replace the 5 registering bodies which up to now have accredited courses run at various schools and colleges.

The normal procedure after qualifying is first to obtain experience as an assistant to an osteopath or at a clinic, then to start one's own part-time practice in addition, and perhaps finally to concentrate entirely on one's own practice.

This is a small profession, but interest in osteopathy is growing steadily.

Training Several courses lead to a degree validated by a university, while others lead to a Diploma. A few are designed for qualified doctors or other health care professionals. Most courses are 4-year full-time or 5-year part-time.

Three main training schools offer full-time courses leading to a degree for those without previous health care qualifications:

1. *The British School of Osteopathy* offers a B.Sc. in Osteo-

pathy. Minimum entry requirements: 2 science A-levels, preferably biology and chemistry, and 3 GCSEs.

2. *European School of Osteopathy*: entry requirements as in (1).

3. *British College of Naturopathy and Osteopathy*: A-level chemistry and biological science and 3 GCSEs in at least 2 of the following: English, maths and physics.

There are special provisions for mature students with other relevant studies or work experience.

These are all accredited by The General Council and Register of Osteopaths. The other registering bodies are: Guild of Osteopaths, Natural Therapeutic and Osteopathic Society, British and European Osteopathic Association and College of Osteopaths Practitioners Association.

The syllabus for all courses includes anatomy; physiology; osteopathic theory; practice and technique; diagnosis; pathology; preventive medicine; biochemistry; dietetics; bacteriology.

There are other, smaller, training organizations. There is also a move within the profession to agree standards so that osteopaths can seek recognition in the EU.

Personal attributes Confidence-inspiring manner; skilful, gentle, yet strong hands; good health; patience; interest in people's lifestyles.

Late start Some relaxation of entry requirements if candidates considered suitable; shortened courses for people with relevant qualifications (e.g. physiotherapy, medicine). Late entrants have no difficulty getting patients once trained. About 20% of students are mature entrants.

Career-break The vast majority of women osteopaths continue working part time from home throughout their career. Post-graduate *refresher* seminars available.

Part time Very good opportunities.

Position of women About 40% of osteopaths are women, and so are about 50% of osteopathy students. Experienced osteopaths say that it is not a job for frail women: they would find some of the work physically impossible. But on the whole women osteopaths have no problem getting patients.

Further information Osteopathic Information Service, PO Box 2074, Reading, Berks. RG1 4YR

Related careers MEDICINE – PHYSIOTHERAPY

Patent Agent (Chartered) and Patent Examiner

Entry qualifications

Minimum 2 A-levels for Foundation exam, but in practice a science or engineering degree; working knowledge of French and German very desirable.

Patent Agent

The work

Patent agents work in the field of intellectual property. Put very simply, a patent is the right to stop a product, process, trademark, design or written material that has been invented or originated by one person from being copied or developed by another for a certain number of years. It is a mixture of legal and scientific/technological work. A patent agent advises inventors, and others concerned with inventions, on the validity and infringement of patents at home and abroad. Until recently only patent agents registered with the Chartered Institute of Patent Agents had the right to submit patents. A change in the law means that now anyone can do the work of a patent agent but cannot be called a 'patent agent' unless registered. (They may be called 'consultants'.)

Patent agents make 'searches' for clients to ensure that their inventions really are new, and prepare detailed specifications, descriptions and formulations of claims which 'cover' the invention. They file and negotiate the application for patents on behalf of their clients at the Patent Office. Having assisted in the creation of a patent, they may deal with its commercial application. They deal not only with patents for processes and products, but also with 'Registered Designs', 'Registered Trade Marks' and Industrial Copyright.

The majority of agents specialize in a particular type of work, e.g. in chemical or mechanical inventions, or in electronics – a very important area – or in designs and trade marks. Most firms of patent agents are trade mark agents, but there are also independent trade mark agents.

Patent agents work in private practice or for industrial organizations. It is usual to start as an assistant doing searches in the Patent Office and other libraries.

Patent agents' work has increased in scope and complexity since the coming into force of the European Patent Convention. In addition to preparing and processing patent applications in this country and corresponding with patent agents abroad to obtain similar protection for clients' inventions there, patent agents who are suitably qualified draft patent applications for submission to the European Patent Office in Munich. There are reasonable opportunities for travel to Europe and other countries.

Although this is a small profession there is increasing scope.

Training

The Chartered Institute of Patent Agents introduced new training regulations in 1991. There is now a Foundation and an Advanced level, with separate exams for the Patent Agents and Trade Marks Registers.

There is no longer a minimum training period before passing the exams, but trainees must have 2 years' professional experience after passing the exams before being registered. Most are expected to go on to take the exams of the European Patent Institute in order to qualify as European Patent Attorneys, eligible to submit patents to the European Patent Office.

Preparation for examinations is mainly by private study; some firms sponsor trainees on a 3-month full-time course for the Foundation Stage. The Chartered Institute arranges lectures and tutorials. Some technical assistants never qualify yet nevertheless do very well, but they cannot become partners in private practice firms.

Personal attributes

Curiosity; an analytical mind; a good memory; a scientific bent; the ability to assimilate facts quickly and to reason and speak clearly; ability to write clearly and unambiguously; liking for concentrated desk work.

Late start

Entrance requirements may be waived for people with relevant experience, but there are difficulties getting training vacancies.

Career-break

Return possible only for those who have kept up with legal and technological changes/developments.

Part time

Some opportunities; it is also possible for experienced patent agents with good contacts to run a small private practice from home. Job-sharing should be possible.

Position of women   Women make up 10% of Institute members. Nearly 7% of Chartered patent agents and 29% of students are women, so numbers are increasing. Few women tried to enter this profession until recently; there is no discrimination.

Further information   Chartered Institute of Patent Agents, Staple Inn Buildings, London WC1V 7PZ

Patent Examiner

Entry qualifications   First- or second-class honours degree in a scientific, engineering or mathematical subject; ability to read French and German is very important.

The work   Patent examiners work in the Patent Office in Newport, Gwent, and examine applications for patents. The Patent Office is now an executive agency of the Department of Trade and Industry. An examiner's work involves detailed examination of the description of an invention; making a search through earlier specifications to ascertain the novelty of the invention; classifying and indexing the features of the invention; writing a report embodying the findings; and, if necessary, interviewing the inventor or the inventor's agent to discuss any problems. The work requires an analytical and critical mind. Each examiner works in a specialized field. Training is on the job and includes a 2-year probationary period. Vacancies arise very rarely.

Personal attributes   As for Patent Agent.

Late start   Very rare, but occasionally possible for people with relevant (technological) degrees and experience.

Career-break   Presents problems – few vacancies; need to keep up with developments; competition from new graduates.

Part time   Possible for established examiners. No reason why job-sharing should not work. (See CIVIL SERVICE, p. 123.)

Position of women   Approximately 10% of examiners are women. The Patent Office is trying to attract more women to join.

Further informa- tion   The Patent Office, Concept House, Cardiff Road, Newport, Gwent NP9 1RA

Related careers   CIVIL SERVICE – ENGINEERING – SCIENCE

Personnel/Human Resources Management

Entry qualifications

For Institute of Personnel and Development's Professional Education Scheme: *either* 2 A-levels and 3 GCSEs (A–C) and minimum age 21; *or* at least 2 years' relevant work experience. About half of all entrants are *graduates* and many have BTEC HND Business Studies (see p. xxi). See 'Training', below, for alternative method of entry.

The work

Personnel officers are part of the management team. Titles vary and are not necessarily any indication of scope and level of responsibility. The term 'human resources manager' is now often used. Their primary aim is always the efficient use and development of people's talents. The Institute of Personnel and Development says that personnel management is not a job for people who merely want to 'work with people'. Personnel managers' main job is 'to provide the specialist knowledge or service that can assist other members of the management-team to make the most effective use of the human resources – people – of the organization'.

Personnel management used to be considered an offshoot of social work; it is certainly that no longer. The average personnel officer does not necessarily spend more time in one-to-one discussions with individuals who need advice than do, for example, solicitors or accountants. 'Personnel' is a 'management function', like buying, marketing and production. Its challenge is to interpret conflicting views and objectives to people at various levels in an organization, some of whom have divergent interests.

Personnel officers are employed not only in industry, but also in hospitals, local and central government: the efficient use of human resources is equally vital to profit-making and to non-profit-making organizations. The range of jobs is very great indeed. In a large organization, employing say 70,000 people at several sites, a personnel director may have a staff of 70, some of whom specialize in one aspect of the work; in a small organization 1 or 2 people might do everything.

Main (overlapping) personnel specializations:

Recruitment, training and management-development: Devising, monitoring and applying selection procedures, possibly selecting the most suitable of various psychological testing and assessment methods for all levels of staff; identifying individuals' potential and planning their education, training and career development. This involves reconciling individuals' needs and aims with the employer's requirements for staff with specific skills at specific levels of responsibility. It is a very important specialization now because of the emphasis in the last few years on the need for a more highly skilled workforce at all levels from operatives to management. This department may include the formation and implementation of equal opportunities policies.

Management of change: Personnel people may or may not be responsible for masterminding this – see MANAGEMENT, p. 275 – but they are invariably involved. During the introduction of new technologies or structures personnel people work closely with systems analysts/designers, with, perhaps, technologists, occupational psychologists and other specialists and with union officials, ironing out problems arising when changes in traditional working patterns are proposed and implemented. This requires personnel people to have thorough understanding of individuals' present tasks, of their place in the hierarchy, and of how proposed changes will affect individuals' jobs.

Reward management: Covers job evaluation and equal pay for equal work administration. It involves systematic study of the tasks that make up individual jobs within the organization, in order to establish their gradings. Reward management sounds misleadingly like a desk-bound routine job, but it can be one of the most non-routine and controversial specializations.

Employee relations: Establishing and maintaining lines of communication between an organization's various interest groups. It involves discussing, with shop stewards and management, 'worker participation' schemes; implication of new legislation (of which there is a constant flow); mergers; implementation of new technologies; dealing with consequent redundancies, and planning reallocation of tasks and retraining schemes.

Employee services is concerned with matters of health and safety and all welfare aspects. It may include personal counselling services (see 'Counselling', p. 410); responsibility for canteens, etc., as well as sophisticated job satisfaction improvement schemes and co-operation with manpower planning, training and other personnel specialists.

Not all personnel departments divide personnel functions in the same way; there are many variations on the 'effective use of human resources' theme.

Personnel workers who get to the top normally have had

experience in several specialist fields, but there are few hard and fast rules. A specialist training officer in a large and/or progressive organization may have greater scope, responsibility and status (and salary) than a personnel director in charge of all specialist functions in another organization. It is impossible to generalize about career-paths, but it is probably best for those aiming at top jobs to get experience in large organizations, where they have the chance of working on a wide range of problems using a variety of personnel techniques.

Many organizations with establishments in different towns expect personnel officers to move around the country. It is quite usual to move from one employer to another, not necessarily remaining in the same type of organization, for example from factory to hospital, store to local government, etc. However, with the introduction of new technologies more personnel people stay either in manufacturing or in service industries.

Training   The Institute's Professional Education Scheme is divided into Stage 1 (Professional Management Foundation Programme) and Stage 2 and leads to graduateship of the Institute. Students take a 1-year full-time, or a 2–3-year part-time course, normally while in relevant employment (but see 'Position of women', below). Following the merger of the former Institutes of Personnel Management and Training and Development to create the Institute of Personnel and Development in 1994, a new Professional Education Scheme is being introduced (by September 1996).

BTEC/SCOTVEC Higher National award holders (see pp. xxi, xxii) and graduates may qualify for partial or total exemption from Stage 1, depending on the relevance of the subject studied for the previous qualification.

It is possible to prepare for IPD exams by correspondence course, preferably, but not necessarily, while in relevant employment. The Institute offers its own flexible learning version of Stage 1 and Stage 2.

Those not qualified or experienced enough to follow the Professional Education Scheme may take a Certificate in Personnel Practice. Study is part time and is suitable for students from a variety of backgrounds, including clerical, secretarial and line management, who will acquire practical personnel skills to help them in their job.

NVQs and SVQs level 4 and 5 in Management and at level 3 and 4 in Training and Development are recognized by the IPD for membership. NVQs/SVQs levels 3, 4 and 5 in Personnel Management are being introduced.

Graduates with a business studies or social/behavioural science degree or post-graduate qualification may get on well without IPD qualifications if they have acquired the necessary knowledge (legislation, training techniques, industrial relations procedures, etc.). Some employers do not mind whether staff have IPD qualifications or not. In fact, some heads of department positively prefer graduates, preferably with social/behavioural science degrees *and/or* with relevant experience acquired in *any* capacity – as secretary, technician, junior manager/supervisor, etc. – who do *not* have IPD qualifications. However, qualifications *are* increasingly required by many employers, and they are valuable for women who want to return to work after the child-rearing gap.

Personal attributes   A flair for seeing all sides of a problem and interpreting each side's point of view to the other; a good memory for names and faces; at least an absence of dislike for figure-work, preferably a liking for it; interest in profitable management and in change; lack of prejudice; tact; detachment; an understanding of people of all types, ages, races and backgrounds, and the ability to gain their confidence and respect; organizing ability.

Late start   Some opportunities for mature entrants who have had relevant experience.

Career-break   Personnel workers are able to return to the work if they have kept up with legislation and other personnel developments. They can take part-time or correspondence *refresher* courses (see 'Training', above) to update their knowledge. A career-break information pack is available for personnel managers.

Part time   Very few opportunities, but recently some determined returners have convinced employers that part time works. Job-sharing (see p. xxviii) is possible with more progressive employers.

Position of women   There were proportionately far more women personnel managers in the past, when personnel work was largely concerned with welfare. As emphasis changed from 'dealing with people' to improving the efficient working of an organization, men took over top jobs and it became customary for women simply to look after women personnel, i.e. women only remained in top jobs, if at all, in stores and other places where most of the staff were female. Statistics are misleading because job titles give little indication of level of responsibility, but women are now known to be in the minority at head of department level. However, many do well as specialists in training and management development and in management of change. They also have good scope in small and medium-sized organizations where there is little personnel-function specialization. There are very few women with industrial relations experience, which is essential for most senior jobs in large organizations. Women who have got to the top of the profession say that the opportunities are there – it is the lack of role-models, and women's lack of confidence to apply for senior posts, which is keeping numbers in senior jobs so low. Over half the qualified members but only a quarter of student IPD members are men.

Further information   Institute of Personnel and Development, 35 Camp Road, London SW19 4UX

Related careers   CAREERS WORK – HEALTH AND SAFETY INSPECTORS – MANAGEMENT – RETAIL MANAGEMENT

Pharmacy

Pharmacist

Entry qualifications

3 A-levels including chemistry and 2 chosen from a mathematical subject, physics and a biological science. The subject not offered at A-level should be offered at GCSE. In practice, an English GCSE (A–C) is essential. Some schools of pharmacy will accept BTEC awards (see p. xxi) in place of A-levels.

The work

Pharmacists work in 3 distinct fields: *community*, *hospital* and *industry*. Students do not need to decide which branch of pharmacy they want to go into until after qualifying.

Community Pharmacists (usually called 'chemists' – a title pharmacists discourage)

Pharmacists dispense or supervise the dispensing of prescriptions. They act as a link between doctors and their patients, by explaining the effects and the correct use of medicines.

Most medicines are now available ready-made but pharmacists still make up the occasional prescription in the dispensary. They are also responsible for the safe and correct storage of a variety of medicines and some chemical substances. They are legally required to keep records such as the 'controlled drug' registers.

Pharmacists may also deal with the buying and selling of cosmetics, toiletries, etc., and the training of shop staff. In larger pharmacies, and particularly in chains of pharmacies, the pharmacist has the choice of remaining involved with the dispensing and sale of medicines, or of becoming more involved with the commercial side.

The role of pharmacists is changing. As more and more new drugs come on the market, both doctors and patients are making more use of pharmacists' thorough knowledge of the composition, action and interaction of new drugs. Many doctors ask pharmacists' advice – or at least their views – on the best way to use new drugs for particular conditions. Pharmacists have more time to keep up with pharmaceutical developments than doctors. Also, patients increasingly ask pharmacists' advice for minor ailments and their opinion on whether they should consult their doctor. Pharmacists are well qualified to know when medical advice must be sought and when a simple remedy (which may be cheaper than one on prescription) is all that the patient needs.

Because pharmacists are becoming more involved with community health care (they may, for example, visit residential homes) their professional body is now trying to change the traditional term 'chemist' to 'community pharmacist'.

Pharmacists are now more often managers of pharmacies or of dispensing departments than owners of their own business.

Abroad: Qualified pharmacists can practise and get jobs fairly easily in some countries of the Commonwealth; harmonization of qualifications within EC countries has been agreed.

Hospital Pharmacists

The work Particularly suitable for those interested in the science of pharmacy. Hospital pharmacists dispense – and supervise the dispensing of – prescriptions for out-patients; they advise patients on the proper use of their medicines; they issue medicines for use within the hospital and they work closely with doctors and nurses to ensure that medicines are used safely, correctly and economically. They advise on doses and side-effects of drugs and are often involved in clinical trial work on new drugs. Most medicines used in hospital are ready-made, but some preparations are made up in the hospital pharmacy. They also have a teaching role – they assist with the training of student pharmacists and student pharmacy technicians; and they lecture to doctors and nurses.

Some hospitals offer a 24-hour pharmacy service, provided by pharmacists who live in when on duty.

Hospital pharmacists' role is also changing. Pharmacists may accompany consultants on ward rounds and may be consulted on the best drug to use in any particular case. Young doctors often ask pharmacists' advice and pharmacists may be asked to check patients' drug-charts to look for adverse reactions if patients take several different kinds of drugs; so there is more patient-contact than in the past.

Hospital pharmacists have a definite career structure. There is work which involves contact with people, and backroom work. Hospital pharmacists work in a community, with the opportunity of meeting people in similar jobs.

Industrial Pharmacists

The work They work in laboratories of pharmaceutical and related firms and on the production and development of new drugs and the improvement and quality control of existing drugs. As in other scientific work (see p. 438), pharmacists work in teams, often together with scientists from other disciplines. Some jobs involve mainly desk-work such as providing information to doctors and the preparation of data on new products for the Licensing Authority. Those with a bent for salesmanship can become representatives, visiting doctors in their surgeries and in hospital, providing information on their companies' products (and they may become marketing executives, an expanding area).

There is therefore scope for the quiet backroom type content with semi-routine work, for the team leader with a bent for pursuing new lines of thought and for those who want to go into general management, marketing and pharmaceutical sales.

Training 3-year degree course. The syllabus includes *pharmaceutical chemistry* – the origin and chemistry of drugs; *pharmaceutics* – the preparation of medicines; *pharmacology* – the action and uses of drugs and medicines in living systems; *pharmacy practice* – dispensing and counselling skills, pharmacy law and ethics.

After graduating, students must obtain 1 year's pre-registration experience in pharmacy, which must include at least 6 months in community or hospital practice, and pass the Society's registration examination, before they are eligible to apply for registration as pharmaceutical chemists.

Personal attributes *For all pharmacists*: A strong scientific bent; meticulous accuracy; a strong sense of responsibility; a calm, logical mind; ability to concentrate; organizing ability.

For community and industrial pharmacists: A flair for business; ability to deal with semi- and untrained staff; a liking for people.

For industrial pharmacists: An inquiring mind; ability to work as one of a team; infinite patience.

Late start No upper age limit for training or jobs, but there is no relaxation of entry requirements.

Career-break Should be no problem. Several schools of pharmacy run short *refresher* courses to help returners update their knowledge and dispensing skills. In some cases the Department of Health will even pay costs of refresher courses. Some large multiple pharmacy groups also offer re-training. There are also some distance-learning courses.

Part time   Good opportunities (although in hospital promotion prospects poorer than for full-timers). Job-sharing is becoming accepted in hospital and in community work.

Position of women   This is a very promising career for women; 45% of registered pharmacists are women and 59% of students starting university pharmacy degrees in 1994 were women. Proportionately more women work in hospitals than in community and in industry. But that is by choice: they are welcome as community pharmacy managers (the majority of clients are women) and also in sales and marketing and have equal promotion chances. The National Association of Women Pharmacists sends useful free pack, *Women in Pharmacy*, on request.

Further information   Royal Pharmaceutical Society of Great Britain, 1 Lambeth High Street, London SE1 7JN *or* 36 York Place, Edinburgh EH1 3HU
National Association of Women Pharmacists, c/o Office Manager, Royal Pharmaceutical Society, London address

Related careers   MEDICINE – *Pharmacy Technician (see below)* – SCIENCE: *Chemistry*; *Biochemistry* . . .

*

Pharmacy Technician

Entry qualifications   Depend on type of work and employer, see 'Training', below.

The work   This varies according to whether the job is in *retail* (*community*) pharmacy, *industry* or the *NHS*. In *retail*, technicians may spend time on the selling side when not assisting the pharmacist with dispensing (but they work always under the supervision of qualified pharmacists who must check prescriptions, etc.). In *hospitals* and *industry*, technicians have more chance to do responsible and varied work. They assist with experiments, with interviewing patients, and they may liaise with other departments, etc. The role of the technician in the NHS and in industry is changing: as in other science-based jobs (see SCIENCE, p. 438) technicians now often do jobs which overlap with graduates', but there will always be a considerable difference between the project-leader type and level of work, and that of technicians who implement proven techniques. While using their judgement and expertise, they do not take ultimate responsibility or do original research.

Training   *For NHS and most industry jobs*: BTEC/SCOTVEC National Certificate in Science (Pharmaceutical). Entry requirements: 4 GCSEs (A–C) including a science, or BTEC First Certificate (see p. xxi) in 2 Sciences. SCOTVEC requires 3 S grades including chemistry. The 2-year day-release National Certificate course is for people in relevant employment and subjects include broad, basic sciences, human physiology, action and uses of drugs, and quality control.

Community pharmacy technicians have another choice: they may take *either* companies' own training scheme *or* the National Pharmaceutical Association's correspondence course. Most employers allow students up to 5 hours a week for study. There are no rigid entry requirements, but students without a GCSE in a biological science will find the course difficult.

NVQs are being developed and should be available in 1996.

Personal attributes   Meticulous accuracy; a scientific bent but not necessarily great academic ability.

Late start   Depends on local supply and demand position. Entrance requirements may be waived; but school-leavers may be given preference.

Career-break   Returners' opportunities depend on supply and demand position.

Part time   Fair opportunities.

Position of women   The vast majority of technicians are women.

Further information   National Pharmaceutical Association, Mallinson House, 38 St Peter's Street, St Albans, Herts. AL1 3NP

BTEC, Central House, Upper Woburn Place, London WC1H 0HH

Related careers   RETAIL MANAGEMENT – SCIENCE: *Science Technician*

Photography

Photographer

Entry qualifications

No definite educational requirements for photography as such, but see individual course requirements under 'Training', below.

Photography covers over 30 specializations, but many photographers combine several of these. London photographers tend to be more specialized than those in the provinces. Many freelance photographers take on any work which is offered, in order to earn a living. 'Bread and butter' jobs can help pay for more creative, but less well-paid, assignments.

Creative Photography

The work

General practice

Approximately half of all photographers work in general photographic studios. The bulk of their work consists of portraiture, group photographs and commercial services. Portrait subjects include, increasingly, pets; some photographers specialize in children.

Photographers prefer their subjects to come to the studio to be photographed, because it is easier to arrange the lighting there. However, there is an increasing demand for portraits in the home, garden or workplace, especially in the case of children's portraits. The 'natural' portrait is much more popular today than the formal one. To produce not just a good likeness, but a characteristic portrait, photographers must have considerable understanding of, and insight into, human nature; they must be able to put sitters at ease so that their expression is natural.

Weddings and other group photographs (e.g. sports and social clubs) form another important part of the work. Wedding photography now offers more scope for 'creative' pictures in a less formal style than it used to. Commercial work is mainly for publicity purposes – for local companies, estate agencies, architects, etc. who do not have enough work to employ a staff photographer.

Opportunities are reasonable. One way in for the keen amateur is to help a busy studio with Saturday weddings.

Advertising

Very varied. Although advertising photographers are often given exact instructions about what to photograph and what effect to aim at, they are also expected to suggest their own ideas for new angles. Many advertisements are records of everyday life – whether it is of a child eating breakfast, or a woman getting out of a car – and involve both work with models, and persuading ordinary people to agree to be photographed.

Advertising photographs are taken either by the photographic departments of advertising agencies, by photographic studios (i.e. several photographers working as partners, sharing darkroom and office facilities, or salaried photographers and assistants working for an employer), or by freelance photographers. Most do some catalogue work; some studios specialize in *mail-order* photography (and may be owned by the mail-order company).

This is the best paid and hence a very competitive branch; success depends entirely on ability, efficiency and the right personality.

Fashion

Although advertising includes fashion photography, some photographers specialize in fashion. Most fashion photography is done by specialist studios or freelances who are commissioned by editors, fashion houses or advertising agencies; they usually work under the direction of a fashion expert.

This is the most sought-after branch and hence *very* difficult to enter.

Photo-journalism (feature photography), press and editorial photography

Photo-journalism is, essentially, telling a story in pictures, and therefore a journalistic sense is needed. *Feature photographers* may work with reporters as a team; they may be freelances, or work for studios. Only a tiny minority are on editorial staffs. It is very varied work, and leads to assignments at any time and in any place – photographing VIPs at home, or life in foreign parts, or schools at work – anything that makes a story. Hours are irregular.

There is more hard, hurried work than glamour in *press photography*, which consists almost entirely of single news pictures. Press photographers must be versatile in taking all kinds of subjects.

They must know what makes a good news picture; be able to write accurate captions; work well with reporters; be very quick and often work under difficult conditions. Hours are irregular.

Editorial photographers work mainly for magazines, nearly always as freelances. Work can be very varied, depending on the article or report which needs illustrating. It varies from shots of a TV star at home with children/pets to a travel feature; from contestants in a cookery competition to action shots of a parachute jump.

Prospects are fair, but competition is stiff. The market for photo-journalists is small. Most work as freelances and may specialize, e.g. in travel. For press photography there are always more candidates than jobs. Some possibilities for photographers in other branches to sell work to newspapers or press agencies. Editorial photography depends on building up good contacts and a reputation for reliability.

Industrial and Scientific Photography

The work This is the most varied branch of photography and has the most openings. Clients include manufacturing companies, research organizations, government departments, higher education establishments, the police and HM Forces. Examples of the work: making photographic progress reports in laboratories; recording the various stages of manufacturing processes; photographing building sites. Industrial photographers also take pictures for house magazines, exhibition stands and instructional purposes. Most of these photographers are salaried employees; some work as freelances or for studios (see 'General practice', above, p. 378).

Medical Photography

The work Most teaching hospitals and medical research institutions employ medical photographers, sometimes as part of a medical illustration team with medical artists and audio-visual technicians. They make still and cine records of work done in operating theatres and research laboratories, and of particular cases among patients. They also illustrate health care guides for patients and teaching material for student nurses and doctors. Medical photographers must not be squeamish.

Of all careers in photography this is the least hectic, least tough, most companionable and worst paid. There is some demand for medical photographers.

Training   *All photography*

Study can be part time, while working as a junior in a studio, or, increasingly, full time. The main courses recognized by the British Institute of Professional Photography are:

1. With, preferably, GCSEs (A–C) in English and maths: 2 years full time or 3 years part time for City and Guilds Photography scheme. Students are sometimes encouraged to study full time for the first year, then to work for a photographer for a year and return to college as either a full-time or a part-time student. Some centres now offer NVQs level 3 and 4 in photography.

2. With 4 GCSEs (A–C), normally including English language, maths and/or a science: a full-time 2-year course for BTEC National Diploma in Design (Photography).

3. With 1 or 2 A-levels, *or* BTEC/SCOTVEC National award, *or*, in some cases, City and Guilds certificates: 2-year full-time course for BTEC/SCOTVEC Higher National award.

This can be followed by a further year leading to the BIPP's *Professional Qualifying Examination* (*PQE*).

There are a few part-time courses leading to BTEC/SCOTVEC National Certificate and Higher National Certificate.

4. With 2 A-levels and 3 GCSEs (A–C), or for some courses an art and design Foundation Course: a degree in photography or photography, film and television or photographic science and technology. Several art and design degrees (see ART AND DESIGN, p. 54) have photography options.

Press photography

Either: 1-year pre-entry course organized by National Council for Training of Journalists (see JOURNALISM, p. 234): Entry requirements: 4 GCSEs (A–C) plus 1 A-level, including English.

Or the NCTJ's traineeship (see JOURNALISM, p. 234): Entry requirements: 5 GCSEs (A–C) including English.

NVQs/SVQs have been introduced by many newspaper companies.

Medical photography

With GCSEs or preferably A-levels, or after general photography course, entry as trainee in a hospital medical photography department. Then *either* private study for BIPP Qualifying Examination in medical photography and the Pre-Fellowship examination in medical photography, *or* part time or block-release for the Primary Certificate of Institute of Medical and Biological Illustrators, leading to the Diploma in Medical Illustration.

Photographic Technician

The work   The processing and printing of films is an extremely important aspect of photography and one in which backroom types are happiest. They may work in 'photofinishing' companies which process film taken by amateurs (e.g. holiday snapshots) or in laboratories which service professional photographers. Most work nowadays is in colour and is increasingly automated. The work requires considerable concentration and technical knowledge, especially of the complex chemistry of colour film; without these skills a photographer's assignment worth hundreds or even thousands of pounds could be ruined. Technicians may take turns at all the jobs: processing, transparency-making, enlarging, printing and mounting, or may stick to one or two. Experienced technicians can learn more specialized skills, e.g. retouching or making duplicate transparencies.

There is a shortage of good technicians; there is a greater demand for technicians than for photographers. Photofinishing offers most openings to school-leavers.

Training   Usually starting as a junior or trainee in a photographic laboratory, and studying by day-release and/or evening classes for City and Guilds examinations (see p. xxii). Also, some in-service courses provided by laboratories and manufacturers of photographic materials. Some large laboratories are approved assessment centres for NVQs in photographic processing.

Personal attributes   *Needed by all photographers in varying degrees*: Visual imagination; eye for detail and composition; patience; perfect colour vision; artistic sensitivity; creativeness; trust in their own judgement (photographers, unlike other craftspeople and artists, do not usually know whether they have done a good job or not until it is too late); good powers of observation; ability to work quickly, under pressure, surrounded by crowds – in all kinds of unfavourable circumstances; ability to work well with others while keeping to their own individual style; originality; unusual inventiveness (for advertising and fashion photography); business sense (for arranging appointments, sending out bills etc.), as very few can afford secretaries; willingness to 'sell' themselves; a manner which encourages people to co-operate.

Press photographers: News sense; ability to remain calm and unmoved, however tragic or unpleasant the circumstances.

Medical photographers: A scientific bent; tactful and reassuring manner; total lack of squeamishness.

Technicians: A scientific bent; manual skill; an eye for detail; patience.

Late start Press photography: upper age 24. A number of photographers have worked in other fields before taking up photography. Some colleges waive entry requirements for mature students. The main drawbacks are intense competition from college-leavers and poor salaries of trainee or assistant photographers.

Career-break Depends on stage reached before the break and type of work done. Possibly difficult to return to best-paid and most competitive fields, but it should be possible to return to some kind of photography and/or to do some freelance work even while raising a family. The BIPP may offer reduced subscriptions for women on a maternity break.

Part time Fair opportunities, especially as freelances.

Position of women Only 9% of BIPP members are women, but about 40% of college applicants are women. There are now a fair number of well-known women photographers, although very few have reached the top in the advertising field. Women still have a little more difficulty than men getting in, especially to press photography.

Further information British Institute of Professional Photography, Amwell End, Ware, Herts. SG12 9HN

City and Guilds of London Institute, 1 Giltspur Street, London EC1A 9DD

BTEC, Central House, Upper Woburn Place, London WC1H 0HH

Institute of Medical and Biological Illustration (IMBI), 27 Craven Street, London WC2 5NX

Related careers ART AND DESIGN – FASHION AND CLOTHING – JOURNALISM – TELEVISION, FILM AND RADIO

Physiotherapy

Entry qualifications

5 GCSEs (A–C) including maths, English and 2 science subjects taken at one sitting and 3 A-levels at minimum grade C; or Scottish Highers with minimum 2B and 2C grades taken at one sitting. Highers should normally include English and either maths or physics plus another science.

Alternative qualifications are BTEC National Diploma in Health Studies (Science) with distinctions/merits in all units, a Higher National Diploma, the International Baccalaureate and certain Access courses. At present the Advanced GNVQ/GSVQ in Health and Social Care does not have a strong enough science base for entry to a physiotherapy degree, but may be considered alongside a science A-level grade C.

The work

Physiotherapists use exercises and movement, electrotherapy – the use of heat, high frequency currents and ultrasonics – manipulation and massage to treat the injured, disabled, sick and convalescents of all ages for a large variety of conditions. They are responsible for assessing and analysing patients' conditions and for planning their treatment. Most patients are referred by doctors who give physiotherapists the information they need to devise suitable treatment, but physiotherapists in private practice also treat self-referred patients.

Patients too ill to be moved are treated in bed; others, such as post-operative patients, may have to be helped to walk properly again. Stroke patients are taught to make their healthy limbs or muscles do the work, as far as possible, of paralysed ones, and how to use paralysed limbs.

Some patients do exercises in water and the physiotherapist works with them in heated swimming pools.

Some patients are treated in groups, but most individually. In all cases, physiotherapists must use their judgement. They must know how far to coax a patient into doing an uncomfortable exercise, and must adapt treatment to suit each patient. They use tact and encouragement together with specialist knowledge when, for example, explaining to a patient why it is important that exercises are done regularly at home, or when persuading children to co-operate; or when allaying patients' fear of electrical treatment.

The work can be physically strenuous as it involves lifting and supporting patients, but physiotherapists learn to lift heavy weights without strain. ('Lifting' is one of the things they teach: patients needing treatment for strained backs are taught to lift correctly.)

The majority work in hospitals. After usually about 2 years' work, gaining all-round experience, they may specialize, for example in work with the elderly; in orthopaedic, chest or neurological conditions; and, increasingly, in work with mentally ill or handicapped children and/or adults. Work outside the hospital in the community is increasing. This may be giving treatments or preventive health education work; advising in factories, hospitals etc. on how to deal with carrying heavy weights etc. Physiotherapists also work with expectant mothers in clinics. There is also room for physiotherapists who want to do only preventive work: sports clubs employ physiotherapists (often part time) to keep their members fit, and to treat minor injuries; large industrial and commercial organizations employ physiotherapists to see that office desks are the right height for comfort, health and therefore efficiency; to show staff how to sit without strain; to teach sales assistants to relax while standing; to teach porters to carry without strain, and so on. Health farms and, sometimes, keep fit classes also employ physiotherapists.

There is a world shortage of physiotherapists, and of physiotherapy teachers and specialists, but promotion prospects vary. Increasingly experienced physiotherapists set up in private practice, treating patients either in their own treatment rooms or in patients' homes. But this needs good contacts with local doctors and capital to buy equipment and see them over the first few months. Qualifications are recognized in the EU and in many countries abroad, but in the USA and some other countries physiotherapists may have to take additional examinations.

Training   All courses now lead to a degree. Courses are at universities working closely with hospitals. Degree holders are eligible for membership of the Chartered Society of Physiotherapy, and for State Registration which is essential for work in the National Health Service, as well as for most other jobs.

The first year is always pre-clinical (theoretical); subjects studied include anatomy, physiology, physics, behavioural sciences, pathology and technical treatment skills. From the second year theory is combined with working with patients.

There are, in specialities such as sports physiotherapy and in teaching, post-graduate courses which are open to all physiotherapy graduates. There are opportunities for blind and partially sighted people to become chartered physiotherapists.

Personal attributes   Enough interest in science and medicine to keep up to date with new developments; a sympathetic yet objective approach to the sick and disabled; ability to work as one of a team and to take responsibility; good health; enthusiasm.

Late start   Most colleges now welcome mature students up to about 35. Entry qualifications are not rigidly enforced; applicants' work and life experience are taken into account; but for those who do not have the usual qualifications, evidence of ability to cope with degree-level study (including science) is required. An Open University credit or similar post-school study is useful. (Applicants may be advised to take an A-level science or Access course, see p. xxxi, and reapply later.) See *Guidelines for Mature Entrants*, below.

Career-break   Returners are welcome; *refresher* training arranged by hospitals or health authorities; it is essential after a break of more than 2 or 3 years.

Part time   Excellent opportunities, increasingly even in senior jobs. Job-sharing is encouraged.

Position of women   The vast majority (86%) are women. Women head most schools of physiotherapy, which used not to be the case. A growing proportion of entrants are men.

Further information   Chartered Society of Physiotherapy, 14 Bedford Row, London WC1R 4ED (*Guidelines for Mature Entrants* available free)

Related careers   OCCUPATIONAL THERAPY – SPEECH AND LANGUAGE THERA-PISTS – TEACHING

Police

Entry requirements

Vary slightly from force to force. In general, candidates must be at least 18½ and have good health and eyesight. *All* entrants sit an initial recruitment test. There are also nationality restrictions. (In Scotland, age and height restrictions may still apply.) There is also graduate entry.

The work

The primary purpose of the police is to protect life and property and enforce law and order. Notions of how best to serve that purpose change from time to time as society becomes more complex and its demands change. The emphasis today is on community policing, responding to the demands of the public. Surveys have shown that the public want to see their police and expect them not just to solve crime, but to prevent it. On one level this is reflected in the traditional role of the PC on the beat, getting to know the community, keeping an eye out not only for trouble but for potential sources of trouble. But there are also broader initiatives through which the police forge links with and respond to the community. Community liaison officers, for example, might work with a range of community groups from schools to old age pensioners.

The 43 police forces in England and Wales and 8 in Scotland are run independently and their organization will vary. Within a force, too, different areas will have different policing needs. The problems of the inner city are not the same as those of a rural area or middle-class suburb. Whatever the situation, the police need to establish channels of communication so that problems can be evaluated and means established to reduce and prevent crime. A serious drugs problem might involve links with the local youth and community workers, while tackling car theft and vandalism in a town centre car park involves liaison with town planners and other local authority officers.

Within a typical large station you might find: the uniformed officers who patrol the community, some on foot, some in ordinary cars, some in fast cars; crime prevention officers, who, for example, advise individuals on safeguarding their homes and property; community liaison officers; juvenile liaison officers, who enforce the policy on dealing with juveniles; the custody officer, responsible for ensuring that arrests are lawful; CID, who work together with uniformed officers on the detection of crime. In the control room, staff are responsible for the operation of the computerized command and control systems, sending the right officers to the right jobs. Flexible shift working patterns enable the police to respond better to the community's needs, which are obviously not the same at 11 a.m., 11 p.m. and 4 a.m.

Other areas of specialization are *traffic*, with responsibilities ranging from planning and operating large-scale traffic control systems to dealing with major accidents, and *mounted*, *dog-handling* and *river* police, all very small. Within the CID, specializations can include fraud, special branch and serious crime. Police do not specialize permanently; promotion often involves a move to a new area of specialization and/or a new force.

Promotion is through the ranks. Everyone starts out as a PC, gaining experience in various areas of police work, from communicating with the public to dealing with a traffic accident, from sorting out a domestic disturbance to dealing with a riot. Even those on accelerated programmes (see 'Training', below) spend at least two years in this rank. Those promoted, after a qualifying exam and further assessment, to Sergeant take on a more supervisory role with responsibility for a team of PCs. An Inspector's time is divided between operational and managerial roles. Chief Inspectors, Superintendents and Assistant Chief Constables take on progressively more managerial responsibility and become more involved in strategic and policy issues. The Chief Constable's responsibilities include financial planning and budgetary control, training and recruitment policy, and development of the force within the community. Some constables choose not to go in for promotion because they enjoy grass-roots uniformed police work and the contact with the public which it involves.

Training   1. *Probationer training* for all new recruits is provided partly at six regional centres and partly in-force. (The Metropolitan Police runs its own recruit training at Hendon Training School.) Subjects covered include law, liaison with social services, courts and policing procedures, and crime prevention. Role-playing exercises are carried out to teach, for example, how to deal with traffic accidents, street disorder, domestic disputes, hooliganism, self-awareness, interviewing skills (e.g. how to take statements from shocked suspects or rape victims). Courses also include some sociology, psychology and training in community relations to enable officers to understand the underlying causes of contemporary problems, such as racial tension and vandalism and how to deal with them. Self-defence and physical education also play an important part in training. *Further training* is organized by forces and includes a wide range of courses on specialist subjects.

2. Officers with ambition, ability and the potential to achieve high rank may be sent on the *Accelerated Promotion Course* at the Police Staff College. At present this consists of a 2-month residential course followed by up to 3 years in-service 'developmental' training, then a further 2 months at the College. Those who have completed this course should be strong contenders for Chief Inspector Rank 2–3 years later.

3. *The Accelerated Promotion Scheme for Graduates* is designed to seek out the most capable graduate entrants, give them a thorough grounding in the basics of police work and promote them quickly to the higher ranks. It includes attendance on the Accelerated Promotion Course, usually after 3–4 years' service. Graduate entrants can reach Chief Inspector within 7 years of joining, and promotion prospects after that are very good. Some graduates are selected for APSG on entry; others join the fast stream after standard entry.

Personal attributes   Maturity; honesty; courage, both physical and moral; sense of humour; flexibility; reliability; real desire to help people; resilience; an observant eye and a cool head; understanding of and sympathy with human weakness; ability to accept both authority and discipline and a high degree of personal responsibility; good health.

Late start   No upper age limit (within reason).

Career-break   Some forces allow career-breaks and run 'keep in touch' schemes.

Part time   Most forces run part-time schemes.

Position of women   Women account for 1 in 7 police officers but a considerably higher proportion of new recruits. Women enter and compete for promotion on exactly the same terms as men and the abolition of the minimum height and maximum age restrictions is of clear benefit to women, as is the introduction of part-time and job-sharing schemes by most forces. As a result of a collaborative exercise by the Metropolitan Police and the Equal Opportunities Commission, which uncovered examples of, primarily, indirect discrimination detrimental to women's prospects, considerable efforts have been made to ensure that women now receive equality of opportunity in all respects. In 1989 the government issued guidelines on equal opportunities in the police, the implementation of which is regularly monitored. The Home Office claims that, since the guidelines were issued, good progress has been made and that opportunities for able and committed women are excellent. Still, women account for less than 2% of Superintendents and Chief Superintendents, but in 1995 the first woman Chief Constable was appointed.

Further information

Any police force recruiting department

Police Department, Room 516, Home Office, Queen Anne's Gate, London SW1H 9AT

Graduate Liaison Officer, Room 553, Home Office, Queen Anne's Gate, London SW1H 9AT

Police Division, Scottish Home and Health Department, Room 364A, St Andrew's House, Regent Road, Edinburgh EH1 3DG

Related careers

ENVIRONMENTAL HEALTH OFFICER – HEALTH AND SAFETY INSPECTORS – PRISON SERVICE – SOCIAL WORK

Politics

This is not a career in the usual sense; with some notable exceptions prospective politicians must usually first prove their ability in some other area before they stand any chance of attracting votes. Politics is included here simply because so many young people want to know how to get into it.

Entry qualifications

An interest in people's problems and in forming legislation. It helps to have been politically active, e.g. doing part-time voluntary work in constituency parties or serving on local councils (see 'Training', below).

Member of Parliament

The work

There are 651 MPs. The House of Commons sits in the afternoon and evening for an average of 35–40 weeks a year. Sessions often last late into the night. MPs spends much of their time listening to and, if they wish, participating in debate. Mornings are spent in committee (where much of the most important parliamentary work is done), answering constituents' letters, seeing visitors, researching. If at all possible, MPs spend a day (usually Fridays) a week or frequent weekends in their constituencies, holding 'surgeries', arranging and holding meetings. They must find time to attend social functions, open bazaars, be interviewed by the press, TV, radio, and attend weekend meetings.

Many MPs carry on with some kind of job which can be fitted in with their busy parliamentary schedule; many are journalists, some lawyers, trade union officials, business people. MPs have very little free time indeed. Though vacations are long, they have to attend to constituency matters all the year round.

Prospects are impossible to predict. There are usually far more candidates than constituency vacancies. When elected in a marginal constituency, an MP is very insecure; even in a safe seat the unexpected can happen at the next election; MPs may also fail to be re-adopted by their constituencies. Most MPs hope to hold ministerial office eventually, but only a small proportion ever do so. It depends partly on their ability and hard work, but also on luck – mainly whether their party is in office, and whether their views on particular issues are acceptable to the party leader.

Selection and training

Candidates must normally have been members of their party for at least 2 years. Many learn the business of politics – debating, dealing with constituents' problems, canvassing, collecting relevant facts, making speeches – by being (unpaid) local councillors. Prospective Labour candidates must be members of an appropriate trade union, if eligible. Some start their political life in their party administration or research departments. A background in student politics is also helpful.

The methods of selection are, with minor variations, basically the same for the 3 main parties. In general, candidates must first be approved by the central or regional party organization. All candidates submit their applications and credentials to the selecting constituency. If successful they are called to interview and, if approved, put on a shortlist of, normally, 3, from which the candidate is selected.

First-time candidates tend to be given hopeless seats to fight, so that they gain experience and prove that they have the enthusiasm needed to campaign successfully.

Personal attributes

Strong political faith and convictions; self-confidence; resilience; considerable public speaking skills; great physical stamina; willingness to work unsocial and long hours and to give politics priority over other interests/activities; thick skin to cope with personal attacks.

Late start

Politics is really a second career and maturity is an asset, but a *woman* candidate of 40 who competes for adoption with a man of 30 is probably at a disadvantage.

Position of women

Nothing like as many women as men put themselves forward as candidates, even though women are very active as voluntary party workers. Women MPs numbered between 20 and 30 for many years. However, in the 1987 election there were many more women candidates than ever before, and 41 were elected. At the time of writing there are 63 women MPs, including the Speaker. There are 2 women in the Cabinet, and approximately 10 women are ministers.

The Labour party has introduced into its constitution a scheme whereby there are women-only shortlists in 50% of winnable seats. The Liberal Democrats aim to have at least one third of women and one third of men on all their decision-making committees, including selection committees.

The long hours, the need to be absent from home and the lack of crèche facilities make politics a difficult career for women with children and/or with husbands who are not equally committed to politics or at least to running home and family in their wives' absence. It is in any case harder for women to be adopted in the first place: a woman candidate has to be of better calibre than a man to stand equal chance of adoption. There is no indication that women candidates fare worse than men in parliamentary elections (which may of course be due to the fact that women candidates generally are of above-average ability). Once in Parliament, women are very successful in terms of holding office in relation to their numbers, and they are very active on committees.

Proportions of women in politics have not changed much over the years. Still only 9·6% of MPs are women; approximately 25% of local councillors are women; 19% of Britain's European Parliament Members are women. The 300 Group (formed in 1980) is trying hard to persuade more women to enter politics (its name was chosen to indicate that at least 300 MPs ought to be women). The Group is supported by all parties and by prominent men and women in public and professional life who are not politicians but see advantages to be gained by everyone if more women were in decision-making positions. The Group runs seminars, provides speakers for schools, clubs and associations, and individual advice, also by letter, to anyone (also men) who wants to get into politics at any level, in any party.

Constituency Agent

The work Agents are paid or unpaid constituency officials (not all constituencies have agents). They are responsible for efficient constituency organization, for checking electoral registers, for membership and fund-raising drives, for organizing meetings and MPs' visits and general local party matters. They normally have mainly voluntary helpers.

Selection and training Potential full-time agents must have worked for the party for at least 2 years. Before being eligible for appointment, Labour Party workers take a correspondence course and an examination for the Diploma in Electoral Law and Party Organization. Tory workers have a minimum of 15 months' training working with a qualified agent while taking the examinations for the Associate Membership of the National Society of Conservative and Unionist Agents. Liberal Democrat Party training is less formal, but their agents also have to learn relevant law and organization during a residential crash course.

There are not many posts, but all parties welcome more applicants. Promotion can be either to a key constituency, or to a regional or central office post. Agents' work is grist to the mill for anyone wanting to become an MP eventually, but a certain period of time has to elapse before agents may stand as candidates in constituencies in which they were agents.

Personal attributes Much as for MPs, plus considerable organizing ability, and ability to make volunteers work hard.

Late start No problem.

Part time Possible in theory; in practice part-time agents tend to be volunteers.

Position of women In the Liberal Democrat party, about half the agents are women, rather fewer in the Labour and Tory parties, but this is entirely due to the proportion applying. There is no discrimination in this (usually badly paid or voluntary) work.

Further information Local or central party organizations
The 300 Group,   Telephone answering service: 01985 812229

Related careers DRAMA – ECONOMICS – JOURNALISM – LAW

NOTE: *On the fringes of politics*: *Researchers* in political parties and trades unions are recruited from graduates, mainly in relevant disciplines, such as economics, politics, sociology. All but the Conservative party have very small research staffs.

Trades union organizers are mainly recruited from unpaid union officials; but occasionally graduates are taken on.

Reporters and *transcribers* record the proceeding of both Houses of Parliament, as well as the various Standing Committees. Competition for traineeships is very stiff and preference is given to candidates with good shorthand speeds. Most, but by no means all, are graduates.

Printing

Entry qualifications	See 'Training', below
The work	Printing is concerned with graphic communication. It has been called the 'meeting place of art and science', but above all it is an industry. It uses a variety of technological processes to create a product of visual impact; it is always a form of communication. The product may be books, newspapers, theatre tickets, posters, packaging, stamps, circuit boards, manuals, record sleeves, credit cards, or reproductions of old masters. The printed materials include paper, card, plastic, metal, textiles. Some printing processes are centuries old, but printing technology has changed enormously in the last few years and continues to change. For example, traditional letterpress is much less common than it was, having been largely replaced by lithography, especially offset litho. Screenprinting is widely used for non-paper materials. Most text is produced by computer-aided typesetting using DTP software. This enables an operator to turn all the elements of text and graphics into complete made-up pages which are then put on film ready for the platemakers. Special typesetting programs can 'convert' different sorts of word-processing programs used by writers so they are ready for typesetting. Electronic scanners are used in the production of both black and white and coloured illustrations; and holograms can be printed on credit and identity cards. Transmission of text and illustrations by satellite for printing in another continent is now common.

(DTP software allows individuals and organizations with the right computer and a laser printer to do their own good-quality printing of 'short-runs'; alternatively, they can give the disk to a printer who can then very quickly print large quantities.)

There are several main types of printing organizations: large and small *general commercial printers*, *specialist packaging printers*, high-quality *book printers*, *magazine printers* and the high street *instant print shops*. Newspapers now form a very small part of the industry, as changing technology has reduced the numbers of jobs. The *production manager* (or *planner*) decides with the client on the most advantageous and economic method of production for each item; this means weighing up factors such as efficient use of machines, materials, speed, cost, quality, eventual use and appearance.

Training   *Technologists and technicians*: while increased technology in some parts of the industry has led to the loss of some jobs, in others it has meant greater demand for highly skilled people. There is a move to increase the number of graduates in the industry. As well as a sound knowledge of chemistry and materials science, they need to know all about computer graphics, laser scanning, computer-controlled printing and converting systems. Some work in production, some move into management, others work in research and development of printed products and on new machinery, paper, inks. Although craft and technician work sometimes overlaps and it is possible to be promoted, anyone with the educational qualifications to undertake a full-time course before joining the industry would be well-advised to do so. Most common routes are:

1. With 2 or 3 A-levels including at least 1 science (preferably chemistry): 4-year honours degree in Printing Technology *or* 3-year B.Sc. in Printing and Photographic Technology.

2. With A-level mathematics, physics or chemistry or equivalent: part-time or sandwich study (2–3 years) for BTEC/SCOTVEC Higher National award.

3. With (usually) 4 relevant GCSEs: full-time course for BTEC National Diploma in Printing (or SCOTVEC equivalent, see p. xxii) or part-time course for National Certificate.

4. With individually specified examination passes, courses leading to college diplomas, e.g. 2-year full-time course for London College of Printing Diploma in Graphic Communications.

5. Art school training (see ART AND DESIGN, p. 54) with specialization in *Graphic Design* or *Typography* can also lead to printing jobs.

Craft: Trainees learn one of the following recognized skilled occupations: origination (preparation for print, which includes typesetting and platemaking); machine printing; print finishing (includes operating cutting and folding machines); bookbinding; carton manufacture; or manufacturing stationery. NVQs/SVQs at level 3 in a large number of printing skills are in the process of being introduced; trainees in future will work for these and/or the City and Guilds Graphic Communications Certificate.

Instant print and small printing units (for example, in-house) train mainly on the job, but may give day-release for the City and Guilds certificate in Reprographic Techniques. Most recruit experienced people.

Personal attributes	Depends on type and level of work, but generally some visual imagination; interest in machinery; practicality; some dexterity.
	For managerial jobs: organizing ability; ability to work under pressure; being a self-starter.
Late start	About 20% are late entrants. Credit given for prior learning (see APL, p. xxxiii) and shorter training possible.
Career-break	Return to work is likely to be difficult because of technological changes and shortage of jobs. A few retraining courses exist.
Part time	Few opportunities in printing: possibly as freelance typographer.
Position of women	Once one of the most traditional industries, printing now employs increasing numbers of women in skilled occupations. However, employers would like to see many more women coming into the industry, particularly as the flexibility of the new training scheme and changes brought about by new technology have improved women's prospects. At the technology level there is no valid reason whatever why women should not succeed; they have no difficulty getting on to degree or HND courses. Art-school-trained women are doing well in typography and production/design. There are now national agreements between employers and printing unions containing provisions for women's rights and equal opportunities.
Further information	British Printing Industries Federation, 11 Bedford Row, London WC1R 4DX
	Institute of Printing, 8 Lonsdale Gardens, Tunbridge Wells, Kent TN1 1NU (publishes *Guide to Educational Courses in the Printing Industry*, cost £5)

Related careers	ART AND DESIGN – ENGINEERING – PUBLISHING – SCIENCE

Prison Service

Entry qualifications

Minimum age 20. Minimum height for men, 5ft 6in. (167·7 cm) (in Scotland, 5ft 7in. (170 cm)); for women, 5ft 3in. (160 cm). No specific academic requirements. Selection is by aptitude test and interview. Also graduate entry to Accelerated Promotion Scheme. (Private contractors may have their own requirements.)

The work

The work of a prison officer goes far beyond locking and unlocking cells and patrolling corridors. One of the responsibilities of the prison service as set out by the Prison Board is 'to provide for prisoners as full a life as possible, to care for physical and mental health, advise and help with personal problems, work, education and training, physical exercise and recreation, and an opportunity to practise their religion'. What this means in practice is maintaining a community where prisoners eat, sleep, work, train, learn, play and so on. Prison officers are concerned with care as well as control, well-being as well as security. They are also concerned at senior levels with the management of staff and resources.

Prison officers (prison custody officers with the private contractors who manage some prisons and undertake court escort services in a few areas) supervise inmates in the activities mentioned above, escort them to and from courts and hospitals, accompany visitors to the visiting room, receive new prisoners. Whatever tasks they are involved in, they must try to work through co-operation with prisoners. An important part of their role is rehabilitation, helping to prepare prisoners to return to the outside community as law-abiding citizens. This involves helping them to develop skills, confidence and self-respect. Partly this is done through activities, but also through building up a relationship. Prison officers can be involved in motivating prisoners to improve their education, whether it be learning to read or studying for an Open University degree; providing a shoulder to cry on when someone gets a 'Dear John' letter; reasoning with someone threatening violence. They must recognize and know how to deal with prisoners who are having to cope with feelings of anger, anxiety or shame, with those who are troublesome and those who are extremely worried or depressed. It may be important to know how physically to restrain a violent and abusive inmate, but it is equally important to understand how such situations arise and how to re-establish communication and co-operation.

Many prisons are old and over-crowded; prisoners' frustrations can lead to tensions that sometimes explode in violence. Most prisoners reoffend. Many are unappreciative, some abusive. Prison work can be frustrating, even depressing, but it offers more scope for personal initiative, individual responsibility and the development of interpersonal skills than is commonly realized. Like social work, it can be very rewarding and is a vital service to the community.

The demands and routines of prison work will vary according to the type and size of institution. These include remand centres, which are mainly for young offenders and those awaiting trial; prisons where high-security prisoners are dispersed; open prisons for those requiring a lesser degree of security; Young Offender Institutions, which place a great emphasis on teaching inmates useful skills; local prisons, which are often multi-purpose with separate sections for different categories of prisoner. Prison officers must be prepared to serve in any kind of institution, in any part of the country, though preferences are taken into account whenever possible. 'Opposite-sex posting' (i.e. female officers in men's prisons and vice versa) is possible, though voluntary, but most officers will for the time being continue to serve in same-sex postings.

All prison officers begin 'on the landings' (the equivalent to 'on the beat' for police constables) as part of a team. On promotion, for which it is often necessary to move, officers take on increased responsibility – for a team, a wing, a function or service (e.g. inmate activities, staff training), ultimately a whole establishment. There is an accelerated promotion scheme (see 'Training', below) for experienced officers and graduate entrants with top management potential. There are also opportunities, after basic experience, to specialize as, for example, a hospital officer, a physical education officer or a trades officer (teaching a skill or trade).

Training   Training lasts about 1 year and takes place on-the-job, under supervision, and at the Prison Service College. There is an *Accelerated Promotion Scheme* for graduates and other particularly able candidates which grooms them to reach an upper middle management position in less than 5 years. Private contractors are responsible for training their staff to standards laid down by the Home Office.

Personal   Leadership; a sense of right and wrong, without being censorious;
attributes   a genuine desire to help people in trouble and the ability to

understand and sympathize with people's failings without necessarily condoning them; the ability to find the right approach to all types of people; immense patience with people at their most unbearable; interests entirely outside prison work to help keep a sense of proportion; a friendly, naturally happy disposition; sense of humour.

Late start Entry up to 49½ (normally under 42 in Scotland).

Career-break No problem (if there is a local prison).

Part time Virtually none.

Position of women As there are relatively few women's prisons, the development of 'opposite-sex posting' should open up more promotion prospects for women.

Further information Home Office, Freepost, London SW1E 5BX
Scotland: Scottish Prison Service Recruitment, Calton House, 5 Redheughs Rigg, Edinburgh EH12 9HW

Related careers PERSONNEL/HUMAN RESOURCES MANAGEMENT – POLICE – SOCIAL WORK

Psychology

Entry qualifica-tions

2 or 3 A-levels plus maths and English at GCSE (A–C) if not at A-level. Requirements are flexible, but students need to be able to handle scientific concepts, to be numerate and able to write well. Useful A-levels are biological sciences, maths and humanities.

The work

Psychology is the scientific study of human and animal mental processes, behaviour and experience. Psychologists study individuals' development and how individuals interact with one another. They use observation and experimental and other methods (e.g. surveys, intelligence tests) to assess and measure all kinds of cognitive (mental) processes, attitudes and emotions. (They must not be confused with psychiatrists, who are *medically qualified* specialists who give treatment to the mentally sick and disturbed.) Psychologists must understand the difference between 'normal' and 'abnormal' behaviour and use their knowledge and skills to solve (or alleviate) a wide range of problems. Although psychology is a science, it is a young science and still offers few cut-and-dried answers to the questions it poses.

The British Psychological Society now has a Register of Chartered Psychologists; people wanting to be Chartered Psychologists and who are eligible (i.e. have taken training approved by the BPS) can belong to one of the following specialist psychology divisions: clinical; educational and child; occupational; criminological and legal. Counselling psychologists involved wholly in teaching and/or research can also belong.

There is a small but steady demand for psychologists (see 'Training', below, for need for post-graduate training for specializations). Although only a small proportion of psychology graduates become practising psychologists, a psychology degree is a useful preparation for employee relations and other personnel functions, for social work, and generally for jobs in organizations where 'dealing with people' is important.

Clinical Psychology

Clinical psychologists help people to come to terms with various kinds of problems. Therapeutic work is carried out with children and adults, in individual counselling sessions and in groups in hospitals (see 'Psychotherapy', p. 408); in therapeutic communities (see 'Mental Health Nurse', p. 339); at day-centres (see SOCIAL WORK, p. 476); and in family groups. The wide range of problems treated includes physical and mental handicap; phobias (including children's inability to face school); neurological and obsessional disorders; brain damage; sexual difficulties; reading and writing difficulties.

Clinical psychologists organize, co-ordinate and co-operate in vocational guidance for the handicapped, rehabilitation, training and retraining programmes for patients with physical handicaps or learning difficulties. They set up systems for job analysis, assess and evaluate the work potential and the progress of patients. The broad types of therapeutic work undertaken are behaviour therapy, psychotherapy and counselling (see PSYCHOTHERAPY AND COUNSELLING, p. 408), rehabilitation and training. Most clinical psychologists work in hospitals, some in child guidance clinics. They work in close collaboration with neurologists, psychiatrists and other specialists. There is a new specialization, health psychology, which involves working in general hospitals with patients undergoing stressful procedures, e.g. surgery or AIDS screening.

Some clinical psychologists spend most of their time on individual case work, while others are more involved in teaching other professional groups, e.g. nurses. The great majority work in the Health Service, but there are opportunities also in private practice and as consultants, e.g. to private clinics.

Educational and Child Psychology

Educational psychologists advise teachers, parents, doctors and social workers on children's and young people's adjustment and learning problems. They are responsible for making formal recommendations (Records or Statements of Special Educational Needs) for the education of children with learning difficulties. Assessment involves sessions with the 'problem' child as well as, usually, its parents and teachers, and a thorough study of the individual's background and environment. Various established techniques, such as ability tests and 'personality schedules' are used. Treatment (called 'intervention') may include individual counselling sessions with child and/or parents and advice to parents and teachers on the 'management' of the problem. Apart from helping individuals when problems have arisen, educational psychologists work with 'systems' or organizations: whole schools, families, groups of teachers or social workers, school classes, youth clubs. Running in-service courses for different groups is an important part of their work. They are largely employed by local education authorities and work in school/county psychological services and child guidance clinics, while a growing number work as independent or private consultants.

Occupational Psychology

Occupational psychologists deal with people as workers. They advise on how people can both enjoy and be efficient in their work by giving vocational guidance to both children and adults. They set up selection procedures for employers and develop training schemes; they help in the organizing of work itself by devising new methods of doing jobs; and they advise on the design of tools and machines so that they are easy to use ('ergonomics'). They also research into and advise on psychological implications of organizational structures and proposed changes, aiming at improving both job satisfaction and the organization's effectiveness.

Occupational psychologists have developed techniques for collecting information from people about what they like doing and what they are good at, as well as what they find difficult and unpleasant. They match this information against that collected by detailed studies of the actual work involved in the jobs concerned. They are very much involved with 'managing change' of working practices in offices and manufacturing, e.g. when new technologies are introduced (see MANAGEMENT, p. 275).

Other occupational/social psychology specializations are concerned with retirement: pre-retirement counselling and training and generally looking into problems connected with the growing proportion of retired people in the community; with mid-career changes necessitated by changes in job opportunities; with problems connected with women's changing career patterns and aspirations; with stress management.

The main employer of occupational psychologists is the Civil Service, mainly in the Home Office (Prison Department), Ministry of Defence and Department of Employment. Opportunities are increasing in industry and commerce, especially in personnel/ human resources departments.

Criminological and Legal Psychology

Psychologists are employed in the Prison Department or by Regional Health Authorities to work both with prisoners and with those who look after them. They work in all kinds of prisons, including institutions for mentally abnormal offenders and in regional secure units. They may run training courses for prison officers and therapy sessions for prisoners and their families, as well as carrying out case work with individuals and preparing psychological reports to help judges decide on sentencing.

Criminological and legal psychologists often collaborate with professionals in other related areas; police officers, probation officers and lawyers are turning more and more to psychology to aid their work.

Counselling psychology

Counselling psychology is an increasingly developing area. Most counsellors enter formal training after a period of work in some other field such as social work, teaching, health visiting or psychiatry. Client groups are diverse: they could be young couples (as in marriage guidance), younger people who have suffered bereavement, groups such as nurses who have emotionally stressful jobs, or patients in a hospice.

Other Opportunities and New Developments

Some psychologists teach in further and higher education; a few are involved solely in research, but most research is carried out by lecturers as part of their work. For research it is usually necessary to take a Ph.D. in a specialist subject. Research may be commissioned by government departments, the police, industrial organizations, research institutes. Research fields vary widely; as well as the mainstream areas – clinical, educational, etc. – there are other specializations; for example:

Social psychology
Concerned with the attitudes and interaction of individuals and groups: what causes whom to behave in what manner; what effect do events, media presentation, individuals' and groups' actions have on other individuals and other groups within the community? They investigate, for example, the causes of, and possible cures for, football hooliganism; or the voting behaviour of individuals and groups. They look into the effect of television on different groups in the community, and they may look into the problems of integration of ethnic minorities into the community, and into the attitudes to, and effect of, class differences among adults and among children.

Neuropsychology or physiological psychology

Concerned with trying to discover the relationship between biological processes and behaviour. For example, how do drugs affect memory and personality? What area of the brain controls speech?

Experimental psychology

Research psychologists who specialize in experimental psychology work in most psychological disciplines to help solve a wide range of problems. They use special experimental methods that have been developed to study human and animal behaviour. They may be given a particular problem to solve: they would then plan the experiment, collect and analyse information, and draw conclusions to enable someone to make decisions. In addition experimental psychologists are always trying to extend the scope of psychology by carrying out experiments to find out more about people and how the human brain works. They may work with animals. Experimental psychologists usually work in teams with other scientists, mainly in government and university research, often on short-term contracts.

Psychology is developing all the time. Two new areas have opened up in recent years:

Health psychology

This does not yet have a clearly defined career path. The majority of health psychologists will be either research workers, typically in university posts, or qualified clinical psychologists, or perhaps occupational psychologists who are concerned with the general issues of promoting mental health and developing healthy lifestyles. One does not yet see many jobs specifically advertised for health psychologists, but it is a field where the application of psychology is gaining recognition. Some Masters degrees in health psychology are available.

Sports Psychology

This is another developing area in which there is no approved route to qualification as a chartered psychologist. Most psychologists who have the expertise to offer a service in sports psychology have taken a postgraduate research degree or have trained in another area of applied psychology.

Training   3-year (sometimes 4-year) degree course. The composition of the courses varies: some lead to BA, some to B.Sc. Topics usually covered include: experimental study of such cognitive processes as thinking, memorizing, learning and perceiving; biological basis of behaviour; animal behaviour; development of children; social relationships and their effects on personality; mental disorders; abnormal development; applications of psychology to the study of society, industry and education; techniques of testing and experiment; counselling skills. There is considerable emphasis on statistics and, increasingly, computers are used.

There is no need to decide which branch of psychology to specialize in till after the course. Post-graduate courses are essential: approved post-graduate training courses are listed in the *Compendium of Post-graduate Studies* published by the BPS.

Clinical psychologists take either a 2–3-year Master's degree course or a 3-year in-service Diploma training course.

Educational psychologists must first take a post-graduate certificate in education (PGCE) and gain at least 2 years' teaching experience (not a requirement in Scotland); they then take a Master's degree course normally lasting 1 year (2 in Scotland). Southampton University offers a combined PGCE and Master's course. Alternatively, qualified teachers can become educational psychologists by taking a psychology degree followed by the specialist Master's degree.

Occupational psychologists may take a degree in their specialization and go straight into a job, or take a more general psychology degree followed by a 2-year full- or part-time Master's degree or Diploma course. (This may be done after several years' work experience, except in the case of ergonomists, who need specialized training immediately after graduating.)

Criminological and *legal psychologists*: some go straight into the Prison Department after a first degree, others first train in a specialization such as clinical or occupational psychology, or take a (new) Master's degree in applied criminological psychology.

Counselling psychologists can take the Diploma in Counselling Psychology at an institution approved by the BPS. At present the BPS has approved only one, run by the University of Surrey, although other institutions are currently applying for approval.

Personal attributes   A detached interest in individuals' and communities' behaviour rather than personal involvement; an interest in scientific method; the ability to work well on one's own, but also to work as part of a team and to co-operate with people from different backgrounds; patience; numeracy. For most jobs, especially in education, a warm and easy manner.

Late start   No problem for qualified late entrants to degree courses; maturity and relevant work experience can be an asset. Owing to competition, and the length of training, mature applicants without normal entry requirements may have difficulty finding a place. Proof of an adequate knowledge of maths at least is essential. An Open University degree in psychology may be the best bet.

**Career-
break**

Depends on competition from newly qualified people (particularly for academic posts). Most psychologists manage to work full or part time while raising a family.

Part time

Some opportunities; and job-sharing exists.

**Position
of
women**

Over 50% of British Psychological Society members and approximately 75% of psychology undergraduates are women. Women have no more difficulties in getting jobs than men.

**Further
informa-
tion**

The Hon. General Secretary, The British Psychological Society, St Andrew's House, 48 Princess Road, Leicester LE1 7DR

**Related
careers**

PERSONNEL/HUMAN RESOURCES MANAGEMENT – NURSING: *Mental Health/Learning Disabilities* – SOCIAL WORK – SOCIOLOGY – TEACHING

Psychotherapy and Counselling

Psychotherapy and counselling are included in this guide because of the interest in and confusion about these occupational areas. The explanations given do not fit into the format used in the rest of the guide.

Psychotherapy

The term *psychotherapy* has two meanings: it is an umbrella term for various forms of treatment of patients with emotional or psychological problems through dialogue with a skilled practitioner. Its aim is to help patients change the way they manage their problems. In this context, psychotherapy covers several methods which differ in intensity and underlying philosophy. The term *psychotherapy* is also used to define an occupation, but one without agreed entry requirements, qualifications or career structure (except for *child psychotherapy*, see below). It is *never* a career option for school or college leavers but invariably a 'second' or 'late start' career for people with relevant qualifications, work and life experience.

Persons with a range of qualifications (or none) practise psychotherapy:

1. *Psychiatrists*: They are medically qualified doctors (see MEDICINE, p. 303) who have subsequently qualified for membership of the Royal College of Psychiatrists. Psychotherapy is only one of a range of treatments they use (drug therapy is another). Most psychiatrists work in the NHS, some work partly or entirely in private practice.

2. *Psychoanalysts*: They normally have a medical degree or comparable qualification (some are also qualified psychiatrists); they have undergone lengthy personal analysis and then taken an approximately 4-year (part-time but very time-consuming) training in Jungian, Freudian or similar psychoanalytical method. Although not a registrable profession, it is generally agreed that in this country only people who have qualified for membership of the Society of Analytical Psychology or the British Psycho-

analytical Society are entitled to call themselves psychoanalysts or analysts. *Very* few analysts work in the NHS; most are in private practice with, possibly, some sessional work for voluntary advice centres.

Psychiatrists who practise psychotherapy, analysts and those clinical psychologists (see 'Clinical Psychology', p. 401) who do some psychotherapeutical work are all sometimes called psychotherapists – which is the reason for the confusion surrounding the term.

3. *Psychotherapists*: At present anyone, whatever their qualification (if any), may use the title 'psychotherapist', a fact which rigorously trained psychotherapists very much regret. There are so many psychotherapy organizations and philosophies that agreement on a common training or accreditation scheme is very difficult. However, there are now two self-regulatory and registration bodies: the British Confederation of Psychotherapists (BCP) and the United Kingdom Council for Psychotherapy (UKCP). Although registration has not yet been made mandatory, both bodies are in discussion with the government. The mainstream organizations, however, base their treatment on psychoanalytical methods. Their professional bodies accept for training only candidates with relevant degree or comparable qualifications and experience; require them to undergo lengthy personal analysis or therapy and then train them much as do psychoanalytical organizations. Courses last a minimum of 3 years part time. In fact psychoanalysts' and psychotherapists' training and work shade into each other (though psychotherapists more often than analysts also treat people in groups – families, couples, fellow-sufferers such as addicts, phobics, etc.). About a dozen universities now run courses for psychotherapists. Some are broad-based; some are run in partnership with professional associations.

There are virtually no jobs for *psychotherapists* in the NHS (except for *child psychotherapists*, see below); they rely on private patients and – very few – voluntary organizations' clinic sessions.

Because there is a growing demand for help from people with problems, a vast number of self-styled psychotherapy organizations have sprung up over the last few years. Some are experimenting with new methods of 'alternative psychotherapy' in good faith, but the methods and the credentials of some organizations are dubious. Before signing up for training (often expensive, and/or too short and not rigorous enough to be of any value) potential psychotherapists must thoroughly check organizations' claims.

The above refers to what is called 'adult psychotherapy'. *Child psychotherapy* is a recognized profession (though a very small one). Child psychotherapists treat children for psychological disturbances of behaviour, thinking and feeling. The work is focused on the relationship established between the psychotherapist and the child, through which insight into the problem is gained. Children, adolescents and parents are seen, usually individually, sometimes in groups. Child psychotherapists work in child guidance clinics, young people's advice and treatment clinics, and in private practice. To be accepted for training with one of the four accredited organizations, candidates must have a psychology degree or comparable qualification and experience of work with normal children. Training, a mixture of theory and practice and including extensive observation of young children, takes 4–5 years. There is a growing demand for child psychotherapists in the National Health Service, especially outside London, e.g. in the Midlands, the South-West and Scotland. Full-time and sessional work is available.

Counselling

This is a much over-used and therefore vague term. It is best defined as the skill of helping normal people, through discussion, to decide how best to cope in specific situations. By listening attentively and without passing judgement the counsellor gives clients the opportunity to explore, discover and clarify how and why they feel as they do; they (the clients, not the counsellors) may then be able to make choices and decisions about their situation which they were incapable of making before.

While psychotherapists may try to change patients' personalities, or at least their attitudes, sometimes over a long period; counsellors tend to deal with immediate, often practical problems, e.g. redundancy or alcohol addiction. Yet psychotherapists' and counsellors' work may overlap, as they use similar methods. Psychotherapists more often deal with severe psychological disorders, especially if working in hospitals, but in private practice both may see patients with similar problems.

Counsellors work in many settings – schools, colleges, GP practices, clinics, counselling centres, staff welfare departments, as well as in private practice. There are counselling services that specialize in particular groups, e.g. young people or ethnic minorities, or in specific problems, such as drug addiction or AIDS. The number of full-time posts is increasing, but there are more trained counsellors than there are jobs. Many combine part-time work with social work, welfare rights work and administration.

There are a few full-time training courses for teachers, social workers and others working in the field. There are many more part-time courses leading to a certificate or diploma. These mostly expect people to have a degree or a professional qualification. The British Psychological Association now has a counselling psychology division and accredits courses (see p. 404). For people hoping to do counselling as volunteers and not looking for a vocational qualification there are part-time introductory courses, courses in counselling skills, and specialist courses in bereavement, cancer, child abuse, etc., counselling.

Although there is no legal requirement for counsellors to be properly trained, people interested in the work are advised to contact the British Association for Counselling for advice (address below).

Further information

British Association of Psychotherapists, 37 Mapesbury Road, London NW2 4HJ

London Centre for Psychotherapy, 19 Fitzjohns Avenue, London NW3 5JY

Tavistock Clinic, 120 Belsize Lane, London NW3 5BA

Association of Child Psychotherapists, Burgh House, New End Square, London NW3 1LT

British Association for Counselling, 1 Regent Place, Rugby, Warwickshire CV21 2PJ

The British Psycho-analytical Society, Mansfield House, 63 New Cavendish Street, London W1M 7RD

Related careers

PSYCHOLOGY – SOCIAL WORK – TEACHING

Public Relations

Entry qualifications

95% of new entrants to the Institute of Public Relations are now graduates.

The work

Public relations officers (now often called 'public affairs' officers or executives) advise on ways to develop relationships with sections of the public whose support and goodwill is essential for the success of an enterprise. Public relations is part of the marketing mix, but is specifically about protecting and promoting reputation. Public relations is more than a publicity tool – it is an essential part of successful management in an increasingly competitive environment. Public relations officers provide factual stories about clients or their product to newspapers, magazines and television, thus keeping the product or the service in the news and creating a 'favourable climate or image'. They answer journalists' questions about their client's product, views or services, and may take journalists to see the client's product or service. They arrange receptions, exhibitions and other projects to 'put over' a client or promote a cause, and give talks to interested groups – schools, women's organizations, etc. They deal with inquiries (and also complaints) from the public.

Public relations officers work either in public relations consultancies (several partners each with their own accounts and a shared office and staff), or in public relations departments of advertising agencies, or in separate press and public relations departments of individual organizations. More and more organizations employ PR specialists to advise on and put into action ways of communicating the organization's functions and activities to relevant groups. Today, local authorities, employers' federations, charities and professional organizations such as the British Medical Association employ public relations or information officers. In the Civil Service they are called information officers and work in nearly all departments, where they usually specialize in either press or publicity work. Hospitals, schools and universities increasingly make use of PR. An important area now is financial PR; some sporting and TV personalities also use public relations officers to help further their careers.

Entry into PR is highly competitive; far more people want to do this sort of work than there are opportunities, although really talented people are sought after. There has been a growth in the number of small, independent consultancies in the last few years.

Training   Competition for jobs is such that it is now very difficult to get into PR by working oneself up from a junior position, such as secretary. The following are all possible entry routes:

1. A sideways move with a degree and work experience in a relevant discipline or industry (e.g. engineering or science). Traditionally many PR people moved sideways from journalism and this is still a possible route.

2. As a trainee with a PR firm or in a PR department with a non-specialist degree. Useful degree subjects are business studies, economics, languages, communication, but employers will take promising people from any discipline.

3. With a degree or post-graduate degree course in PR. The IPR recognizes several university and college courses as leading to awards qualifying the holder to full membership of the Institute.

Training is usually on the job with part-time study for the examinations set by CAM (Communication, Advertising and Marketing Education Foundation). Study can be full time, part time, by correspondence or private.

Entry requirements for CAM Certificate: 3 GCSEs and 2 A-levels (including English language); or BTEC or SCOTVEC Higher National award in Business Studies (see pp. xxi, xxii); or London Chamber of Commerce and Industry Third Group Diploma in Marketing or Public Relations; or 1 year in full-time employment in the communication business and 5 GCSEs (A–C) or equivalent, including English language.

The Certificate covers marketing; advertising; public relations; media; sales promotion and direct marketing; research and behavioural studies; It normally takes about 2 years' study, usually at evening classes, occasionally by day-release or distance-learning.

To qualify for membership of the IPR, certificate holders go on to take the CAM Diploma. This examination is in 3 parts: public relations practice; public relations management; and business management strategy and practice.

Partial exemption may be granted on a subject-for-subject basis from the Certificate to holders of related awards, certain professional or academic qualifications.

West Herts College, Watford Campus, offers a 1-year full-time post-graduate Diploma in International Public Relations.

NVQs in Public Relations levels 2, 3 and 4 have been introduced and may provide another route to IPR membership.

Personal attributes   Ability to get on exceptionally well with people of all kinds, whether hard-hitting journalists or less confident members of the public; enterprise and initiative; good news sense; sense of sales-manship; a calm temperament; analytical powers; ability to write and speak well and persuasively; imagination; tact; ability to keep polite under provocation and/or pressure.

Late start   Only advisable for people with special expertise/experience. Approximately a quarter of CAM students are aged 30 + .

Career-break   No problem for women who were firmly established before the break. Many work from home, perhaps having only one client for a year or so, then gradually increasing their workload.

Part time   Fair opportunities, especially working from home or for small, non-commercial (i.e. usually voluntary) organizations.

Position of women   Women do very well in PR; 60% of practitioners are women and they hold some of the top jobs. But, while women account executives outnumber men 2 to 1, only one-third of directors are women. Starting as a secretary used to be a useful way in, but this is no longer advisable.

Further information   Institute of Public Relations, The Old Trading House, 15 North-burgh Street, London EC1V 0PR

CAM Education Foundation, Abford House, 15 Wilton Road, London SW1V INJ

Public Relations Consultants Association, 1st Floor, Willow House, Willow Place, London SW1P 1JH

Scottish Public Relations Consultants Association, Campsie House, 17 Park Circus Place, Glasgow G3 6AH

Related careers   ADVERTISING – FASHION AND CLOTHING – CIVIL SERVICE: *Information Officer* – JOURNALISM – MARKETING AND SELLING – SECRETARIAL AND CLERICAL WORK

Publishing

<table>
<tr>
<td>Entry
qualifica-
tions</td>
<td>In practice a degree or comparable qualification and/or specialist knowledge/experience; design training for some aspects of production. In specialist publishing, such as educational, scientific or art, editorial assistants normally have a degree in a relevant subject. In general publishing, the degree subject is normally irrelevant.</td>
</tr>
<tr>
<td>The work</td>
<td>Publishing is an industry (one of the smallest in the country), not a profession. It requires business acumen and an interest in marketing (see p. 297) as much as creativity and literary flair. The function of publishing has been described as extending the author's idea into a finished book and getting it into readers' hands – in other words publishing involves the organization of production, marketing and distribution as much as (and in many cases more than) literary effort.</td>
</tr>
</table>

Publishing houses vary greatly in size, from large ones with overseas branches and several 'imprints', producing hundreds of titles a year, to those run on a shoe-string with a handful of employees and a small yearly output. The trend is towards 'conglomerates' with large houses buying up smaller ones, but keeping their identities fairly separate. Many are now owned by United States companies. Some publishers specialize in educational, scientific, art books, or paperbacks. *Desk-top publishing*, in which editor, designer and production staff handle text and illustration on disk at different stages, is widely used. Many organizations use DTP to produce publications for their own use and also for books which have very limited sales. In some cases one person can carry out all the tasks from start to finish.

Publishers select and commission manuscripts, design the appearance of the books, have them printed and bound, and promote and sell the finished copies, but the internal organization of 'houses' varies. The process is usually divided into 3 main departments (apart from the usual commercial ones such as accounts). The division of work is more rigid in some houses than others; in small houses everybody may have to do anything that needs doing (a good way of learning). The increase in DTP has tended to break down demarcation barriers.

The 3 main publishing departments or 'functions' are:

Editorial

Main duties are identifying publishing opportunities and commissioning authors. Increasingly agents working for authors play a large part and fewer books are commissioned from scratch. Editors are responsible also for getting outside specialist readers' opinions; preparing typescripts (or disks) for the printer; liaising with authors, possibly suggesting changes; dealing with contracts, copyright, subsidiary rights (these may be separate departments). Editorial departments also deal with new editions of existing books.

An editorial director or chief editor (titles and responsibilities involved vary greatly in different houses) is usually in charge. Individual editors may each be responsible for books on a special subject, or for a range of subjects. They may initiate a book on a special subject, select the author and deal with the project right through. The number of books one editor deals with at any particular moment varies according to type of firm and type of book, and so does the amount of contact the editor has with the author.

Editorial assistants or 'copy-editors' deal with 'copy preparation'; checking facts and references, spelling, punctuation, and possibly doing some rewriting, proof-reading and correcting. Again, responsibilities and duties vary greatly. Increasingly this work is done by out-of-house freelances under the editor's management.

Design and Production

In larger publishing houses there may be a separate art department. In others designers work in the production department. The production department receives the edited typescript and decides in consultation with designer and editor on the appearance of the book, on the shape, typeface, paper, illustrations, etc.; the production department deals with printers, paper merchants, binders etc. Staff must understand all aspects of costing and marketing and of the various types of illustration and typography. But above all they must understand the new printing and production technologies which are drastically changing established production methods. Technical and textbook publishers may employ their own illustrators, but most artwork, including illustrations and book jackets, is commissioned from freelances and outside studios.

Marketing (includes Sales)

In some ways the most important publishing activity, marketing or 'promotion' is responsible for planning, researching for and preparing review lists, sales campaigns, writing 'blurbs', and for the representatives who call on bookshops, schools, libraries, etc. to give information on forthcoming books and to collect orders. Marketing staff make representations to key accounts and there is a heavy emphasis on public relations. In addition, marketing people in many houses now often initiate projects, based on feedback gained by the sales representatives when they visit bookshops. On the basis of a 'feasibility study' – mainly researching the market and costing – it is decided whether to go ahead and, jointly with editorial, get the book commissioned, or whether to abandon the idea. This is a good department in which to learn how publishing works.

There are many more posts in non-editorial than editorial departments.

Other Kinds of Publishing

Book Packaging

A small, but growing development outside traditional publishing is book 'packaging'. Packagers are *marketing* people. They find an idea which is likely to be profitable, commission an author and artwork and produce a dummy copy of the book. They then offer it to publishers, usually in several countries. 'Packages' are usually highly illustrated; a 'bank' of pictures is printed separately and then overprinted with the translated text with the minimum production expense. Promotion, selling and distribution are done by the publishers who buy the packaged book.

Packagers' overheads are lower than traditional publishers' and it is therefore easier to start up as a packager than as a publisher. But good contacts, publishing experience and ideas are essential.

Electronic Publishing

This has much more in common with *information technology* (see p. 138) and with information work (see p. 227) than with 'literary' publishing – at least for the present. It was initially used to provide databases or 'on-line information services' and is in fact sometimes called 'database publishing'. It produces such services as Ceefax and individual organizations' and professions' computerized research bases/libraries. The growth area now is in multimedia publishing on CD-Rom, in which most large publishers are already, or are about to become, involved. *Computer specialists, information scientists* and *librarians*, as well as experts in the appropriate field (i.e. anyone from accountant to zoologist), might work in electronic publishing, but it is at present a very small job area.

Magazine Publishing

This is quite different from book publishing. *Feature editors* need to be able to write original copy; *editorial assistants* must be able to 'sub' (reword, shorten, etc.) other people's writing. They all need to know something about layout and production, as well as to understand the business side of magazines (including advertising). Some editors started as secretaries, others as freelance or staff journalists (see JOURNALISM, p. 234). Most magazines have a 'publisher' responsible for the business side: the usual background is in advertisement selling, but some publishers are ex-editorial staff.

*

There are very limited opportunities on the editorial side of publishing, which attracts the most applicants, especially in general publishing; more scope in technical, scientific, educational. First editorial job is usually as editorial assistant ('assistant editor' may mean the same thing). Opportunities are slightly better in other departments, especially in sales and marketing and production.

Training   Nothing specific; degree in any subject advisable. See 'The work', above.

There are a small number of pre-entry courses, some of which are for graduates, and there are several degree courses in publishing. There are training courses in book production and design, and some art and design courses include book design and production (see ART AND DESIGN, p. 54). Pre-entry training is recommended especially for these departments. A few firms run their own training schemes, but most rely on short in-service courses provided by, for example, the Book House Training Centre. Some of these courses are also useful to prospective applicants. NVQs have been introduced but take-up in the industry has been very slow.

Previous bookselling or other sales experience is useful.

In the past many editors came up the secretarial ladder; this still occasionally happens, but there are far more graduate secretaries working for publishers and hoping to make the break than there are editorial jobs.

Personal attributes   Creative ability; interest in social and economic as well as literary trends; ability to see books as a marketable commodity; some writing ability; critical judgement; common sense; resilience; good business sense; willingness to take responsibility and make decisions; ability to get on well with a wide variety of types of people.

Late start   Difficult because of the competition from young graduates, but possible in technical and educational publishing for people with technical/scientific background.

Career-break   It should be possible (and it is advisable) not to give up completely, even temporarily.

Part time   Experienced proof-readers, copy-editors, editors may be able to do freelance work.

Position of women   *Book publishing*: There are far more male than female editorial directors and publishing house board members, but a handful of women have now reached the top. Many women have done well in 'senior middle' jobs, especially in marketing, also as children's and educational book editors. Among copy-editors and editorial assistants women greatly outnumber men. Many women go into publishing as secretaries hoping to become editors; some do, although far more remain in junior editorial jobs.

Magazines: Women have little problem reaching senior positions.

Further information   Publishers' Association, 19 Bedford Square, London WC1B 3HJ
Scottish Publishers' Association, 137 Dundee Street, Edinburgh EH11 1BG
Book House Training Centre, 45 East Hill, Wandsworth, London SW18 2QZ
Individual publishing houses

Related careers   ART AND DESIGN – BOOKSELLING – INFORMATION WORK – JOURNALISM – PRINTING

Purchasing and Supply

Entry qualifications

For professional qualification: 2 A-levels, 3 GCSEs (A–C), including English language and a quantitative subject; or BTEC/SCOTVEC National award. Also *graduate* entry. No specific qualifications for mature entrants with relevant work experience (see also 'Late start') but see 'Training', below.

The work

Purchasing and supply is a broad-based function covering the whole business of 'managing materials'. It is, therefore, closely linked with Logistics and Distribution Management (see p. 269). Purchasing and supply staff work in private industry – manufacturing, retailing, distribution – and in the public sector.

There are a number of different purchasing roles and individuals may move from one to another. As purchasing *planners* they are responsible for ensuring regular supplies of materials, tools, components, equipment – anything other departments in the organization may require to function efficiently. This can range from raw materials, office equipment and machine components to medical supplies and disposable towels for hospitals and audio-visual equipment for schools. They work closely with the 'consumers' – for example production managers, medical staff, education officers – who specify exactly what is required. Those working as *buyers* search out ('source') the most suitable supplies and negotiate terms and delivery dates. They may have to decide, at times, when to agree to pay more than budgeted for in order to get supplies which are in short supply; this would probably be decided jointly with production manager and accountant. They are a vital link between the various departments which need supplies, and the suppliers – their success depends largely on maintaining good relationships with suppliers and on negotiating advantageous contracts.

Some purchasing and supply staff travel all over the world and should be able to speak foreign languages; they must be aware of technological, social, economic and political developments which might affect price levels and availability of supplies.

It is often possible to switch from one type of buying to another: commodity knowledge is not always vital as specialists give purchasing officers detailed specifications; for example, machine tools or electronic equipment can be bought by a purchasing officer who previously bought raw materials for a food manufacturer. However, a technical background (engineering for example) is useful in many jobs and sometimes essential.

Those working as *purchasing managers*, in charge of departments, are responsible for stores management and inventory control. Deciding how much stock to hold and how far to let it run down before re-ordering can greatly improve (or reduce) an organization's efficiency and/or profitability. They need to know how far forward supplies can be bought in, weighing up price rises and possible future shortage against possible spoilage and storage costs.

Opportunities have increased as medium-sized organizations where buying used not to be a specialist function now often employ purchasing specialists; purchasing is one of the functions which can lead into *general management* (see p. 275).

Training   The Chartered Institute of Purchasing and Supply is the professional body awarding recognized qualifications. Its Professional Examination Scheme is in 2 parts – Foundation and Professional. Many courses are part-time evening, but more flexible and modular programmes are becoming available, as well as distance learning. There are a few full-time courses. Most Foundation stage students qualify via BTEC/SCOTVEC courses (see pp. xxi, xxii). Holders of business studies degrees and Higher National Diplomas are eligible for some exemptions from the Foundation examination. The syllabus includes accounting, statistics, management and economics. The Professional stage develops general purchasing subjects; students may choose options in marketing, operations management and international factors.

There is a 'second-tier' qualification, for school-leavers with 4 GCSEs (A–C) and mature entrants with at least 2 years' experience in purchasing and/or stores work. Part-time study leads to the Certificates of Purchasing and Stores and these provide access to the Foundation programme.

NVQs/SVQs are being developed.

Personal attributes   Numeracy; organizing ability; practical approach to problem-solving; considerable business acumen and some gambling spirit; ability to establish friendly relationships quickly; judgement to gauge the right approach to individual suppliers; awareness of technological changes and their implications for purchasing.

Late start   Good opportunities. 30% of CIPS students are over 30 (but not all are new entrants). People with previous work experience are welcome. Graduates and others with relevant experience are granted substantial exemption from CIPS exams, and GCSE requirements for those over 26 are waived. CIPS courses are open to those not yet in relevant employment.

Career-break
Should not present problems, but keeping in touch with world economic conditions and commercial law is vital. Short Institute courses can be used as *refreshers*. Temporarily retired women pay reduced Institute subscriptions.

Part time
Good opportunities. Job-sharing is possible.

Position of women
Women have long been established as buyers for retail stores, but it has taken time for them to become established in purchasing and supply. Now they are doing well and they account for 20% of CIPS membership compared with only 4% in 1991.

Further information
Chartered Institute of Purchasing and Supply, Easton House, Easton on the Hill, Stamford, Lincs. PE9 3NZ

Related careers
COMMODITY MARKETS – LOGISTICS AND DISTRIBUTION MANAGEMENT – RETAIL MANAGEMENT – SURVEYING: *Quantity Surveyor*

Radiography

Entry qualifications Degree course requirements. 1 or even 2 sciences, at either level, may be required; BTEC/SCOTVEC awards may be accepted in lieu. It is essential to check with individual courses.

See 'Late start', below, for mature students' entry.

The work Radiography has 2 branches: *diagnostic* and *therapeutic*.

Diagnostic Radiographers

They work in diagnostic imaging teams with radiologists, who are doctors with specialist qualifications. They are involved with the whole range of imaging techniques, including the use of ionizing radiation to produce X-rays, medical ultrasound, magnetic resonance imaging, nuclear medicine and others. Radiographers have to be skilled in the operation of complex equipment. They must understand not only how to use imaging techniques, but the theory behind them. In addition, they have to produce reports on the images obtained to help doctors in their diagnosis. Radiographers, therefore, need a considerable knowledge of anatomy, physiology, physics and radiation science.

They work in hospital X-ray departments and on occasions use mobile equipment in wards. They may also be asked to produce X-ray images during operations, when it is particularly important to obtain fast, high-quality images.

It is likely that there will be increasing opportunities for radiographers to work outside hospitals in primary health care: in particular, fundholding GP practices are being encouraged to develop their own imaging services, for example ultrasound for pregnant women.

Diagnostic radiographers normally see patients only once or twice, but often in traumatic circumstances. They must, therefore, be skilled in patient care techniques, especially in gaining patients' co-operation and explaining procedures.

Therapeutic radiographers

They are a crucial element in the cancer treatment team. They work with oncologists, doctors with specialist qualifications in the treatment of cancer. They carry out treatment by means of ionizing radiation and sometimes drugs.

Treatment is given to seriously ill and worried patients, often over a long period of time. Radiographers must be expert in the giving of the treatment and also highly skilled in how they actually deal with their patients. They must be able to reassure sick and often frightened people without appearing to minimize the seriousness of the illness. Cancer treatment is increasingly being seen in a 'holistic' way, i.e. as treatment of the whole person, not just the illness, and this is affecting the way radiographers work, just as it does other members of healthcare teams. There are some pilot schemes involving Macmillan radiographers, who work with patients in their own homes and take a leading role in the patient's all-round care, with responsibility for other issues such as counselling. The effect of radiotherapy is permanent: once given, it cannot be undone; therapeutic radiographers' responsibility is heavy. They need extensive knowledge of human anatomy and physiology and of radiation physics.

Exposure to X-rays can be dangerous, but X-ray departments are equipped with safeguards which ensure that operators are not harmed in any way. Protective clothing is worn and operators are never within reach of the actual X-ray beams. The controls are operated from outside the treatment rooms so that the radiographer is never exposed to radiation; treatment rooms are lined with material which the X-rays cannot penetrate.

There is a shortage of radiographers, especially therapy specialists. The majority work in hospital. There are a few posts with specialists in private practice; these may be better paid, but the work is lonelier than in hospital. There are also some openings with mobile X-ray units. For both these jobs previous hospital experience is necessary. Radiographers can earn their living in most countries of the world, provided they speak the appropriate language. There is a considerable number of post-graduate courses in the newer techniques of medical ultrasound, nuclear medicine and magnetic resonance imaging (used in both diagnosis and treatment of various diseases).

Training   The Diploma of the College of Radiographers has been replaced by a 3-year (4-year in Ireland) degree at university. About 50% of the course is clinical, i.e. spent within the clinical environment working with patients. Students train as *either* diagnostic *or* therapeutic radiographers.

Personal attributes A strong scientific bent; a steady hand and a sharp observant eye; a genuine liking for people and a desire to help the sick; a cheerful, confident manner; patience; calmness; firmness; ability to take responsibility and to work well with others; good health.

Late start Upper age limit for training is 50. Mature applicants are increasing. Entry requirements are relaxed. See also 'Access courses', p. xxxi.

Career-break No problem, but retraining essential – extent depends on length of break (changes in procedures and equipment are drastic and rapid). *Refresher* courses are available.

Part time No part-time training. At the moment part-time job opportunities are still limited, but there is no reason why work should not be organized on a part-time or job-sharing basis (see p. xxviii), as it is in similar professions.

Position of women Until recently about 90% of radiographers were women; there are still only around 12% men. Men have a disproportionate share of top jobs.

Further information College of Radiographers, 14 Upper Wimpole Street, London W1M 8BN

Related careers PHOTOGRAPHY – SCIENCE: *Scientist*; *Science Technician*

Religious Ministry: Main Religions in Britain

Entry qualifications

Normally 3 GCSEs (A–C) and 2 A-levels. Provisions for those who lack these qualifications, especially mature entrants (see 'Training', below), but must show evidence of ability to undertake academic study.

The work

Ordained ministry: Many duties are common to all denominations and include: holding services, preaching, conducting marriages and funerals. Less formal but equally important is 'pastoral care', such as visiting the sick, comforting the bereaved and helping individuals with their religious and personal problems. Like family doctors, priests receive many confidences and try to help their parishioners come to terms with their weaknesses and circumstances. They must also find time for solitary prayer and study. Rabbis in addition play a large social and sometimes political role in their communities.

Traditionally, ministers have been appointed to one congregation. Nowadays many work in team ministries, particularly in inner cities, within which individuals may specialize, e.g. in youth and community work. Many serve as hospital chaplains and some are responsible for the administration of schools. Others become chaplains in colleges, the Forces, industry, prisons.

The Roman Catholic and Anglican churches have *religious communities*; in some members are committed to a life of prayer and contemplation, in others they help to run schools, hospitals or residential homes.

Lay ministry: Many churches train and employ lay workers, both stipendiary and non-stipendiary (paid and unpaid). They assist ordained ministers in services and pastoral work and may also be responsible for particular branches of the ministry, such as teaching or counselling.

Training

All candidates have to go through a rigorous selection process to assess their 'calling' and suitability. Training is followed by a probationary period and does not lead automatically to ordination.

Church of England (Ordained Ministry)

Graduates under 30: With theology degree, 2 years full time at theological college; with degree in any other subject, 3 years and may include theology degree.

Non-graduates under 30: 3 years full time at theological college, sometimes preceded by 2-year part-time training scheme (the Aston Training Scheme).

Graduates and non-graduates over 30: 2 years full time or a 3-year part-time course.

Stipendiary lay ministry: As for ordained ministry, except for the Church Army, which runs its own 3-year course for trainee officers.

Roman Catholic Church

6-year full-time course of academic study combined with pastoral training. May include theology degree. Course length may be reduced for graduates and mature entrants. Training can take place in colleges abroad.

In the Church of England and the Roman Catholic church *religious orders* carry out their own training.

Church of Scotland (Ordained Ministry)

Under 23: With Scottish university entrance qualification, preferably a degree in any subject followed by 3-year course leading to degree in theology, but alternatively 4-year degree in divinity plus 2 years' further study in divinity.

Aged 23–29: 5-year training incorporating degree (occasionally licentiateship).

Aged 30–39: 4-year training incorporating degree (occasionally licentiateship).

Aged 40 plus: 3-year course for degree or licentiateship.

Lay ministry
Aged 23 plus: Individual training programme, usually involving Diploma level study.

Methodist Church

Ordained ministry
Under 30: With minimum 4 GCSEs (A–C) and Accredited Local Preacher qualifications, 3-year full-time course. Those with university entrance requirements may take degree.
Aged 30 plus: 2-year full-time or (if married) 3-year part-time course.

Ministers in local appointments
As above, but MLAs are normally aged over 30 and remain in their own occupation, carrying out ordained ministry in their leisure time.

Lay ministry
Qualifications for *deacons* (men and women) similar to ordained ministry, but applicants need not be accredited local preachers.
   Lay workers – no minimum qualifications.

Baptist Union

Minimum qualifications: Cambridge Diploma/Certificate in Religious Studies and at least 3 GCSEs (A–C), including English. Details of entrance requirements for various courses of ministerial training from Baptist Union affiliated colleges.

United Reformed Church

Graduates under 30: 4-year full-time course.
   Graduates over 30: 3-year full-time course.
   Non-graduates aged 21–30: With good academic qualifications, 4-year full-time course which may include degree.
   Non-graduates over 30: 3- or 4-year full-time course.

Jewish Faith

Orthodox
Either 3–4-year post-A-level course at Talmudical college, followed by rabbinical training, *or* (more commonly) 3-year degree course at Jews' College followed by 3–5 years' rabbinical training.
   Other training courses: B.Ed. in Jewish Studies for intending teachers; Cantorial course for conductors of services.

Progressive (*Reform and Liberal*)
A degree in any subject followed by 5-year full-time course for rabbinical ordination at Leo Baeck College.

A 4-term part-time teacher training course exists for those wishing to teach at religion school. There is a 1-year part-time course for kindergarten teachers.

Personal attributes Total sense of vocation and conviction that no other kind of work will give personal satisfaction. Desire to share faith with others; good intellect; ability to relate to all members of the church however well or poorly educated. Good health and stamina, mental and physical; open-mindedness and genuine desire to serve others without discrimination; willingness to be continually 'available'; self-discipline and self-sufficiency – although at the centre of the church ministers are always slightly 'set apart'. Emotional stability. Ability to work on own and as part of a team. Administrative skills.

Late start All denominations make provision for mature entrants (see 'Training', above).

Part time Some opportunities.

Position of women The status of women varies widely between denominations. The Roman Catholic and Orthodox Jewish faiths exclude women from ordination. The Progressive Jews ordained the first woman rabbi in 1976. The Church of England now ordains women as priests. The Church of Scotland accepts women and men on equal terms for ordained and lay ministry. Many women seek ordination later in life.

Further information *Church of England*: Advisory Board of Ministry, Church House, Great Smith Street, London SW1P 3NZ

Roman Catholic: Fr Michael Robert, Vocations Director, Allen Hall, 28 Beaufort Street, London SW3 5AA

Church of Scotland: Church of Scotland Department of Education, 121 George Street, Edinburgh EH2 4YN

Methodist Church: The Candidates Secretary (Division of Ministries), 25 Marylebone Road, London NW1 5JR

Baptist Union: The Ministry Office, Baptist Union of GB, P.O. Box 44, Baptist House, 129 Broadway, Didcot, Oxon. OX11 8RT

United Reformed: The General Secretary, The United Reformed Church, 86 Tavistock Place, London WC1H 9RT

Jewish Religion: *Orthodox*: London Board of Jewish Religious Education, Woburn House, Upper Woburn Place, London WC1H 0EP; *Progressive*: Leo Baeck College, The Manor House, 80 East End Road, London N3 2SY

Related careers   SOCIAL WORK – TEACHING

Retail Management

Entry qualifications

Nothing rigid; all educational levels.

The work

Retailing is one of the largest industries in the UK, accounting for about 11% of employment. It is one of the few career areas where getting on does not necessarily depend on passing examinations.

The industry is constantly having to adapt to changing lifestyles and new technologies. For example, the new Sunday Trading laws have increased trading hours. Computerization and 'rationalization' (less personal service; more part-timers for peak-hour work; fewer leisure periods for full-timers) has led to a reduced total workforce but, proportionately, more management opportunities.

No industry-wide career-structure exists. Titles, and responsibilities attached to titles, vary from one company to another, and so do recruiting and promotion procedures. The main types of 'retail outlet' are *hyper- and supermarkets*; *department stores*; *chain stores*; *co-operatives*; *independents*. The categories are not as clear-cut as they used to be. Supermarkets and multiples have 'diversified', i.e. sell more than one type of merchandise; some department stores give houseroom to specialist shops – for example, photographic equipment; some independents have joined together for bulk-buying purposes; some out-of-town centres combine retailing, entertainment and leisure facilities. Out-of-town retail parks have prospered at the expense of high street shops.

A growing type of retailing is *'franchising'*: a group of outlets – at present mainly food and fashion – is centrally controlled and sells to 'franchisees' the right to use its name and image, and to sell its centrally bought merchandise. Within certain guidelines, franchisees then run their own shows. *Mail order* is a growth area, mainly but not only, in fashion and household goods. It divides into two kinds: the traditional 'catalogue companies' which sell through part-time agents; and the more up-market 'direct mail', 'direct response' or 'direct marketing' companies. These sell through advertising in the press and/or through catalogues sent to likely customers. This is a sophisticated, high-risk business, more a marketing operation (see MARKETING AND SELLING, p. 297) than traditional retailing. Success depends on selecting a few sure-fire items for sale, the right advertising media and the right people to send catalogues to.

In traditional retailing, buying and selling organization varies from one company to another. For chain stores, hyper- and supermarkets buying is usually done centrally: identical merchandise is allocated to stores which are also given display and promotion guidelines. In department store groups, buying is also done centrally, but individual outlets still have their own distinctive character and do not necessarily all sell the same merchandise; they target specific customer groups, e.g. sophisticated in Knightsbridge, London, down-to-earth in small northern town.

Traditionally, most people going into retailing hoped to become buyers or store managers. While these positions are still very popular, there are now other sought-after activities in retailing such as merchandising, personnel, marketing, new product development and IT. Nearly always these require people to have A-levels or a degree. Specialists, such as *fashion graduates* (see p. 207), *food technologists* (see p. 462) and *electronics experts* (see ENGINEERING, p. 181) are sometimes recruited as trainee-buyers.

Most people, however, stay in selling and store management. Whatever the eventual ambition, and whatever training scheme the new entrant is on, starting on the shopfloor – the 'sharp end' – is essential to learn about customer-relations and trading principles. There are varying hierarchies from sales assistant, shelf-filler, checkout operator, warehouse clerk, via section, department, specialist (transport, staff, distribution, etc.), deputy to store manager, and after that perhaps area manager. Job titles, and job functions, vary from one retail concern to another. Speed, and likelihood of promotion, varies from company to company, and according to age and ability.

Store managers co-ordinate the various retailing functions: stock control; security; staff deployment; maximizing profit per square metre of premises; dealing with customers' complaints and queries; liaising with head office, etc. Supermarket and department store work differ greatly; supermarkets are much more hectic places with emphasis on fast-moving goods; managers must make their own, quick decisions, whether they are dealing with a staff, delivery or customer problem. In department stores, managers have such 'support services' as personnel, distribution and complaints departments on the premises and there is more emphasis on personal service. Hypermarkets and chain stores again make different demands. Ideally, prospective retailers should decide which type of atmosphere and work is right for them. In practice, there may not be much job choice, but one can switch from one type of retailing to another: basic retail expertise is a 'transferable skill', although it is easier to switch from supermarkets to chain stores than the other way around.

Staff management and training may have its own hierarchy, parallel with store management, and it may be a step on the store management ladder (see PERSONNEL . . . MANAGEMENT, p. 368).

Buying is very different from its image of spending other people's money on items one likes. Buyers work closely with *merchandisers*, who control the budget. Buying consists of selecting from suppliers' existing lines and also, jointly with manufacturers, developing new ideas, and adapting existing lines and prototypes bought or seen abroad or at a competitor's at home. Developing 'own brand' lines is expanding. Buyers work closely with marketing and production specialists and with store managers. Buying policies are based on methodical analysis and interpretation of past sales figures, on economic forecasts, on demographic trends (the present ageing population and the reduction in the number of late-teenagers have important implications for buyers); on lifestyle changes (the trend for more casual than formal clothing; the fashion to drink out of mugs rather than cups; increasingly exotic foreign travel and resultant interest in foreign food and drinks, etc.). Buying is a commercial activity and requires communication and negotiating expertise and number-crunching, as well as flair for guessing next year's preferences. It involves complex decision-making. For example, a buyer may find a very efficient and inexpensive spin-dryer with an unsatisfactory after-sales service. 'Does good performance and competitive pricing outweigh less-than-perfect after-sales service?' is the kind of decision buyers have to take – and be able to justify later, if customers complain.

Merchandisers tend to work at a policy level, forecasting departmental sales and profits and determining the budgets within which buyers operate. The work of both buyers and merchandisers involves constant decision-making and assessment of information. While merchandising is usually a senior head office job, confusingly it can mean different things in different companies. It can also describe people employed by wholesalers or manufacturers who ensure that their employer's products are adequately displayed in retail outlets. And it can describe persons who, working closely with display specialists, are responsible for the display of goods in a store.

Commodity knowledge – expertise in one type of merchandise – used to be all-important; then managerial and commercial expertise determined promotion and buyers easily switched from buying one type of merchandise to another. Now, commodity knowledge, at least in 'high-tech' consumer goods, textiles and food, again seems to matter more; but it varies from company to company.

Head office jobs include *general management* (see MANAGE-MENT, p. 275); *marketing* (see p. 297); *design* (see p. 54); *food and other technologies* (see p. 462); *personnel* (see p. 368); *store planning*; and *retail analysis*: what type of shop/shopping centre is likely to be profitable in the year 2000 – where, and why? How will European competition affect our stores once we are in the integrated European market, and what can we do to remain competitive once European retailers set up their shops in this country in greater numbers? As retailing is becoming ever more sophisticated and professionalized, new specialisms emerge, or traditional jobs are being fined down into separate functions. For example, 'transport management' may be divided into 'vehicle and depot management' and 'operations management' with responsibility for the movement of goods from supplier or port of entry to depot or store (see DISTRIBUTION MANAGEMENT p. 269). These planning/forecasting jobs involve a mixture of crystal-ball gazing, statistics, technological and economic forecasting, psychology and sociology (and are very much a growth area for graduates from any discipline).

Retailing also offers good opportunities to systems analysts and other computer experts (see COMPUTING, p. 138) as more companies adopt computerized 'point of sale' stock-control and 'electronic fund transfer' systems and prepare for computer-based armchair shopping. There are openings for computer science graduates or other computer-literate graduates able to work well in a team designing and modifying databases and making systems more user-friendly.

Fashion retailing is a specialized job for people with experience of fashion (see p. 207) as well as of general retailing. Boutiques, like other small shops, suffered during the recession, and, while popular with people with a fashion or retail background wanting to start their own business, they remain 'high risk' concerns.

A knowledge of a foreign (European) language, together with an understanding of the relevant country's culture, will be a great advantage for retailers from now on.

Food retailing has been called 'recession-proof'. It did well even during the 1990s recession.

Training   Training is patchy and haphazard. Some employers – including most but not all of the well-known chain and department stores – train staff systematically, using outside courses and/or their own in-house training schemes, to produce 'retail professionals' with transferable skills (i.e. trainees who can later use their training in all kinds of retail companies). Other companies give little career training, but teach people to perform specific jobs in their organization. While promotion up the retail hierarchy does not depend on having paper qualifications, the importance of expertise is growing enormously, as technological and management systems are becoming ever more sophisticated; such expertise can, in practice, only be acquired by systematic training. However, there are many ways of training. It is generally agreed that the best way of becoming a retail professional is to learn on the job, with additional off-the-job training and being assessed for NVQs/SVQs (see below). That means finding a job with day-release or similar facilities for taking courses.

The alternatives to a job-with-training are (a) taking any job in retailing and learning by experience and possibly taking a relevant distance-learning course or evening classes or (b) taking a pre-entry course (see below).

Individual companies' training schemes vary greatly. All retailers stress the flexibility of their training schemes and emphasize that no specific qualification or training scheme automatically leads to any specific point on the retail job ladder. Individual patterns vary not only from one company to another, but also from one year to another according to company plans for expansion or consolidation/contraction or change of emphasis, and also according to current views on which type of training (length, outside or in-house course, theory-and-practice mix) is the most cost-effective. Companies may recruit young people at 16 with GCSEs, at 18 with A-levels or a GNVQ, or offer graduate training schemes. Candidates are strongly advised to look at several companies' recruitment literature, to read the small print and, at interviews, ask questions about promotion prospects, etc.

Qualifications are offered at different levels. Retail NVQs/SVQs are awarded by RSA, City and Guilds and SCOTVEC in partnership with the Distributive Occupational Standards Council. Sales staff in many companies now work towards NVQs/SVQs levels 1 and 2 during their training. Levels 3 and 4 are more gradually becoming established at supervisory and management level.

Modern Apprenticeships (see p. xxiv) are being introduced for young people wishing to enter retailing straight from school.

BTEC courses in distribution and retail management are also widely available, both full-time and part-time, for those already working in the industry. Candidates with 4 GCSEs (A–C) can take a BTEC National Certificate (or Scottish equivalent), usually

2 years full-time, or National Diploma, 2 years full-time or 3 years part-time, which are both recognized as an entry qualification for most junior management training schemes run by major stores. For those with the BTEC National or with an A-level, BTEC/SCOTVEC offer Higher National courses in retail management for those aiming at senior-level jobs.

Degrees in retail management are available at a number of universities and are increasingly recognized and requested by large retail companies.

GCSE entrants with only good Saturday/holiday retail experience may be eligible for 2-year training schemes planned for A-level entrants, which may lead to the BTEC Higher National Certificate or Scottish equivalent. Equally, A-level entrants with some work experience may be eligible for graduate training schemes. Graduates are expected to be ready for their first junior management job in 9–15 months; A-level entrants and others with good hands-on experience are expected to take 15–24 months. Degree subject is immaterial, and Higher National Diplomas (BTEC or Scottish equivalent) are usually considered as of equal value to degrees. Training patterns are as varied, and as confusing, as this. Company training policies and candidates' personal qualities are likely to remain more important than paper qualifications. A 16-year-old without any GCSEs but with potential (including the potential to make supervisors notice it!) can catch up with a 21-year-old graduate entrant: when the graduate starts training, the school-leaver has had 5 years' practical experience and is eligible for management training along with the graduate.

Personal attributes   Numeracy; an outgoing personality; an interest in both people and things; organizing ability; communication skills; commercial sense. For *store management*: leadership qualities; ability to delegate and take decisions quickly and to keep calm in crises; physical stamina. For *buyers*: interest in social and economic trends; negotiating skills; objectivity to be able to judge the relevance of one's own taste and gauge that of customers. For *buyers* and *merchandisers*: good mathematical and analytical skills.

Late start   Good opportunities. Most companies positively welcome people who have had work experience, and will train people of up to about 35 for management. BTEC/SCOTVEC courses also welcome mature students and distance-learning courses are available.

Career-break   Most companies encourage returners and provide refresher training.

Part time   Ample opportunities up to supervisor level, and increasingly also at management levels. With lengthening shopping hours, several managers share store management anyway, so it is quite possible to organize part time and job-sharing at management levels. Head office jobs, including buying and merchandising, can also be done at 'less than full time'. So far, job-sharing and part-time work at senior head office levels seem to have been started only when enterprising individuals have taken the initiative.

Position of women   Considering that the vast majority of sales assistants, and of customers, are women, surprisingly few women are in senior management. But the situation has improved in recent years; more women are moving up the ladder faster. In chain store management – until fairly recently a male preserve – women are now doing quite well, and they are also doing well in department stores.

Women *buyers* are no longer confined to fashion and similar areas. There are still very few women in supermarket management. The reason given is that managers may have to help humping heavy goods; however, it is unlikely that there is much work which is too hard for any but the most delicate females. Because retailing is such a diffuse industry, women in retail have no forum as have, for example, women in banking or medicine.

Further information   National Retail Training Council, Bedford House, 69–79 Fulham High Street, London SW6 3JW
Individual retailing concerns

Related careers   CATERING: *Hotels* – MANAGEMENT – LOGISTICS ...
MANAGEMENT – PERSONNEL / HUMAN RESOURCES MANAGEMENT

Science

Scientist

Main functions or activities: Research and development; analysis and investigation; production; technical sales and service; technical writing.

Main branches: Physics; chemistry; biological sciences; environmental sciences and conservation; cybernetics; mathematical sciences; materials science; biomedical science.

Entry qualifications

Scientists and technologists normally need a degree, but the borderline between scientist, technologist and senior technician – BTEC/SCOTVEC Higher award holder (see pp. xxi, xxii) – is often blurred; many of the latter have degrees.

Precise degree course requirements vary from one course to another. In general:

For *physics, cybernetics and applied sciences* degrees, A-levels must include physics and mathematics.

For *some mathematics* degrees, A-levels must include pure and applied maths.

For *chemistry* degrees, chemistry and physics and/or mathematics A-levels are preferred, but other combinations may be acceptable.

For *biological sciences*, biology, a physical science – preferably chemistry – and mathematics are ideal; other combinations may be acceptable.

For *some* science degrees biology may only be accepted as a third A-level: if only 2 A-levels are offered they must both be in sciences more relevant to the degree subject.

The Advanced GNVQ in science (or, for some biological degrees, health and social care) is another route into higher education; as this is a new qualification, students should always check its acceptability with individual institutions and departments.

For *BTEC/SCOTVEC Higher National Diploma*: 1 relevant A-level passed and another studied at A-level (or 2 Highers); for *BTEC/SCOTVEC Higher National Certificate*: *either* BTEC/SCOTVEC National award *or* 2 relevant A-levels passed (but for individual subject Certificate courses requirements may vary).

The work   All jobs are based directly or indirectly on scientific or technological developments. More to the point, all jobs are likely to be affected by today's or tomorrow's scientific developments or their exploitation. 'Scientific literacy' – an understanding of what science is about and how it affects virtually every aspect of industrial society – is an advantage in most jobs, and is essential in many, however remote from schoolroom science.

A science qualification is, of course, often a vocational qualification, but it need not be by any means. The image of the white-coated, lab-based scientist as the only, or even the main kind of, science professional, is quite out of date.

Science practitioners

Scientists can choose: they can become 'science practitioners' or 'practical scientists' and use their scientific training and education in all kinds of science jobs. In research, they can push out the frontiers of knowledge even further – in space and astronomical investigations; interaction of energy and matter in lasers; optical fibres; bioengineering, etc., there is a vast variety of research areas. Then there is work for scientists who want to solve problems thrown up by scientific developments: advances in medical science have led to over-population and food-shortages; excessive use of energy requires alternative sources; chemical industries have led to pollution of the environment. Biotechnologists, chemists and other specialists investigate and try to alleviate undesirable but inevitable side-effects of innovation. And then there is of course the vast, mainly physics-based, information technology industry and its spin-offs, to give just a few examples.

The nature of practising scientists' work ranges from laboratory-centred 'boffin' research to 'people-centred' activities like technical selling (see p. 443) or people-and-technology-centred work in manufacturing (see p. 443) or profit-centred work in marketing and other commercial functions. (See below for details of the various 'functions', and of the main science specialisms or 'branches'.)

The outlook for scientists varies considerably from one branch to another and may change from one year to the next. Physicists are in greatest demand (mainly in the electronics industry, see p. 188), but mathematicians, cyberneticians and some applied scientists (e.g. materials and polymer specialists) are also in demand, followed by chemists, biochemists and microbiologists. Botanists, zoologists and environmental science graduates are least in demand. However, scientists can often switch to another, related field (this may involve a post-graduate course).

Prospects in the various types of work or *functions* vary mainly according to economic climate. In research and development, cutbacks tend to bite much earlier than in manufacturing and analysis and investigation. Technical writing and technical sales are expanding functions. However, scientists only specialize in a function *after* graduation. (But some degree subjects are more likely to lead to one function, some to another: for example *applied* scientists are much more likely to be in demand in manufacturing than, for example, botanists, and a broad-based integrated course is not likely to lead to research.)

Scientists often start in laboratory work (*research and development, analysis, investigation*) and then move into *manufacturing, technical sales and service*, or *writing*; or they may use their science background in *marketing* (see p. 297); in *information work* (p. 227) or in *patent agency* (p. 364) or *operational research* (p. 295). *Teachers* of mathematics and most sciences are much in demand in schools (but higher education teaching prospects are bleak).

Career prospects are generally much better for graduates who have at least a reading knowledge of a foreign language (at the moment especially German or Russian). Anyone who wants to work in EU countries must be fluent in the relevant language and/or have specific experience. Short-term contracts possible in developing countries.

Science as a tool

Scientists can equally choose not to practise as scientists, but to use their understanding of science as a tool with which to do other kinds of jobs – in commerce, industry, the public service – more effectively. People who have scientific curiosity but are not sure whether they want to be scientists, can choose a science qualification confident in the knowledge that their scientific background will be a door-opener into a variety of jobs in many different settings. For example, a scientist who goes into stock-broking or merchant banking is likely to become skilled at market forecasting and better able to assess a new high-technology company's chances of success, or the advantages or disadvantages of a merger between two science-based companies, than someone without a scientific background who has to go by hunch, or someone else's advice. A senior Civil Servant is better at advising ministers on, for example, the implications of rapidly changing technology when discussing the future of, say, transport, or the health service, or defence expenditure, than someone without a scientific background. (The Civil Service very much wants to attract more scientists as Administration Trainees (see p. 124) – the potential high-flyers in the Civil Service – and into the Science Management Training Scheme.) In publishing, to choose a very different example, a scientist will be at an advantage over a non-scientist when judging the possibilities of electronic publishing. There are dozens of similar examples.

In industrial and commercial management (see p. 275) and in marketing (see p. 297), science graduates are welcome. About 40% of all employers' vacancies for graduates are open to graduates from any discipline: the employers buy graduates' 'trained minds' rather than their specific knowledge. Increasingly, when recruiting any-discipline graduates, employers tend to prefer science or technology to arts graduates *provided* they have the other skills they are looking for. The former's scientific literacy is useful at a time when science and technology impinge on so many aspects of every organization. Scientists' analytical approach to problem-solving is invariably useful even when the problem is not a scientific one. Scientists with communication skills are above all badly needed to close the communication gap: to explain basic relevant scientific facts, trends and implications to their scientifically illiterate colleagues (many of them in very high places). Information work (see p. 227) has good openings for scientists. Finally, for people who want to set up in business on their own (see WORKING FOR ONESELF, p. 551), a science background is extremely useful (though it will have to be complemented with business knowhow).

Practising scientists' work can be divided in two ways: by the types of activities or 'functions' and by the various 'branches' or science-specializations:

The Main Functions

Research and Development

Research is the lifeblood of science, enlarging existing knowledge and stimulating the growth of new branches. *Development* translates research findings into new – or improved – products and processes. The two overlap.

The terms 'pure' and 'applied' are often used to describe the type of research undertaken. In this context 'pure' research means increasing knowledge for its own sake and 'applied' research is 'goal-orientated' – directed towards solving technical problems, improving national defence or prestige – or 'wealth creating'. Science research is very expensive to carry out, much of it is sponsored, by industry or government, and is goal-orientated. Some university departments may fund 'pure' research from their resources or through research studentships which lead to higher research degrees (M. Phil. or Ph. D.).

Most research is teamwork, with several scientists, often from several disciplines, and technicians, working under a team-leader. The work may be divided into projects; several scientists are then responsible for their own project within the overall framework.

Personal attributes   Above-average intelligence; enthusiasm; willingness to work patiently for long hours (or even months) and persevere with tricky problems; creativity; ability to work in a team and to take decisions and stand up for them if things go wrong; ability to communicate findings effectively; great powers of concentration; stubborn persistence in the face of disappointing research results. Industrial researchers must be willing to change direction – at however interesting a point in their research – in the interests of the company's profitability.

Analysis and Investigation

Routine tests and investigations are carried out in all fields of science. In chemical research, for example, analysis of intermediate compounds enables scientists to keep track of chemical changes that are taking place. In manufacturing industry, the composition of both raw materials and products is monitored by analysing samples in *quality control* laboratories. In the food industry, regular checks are made on biological and chemical purity of foodstuffs. In pharmaceuticals the safety of drugs, beauty preparations and food additives is investigated. Before such products can be marketed, substances are tried out on experimental animals or by tissue culture to see whether there are any toxic side-effects. In the agrochemical industry, new fertilizers and pesticides are given field trials; the chemicals are used on experimental plots in various parts of the country – and sometimes overseas – so that scientists can determine how performance is affected by different soils and climates.

Many analytical techniques are automated; most routine testing is carried out by technicians (see p. 456). The professional scientist trains and supervises technicians, initiates, organizes and oversees projects and researches into new experimental methods.

Personal attributes Interest in applied science; methodical approach; patience; ability to organize other people and their work; ability to communicate effectively with highly specialized colleagues and with trainee technicians; observation to recognize the unexpected.

Manufacturing Production
(see also ENGINEERING, pp. 185, 191)

The central activity in industry is organizing production. That involves supervising the people who operate the industrial plant. Production managers (titles vary) are a vital link in the chain of command from chargehand to production director, and between production and other departments. Their main function is to see that production runs smoothly and is as efficient as possible. That means they must keep up with technological developments and arrange for and supervise the installation of new equipment as necessary. Hours can be long and irregular, and may include some shift-work – but this is by no means so in all plants. Production managers usually have a small office, but they spend little time in it. The work involves daily contact with other professionals and managers from other departments as well as with shop stewards, etc.

Production professionals are equally concerned with managing people and with the exploitation of new technologies. The largest opportunities are for chemists. Production managers, or whatever the title of persons in charge, are normally graduates; technicians work under them. Production specialists can switch from one type of plant to another; and they can later go into *marketing* or *general management*.

Personal attributes Willingness to accept responsibility and take decisions; ability to keep calm in a crisis; leadership skills to motivate and organize plant operatives; practicality; ability to get on well with people at all levels in the industrial hierarchy; interest in the commercial application of science.

Technical Sales and Service

Two closely related activities: selling a science-based product and providing a technical back-up service for the customer. The product might be a sophisticated scientific instrument, an industrial chemical, a drug or a pesticide. The customer could be a research scientist, an industrial manager of a tiny or a large concern, a pharmacist or a farmer, i.e. a person with a lot of or no scientific knowledge. The technical sales executive or 'rep' needs a thorough knowledge of the product, its uses and limitations. The kind of technical service a company provides depends on the nature of its products. A technical service scientist representing a plastics manufacturer deals mainly with customers who mould plastics into containers and would investigate complaints and answer technical queries (and perhaps suggest new ways of using the material). It is part of the job to act as a link between the research laboratories and the sales staff.

Representatives for pharmaceutical firms visit doctors and pharmacists and inform them about new drugs and also provide feedback to the company on doctors' opinions of its products. In agricultural service industries reps may sell fertilizers, pesticides and animal health products to farmers and give advice about how they should be used (see AGRICULTURE AND HORTICULTURE, p. 20). Reps are usually given a 'territory'; its size depends on what they sell and whether it is a country area or town: some reps may be away from home all week; others come home every night. Many work from home and only go to the office occasionally.

Personal attributes Outgoing personality; liking for meeting a succession of people; a thick skin for the occasional rude customer; sensitivity to gauge the right approach (long-winded, brief, aloof, friendly, etc.); ability to communicate facts effectively to customers who may be much more, and may be much less, knowledgeable than the reps themselves; self-sufficiency for possibly long hours of lone travelling.

Technical Writing

A technical writer assembles a package of scientific or technical information for a particular readership. The work is often done on a contract basis; specialist firms hire out technical writers to client companies for the duration of a particular writing project. This may concern, for example, a set of handbooks and instruction manuals to accompany a complex piece of electronic equipment which is being marketed by an electronics manufacturer. Two 'packages' may have to be written: one in simple language for operatives or chargehands who have only to know how to operate the equipment; and another package aimed at technical managers who want to know more technical details and may need to be able to repair or adjust the equipment. In the pharmaceutical industry, writers prepare 'case histories' of new drugs (experiments done, etc.) for submission to the Committee on Safety of Medicines.

Technical copywriters (see ADVERTISING, p. 14) may write promotional material for science-based products. This is an expanding field, particularly in electronics, engineering generally and pharmaceuticals.

Personal attributes   Wide scientific/technological interests and knowledge; an inquiring mind; ability to search out information and sift the relevant – for the particular purpose – from the irrelevant; ability to explain complex matters lucidly and concisely; a scientific grasshopper mind, to switch from one type of subject to another; liking for desk-work.

The Main Branches of Science

The classification of science into content areas is constantly changing. Most people are familiar with physics, chemistry and biology but as scientific investigation gets more complex, or is applied for different purposes, so different classifications may arise: a 'subset' of one of the main disciplines may be identified for more detailed study (e.g. astronomy – the study of extra-terrestrial systems – or virology – the study of viruses). An overlapping area of two main disciplines may emerge as worth studying in its own right (e.g. biophysics, biochemistry) or an interdisciplinary area may be identified, usually problem-orientated (practical rather than academic) and develop its own concepts and methods of study (e.g. cybernetics, environmental sciences, materials science, biotechnology).

Physics

Physics – the study of matter and energy – lies at the heart of science. It is closely related to mathematics and also quite closely to chemistry; *chemical physics* – the study of materials and molecules – is a subject in its own right. *Biophysics* – the physical properties of living matter – has assumed greater importance as biological knowledge has grown. Many aspects of *engineering* and *materials science* are 'applied' aspects of physics. So the physicist, who always has a sound mathematical background, has a wide choice of occupations and settings in which to work.

Most industrial openings occur in engineering and related industries – especially in electronics, telecommunications, computing and transport; other opportunities exist in chemical and energy industries, e.g. oil, gas, electricity. In the Civil Service physicists work on problems ranging from research into navigation to recycling industrial waste. (See also 'Medical or Biomedical Engineering', p. 190)

The work of medical physicists is increasingly important to medicine. They form part of a team of specialists concerned with the diagnosis and treatment of disease, using radiotherapy and diagnostic radiology, radioisotopes, ultrasonics and many other physical methods to help doctors cure patients. In *occupational hygiene*, physicists help prevent damage to people's health by monitoring potential hazards from radiation, noise, dust and other sources in working environments. (See also 'Environmental Sciences and Conservation', especially *geophysics* and *meteorology*, below.) There are very limited opportunities for physicists (who may or may not have taken a degree in astronomy or astrophysics) and for mathematicians to branch out into *astronomy*. Research into such aspects of astronomy as satellite communications systems or the structure of the universe is done at government, university, and some commercial telecommunications (i.e. electronics) research laboratories. In *computer* design and manufacture, physicists play an important part.

Chemistry

Chemistry – the study of the composition of materials, their properties and how they change and react with other materials – occupies a central position in the sciences. It forms the basis of, for example, the manufacture of metals, pharmaceuticals, fertilizers, paints, synthetic fabrics, dyestuffs, plastics, paper, cosmetics, herbicides, pesticides, foodstuffs and many other products.

It has links with all the other sciences, such as physics, biology and geology and contributes to 'applied' science areas such as *food science*, *forensic science*, *materials science*, *pharmacology* and *pharmacy* and *textile technology*. So someone with an interest in chemistry has a wide choice of employment. The big chemical manufacturers, oil, drug and cosmetic companies are the biggest employers of chemists. In the Civil Service, chemists in the Science Group work on road-surfaces, building materials, nutrition, pollution, and other research; others are employed as forensic scientists (see p. 131); in the general Civil Service they are welcome as Administration Trainees (see CIVIL SERVICE, p. 124), using their expertise in an advisory capacity and as background knowledge. Others work in the public health field, e.g. analysing drinking water, food and drugs, and in hospital laboratories. A few chemists work on restoration and research in museums. (See also 'Biochemistry, microbiology and biotechnology', below.)

Biological Sciences

Biology can be subdivided into 4 major disciplines – the study of: plants (*botany*); animals (*zoology*); micro-organisms (*microbiology*); chemistry of living matter (*biochemistry*). However, as the interdependence of plants and animals is increasingly recognized, more emphasis is being placed on biology as an integration of botany and zoology, e.g. *ecology*. More specialized biological sciences deal with particular groups of living organisms – viruses (*virology*) and insects (*entomology*) for instance – and with particular biological processes such as the functioning of the body's organs (*physiology*) or the mechanisms of heredity and variation (*genetics*).

Botany and zoology

Most opportunities used to occur in the public sector – mainly in the Civil Service Science Group, agricultural (e.g. animal and plant breeding) and medical research, and conservation, but many of these research bodies have been privatized. The Ministry of Agriculture, Fisheries and Food employs marine biologists to monitor fish stocks and pollution levels. A small number of biologists work in the Health Service, for water authorities and museums. In industry there are limited opportunities in pharmaceuticals and agrochemicals.

The most marketable aspects of botany and zoology are those related either to medical and pharmaceutical research (such as parasitology and physiology), or to agriculture and horticulture (such as plant pathology and entomology). Opportunities in *marine* and *freshwater biology* and *general ecology* are very limited. However, concern for the environment has meant an increase in jobs in industry for 'environmental' biologists.

Biochemistry, microbiology and biotechnology

Biochemists and microbiologists have much better career prospects than botanists or zoologists; there is a steady demand from industry (mainly food, drink, pharmaceuticals and agriculture), from medical research and hospital laboratories, specialist research organizations and, to a lesser extent, the Civil Service Science Group.

A *biochemist* working for a pharmaceutical company might study the mechanism of a new drug or (helped by a microbiologist) investigate biochemical aspects of the production of antibiotics by fermentation. *Hospital biochemists* work alongside medical colleagues and technicians as members of a team: they supervise routine biochemical testing (see 'Medical Laboratory Scientific

Officers', p. 452), do research into, for example, the function of hormones or the body's defence mechanisms, and may also teach clinical biochemistry to doctors and nurses. Some use biochemical analysis in clinical diagnosis or in forensic laboratories (e.g. for genetic fingerprinting).

Microbiologists often specialize in bacteriology and virology and become experts in plant or animal diseases. In the food industry and in environmental health laboratories they check samples for pathogenic microbes and investigate spoilage. In oil companies they explore ways of producing synthetic protein by feeding bacteria with the by-products of petroleum refining.

Biotechnology is fairly new as an academic discipline but covers processes which use multi-disciplinary approaches to problem-solving in science-based industries. It is, very broadly, the use of living organisms to perform a useful task. The main uses are in manufacturing industry – particularly brewing and the food, ferti-lizer, animal feedstuffs and pharmaceutical industries – medicine, agriculture and horticulture. It has also been described as 'factory farming of bugs' or microbes – the smallest living organisms – which are then put to industrial uses.

Biotechnologists work in a vast variety of science-based jobs, for example on the development of synthetic proteins; of new strains of wheat; of hormones and drugs. They also work on pollution control (e.g. with biodegradable waste products), and on the generation of new sources of energy from such varied natural materials as plant tissue and animal waste products. The usual way into biotechnology is via a science degree – preferably chemistry, biochemistry or microbiology – followed by post-graduate study, or a biotechnology degree. Genetic engineering – the manipulation, using scientific techniques, of genes – is one aspect of biotechnology. It is increasingly used to produce varieties of crops which are especially resistant to disease or tolerant of poor weather. *Molecular biology* – the understanding of how genetic information is stored and passed on – has opened up vast new areas of research.

Environmental Sciences and Geoscience

The environmental sciences are fashionable. Concern with pollu-tion, dwindling natural resources and threatened plant and animal species has given a fresh impetus to the scientific study of the environment. *Conservation* and *ecology* (the study of how plants and animals interact with their natural surroundings), together with *meteorology*, *oceanography*, *geology* and *geophysics*, are im-portant environmental subjects.

Environmental science is often a *post-graduate* specialization: scientists take a first degree in a traditional subject and then either graft on an appropriate post-graduate course or get trained by employers in environmental aspects of their subject. *Meteorologists* and *physical oceanographers* usually have degrees in physics or maths; biologists normally take a specialist course (for example, in ecology or marine biology) before becoming conservationists. *Geoscience* graduates are the exception: they can go straight into professional work without further training. But there is an increasing number of first degree courses in environmental subjects – either joint honours (such as physics and meteorology) or broad-based integrated courses in environmental sciences. The most useful of these are probably those offering a placement year in which students get 'hands-on' experience. Even graduates with an environmental science degree often need to take a more specialized post-graduate course and / or gain voluntary work experience before applying for paid jobs.

Conservation

Nature conservation used only to mean protecting unusual plants and animals and their habitats. Now, many human activities have a wider environmental impact. Crop protection chemicals, for example, can upset the balance of ecological systems. If herbicides are used to control aquatic weeds, dead plants consume oxygen while decaying. As a result, fish and other organisms may die through lack of oxygen. A pipeline or bypass laid across country may disturb plant and animal life around it; an open-cast mine may leave a permanent scar on the countryside. Modern conservationists, recognizing the importance of protecting flora and fauna, are concerned with the wider problems of preserving the countryside as a whole.

The Nature Conservancy Council – responsible for conserving the wildlife and physiographical features of Great Britain – was superseded in 1991 by separate conservancy bodies for England, Scotland and Wales. Between them, they manage over 100 National Nature Reserves and several thousand Sites of Special Scientific Interest, and advise farmers, landowners, local authorities, industrialists and others on conservation matters. Scientists (mainly biologists, botanists, zoologists, geologists and geographers) are employed as Assistant Regional Officers. The Nature Reserves are run by Wardens (not always graduates) who are experienced conservationists. Environmental research covering land, ocean and fresh water is carried out by the many institutes which come under the aegis of the Natural Environment Research Council (NERC).

Geoscience

Geoscience covers all branches of science concerned with the structure, evolution and dynamics of the earth and with the natural mineral and energy resources that it contains. It comprises *geology, geophysics and geochemistry*. Geoscience investigates the real world beyond the laboratory and is directly relevant to the needs of society. Its study develops a wide range of skills useful in a wide range of careers, with opportunities in the UK and abroad.

Activities carried out by geoscientists include geological mapping, geophysical prospecting, geochemical sampling, borehole logging, chemical analysis of rocks and minerals, rock testing of geotechnical properties, computer processing of data, computer modelling of geological processes and of subsurface geology.

Careers tend to fall into one of the following fields:

Exploration and production: the search for natural resources such as fossil fuels, metals, construction materials and groundwater, and the geological management of their extraction.

Engineering and environmental: the investigation and monitoring of local ground conditions associated with construction, planning, land use and environmental issues.

Geological survey: The systematic collection of surface and subsurface geological information, both onshore and offshore, for the production of geological, geophysical and geochemical maps and databases.

Education and research/conservation: teaching and research posts in universities; school and college teaching; museum posts; scientific posts with nature conservancy bodies.

Meteorology and Oceanography (see also METEOROLOGY, p. 317)

Meteorology and oceanography – concerned with the atmosphere and the oceans – are closely related. The physics and dynamics of atmospheric and oceanographic processes have much in common; the oceans exert a powerful influence on the weather. At honours degree level, *meteorology* and *physical oceanography* are highly mathematical; numerical methods are widely used in modern weather forecasting.

The Meteorological Office also carries out research into such topics as the physics of cloud formation and energy exchange between atmosphere and oceans. Scientists are usually involved either in *forecasting* or in *research*.

Research in physical oceanography is undertaken at the Institute of Oceanographic Sciences (part of the Natural Environment Research Council – NERC). Topics include studies of waves, tides, currents and general circulation of ocean water. NERC also investigates the ecology of deep-water organisms, the composition of the sea-floor, *marine biology* subjects. Oceanographic work is done partly in the laboratory and partly at sea.

Mathematical Sciences

Mathematicians – pure and applied – are much in demand. They work in commerce, e.g. in finance and in actuarial work (see ACTUARY, p. 11), in science-based activities and in computing (see p. 138). They frequently work in teams with scientists and engineers. They may analyse data produced by scientists; they may work on translating problems into mathematical terms (making 'models'), work out solutions and then express the results in non-mathematical form. They make calculations which enable *control engineers* (see p. 192) to make adjustments to the manufacturing process. Sometimes the mathematical models are so complex that a special technique called *numerical analysis* is used to solve them. Some mathematicians specialize in numerical analysis; others become expert in *operational research* (see p. 295).

Statisticians – including mathematicians who have specialized in statistics – work in industry, medical, social and agricultural research, and in the Civil Service (Central Statistical Office and all the departments with a statistics division). They are concerned with the design of experiments, questionnaires and surveys and with the collection, analysis and interpretation of results. In a government department they provide information on which policies can be based; for example they predict the effect of changes in the tax system or the likely demand for energy. Wherever computers are used – and that is in virtually every field of activity, see COMPUTING/INFORMATION TECHNOLOGY (p. 138) – statisticians process and interpret data and help design and improve systems. There is also scope for statisticians in marketing and market research where they design surveys to establish demand for goods and services. The majority of statisticians need a scientific background; some need social science expertise (it is easier to switch with a science background to statistics in social sciences than to switch with a social science background to statistics in science).

Materials Science

Materials science is an umbrella term for sciences concerned with a variety of metallic and non-metallic materials (including *polymers*, *papers*, *ceramics*, *glass* and *textiles*). *Metallurgists* work on the extraction, refining and fabrication of ferrous and non-ferrous metals used in products ranging from aircraft bodies to electronic components. *Textile* technologists work with domestic materials, such as clothing and furnishing fabrics, and with industrial products used for a wide variety of purposes, e.g. insulation, road reinforcement and even the manufacture of artificial veins. *Polymer* scientists and technologists work on all kinds of plastics and other polymeric materials used in products ranging from picnic plates and computer keyboards to gas pipes and gear components.

It is possible to specialize early on in metallurgy, polymers, textiles or one of the other non-metallic materials, but most entrants to these industries have followed a broader course in materials science. There are good opportunities for materials scientists to use their interdisciplinary approach in these industries, as well as in the newer ones concerned with composite materials: polymers reinforced with glass or carbon fibre, for example, and others still in the experimental stage. Physics, chemistry and engineering graduates are also recruited.

Biomedical Science

Most biomedical scientists work in the NHS, where they are known as Medical Laboratory Scientific Officers (MLSOs). They are concerned with laboratory investigations for diagnosis and treatment of disease, and research into its causes and cure. Trainees work under the overall direction of senior staff who have specialized in the application of their particular discipline to medicine. Work is done in hospitals, universities, blood transfusion centres, public health laboratories, veterinary establishments and pharmaceutical firms. In hospitals there may be some contact with patients, depending on the specialization. Scientists may supervise medical laboratory assistants.

The main specializations are: *clinical chemistry*: the analysis of blood and other biological materials; *medical microbiology*: the isolation and identification of bacteria and viruses from patients with infections, or in water and foodstuffs; *haematology and serology*: the study of blood; *histopathology and cytology*: the study of tissues removed during surgical operations and at post-mortem examinations, and in investigations for the early detection of cancer.

Training (all sciences) Normally a degree. Science courses usually consist either of a detailed study of a single subject, with supporting ancillary subjects, or of a study of 2 distinct disciplines in a joint honours course, or of a cluster of several related disciplines, such as biological sciences. The question of whether a broad-based or a specialized degree leads to better prospects is impossible to answer in a general way: it depends on an individual's adaptability, motivation, specialization, on changing economic circumstances and on technological developments. There is a continuing need for specialists, but a 'generalist' scientific education possibly leads to a wider choice of jobs especially for 'non-practising' scientists; its built-in flexibility enables the scientist to change direction if, for example, that should be desirable or necessary after a career-break, or because supply and demand in a specialization have changed.

For *research* a first or upper second honours degree is usually required but research assistants who work part time for a Ph.D. are occasionally taken on with a 2.2. A first degree may have to be followed by a career-orientated post-graduate course. First-degree course emphasis varies greatly. Some courses are very much more practical and vocational in approach and structure than others, and prospective students need to do careful research before applying.

Many degrees are 4-year sandwich courses, with a year spent at work. This may be an advantage to people who want to go into industry: their experience of the work situation during their training reassures employers that the applicant at least knows what a working environment is like.

There is an increasing number of full-time undergraduate courses which are extended to 4 years and lead to a Master's degree, for example M.Sci., M.Chem., M.Phys. Anyone intending to do research would be advised to choose one of these.

BTEC/SCOTVEC Higher awards (see pp. xxi, xxii) or Dip. H.E.s normally lead to senior technicians', not to professional scientists' jobs, but the distinction between scientist and technician is often blurred. Technologists may have an applied science degree or BTEC/SCOTVEC Higher award.

BTEC/SCOTVEC Higher award students can complete their professional training by taking a further 1-year full-time or 2-year part-time (day-release) course leading to the graduate membership examinations of one of the relevant scientific institutes, e.g. the Licentiateship of the Royal Society of Chemistry.

Higher level GNVQs may eventually replace BTEC/SCOTVEC higher awards.

Once in a job, training, or at least learning, continues. This may or may not lead to a further qualification.

Biomedical scientists
For MLSO posts, State Registration is essential, and for this a degree is necessary (the previous alternative entry via BTEC/

SCOTVEC has been closed). Post-graduate education and training depends on the degree discipline. For example, graduates from specifically approved degrees in biomedical sciences do not need to take any further educational qualification during their 1-year training. Those with a degree (single hons. or modular) in related sciences complete either the IBMS Primary examination (1-year day-release) or an approved post-graduate diploma during their 1-year training (related sciences include anatomy, biochemistry, biology, genetics, microbiology, physiology, pharmacy). Those with a less relevant science degree (e.g. chemistry, physics) take the same exams but train for 2 years. After training, graduates can apply for Associate membership of the Institute.

For senior MLSO posts it is normally necessary to become a Fellow of the Institute through examination, higher degree or thesis.

Late start Degree course requirements in terms of GCSEs and A-levels may be relaxed, but candidates' knowledge of maths and science has to be up to date; many late entrants first take evening classes or other preparatory courses to freshen up their school sciences, etc. Opportunities limited.

Career-break Return only possible if one has kept up with developments, and even then some areas, such as research and development, would probably be difficult to get back to. But it is possible to use a science degree to switch to technical writing (see p. 444) or information work (see p. 227) or teaching (science teachers are in great demand). A few firms now provide opportunities for women who want to keep in touch, by arranging regular visits to labs, home-based projects or part-time work. But such schemes are still very few. Individuals can ask for arrangements to be made. Another way of keeping up with developments is by taking a short Open University course (see p. xxxiii). Most professional institutions offer reduced subscriptions for people on a career-break.

Part time Not many opportunities at the moment, except in technical writing (and then it is spasmodic rather than part time) and in science and mathematics teaching (see p. 517), but job-sharing should be possible in many types of work.

Position of women The number of women scientists remains relatively small and there are few in the top jobs in most disciplines. This is mainly due to the fact that fewer girls than boys have been taking science GCSE and A-levels (except in biology). In 1993, 5% of girls getting A-levels passed physics, compared with 21% of boys. 10% passed chemistry (17% of boys), 14% passed maths (29% of boys), but 17% passed biology (only 13% of boys). Under the National Curriculum girls are not able to drop sciences at GCSE, so A-level entries may increase.

The proportion of women taking science degrees is rising even more slowly. In 1994 16% of university students accepted for physics courses, 35% for chemistry, and 36% for maths were women. A much larger proportion of women started biology and zoology degrees (56% and 54%) which carry less weight on the job market. However, 49% of the biochemists were women. When choosing science-based courses women do not assess their chances in the job market as realistically as do men. For example, women made half of the applications for medicine in 1994, entry for which, like veterinary science, is one of the most competitive. The ratio of applications to acceptances for medicine and dentistry combined was 12.8:1. Similarly, women made 56% of biological science degree applications, where the ratio was 9·6:1. Other university science courses are not as over-subscribed. For example, the ratio was 7:1 for physical sciences (but only 32% of applications were from women), 7:1 for mathematical sciences (19% from women) and 7·6:1 for engineering and technology (10% from women). Industry would welcome more women scientists in research, as well as in technical sales, marketing and production. However, a survey by the Institute of Physics revealed that women physicists tended to hold less well-paid and prestigious jobs in industry than their male colleagues.

A growing number of universities now arrange 'conversion' courses, allowing entrants with good science GCSEs but without the usually required A-levels, to prepare for science degrees.

Further information

Biochemical Society, 59 Portland Place, London W1N 3AJ

Royal Society of Chemistry, Burlington House, Piccadilly, London W1V 0BN

Institute of Biology, 20-22 Queensberry Place, London SW7 2DZ

Institute of Mathematics and its Applications, Maitland House, Warrior Square, Southend-on-Sea, Essex SS1 2JY

Institute of Materials, 1 Carlton House Terrace, London SW1Y 5DB

Institute of Biomedical Science, 12 Coldbath Square, London EC1R 5HL

Institute of Statisticians, 43 St Peter's Square, Preston, Lancs. PR1 7BX

Institute of Physics, 76-78 Portland Place, London W1N 4AA (from early 1996)

Geological Society, Burlington House, Piccadilly, London W1V 9AG

Civil Service Commission, Alencon Link, Basingstoke, Hants.
RG21 1JB

English Nature, Northminster House, Peterborough, PE1 1UA

Nature Conservancy Council for Scotland, 12 Hope Terrace,
Edinburgh EH9 2AS

Countryside Council for Wales, Plas Penrhos, Ffordd Penrhos,
Bangor, Gwynedd LL57 2LQ

Natural Environment Research Council, Polaris House, North
Star Avenue, Swindon, Wilts. SN2 1EU

BTEC and SCOTVEC (see pp. xxi, xxii)

Science Technician

Entry qualifications

Nothing rigid. They vary according to the job's and to colleges' requirements; from a few lower grade GCSEs with at least 1 science
to 2 science A-levels or even a degree. (The Civil Service requires 4
GCSEs (A–C) including a science, maths and English language.)
For BTEC/SCOTVEC awards, see pp. xxi, xxii.

The work

*Laboratory technician, assistant, technical assistant, research assist-
ant, scientific assistant, technical officer, assistant scientific officer*
are all titles used to describe people who perform science-related
procedures and techniques under the overall supervision of scientists. As scientific investigations become more complex technicians
become more important and the variety of jobs is growing. They
are essential team-members, not unskilled bottle-washers: they
need to be able to use new technologies and analytical methods,
rather than rely on practical skills. Their tasks range from mun-
dane routine to work which overlaps very much with that of
professional scientists.

They may work in any of the functions and branches described
under 'Scientist' (see above).

Training – general (see also under different branches)

This can be full or part time.

Full time: normally 2-year full-time or 3-year sandwich courses,
leading to BTEC National Diploma (being replaced by Intermediate GNVQs) (or 2 years full time for SCOTVEC equivalent,
see p. xxii). Entry requirements for these courses are, in
most colleges, 4 GCSEs (A–C), including a relevant science,
maths and an English subject. There may be full-time
'catching up' opportunities for students who want to become
science technicians but lack appropriate GCSEs. (See BTEC,
p. xxi.)

Part time: on the job with day- or block-release for BTEC
National award (see p. xxi) in the biological sciences, physics or
chemistry with specialist options to fit in with their work. Techni-

cians can switch specialization by adding option modules to basic Certificates. There is a great variety of options. Not all specialist subjects are available at all colleges – it depends largely on local job opportunities.

Students without the entry requirements for BTEC National can work for a BTEC First Certificate or City and Guilds Science Laboratory Assistant (or Technician, the latter is slightly more theoretical in content) Certificate by part-time study while in relevant employment. With experience, they may then be able to go on to BTEC National Certificate training.

In Scotland students take appropriate modules for the SCOTVEC National Certificate (see p. xxii).

Higher or *senior technician training*: Students with BTEC National Certificates containing sufficient units (see p. xxi) or BTEC National Diplomas can take a BTEC Higher National Certificate (part time) or BTEC Higher National Diploma (full time or sandwich). Again, there are a great many specializations.

Direct entry requirements to Higher National Certificates and Diplomas vary according to main subjects. For example, for the Applied Biology Higher National awards the following requirements now normally apply: A-level study in biology and chemistry or physics and a pass in one of these. For Chemistry Higher National awards: A-level in chemistry plus 2 sciences studied beyond GCSE (normally maths and physics). For Physics Higher National awards: A-level in physics, GCSEs (A–C) in maths and English subject plus maths studied beyond GCSE. (Maths must of course always be offered at GCSE (A–C) if not included in A-levels.) For SCOTVEC Higher National awards entry is at the discretion of colleges, but normal requirements are 5 SCEs (including 2 at 'H' grade) including maths and 2 relevant sciences or appropriate National Certificate modules.

There are 4 main settings: hospitals, industry, education, Civil Service.

Hospitals

Technicians

There is a wide variety of technician jobs in hospitals. Some are physics-based, others require a good knowledge of biology and chemistry. Some consist almost entirely of laboratory work, others involve occasional or regular patient contact. Most technicians are now called Medical Technical Officers. The main groups are: *medical physics technicians* and *physiological measurement technicians*.

Medical physics technicians: Broadly deal with 'imaging' equipment – X-ray machines; scanners; ultrasound; isotopes and similar matters, and with medical electronics generally. They may administer tests, i.e. have some patient-contact; or they may be wholly or largely concerned with the checking, recalibrating, maintenance, development and modification of equipment from lasers to renal dialysis machines – i.e. no or very little patient-contact. The very expensive and advanced imaging equipment is available only in teaching and large district hospitals, hence few medical physics jobs. In some hospitals radiographers have taken over the radioisotopes part of the technicians' work and the maintenance side may be carried out by staff from the works department (see ENGINEERING, pp. 190, 196).

Physiological measurement technicians: Administer a variety of diagnostic tests (i.e. it is work with constant patient-contact) and it is normal to specialize in one type of work. *Audiology* technicians test the hearing and balance of adults and children, using special instruments, and select, fit and adjust hearing aids; *neurophysiological* technicians are concerned mainly with using EEG (electroencephalography) to record the electrical activity of a patient's brain. *Cardiology* technicians measure heart function and electrical activity, using cardiograms (ECGs) and monitor pacemakers. *Respiratory* technicians administer tests on lung function to help in diagnosis and treatment of lung disease.

Other technicians: There are also some types of work which do not really fit into the above categories. *Perfusionists* work in cardiac departments, using an artificial circulatory system to re-route the blood around a particular organ in order to isolate it (necessary for bypass operations). *Anaesthetic* technicians are involved mainly in laboratory research work. *Operating department practitioners* help prepare patients for operations and help look after supplies and equipment in the operating theatre. *Pathology* technicians assist pathologists in examining bodies to establish cause of death and deal with members of the public who come to the mortuary.

Training   Students may be recruited into a particular department and train from the start in, for example, audiology or ECG; or they may be recruited on to a general training scheme which gives them a chance to look at different specializations before making up their minds. Nationally agreed schemes last for 2 years with day- or block-release. Further education is mainly based on the BTEC/SCOTVEC National Certificate in sciences or electronics with relevant options. Students can then go on to take a BTEC/SCOTVEC Higher National Certificate, specializing in medical physics or physiological measurement. Some technician associations run their own education scheme which may or may not be linked with BTEC/SCOTVEC. Pathology technicians work for a Royal Institute of Public Health and Hygiene certificate. Operating Department Practitioners work for an NVQ (see p. xx); NVQs are due to be introduced for other technicians.

Although in theory trainee technicians require only the entry qualifications for BTEC/SCOTVEC courses (see pp. xxi, xxii), in practice they need 2–3 A-levels or a BTEC/SCOTVEC Higher National award to get a hospital job. Many new entrants, especially in medical physics, have physics degrees. At present, non-graduates who want hospital technician jobs have more scope in biology/chemistry-based medical laboratory work than in the fast-changing and developing physics-based area. There are some jobs for assistant technical officers (ATOs) who help MTOs and can apply to join MTO training schemes after gaining experience.

Industry

Very varied work most of which falls into two broad categories: *quality control*, and *research and development*.

In *quality control* ('QC'), during the production of chemicals, detergents, plastics, cosmetics and other manufactured goods and in the food processing industry, technicians test, for example, the purity and/or nutritional value of foodstuffs. In the pharmaceutical industry they help with tests on drugs and medicines. In electronics, technicians may test computer circuitry or the quality of television and radio components (their work overlaps with that of engineering technicians, see p. 195).

In *research and development* technicians assist scientists with all types of research (see p. 441). They may use new equipment and help modify it and they adapt standard procedures to suit particular experimental work.

Education Establishments

Technicians help researchers, teachers and lecturers. They work in science faculties, in research institutes and medical schools, secondary schools and colleges. They prepare work for lectures; and they help generally in the department. Technicians may prepare specimens for lectures in microbiology, histology, zoology, botany or geology, using for example techniques for culturing bacteria, or prepare thin sections or rocks or fossils for microscopical study, etc. In a chemistry faculty technicians are concerned with the assembly, care and maintenance of apparatus, and the preparation of bench reagents used for demonstration and experiment. They may, in research, use such techniques as flame photometry, spectrophotometry, chromatography, or use radioisotopes.

The job of the school or college lab technician used to be rather menial, but conditions and prospects have now improved considerably. The work combines science with dealing with children and young people; it covers preparing, setting out and maintaining demonstration materials and apparatus as well as helping students and pupils in the classroom. In smaller establishments there may only be one technician; in one day the technician could then help in and prepare for classes in physics, chemistry and biology. In large establishments several technicians work under the direction of a chief technician, and there are opportunities for progress, with training, to a more senior post, and to specialize in either biology, chemistry or physics.

Science Group of the Civil Service
(see CIVIL SERVICE, p. 123)

Technicians are called Assistant Scientific Officers. They are part of a team led by a scientist engaged in research in any of the scientific disciplines.

In laboratories scientists carry out fundamental research, investigate new techniques and equipment, ensure that standards of safety are maintained. Technicians provide support to research and project teams. Their work includes making observations of experiments, logging data, summarizing results for interpretation. For example, they may measure jet-pipe temperatures of a helicopter engine; determine the nitrogen content of animal fodder; test for drugs for police investigations; make weather observations at an airport.

Openings vary according to changing situations, geographic area, area of specialization, level of qualification. Best prospects probably for well-qualified physics-based technicians, e.g. in the information technology 'hardware' industries as well as elsewhere. For biology/chemistry-based technicians, fair prospects in pharmaceuticals, agricultural chemicals and similar industries and hospital medical research. People with low school-leaving qualifications but interested in the job should try and improve their qualifications if they cannot get student-technician jobs. On the whole there is a growing range of jobs which are loosely called 'science technician'.

Personal attributes generally Manipulative skill; patience; scrupulous attention to detail; a sense of responsibility; willingness to take orders; ability to work both independently and as one of a team.

Late start Not much scope in most branches, school-leavers tend to be given preference. But adults can take full-time BTEC/SCOTVEC science courses, and there are a reasonable number of late entrants to hospital technician work (see p. 457).

Career-break As this is a rapidly changing area, only technicians who systematically keep up with developments can return, but there are updating opportunities, partly through the Open University (see p. xxxiii). The Department of Health is encouraging health authorities to offer retainer schemes to all their staff. The Institute of Medical Laboratory Sciences has special membership for non-working members.

Part time and job-sharing Fair opportunities at all levels.

Position of women There are about equal numbers of males and females, but far more men are senior technicians mainly because fewer women have physics at A-level. As a result more women go into dead-end low-level technician jobs where they do not get – and often do not ask for – day-release for further qualifications. Women with physics GCSE and A-levels do as well as men.

Further information City and Guilds of London Institute, 1 Giltspur Street, London EC1A 9DD
BTEC, Central House, Upper Woburn Place, London WC1H 0HH
SCOTVEC, Hanover House, 24 Douglas Street, Glasgow G2 7NQ
Regional Health Authorities for information on Medical Technical Officers
The Institute of Science Technology, Mansell House, 22 Bore Street, Lichfield, Staffs. WS13 6LP (This runs mainly work-based courses, including one for its own Higher Diploma.)

Related careers ENGINEERING: *Engineering Technician* – MEDICINE – OPTICAL WORK – PHARMACY – PHYSIOTHERAPY – RADIOGRAPHY

Food Science and Technology

All educational levels, see 'Training'.

The work   *Food science* is concerned with the chemical and biological nature of food and its behaviour under natural conditions, during processing and during storage. *Food technology* is the application of relevant sciences, including engineering, to the processing, preservation and development of raw materials and manufactured foods. Food scientists and technologists work in quality control, product development and production departments (see p. 443) of food manufacturers and retailers. They also work for equipment manufacturers, ingredient suppliers, public analysts, environmental health departments and the Civil Service. Some work in research and development on 'fast foods' and 'systems catering' (see CATERING, p. 96), monitoring the behaviour of foods as new technologies are introduced. Some work together with *biotechnologists* (see p. 447). Some research jobs are for food *scientists*; production jobs tend to be held by *technologists*; but there is no clear-cut division between the two and both types of specialists are found in most job areas. There are jobs for technicians and for graduate scientists and technologists.

The industry is less affected than many by economic slumps. Its diversity provides opportunities to specialize. The broad-based training allows for flexibility. As in other industries, technologists now often move into top general management (see 'Line management', p. 278).

Training   *Technician level*: with 4 GCSEs (A–C) including a science, maths and a subject testing use of English, BTEC award in Food Science/Food Technology with various options. Courses can be part-time day-release (2 years), full time (2 years); or sandwich (3 years).

With 1 science A-level passed and another studied to A-level (more often 2 passed, in practice), one of which should be chemistry and the other either physics, maths or biology, and GCSE (A–C) in maths, or BTEC National, BTEC Higher award in Food Technology (part time, full time or sandwich). For equivalent SCOTVEC awards, see p. xxii.

Graduate level: with 2, or sometimes 3, science A-levels which must include chemistry (precise requirements vary), degrees in various aspects of food science. Degrees vary in title, emphasis and content, so candidates need to study different syllabuses carefully. Some are more commercially orientated (combining food science and marketing for example); some are more science-based; others put more emphasis on relevant technologies; yet others on management.

While food science and technology degrees are strictly vocationally orientated, *science* and *engineering* graduates (see pp. 438 and 181) can also get into the food industries and then take post-graduate qualifications, either by part-time or full-time study. There are post-graduate courses in food science; food analysis and composition; food and management science; food micro-biology; food engineering; biotechnology.

Personal attributes A meticulous approach to technical problems plus an interest in people as consumers and changing tastes and eating habits. For many jobs a real interest in food is desirable, as is the ability to work as part of a team. For *management careers*, ability to organize people and work, to work under pressure and to take decisions.

Late start The proportion of late entrants – 10–20% – is fairly high. Recent study of chemistry is an advantage.

Career-break Provided people stay in touch through professional institutes there should be no problem.

Part time Few opportunities at present, but job-sharing of certain posts should be possible.

Position of women There are more women than men entering this field. They have little difficulty entering all areas.

Further information Institute of Food Science and Technology, 5 Cambridge Court, 210 Shepherds Bush Road, London W6 7NL

Related careers ENGINEERING: *Engineering Technician* – OPTICAL WORK – PHARMACY – RADIOGRAPHY

Secretarial and Clerical Work

Entry qualifications

Various educational levels: minimum usually 4 GCSEs (A–C), including English language; but see 'Training', below.

The work

Office work consists largely of handling information – searching for, producing, passing on (verbally or in print) facts and figures, questions and answers, messages and instructions. 'Information technology' (IT) which broadly describes the equipment and systems used to process, transmit, file or otherwise handle information electronically, has changed the nature of office work. But fear of the unknown has tended to exaggerate IT's effect. The 'paperless office' is not about to take over overnight. The workforce is shrinking – especially at the lower, unskilled end where automation is drastically reducing the scope. But secretaries and people who produce and handle text will still be needed even when all managers have their own desk-top computers on which they can call up information and which they can use to communicate with each other, customers, clients, etc. IT also creates some new jobs.

The main jobs:

Secretary

Titles have no precise meaning: executive secretary, private secretary, personal assistant are used indiscriminately. Some of the most high-powered secretaries prefer to call themselves merely 'secretary'; some 'personal assistants' just do junior executives' typing and telephoning.

The confusion over titles arose because traditionally there was no promotion ladder and career-structure, and no precise definition of the secretary's work nor of the differences between *personal assistant*, *secretary*, *shorthand- or audio-typist*, or *word processor operator* and *clerk*. Differences between these jobs are considerable, but in employers' and employees' minds they are blurred, which leads to disappointment and frustration on both sides of the desk. However, with the wider choice of career opportunities for women, fewer able women are now willing to stay in jobs without prospects of advancement (and there are still *very* few male secretaries). Mainly for that reason some organizations are now introducing something resembling career-structures (see below). For example, the difference between 'personal assistant' and 'secretary' is now often being taken seriously. Secretaries follow their boss's instructions; when they fully understand the department's work, they become a 'personal assistant' and in that capacity make their own decisions. For example, a sales manager's secretary would, if a sales representative falls ill, ask the boss to whom the sick person's work should be allocated. A personal assistant would simply reallocate the work, without asking the boss.

Another development which is changing the secretarial scene is 'team secretaries' (in another office, they might be called 'administrative assistants'). They 'manage' a group of, say, several junior architects in an architectural partnership, or overseas marketing people in an export department. They organize appointments, travel schedules, etc. and keep track of the department's various projects and assignments. If the head of the department or partnership wants to know where X is, or how project Y is progressing, the team secretary knows the situation.

Both personal assistant and team secretary are in fact junior/middle management jobs but they are not necessarily recognized as such (see MANAGEMENT, p. 275 and 'Position of women', p. 475).

The traditional secretary usually still works for one person or, increasingly, more than one. (This is of course the 'office' secretary, not the administrator in charge of an institution, learned society or similar organization (see CHARTERED SECRETARY, p. 110). It is the secretary's task to husband the boss's time and energy so that he or she can concentrate on whatever the job is at that moment.

Secretaries act as buffer between the boss and callers and phone calls, and take minor decisions on her/his behalf. They must understand their boss's work well enough to know when to act on their own initiative and when to ask for instructions. This is one of the most challenging secretarial skills. Secretarial duties may also involve:

1. Acting as link between individuals and various sections in an organization; this could be departments in a university, company or store, or individuals in a management-team, and may involve writing memos, ringing people up, going to see them.

2. Collecting information from a variety of printed and personal sources – this involves knowing where to go for whatever

the information required, perhaps telephoning trade associations or government departments.

3. Preparing agendas for meetings and collecting documents supporting the various items, distributing the papers at the right time to the right people; taking minutes at meetings, editing them and writing them up.

4. Looking through the day's mail and deciding which letters the boss has to deal with personally and which ones to cope with independently; summarizing lengthy letters and documents; drafting replies to some letters and presenting them to the boss for approval and signature.

5. Making travel arrangements and arranging meetings, at home or abroad, for several busy people: this is a time-consuming task which requires meticulous attention to detail and may involve international trunk calls and lengthy correspondence until finally a time and place suitable to everyone has been agreed upon.

The amount of typing or word processing secretaries do varies. In large offices they may deal only with their boss's confidential correspondence, other matters being dealt with by a 'junior secretary' or someone from the typing-pool or word processing unit. Secretaries may be in charge of one or several juniors, or cope single-handedly.

The extent of automation still varies from one office to another, but it is increasing everywhere. The new technologies mean that secretaries and bosses both have access to numerous types of computerized equipment. As well as enabling bosses to do *their* job more effectively, secretaries are able to perform many administrative tasks more effectively than hitherto. They are also able to relieve their bosses of administrative tasks, and possibly take over part of the boss's main task. The availability of data processing equipment – and opportunities to use it – should, in theory, enable capable secretaries to take part in executives' decision-making tasks, e.g. financial forecasting and analysis and production progress charting; or assessing customer response. The *potential* for merging the two roles – that of the manager/executive and the secretary – now exists. How much, in practice, the secretary will be able to exploit the potential depends on the boss's willingness to let go of responsibilities, the secretary's initiative, and a host of imponderables.

Traditional secretarial tasks which are, increasingly, computerized, include arranging meetings; booking conference rooms; recording and instant dispatch of voice and text messages; maintenance of lists, e.g. personal addresses, business contacts (with background information), internal telephone directories; 'unstructured information', e.g. product descriptions; training records; filing and retrieval; travel arrangements.

Invariably, being a secretary is a self-effacing job. Good secretaries rarely get the kudos they deserve when, thanks to their efficiency, crises are avoided, but they are likely to be blamed if things go wrong – if they forget to remind their boss of an appointment which she/he too had forgotten and which is written down in the appointments diary.

There are good opportunities for 'real' secretaries. They can pick and choose the environment they want to work in, whether the City, a public institution or a professional office – say, accountants' or solicitors'. There are some possibilities in fashion, in travel, employment and estate agents – in areas where specialist training is not expected – for going up the management ladder. *Very* few secretaries in television manage to jump the abyss between secretarial and creative work.

Secretarial work used to be the best way into management generally, but there are much better ways now (see MANAGEMENT, p. 275). The vast majority of secretaries remain secretaries throughout their working lives. Promotion usually still means becoming secretary to someone higher up in the hierarchy – e.g. from secretary to sales manager to secretary to finance director to secretary to managing director to secretary to chairman. In this promotion system, expertise gained in one job tends to be fairly useless in the next, therefore the opportunities for independent work, for becoming PA (or acting as PA at least) or executive, tend to be less in the new job than they were in the previous one. Many secretaries find that the higher up in the hierarchy their boss, the less the boss is likely to delegate. So secretaries who want a career and not a job need to find out far more details about what an advertised job involves than do people who go into structured careers with accepted work-content, qualifications, promotion prospects, etc.

Secretaries who have word processing experience can become *supervisors/co-ordinators/trainers*. They are the buffer between the users ('text originators') and the operators; they schedule work as it comes in and they appease users whose text cannot be dealt with instantly. They may also diagnose and possibly deal with minor equipment faults and deal with the equipment suppliers if things go seriously wrong. This job can lead to, or be combined with, 'in-house training' – work which involves training new word-processor operators and persuading managers to learn what the equipment can and cannot do; writing manuals; advising office managers by evaluating the many different types of machines when new ones are to be bought. This type of job is still evolving. It always involves contact with a large variety of people; its exact content varies accórding to size, type and ideas of the employing organization.

Secretaries who want to get out of the office atmosphere and yet use their work experience can become *customer support representatives* with manufacturers. They demonstrate equipment to prospective clients and later provide a 'hand-holding' and trouble-shooting service for companies which have bought their equipment. This work, in turn, can lead to selling and marketing (see p. 297) for word processing equipment manufacturers. (See also WORKING FOR ONESELF, p. 551.)

Specialist Secretary

Though there is no need to decide on any specialization before training, there are 3 specializations for which special training is useful but not essential.

1. *Medical secretaries*: They work in hospital, for one or several consultants; in consultants' private consulting rooms; or for general practitioners. They require knowledge of medical terminology and of health and social services organization. In hospital, secretaries have less contact with patients than in consulting rooms and general practice, but they have more companionship. In GPs' group practices the work involves organizing/administration.

2. *Farm or agricultural secretaries*: They deal with the paperwork which modern farming entails. They fill in forms, keep accounts, keep and analyse records, and deal with correspondence, often on their own initiative. Only very big farms employ fulltimers; most need part-time help. So farm secretaries either work as freelances, spending a number of days a month on different farms, or they are employed by farm-secretarial agencies and are sent out to different farms. The work is varied, as it involves working on different types of farm; and it requires experience and self-confidence because farmers, unlike other employers, usually know less about the work to be done (accounts, filling in VAT and other forms) than their secretaries. Specialist training is a great advantage.

Both medical and farm secretaries now often use computers; doctors' secretaries to keep patients' records; farm secretaries to record, for example, cows' milk yield in relation to expenditure on various foodstuffs.

3. *Bi- or multilingual secretaries*: They translate incoming mail; they may compose their own letters in a foreign language from notes dictated in English, but most outgoing mail is written in English. They sometimes read foreign journals and search for and

translate or summarize relevant articles. Occasionally they may act as interpreter. Their scope varies: some secretaries hardly use their languages at all; others are relied upon totally by their mono-lingual bosses. Foreign Office secretaries must be proficient in 1 language but many never use that knowledge even when working in embassies abroad. There are commercial opportunities abroad for truly bilingual secretaries with, occasionally, the relevant shorthand. International organizations usually require previous senior secretarial experience. Overall, the greatest demand is for French/English, German/English and French/German/English, mainly in international marketing and in export. There is a small, steady demand for Spanish, for other European languages, and for Russian and a growing demand for Japanese and Arabic.

At home, foreign shorthand is rarely required; in order to master it, it is essential to be *absolutely fluent* in the language(s) concerned. For most linguist-secretary jobs a grasp of the relevant country's economic and social set-up is far more important than shorthand and 100% speaking and writing fluency.

They get jobs easily, but not necessarily with much scope for using their language proficiency. Graduates are often overqualified. GCSE or A-level language plus knowing how to use a dictionary is often all that is needed, even when the job was advertised as for a linguist. There are more secretaries who want to work abroad than there are jobs available. However, good linguists with about 3 years' secretarial experience can get jobs in EU countries and elsewhere, mainly in British or multinational companies' offices.

Shorthand- and Audio-Typist/ Word-Processor Operator

Many so-called secretaries are really typists or word-processor operators. They work for a number of people, often in a central word-processing unit or 'station', and not for individuals as secretaries do. Their job is far more impersonal, concerned with producing texts efficiently and economically rather than dealing with people and all the various jobs the secretaries cope with. It is work for people who like getting on with the job without having to talk much to their bosses; but it can be a step to secretarial work too.

The demand for *shorthand*-writers is still great though diminishing. There are still many executives who insist on dictating to an individual rather than into a machine.

Copy-typists have virtually disappeared. Offices now either use photocopying or similar machines or word processors (WPs).

Clerk

This may involve some typing and/or word processing and/or using computers (see COMPUTING, p. 138). Clerks' work varies even more than secretarial work. Some clerks work on their own all day; others are in constant contact with colleagues and/or the public. Clerks in travel agencies may send out brochures to customers or hand them out over the counter; in a mail order firm, however computerized the system, they may check incoming orders to see whether the right postal orders are enclosed; in a hospital or commercial office a junior may do nothing but photocopy. Clerks may work in post-rooms, collecting and distributing mail from and to various departments and individuals. In personnel departments, they may work on computerized staff records, entering details about absence, wage increases, etc. In large organizations, whether town hall, store or manufacturing company, there is often a computerized filing system. In a small office a clerk may still do 'old-fashioned' filing, answer the telephone, make the tea and do some typing/word processing. The extent to which clerks' work has been affected by the introduction of computerized equipment varies enormously but job opportunities have lessened. At the moment, many offices still rely largely on the old-fashioned methods of entering and updating facts and figures, transmitting messages, collecting and distributing information. But this is changing. For example in insurance offices, when updating clients' policies, clerks first had to look for the file, then re-type part of the policy and file it again. With computerized equipment however, the clerk keys in the reference code, the policy is 'called up' (appears on) the video display unit, the clerk keys in the necessary amendments and, at the press of a few buttons, the policy is amended as required, printed, and stored in the equipment's memory – the electronic file. Any telephone inquiry dealt with by clerks, whether from a supplier in a manufacturing industry or an airline customer, is dealt with now by keying in the question and getting the answer instantly on the VDU.

Clerks may also become telephonists or receptionists. The receptionist's job may be rather more complex than it appears – receptionists are expected to have a good knowledge of who does what in the organization so that they can direct callers to the right person or department. Hotel receptionists (see CATERING, p. 98) may do behind-the-scenes accounts work as well as dealing face-to-face with clients and staff.

Training   No set pattern. Secretaries should still learn shorthand, at least at

90–100 words per minute (and transcribe it adequately), and audio-type at 50 words per minute. They must be able to spell. They must know how to use, and where to find, sources of reference. They need a good grasp of who does what in the commercial world, in the community, in government. They must be able to draft and summarize letters, reports, etc. – both verbally and in writing.

Where, and how, they acquire the 'secretarial core skills' is totally immaterial. Certificates and Diplomas awarded by colleges, the Royal Society of Arts, the London Chamber of Commerce and Industry, Pitman's, for example, and specialist ones by the Association of Medical Secretaries, are useful when there are more applicants than vacancies. Qualifications secure a first interview, but they count for far less than impression made at interview.

A sixth-form education, A-levels in such subjects as geography, English, economics, and intensive courses in shorthand, typing and then word processing, are far more useful than leaving school at 16 and taking a 2-year secretarial course. GCSE (A–C) English language is essential: a degree is rarely an advantage. Even when an employer specifies 'graduate secretary', an intelligent, well-informed sixth-form leaver is usually acceptable. There are so many graduate secretaries simply because some arts graduates cannot think of anything else to do – not because many secretarial jobs are so intellectually demanding that only graduates could fill them. Graduate secretaries do not even have significantly greater chances of getting into management than sixth-form leavers.

There is a tremendous variety of secretarial courses, but there is no pecking order, no 'best buy'. Much education and training for secretarial/general office work and word processing is sadly disorganized and out of date, with several overlapping qualifications. Certain qualifications, such as the Royal Society of Arts', are well known and carry considerable weight, but individual colleges, teaching methods and equipment vary enormously. At this stage in the 'office revolution', when new office equipment and routines are being widely introduced, a course for a good qualification at a college with antiquated equipment, and teachers who know little of present-day office practice, may be less useful than a course in a college which arranges visits to modern offices, and which has teachers who understand 1990s office technology, even if the college only awards its own diploma.

One cannot even judge the usefulness of secretarial courses by their entry requirements. There are some courses which only accept entrants with at least 2 A-levels (some even insist on a degree) which may lead fairly quickly to senior secretarial jobs.

But it is quite likely that students who take these courses would have got equally far, equally quickly, if they had merely taken a short sharp typing/word processing-only course. NVQs/SVQs levels 1–3 in Administration have been in place since 1989, but in 1995 the Administration Lead Body revised these to make them applicable to a wider range of people across different levels and with a clearer progression from one level to another. Some are designed for secretarial, some for clerical staff, including receptionists, and others for administrative staff. Also in 1995 a level 4 was introduced. These NVQs/SVQs are awarded by a number of different bodies, including BTEC, City and Guilds/Pitman's Examinations Institute, LCCI and RSA.

Courses fall into broad categories, each with many variations; and often with various optional subjects:

1. Courses for students with 2 A-levels or with degrees or comparable qualifications, lasting between 3 and 9 months; a 3-months' crash course, learning the core skills, should be sufficient.

2. 6-month to 2-year courses for students with 4 or 5 GCSEs (A–C). Unless 2-year courses include something like medical, legal, farm or linguist secretarial work, or A-level study, 2 years is unnecessarily long.

3. 1- or 2-year courses for students with 3 to 5 GCSEs (A–C). They often include GCSE (or A-level) study. Courses are likely to lead to clerical rather than secretarial jobs in the first instance.

4. Courses for students with 'a good general education' (no specific passes). These are not strictly speaking *secretarial* courses (whatever their title). They should last 2 years and include general educational subjects if they are eventually to lead to secretarial work.

5. 1-year courses in English, shorthand, typing, word processing, office routine, lead to *clerks'* and *typists'* or *word processors'* jobs (also applies to commercial courses at school).

6. BTEC (see p. xxi) courses, part time or full time. BTEC National Certificate (normally part-time) in Business and Finance and the BTEC National Diploma will eventually be replaced by GNVQs.

However, adequate word processing is not available at all colleges. Many lack up-to-date equipment or have too little of it. Applicants with good typing skills can still get jobs: they may then be given in-house word processing training. However, as employers are often in a buyers' market now, applicants who are familiar with word processors are at a distinct advantage in the job market. For that reason, private word processing schools have proliferated over the last few years. Their courses vary enormously in quality; some use out-of-date equipment and/or

Secretarial and Clerical Work

provide insufficient 'hands on' WP experience and/or are unnecessarily long. Most good courses normally last only about 1 week full time (or longer part time/evenings only) *and they only accept students who can type*. So before signing on for a private school WP course, it is essential to make sure that it is a good one. On the whole, courses attached to well-known secretarial agencies are a wise choice. Most of them have been started to ensure the agency has a pool of well-qualified people on its books rather than to make a profit; they are run 'at cost'. Courses normally teach on the two or three types of machines in widest use. Word processor operators who then get jobs where they have to use a different type of machine, get short 'conversion training' on the job. In any case on-the-job training goes on for some time: it takes quite a few months for a word processor operator to be really proficient at the job.

Specialist training

Bi- or multilingual secretary: Entry requirements from 'good GCSE pass' or 'A-level standard' in the relevant language to language degree. Most courses last 2 years. Prospective secretary-linguists who intend to take a language degree should look out for degree courses including 'area studies' – which means the course covers the relevant country's history and social and economic institutions, etc. That type of knowledge is also very important for getting jobs abroad with commercial firms and international agencies.

Medical secretary: With 4 GCSEs (A–C) including English language, 2-year full-time course; with 1 A-level, 1-year full-time course for *Diploma for Medical Secretaries*. With two GCSEs (A–C) one of which must be English language: 1-year full-time (or longer part-time) course for *Diploma in Health Service Reception*. Distance learning courses are available.

Part-time courses leading to the *Diploma in Practice Administration* (approved by the British Medical Association and the Royal College of General Practitioners) are available for persons holding the Certificate in Medical Reception plus at least 1 year's experience; for those holding the Diploma; and for experienced secretaries who have not taken the Certificate or Diploma examination but have several years' experience of the work and hold a 'Letter of Recognition' (from the Association of Medical Secretaries).

Details from Association of Medical Secretaries, Tavistock House North, Tavistock Square, London WC1H 9LN.

Farm secretary: National Certificate or BTEC National Diploma courses for farm secretaries are run at some agricultural colleges.

Personal attributes   *Secretaries* who hope (probably in vain) to become executives: exceptional organizing ability, self-confidence, determination and ambition, a logical brain, business acumen, willingness to take responsibility and willingness to take orders; ability to communicate easily with people at all levels of education and status in the organization; willingness to work long hours.

Personal assistants: The above qualities without the ambition and business acumen; willingness to take responsibility must be coupled with willingness to remain in a supportive role; a sympathetic manner, a desire to be of use to others; ability to ignore getting undeserved blame when things go wrong and not getting well-deserved praise; indifference to seeing less able 'executives' have higher status and pay, and more responsibility.

Typists/word processor operators: Wanting to get on with one's work without involvement with people and in the organization's business; accuracy.

Clerks: depends on type of job – some require a liking for quiet backroom work dealing with paperwork; others a liking for dealing with people; most require attention to detail and willingness to do as told.

Late start   Secretarial work is easy to start late. While there are some employers who will not consider anyone over 35, there is a growing number of employers who prefer the over 35s. Some courses geared to mature students are available under Training for Work (see p. xxv) (including specialist secretary's courses).

Career-break   Should be no problem for secretaries with word processor operating experience. Numerous courses are available for those wishing to update their skills.

Part time   Good opportunities for word processor operators. Not quite as good for secretaries, who are expected to be available whenever the boss wants them. However, even here part-time work and job-sharing is gradually becoming accepted, but part-timers are never likely to have as wide a choice of jobs as full-timers. The fewer the hours they are willing to work, the more restricted the choice of job.

Part time can be anything from 6 hours a week, to 4 full days; 2 or 3 full, or 3 or 4 half days are the most usual. A flexible number of hours, to suit both secretary and employers and varying week by week, is sometimes possible. There are a few jobs which can be done in term-time only, leaving mothers free during the children's

475   Secretarial and Clerical Work

holidays; and occasionally some 1 week (or fortnight) on, 1 week (or fortnight) off jobs.

'*Temping*' is a kind of part-time work. It is particularly suitable for actors, artists, models, etc., people who have to 'fill in' while waiting for their own kind of work; for mothers who cannot get a term-time-only job, and for secretaries, WP operators and typists who prefer a frequent change of environment to getting involved with one set of people and one type of work. Temps normally work for agencies who send them to employers on a weekly or daily basis; only those with very good contacts and experience can work as freelances.

Position of women

This is still almost entirely women's work, but younger men are increasingly taking up secretarial, clerical and office administration jobs – 1 in 6 according to a recent survey. Some word-processing unit supervisors and customer support representatives are male graduates who come into the organization with computing experience or as management trainees.

Further information

No central organization. Local education authority for lists of local courses (and see 'Medical secretaries', p. 473).

Related careers

CIVIL SERVICE – CATERING: *Hotel Reception* – COMPUTING/IT – HEALTH SERVICES MANAGEMENT – LANGUAGES – MANAGEMENT – PERSONNEL/HUMAN RESOURCES MANAGEMENT – PUBLIC RELATIONS – WORKING FOR ONESELF

Social Work

Entry qualifications
For entrants under 21, 2 A-levels and 3 GCSEs (A–C) in different subjects *or* 5 passes in the SCE, including 3 at Higher level, *or* approved alternative. For entrants over 21, evidence of ability to cope with course. For post-graduate courses, a degree.

The work
Social workers help people to overcome or adjust to a wide variety of social or personal problems. They work in a variety of settings: in local authority social services departments, dealing with the problems of families and children, the elderly, those with physical and mental disabilities and the homeless; in hospitals and other health settings, dealing with those who are ill and their families; in probation and after-care, dealing with offenders, prisoners, ex-prisoners and their families; in education departments, with children who are having problems which affect their education; in voluntary agencies which supplement the work of statutory services, sometimes with particular groups, e.g. the elderly or disadvantaged children.

The training of social workers is 'generic', i.e. it equips them to deal with all kinds of social problems, in various settings, with all age and client groups. Nevertheless there is scope to specialize in work with particular client groups, e.g. children or the elderly.

Fieldwork

Field social workers work with people who live in their own homes, as opposed to in residential care. Most local authorities' social services departments (social work departments in Scotland) organize their field workers into area teams, providing a full range of services across the spectrum of client groups in a given geographical area. Within the area team there may be specialist workers or teams dealing with particular groups. Organization and balance between 'generic' workers and specialists vary. Some generic workers become virtual specialists simply by the balance of their case allocation. The nature of the area also affects social workers' caseloads; problems occur in some areas (e.g. a large refugee population) which are non-existent in others.

The work is a mixture of counselling, liaison, mediating, monitoring and practical problem-solving. Some people who turn to social services for help have immediate problems which can be sorted out fairly quickly. For example, a family with a young baby might need a social worker to negotiate on their behalf with British Gas so that their supplies are not cut off. Other problems require a longer-term relationship in which the social worker provides both practical assistance and counselling, helping individuals or families to identify both their problems, which are often complex and interrelated, and ways in which they might cope with them. The problems are very varied, from the stresses and problems of intractable poverty or long-term ill-health to the strains of caring for elderly relatives or handicapped children.

Social work is very much more complex than simply offering a sympathetic ear and practical help. There is a great deal of legislation which gives social workers both responsibility and powers to act in cases where people are at risk. The most obvious example is child protection, which is a top priority at present and which can take up a large proportion of a social worker's time. Social workers must assess and monitor families at risk of neglecting or abusing their children, visiting regularly and giving support, keeping an eye on how they handle their children, perhaps referring them to a family centre to learn childcare skills and discuss their problems. Sometimes, of course, social workers decide that it is not in the children's best interests to remain with their families and must take the necessary action and provide the proper supervision. The mentally ill are another group over whom social workers have powers of removal if they become a nuisance or a danger to others or to themselves.

Social workers do not just sort out problems: they try to prevent their getting worse or leading to other problems. For example, the isolation and poverty of young mothers can lead to child abuse. Social workers' preventive work can take the form of individual counselling and support, work with whole families or group work, where people with similar problems are brought together for mutual support.

The day-to-day work of a field social worker is very varied. Much time is spent visiting clients, listening to their problems, offering support and encouragement and monitoring those at risk. Most team members will have a day as duty officer, seeing clients who come into the office (e.g. seeking advice on benefits or without money to pay overdue bills) and taking calls (e.g. from a neighbour or teacher concerned about a child with unusual bruising). Time is also spent on paperwork, keeping detailed case notes, and writing reports, e.g. on a juvenile offender or for an adoption hearing. Liaison with other professionals or organizations is very important and time-consuming. For example, a social worker might have to arrange for an elderly client to have a home help, find residential accommodation for someone unable to cope alone, or track down additional complementary support from a voluntary agency.

Some field social workers within area teams specialize in, for example, adoption or child abuse cases. Others do more specialized work in a variety of other settings. *Social workers in hospitals* help with the problems that can arise through illness. For example, children might need to be looked after while their mother is in hospital; a family might need advice on financial assistance when the main breadwinner is unable to work; a pregnant teenager might need support and advice before, during and after the birth of her baby. Some social workers are attached to special units, such as clinics for the treatment of those dependent on drugs or alcohol, and some work in general practices or health centres alongside the family doctor, nurse, health visitor, community midwife and district nurse.

Social workers also work in day centres, adult training centres, social education centres, child guidance clinics and intermediate treatment, which involves working in the community with young people at risk. *Community social workers* (there is debate about to what extent they are a part of mainstream social work) work in the community to help people identify their common problems and work together to solve them, e.g. by setting up a mother and toddler group or establishing a community social centre. (With cutbacks in public expenditure this type of work has virtually disappeared in some areas.)

Education Welfare Work

Education welfare officers or *education social workers* deal with the problems which prevent children benefiting fully from their education. The problems can be very wide-ranging, from inadequate transport in a country area to complex family problems leading to truancy or behaviour problems, to material or emotional deprivation. The social workers work with schools to identify the problems, establish links with the home and devise ways of overcoming the problems. Most education welfare officers are employed by local education authorities, but some are with the social services department.

Probation Service

In England and Wales the probation service is organized into 56 areas responsible to the Home Office; in Scotland probation is part of local authority social work departments.

Like other social workers, probation officers have a dual role of care and control. It is their job to supervise offenders in the community and to 'advise, assist and befriend' them. The involvement begins before sentencing when the probation officer may be asked to prepare a social inquiry report to be taken into account when deciding on a suitable penalty. The probation officer develops a picture of the offender through interviews with him or her, the family, employers and so on, and tries to establish any circumstances relevant to the offence and whether it might happen again. A recommendation is then made to the court about suitable penalties.

Offenders may be released into the community on probation orders, community service orders or suspended sentence orders. The probation officer supervises them, making sure they understand the nature of the order and comply with any conditions.

Probation officers try to help offenders develop self-knowledge and self-discipline and regain self-respect. They might help with accommodation, work, developing skills, getting treatment for a psychiatric problem or social adjustment. Some offenders welcome the sympathy, interest and assistance offered by probation officers, but others are hostile to any figure of authority. Probation officers have to find the right way of gaining cooperation, but can always ultimately refer back to the courts.

Residential Care

Some people have problems that cannot adequately be dealt with in their homes with their families, even with the other help available. These people may need residential care on a long-term or temporary basis. Residential homes vary in size, purpose and client group. They may be run by local authorities or by voluntary agencies. They may cater for the elderly, the physically or mentally handicapped, ex-prisoners, single mothers or children.

The work varies greatly according to the type of home and client group. It can range from complex assessment and care in conjunction with other professionals to arranging birthday and other celebrations, to helping with basic day-to-day tasks such as dressing, feeding, shopping and so on. Counselling is also part of the job and may arise from many everyday occurrences. The aim is to help the residents to as much stability and independence as possible, whether they return to their own homes or remain in care. Good residential care depends on developing good relationships with residents and effective team-work with colleagues.

Residential care workers do not necessarily need to live in, but may be required to do so on a shift basis. Even those who live on site are not required to be on call all the time. A high proportion of workers in residential care are not qualified social workers. There are NVQs (see p. xx) available for care assistants.

Training   The professional qualification for social workers is the Diploma in Social Work. Programmes leading to the qualification last at least 2 years (many are longer) and are planned and run by educational institutions and social work agencies working together as programme providers. The Dip.S.W. is a generic qualification but students have the opportunity for an extended placement and associated study in one particular practice setting. Students may begin courses at 18, but the Dip.S.W. is not awarded until the candidate is 22 (most entrants are older). (Probation training is under review and in future may not be covered by the Dip.S.W.)

Programme content includes: knowledge and understanding of human growth and behaviour and of a range of human needs; the process of observation and assessment; transcultural factors; aims, methods and theories; social work settings; administrative and legal systems which provide the framework for social work practice. Students also learn about the rights of clients and examine the ethical issues which confront social workers, as well as developing skills in, for example, making decisions, using resources and compiling social histories.

Programme structures vary to meet the needs of those entering at different points. Most programmes lead to an academic award (e.g. Dip.H.E., degree, post-graduate degree or diploma) as well as the Dip.S.W. Some students are employment-based; others are college-based. Employment-based students are already employed in the personal social services, are admitted to a programme with the agreement of their employers, keep their jobs and continue to be paid a salary. College-based students are often required to have had relevant paid or voluntary experience.

The main patterns of training are:

1. Non-graduate route: 2-year full-time courses leading to Dip.S.W.; many courses also award Dip.H.E.; some 3- or 4-year part-time courses available.

2. Degree route: 3- and 4-year full-time courses leading to Dip.S.W. and degree in relevant subject.

3. Post-graduate route: 2-year full-time courses leading to Dip.S.W. and a relevant post-graduate degree or diploma.

NOTE: NVQs are widely available in this field, but CCETSW were unable to provide details by the time of going to press.

Personal attributes The desire to help people irrespective of one's own personal likes and dislikes; the ability to communicate with every level of intelligence, cultural or social background or emotional state; perseverance in the face of apparent failure when clients/groups show no sign of improvement or appreciation of efforts made for or on behalf of them; stability; a ready understanding of other people's way of life and point of view; sympathy and tolerance of human failings; belief in individual's potential to do better; good verbal and written skills to record and report; the ability to take an interest in other people's problems without becoming emotionally involved; a sense of humour; wide interests unconnected with social work (to keep a sense of proportion); patience and empathy.

Late start Maturity is essential. In 1993, 44.2% of Dip.S.W. students were between 25 and 35; 28.8% were between 35 and 44. Some programmes are specially designed for those with family commitments.

Career-break Returners are welcomed back. Some authorities may have formal schemes.

Part time Part time and job-sharing available.

Position of women About three-quarters of social workers are women. A much smaller proportion of senior jobs is filled by women, but their position is improving. 21 Directors of Social Services are now women (out of 132).

Further information CCETSW Information Services: Derbyshire House, St Chad's Street, London WC1H 8AD; 78–80 George Street, Edinburgh EH2 3BU; 6 Malone Road, Belfast BT9 5BN; St David's House, Wood Street, Cardiff CF1 1ES

Related careers CAREERS WORK – NURSERY NURSE – NURSING – POLICE – PRISON SERVICE – TEACHING – YOUTH AND COMMUNITY WORK

Sociology

Entry qualifications
2, or more often 3, A-levels and 3 GCSEs (A–C); usually maths or statistics and English at either level.

The work
Sociology is sometimes confused with social work, but there is a vast difference between the two. Social workers deal with individuals with problems (see SOCIAL WORK, p. 476); sociologists try to examine the way society functions: they study the conditions under which problems arise to understand why they do so. Sociologists research and develop theories and 'concepts', and try and find solutions or at least ameliorations to problems. Social workers need some understanding of sociology; but sociologists do not need the professional social workers' skills of coping with individuals' problems.

Sociologists research and develop theories about the social relationships that make up society and how these change or remain constant over time. They look at the interactions between individuals, between groups, and within and between whole communities. For example, sociologists who study schools may investigate what happens when teachers and pupils meet in different institutional settings – in class, on the sports field, in the street. From such investigations theories about the structure of school life, its importance to society and the problems that arise during education can be constructed.

Sociology covers every area of human social activity, e.g. race relations, interaction between the sexes, union–management disputes, the doctor–patient relationship, problems caused by homelessness, poverty and unemployment. Sociologists examine the institutions which make up society's legal, political and economic systems, the workplace, the family, and both urban and rural communities.

Virtually every aspect of modern life is of interest to sociologists. They are usually concerned with highly topical issues. In recent years these have included the impact of technological advance; the sociology of science and medicine; child sexual abuse and its detection; the treatment of people suffering from AIDS and understanding the social factors involved in stopping its spread.

Sociologists hope that by understanding the complexities of society they can avert some problems. An example is where new technology innovations change the nature of available jobs in a city and older male workers find themselves out of a job. Sociologists recognize that for some men unemployment can strain relations between them and their families, leading to potential domestic violence or suicide. Because sociology has devoted much research to the key concepts of class and gender, it can suggest which groups might find the strain greatest. Therefore advice can then be offered to employers, councils and government on the consequences of changing employment patterns.

Sociologists collect information in a variety of ways, mainly by the fieldwork techniques of observation and interviewing. Observation may involve participating in the work of an institution or an organization such as a factory or a youth club, or it may mean moving into an urban or rural community and joining in the life of that community. A particular study may take months or years. Interviewing can sometimes be combined with observation, but is often carried out independently using systematically prepared sets of questions. Different kinds of research call for different styles of survey. Apart from this fieldwork, there is the collation, analysis, interpretation and presentation of the information collected. Statistics and computers are used extensively. For some sociologists the important part of their job is the development of theory and concepts which can then be used as starting-points for new investigations.

Sociology is closely allied to and overlaps with other social sciences, especially social anthropology, social psychology (p. 404) and economics (p. 178).

There are far more sociology graduates than jobs/training as sociologists. Careers in research and higher education have become very scarce. While a sociology degree is never a vocational qualification, it can be the basis for further specific training and for many kinds of jobs with on-the-job training. There are reasonable opportunities within health and social services and with voluntary agencies for jobs involving a substantial amount of applied research. Now, more sociologists go into industry, to work in *industrial relations* or other *personnel specializations* (see p. 368) and generally on questions related to organizational and technological change. There are some opportunities in *market research* (see p. 16) and *marketing* (see p. 297). The *police* (see p. 387) welcome sociologists' understanding of human behaviour.

Training   Honours degree in sociology or a combination of social sciences. There are also some courses which combine sociology with arts or with modern languages. On some business studies degrees sociology is a major option. There are also a few courses where sociology can be combined with physics and/or maths, engineering, education, management studies, computer studies. Modularization of degree courses gives wider scope for students of all disciplines to study some sociology.

The choice of the right course is important, and complicated: the wording used to describe courses varies, and the combination of subjects covered and the emphasis given to the different aspects of sociology cannot necessarily be deduced from the title given to a particular course. It is essential to study up-to-date prospectuses, and to consult the *CRAC Degree Course Guide* before choosing a course. It is not wise to go by the experience of people who read sociology even recently, because of the many changes and innovations in this field.

During their first year, students study the rudiments of the social sciences generally: economics, politics, social institutions, social and/or economic history, psychology, statistics, geography. During the second and third years they concentrate entirely on sociology or choose 2, occasionally 3, subjects from among: sociology, economics, geography, social administration, politics, philosophy, and statistics.

Personal attributes   A deep but detached interest in how people live, think and behave; a rigorous scientific approach to contemporary social problems rather than emotional responses; the ability to get on well with all kinds of people at all levels of intelligence, at least sufficiently well to interview them successfully; ability to recognize one's own biases; an analytical, logical brain; the ability to discuss and write lucidly, and some mathematical ability.

Late start   Many mature students study sociology. Maturity helps in work which centres around understanding human behaviour, but as jobs are scarce young graduates tend to be given preference.

Career-break   Should not cause any problems as long as people keep up with developments. Reduced fees for British Sociological Association.

Part time   Occasional research assignments. Job-sharing possible.

Position of women   Depends entirely on type of job: on the whole women sociology graduates do not encounter special problems. As the degree is a preparation for a wide variety of jobs, it could be a useful preparation for women who intend to return to work after a break and who are not quite sure what they want to do eventually. More women than men take sociology degrees.

Further information	British Sociological Association, Unit 3 G, Mountjoy Research Centre, Stockton Road, Durham DH1 3UR (send s.a.e.)

Related careers	ADVERTISING: *Market Research* – ECONOMICS – MANAGEMENT SERVICES: *Work Study* – NURSING: *Health Visitor* – PERSONNEL / HUMAN RESOURCES MANAGEMENT – POLICE – PSYCHOLOGY – SOCIAL WORK

Speech and Language Therapists

Entry qualifications

Degree course requirements. Subjects should normally include English, a science subject, maths, a foreign language. Some courses specify certain sciences or other subjects at A-level.

The work

Speech and language therapy is concerned with communication difficulties. Speech and language therapists assess and treat all kinds of voice, speech and language defects. Children may have an articulation problem or be excessively slow in learning to talk. Stammering can afflict people of all ages. In hospital clinics therapists work with children and adults who may have lost the ability to speak through brain damage (e.g. a stroke) or disease. Patients who have had their larynx or voice box removed have to be taught an alternative method of sound production.

Every patient needs a different approach – in helping each case, therapists must apply their knowledge of phonetics, psychology, anatomy and physiology, neurology and acoustics, and their common sense.

Speech and language therapists work in clinics, special and mainstream schools or in hospitals. Some patients are treated in groups, most individually. Some speech and language therapists work on their own, many as members of a team. In rural areas considerable travelling may be necessary.

A speech and language therapist meets a great many people – teachers, social workers, doctors, psychologists, as well as patients. The work is very demanding and responsible.

There is a steady demand for therapists, but jobs are not necessarily available just where they are wanted. There are some opportunities in the Commonwealth and other English-speaking countries.

Training

This is now an all-graduate entry profession.

3- or 4-year degree course syllabus includes: speech pathology and therapeutics; phonetics; linguistics; anatomy and physiology; psychology; neurology. Students are also given insight into other relevant subjects including acoustics, audiology, ENT disorders, education, orthodontics, plastic surgery, psychiatry, reasearch methodology and statistics and sociology. During practical work in hospitals, schools and clinics students first observe then assist with treatments.

There are 2-year post-graduate courses for graduates in psychology, linguistics or other relevant subjects which can lead to a Masters qualification. Both methods are equal in job-getting terms.

Personal attributes Understanding of people, whatever their age, temperament, background, and mood of the moment; desire to help; ability to detect personal problems which may have a bearing on the cause and treatment of the defect; tact; unlimited patience. Because much of the work is with children, and sometimes with emotionally disturbed ones at that, the knack of gaining children's confidence; a pleasant voice – young patients are apt to imitate; a sensitive ear to detect slight sound differences; a calm manner and stable temperament; good command of concise written English for reports and notes to guide parents. *For senior posts*: organizing ability.

Late start Possible: over-21s may be accepted with non-standard entrance qualifications. Jobs should be no more difficult than for the young entrant.

Career-break Should be no problem. *Refresher courses* and individual re-introduction programmes available.

Part time Some opportunities, but not usually for head of department jobs. Job-sharing is increasing, even at senior level.

Position of women This used to be an all-female job, but now an increasing number of men are entering the profession. They now account for about 5%.

Further information Royal College of Speech and Language Therapists, 7 Bath Place, Rivington Street, London EC2A 3DR

Related careers DRAMA – SOCIAL WORK – TEACHING: *Special Needs Education*

Sport

Entry qualifications
No formal educational qualifications. For degree courses in sport or recreation studies: 2–3 A-levels.
NOTE: an A-level in Sport Studies and Physical Education is now widely available.

The work
Sport can be divided into 3 main career areas, although many people combine 2 or more:

    1. *Players* or *participants* who are paid professionals. This guide is concerned only with those sports in which it is possible to earn a living, but the professional/amateur distinction is frequently blurred or has disappeared altogether.

    2. *Teaching* or *coaching* children or adults.

    3. *Administration* (which overlaps with LEISURE/RECREATION MANAGEMENT, see p. 261).

Professional Players

In most cases those with sufficient talent will have been spotted well before they leave school. People whose job it is to find and nurture talent will have discovered potential players through schools, youth clubs, local and county teams. In general it is too late to start serious training for a sporting career after leaving school (exceptions are horse and motor racing which cannot be started while at school). For most people sport has to remain a recreation.

Training
Football (boys only)
Most begin at 14 (can be 13 in Scotland) as Associated Schoolboys with a professional club. At 16 they may be invited to become full-time trainees on a 2-year Youth Training programme. The first year of the scheme is broad-based: on-the-job training includes football training and coaching, work experience in various aspects of running and maintaining the club. Trainees follow a day-release course at college, working towards NVQ Level 2 Leisure and Tourism and following an Information Technology course. After the first year they are assessed: the majority stay on at the football club and continue their football training and

day-release course. Others may choose to concentrate on another area of work within the club or transfer to a more appropriate YT. At the end of the 2 years, the club decides whether or not to offer a professional contract: the majority are not good enough and leave the game by their early 20s.

In Scotland, professional footballers are encouraged and given financial help to continue with educational courses throughout their careers to prepare them for life after football.

Cricket (boys only)

Most county cricketers are recruited straight from school, having already played trial matches. For a few seasons they play in club and second XI matches. If they are considered to have first-team potential they may be offered a contract by the county: they agree to play exclusively for the club. The MCC runs a Young Cricketers Scheme for promising boys aged 16 to 18. Successful candidates for the scheme may choose between 2 different contracts: (A) Summer only, renewable annually or (B) 3 summers of cricket and 2 winters of education. Those on (B) who have 4 GCSEs (A–C) can study for the GNVQ Advanced in Leisure and Tourism at City of Westminster College; this specially provided 2-year course runs from October to March only, so as not to disrupt the summer playing programme. Those with lower qualifications on either contract can instead work for NVQs. About 50 county players each year find cricket jobs overseas during our winter, playing cricket or coaching. The rest have to find other employment in the close season (a few play professional football). Most have stopped playing by the age of 40, although top players may stay in the game as coaches, umpires or managers.

Tennis (boys and girls)

Most aspiring players will have started playing at age 7 to 9 (usually short tennis at school, club or sports centre). They progress by playing in 'starter' tournaments and other competitions at local club level and may be selected for county training. The most promising 150 boys and girls aged between 11 and 17 are selected for the Rover National Training programme run by the Lawn Tennis Association; this is managed by 10 coaches on an area basis; or at the LTA Rover School at Bisham Abbey, Bucks. Some become full-time players by age 16–17, often joining one of the LTA's national squads. A few gain scholarships to the United States at 18/19 years. The LTA organizes and helps finance a comprehensive national tournament programme as well as international experience for these players throughout their development.

In any one year only around a dozen men and women players make a full-time living, with those in the world's top 100 earning very large sums.

Golf (boys and girls)
There are 2 distinct kinds of golfing professional: (1) the *club professional* (belonging to the Professional Golfers' Association) and (2) the *tournament player* (belonging to the PGA European Tour and, for women, the WPG European Tour). Although some professional golfers have become successful in both areas, this is not recommended for newcomers, since intense competition within each branch requires single-minded dedication to one only.

1. *Club professionals* (around 4,000): Work at a club, running the shop, repairing equipment and giving lessons. The job requires a high level of playing ability (they have their own tournaments organized by the PGA), business flair and organizing ability. In golf there is a very clear distinction between amateur and professional status and aspiring club pros should first seek advice from the PGA before taking the plunge and forfeiting their amateur status. Before being registered as trainees, potential professionals (men and women) must first spend a minimum 6-month probationary period with a PGA approved training establishment. During this they retain their amateur status and aim to reduce their handicap to 4 or less. They then take the PGA entrance examination (unless they have GCSEs A–C in English and maths), sign a contract and become professional. They follow a 3–4 year planned programme of work (covering all aspects of the business) with on- and off-the-job instruction (including residential courses), leading to a final exam. They must be prepared to work long hours, and earn very little while learning.

All potential pros must have a handicap of 4 or less, before starting.

2. *Tournament players*: aspiring professional men players have to qualify the first season for 1 of the 50 available Player's Cards by competing in a pre-qualifying school (tournament), then in the qualifying school held in Europe. To retain their Card they need to finish in the top 125 in the European tournaments that season. Only a handful of tournament players are successful enough to earn large sums through winnings and commercial sponsorship.

Women's golf is a growth area and women have their own association. Applicants for probationary membership of the WPG European Tour must be aged 18 or over and, if amateur, have a current handicap of 1 (without star). Existing professionals may also apply, provided they are members of a recognized Ladies'

Professional Golf Association/Tour. All applicants must be proposed and seconded by members of the Tour.

Horse racing (boys and girls)
There are 2 kinds of races – flat and National Hunt (over jumps). Increasingly, training of stable staff for both kinds of racing stables is carried out by the British Racing School, Newmarket, and the National Racing School, Doncaster, rather than by trainers themselves. School leavers can either apply direct to the Racing and Thoroughbred Breeding Training Board (RTBTB) or to individual trainers who will then send them to the School after some practical experience in the stables. Pupils must be 16/17, around 9 stone or under. Previous riding experience is not essential but helps.

Basic courses at the British Racing School, Newmarket, last 9 weeks, those at the Northern Racing School 12 weeks. Boys and girls are then placed with trainers or thoroughbred stud owners as stable 'lads'. Courses cover riding, grooming, mucking out and basic care of horses, plus lectures on racing topics. The training is for stable staff, not jockeys. Trainees work towards a vocational qualification in Racehorse Care and Management. (The awarding body is the RTBTB.) A tiny minority become apprentice jockeys – the great majority remain as stable 'lads' (there are 50 'lads' for every jockey). National Hunt 'lads' are heavier (up to 9/10 stone); they need to gain experience first with a National Hunt trainer, who will send them to the British Racing School if they think they are suitable (in which case the weight restrictions are waived). A very small number become 'conditional' jockeys (the National Hunt equivalent to apprentice jockeys). There is a clear distinction between *amateur* and *professional jockeys*, with many more races for professionals.

Women have done well over jumps and on the flat but their racing history is comparatively short. They have only been allowed to ride as professionals on the flat since 1975 and over jumps since 1976. The problem is that only those considered likely to ride winners are given rides; so until they have had success and proved themselves, they are unlikely to be chosen, which makes it hard for them to get started.

Teaching, Coaching/Instructing

For *PE teaching*, see TEACHING, p. 517.

Coaches and instructors in individual sports work at varying levels and in different settings, from national teams to youth clubs, from private sports clubs to local authority leisure centres.

A great many coach part time and/or voluntarily, while following another paid occupation. Full-time paid coaches are nearly all ex-professionals or leading amateurs. Some combine playing with coaching. As well as having great technical expertise they need the ability to get the best from players, to know when to sympathize and when to put on pressure. The relationship between player and coach is crucial to success. All the sports' governing bodies run courses for coaches and instructors, e.g. the LTA Coach Education Programme.

NVQs in coaching, teaching and instruction are being introduced. There is also a Community Sports Leader award scheme run by the Central Council for Physical Recreation (CCPR); although not a vocational course, it may provide a starting-point.

Sports Administration
(excluding Leisure/Recreation Management – see p. 261)

Most sports governing bodies have a very small paid staff. Apart from the usual secretarial and clerical posts, the administration of organizations such as the FA or Lawn Tennis Association is carried out by people with relevant expertise, either as former players or managers, or in business or public relations which could help to bring in sponsorship. There are occasional openings for people with degrees in sports science or recreation management. (The LTA runs a Diploma in Tennis Management.)

Active sports careers are necessarily short. After this a minority manage to find work in some way connected with their sport (coaching, managing, promoting products), while the majority have to look elsewhere for employment. Therefore it is essential that those considering a sporting career should look ahead and reach as high a standard academically as possible while at school or college to enable them to take up another training later. This may mean combining a course of further or higher education with part-time playing (e.g. as some cricketers do).

Personal attributes   Total dedication and single-mindedness; strong competitive urge and will to win; high level of physical fitness and mental and physical stamina; ability to respond positively to criticism; resilience and will-power to cope with injuries and setbacks.

**Position
of
women**

Sport is different from any other work area. Private clubs are excluded from the Sex Discrimination Act altogether and, as most sport is organized by clubs, those who choose to can refuse women as members; also sporting competition may be confined to one sex where the 'average' woman is at a physical disadvantage to the 'average' man (i.e. in football, not darts or horse racing). Even the outstanding girl or woman who is good enough to merit a place in a male team and who may be the best available player can be barred and so is unable to experience the highest level of competition. All too often girls who are good at sport at school are considered rather unfeminine, while boys who are good at it are highly valued. Girls are often automatically assumed to be worse at sport whereas certainly at primary school sex differences are negligible (and it is at this age that serious interest and training in most sports needs to start). Men's events are generally more prestigious, better sponsored and carry higher prize money than women's. Very importantly, the media takes very little notice of women's sporting achievements, whether amateur or professional. However, the situation is improving little by little and no potentially outstanding sportswoman should be put off. In certain sports the gap is narrowing between male and female achievements and each year sees a new 'first' for a woman.

**Further
informa-
tion**

The Sports Council, 16 Upper Woburn Place, London WC1H 0QP

The Central Council of Physical Recreation (CCPR), Francis House, Francis Street, London SW1P 1DE (for list of courses)

Institute of Professional Sport, same address as CCPR (send A5 s.a.e. for careers booklet 'Playing at the Top')

Women's Sport Foundation, Wesley House, 4 Wild Court, London WC2B 4AU (produces booklet aimed at promoting careers in sport for young women, 'Enjoy sport? Why not work at it!'. Send £2 plus large s.a.e. (29p))

The Footballers' Further Education and Vocational Training Society Ltd, 2 Oxford Court, Bishopsgate, Manchester M2 3WQ

Test and County Cricket Board, Lord's Cricket Ground, London NW8 8QN

The Lawn Tennis Association Trust, The Queen's Club, West Kensington, London W14 9EG

Professional Golfers' Association, National Headquarters, Apollo House, The Belfry, Sutton Coldfield, West Midlands B76 9PT

The PGA European Tour, The Wentworth Club, Virginia Water, Surrey GU25 4LS

Women Professional Golfers' European Tour, The Tytherington
Club, Macclesfield, Cheshire SK10 2JP

Racing and Thoroughbred Breeding Training Board, PO Box
21, Newmarket, Suffolk CB8 9BL

Related careers	LEISURE/RECREATION MANAGEMENT – TEACHING

Stock Exchange and Securities Industry

The London Stock Exchange is the central market place through which investors, both individuals and institutions, buy and sell securities, i.e. stocks and shares. These securities are a means by which companies and government raise finance. As well as the Official List of securities quoted on the Exchange, there are also: AIM, the new market for smaller and growing companies keen to raise public finance and have their shares more widely traded; and the London Traded Options Market – an option is the right but not the obligation to buy or sell a set amount of security, at a set price, within a set period of time; it is also a 'contract' which can itself be traded.

Recent years have seen enormous changes in the operations of the London Stock Exchange. Trading on the market floor has been replaced by the computer screen and telephone. (Options are still traded on the floor but this is due to change.) Rules governing membership of the Exchange were changed and securities dealing now takes place in merchant banks, clearing banks and investment banks, as well as the old stockbroking firms. All buying and selling of securities is carried out by member firms of the Exchange. Prices for securities are quoted on SEAQ (Stock Exchange Automated Quotations system) which is displayed in firms' offices. The term 'securities house' is frequently used.

Though London and its London Stock Exchange are a major world centre for the trading of domestic and international securities, the securities industry is truly international, with trading a 24-hour activity.

Following the changes known collectively as 'Big Bang' in 1986 and the resultant explosion in securities trading activity, it became clear that the financial rewards could be extremely high. More recent years have made equally clear that the risks are high as firms have cut down or pulled out of trading activities – and got rid of large numbers of highly paid staff.

Entry qualifications
Nothing rigidly laid down, but at least GCSE (A–C) maths and English normally expected. Most employers have substantial *graduate* recruitment. Most analysts/researchers will be graduates.

The work   Since 'Big Bang' did away with the separate and distinct functions
of the stockbroker and jobber and established broker/dealers,
some of the terms have come to be used loosely. A broker/dealer
may be a firm or an individual; an individual may be just a
broker or just a dealer, or combine both roles; some firms specialize in one or other activity or segment of the market, others offer
a complete service.

Researchers, or analysts, provide the information on which to
base advice to clients. They usually specialize in a particular
industrial sector or group of companies. They develop a thorough
understanding of their area by studying company reports, meeting
managers, seeking out any information of relevance to the industry and keeping up to date on any news likely to affect it,
analysing past, present and future indicators and forecasting
future performance.

Brokers, or salesmen/women, take the results of the research
and try to persuade their clients to buy or sell shares. Some deal
with institutional clients, developing long-term relationships with
their fund managers. Brokers dealing with private clients may
have to deal with many more clients and many more securities,
since small investors may be interested in a range of companies
too small to be considered by the institutional investors. Some
clients follow the market themselves and require only an execution
service. Others require advice on investment and brokers or
salesmen/women must thoroughly understand their clients' circumstances in order to give appropriate advice.

Dealers, or traders, carry out the technical side of deals. They
may act for brokers and their clients, negotiating the deal with
other 'market-makers' (who are specialized dealers) or a third
party, or they may act on their own account as principals, seeking
to make a profit out of buying low and selling high. (Strict
regulations ensure that clients get the best price available.)

Settlement staff process the transactions arranged by the dealers. Routine work is done by computer; the rest is highly specialized and involves the preparation of documents and calculating
and arranging payment of commission and taxes. (The Bank of
England is now working to introduce a computerized automatic
execution system for the transaction of smaller orders, as well as a
method of 'paperless transfer'.) Settlement staff with the right
skills can move into sales or dealing.

Training   On-the-job training has always been a feature of the London
Stock Exchange work and continues to be. This, however, can
mean a very sophisticated graduate training programme. While
training, perhaps by a 'Cook's Tour' of several back-room depart-

ments, recruits who plan to deal in securities or give investment advice normally study for the exams of the Securities and Futures Authority Limited. These must be passed before one can become a *registered trader* or *registered representative*, which is mandatory for those who trade or advise. Study may be by evening classes, distance learning or in-company tuition.

These exams are tests of basic knowledge; there are more specialized exams leading to the Securities Industry Diploma.

Administration of the London Stock Exchange: the Exchange itself employs staff in a variety of roles. Many of the vacancies are for computer-trained staff to help in the design, development and running of the various automated systems. People with accountancy, legal, company secretary and general management skills are also recruited. Each year the Exchange takes a number of graduates with good honours degrees and management potential on to the Graduate Training Scheme.

The Exchange also manages a YT scheme. There is a very high success rate in permanent placements for those completing the scheme.

A large number of staff are employed in general clerical and administrative work and there is good scope for promotion from within the organization.

Personal attributes   For *researchers/analysts* – numeracy, ability to assess long-term trends, analytical skills; for *brokers/salesmen/women* – affability, the ability to develop good relationships with clients and inspire confidence; for *dealers* – stamina, willingness to take risks, ability to make quick decisions, high powers of concentration, exceptional self-confidence, memory for people and figures.

Late start   Opportunities mainly for those with professional qualifications in, for example, accountancy, economics, computing, general management. Analysts often have previous experience in industry. Dealing is a young person's job.

Career-break   Possible in research, analysis, computing and management areas.

Part time   Rare. Possible in administrative areas.

Position of women   Opportunities are increasing for women willing to break down traditional barriers. Proportions of women at junior levels and among graduates in research and analysis are growing.

Further information Public Affairs Department, the London Stock Exchange, London EC2N 1HP

Related careers ACCOUNTANCY – BANKING – BUILDING SOCIETY WORK – ECONOMICS – INSURANCE

Surveying

Surveyor

Entry qualifications

For membership of the Royal Institution of Chartered Surveyors: enrolment on an RICS accredited degree or diploma. For many courses, specific A-levels or A-levels from a group of subjects are required. For example maths, or geography or economic geography or a physical science may be asked for.

For membership of ISVA: 5 GCSEs (A–C) or equivalent, including English language and maths.

The work

The work is not *necessarily* mainly technical: in many surveyors' jobs the commercial element is greater than the technical; but technical expertise may be essential background knowledge. The variety of jobs is very great.

Surveying is an umbrella term for jobs which are, in varying degrees and in varying proportion, concerned with, to quote the RICS, 'the measurement, management, development and valuation' of virtually anything: oceans, rivers, harbours, earth's surface, all land, and anything that is in or on land or water, whether natural or man-made. Many surveying jobs are also concerned with protecting or improving the urban and rural environment and the efficient use of resources. However, most surveying is a commercial activity rather than an environmental subject.

The various surveying branches each involve a different mix of technical, commercial, practical and academic ingredients, and different amounts of time spent on dealing with clients, dealing with other professionals, and on office and outdoor work. Each branch, therefore, suits people with different temperaments, interests, aptitudes. For example, the urban estate agent-surveyor has little in common with the hydrographic surveyor charting oceanic depth, or with the planning surveyor doing research into shopping centres, although they do share core skills such as law, economics, valuation and management.

The professional surveying specializations are grouped into 'Divisions' by the Royal Institution of Chartered Surveyors. These are, in order of size: general practice which covers valuation, estate agency, auctioneering and urban estate/housing management; quantity surveying; building surveying; land agency and agricultural surveying; planning and development; land and hydrographic surveying; minerals surveying.

The Incorporated Society of Valuers and Auctioneers' qualification covers much the same ground as the RICS's General Practice Division *except* housing management. (See also HOUSING MANAGEMENT, p. 223). The ISVA divisions also include fine arts and chattels, agricultural practice and plant and machinery.

The main surveying branches:

General Practice Surveyors

Valuation surveyors (also called valuers, or simply surveyors)
They assess the value of any type of property at any particular time. It may be in connection with rating, insurance, death duty purposes, as well as for general commercial and, these days, for investment purposes. Some specialize as *investment surveyors*. There are various valuation methods; the most commonly used is the 'comparison' method. This is an intricate mixture of basing judgement on ascertainable facts – value of property in the neighbourhood or other similar property; quality, etc. – as well as on 'getting the feel'. When assessing the value of residential property, or a row of shops, for example, factors taken into account include possible future development in the area (motorways, one-way traffic schemes, housing estates, parking restrictions); amenities (open spaces; swimming baths; entertainment facilities generally); proximity to schools, shops, transport; noise; as well as type of neighbourhood and informed guesswork as to whether the area is likely to go down/come up or whether it has any feeling of community (which might affect quality of school or be of interest to the elderly, etc.).

Valuers may also assess contents of houses. Though they may be able to tell a Rembrandt from an amateur's efforts, valuers do not normally assess the value of works of art but call on an expert in that field as necessary (who may be a colleague qualified in the chattels section of the RICS General Practice Division or ISVA's Fine Arts and Chattels Division). If working for a property developer or local authority they may value land. They may inspect, for example, a plot of land which is up for sale, assess its potential in terms of houses, shops, flats, etc. to be built there, and do a rough 'costing' of whatever type of building is being considered. They may also value all kinds of plant and machinery.

Apart from working for estate agents, local authorities, property developers and other commercial concerns, valuation surveyors also set up in private professional practice. Work for property developers requires a certain amount of gambling instinct and very pronounced business acumen; local authority valuers' work is more concerned with valuing according to laid-down criteria.

Estate agents

Valuation surveyors (as described above) may be estate agents, but estate agents are not necessarily valuation surveyors. Within surveying, estate agency is the most commercially and least technically oriented specialization and probably the largest in terms of opportunities. There is at the moment no need for estate agents to have particular qualifications (but this may soon change). However, most firms of estate agents have at least one RICS-, ISVA- or NAEA- (see p. 509) qualified partner. Estate agents negotiate the sale, purchase, leasing of property – not only of houses but also of industrial and commercial premises, agricultural and other land. They arrange and advise on mortgages and on implications of rent acts, and on relevant law generally. As *managing agents* they manage property for clients, which involves drawing up leases, collecting rents, responsibility for maintenance, etc.

Estate agents' clients may be property managers of vast commercial empires, or first-time house purchasers who need to be guided through the complexities of making the most expensive purchase of their lives. Estate agents may specialize in one type of property (residential, or commercial or industrial), or they may deal with a mixture of types of properties. *Negotiators*, who deal with clients, often specialize in dealing with one type of client, for example with house purchasers, helping them to sort out priorities: few can afford their dream house, i.e. what they want exactly where they want. Negotiators help weigh up advantages of, say, sunny garden or 'good neighbourhood'; solidly built but no garage; not-so-solid but near shops/school/transport/parks, etc. Or they specialize in dealing with industrial property: are there goods transport/loading facilities; planning restrictions? Is there a supply of skilled labour?

Estate agents advise vendors on the price to ask, so they have to understand something about valuation, even if they are not professionally qualified valuers. The work involves a lot of client-contact, of getting about and getting to know an area and being aware of changes in type of locality and its effect on property values.

Auctioneers

Most estate agents are also auctioneers. (Normally estate agents employ different people as negotiators and as auctioneers, but in small firms everybody might do everything.) Some firms specialize in auctioning commercial, industrial, residential or agricultural property; others specialize in furniture, machinery, works of art. (The few well-known auction rooms where paintings etc. are auctioned are staffed by art specialists who have learnt about auctioneering as well as by the estate agent-valuer-auctioneer.) An auctioneer outside London may well auction the contents of a house one day, cattle in the local market-place the next, and a row of shops the day after that. Work varies according to whether done in country town or big city. The actual auctioneering is only part of the work: it also involves assessing value and advising vendors on 'reserve price', and it involves detailed 'lotting up' and cataloguing items to be sold.

While some firms of auctioneers, especially in the country, engage people specially for auctioneering and teach them the necessary skills and techniques, it is advisable to train as valuer (see above) as well.

Quantity Surveyors

Quantity surveyors are also called 'building economists', 'construction cost consultants', 'building accountants'. Quantity surveyors are essential members of the design team on building projects of any size. They translate architects' or civil engineers' designs into detailed costs – of labour, materials, overheads; and they break down all materials and processes to be used into detailed quantities and timing. They evaluate alternative processes and materials and may suggest alternative design technologies and materials to those suggested on the original design. Their thorough and up-to-date knowledge of new construction technologies and materials enables them to find ways of getting work carried out in the most speedy, economical and efficient way, without impairing the design. Calculations involved may be very complex – for example, future maintenance costs have to be considered when evaluating the use of alternative materials and processes. Calculations are usually done with computers.

Quantity surveyors are normally appointed by the designer of the project, i.e. the architect or civil engineer. Because of soaring costs and constantly changing technologies, the quantity surveyor's status in the design team has risen enormously in the last few years. Although the architect/civil engineer still has the last word, the quantity surveyor's suggestions for modifications are taken very seriously indeed.

Quantity surveyors are responsible for cost control during the whole project. They advise on cost implications of any proposed variations to the design, make interim valuations of completed work, check contractors' interim accounts and settle final accounts. They are also involved with financial administration of contracts for mechanical and electrical engineering and similar services and may be responsible for overall project management.

Quantity surveyors' work is a combination of straightforward figure work, complex calculations and negotiating skills. They must be able to deal with colleagues from other disciplines, contractors, clients. They spend more time at their desks doing calculations or writing reports and at negotiations than on the building site, but the time spent on the various ingredients of the job varies from project to project, and according to the type of employer and method of working.

About 60% of quantity surveyors are in private professional practice; others work for contractors, consultant engineers, in government departments, local authorities, commercial and industrial firms.

Building Surveyors

Building surveyors make structural surveys of and diagnose defects of buildings of all types, for prospective purchasers, vendors, owners, building societies. They assess maintenance costs and control maintenance programmes; they prepare plans for conversion and improvements. They draw up plans and specifications, go out to tender, and may supervise contractors' work and check accounts. They advise on building, planning, health and safety regulations, and they may also be involved with restoration or maintenance of ancient monuments and historic buildings. They spend a good deal of time clambering about on buildings to check roofs, lofts, drains, fire escapes and general structural soundness, so their work requires agility.

Many work in private professional practice; others are employed by any type of organization which owns, sells, buys, builds, manages property. This includes housing associations, building societies, all types of industrial and commercial firms, local authorities and central government. This is the most practical specialization, with the least office work.

Rural Practice Surveyors (formerly Land Agents/Agricultural Surveyors)

Terms are confusing as they have changed in recent years. Traditionally, land agents (called factors in Scotland) were (usually resident) managers of farms or other rural properties. More usually now their work is done by firms of agricultural surveyors (now called by the RICS rural practice surveyors), who manage a

number of farms and estates on a contract basis. They do much
the same work in rural areas as general practice surveyors do in
towns. They may do valuation (including livestock and agricultural plant), estate agency, auctioneering, or they may concentrate
on farm management (see AGRICULTURE AND HORTICULTURE,
p. 20). Increasingly they also advise on alternative uses of land,
for recreational purposes such as country parks, caravanning and
camping sites, country trails, long-distance footpaths, nature reserves. They would then also implement changes.

Rural practice surveyors may also conduct sales and auctions
of country properties, contents of country houses, livestock, agricultural machinery, plant, forests and forest products.

Many are in private professional practice. According to the size
of the practice, other specialist surveyors (valuers, building surveyors) may be employed. Rural practice surveyors sometimes now
do farm business management as well, perhaps employing specialists to advise on mechanization, diversification (see alternative
land use above) and other ways of improving farm profits. They
are also often involved with conservation issues, trying to reconcile
landowners' and conservationists' sometimes conflicting interests.

They also work for MAFF (see AGRICULTURE AND HORTICUL-
TURE, p. 20), local government, the National Trust and other
bodies which own/manage land.

Rural practice surveying is an unusual combination of business,
technical, environmental and agricultural work, and is one of the
few professional jobs which include getting about the countryside.

Planning and Development Surveyors

The work overlaps with TOWN AND COUNTRY PLANNING (see p.
539).

Planning surveyors are concerned with the efficient allocation
of resources in planning and with planning economics and planning law. The work is largely desk research (including statistics)
and communicating with other specialists concerned with planning. A planning surveyor, for example, investigates the economics
of a proposed shopping area. That would involve collecting facts
and figures from various sources, assessing their implications and
writing up the findings. Another project might mean having to
find a suitable site for an industrial plant which has to be
somewhere within a given area, must be near an inland waterway,
near transport and must not be within an area of scenic value.
That would not necessarily involve travelling, but consulting
maps and relevant organizations.

The planning surveyor also advises clients on planning implications or proposals to buy and develop a property. This could involve visiting the site, taking photographs, and then appraising the proposal from a civic design point of view. They are also involved in marketing completed properties.

Planning and development surveyors work for planning consultants, local and central government, or as specialists in general practice surveying firms.

Land and Hydrographic Surveyors

Land surveyors must not be confused with land agents/agricultural surveyors. Their work is quite different and much more 'technical'. They use sophisticated technologies (including satellite positioning systems and laser alignment devices) to measure and plot the precise shape and position of natural and man-made features on land for the purpose of map-making, including large-scale maps which are used for engineering constructions. (Before motorways can be sited, for example, or bridges built, the minutest physical details of the area have to be plotted and mapped. Their expertise was essential in planning the Channel Tunnel.)

Land surveyors do not draw maps; that is done by cartographers (see p. 92). Land surveyors work in private practice, or for the government (Ordnance Survey, Ministry of Defence mainly), or for consulting engineers and big contractors. Some work for the Directorate of Overseas Surveys which sends (experienced) surveyors to the developing – and other – countries to survey land, some of which has never been surveyed and mapped before. Some go into Archaeological Surveying (see ARCHAEOLOGY, p. 38).

Hydrographic surveyors are the smallest and most scientific branch, although the recent growth of off-shore oil and gas industries has widened their scope. They survey oceans, waterways, harbours and ports for purposes of producing nautical charts which show the precise shape, size, location of physical features of the sea bed, etc. and hazards, currents, tides, sunken wrecks. They supervise the dredging of ports and channels. The information sent by hydrographic survey ships operating in most parts of the world to the Navy's Hydrographic Department is being continuously revised. Collecting and interpreting information is done with highly sophisticated electronic equipment. British Admiralty Charts are used by seafarers all over the world, and by North Sea oil and gas engineers.

Many hydrographic surveyors are also naval officers. This is fairly tough outdoor work, combined with high technology.

Minerals or Mining Surveyors

This is the smallest specialization. Mining surveyors are responsible for mine safety and for mapping mineral deposits, and are
involved with the potential use, value, properties, management
and exploitation of mineral deposits, which means combining
technical, scientific, managerial and commercial aspects. They are
also responsible for minimizing environmental damage to the
countryside where mineral deposits are mined.

In this country, mining surveyors are concerned mainly with
coal mining, but minerals surveying overseas covers a variety of
other minerals.

Prospects for chartered surveyors of all kinds vary according to
economic conditions, but are mostly reasonable, especially as a
wider range of organizations now employ surveyors, for example
financial institutions; best opportunities are for general practice,
quantity, and building surveyors. Some opportunities in EU
countries (for those who speak the relevant language fluently),
especially for quantity surveyors, who are also in demand in
Africa and the Middle East.

Training   For membership of the Royal Institution of Chartered Surveyors
(any surveying specialization) about 70% take 3-year full-time
(or 4-year sandwich) degrees or diplomas in surveying; others
study while in appropriate employment, which takes 5 to 6 years
of part-time study (or 4 years for the 'distance-learning' diploma
course run by the College of Estate Management). Day-release
is often granted in public sector employment. In the private
sector, students usually have to study in their own time by correspondence course and evening classes.

Choosing a course needs careful research. Some courses allow
students to choose between several allied specializations during
the second year. It is essential to study the RICS and ISVA up-
to-date lists of accredited degrees and diploma courses in each
division. Course titles, especially for general practice, vary and
are often misleading. For example there are several different titles
for courses leading to General Practice Division exemptions; nor
are the titles necessarily an indication of course emphasis.

Though it is usual to work initially in the specialization in
which one qualified, it is quite possible to switch specializations
later. In practice some specializations (such as, for example,
building and quantity surveying) are more easily interchangeable
than, for example, general practice and hydrographic.

General practice surveyors (i.e. valuers, estate agents, auctioneers) can train *either* for the RICS General Practice Division, as above, *or* for membership of the Incorporated Society of Valuers and Auctioneers (see 'Entry qualifications', above). ISVA training is *either* by 3-year full-time course (courses at only a few colleges); *or* by day-release; *or* (the most common method) by correspondence course, taking 4 to 6 years, while in approved employment.

Graduates from any discipline may take a post-graduate conversion course. Alternatively, they may take the 'distance-learning' diploma course (see above). Though theoretically an arts graduate could qualify in any of the specializations, most opt for the General Practice Division. Science/engineering graduates might opt for Building or Quantity Surveying RICS divisions. History of art graduates might choose the Fine Arts and Chattels division of ISVA. Graduates with related degrees, for example in building or planning, qualify for partial exemption if they opt for the Building or the Planning and Development Divisions. There is 1 3-year Diploma in Fine Arts and Chattels Valuation for people with 2 A-levels or experience in valuation.

Personal attributes Practical approach to problem-solving; ability to inspire confidence in clients; ability to take complex decisions on own initiative and work as one of a team as well; for some jobs ability to handle labour. For *consultancy* and *estate agency*: business acumen; liking for being out of doors.

Late start Possible, but requires very strong motivation. No problem getting training, but first job may be difficult for over-30s. Depends on previous experience. Normal entry requirements may be waived by ISVA.

Career-break Should not be difficult in, for example, general practice surveying; possibly more difficult in areas where technologies change rapidly, but here keeping up with developments by reading journals and attending meetings should help. No *refresher* courses so far. Reduced membership fees of ISVA.

Part time Not very common, but the profession is looking at ways to promote it. No reason why established surveyors should not suggest to their employers that part time with flexible hours or job-sharing should work well.

Position of women There is no logical reason whatever why there should be so few women surveyors. Just under 14% of newly qualified and student members of the RICS are women. ISVA has about 4% qualified and 15% student women members.

The few women in the profession are doing well, although some have changed employers rather often because promotion was blocked for them. The majority have gone into general practice, fine arts and chattels, and management or teaching (one polytechnic has a woman as head of the surveying department); fewer choose quantity or building surveying.

The first woman chartered minerals surveyor qualified in 1986. Mining surveyors during training must visit mines (women have only recently been allowed to work as miners) and hydrographic surveyors are trained, partly, by the Navy, on naval vessels. These two are, in any case, a tiny minority of surveyors. No other surveying makes demands on physical strength or presents any hazards with which most women, however traditional in outlook, cannot cope as well as men. (Building surveyors go up scaffolding, but women have no worse heads for heights than men.)

In fact, much surveying work is concerned with improving the environment and generally the quality of life, and much of it involves dealing with people: even the most traditional-minded women should find something to their liking in surveying. It is lack of knowledge of what surveyors actually do which keeps women from entering this many-sided profession in greater numbers.

Further information

Royal Institution of Chartered Surveyors, Education and Membership Department, Surveyor Court, Westwood Way, Coventry CV4 8JE

ISVA, 3 Cadogan Gate, London SW1X 0AS

College of Estate Management, Whiteknights, Reading RG6 2AW

Related careers

AGRICULTURE AND HORTICULTURE – ARCHITECTURE – CARTOGRAPHY – ENGINEERING – HOUSING MANAGEMENT – SURVEYING: *Technician* – TOWN AND COUNTRY PLANNING

Surveying Technicians
(includes managerial jobs in the construction industry; see BUILDING, p. 79)

Entry qualifications

Either 4 GCSEs (A–C) including maths, a science and a subject proving competence in the use of English for BTEC National awards (see p. xxi); *or* 1 A-level passed and another one studied

for direct entry to BTEC Higher National awards. For
SCOTVEC equivalents see p. xxii.

The work   Most specializations overlap very much with supervisory and
management jobs in the building industry (see p. 79). Titles vary:
the term 'technician' may not be used, even when the qualification
required is a technician qualification.

Individual technicians' work varies enormously: some are desk-
bound draughtspersons, some are out and about; all now use
computerized procedures and equipment. Some have a great deal
of client-contact, some have none. Almost invariably they are
part of a team.

The majority work under the overall direction of surveyors,
architects, civil engineers or planners. Some of their work is
indistinguishable from that done by chartered surveyors: until
some years ago, chartered surveyors qualified almost exclusively
by on-the-job plus part-time training, and they had only slightly
higher entry qualifications than technicians often have now. While
chartered surveyors' training is certainly much more demanding
academically than technicians', many tasks are still the same as
they always were and do not require the chartered surveyors' in-
depth training. Technician-level qualifications are sufficient for
the majority of those 'surveyors' who, while wanting responsibility
and professional training, do not aspire to initiate and take
charge of complex projects.

Surveying technician specializations:

Building Surveying Technicians
(see 'Building Surveyors', p. 503 and 'Building
Managers', p. 80)

Subdivisions cover construction and assessment of structures;
administration of building regulations; preparations of plans;
specification for and organization of work to be carried out by
contractors; estimates of cost before projects start; dealing with
tenders and contracts and checking and passing contractors'
accounts; advising lay public on soundness of construction of
property they consider buying (while ultimate responsibility for
such advice lies with the employing chartered surveyor, the actual
surveying on which surveyors' reports to clients are based is often
carried out by technicians – the customer is not necessarily aware
of this); advice to property owners on maintenance and repair.
This may include drawing up schedules for redecoration, advice
on eradication of damp, dry rot, etc.

Building surveying technicians work in a great variety of settings – and under a great variety of titles (for example *building manager*, *building surveyor*, *building inspector*). They are employed by virtually any type of organization which owns or is responsible for the building and/or maintenance of property, and by firms of consultants. When they work for building contractors, they may also be called *planning* or *contracts manager*, or *contracts surveyor*. Their work may be mainly organizational – ensuring that manpower and equipment are used efficiently; this means planning all the operations which are involved in completing a contract to build whatever it is. For example, if a firm of building contractors is engaged simultaneously on converting several houses into flats and building office blocks, the contracts planner or manager has to estimate for how long how many workers and which equipment will be required on each job and when the various specialists, such as heating engineers, plasterers, electricians, should be where.

While in the past only very large contractors had contract planners, now middle-sized firms often engage such staff (under various titles, and not necessarily only engaged on this type of planning).

Another job for building surveying technicians is as *site managers*. They are responsible for organization of the sequence and smooth working of operations on site.

Technicians who prefer desk-bound work can become draughtspersons and eventually be in charge of a drawing office. But drawing offices now have fewer vacancies as so much work is computerized and completed more quickly. Many work for estate agents, where they meet the general public (see p. 501).

Quantity Surveying Technicians
(see 'Quantity Surveyors', p. 502)

They form part of the surveying team concerned with the costing and financial management of all types of building work. They may use computers and word processors. There are three main, but interrelated subdivisions (with rather quaint traditional titles).

1. *Takers off*: They abstract and measure from architect's, surveyor's or engineer's drawings every item of labour and materials to be used on a project, and list them in recognized terms. The information is needed to produce a 'cost plan' or Bill of Quantities. The job is usually office-based, and involves liaison with architects and other specialists, often as part of a technician team.

2. *Workers up*: They work out volumes, quantities and areas of

all the items which have been measured by the taker off, and record them in a way which can be understood by all construction workers. These are then presented on the Bill of Quantities used by the quantity surveyor in deciding the most economical means of construction. Workers up are entirely office-based; they may be responsible for a part or whole of a project.

3. *Post-contract surveyors* and *site measurers*: They divide their time between office and site. Work includes monitoring work done so that interim payments can be made to contractors. They may discuss the implications of variations on the plans with sub-contractors employed on the site and must understand contracts. Post-contract surveyors may be physically measuring work on site one day, attending a site meeting with a number of colleagues from different building-work spheres the same afternoon, and negotiating final payment with a subcontractor the next day. Usually they will have been workers up and takers off before becoming post-contract surveyors. Their job overlaps very much with that of chartered quantity surveyors.

General Practice Technicians
(see 'General Practice Surveyors', p. 500)

This division covers the work done by chartered general practice and planning surveyors. (At chartered level, there is a separate Planning and Development division.)

General practice technicians may specialize in valuation, estate agency, estate and property management, housing management, town and country planning (see p. 539). Openings are the most varied, ranging from suburban estate agency's or international property company's *negotiator* (see p. 501) to Inland Revenue or insurance company's valuation technician. This specialization offers scope both to those who are mainly interested in meeting members of the public and to those who want to do mainly drawing or other office work and are interested in combining technical and commercial work.

Land Surveying Technicians
(see 'Land and Hydrographic Surveyors', p. 505)

These work with chartered land surveyors. The work has changed considerably in the last 10 years with the use of electronic distance-measuring equipment and digital coding and modelling of land shapes. There are also opportunities in photographing and tracking man-made satellites, and in aerial photography.

This is one of the most adventurous of technician specializations, with work for oil companies and air survey companies at home or abroad, including Third World countries.

Minerals Surveying Technicians
(see 'Minerals or Mining Surveyors', p. 506)

This is a small division and involves the preparation of accurate plans in connection with safety, operation and development of mines, and geological formations in connection with mineral deposits. Much of the work is underground.

Hydrographic Surveying Technicians
(see 'Land and Hydrographic Surveyors', p. 505)

Making and updating charts of seas and coastlines, and profiles of sea beds; 'sign posting', on charts, of shipping lanes. This can be arduous outdoor work on survey ships and requires practical seamanship; only few draughtsmanship, office-based jobs.

Agricultural Surveying Technicians
(see 'Rural Practice Surveyors', p. 503)

This work overlaps with agriculture (see p. 20) and land agency. Main employers are local authorities and public bodies such as gas and electricity boards.

Surveying technicians generally are in demand but especially in quantity, general practice, land surveying and building surveying where their work often overlaps with that of chartered surveyors. In these specializations there are often more opportunities for technicians than for chartered surveyors. Experienced technicians have some opportunities in EU countries if they speak the relevant language fluently.

There is a 'bridging arrangement' which enables qualified technicians to attain RICS membership and become chartered surveyors.

Training (all technicians)

Students choose courses according to the type of work they are in or want to do. However, BTEC/SCOTVEC courses are flexible and, within related areas, it is usually possible to switch from one specialization or division to another; possibly adding course units.

The main surveying divisions are now covered by two 'generic' course categories:

1. *Building Studies*: This covers *building surveying* and *quantity surveying*.

2. *Land Administration*: This covers *general practice surveying* (incorporating valuation and property management/estate agency); *land surveying* (incorporating land, sea and air surveying; cartography); *planning* (incorporating town and country and regional planning).

Then there are specialized courses: *minerals surveying* technicians take *mine and mining surveying* courses; *hydrographic surveying* technicians train either at the Royal Navy Hydrographic School, Plymouth (residential) or take special options in BTEC *land surveying* courses. There are few training vacancies (and jobs) for mining and hydrographic surveying technicians. *Agricultural surveying* technicians normally take the National Diploma in Agriculture (see AGRICULTURE AND HORTICULTURE, p. 24).

BTEC courses are normally taken *either* by day- or block-release, and last 2 years for the BTEC National Certificate and a further 2 years for the Higher National Certificate, *or* they are taken by 2-year full-time study for the BTEC National Diploma, followed by a further 2 years' full-time or 3 years' sandwich study for the Higher National Diploma. It is possible to switch from part-time National to full-time/sandwich Higher National and vice versa. (And there are plenty of opportunities, for the less ambitious, with National rather than Higher National awards.) Entrants with 1 relevant A-level and another subject studied at A-level can go straight into the Higher National Diploma course or into the second year of the National Certificate course. In Scotland, students take relevant SCOTVEC National Certificate modules (see p. xxii) and then take the Higher National award. They can then take the Joint Test of Competence run by the RICS and SST.

For the majority of jobs, Higher National awards are as marketable as degrees. For some jobs in the building industry they are in fact preferred because of their practical content and approach.

The Chartered Surveyors Training Trust runs a technician training scheme for school-leavers in the London area and West Midlands. Trainees are placed with employers and study part time for the BTEC National Certificate.

The National Association of Estate Agents offers 2 correspondence courses. One is for junior negotiators and leads to a Certificate in Residential Estate Agency. The other is for those hoping to become branch managers and leads to a Certificate of Practice in Estate Agency.

Personal attributes Some mathematical ability; interest in finding practical solutions to technical problems; liking for outdoor work; ability to work as one of a team and also to take responsibility, coupled with willingness to work for people more highly qualified than oneself; meticulous accuracy; ability to supervise building site workers.

Late start There is no reason why people should not start in their twenties or thirties, especially if they have had some related experience or training, e.g. a geography degree or work experience in estate agency, on a building site, with computers.

Career-break It is too early to know how returners would fare but, if they have kept up with developments, there is no reason why experienced technicians should not return to work. It would probably be easier in general practice and quantity surveying than, say, in agricultural surveying.

Part time Not at the moment, except, perhaps, in quantity surveying but no reason why experienced technicians should not try and make their own part-time or job-share arrangements, especially in estate agency work.

Position of women The proportion of women members of the Society of Surveying Technicians is minute (though there have been draughtswomen for a long time), well below 1%. However, especially in planning, estate agency (general practice) and quantity surveying, there are good opportunities for women, but very few are applying for training or jobs. Only tradition is keeping this area of employment virtually a male preserve.

Further information Society of Surveying Technicians, Surveyor Court, Westwood Way, Coventry CV4 8JE

BTEC and SCOTVEC (see pp. xxi, xxii)

The Chartered Surveyors Training Trust, 9 Bentinck Street, London W1M 5RP

National Association of Estate Agents, Arbon House, 21 Jury Street, Warwick CV34 4EH

Related careers ARCHITECTURE: *Architectural Technician* – BUILDING – *Chartered Surveyor* (*above*) – HOUSING MANAGEMENT

Tax Inspector

Entry qualifications

First- or second-class honours or post-graduate degree in any subject or equivalent. (Opportunities also for those starting as Tax Officer, see 'Executive Officers', p. 126).

The work

Tax Inspectors work in the Inland Revenue department of the Civil Service. Their main duty is to investigate the accounts of business concerns in order to agree the amount of profits for taxation purposes. By examining accounts and interviewing individuals they aim to spot any cases of tax evasion or fraud. They also advise taxpayers on tax and business law. Their work brings them into contact with the whole range of Britain's industry and commerce in their own district.

They deal with many kinds of people – accountants, lawyers, industrialists, farmers, small shopkeepers – by personal interview as well as by correspondence. They also represent the Crown before an independent tribunal when they and the taxpayer concerned cannot agree on the tax assessment.

There are District Offices in all areas. Promotion prospects are best for people willing to move to where there happens to be a vacancy. Opportunities also exist outside the Civil Service as tax advisers to companies and individuals.

Training

On the job. During the 3 years' initial training inspectors take part-time and residential courses to a professional standard and have to pass examinations which qualify for promotion.

Personal attributes

Common sense; judgement; administrative ability; keen intellect; the ability to sum up people and situations; impartiality; equanimity; enjoyment of responsibility.

Career-break

See CIVIL SERVICE, p. 136.

Late start

See CIVIL SERVICE, p. 136.

Part time

Some opportunities. See CIVIL SERVICE, p. 136.

**Position
of
women**   See CIVIL SERVICE, p. 136.

**Further
informa-
tion**   Graduate and Schools Liaison, Room 127/2, Horse Guards Road,
                London SW1P 3AL

**Related
careers**   ACCOUNTANCY – ACTUARY – BANKING – INSURANCE – CIVIL
                   SERVICE

Teaching

The image of teaching has suffered in recent years. Though there sometimes seems little consensus about what schools are actually for, they are blamed for failing to deliver. Constant change and criticism have undoubtedly taken their toll. Teachers admit to feeling over-stressed, underpaid and undervalued. They are charged with falling standards of achievement and discipline. Some of the continuous changes they are required to implement they disagree with; others they support but are forced to carry out without adequate time, support or resources.

Yet there are still plenty of people who can make a good case for teaching as a career. Two points are clear: good teachers are the key to any worthwhile educational reform and national prosperity, and for many teachers their rewards stand up to comparison with many more glamorous, less beleaguered professions.

It is vital overall that first-class teachers be recruited and retained, but supply and demand does vary from subject to subject. There is great competition to recruit graduates with backgrounds in maths, science, technological subjects and modern languages. The requirements of the National Curriculum will exacerbate many of these shortages as children who would have dropped subjects are compelled to carry on with them. To combat shortages, the Teacher Training Agency will be running a 'Priority Subject Recruitment Scheme' for maths, technology, science, modern foreign languages and religious studies. The demand for primary teachers is increasing and many parts of the country are particularly short of 'early years' teachers. Primary teachers with special knowledge and skills in areas of the National Curriculum such as science and technology are likely to have excellent prospects.

Entry qualifications

A degree plus GCSE A–C (or equivalent) in maths and English language. (A pass in a science subject will be required for intending primary teachers born on or after 1 September 1979 and beginning training after 1 September 1998.)

Primary Schools
(including Nursery)

The work   Primary schools are generally organized in two broad categories, infant and junior or first and middle. The age ranges vary slightly; sometimes the break is made at 7, sometimes at 8. Most children go on to secondary school at 11, but some remain at their primary/middle school until 12 or 13. Sometimes the younger and older primary children go to separate schools; in other cases a single school deals with the whole primary range. Some schools have attached nursery units, taking children at 3 or 4. (N.B. To teach in a state-maintained nursery school you must be a qualified teacher, though there may be unqualified assistants.)

The precise organization of primary education varies from one local education authority to another. Schools also vary greatly in size, location and catchment area. Some schools will have as few as 2 teachers, others as many as 30. In the former case each teacher will teach several age groups; in the latter several teachers will share responsibility for an age group, sometimes through 'team teaching'.

Nursery and lower primary children learn largely through play and activity, which are planned and supervised by the teacher to achieve certain goals. So a bright child might be 'playing' in such a way that will develop manipulative skills which lag behind his or her reading, while a listening game might be devised for those children who have poor concentration. The teacher is observing all the time to recognize which areas need working on for each child. Children of this age are extremely demanding, able to work independently for only very short periods of time, demanding attention and cuddles and asking endless questions of the person who is usually next to Mummy and Daddy in importance in their lives. (And of course some children don't have a Mummy and/or Daddy.)

Formal teaching in the primary school is introduced gradually. Much work remains individual. The teacher fosters the growing ability of the children to work independently, both as individuals and in groups. Much work is integrated into multi-disciplinary topics or projects with the emphasis on stimulating children's natural curiosity and enthusiasm and widening their experience. The teacher has to plan the topic, relating it to the age group; make sure all the necessary resources are to hand; check that it meets the National Curriculum attainment targets in the appropriate subjects and record them; see in which areas of the curriculum the topic isn't working and go back to those subjects.

One of the primary teacher's most important skills is classroom management. It includes timetabling, the grouping of children and the organization of the classroom. Learning time is wasted if the most boisterous child sits with those of his or her peers least able to cope, or if children involved in a messy activity have constantly to move among children quietly engaged to get to their materials.

Primary teachers normally take their classes for all subjects, all day. The demands of the National Curriculum and the introduction of new subjects have led many teachers to take additional in-service specialist training to enable them to act as advisers or co-ordinators for a particular subject within their schools. Primary teachers do not have as much marking as the teachers of older children, but lesson preparation can take up a good deal of time. Time is also spent on assessment and recording, organizing displays, extracurricular activities and maintaining good relationships with parents.

Secondary Schools

The work   Commonly at the age of 11, but sometimes at 12 or 13, children transfer to secondary school. Most children go to comprehensive schools, which cater for the whole range of ability. Some authorities, however, have retained a selective system with the more academically able children going to grammar schools. In some authorities children remaining in full-time education at 16 + go to sixth-form colleges, some of which offer a traditional sixth-form curriculum, while others offer a more diverse range of courses.

Unlike primary teachers, secondary teachers teach a limited number of, usually, closely related subjects to many different age and ability groups throughout the day and week. Within the framework of their specialist knowledge, they need the teaching skills to establish working relationships with, for example, the unmotivated, the slow learners, the young pupils who look to the teacher for everything, and the sixth-formers who test them with profound questions. They must try to stimulate the interest of all pupils and help them to achieve the best they can, whether it be 2 hard-earned GCSEs or 3 top grade A-levels. This demands enthusiasm and flexibility.

Secondary teachers obviously need a good grounding in their subjects, but they do not need to know it all. Modern education is about learning how to learn, handling data, developing thinking and problem-solving skills. These are skills and challenges for teachers as well as pupils.

Secondary teachers spend a good deal of time (much of it out of school hours) on preparation and marking. They must be clear what they are going to achieve in each lesson, following the scheme of work as planned in the syllabus, and have the necessary material ready at each point, in each lesson, every day of the week. Good organization is vital. Formal assessment and recording have, in recent years, involved teachers in a good deal of additional administrative work, but much assessment is intuitive and goes on all the time with teachers watching to see if their pupils are keen, interested, responsive and so on.

Most teachers have responsibilities in addition to their subject teaching. Personal and social education, for example, is often a shared responsibility. Time is taken up in registration, form time, assemblies, administration, departmental and other meetings with colleagues, contact with parents. Many teachers get involved in a range of extracurricular activities, from sport to drama, to chess or other special interest clubs, which can take up considerable time. Some plan and accompany children on trips. In addition, everyone on the staff shares responsibility for standards and so is effectively 'on duty' throughout the day, watching out for, preventing and dealing with problems.

It is a fallacy that, once established, a teacher can do the same things year after year. New subjects are introduced; old subjects develop and are approached in new ways; teaching and examining methods change; each class is different. Good teachers need to update and evaluate their work constantly, deciding what to change, what to repeat, finding the right method for a particular pupil or group.

Special Needs Education

Children may have special educational needs for a variety of reasons ranging from emotional or behavioural disturbance, through specific learning difficulties, to complex multiple physical and/or mental handicaps. Increasingly, such children are, whenever possible, educated in ordinary schools. Depending on circumstances the child might be integrated into an ordinary class but have special help or be in a special unit or class attached to an ordinary school. Some children still need to go to special schools, sometimes for the whole of their schooling, sometimes only for short periods.

The work is emotionally and physically demanding. The teacher is involved not only in teaching academic subjects but also has to help pupils to overcome problems in a range of day-to-day activities, such as eating or playing. The teacher needs to build up a good relationship with the child, but also with the others concerned with the child's welfare and development, e.g. doctors, social workers, speech and language therapists, physiotherapists, psychologists.

Apart from teachers of the blind, deaf and partially hearing, special needs teachers do not need special qualifications. It is usual to gain teaching qualifications (see below) and experience of teaching 'normal' children before moving into special needs work and taking in-service training courses.

Independent Schools

Independent education covers a very wide range of institutions, from the renowned public schools to Montessori nursery schools. Some are based on a traditional academic approach while others are very 'progressive'. Many have outstanding records in preparing their pupils for external examinations and higher education, while others compare unfavourably with good state schools. Some pay their teachers considerably more than the scale for teachers in the maintained sector while others fall far short.

Teachers in independent schools do not need to be professionally qualified. A good honours degree is usually the required qualification. However, many independent school teachers do have a professional teaching qualification which enhances their flexibility in the jobs market. There are courses and qualifications of interest to particular sectors of independent education (e.g. Montessori and Rudolf Steiner), but these do not qualify one to teach in state schools.

Further Education

Many of the courses offered in the further education sector have a vocational bias. Some colleges are devoted to one particular field, e.g. agriculture. However, colleges also offer a broad range of other courses, from GCSEs and A-levels (which many students take in conjunction with vocational studies) to leisure interests such as painting, foreign languages and keep fit. Increasing numbers of school-leavers are continuing their education in FE colleges and some local education authorities are making them the focus of 16 + provision.

You do not need a professional teaching qualification (see below) to teach in further education. What is important is experience and/or qualifications in the field you wish to teach. However, a few colleges offer training for FE teachers, and other qualified teachers do compete for jobs. What precisely is required is likely to depend on supply and demand and the subjects involved. For example, a PGCE (see below) is likely to be more of an advantage for a teacher of a GCSE course than for someone teaching a BTEC in engineering.

Higher Education

In higher education, a higher degree is normally required for teaching. One's academic qualifications are far more important than certified teaching skills. The role of higher education institutions is not merely to pass on knowledge, but to extend it, so research is an important element of work in this sector. Administration is another key task. Higher education is facing a period of growth and diversification.

Training

There are 2 main methods of initial teacher training leading to Qualified Teacher Status (QTS):

1. Bachelor of Education degree (B.Ed.). Entry qualifications are 3 GCSEs (A–C) or equivalent, including English language and maths, plus 2 A-levels or equivalent. Courses normally last 4 years and include classroom work, professional practice (theory of education, child development, etc.) and subject study. Students normally specialize in the teaching of certain age ranges and subjects, but they are not restricted to those in their subsequent careers. Most primary teachers qualify by this route. Not all secondary subjects are available on B.Ed. courses, so most secondary teachers qualify by method (2) below.

2. Post-graduate Certificate of Education (PGCE). Entry qualifications are an appropriate degree plus GCSE (A–C) in English language and maths. Courses normally last 1 year and do not concentrate on subject knowledge but on professional skills. Course structures vary, but all must include 24 weeks (out of 36) in schools.

A number of variations on the PGCE theme are evolving. There is a small but growing number of *2-year part-time PGCE courses* in certain subjects. There are also *2-year conversion PGCE courses* for graduates wishing to teach a subject which was not the subject of their first degree; subjects available include maths, physics, chemistry, modern languages, CDT (craft, design and technology) and music. There is also an *Open University PGCE course*, which lasts 18 months and combines distance-learning and teaching practice under the guidance of a local tutor.

Under the new SCITT scheme (School-Centred Initial Teacher Training Scheme), consortia of schools organize 1-year's school-based training for graduates which leads to QTS.

There are a number of other 4-year degree courses which lead concurrently to a teaching qualification. For additional schemes aimed mainly at mature entrants, see 'Late entry', below.

NOTES ON THE SCOTTISH SYSTEM: To be eligible for permanent teaching appointments in maintained schools in Scotland, teachers must be registered with the General Teaching Council for Scotland. To be eligible to register one must hold a Teaching Qualification, in either Primary Education, Secondary Education or Further Education.

The patterns of qualification are similar to those in England. Unlike in England, however, one is registered to teach a particular age range and, in the case of secondary education, a particular subject or subjects. *Primary teachers* may take *either* a 4-year B.Ed., for which the normal entry requirements are 3 SCE Higher passes and 2 Standard or O-Grade passes (English must be passed at H-grade, maths at either grade), *or* a 1-year post-graduate course for which a UK degree plus H-grade English and Standard or O-grade maths are required. *Secondary teachers* usually take a 1-year post-graduate course in specific subjects following first degrees with sufficient specified achievement in the relevant subjects. There are secondary B.Ed.s in physical education, music and technology.

As in England, alternative equivalent qualifications may be acceptable for entry. Mature students may get some concessions, but the requirement for maths and English must be met. Teachers who have trained outside Scotland and who have suitable qualifications may be admitted to the register, in some cases after additional training.

Teachers in further education do not need to be registered. The course for registration is open only to serving teachers seconded by their authority.

Personal attributes Liking for children and young people; patience; sense of humour; enthusiasm; flexibility; fairness and consistency; confidence; optimism; organizing ability; sensitivity; good communication skills; ability to work on one's own and as part of a team.

Late start There are good prospects. In 1993 1 in 3 of all students on initial teacher training courses was over 26. There are a number of initiatives for such students:

1. Shortened B.Ed. In a number of subjects (maths, chemistry, physics, modern languages, music, business studies and CDT) there are shortened 2-year B.Ed. courses for those who already

have appropriate technical or professional qualifications and experience.

2. Licensed teacher scheme. LEAs have discretion to take on suitably qualified candidates who are employed as classroom teachers and trained on the job. The period of training normally lasts 2 years, but may be shorter for those with some teaching experience. Licensed teachers must be at least 24, have GCSE (A–C) or equivalent in English language and maths, and have successfully completed at least 2 years' full-time (or part-time equivalent) higher education.

3. Teacher training colleges may be able to offer alternative tests or recommend 'access' (see p. xxxi) courses for those who do not have the specified formal qualifications for entry to an appropriate course.

Career-break

The education authorities are keen to attract teachers back from the 'PIT' (pool of inactive teachers). Initiatives include special courses for returners and 'keeping in touch' courses and the encouragement of flexible working arrangements such as supply work, part-time work and job-sharing. The Information Section of the Teacher Training Agency provides a directory of courses and guidance notes for returners. Teachers who return on a regular full- or part-time basis are entitled to be paid at a point on the standard national scale no lower than the point on which they were last regularly paid. Employers can take into account any experience or qualifications gained during the break in deciding whether to appoint at a higher point.

Part time

Depends on local situation, subjects offered and so on. Supply work, part time and job-sharing are all possibilities.

Position of women

Teaching offers many women something they want: the opportunity to do a professional job but work school hours and term-time only. A career-break can be relatively easily fitted in as well. Of course, that is only part of the story. While a woman teacher can certainly be home during the school holidays, the normal workload extends far beyond the formal end of the school day. Women's inability or unwillingness to take on additional responsibility because of family commitments and the time and experience lost during a career-break are two factors in women's under-representation at the higher levels of the profession. The male-dominated education establishment and indirect discrimination are claimed to be other factors. In primary schools, where about 80% of teachers are women, men are 4.4 times more likely to be heads. In secondary schools, 60% of teachers are women, but men are 3.3 times more likely to be heads. These figures are little changed since 1988, though women's chances in secondary schools have improved marginally.

Further information

The Advisory Service on Entry to Teaching in Scotland, 5 Royal Terrace, Edinburgh EH7 5AF

Information Section, Teacher Training Agency, Portland House, Stag Place, London SW1E 5TT

Related careers

CAREERS WORK – NURSERY NURSE – PERSONNEL/HUMAN RESOURCES MANAGEMENT – SOCIAL WORK – YOUTH AND COMMUNITY WORK

Television, Film and Radio

Entry qualifications

Very varied but marked trend towards graduates. IT skills are almost essential.

This whole area is going through a period of unprecedented change, both technological and organizational, with a dramatic impact on career and training opportunities. Large numbers of staff have been shed as, increasingly, IT franchise holders will buy in, rather than originate, programmes, and so have no permanent production staff or facilities. The BBC, too, has been cutting back on staff, recruitment and training, and, in common with ITV companies, is required to commission 25% of its output from independent companies. It is in the independent, non-broadcast sector that there is likely to be most growth. The whole industry relies increasingly on freelances. Most 'career' opportunities lie in management/administration/sales.

TV, Film and Video

The industry consists mainly of the 'terrestrial' (as opposed to satellite) broadcasting companies and independent companies producing for broadcast, the corporate sector (e.g. training and corporate image promotional film and videos), commercials, music promotion and feature films. There are also production facilities in educational establishments and community-based units. Satellite and cable have gone into production in a limited way, but they still buy in most of their programmes and offer most job opportunities in sales and marketing and on the technical side. The boundaries between the sectors of the industry are becoming increasingly blurred. Independents commonly work in more than one sector, e.g. both making programmes for broadcast and doing corporate work. The broadcast companies are also diversifying into, for example, corporate work or making programmes for satellite and cable.

A wide range of jobs is involved. In 1989 the Institute of

Manpower Studies undertook a study into the industry. They identified more than 100 jobs in the different sectors, but the terminology and job content can vary considerably. Job titles are not clear-cut. In addition, there is an industry-wide trend towards 'multi-skilling'. Sometimes this is the result of technical development when, for example, 1 piece of equipment and operator can do what previously took 2 pieces and 2 operators. Another impetus is the need for a more flexible workforce; film editors learn video editing in order to survive.

Put simply, activities can be divided into pre-production, production and post-production. Each has a range of different jobs involved, but people tend to be employed (as freelances) not until, and then only while, they are needed. Also, distinctions between jobs are blurring as people need to do more to keep employed.

Below are some of the programme-making jobs involved in broadcast TV. They are based on the BBC, but similar jobs are needed elsewhere in programme production, including the growing independent sector. Where possible indications of the kind of qualifications and training normally needed are given, but see 'Notes on entry and training', p. 536.

Production Staff

Producers/directors

The work   Exact functions vary. Producers are usually responsible for initiating, budgeting, casting, and the shape or 'treatment' of programmes. Directors are responsible for interpreting the idea and actually making the programme. These top jobs are very responsible and are done by specialists in particular fields, such as current affairs, drama, education, science or technology, who have long, often technical experience in the medium. Many work on contracts for particular projects.

Production assistants

They provide organizational support to a programme. They may do some research, make bookings, arrange meetings, sit with the producer in the gallery checking on timing, cue the inserts of film or tape and are normally responsible for continuity. They have considerable contact with people both inside and outside TV. Where there is no production secretary in a department they perform any necessary secretarial duties. They are normally recruited from among *production secretaries*.

Production secretaries

Entrants who start as secretaries may become secretary to a producer, if they are lucky and have exceptionally good secretarial skills. They see to it that the right instructions about make-up, costumes, sets, rehearsal times and studio bookings go to the right people. They type (and often re-type) the shooting script. Not all programmes (e.g. drama) have a secretary, but, especially in the independent sector, this is a good career route for men as well as women.

Floor managers (known as 'stage managers' in outside broadcasts)

They may be involved at the planning stage in advising on design, sound and props. During recording they control the studio floor. They are responsible for discipline on the floor and for safety of staff and artists. Duties include relaying the producer's/director's instructions to actors and presenters, using headphones to keep in touch with the gallery. They are responsible for cueing the actors, which can be a complicated task as they are often working on different sets and cannot see each other. The floor manager has to move around the sets while keeping out of camera shot. A diplomatic, pleasant personality is essential. In outside broadcasts they have to liaise with the general public.

Entry   Nearly all from the ranks of assistant floor managers or other production posts.

Assistant floor manager

Similar to assistant stage manager in the theatre. Work varies according to size and type of production, but usually includes making sure that all the props are available, taking charge of the prompt book and mark-ups during rehearsals. Assistant floor managers usually start their on-the-job training with the easier talks and discussion programmes before going on to drama series etc.

Entry   Candidates are expected to have experience in professional stage management, in theatre, film or TV.

Researchers

The majority of researchers are freelance. Research may be anything from looking through newspaper cuttings and finding a suitable person to be interviewed – not by researcher but by interviewer/presenter – on a news programme, to spending several months researching the background for a documentary or drama series. Researchers must be good all-rounders, able to pick out relevant facts from a mass of material. They usually write 'briefs', which may range from a few questions which an interviewer is to ask on a programme, to exhaustive background material for a documentary scriptwriter. Researchers in current affairs must also be able to think up programme ideas and to work under tremendous pressure. Specialist researchers, for example for scientific or medical programmes, are often freelances.

Entry   Usually graduates and/or ex-journalists, or by promotion from within.

News staff, presenters, interviewers
Newsroom staff compile and write scripts for the *presenters*; *reporters* and *correspondents* 'get the stories' and present some themselves. The essence of broadcast news is brevity. *TV and radio journalists* (there is a trend for all journalists to have to work in both media) must be instant fact-selectors and decision-makers. They may be sent anywhere at any time. *Editors* are senior staff responsible for piecing a programme together.

Entry   Entrants are almost invariably graduates (any subject) with keen interest in current affairs, but 'general education' plus proven journalistic ability (i.e. good job on a good paper) can also lead in.

Design

Set designers
They are responsible for designing the sets down to the smallest accessories in accordance with the producer's concept. The producer calls in the designer when the idea is beginning to take shape. The designers' interpretation of the atmosphere the producer has in mind and their own suggestions are vitally important to the success of the production. They must have a good grasp of the technicalities of production.

Design assistants work with the designer on the technical, rather than creative, tasks. They draw ground plans and make working drawings; draw up specifications; make models of sets; and make or search for props.

Graphic designers and their *assistants* create credit titles, 'linking material', captions, maps and general illustrations. This is now frequently done using computers, but nevertheless it is still essentially creative work.

Scenic artists and *assistants* paint backcloths and decorative features such as curtains, carpets and portraits.

Visual effects designers and *assistants* devise, make and operate a wide variety of visual effects and 'illusions'.

Entry   Whatever the level of entry qualifications, all first appointments are to the post of assistant. Generally speaking, progress to designer is from design assistant. All design assistants need degree level qualification in relevant art discipline. Additionally, graphic design assistants normally need commercial art experience (e.g advertising) following a degree or diploma; scenic artists need wide knowledge of painting, history of art and architecture and interior design; visual effects staff need to be able to work in all kinds of materials, make models and have a basic grasp of physics. Most design is 'outsourced', that is, done by freelances or those working in facilities houses. Some companies employ designers as project managers.

Costume designers (also called 'wardrobe')
They are in charge of hiring, designing and adapting up-to-date and period costumes. They are called in on new productions at an early stage to discuss the costumes and to advise on whether to hire, make or adapt, and to arrange for this to be done. Later they liaise with other designers and make-up staff. They need a thorough knowledge of period styles, but further research is often needed to make certain of representing the exact year or season. Assistants help designers in all aspects of their work and may stand in for them, e.g. when filming on location.

Entry   Preferably with a theatre or textile design degree and considerable experience in theatre or film costume. All entrants start at assistant level, from which designers are promoted. Assistants must be at least 19 with an A-level standard of education and a good knowledge of costume design and history (a degree or diploma is essential for promotion to designer). Virtually all work is done on a freelance or short-contract basis.

Dressmakers make up costumes under the supervision of designers and make alterations to costumes which are hired or from stock.

Entry   With BTEC/SCOTVEC Higher National Diploma in Fashion and a minimum of 2 years' experience in the theatre or with a theatrical costumier. Knowledge of history of costume an advantage.

Dressers work on last-minute ironing and maintenance of costumes and help actors to dress for performance.

Make-up artists/designers
Television make-up is highly skilled. It requires the ability to understand and defeat the camera's often unkind effects on faces.

It also requires a thorough knowledge of period hairstyles. An experienced senior assistant is usually in charge of each dramatic production and makes up the star actors. Juniors see to the rest of the cast and also look after the simpler make-up required for non-dramatic productions. Tact and diplomacy are essential.

Entry   Most make-up artists train privately, which is expensive.

Technical Operations

These concern the technical interpretation of the director's instructions and producing the required sound and vision effects which are finally seen and heard. Most TV programmes are pre-recorded. When recording a programme as well as during 'live' transmission, previously recorded and/or filmed material may be slotted in. The operational and technical sides of creating programmes and getting them on to TV screens are highly complex and require creativity, technical expertise and an unflappable temperament.

Camera operators help in setting up and operating electronic cameras and associated equipment in studios and on outside broadcasts. Promotion is to assistant and later cameraman/woman, vision supervisor, vision controller and ultimately possibly to technical manager responsible for lighting (various titles).

Sound assistants help in setting up and operating sound recording and reproduction equipment; they 'collect sound effects', and may eventually become sound supervisors responsible for control and balance of the various sound sources which are combined for final transmission. They are London-based in the BBC.

Audio assistants do similar work to sound assistants but they work in the regional (smaller) centres, and are also involved in the operation of radio sound equipment in joint radio/TV centres.

Recording operators control the increasingly sophisticated videotape and telecine (the film equivalent) equipment. They set up and run the recorders and must respond instantly to the producer's requirements. Recordings may be for instant replay or later transmission.

Entry and training   Minimum age 18. GCSEs (A–C) in English language, maths and physics. Applicants for training courses should also have a keen interest in, and some 'hobby experience' of, hi-fidelity reproduction, tape-recording music, colour photography or lighting for amateur dramatics, and, for sound operators, ability to read a musical score. A strong interest in current affairs and IT skills are also very useful.

Vision-mixer

Up to 6 cameras may be in operation during a production. The producer in the control room decides which camera's picture to send out to the audience, and tells the vision-mixer, who switches to the selected camera as the order is given. This needs concentration and quick reflexes.

Training   Mostly on the job for existing TV staff.

Engineering

Some TV engineers work in studios, outside broadcasting, coping with emergency repairs and sudden equipment failure, generally acting as technical 'back-up'. Others are responsible for operation and maintenance of equipment used to route, control and distribute signals from various sound and vision programme sources. All this work can be hectic and needs quick decision-making and a cool head. Other departments are concerned with research, development, planning, installation of a variety of complex equipment (see ENGINEERING, p. 181, for engineering functions). In a time of changing technology they must be prepared to update their knowledge and assimilate new ideas quickly. Currently, this is one of the areas being reduced, with a blurring of distinctions between traditional engineering and IT skills.

Entry and training   Increasingly, employers are favouring some specialist degree courses.

Filming for TV

Film camera and sound staff are quite distinct from TV camera and sound staff. A considerable amount of television material is filmed (although most is on videotape); whole programmes are filmed, e.g. schools broadcasts, documentaries; film is also used as an important ingredient in all kinds of programmes – light entertainment, current affairs, children's programmes, plays and series. Camera crews travel a lot and at short notice. There are three basic jobs: *editing*, *camera*, *sound* (titles may vary).

Film editors work entirely in the cutting-room, 'editing down' material shot in the studio or on location. A great deal of their work is done on their own initiative, as directors do not have time to be with editors all day. The job is highly creative as it is the editor who shapes and fashions the final programme which audiences see, but very few editors work purely with film. Editing can lead to directing.

Film camera crews usually consist of 2–4 people. The head of the camera crew is in charge of lighting; works in close co-operation with the director; knows the script thoroughly and arranges the all-important lighting and camera angles for each individual shot, so as to achieve the atmosphere the director wants. Lighting cameraman/woman can be an important step to directing film.

Assistant camera crews load and change magazines, make sure the right equipment is available at the right time and place and in working order, and they learn how to operate cameras and lighting equipment. Promotion is pretty slow – it takes about 10 years to reach lighting cameraman/woman status.

Rostrum camera crew record on film and tape the artwork produced by the *graphic designers* (see p. 529).

Film sound recordists/sound technicians are concerned with dubbing, sound-transfer and above all with mixing sound from various sources. This may include location recordings on tape, and sounds produced by effects machines. Achieving the correct balance, controlling the 'input' from various sources, is a highly skilled job, requiring great technical skill and musical creativity.

Assistants manipulate microphones and other recording equipment and learn by watching. Far fewer apply for sound than vision jobs so chances of acceptance are better.

Projectionists (or *film assistants*) operate projection equipment and may also work on dubbing.

Entry qualifications and training (TV film)

Interest and 'hobby experience' are crucial. There are a number of film/TV courses at art schools, either as part of an art and design degree course, or 2–3-year BTEC/SCOTVEC Diploma courses, or at post-graduate level. Course emphasis (and entry requirements) vary enormously: for example on closed circuit educational television films; on feature or instructional films; with technical or creative bias, etc.

Film and Video Industry

Feature film making has for several years been a depressed part of the industry in Britain. The future demands of cable TV and the home video market should provide greater opportunities than the recent past. However, entry into cinema film making will remain very highly competitive. The only real job prospects lie with the growing number of often very small production companies which combine TV film making and, very occasionally, cinema, with the whole range of other productions, e.g. training and advertising films.

Video recorders, while not offering the same 'creative' scope as film cameras, have very wide and growing applications: sales promotions (e.g. for pop records and at 'point of sale' in shops), training of all kinds, recording ballets for a dance company's repertoire, monitoring the performance of racehorses during meetings. Many companies use only freelance staff as and when they need them and many of these specialize, e.g. in making wildlife or travel films. Studio facilities and sophisticated equipment are often hired from 'facility houses' which do not themselves make programmes.

Entry and training
There is no essential difference between filming for TV and making non-broadcast films. Similarly, people employed in video production do much the same work as those in films.

There are no jobs which can be done straight from school. Entry is normally via one of the following:

1. TV training and experience.

2. An appropriate diploma, degree or post-graduate course at film school or art college (titles and content vary, so it is essential to study prospectuses carefully).

3. An electronic engineering course (all levels) plus in-service training.

4. The FT^2 scheme (supported by all sides of the film and TV industry) started in 1985 as JOBFIT to co-ordinate new entrant training in the *freelance film industry*. Candidates are considered not only on the basis of academic qualifications, but also on a proven commitment to the industry (i.e. through amateur film and video-making). The scheme lasts 2 years. Year 1 is general, with attachments to editing, camera, sound or art departments. Trainees then choose their specialization and spend the second year in their chosen area.

5. Specialized knowledge leading to making videos on a particular topic.

6. Very occasionally, extensive amateur experience.

There is more scope for versatility in video than in film making: people tend to work 'cross-sectorally', that is, move from one type of work to another fairly easily. Technicians need to be able to work in both film and television. There is always room in this expanding industry for really good technical people.

Radio

Independent radio has more than 50% of the listening audience. They therefore account for the bulk of jobs – and most of those are in sales or advertising.

Entry routes differ between BBC network, BBC local (which has made a positive decision to become journalism-based) and independent local radio. Once trained it is possible to move from one to another. Below are some examples from network radio.

Production

Producers are responsible for initiating and developing programme ideas. They need an interest in the creative use of radio, a journalistic approach, some experience in relevant subject areas, e.g. the arts, science, medicine, social issues, drama, comedy, popular music, etc. and good technical skills. Work formerly done by studio managers is now done by producers. Producers are recruited from within the BBC – from local radio, researchers, studio managers, and radio production assistants, for example; by direct advertising in the press; via the radio production trainee scheme.

Radio production assistants help producers by providing all-round administrative back-up for a programme, varying from typing scripts to helping in the studio. They are recruited from secretarial and clerical staff within the BBC or direct from outside.

Researchers work on individual programme strands. They will have specialist knowledge and skills. They may be recruited by direct advertising in the press and work mainly on short-term contracts which can vary from 1 month to 1 year.

Continuity announcers/newsreaders are recruited from existing broadcasters in local radio or from other employees with good, clear voices. They work on their own and need to be good at problem-solving. Occasionally jobs will be advertised in the press; previous broadcasting is generally required.

Sports assistants and correspondents often come from local radio, or have experience as sports journalists on newspapers. They need a good broadcasting style, an all-round knowledge of sport and more detailed commitment to one or more sports.

Reporters who work on all the main 'magazine' programmes from *Woman's Hour* to *Kaleidoscope* are freelances who generally started their careers on local or independent radio.

NOTES ON ENTRY AND TRAINING (TO THE INDUSTRY GENER-
ALLY)

The uncertainty in the industry in recent years has meant that
training schemes in independent television have virtually ceased.
The BBC continues to run many of its training schemes, but they
are likely to take fewer people and run not on an annual basis but
according to operational need. These schemes are an excellent
way into the industry but they are intensely competitive. As far as
the numbers entering are concerned, they have only ever been the
tip of the iceberg. For example, in 1990 the BBC recruited about
3,500 permanent staff (i.e. those not on short-term contracts).
Only 6% of those – about 200 people – were trainees (across the
board in all areas). 31% were secretarial/clerical staff. The remainder covered all other areas, including finance, law and personnel.

Some of those secretaries will make it to production (many will
not) because this is still a foot-in-the-door industry. The IMS
survey (see pp. 526–7) looked at first jobs in the broadcast TV
industry and where they led. More than two-thirds of employees
had started in one of 7 first jobs: engineering technician, technical
assistant, secretarial/administration, sound assistant/trainee,
camera assistant, trainee editor and assistant floor manager. Many
of these led to a diverse range of careers. For example, nearly half
the technical assistants had become engineers, but more than half
were in sound, camera, light, post-production, production and
producer/director jobs. Looking back to first jobs, 158 producers/
directors reported 27 different first jobs: 13% had started as
production assistants, 12% in secretarial/admin work. Though
53% of those in camera grades had started as camera assistants,
6% had started in secretarial/administration.

Clearly, the 'take-any-job-do-anything' strategy can work. But
it is not easy to get these first jobs. On the operational side you
need to get skills and that means you need to be enterprising.
Hospital and local radio often need volunteers and can offer
'hands-on' experience. Get involved in amateur theatre or make
your own videos or recordings. Watch television and become
aware of companies' output.

Independent production and facilities companies, corporate in-
house production units, major educational and franchise workshops are likely to be growth sectors and can provide experience
that can take you into the broadcast companies as permanent
staff or on a freelance basis (*all* sectors increasingly use freelances).
They are also career outlets in themselves. Most are very new
(formed since 1981) and very small. Probably about three-quarters
of them have 10 or fewer employees. Recruitment and training
patterns are haphazard, but a small organization can often offer

all-round experience. Corporate in-house production units offer employment to only a very few people, but they often have state-of-the-art equipment. Try knocking on doors – people have been known to get jobs this way, turning up just as someone was needed, or trying again and again and again *until* someone was needed. Consider taking a job as a 'runner' (most of whom are graduates in their 20s) – the person who makes the tea, does deliveries, deals with the post and answers the phone can really find out how the industry works and who does what, which is vital. Trade directories like the *BFI (British Film Institute) Directory* can be very useful sources of information.

Increasing numbers entering the industry, especially on the production side, are graduates. Relevant degrees in, for example, film and media studies are very popular, but they do not necessarily give candidates a head-start. What employers are looking for is a lively interest in current affairs and broadcasting, and evidence that you have got practically involved in a way to complement your interests. Nevertheless, some courses are favoured by employers. Before taking any 'relevant' course, question in what ways it will stretch your mind and help you to develop wide interests. Ask to see details of what previous graduates have done and whether NVQ accreditation is available.

Once in, most people develop their own careers. They may pick up new skills informally, by following around someone more experienced or experienced in a different area, or formally, as through the BBC's system of 'attachments' whereby staff can try out other jobs. The industry recognizes the need for more structured training, especially as the need for freelances increases, and is introducing NVQs (see p. xx). More than 30 will be available and they will cover every level up to senior technical, production and management grades.

Even when particular training is useful or essential, getting that training doesn't guarantee a job. Since it is recognized that the vast majority of listeners and viewers are not ABC1s, there is a trend towards recruiting from a wider background (i.e. not just middle-class Oxbridge graduates). Good team skills are essential; this is *not* an industry for prima donnas. Specific skills, for example the ability to speak Welsh or highly developed IT skills, can give you a head start. But, as ever, much depends on being the right person in the right place at the right time. The more you know about the industry, the nearer you are to being the right person – and the better able to find the right place.

SKILLSET is the industry's training organization. It is *vital* that anyone considering working in this complex and rapidly changing field contacts them. They have an excellent careers pack

538   Television, Film and Radio

on the shape of the industry – the employers, the jobs, the courses – with good advice on planning a strategy. They also maintain a database of training provision.

Personal attributes
Creative imagination; wide interests generally, a special interest in a particular subject; a clear, quick, logical mind; appreciation of what audiences want; a strong constitution; the ability to work as one of a team and to take responsibility; a sociable nature; a fairly thick skin; tact; calmness in crises; speed of action; self-confidence; determination and persistence; desire to communicate ideas; ability to take criticism; temperament and skills to be self-employed.

Late start
Scope mainly for people with relevant experience and qualifications, especially for experienced journalists and engineers. In general, people in this insecure, heavily freelance industry are getting younger.

Career-break
Depends on how well established before, but in some areas return presents problems. Companies are generous over maternity leave but it is essential to get back to work as soon as possible as there is so much competition. The National Film and Television School runs courses to update skills in the light of new technology.

Part time
The BBC is encouraging flexible working arrangements, including job-sharing. Many staff in the industry are freelance and work on short-term contracts.

Position of women
Women can do well. There are few institutional barriers to break down, and women's talents have long been recognized and rewarded. They are, in fact, in a tiny majority. There are good opportunities in management, and those working in the BBC benefit from some very advanced 'positive action'. HOWEVER, the hallmarks of this industry – for everyone – are competition, stress, long hours, lack of security, need for mobility – all distinctly 'mother-unfriendly'.

Further information
SKILLSET, 124 Horseferry Road, London SW1P 2TX

Related careers
ADVERTISING – ART AND DESIGN – DRAMA – JOURNALISM – MUSIC – PHOTOGRAPHY

Town and Country Planning

Entry qualifications

Degree or post-graduate qualification accredited by the Royal Town Planning Institute (see also 'Training', below).

Town Planners

The work

Planners aim to reconcile the community's desire for a high standard of environment for work, home and leisure with the conflicting demands for land from industry, traffic, etc. They are concerned, in broad terms, with civic design, urban renewal, land-use and transportation systems. The majority work in local authorities, some in the Civil Service and some in private consultancy firms. In recent years planning emphasis has changed. Planners have learnt from past experiments; for example instead of large-scale slum-clearance schemes which dispersed long-established communities, planners now recommend rehabilitation of existing houses, to keep 'urban villages' intact; or help revitalization of inner-city areas: as factories and inhabitants move out, small workshops are being created out of derelict warehouses and factories to attract light industry and create local jobs. Altogether, the social and economic consequences of planning are researched and considered much more thoroughly now than they were only a few years ago.

The planning process may be broadly broken down into two separate but interrelated functions:

Survey, analysis and research
Involves devising and conducting surveys of the structure, functioning, wishes and needs of communities and assessing problems and aims of urban and regional development. This is social research (see SOCIOLOGY, p. 482). Physical planners' final plans are based on the outcome of these findings.

Physical planning
Drawing up development plans and implementing them. When, for example, a twilight area is redeveloped, planners draw up plans for new road networks, for shopping precincts, leisure and

recreation facilities, the number and types of schools likely to be needed, etc.

Each county (see LOCAL GOVERNMENT, p. 265) is covered by a *Structure Plan* which outlines planning policy for that area in relation to neighbouring counties' Structure Plans. This is 'regional planning'. A county council planner might collate and analyse information in order to predict, for example, likely levels of need for transport, leisure facilities, schools, if plan 'A', proposing plans for increased industrial development, is implemented.

Structure Plans are mainly written policy statements. District planning authorities draw up *Local Plans*. These fit into a Structure Plan, and go into much more detail. They consist largely of maps and drawn plans. A Local Plan would show, for example, streets which are designated conservation areas; or a plan for small workshops and a shopping precinct. Local planners are also concerned with development control – dealing with planning applications from the public. Very broadly, there is more scope for improving the environment at Structure Plan-level planning; but more contact with the general public and such immediate environmental matters as closing roads and rerouting traffic, rehabilitating old houses rather than pulling them down, at Local Plan level.

Jobs are very dependent on public authority spending levels, although there are increasing opportunities in the private sector. There are occasional openings for experienced planners in developing countries, mainly on a short-contract basis.

Training   *Either*: 4-year full-time, 6-year part-time or 5-year sandwich degree accredited by the Royal Town Planning Institute; *or*: a degree in any subject followed by a 2-year full-time or 3-year part-time course accredited by the RTPI. A few schools of planning offer preparatory courses for people without the normal degree or professional qualifications (e.g. some BTEC Higher National award holders) which then give entry on to their accredited post-graduate courses.

After 2 years' practical planning experience, candidates who have fulfilled the academic requirements of the RTPI qualify for election to membership as Chartered Town Planners.

Sociologists, geographers, economists, architects, landscape architects and other specialists concerned with the various aspects of planning also work in planning departments, particularly in counties and big cities. For work concerned with overall strategic planning problems and policy, i.e. for senior posts, however, a planning qualification is essential.

See also ARCHITECTURE, 'Training' (p. 42).

Personal attributes   A keen interest in other people's priorities and way of life; powers of observation; creative imagination; patience for painstaking research; the ability to work as one of a team as well as to take responsibility; interest in social, economic and environmental developments.

Late start   Graduates with relevant degrees (geography, social science, engineering) could start post-graduate training. There is no specific upper age limit. An RPTI accredited 'distance-learning' course is available for people (graduates or non-graduates) who want to switch to planning from related careers (architects, geographers, engineers, etc.) in mid-career. It should also be useful for people returning after a *career-break*.

Career-break   Planning priorities and legislation change constantly, so planners must keep up with developments. There are 'mid-career' updating courses and seminars for all planners, which could be useful as *refresher* courses (see 'Late start', above). Returners can also take additional courses, for example in traffic engineering/planning at the returning stage. Reduced RTPI subscriptions available.

Part time   Experienced planners increasingly do freelance work. Some local authorities have job-sharing schemes. Part-time courses available (see above).

Position of women   About 20% of qualified and 42% of student members of the RTPI are women. Women do well up to middle-level jobs; very few are Chief Officers in local government planning departments.

Further information   The Royal Town Planning Institute, 26 Portland Place, London W1N 4BE

Planning Technicians

They are the support staff, carrying out various technical and practical tasks. These include drawing up of plans; preparing maps and diagrams; conducting surveys and interpreting results; dealing with inquiries from the public. They use computers for the various activities and may be in charge of a department's computer system.

Entry qualifications   4 GCSEs (A–C) including maths and a subject involving written English.

Prospects are not good at the moment as much technician work is done by graduates who cannot get higher level jobs, especially in the public sector.

Training   On the job with day-release for the BTEC National Certificate in Land Administration (or SCOTVEC Certificate in Planning) (see pp. xxi, xxii), which takes 2 years, with a further 2 years for the BTEC/SCOTVEC Higher National award. It is possible, but not usually recommended, to cross over to professional membership of the RTPI by taking a town planning degree after the BTEC National Certificate.

Late start   Few opportunities

Career-break   Could be difficult as no *refresher* training.

Part time   Very limited, but job-sharing should be possible.

Position of women   A growing number – 26% – of Society of Planning Technicians are women.

Further information   Society of Planning Technicians, 26 Portland Place, London W1N 4BE

Related careers   ARCHITECTURE: *Architectural Technician* – CARTOGRAPHY – ECONOMICS – ENGINEERING – HOUSING MANAGEMENT – LANDSCAPE ARCHITECTURE AND DESIGN – LOCAL GOVERNMENT – SURVEYING: *Auctioneers*

Trading Standards Officer

Entry qualifications

For the Diploma in Trading Standards: normally 2 A-levels, 3 GCSEs (A–C), including English, maths and physics at either level. *Graduate* entry about 60%. For the Diploma in Consumer Affairs: 5 GCSEs, including English language, or relevant experience.

For degree in consumer protection: 2 A-levels (no specific subject requirement, but GCSEs must include English, maths and science).

The work

Trading standards officers (TSOs) are employed mainly by local authorities to ensure a fair system of trading between consumers and traders and between traders themselves. They are responsible for the enforcement of a vast array of consumer protection legislation designed to protect the consumer from, for example, unsafe electrical products or short-weight goods. At the same time they try to ensure that no other trader suffers from the effect of such unfair trading practices. TSOs are interested in subjects as wide-ranging as food safety, metrology (science of weights and measures), animal health and welfare, consumer credit, misleading advertising, counterfeit goods and sales of restricted products to under-age children.

There are two main aspects to the work. The first is routine checking and inspecting to see that, for example, the motorist gets the amount of petrol indicated on the pump, that foods are properly labelled (the actual testing of food composition is carried out by public analysts), that heavy goods vehicles are not dangerously overloaded, that video films are correctly classified and labelled. Much of this is done openly, but test buying is also done. The other aspect is investigating complaints from consumers and traders. These may claim that a holiday brochure was misleading, that a 'pre-shrunk' shirt has shrunk two sizes in the wash, that a toy contained a dangerous sharp part, that the mileage on a second-hand vehicle was not what it was claimed to be, or that goods were over-priced. In each case the TSO has to gather the facts and, in the light of these, to decide whether or not the law has been broken. If it has, the TSO makes out a report and eventually decides whether to take the trader to court.

The establishment of a Single Market within the EU means that trading standards are having to be established to ensure fair competition within that market place. The result is a growing number of rules and regulations that must be monitored by TSOs.

The work is diverse and mainly carried out away from the office. It also involves working some unsocial hours. TSOs meet a great variety of people and have much scope for decision-making. Most authorities offer a good career structure within the constraints of local govenment spending. There are now increasing opportunities for TSOs to be employed by traders to ensure that they do not inadvertently break the law.

Training

The Diploma in Trading Standards is a statutory requirement for TSOs responsible for overseeing weighing and measuring legislation. The syllabus includes relevant civil and criminal law, metrology, statistics, trading practice, quality assurance, enforcement and advice.

Trainees *either* work in a trading standards department with block-release for study (normally 3 years) *or* take one of the few degrees in consumer protection, which give exemption from most of the written papers of the DST, followed by practical training in a department.

The Diploma in Consumer Affairs is a recognized qualification for people not involved in weighing and measuring, but who are employed for specific enforcement roles. They may work, for example, in consumer credit (including debt counselling), animal health inspection and food safety checking. Trainees learn on-the-job with distance-learning or, increasingly, day-release for study. They take 'core' subjects, such as investigation techniques and structure of trade, and modules on specific subjects. They can add other modules during their career.

Personal attributes

Ability to grasp a great many facts and apply them in a practical way; good communication skills, written and verbal; scrupulous attention to detail; self-confidence and ability to work on one's own unsupervised; ability to explain technical points clearly to traders and consumers; diplomacy.

Late start

In theory, people with a background in business or law should have reasonable chances. In practice, when vacancies for trainees are limited, as now, young graduates are often given preference.

Career-break

The steady demand for qualified officers means that it is becoming easier to take time out.

Part time Increasingly possible.

Position of women It used to be an all-male preserve, but this is changing rapidly. Currently 15% of TSOs are women, but they account for 55% of trainees. In associated areas such as consumer advice there are more women than men.

Further information Institute of Trading Standards Administration, 3–5 Hadleigh Business Centre, 351 London Road, Hadleigh, Essex SS7 2BT (or contact the local Trading Standards Office)

Related careers ENVIRONMENTAL HEALTH OFFICER – HEALTH AND SAFETY INSPECTORS – HOME ECONOMICS – LAW

Travel Agent/Tour Operator

Entry qualifications None specified, but entrants to travel agencies usually have several GCSEs. GNVQs/GSVQs (see p. xix) in Leisure and Tourism offer a travel and tourism option. Also increasing *graduate* entry (mainly tour operators). Foreign languages especially useful for incoming tourism.

Travel and tourism form the UK's biggest growth industry, employing 1·5 million people. It overlaps with the growing leisure industry and is essentially concerned with providing services for people who are away from home, on business or on holiday. These may be UK residents travelling within Britain or going abroad or 'incoming' tourists who make a substantial contribution to the UK economy. Both business and leisure travellers increasingly seek a broader range of services and more sophisticated or unusual ways of spending their time and money. The business traveller may want sports facilities and saunas. The holiday-maker may want to try hang-gliding, hill-walking, wine-tasting, bird-watching or painting.

Many jobs in tourism are concerned with providing accommodation and food – whether for farm-based holidays or international conferences. Other jobs are in transport operations – from hire car fleets to coach companies, airline operators to Caribbean cruise ships. Others are in entertainment and visitors' attractions, tourist information services and – increasingly important – marketing and promotions. Tourist information is both general and specific, ranging from selling Britain to potential visitors all over the world to helping a family find bed-and-breakfast accommodation in Northumbria.

As the industry becomes more complex and competitive, so it needs better-trained people who are adaptable, creative and thoroughly professional.

This section deals with 2 distinct sections of the industry: travel agencies and tour operators. A few large companies own agencies, operators and airlines.

Travel agents are the retailers. They sell tour operators' holidays, plan trips for people within the UK and abroad, and sell tickets for rail, air, ferry and coach travel. Some specialize in business travel, arranging travel and accommodation for company executives. *Tour operators* usually specialize in either incoming or outgoing operations. They put together and organize package holidays – anything from self-catering cabins in the Scottish Highlands to trekking in the Himalayas. Tour operators concentrate on planning – and selling – their holidays, with such subdivisions as British and foreign; summer and winter; business and holiday; party and individual packages. Although the bulk of the package holiday business is controlled by a few huge operators, there has been a growth in small companies catering for special interest holidays, for example cycling and art history tours.

Travel Agents

The work   *Counter work*

This is essentially selling. Clients (never called customers) may know what they want and simply buy a ticket for a train journey, or book a world tour, or want some travel literature. But most have no idea of what they want. Their leisure-time tastes must be summed up, and 'channelled' into what the counter-clerk thinks is the holiday they will most enjoy in a price range they can afford.

Counter-clerks usually have not been to the places they suggest – but they should know, from travel literature, from colleagues or training courses, as much about the holidays they recommend as possible. They must take trouble with each client; their responsibility is far greater than that of most other sales assistants. Most people 'buy' only one holiday a year, and if this one is not a success, they will go to another agency next year.

Business house clerks deal with companies, mainly over the telephone, making travel arrangements for their staff. In smaller agencies staff may share all the tasks.

All clerks perform a range of tasks behind the scenes and may spend many hours on the telephone. They keep elaborate filing systems with cross-references; every member of staff must be able to find quickly details about block and individual bookings. Much of this is now computerized. Each booking involves filling in forms, sending them out, filing, checking and possibly dealing with detailed correspondence. Itineraries and currency-conversion have to be worked out; timetables checked. Minor clerical errors can have disastrous consequences for clients' holidays and trips. Nearly all agents now use Prestel.

Managers co-ordinate the work of clerks and select those tour operators' brochures which they think will offer their clients what they want. As their profit is made from selling packages, travel agents must have good knowledge of tourist areas and also know how to advertise and promote their services to existing and potential clients.

Opportunities in travel agencies have levelled out in recent years. There is a high proportion of junior to senior staff, so promotion prospects are not very good.

Tour Operators

Planning

This is done by directors and 'travel technicians' (i.e. experienced clerks). 'Planning trips' last from 1 to 8 weeks twice a year and are exhausting. 2 or 3 resorts and perhaps 12 hotels may be investigated in a day. Local transport, garage facilities, food, amusements, beaches will be checked and local tourist officials consulted. Planning of the tour later involves checking timetables and maps, costing, and conferring with transport and accommodation services suppliers. Costing is crucial and the success of operators depends largely on ability to negotiate discounted prices with hotels, villa companies, airlines, etc. All this has to be done up to 2 years in advance, which adds to the difficulties, as the information supplied must be accurate.

Sales

Sales people visit travel agents to make sure brochures are on display. Those companies specializing in school parties (for example to ski resorts) have a sales team which visits schools to try to win their custom.

Reservations

Reservations staff take bookings from individual travellers and travel agents. However, increased use of computerized reservations systems is reducing the size of these departments.

Representatives or couriers

Many are freelance and are employed for the summer or winter season (occasionally both) by individual companies. The majority work with incoming tours, i.e. with overseas visitors to Britain. A minority work overseas, either travelling with groups from Britain to their holiday destination or based at a resort. Some may do secretarial work and/or planning off-season. This is not a career as such but rather a pleasant change for competent secretaries/ linguists or simply good organizers. Training is mainly provided by the company (although 1 or 2 private organizations run short courses for people hoping to become couriers).

Most travel staff work long hours and most Saturday mornings.

Training   Training can be full- or part-time or by distance learning. NVQs/
SVQs are well established.

    1. The Travel Training Programme run by the Travel Training
Company is the main way into travel work for school-leavers.
There are no set entry requirements, but in practice many trainees
have 3–4 GCSEs. Most openings are in travel agencies, but there
are also a few in business houses, with tour operators and with
airlines. Trainees are expected to reach NVQ/SVQ levels 2 and
3 by the end of 2 years and they study either business travel, tour
operations or – the most popular – retail travel.

    2. There are a number of other specialized courses and qualifica-
tions which can be either 'stand alone' or contribute towards an
NVQ/SVQ. One example is the qualification awarded by IATA
(the International Air Transport Association) required by staff in
agencies selling airline tickets. Another is the ABTA Travel
Agents Certificate (ABTAC) introduced in 1995 to replace
COTAC, which had been the recognized qualification for travel
agencies. ABTAC is available at 2 levels – Primary and Advanced
– and candidates sit a written test. Then there is the *Certificate for
Overseas Resort Representatives* (2 written tests and assessment)
and the *Certificate in UK Tourism.*

    People aiming at management can study for the *Certificate in
Travel Agency Management.* This in turn leads to the *Diploma in
Advanced Travel Skills* (NVQ level 4).

    3. BTEC National award (see p. xxi) in Travel and Tourism
or in Leisure with tourism option (or SCOTVEC equivalent).

    4. BTEC/SCOTVEC Higher National award in Business and
Finance, Travel, Travel and Tourism, Travel and Tourism
Management.

    5. 'Vocational' degrees in travel and tourism, 3-year full-time
or 4-year sandwich. Some other degrees, for example in tourism
studies, business studies and leisure management, offer relevant
options. Potential applicants should study course syllabuses carefully. Other graduate entry to the industry is possible with qualifications in, for example, marketing or accounting.

    6. There are some *post-graduate courses* and some of these may
also accept HND holders. At graduate and post-graduate level
tourism and *hospitality management* and *leisure management* training and work may overlap.

    7. The Institute of Travel and Tourism no longer runs its own
examinations for new entrants. Instead it accepts for the appropriate membership grade holders of approved ABTA, BTEC/
SCOTVEC awards or NVQs/SVQs. Experienced staff over 21
without these awards can still take the Institute's own
examination.

Personal attributes

Aptitude for figure work; good judgement of people; a friendly manner; accuracy; organizing ability; common sense; a good memory; a liking for selling.

Late start

Little opportunity in travel agencies, as most posts filled by school- and college-leavers. Some opportunities with tour operators. It is possible to prepare for entry, or to update skills or retrain, by using The Travel Training Company's Self-Study training packages.

Career-break

Opportunities for returners depend on contacts, on having kept up with changes in the industry. See Self-Study packages under 'Late start'. Suitable updating courses also available. Check with your local TEC (see p. xviii).

Part time

Sometimes available.

Position of women

Although more women than men are employed in travel agencies, only about 1 manager in 8 is a woman. In large tour operating companies, women are beginning to do well, though they have to have more paper qualifications (and languages) than the men with whom they compete.

Further information

The Travel Training Company, The Cornerstone, The Broadway, Woking, Surrey GU21 5AR

Institute of Travel and Tourism, 113 Victoria Street, St Albans, Herts. AL1 3TJ (enclose £3 and s.a.e.)

Related careers

CATERING: *Hotels* – CIVIL AVIATION: *Cabin Crew*; *Ground Staff* – LANGUAGES – LEISURE/RECREATION MANAGEMENT –SECRETARIAL AND CLERICAL WORK

Working for Oneself:
Mini-Entrepreneurship

Creating one's own job has now established itself as an 'alternative career'. Potential mini-entrepreneurs can get encouragement, advice, and sometimes financial help, from various sources, but their business plan has to stand up to severe scrutiny.

Entry qualifications

See 'Personal attributes' and 'Training', below.

The work

The variety of self-generated work is unlimited. It can be broadly divided into three overlapping types of activity: *providing a service*; *selling*; *making*. Most enterprises combine two activities, one of which is usually the crucial one. Deciding which type of enterprise to choose requires a great deal of research, because setting up a business is an uncharted area in conventional career terms. First impressions of what is involved in, say, running a sandwich delivery or motorbike messenger service, or a musical instrument repair or manufacturing workshop, tend to be misleading. They conceal any number of pitfalls – the need for unexpected areas of expertise, or for much more capital than bargained for, for example.

Providing a Service

This requires least capital, involves least risk, covers a vast range, e.g. babysitting, window or office cleaning, running a bicycle delivery service – activities based on using one's time, basic skills and possibly basic equipment; or repairing videos or motor-bikes, cooking directors' lunches in offices, running a word-processing or computer programming service, i.e. using specific skills plus equipment and, possibly, premises – kitchen, garden shed, living-room.

Professionals – in law, accountancy, systems analysis, etc. – with considerable experience, may set up their own computer-ized service and sell their expertise to companies for specific projects. This is still very much in its infancy but is likely to be a growth area. It enables professionals to be their own boss, working from home, while retaining links with previous employers and at the same time also working for new clients. Companies like it because using people who work from home saves overheads.

Selling

This usually overlaps with *providing a service* or with *making*, or it depends on 'buying-in' goods to sell (or collecting them from friends, etc.). It includes, for example, making sandwiches at home and delivering them to regular customers, running a second-hand clothes or clutter stall, selling 'bought-in' groceries from a mobile shop (probably a battered old van). This kind of selling could be a run-up to opening a shop, restaurant, mail-order business. Selling involves more initial organization and business know-how, capital and risk than *providing a service*.

Making

This usually overlaps with *selling* and covers anything from making children's clothes to assembling car roof-racks to manufacturing high tech components for the computer industry or electric guitars. It ranges from using talent plus basic skills to using sophisticated skills acquired by a range of levels of training, from YT to degree and post-graduate course, plus equipment. It requires some capital and probably premises. But if the idea is viable (see below) and the skills are there, finance and other help is available (see below).

*

The Law

Far fewer formalities have to be complied with than would-be entrepreneurs tend to fear. Mini-entrepreneurship is fashionable and a Good Thing in bureaucracy's eyes. The spirit rather than the letter of by-laws has to be observed. It is not permissible to run a saw-mill in one's garden because the noise would annoy the neighbours. It is unlikely that the Environmental Health Officer (from the Town Hall) would forbid sandwiches for sale being prepared in one's kitchen as long as that is clean. Local authorities must be consulted about planning and other regulations, but permission to go ahead is rarely 'unreasonably withheld' in the present climate of encouragement for so called 'start-ups' – small businesses. Even the Inspector of Taxes and the Department of Social Security, which have to be told, advise, inform and encourage rather than hinder. (Many people, for example, fear they will have to cope with VAT if they want to set up in business. In fact few people will reach the annual turnover limit necessary for registration in the first few years.

Business Format

Again, far fewer formalities have to be observed in the initial stages than generally believed. The basic formats are (a) *Sole trader*: The Income Tax and DSS merely have to be informed that the business exists; (b) *Partnership*: If two or more people set up a business jointly, a solicitor draws up a straightforward agreement. Both sole traders and partnerships are liable for all the debts they incur should the business fail; (c) *Limited company*: Requires slightly more formalities, but once set up persons involved are only liable for the money they put into the business should things go wrong; (d) *Co-operatives*: Various types; to set one up, solicitors' or special agencies' advice is essential (see 'Further information', below).

Training   No formal training structure as for conventional careers exists, but for most businesses mini-entrepreneurs need special skills. Welders, beauty therapists, typographers, software engineers, electronics engineers (technicians and graduates) or whatever, must first acquire the skill they intend to 'sell', i.e. which they want to use as the basis for their business. (See under individual career headings how to acquire such skills.) But to survive in the tough business world, basic business know-how is absolutely essential, too. The meaning of such terms as cash-flow, balance sheets, mark-up and, say, the difference between marketing and market research must be understood. The overall failure rate of new mini-ventures is fairly high. However, the failure rate can be linked closely to the level of research done and specialist advice/ training taken prior to starting up. Statistics are misleading because there are so many variables which affect success or failure, but there is general agreement among experts that successful entrepreneurship requires several indispensable ingredients:

1. *A marketable idea*: No idea is good in a vacuum. It must fill a gap in a given market. A bike repair service in a seaside suburb mainly inhabited by retired people would fail; one on a new housing estate some miles from shops and offices, etc. stands a good chance (as long as there is no efficient competition or, if

there is, the competition has more work than it can cope with
and/or the local market is expanding); a mobile grocery-van on
that housing estate where few shops have yet been opened sounds
a good idea; a mobile grocery-van near a large shopping centre
does not; a small-van removal service might flourish in bedsitter-
land; it would not in a large-one-family-houses suburb. Researching the market and making a marketing plan are probably the
most essential tasks when preparing to go it alone.

2. *Motivation and commitment*: Mini-entrepreneurs have to be
willing to work harder, and more irregular hours, than employees
usually do (see 'Personal attributes', below).

3. *Resources*: If the idea fills a gap in the market and the
commitment is there, advice, possibly financial assistance and
help with finding premises (if kitchen/garden shed/living-room are
insufficient/unsuitable) are available.

Because the powers-that-be agree that in business small is
beautiful (at least to start with) and that an increase in self-
generated jobs will reduce unemployment, a plethora of agencies
to help 'start-ups' have sprung up over the last few years. Many
of these have since disappeared, but there are still several sources
of help, advice and training which can help those starting a new
business to avoid some of the more obvious pitfalls and to
maximize their chances of success. The main change has been the
replacement of national schemes by more locally based initiatives
(see 'Training', below).

The 2 main points of contact for new entrepreneurs are:

1. *Training and Enterprise Councils* (TECs) in England and
Wales and *Local Enterprise Companies* (LECs) in Scotland.
These receive money from central government to fund local
services and it is they who decide who should get what. They are
required to provide a business information advisory and counselling service; in most cases this should include help for people
wanting to start businesses. (They have taken over responsibility
for this aspect from the national Small Firms Service.) There are
local variations: for example, some TECs will make an initial
training course a condition of financial help, while others will
make it voluntary. Some TECs provide a range of training
sessions on various aspects of running a business and some place
considerable emphasis on helping people for a period after they
have actually started their business. TEC advisers explain what
training and financial/business support schemes are available, and
for what, in their area. These take into account local needs and
possible gaps in the market. Potential business start-ups will be
very closely scrutinized – a proper business plan is essential – and
backing only given where the TEC think there is a good chance

of success. TECs also administer financial schemes such as Enterprise Allowance. The local Jobcentre can give the address of the nearest TEC or LEC.

2. *Local Enterprise Agencies* (Enterprise Trusts in Scotland): there are several hundreds of these, privately run, and many work closely with TECs. They help with information on the local business scene, with forming a business plan and with business counselling generally. They can give advice on tax, marketing, law, etc. The London Enterprise Agency (LEntA) runs 1-day sessions for anyone thinking of starting up their own business. (These are called 'Invest a Saturday' and cost £100, which includes a guide and some counselling.) Similar introductory courses may be available in some other areas. *Business in the Community* is the umbrella organization for these agencies and keeps an up-to-date list.

At the time of writing most of these services are free. Other useful organizations are:

3. The *Scottish Business Shop* provides a range of advisory services to small businesses throughout Scotland, including an information pack, a database of factual information and 3 free counselling sessions.

4. The *Rural Development Commission* (formerly CoSIRA) gives advice and help to people intending to set up in business in rural areas.

5. The *Crafts Council* will advise people thinking of setting up a pottery, weaving or similar crafts workshop.

6. The *Prince's Youth Business Trust* and *Livewire* advise and help young people (under-25s usually) who choose the self-employment option.

7. Some business studies degrees, post-graduate courses, BTEC and SCOTVEC awards (including BTEC Continuing Education units) have self-employment options.

8. *Open University* (p. xxxiii) *Start Up Your Own Business course*: It includes tuition by correspondence material (cassettes, work assignments, etc.).

9. *Some local colleges* run courses which, though not necessarily planned for potential entrepreneurs, are very useful – e.g. in bookkeeping, marketing, basic computer application. Some are evening classes, others are day-time courses organized under the '21 hours rule' which means unemployed people can draw benefit while attending college for a maximum of 21 hours a week.

Personal attributes   Unquenchable resilience; tenacity; decisiveness; organizing ability; being a bit bossy; exceptional stamina; business acumen; enjoying risk-taking – being a bit of a gambler; ability to put up with temporary hardship; resourcefulness; self-confidence bordering on conceit; true enjoyment of hard work; ability to get on well with other people however unreasonable their requests/criticisms/impatience; imagination; ability to work under pressure; interest in economic and social trends. (Extent of these qualities depends on extent of venturesomeness of enterprise contemplated.)

Late start   Age is a positive advantage in this 'alternative' career. Anyone who has had experience of the world of work scores over school/college-leavers when it comes to applying to banks, etc. for funds or to other agencies for premises or other help. Career-changers and returners are welcome on courses.

Career-break   Might present problems. It is too early to say at what stage in this particular work area a complete break would be least harmful. Most women entrepreneurs at present have either not yet reached the career-break stage, or they started their enterprise when there was no longer any need for a career-break.

Part time   Only possible by running small home-based businesses, or by being part of a well-organized co-operative.

Position of women   Women were slower than men to start choosing the self-employment option (24% of self-employed people in 1993 were women) but they are catching up fast. But figures are misleading because more women than men run small-scale enterprises from home – anything from catering to word-processing and cosmetics manufacturing – which do not necessarily show up in the statistics. The failure-rate among women entrepreneurs is believed to be smaller than that among their male counterparts – probably because to get bank loans women have to produce a more thoroughly researched business plan than men. Bank managers realize that women are less likely than men to have the unpaid 'back-up' help which male entrepreneurs tend to get from wives, and that women have more difficulty than men persuading suppliers that they are creditworthy. So the women who have managed to get the necessary start-up finance tend to succeed.

Self-employment can be the answer both for women who want to combine work with looking after a family by running small-scale enterprises from home, and for women with managerial ability who feel thwarted in the male-dominated business world. However, many women lack the necessary self-confidence to start.

**Further
informa-
tion**

Local TEC or LEC (ask at Jobcentre or look in telephone
directory)

Rural Development Commission, 141 Castle Street, Salisbury, Wilt-
shire SP1 3TP (England and Wales only)

Scottish Business Shop, 21 Bothwell Street, Glasgow G2 6NL

Crafts Council, 44A Pentonville Road, London N1 9BY

London Enterprise Agency, 4 Snow Hill, London EC1A 2BS
(write for useful booklet, 'Getting Started')

Business in the Community (for addresses of local enterprise
agencies), 8 Stratton Street, London W1X 6AH (for England
and Wales); Romano House, 43 Station Road, Corstorphine,
Edinburgh EH12 7AF (for Scotland)

Livewire: Freepost Livewire, Newcastle upon Tyne, NE1 1BR

The Prince's Youth Business Trust, 5 Cleveland Place, London
SW1Y 6JJ

Small Business Bureau, Curzon House, Church Road, Windle-
sham, Surrey GU20 6BH

Several high street banks have useful booklets on running your
own business

**Related
careers**

MANAGEMENT

Youth and Community Work

Entry qualifications   Depend on age and experience. See 'Training', below.

The work   Youth and community work has elements in common with education and social work. A primary concern is the social education of young people, helping them to explore their strengths and weaknesses, develop physical, intellectual, moral, social and emotional resources, and facilitate their growth from childhood to adulthood. Recent years have seen increased 'targeting' of disadvantaged groups, but current debate sets that against the need for more mainstream work. Many young people stay at home these days in rooms full of TVs, videos, stereos and computers – all essentially passive entertainments – and miss many opportunities for social development.

Job titles vary. People with different titles can be doing substantially the same work, while the work of people with the same title can vary greatly. *Youth workers* or *youth and community workers* may be club- or centre-based, 'detached' or community-based. In a club or centre the youth worker plans activities to appeal to a wide range of ages and tastes. They give young people the means to mix socially and organize themselves, to develop confidence and skills, both practical (e.g. in sport or drama) and social (e.g. co-operating as part of a team), to channel their energies in a constructive way. Forming relationships with young people is a very important part of the work and may involve the youth worker in counselling or unofficial social work. For example, the youth worker may be the first person to recognize signs of drug abuse or the bottled-up effects of a family break-up.

In some centres activities are organized for other groups within the community, e.g. mother-and-toddler groups, pre-school play-groups, leisure interest classes, literacy classes or English for immigrants. Sometimes the youth and community worker is responsible for such activities; sometimes the role is one of liaison with other groups. The balance between 'youth' and 'community' varies greatly; in some areas local authority services that changed their name from Youth Service to Youth and Community Service are now changing back.

Many youth and community workers are 'detached', i.e. they do not work from a fixed base. Some go out into the community to make contact with young people who do not come to clubs to identify their needs and help develop community solutions. Others do project work on, for example, drug abuse, unemployment or health education. Some youth workers are attached to schools (they usually need teaching qualifications) and a number work in social services departments with 'at risk' young people.

Youth work is very dependent on part-time, often voluntary workers. Even in a large centre there may be only 1 qualified worker, and, increasingly, qualified workers are given area responsibility for a number of clubs or centres. This means that qualified youth and community workers have less face-to-face contact with young people. Their job includes lots of administration, organizing of events and activities, recruitment, training and support of part-time workers, management of budgets and premises, liaison with the management committee and other groups, and seeking grants, sponsorship and other material support.

Youth and community workers are employed by local authorities (the Youth or Youth and Community Service is usually part of the education department, but sometimes comes under the leisure department), or by voluntary groups; it is estimated that 80% of youth work is provided by the voluntary groups (e.g. churches and organizations like Guides and Scouts). There is, however, a great deal of co-operation between the statutory and voluntary sectors.

Training   This is flexible and ensures that suitable people, whatever their age and educational qualifications, have a chance of qualifying. Though applicants for courses are normally expected to have 3 GCSEs (A–C) and 2 A-levels plus experience of voluntary or paid (for example, *playleader*) work with young people and/or other community work, applicants whose practical work experience has shown that they are suitable for the work may be accepted with lower educational qualifications. Minimum entry age varies from one course to another and again depends on individuals' experience and maturity.

There is a range of courses endorsed by the National Youth Agency as leading to qualified youth worker status. These include 2-year full-time Diploma in Higher Education courses, 3-year degree courses and 1-year post-graduate courses. Part-time courses and a distance-learning course are also available.

People without formal qualifications can apply for apprenticeship or employment-based schemes which combine employment with study. Experienced youth workers can in some areas become qualified through the Validating Learning from Experience scheme.

The NYA publishes a *Guide to Initial Training Courses in Youth and Community Work.*

In Scotland 3-year full-time course; may be reduced to 2 years for mature entrants with appropriate experience. Graduates and those with certain appropriate professional qualifications take a 1-year course.

Personal attributes   An outgoing personality; ability to communicate easily with people who may need 'drawing out'; patience; imagination to put oneself into the shoes of people who feel alienated from society; wide interests in current social and economic trends and problems; organizing ability; feeling at ease with people of all ages; creativity to think up activities (see also SOCIAL WORK, 'Personal attributes', p. 480).

Late start   Mature candidates are welcome on courses. This can be a suitable 'second career' for people changing direction in their twenties or thirties, if they have relevant experience.

Career-break   Should not present any problems.

Part time   Ample opportunity in youth work. Job-sharing is beginning to appear.

Position of women   There is no reason why women should not do well in this career and the number of women on courses has risen.

Further information   National Youth Agency, 17–23 Albion Street, Leicester LE1 6GD
Scottish Community Education Council, Rosebery House, 9 Haymarket Terrace, Edinburgh EH12 5EZ

Related careers   LEISURE/RECREATION MANAGEMENT – SOCIAL WORK – SPORT – TEACHING

Index